# College Radio Days

Also by Tim Brooks

*Lost Sounds: Blacks and the Birth of the Recording Industry, 1890-1919*

*The Complete Directory to Prime Time Network and Cable TV Shows, 1946-Present* (with Earle Marsh)

*Survey of Reissues of U.S. Recordings* (monograph)

*The Columbia Master Book Discography, 1901-1934* (with Brian Rust)

*Little Wonder Records and Bubble Books* (with Merle Sprinzen)

*The Complete Directory to Prime Time TV Stars*

# College Radio Days

# 70 Years of Student Broadcasting at Dartmouth College

by
Tim Brooks

ISBN: 978-0615893204


**Glenville Press,** P.O. Box 31041, Glenville Stn., Greenwich, CT 06831

Timothy Brooks LLC

Website: **www.timbrooks.net**

10 9 8 7 6 5 4 3 2 1

Cover design by Anne Fink
Photo credits. Pages 155-158:  courtesy of Robert R. Gitt (1946, 1948, 1962), Harold Levenson, Heath Cole (1960), Dartmouth College Library (1959, Robinson Hall). Pages 299-302: Heath Cole/Dartmouth Broadcasting (1979, 1982, 1995, 2009, 2013), Deborah Wassel (2007), Eli Burakian, Dartmouth College (2012). Author biography photo: Richard J. Garfunkel.

# Contents

# Preface and Acknowledgments

The original version of this manuscript was written in 1964, as I was about to graduate from Dartmouth—and from WDCR. It was not done for credit, or as course work, but simply because I thought the station needed some sense of its history. Since then that manuscript has been accessed for numerous purposes, and in 2008, as the station approached its 50th anniversary, someone said "why don't you bring it up to date?" I agreed, intending to find a few people with a broad overview of developments since 1964, and scan the pages of *The Dartmouth*, to find out how the stations had changed over the last 40-plus years.

Then, reality got in the way.

No one seemed to have any real knowledge of how these remarkable stations had evolved over time. Even long-time faculty and administration members remembered only vaguely, or selectively, what happened and when. It was, after all, only part of their world. Most alumni could speak only about their own four years—which they did, enthusiastically—but had no idea what transpired before or after that. As for the written record, coverage in *The Dartmouth* and elsewhere was highly uneven, intense at times, non-existent at others. Since the 1990s the stations have received very little press attention. Most surprising were the station's own files, to which I was given generous access. They contain a fair number of documents from the 1960s to the 1980s, but very little after that. Even documents cited in my 1964 history are now gone.

Therefore much of what you will read here is based on the recollections of station members and others. I interviewed or corresponded with nearly 200 of them during 2008-13, and their enthusiasm for the stations was contagious. Nearly everyone contacted was happy, indeed eager, to share their memories, and in some cases memorabilia too. Again and again alumni said that their time at the station was one of the most rewarding and important—or *the* most rewarding and important— part of their Dartmouth education, and important to their subsequent careers as well. The story of Dartmouth radio turned into a story of changes in campus life over the 70-plus years, as well as the broader story of college radio in the U.S. I made new friends, and learned what an inclusive and enthusiastic group the Dartmouth radio fraternity really is. In fact it was so interesting to talk with students and alumni ranging in age from 19 to 90, that at times I didn't want the research phase to end.

But now it's time to share the story. Sources have been footnoted fairly thoroughly, both as documentation and to show appreciation to those who have contributed so willingly to this project. A small amount of information given in confidence, or drawn from documents which might reasonably have been expected to be kept private, is not sourced; such information was used only if it was essential to the narrative and confirmed by multiple sources. Another convention is that the class year of students is generally given only with the first mention of their name in a chapter. If you want to find additional citations for them check the name index.

Special mention should be made of several people, among them George Whitehead '61, former General Manager and recent Overseer and station volunteer. In addition to helping greatly with this history George has rolled up his sleeves, rebuilt consoles, salvaged transmitters, and pitched in wherever necessary to refurbish the station's technical plant. Dartmouth is lucky to have dedicated alumni like him. Entrepreneur/d.j. David Marston '74 has also been most helpful throughout, providing an unusually broad view of the station throughout the 1970s and helping reconstruct the sequence of professional sales staff. Tim Reynolds '91, chairman of the overseers from 1996-2008, was helpful in the early going, and longtime overseer and College treasurer's representative John Bryant helped both in 1964, when he was a young administrator, and in 2008, by which time he had retired. I'm sorry he did not live to see the final product.

Also extremely helpful in locating materials have been College Archivist Peter Carini and the staff of Rauner Special Collections at the Dartmouth College Library, especially Sarah Hartwell, and current station operations manager Heath Cole, who has cheerfully answered questions at every turn. Among alumni, Maura Harway '77 produced a veritable treasure trove of newsletters, tapes and other materials from the mid 1970s, while Guy MacMillin '64 offered a nearly complete run of the extraordinary series *Tales for the Midnight Hour* from the 1960s, and Bill Gitt '53 produced audio he'd saved from the 1950s, including the legendary *Hunky Dorey Hour*. Guy also deserves enormous thanks for volunteering to copy edit the entire manuscript.

Many, many others have also been extremely helpful. Alumni whom I've interviewed or with whom I've corresponded include Sandy Alderson '69, Henry Allen '69, Bill Alpert '45, Martin Aronson '55, Frederick Asher '63, Phil Augur '95, Jennifer Avellino '89, Bill Aydelott '72, Edward Bardusch '76, Larry Barnet '68, Roderick Beaton '03, Jack Beeler '73, Karli Beitel '10, Gino Beniamino '04, Rick Beyer '78, Abdhish Bhavsar '87, Grant Bosse '94, Chris Brewster '72, Rob Brown '59, Keith Burdette '03, Sean Byrnes '00, Craig J. Cain '45, Walt Callender '78, Allan Cameron '60, John Catlett '66 (Tuck), Neel Chatterjee '91, Phillip Cheung '97, Bill Cogswell '61, David Cohen '94, Bob Cohn '66, Gerrett Conover '87, Dan Daniels '84, John D'Auria '74, Chris Davidson '76, Kathy DeGioia (Eastwood) '76, Ben DeWitte '02, John Donvan '77, Sturges Dorrance '63, William Downall '72, David Dugan '52, Donald Elitzer '69, Schuyler Evans '10, Tom Farmer '81, Robin Felix '75, Arthur Fergenson '69, Wallace Ford '70, Geanette Foster '14, Gregg Fox '13, Fred Frawley '73, Paul Gambaccini '70, Ted Gerbracht '64, Ed Gerson '35, Pam Gile '76, Robert Gitt '63, William Gitt '53, Henry Goldsmith '62, Robert L. Grant '43, David Graves '70, Robert Gray '83, John Gridley '64, Lucretia Grindle '83, Robert Hager '60, Bob Hargraves '61, Richard Harris '58, Rob Hartford '65, Maura Harway '77, Carey Heckman '76, Buck Henry (Buck Zuckerman) '52, Mike Henry '98, Alfred Hill '65, Joe Hirschberg '43, Michael Hobbs '62, Richard Hollands '50, Priscilla Huff '91, Norman Jacobs '69, Erin M. Jaeger '11, Allan "Bic" Jayne '73, Paul Jones '65, Richard T. Kanter '44, Ron Kehoe '59, Jeff Kelley '69, Richard A. Kelly '46, Dan King '02, Eric Kintner '67, Bob Kirkpatrick '72, Paul Klee '66, Jason Klein '82, Tony Knapp '63, Kevin Koloff '77, Beth Krakower '93, Brent Laffoon '98, John Landrigan '84, Vivian J. Lee '97, Harold Levenson '61, Guy MacMillin '64, Dwight Macomber '70, Stu Mahlin '63, Richard

Mark '77, David Marston '74, Ted Mascott '62, John May '85, Eric McDonald '04, Alan McKee '64, Tim McKeever '72, Scott McQueen '68, Alex Middleton '06, Justin Mohr, '03, Bill Moyes '70, Katie Mulligan '85, Randy Odeneal '68, Mike O'Donnell '02, Eric Overton '87, Jeff Panitt '65, Todd Piro '00, Bob Ponce '80, David Prentice '69, Charles Quincy '11, James Rayton '65, Vikash Reddy '05, Robert Reich '68, Barbara Reinertsen '77, Tim Reynolds '91, John Rockwell '72, Jordan Roderick '78, Seth Rosenblatt '89, Jim Rosenfield '52, Larry Russell '54, Paul H. Samek '45, Phil Schaefer '64, Leonard Schulte '74, Harriet Schwartz '78, Andy Shapiro '88, Jeff Shapiro '83, Robert Shellard '69, David Shipler '64, William Sigward '74, Seth Skolnik '89, Lonna Slaby (Saunders) '74, J. Charles Smith '73, Margaret Smith (Lamunde) '82, Pavel Sotskov '09, Mark Stitham '72, Carl Strathmeyer '70, Jeffrey Sudikoff '77, Jerry Tallmer '42, Peter Threadgill '77, John Van de Kamp '56, Thomas VanBenschoten '74, Jim Varnum '62, Richard von Riesen '80, Mark Wachen '89, James Washington '77, Deborah Wassel '07, Eric Wellman '91, Doug White '75, George Whitehead '61, April Whitescarver '96, Royce Yudkoff '77, Chris Zhao '13, Steven Zrike '71, and Stu Zuckerman '70.

I also want to thank quite a few faculty and others. These include Rick Adams, Prof. Jordan Baruch, Rich E. Brown, John Bryant, Dean Katherine Burke, Laura Canada, Prof. John Carey (Fordham), College Archivist Peter Carini, Dean Joe Cassidy, Carl Chen (Yale), Cary Clark, Heath Cole, Dr. Tom Evans, Leona Fiske, Jeff Haley (Radio Advertising Bureau), Prof. Eric Hansen, Prof. Jeffrey Hart, Sarah Hartwell, Prof. Ernest Hebert, Tim Hoehn, Evelyn Hutchins, Prof. Almon Ives, Julie Kaye, Dean Linda Kennedy, Prof. Thomas Kurtz, Martha Luehrmann, Sean Owczarek (Yale), Prof. Rob Quicke, Chris Robinson, Dean Holly Sateia, Prof. David Sices, Bob Smith (Cornell), Elizabeth Stauderman (Yale), Dean April Thompson, and Prof. Peter Travis.

Although I've tried to verify factual statements much of this history has been pieced together from imperfect recollections and bits of information, and there are bound to be mistakes. For those I take responsibility. If you see any errors let me know (at **tim@timbrooks.net**), and please include documentation if possible. Memories, including mine, can be faulty!

*Tim Brooks*
*Greenwich, CT*

# Introduction

# A History of College Radio in the U.S.

The president was skeptical. A faculty committee stood ready to nix the idea on the grounds that it might create a riot danger in the dormitories. As one student put it, "We had to go in and face the most hostile group... who saw no reason to have a radio station at Dartmouth College. We collected all the evidence we could, and we summoned forth the essays on freedom of speech and God knows what... and we sat there and banged the table!"[1]

President Ernest Martin Hopkins had reason to be skeptical. Seventeen years earlier, in 1924, he had reluctantly approved a proposal by the radio club to launch a student-run AM broadcasting station at Dartmouth. It operated for about a year. Then in October 1925, the story goes, as the station was about to resume operation with a special broadcast, Hopkins had been introduced to give his opening speech. An engineer threw a switch the wrong way and instead of Hopkins out over the airwaves went a string of expletives. "Shut that God-damn door!" Furious, Hopkins shut the station down and refused to consider another for many years.

But undergraduate Dick Krolik and his friends banged the table long enough in the spring of 1941 to persuade him to finally give it another try. Little did anyone imagine the long and fascinating journey that station would take in the years to come.

The birth pains of radio at Dartmouth were replicated, in one way or another, on campuses across America, over many years. College radio has been around as long as radio itself, appearing in the early 1920s at the same time as the first professional stations. In fact, if you count early experimental amateur ("ham") stations, communicating with other experimenters, it began even before that, in college physics departments during the days of Marconi. College stations eventually grew into a vital part of the media world, involving tens of thousands of students, providing invaluable experience for the leaders and communicators of the future, and bringing listeners, both on and off campus, programming found nowhere else on the dial.

Amazingly, no comprehensive history of this influential medium seems to have been published.[2] Nor have there been in-depth studies of individual stations, and how they operated. This book is for those involved with the Dartmouth stations, but also for anyone interested in the development of this unique and influential part of the media landscape. The journey of Dartmouth radio in many ways mirrors the history of college radio in the U.S.

# I

## A Short History of College Radio

Radio was one of the wondrous, and life-changing, inventions of an era that brought us many of them—the electric light, the telephone, automobiles, airplanes, motion pictures, sound recordings, and so much more. Colleges were very much involved in the early development of radio, following Guglielmo Marconi's demonstration in 1901 of the practicality of long-range point-to-point radio communication using Morse Code. Experimental "broadcasting" (one audio signal to many receivers) began a few years later, mostly by individual experimenters. Broadcasting had many fathers and there is little agreement on who was first, but experimental stations were on the air, intermittently at least, as early as 1907 (Robert Karlowa in Rock Island, Illinois) and in 1909 by electronics teacher Charles "Doc" Herrold of San Jose, California, whose long-running station eventually morphed into KCBS, San Francisco. Herrold coined the term "broadcasting," and presented what he claimed was the first disc jockey, who played 78 rpm discs from a local record store.[3]

College faculty members and students soon became actively involved in the new, and still experimental, medium. Cornell University began radiotelephone experiments in 1910 as did St. Joseph's College in Philadelphia in 1912. Federal licensing began in 1913, and when the first list of licenses was released by the U.S. Commerce Department, nearly half were assigned to colleges and other schools, including Harvard. In 1915 the University of Wisconsin-Madison received a license for experimental station 9XM, which became WHA, possibly the first educational station in the U.S. The University of Iowa's 9YA (1915) is believed to have been the first station broadcasting on a regular schedule west of the Mississippi. Other early stations included those of Ohio State University, the University of Illinois, Purdue University and Tulane University. WRUC at Union College in Schenectady, New York, claims to have been the first student-operated station in the nation, signing on October 14, 1920.[4]

Dartmouth ham operators were active as early as 1908, listening in on an early receiver, and by 1914 they had their own transmitter. Their experimental station 1YB (later W1ET) was operating by 1919, and in 1924-25 the radio club tried its hand at standard AM broadcasting, as will be explained in this book.[5]

The 1920s were an exciting time for radio. With the broadcast, famously, of the Harding-Cox election results on newly licensed KDKA in Pittsburgh in November 1920, commercial broadcast stations began to spring up all over the country. Radio, once the province of engineering geeks and laboratories, moved into homes across America. Ordinary citizens had never seen anything like this new medium. An ever-changing vaudeville stage, and a lecture hall, right in your own home!

## Colleges Get Pushed Aside

For the first few years college owned and commercial stations co-existed, but as radio became big business commercial interests began to covet the educational frequencies. The government was all too happy to oblige them, and one by one colleges found themselves forced to share their frequencies, or give them up, to businesses. In addition the regulatory regime pursued by the Commerce Department and its successors the Federal Radio Commission (1927) and the Federal Communications Commission (1934) was one of constantly changing rules, frequency reassignments, and changing reporting requirements. The bureaucratic harassment was just too much for many institutions, which simply abandoned the field. As early as 1925 colleges with stations banded together to form the Association of College and University Broadcasting Stations, to try to fight back against the growing commercial encroachment. In 1934 it reorganized to become the National Association of Educational Broadcasters (NAEB). However the educators were clearly outgunned by the powerful and well-connected commercial interests, including the thriving radio networks. More than 200 AM broadcast stations were licensed to educational institutions between 1920 and 1936; however by 1937 only 38 were still on the air.[6]

## FM Broadcasting

During these dark days for college broadcasting there was one glimmer of hope, although it would take a long time to reach fruition. FM radio, developed in the 1930s, offered an alternate avenue for college and educational broadcasters and when the Federal Communications Commission (FCC) announced its first assignment of FM frequencies in 1940 it reserved five channels out of the total of 40 (from 42-50 MHz) for educational non-commercial use. When the FM band was shifted in 1945 to the 88-106 MHz band we know today, 20 channels from 88 to 92 MHz ("the left hand side of the dial") were set aside for such stations.[7] The main drawback, of course, was that hardly anyone owned an FM receiving set.

Among the first educational FM stations were KSUI at the University of Iowa and WILL of the University of Illinois (1941). In early 1948 Syracuse University was given authority to operate a experimental 2.5 watt FM station, WJIV. This became the prototype for low power FM broadcasting, which became a standard type of license for many colleges (the standard power was later set at 10 watts), although Syracuse itself soon traded up to full power WAER-FM.[8] The advantages of low power FM were many: a relatively modest investment by the institution, coverage that was wide enough to cover most campuses but not so broad as to interfere with commercial broadcasters, and relatively lenient regulations allowing, among other things, no engineer to be on duty and no minimum number of hours on the air each day (allowing stations to shut down during vacations). Still, the real boom in college-based 10 watt FM stations did not begin until the 1960s, by which time FM had also developed the ability to broadcast in stereo.

## Carrier Current AM

Meanwhile many colleges, seeking a way to cover the campus and not interfere with commercial stations, had adopted a third mode of transmission, carrier current broadcasting. With this system an AM signal is distributed via the electrical wiring in campus buildings, and can normally be heard within 200 feet or so of such wiring. As a supplement, small transmitters are sometimes placed in individual buildings capable of boosting the signal in the immediate area. It is inexpensive, low power (usually five to 30 watts), campus-limited, receivable on normal AM radio sets, and not subject to FCC regulation. It can be commercial or non-commercial, broadcast on whatever frequency (or frequencies) it wishes, and choose its own call letters, even if they are in use by another station—all because of its very limited reach. It does have many technical challenges, however, including signal leakage, difficulties passing its signal through transformers, and often poor signal quality. The Dartmouth station, which was a carrier current operation from 1941 to 1958, encountered all of these problems.

The history (and even the current state) of carrier current broadcasting is poorly documented, in part because of the lack of licensing. However the earliest examples appear to have been in the late 1930s. A colorful book titled *The Gas Pipe Networks*—so named because the wiring for these stations often ran through the steam tunnels under the buildings, and students joked that the signal was coming from the plumbing—describes the origins of one of the earliest installations, at Brown University in Providence, Rhode Island. In 1936 two freshmen, George Abraham and David Borst, ran a wire between their dorm rooms, which were in different buildings, so that they could "broadcast" to each other. Soon other students asked to be connected and Abraham and Borst began to string wires all over campus, linking back to master control in Abraham's room. Each subscriber had a wire connected to his radio set, and also a microphone. The primitive system proved its worth when a Vigilance Committee of sophomores set out to conduct their traditional hazing of freshmen. They were unaware that a special "line one" of the wired system had been reserved solely for freshmen to communicate with one another. The freshmen were able to report on the movements of the sophomores so that when the sophomores approached a dormitory they were met with a barrage of water balloons and forced to make a hasty retreat.[9]

Besides allowing for campus hijinks, the Brown Network also broadcast news coverage and music. It was soon allowed to build studios in the student activities building and switch its distribution system to the campus wiring grid. A visit to the college in 1939 by RCA's David Sarnoff, who was much impressed by the students' industry, brought the operation considerable publicity. Other eastern colleges began to pick up on the idea with their own carrier current systems, including Wesleyan, Williams, the University of Maryland, Swarthmore, Cornell, Princeton, Harvard, and, in 1941, Dartmouth.

### Post World War II

In the late 1940s colleges were flooded with veterans returning from World War II, many on the G.I. Bill, and many having had electronics training during the war. This rich pool of relatively experienced students gave rise to radio stations on many campuses. They were inspired by the commercial radio industry that by then blanketed the country. (Mass television was still a few years away.) At Dartmouth, as at other campuses, student stations were either started, or re-started, using one of three principal distribution methods: carrier current, low power FM, or full power AM or FM. The latter were subject to the full licensing requirements of the FCC, and generally run by professionals with students serving as interns. The first two, being campus-limited, could be run by students alone.

Dartmouth's post-war route was carrier current, although it had perhaps an unusual degree of autonomy and professionalism in its operation. In 1948 it banded together with four other Ivy League stations—those of Harvard, Yale, Princeton, and the University of Pennsylvania—to form the Ivy Network, which sold national advertising on all five stations. Meanwhile the Intercollegiate Broadcasting System, which had been founded by Brown's George Abraham and David Borst in 1940, represented a wider range of college stations, and also attempted to sell time on them to national advertisers.[10]

The 1950s and '60s were a period of steady growth for college radio. Many stations that had been carrier current switched to either low-power FM or, in a few cases, full power in order to enhance their signal quality and coverage. (Dartmouth switched to a full-power AM station in 1958). There was a considerable upheaval going on in the radio industry at this time, as television swept the nation and the once-mighty radio networks rapidly disintegrated. Individual radio stations survived, and in some cases thrived, by becoming music stations, particularly those that catered to youthful audiences by featuring the new rock 'n' roll music. The era of Top 40 radio and garrulous disc jockeys had arrived. This dovetailed nicely with the interests of students, who were delighted to play the music of their own generation.

There was still considerable resistance by commercial stations to encroachment on their turf by mere students, however, so full-power college stations were relatively uncommon. This was particularly true in large markets, where frequencies were scarce, but even in small town Hanover, New Hampshire, the one commercial broadcaster in the area fought fiercely to prevent Dartmouth College from launching a student-run AM station. Most of the college stations that transitioned away from carrier current shifted to low power FM, which could cover the campus without antagonizing local commercial stations. With FM receivers gradually becoming more common, this was increasingly practical.

A major development of the late 1960s was the passage of The Public Broadcasting Act of 1967, which created the Corporation for Public Broadcasting and (in 1970) National Public Radio. These channeled funds and programming to public stations, which were starving for both, and some college stations signed on to become NPR affiliates (which effectively meant they were no longer student-run).

As FM grew in popularity commercial broadcasters once again began to come after the college frequencies, and in 1978, after heavy lobbying by the National Association of Broadcasters and public broadcasters, the FCC ceased issuing 10-watt ("Class D") licenses. Eventually it instituted a new class of low power FM (LPFM) licenses, which could range up to 100 watts, but with significant restrictions insisted on by the NAB to "protect" commercial broadcasting. After many protests the Local Community Radio Act of 2010 loosened these restrictions somewhat, however the subject of low power radio, a mainstay of college broadcasting, remains controversial. Advocates feel that it is essential to promote localism and minority formats in an era of corporate and format consolidation, while commercial opponents fear it will cause signal interference and use up frequencies that they would like to have for low-power repeaters to enlarge their coverage areas.[11]

## II

### College Radio Today: The Ivy League Stations

The eight Ivy League stations illustrate the path followed by many student-run college stations. All began as AM carrier current stations, mostly in the early

1940s; seven out of eight transitioned to FM in the 1950s or '60s; and nearly all now have some professionals on staff working with the students, particularly in sales. Beyond that, their stories differ somewhat.

Brown University, which arguably started it all with a primitive wired distribution system in 1936, soon switched to carrier current and the call letters WBRU. Today this is an Internet-only station. A second station, WBRU-FM/95.5, was launched in 1966 using a donated commercial license, which allowed it to broadcast with a rather powerful 20 kw of power and be heard throughout Rhode Island as well as in portions of Massachusetts and Connecticut. The FM station now has a paid sales and programming staff, and brings in substantial revenues ($1.5 million in 2011). It features modern rock music and it has "broken" many emerging artists over the years, while winning awards as Best College Station. It is owned by Brown Broadcasting Service, Inc., a non-profit association governed by a combination of students and alumni.[12]

Columbia University is the birthplace of FM radio. Major Edwin Armstrong, the father of FM, was for many years a professor there, and developed the technology in a Columbia laboratory. Nevertheless its first student station, launched in 1941 with the encouragement of Armstrong, and soon called WKCR, was distributed by carrier current. It was non-commercial and featured lectures and classical music, along with rebroadcasts from Armstrong's experimental FM station, W2XMN. In 1956 the University launched WKCR-FM/89.9 which also broadcast educational and public affairs programming, until 1968, when it shifted to jazz and avant-garde classical music. Originally a 10-watt FM station (i.e., campus-limited), it now has somewhat greater power and can be heard in much of New York City. The station is owned by the University.[13]

Cornell University launched its student carrier current station in 1940, at first designated WCRG and later WVBR ("Voice of the Big Red"). The student radio club raised money in 1958 to build WVBR-FM/93.5, initially with 175 watts of power, growing to 3.0 kw by the end of the 1960s. Today it is a commercial, student-run station featuring tightly formatted album-oriented rock music, which draws a significant audience in the community. Studios and transmitter are off campus. WVBR-FM is owned by the Cornell Radio Guild, a non-profit membership corporation governed by students, resulting in some tensions with the University. Cornell itself has owned a number of professionally run stations over the years, beginning with educational WEAI in 1923, commercial WESG in 1932, and commercial WHCU from 1941. It sold these broadcast holdings in 1985.[14]

Dartmouth, as will be detailed in these pages, launched a carrier current student station in 1941 and switched to a full power commercial AM station (then the most widely used medium) in 1958. For many years WDCR was believed to be the only completely student-run commercial AM station in the nation. However with AM in decline in recent years, WDCR switched to Internet-only distribution in 2008. Meanwhile Dartmouth added a student-run FM sibling, WFRD-FM/99.3, in 1976. With 6.0 kw power and tightly formatted alternative rock programming, it is today one of the most popular stations in its market. The stations are owned by Dartmouth College and run by a combination of students and professional staff.

The Harvard University newspaper *The Harvard Crimson* launched student station WHCN on carrier current in 1940. The station broke away from the paper in 1943 and became WHRV and later WHRB (1951). In 1957 it switched to FM as

WHRB-FM, first on 107.1 and then on 95.3, with 300 watts of power (later raised to 3.0 kw). Today it brings to the Boston market a mix of jazz, classical music and other genres underserved on commercial radio (e.g., "Hillbilly at Harvard"), and is famous for its "orgies"—musical marathons of single composers, labels or genres which can last as long as a month. It is a commercial station and is owned by Harvard Radio Broadcasting Co., Inc., a non-profit corporation run by students and alumni. WHRB alumni are called "ghosts" in station vernacular, referring to their tendency to "haunt" the station after "death" (graduation).[15]

Princeton University opened student station WPRU in 1940, operating on carrier current. This transitioned to WPRB-FM/103.3 in 1955, originally with 250 watts of power but increased to a powerful 14 kw in 1960, with a listening area stretching from the outskirts of New York City to Wilmington, Delaware. It is a commercial station offering listeners an eclectic mix of classical music, jazz and independent rock, along with public affairs and sports. It is financed by a combination of advertising revenue and listener support, and owned by the Princeton Broadcasting Service, Inc., a non-profit governed by students and alumni.[16]

The University of Pennsylvania was the last Ivy to permit student broadcasting, launching WXPN on carrier current in 1945. This became WQHS in 1980 and transitioned to Internet-only distribution in 2003. Meanwhile non-commercial WXPN-FM/88.9 (later moved to 88.5) went on the air in 1957, with a campus-limited 10 watts of power. Later this was raised to 5.0 kw, giving the station community coverage as well. Its programming is an eclectic mix of jazz, blues, alternative rock, and various features not likely to be heard on commercial radio. Perhaps its best known program is *World Cafe*, featuring live performances and interviews and syndicated by NPR. The station is owned by the University and was originally operated by a student staff. However an obscenity scandal in 1975 (which resulted in license revocation and a long legal battle with the FCC) led the University to place professionals in charge.[17]

Yale University's student station was established in 1941 as WOCD, financed by alumni contributions and operated by the *Yale Daily News*. Like the other Ivy stations, it was distributed to the campus via carrier current. In 1945 it broke away from the newspaper and was renamed WYBC. In 1948 the non-profit Yale Broadcasting Company was incorporated to manage the station, as well as other ventures including a brief flyer into television in the mid 1950s (WYBC-TV). WYBC radio continued to operate until the early 1980s. Meanwhile in 1959 WYBC-FM/94.3 was launched as a commercial FM station, with 300 watts of power, eventually increased to 3.0 kw. During the tumultuous 1960s it became quite activist and aligned with the counterculture movement, as well as the minority communities of New Haven, to the extent that it was used as the model for the fictional "WBBY," a parody of a laid-back, liberal student station in the Doonesbury cartoon. Following financial difficulties that began in the 1980s the station was taken over by a professional staff in 1992. As of 2013 WYBC-FM was managed by Cox Broadcasting and had a urban adult contemporary (black) format. In order to give students an outlet YBC purchased a bankrupt AM station in 1998 and converted it to WYBC-AM, operated by a mixed professional and student staff. However students were already abandoning AM radio by this time and in 2010-11 the experiment was ended, with students assigned to an Internet-only station (WYBCX), while WYBC-AM became an NPR station managed by Sacred Heart University. The licenses are held by a non-profit corporation governed by three boards consisting of students, alumni, and community representatives.[18]

## Other Top College Stations

Of course there are hundreds of other college stations operating in the U.S., many of them quite successful. Radio-Locator, a principal source for information on licensed broadcast stations in the U.S. and Canada, lists 467 licensed college stations, and there are hundreds more that are unlicensed because they use carrier current or Internet-only distribution.[19]

According to Radio-Locator, the three most listened-to college stations in 2012 were KTSU-FM/90.9, an 18.5 kw jazz station operated by Texas Southern University that blankets the Houston market; KEXP-FM/90.3, a 4.7 kw station featuring alternative rock (including live performances) and operated by the University of Washington in Seattle; and WERS-FM/88.9, a 4.0 kw station with a eclectic music format owned by Emerson College and serving the greater Boston area. All three are non-commercial.

There are a number of awards each year for "best college station," each subject to its own biases, but it is interesting to see what a wide variety of stations have been recognized in recent years. The oldest college station association, the Intercollegiate Broadcasting System (IBS), presents an annual "Abraham and Borst Award" (named after its founders) to the "best college station in the nation." Candidates must submit sample tapes which are screened by a panel of judges. Recent winners have included:

- WUTM-FM/90.3, a 185 watt contemporary hits station at the University of Tennessee (2012);
- WGCS-FM/91.1, a 6.0 kw eclectic music and sports station at Goshen College in Indiana (2011);
- Radio DePaul, the Internet-only eclectic music and talk station of DePaul University in Chicago (2010).

The MTVU cable television network, which targets the college audience, presents its own Woodie Awards each year in a nationally televised ceremony.[20] These are voted on by students nationwide, and have been the subject of much lobbying by some stations (one winning station posted a "how to vote for us" video on YouTube). Recent winners of this popularity contest have been:

- WASU-FM/90.5, a 200 watt alternative rock station at Appalachian State University in North Carolina (2012);
- WVUM-FM/90.5, a 1.3 kw eclectic music (classical and rock), sports and public affairs station at the University of Miami-Florida (2011);
- KUPS-FM/90.1, a 100 watt alternative rock station at the University of Puget Sound in Washington (2009)

CMJ, a college music trade publication, presents a "best station" award at its conference each fall, at which student representatives gather to learn about the industry. The award is voted on by attendees at the conference. It has recently gone to:

- WKDU-FM/91.7, the 800 watt free-format student station of Drexel University (2011, 2010);
- KUSF in Exile, the Internet-only successor to KUSF-FM which was sold by the University of San Francisco (2011);
- CJLO-AM/1690 kc, a 1.0 kw AM music and talk station at Concordia University in Montreal, Canada (2010);
- KSSU, the free-format carrier current station at California State University in Sacramento (2009).

Another well-publicized award is presented by *The Princeton Review* as part of its annual survey of students at nearly 400 colleges and universities. Some 122,000 students are surveyed and among the questions they are asked is "how popular is the radio station [on your campus]?" Thus this award is a measure of how well known stations are on their respective campuses. Recent winners have been:

- WERS-FM/88.9, at Emerson College in Boston (2013);
- WSBU-FM/88.3, a 165 watt alternative rock station at St. Bonaventure University in New York (2012);
- WGRE-FM/91.5, an 800 watt alternative rock, news, and sports station at DePauw University in Indiana (2011);
- WICB-FM/91.7, a 4.1 kw alternative rock, news, and sports station at Ithaca College in New York (2010).[21]

An analysis of the winners of these awards reveals several interesting facts. No one station (or small group of stations) dominates the "best station" lists. The 15 awards listed here went to 14 different stations. The winners are predominantly FM stations (10), with one AM, one distributed via carrier current, and two Internet-only. The FM winners are generally low power (less than 1.0 kw). Nearly all are non-commercial (supported either by donations or their universities), and are staffed largely, though not exclusively, by student volunteers. Alumni are heavily involved in many of them. In terms of their histories, many began as carrier current and/or low power (10 watt) FM stations, and later, with the backing of their institutions, won power increases.[22]

College radio is indeed a large and diverse universe, one that adds considerable variety to the radio dial.

### Bringing Diversity to Radio

As can be seen in the preceding examples, college radio typically provides programming that is hard to find on commercial stations, such as jazz, world music, reggae, classical, and numerous strains of non-mainstream rock. Often it is the music of a young and musically adventurous generation. This is where you are most likely to hear new artists, local artists, and music genres not encountered on more tightly formatted commercial stations, or even on public radio. In the 1980s college stations launched or boosted the careers of bands like U2 and R.E.M., and later those of Nirvana, Pearl Jam, Soundgarden, White Stripes and Coldplay. Adelphi University's WBAU, located in a suburb of New York City, was one of the first to play rap music, "before mainstream stations got close to touching it." Among its personalities were the youthful Dr. Dré, Wildman Steve, Chuck D, and Flavor Flav.[23]

Other college stations have specialized in talk and specialty shows, often with a strongly local flavor. Some have excelled in public affairs. The Dartmouth stations' massive coverage of the quadrennial New Hampshire presidential primary was syndicated throughout the Northeast and internationally in the 1970s and '80s. Since college stations do not (usually) have to worry about audience ratings, they are free to experiment in ways that profit-making stations are not. Even NPR stations have to keep an eye on audience levels in order to attract enough listeners to raise money during fund-raising marathons.

Another misunderstood aspect of college radio is its role as a training ground. The common belief is that college stations "train students to be broadcasters." However the Dartmouth case study reveals that very few of the student managers there subsequently went into radio. The vast majority became marketers, lawyers, financiers, entrepreneurs, educators, or other professionals. No matter what career they went into nearly all give enormous credit to their college radio experience as having given them hands-on experience, at a young age, in how to run a real business. At Dartmouth, at least, the campus station was not simply a "radio school." It taught organization, leadership, speaking, communicating, persuading, reporting, selling, and, most of all, accountability, all in the context of a realistic business setting that no classroom could duplicate. Those interested in political and social issues learned about them first hand as part of the active news and public affairs department, which often gave them access to politicians and other decision makers that only a broadcast station could command. Those committed to public service used the wide coverage of the station as a platform for pro-social campaigns such as *Let's Help*, and more recent efforts to support food kitchens and flood relief. Those who wanted practical experience in technology found it working on the station's technical and IT infrastructure. The students were given considerable autonomy to run a relatively large, federally regulated commercial business. The result was valuable training for their future careers, no matter what those careers might be.

### A Medium Under Siege

College radio has always had an uneasy relationship with commercial broadcasters, who often belittled their young competitors as "just a bunch of kids" and sometimes coveted their frequencies. Despite the contributions college radio has made in programming and training, in recent years an alarming number of colleges have shut down their stations, sold off their licenses, and/or minimized them as student activities. AM and FM licenses are often valuable, and if a station is going through a period of suboptimal operation it may look like easy pickings for a cash-strapped administration. Even a campus-limited station that has no market value may be seen as a drain on the college's finances.

There have been a number of station closings in recent years. Instead of helping their stations transition into the new technological age, and allowing students and community to continue to benefit from the programming and training they offer, a few schools have sold them and cashed the check. Three widely publicized cases occurred in 2011: Vanderbilt University's WRVU was shut down abruptly (despite a reported audience of 30,000 listeners per week) and its license sold to a local NPR station for $3.4 million; Rice University's KTRU, a 50,000 watt FM station, was sold to a local NPR outlet for $9.5 million; and the University of San Francisco's KUSF was sold for $3.8 million to an NPR outlet that wanted its frequency. The KUSF situation was particularly bizarre. The signal was literally cut in the middle of a recording, the volunteer staff was escorted off the premises, and locks were changed on the doors. A group of staffers then approached a University official, with cameras rolling, to seek an explanation. He closed the door in their faces. The video can be seen on YouTube.[24]

In all three cases there were widespread student protests, and in Vanderbilt's case a lawsuit following the sale. However the FCC declined to stop the sales, and the stations were switched from their eclectic student-driven format to more generic formats run by professionals. The students were told they could "go online," where of course there were far fewer listeners and would be little real-world business experience.

Adelphi University's pioneering WBAU, mentioned earlier, was shut down abruptly in August 1995 and its license sold by a president who was later ousted for financial mismanagement.[25]

*The New York Times* reported in late 2011 that "in the last two years 14 stations have been sold or have pending sales..." Many went to NPR stations or to religious broadcasters.[26]

One rationale given is the false notion that "radio is dead." I've heard this often from people who don't pay particularly close attention to the media industry, or even to what's around them, and who think radio is on the way out. It isn't. Commercial measurement services such as Arbitron and Nielsen report that radio listening remains at or near all time high levels. Unlike newspaper publishing, this is not an industry suffering from structural decline. What has actually happened is that radio has shifted from being a foreground medium, which it was in the days of brassy, in-your-face Top 40 Radio, to a background one. It is part of our environment.[27]

Recently I helped field a $3.5 million study of media usage in which trained observers followed ordinary people around for a full day, recording every interaction they had with media of any type. Seventy-seven percent of adults were exposed to broadcast radio during a typical day, second only to live television, more than internet use, and far more than magazines (35 percent) or newspapers (27 percent). Only about 10 percent used "other audio" (CDs, tape, mp3 players). The average duration of radio listening was slightly under two hours per day. Interestingly, in a follow-up survey the next day slightly under 60 percent of the same respondents *thought* that they had listened to the radio on the measured day. Radio listening is so common we don't even notice that we're doing it.[28]

Radio, which can be thought of more broadly as curated audio entertainment and information, is exactly what is needed in certain circumstances, such as in the car, at work, in a store, or in the background at home. Nor is radio heard only over-the-air. Increasingly it's delivered by satellites and the Internet. What is changing is radio's demographics. Teens and young adults, including those of college age, now get their music from iPods and online services like Spotify and Pandora. Few students have radios in their dorm rooms.

So where are the listeners to college stations? A few are still on campus, listening on the ubiquitous laptops and mobile devices (most stations stream on the

Internet, either exclusively or to augment their terrestrial signal). If you want to have your school's away game on in the background while you're studying, it's easy enough to do—simply go online. But most of the listenership to non-campus limited stations is in the surrounding community. Since the Dartmouth station began AM broadcasting in 1958, the majority of its audience has always been off campus. The earliest listenership surveys document this, and the station's business model has always been based on delivering a community audience.

College FM or AM stations can be very viable businesses (which is why the licenses are valuable). Running one is an excellent learning experience for students. The stations' greatest challenge, as evidenced by the experience at Dartmouth in recent years, is attracting and holding staff, since the students themselves don't listen much anymore.

Campus-limited stations have a different problem, because their audience *is* largely confined to the campus. Online streaming has been advanced as a solution for this, and it may be, in the long run. *The New York Times* reported that 40 percent of the 350 average daily online listeners to WDVL, the student station of the State University of New York at Fredonia, in upstate New York, live in the New York City area, almost 300 miles away. Only four percent live on or near campus. Other clusters of logged-in listeners are located in Los Angeles and the Czech Republic.[29]

However at the moment online streaming is a poor substitute for terrestrial broadcasting. There is simply too much competition. There are thousands of stations online, which various aggregators conveniently organize by genre for easy access. There are lots of stations on the radio dial too, but the more successful ones advertise and brand themselves in order to create loyal listeners. Online stations, by and large, do not advertise. (The following case study describes the various ways in which the Dartmouth station and its d.j.'s have attempted to promote their shows.) As one newspaper story noted, students are "lucky if a streaming show draws 20 listeners." That is consistent with Dartmouth's streaming experience.[30]

### The Future of College Radio

Properly managed, college radio can offer a unique programming service, provide valuable management training, and in some cases even pay for itself. It is a part of our media landscape that should not be lost. Some are trying to make sure that does not happen.

Internet distribution holds the potential, at least, to broaden the reach of college radio and is slowly becoming more prevalent. The very first radio station ever streamed over the Internet was a college station, the University of North Carolina's WXYC-FM/89.3 in Chapel Hill, in 1994. The addition of college stations (including Dartmouth's) to Clear Channel's heavily marketed iHeart platform was a breakthrough in 2012. Many other aggregator sites that facilitate radio listening on a PC also include college stations. These include shoutcast.com, live365.com, tunein.com, streema.com, live-radio.net, onlineradiostations.com and even the built-in (on some computers) Windows Media Player and the widely used iTunes software. Most include "college radio" as a genre. Shoutcast reports more than a million streaming listeners per month to its top station in the college category (KCRW, an NPR affiliate), and several student-run college FM stations that utilize streaming add 10,000 to 100,000 listeners to their monthly audience this way.[31]

However record companies and other rights holders are constantly lobbying the government to let them charge stations steep fees to stream their material online, even if makes online distribution by smaller stations impossible. It is another example of how U.S. copyright laws have been used by large corporations to protect incumbents and squelch innovation. Because of this, the future of internet broadcasting for niche broadcasters like college stations is uncertain.

College stations have two principal trade associations. The oldest and largest is the Intercollegiate Broadcasting System, founded in 1940, while a more recent entry is College Broadcasters, Inc., founded in 1998. Both hold useful annual (or semi-annual) conferences at which student broadcasters learn about the field, and both also engage in negotiations and sometimes litigation with the government on behalf of their members (for example, on rates for streaming copyrighted material). Neither has been very successful in fighting legislation and FCC rulings that typically favor corporate broadcasters over smaller stations such as those on college campuses. Nor have they done much to build public support for college radio as a whole.[32]

In April 2011 CBI did call for a moment of silence on college stations across the country, to draw attention to the rash of sales of student stations by universities then taking place. If the object was to gain attention for the value these stations contribute to their communities and to education, it had little effect, and was little noted in the media.

A more successful effort was College Radio Day, launched in 2011 by assistant professor and station manager Dr. Rob Quicke of William Paterson University in Wayne, New Jersey. The idea quickly caught on and on October 11, 2011, 350 stations across the country aired pre-recorded spots, interviews and features celebrating the contributions of college stations everywhere. Thanks to careful advance planning, College Radio Day generated stories in *The New York Times, The Washington Post*, the New York *Daily News*, *USA Today* and many other mainstream newspapers and newscasts. An advisory board and funding was established, and College Radio Day 2012 was even bigger. It was planned to be an annual event, raising public awareness of the considerable contributions of college radio.[33] According to the project's web site,

> The aim of College Radio Day is to raise a greater, national awareness of the many college and high school radio stations that operate around the world by encouraging people who would not normally listen to college radio to do so on this day. It is hoped that those people who do tune in like what they hear and become regular listeners. The organizers of College Radio Day believe that college radio is one of the last remaining bastions of creative radio programming, free from the constrictions of having to be commercially viable, and a place where those involved in its programming believe passionately in its mission.[34]

Most alumni of college stations hold fond memories of their time at those stations, and credit them as an exceptional learning experience that served them well in their later careers. That was abundantly true of the Dartmouth station alumni I interviewed. However college radio alumni are usually familiar only with their own particular station (which was, of course, "the best"), and with the specific years they were there, nothing before or after. In this book we will look at a much broader canvass, basically the whole history of the medium from the 1920s to date, through the lens of one particular institution.

Admittedly, Dartmouth's WDCR and WFRD are somewhat unusual in that they were completely student-run commercial stations for much of their history. But they also passed through practically all of the stages of college broadcasting in the U.S., from the short-lived AM experiments of the 1920s to internet distribution in the 2000s. They have also been, at various times, under strict college control, completely student-run, or run by a combination of students and professionals. They serve as an example of how these various models can work, as well as what college broadcasting can achieve.

III

## Radio at Dartmouth College

Dartmouth College, one of the oldest and most elite colleges in the U.S., has a long history of rugged individualism.[35] For nearly fifty years its remote but beautiful campus in northern New England was home to a unique brand of college radio. In 1958 the College opted to obtain a full-power commercial license and turn it over to students to run, lock, stock and barrel. The students were responsible for everything, technical operation, programming, staffing, and all other functions, including advertising sales. They learned by doing, and everyone in the region could hear them do it. The College was of course in the background to help (or end the experiment) if they got into serious trouble, but the success or failure of the enterprise rested essentially in their inexperienced hands. It was an experiment in setting students loose and letting them learn by running a real business. The lure of real responsibility at such an early age proved to be not only a powerful motivator for the students to do well, but also an effective teacher.

Dartmouth's unusual approach to student broadcasting was not the result of a grand decision by the College to make broadcasting an educational objective, but rather in reaction to a proposal brought forth by a few ambitious students backed by some sympathetic faculty members. To this day there is no communications major or journalism school at Dartmouth. A cynical view might be that the trustees knew they needed to have a campus station (most schools had one), and this was a cheap way to do it by letting it pay for itself. A more charitable view would be that they recognized that, if managed correctly, it could be an excellent learning lab for the business leaders and communicators of tomorrow. The trustees' unwavering support for the experiment over the years suggests that they took both factors into account. Also critical to the growth of the station was the strong support of two Dartmouth presidents, John Sloan Dickey (1945-70) and John Kemeny (1970-81), both of whom supported student independence on many occasions.

There would be many challenges in operating a student-run commercial station, challenges that have no doubt deterred other institutions from even trying. They are raised as objections today by those who maintain that such an approach can't work. For one thing local commercial stations would no doubt scream bloody murder at the idea of a student station with non-paid staff and the backing of a large university competing for their advertising dollars. There was only one station in the market when Dartmouth proposed its AM station, but that station fought fiercely to scuttle the plan, predicting financial ruin for itself if the College was allowed to go forward. Second, there would be constant tension over what kind of station the College should have. Some faculty, secure in their tenure, wanted an educational station serving their idea of what the public should hear, not what it wanted to hear. A non-commercial station could conceivably do this, but one expected to support itself would have to provide programming people would actually listen to. This tension between noble intentions and commercial viability has been a constant over the 70-plus years of Dartmouth broadcasting.

Another issue was how a student-run commercial station would meet the unique and rigorous requirements of a federal license, which required among other things on-staff technical expertise and specified hours of operation. This was an important issue during the years when technical licensing exams were mandatory, and students were not available to keep the station on the air during intersession and summer breaks.

Then there has been the challenge of financial stability. Despite the free staff, student salespeople are less experienced than their commercial competitors and not in place long enough to build the personal relationships that are so important to local sales. This has perhaps been one of Dartmouth Broadcasting's greatest challenges over the years, one that has been met by varying approaches as we shall see.

The issue of staffing has also been an issue. By definition no one (well, hardly anyone) remained at the station for more than four years. Many were on staff for less than that. Experienced senior leaders were generally juniors or seniors, so there was constant turnover at the top. How could a student-run station expect to have any kind of continuity, and how in fact was competent top leadership even chosen if students were truly running the show?

So how did Dartmouth do it?

## Dealing with Commercial Competitors

The sole commercial station in the market when a Dartmouth AM radio station was proposed tried hard to kill the idea. However its predictions of financial ruin were vastly overblown. The market proved well able to support two stations, and in fact now has more than 20. The FCC dismissed this objection quickly, pointing out that competitive considerations played no part in licensing decisions, only service to the public. As in most such situations, competition benefited the public. A more serious consideration was whether the Labor Department would require that all station staffers be paid minimum wage, which would have bankrupted it considering how many staffers there were. However the department ruled that as long as the station was not intended to make a profit, did not put anybody out of business, and had less than five paid staff, it was exempt from this rule.

## Programming: Noble Intentions vs. Commercial Viability

The tension between noble programming intentions and commercial viability has played out in many ways. At first, in campus-limited days (1941-58) and in the early years of AM broadcasting (1958-1960s) the station had a segmented schedule, with disc jockey programs in the afternoon and late night (after study) hours, and educational fare during the evenings. The latter included such stalwarts as *Inter-*

*Fraternity Quiz*, discussion shows, and the long-running classical program *A Little Night Music* with genial Professor Robin Robinson. When an FM station was added the model that evolved was campus service on AM, and a purely commercial operation (to pay the bills) on FM. This did not entirely stop criticism—some people wanted both AM *and* FM to be programmed to their taste—but it served as a workable compromise for more than 30 years.

With the abandonment of broadcast radio by students in the 2000s it remains to be seen whether the bifurcated model can endure. The AM station now exists solely on the Internet.

### The Challenges of an FCC License

Unlike most businesses, a federally licensed radio station comes with fairly stringent technical and operational requirements. Could students be entrusted with that kind of legal responsibility?

In fact, this has not been much of problem. If anything, Dartmouth Broadcasting had more trouble with the FCC in the 1950s, when its supposedly campus-limited signal leaked out into the community, than it had after converting to full-power AM-FM. In the early years of AM at least one student staffer held the required First Class Radiotelephone Operator license, and there were always the helpful professors of Dartmouth's Thayer School of Engineering to fall back on for advice. The FCC waived the hours of operation requirement to allow the station to go silent in the summer and during intercession. By the late 1960s the waiver was no longer necessary as the station found ways to broadcast year-round.

The FCC's technical requirements gradually eased over the years (a First Class Licensee no longer needs to be on duty), and consulting engineers were retained when necessary for upgrades such as the studio reconstruction of the 1990s. In addition dedicated alumni engineers have generously pitched in to help the students.

### Financial Stability

The goal of financial stability and self-funding has been a vexing one throughout Dartmouth Broadcasting's history, although it appears that over the long run advertising revenue has offset most or all of the expense of running the stations. That clearly would not have been the case had it been a non-commercial station, or one with such limited range that ad revenues would have been minimal. Revenues have varied from year to year, and most major capital investments (e.g. the transition to AM, the launch of FM) have been borne by the College, often in the form of loans which the station repaid.

As with most businesses it has been an uneven ride. Some student sales staffs were very aggressive and successful, others (even though trained by their predecessors) were not. With the establishment of a College-dominated Board of Overseers in 1966 increasing pressure was placed on the station to meet its financial goals, and in 1975 a significant decision was made to hire a professional sales manager to carry out this function. This was not a panacea. Some of the hired salespeople weren't very good, and there was at first a good deal of turnover, but in the long run it does seem to have stabilized income. One downside of course was that it took an important component of the "all student run" experience out of student hands. There were attempts to include students in the selling process, working alongside and under the tutelage of the professionals, but this soon petered out. The goal of salespeople, and the basis of their own compensation, is to sell, not to teach.

Interestingly the introduction of a paid sales staff replacing students did not diminish student independence in other areas. Station managers I spoke with from the 1970s to the 1990s felt that they were very much in control, and ran the station on their own, with little interference from the College, despite the fact that ad sales was now a separate function. The main loss was in the training of salespeople, and in the important lesson for general management that they too were financially accountable, as they would someday be in the real world. As one former staffer who later became a successful businessman remarked, "Students learn to spend money, not make money."[36]

## Has the Station Achieved Its Programming and Training Goals?

Early on the College laid out two formal goals for its station, first to provide a worthwhile programming service, and second to provide a practical training ground for students interested in broadcasting.

There have been striking programming accomplishments over the years, especially in the area of news coverage. The crowning achievements were probably the election night spectaculars staged in presidential and midterm election years from 1956 to the 1990s. A large auditorium on campus was wired by student engineers as "election central" and scores of staffers participated in the carefully planned multi-desk coverage, with reports called in by students stationed at polling stations and campaign headquarters across the state. The quadrennial New Hampshire first-in-the-nation presidential primary lent itself to this. The eyes of the nation were on New Hampshire and the students' campaign interviews and extensive primary night coverage were heard far and wide. At its peak in 1976 and 1980, The Dartmouth Election Network was syndicated to nearly thirty stations and internationally via the Voice of America, and heard by as many as 10 million listeners on primary night. Not only did this provide excellent training for station members (as reporters and future citizens), it was a public relations bonanza for the College.

Industrious station newsmen scored many coups over the years. In some years press credentials were obtained and student reporters sent to the national political conventions; there were remotes from Washington, D.C., covering the anti-war demonstrations in 1969 and 1970. Candidates, public officials and regular citizens were almost always willing to speak with an articulate college student with a microphone in hand, and the auspices of a broadcast station usually ensured access to newsmakers. In 1992 candidate Bill Clinton bounded up the steps to the third-floor studios uninvited, and talked his way on to the air.

Another highlight of Dartmouth Broadcasting's programming history has been its public service campaigns, ranging from the months-long *Let's Help* campaigns of the late 1960s and early '70s to the year-end 99-hour marathons of the 1980s and 1990s, all of which raised money for local charities. Fundraising campaigns have continued under the current professional manager, Heath Cole.

The station encouraged scripted and unscripted series when motivated students could be found to take advantage of a broadcast platform to express their creativity. There were many dramatic productions in the 1940s and '50s, when the station was closely allied with The Dartmouth Players. Later notable original series have included *The Hunky Dorey Hour* (comedy, 1950s), *The Ed and Charley Show* (comedy, 1960s), *Tales for the Midnight Hour* (horror anthology, 1960s), *Dartmouth Inquiry* (great issues, moderated by future Secretary of Labor Robert Reich, 1967), *Midnight Mulch* (comedy, 1970s), *Pooh Corner* (an award-winning children's show, 1970s), *The One AM Report* (improvisation, 1970s), *Dartmouth Dialectic* (issues, 1995), and *The Steve and Doug Show* (comedy, 1997), among many others.

There is no doubt that Dartmouth Broadcasting achieved its goal of providing a training ground for students. A few station leaders went directly into broadcasting and became highly successful, whether as newscasters, sportscasters, or station owners. These include James Rosenfield '52, president of the CBS Television Network, Reese Schonfeld '53, president of CNN, Herb Solow '53, a major TV production executive (*Star Trek, Mission Impossible*), NBC newsman Robert Hager '60, BBC personality Paul Gambaccini '70, radio station group owners Herb McCord '64, Scott McQueen '68 and Jeff Shapiro '82, and ESPN sportscaster Brett Haber '91, to name a few.

No matter what field alumni went into, nearly all that I spoke to credited Dartmouth Broadcasting as an important part of their education. Judging by the testimony of its alumni, at least, Dartmouth's experiment in using a broadcast station as a training ground has been enormously successful.

### Staffing Challenges

Although Dartmouth's unusual term scheduling ("the D-Plan"), with its irregular student schedules, was instituted in 1972, the issue of station staffing—i.e., finding dedicated students to run the station on an ongoing basis—did not become a serious issue until the 2000s.[37] In the 1980s and '90s a custom of acting or temporary news directors, program directors and even general managers was adopted to allow replacements to fill in during terms when the regular occupant of the position was away. Some of the absent managers kept in touch with their replacements, but even when they didn't things continued to run smoothly, most of the time.

More serious blows during the last decade have been a decline in the glamour of radio broadcasting among students, and a decision by the College to encourage students to engage in more extra curricular activities and spend less time with each. Traditionally Dartmouth Broadcasting was run by a relatively small core of dedicated students (sometimes *too* dedicated), surrounded by a larger number of less intensely involved staffers. This is the structure in most volunteer organizations. There are still strong and dedicated general managers, but by the 2000s fewer students could be found who were willing to put in the time to become part of that dedicated core.

There is another factor that I believe has created the staffing crisis at Dartmouth radio. It is little recognized when looking at the station at a point in time, but more apparent when looking at its whole history. That is the serious erosion of student control during the 2000s. Hiring a professional sales manager who worked at the station had not seriously impacted the culture of student independence. However in 2001 the College decided, unilaterally, to move the entire sales operation off premises and contract it to a competitor, Jeff Shapiro, who operated several stations in the market. There was supposed to be an educational component to the arrangement, with students offered seminars and training by Shapiro's operation, but like most such arrangements that never really worked out.

In addition sales and fulfillment were unsatisfactory, so in 2006 Shapiro terminated the arrangement and the overseers decided to return to an in-house professional sales staff. But this time they designated a professional day-to-day operations manager, who also began to fill air shifts. Later in 2006, to insure a reliable air product, a professional announcer was hired to handle the important morning shift and professionals were hired to lead the station's signature sports coverage as well. Perhaps this was all necessary, as students were not satisfactorily filling those roles, but it became obvious that students were not in control in the way they had been in the 1990s. It was also quite clear who was making major decisions regarding the station. The administration's "light touch" of earlier decades had given way to much firmer control. That made it all the more difficult to attract student hard workers who had historically been drawn by the lure of real responsibility.

Finally, alumni have traditionally not been involved in station operation to nearly the degree they are on other campuses. At Brown, Harvard, Princeton, and Yale the student stations are owned by a separate non-profit corporation run by students and alumni. At Dartmouth, the Board of Overseers, established in 1966 as an advisory body, did not include a significant number of alumni until the 1990s. In the late 2000s a small group of alumni who were experienced engineers volunteered to help the station deal with some difficult technical challenges, but once those problems were solved the group disbanded. Today it is clearly the college administration that calls the shots. Alumni are given little opportunity to become seriously involved in the operation of the stations and are rarely solicited for support.[38]

### Can Other Institutions Learn from Dartmouth's Experience?

Every situation is unique, but that cliché can of course be used either as a starting point for fresh thinking or as an excuse to maintain the status quo. The students and administrators who allowed this experiment to begin in the 1940s and flourish in later years did not do so by clinging to the safety of what everyone else was doing. The history of the Dartmouth experiment would seem to indicate that while it was not necessarily easy, it did indeed prove possible to:

1. Give students real, independent responsibility to run a full power broadcast station;
2. Reap clear benefits in terms of training future leaders and thinkers; and,
3. Offer a differentiated programming service to the community. In today's world of increasingly homogenized, packaged, corporate-controlled radio programming, even a modest amount of creativity on the airwaves should be encouraged.

### The Past and the Future

Although WFRD is now run largely by a small professional staff with strong oversight by the administration, students still play a very important role in the station. The general manager and other Directorate member are still students. The Board of Overseers is a large (12 members or more), diverse group, and very dedicated to working on behalf of the station. Its members today include College administrators, faculty, and alumni who have gone on to broadcasting careers. The latter have been extraordinarily willing to "give back" by helping the current student management in any way they can, when asked, including holding think tanks on the future of the station and seminars on the practical matters of station operation.

Those now making decisions for Dartmouth Broadcasting will need all the wisdom they can muster to guide it through this new era. Hopefully, as they do so, the station will not lose the unique educational value it has provided to so many graduates during the past 70 years.

# Chapter 1

# The Twenties

Radio during the first two decades of the 20th century was an experimental science, with its potential for mass entertainment scarcely dreamed of. Wireless telephony was adopted early and enthusiastically by hobbyists, however, and hundreds of amateur transmitters were in use by the end of World War I. Dartmouth "hams" had been active since before the war. A code receiver was installed in 1908, a transmitter in 1914, and by 1917 operators were numerous enough to organize an amateur radio club, the predecessor of today's W1ET. Their organization grew fast, and in the spring of 1923 money was obtained from the College to purchase new, powerful equipment and construct twin antenna towers atop Wilder Hall.[1]

Enthusiastic club members had the 90 foot steel towers up in 10 days flat, during early May 1923 (for their efforts they received athletic credit). A new 1000-watt transmitter was also installed, making Dartmouth's "1YB" one of the most powerful amateur ham radio stations in the country. It was also one of the most active. Sending messages in code on the 60-meter short wave length, Dartmouth operators reached literally all four corners of the globe. During 1923 and 1924 contact was made with such distant points as Norway, England, Mexico, New Zealand, the polar ice cap (to the MacMillan Expedition heading for the North Pole), and even "an Italian ship anchored in the harbor of Barcelona, Spain."[2] As a club service, students at large were offered the chance to send messages to their homes, "anywhere in the East."

With such success in the ham field, club members soon began to lay plans for another project – to use their versatile equipment to transmit broadcasts of games and other Dartmouth events to home listeners throughout New England, on the standard broadcast band.

They could take as an example the commercial broadcasting stations which were springing up around the East during the early 1920's. Beginning with Pittsburgh's KDKA in 1920, Westinghouse and other electronics companies had set up radio stations in most major cities, and even in the wilds of Hanover there were fascinated listeners. An expensive radio receiver, donated by an alumnus, had been installed in the living room of College Hall, in the fall of 1922. It was operated nightly by radio club members or physics professors for the entertainment of those who came to hear the music and talks emanating from Boston, New York, Pittsburgh, Chicago and other metropolitan centers.

### Official Hesitation...

The radio club's plan was laid before President Ernest Martin Hopkins in the fall of 1924, by the club advisor, Professor Gordon Hull. Hopkins agreed that such broadcasts would be good publicity for Dartmouth and a service to alumni, but he was extremely wary of entrusting them to students. "I think it is pretty definitely the impression of the trustees," he wrote in early October, "that no undergraduate organization is likely permanently to be responsible enough to accept the responsibility for doing broadcasting and doing it well … Even (if) an organization is found, there will always be some irresponsible individual who will crave the opportunity of getting himself and his voice on to the air, and who, at the same time, will sufficiently lack either knowledge of grammar of knowledge of the fitness of things, so that the broadcasting will become a liability to the College at a point where it cannot well accept a liability."[3]

President Hopkins had another objection too. He had been tuning in on broadcasts from St. Lawrence University and Rensselaer, and looking into other colleges' radio activity, he said, and had come to the conclusion that so far "broadcasting had been largely a monopoly of the less good and less well known colleges of the country, and that colleges of the class in which we believe we belong have taken it up very little …"

He would not forbid student-run broadcasting, but he would attach to it strict conditions: (1) permission was tentative, and might be withdrawn at any time; (2) the experiment must have qualified and responsible men in charge; (3) each broadcast must be approved in advance by a faculty committee representing all departmental interests. In general, he wanted assurance that "the station might not become a nuisance … that whatever went out should always be creditable to the College … and that we should always have a control which precluded either irresponsible or undesirable use of the apparatus." Only then would he be "willing to see this matter developed as an experiment."

### WFBK is Founded

With this hesitant go-ahead the radio club applied to the Commerce Department for a Class A, Limited Commercial license. These were easy enough to get in 1924, and on October 18 the permit was issued, providing the following:

> 1. The station would operate on the 256-meter wave length (1170 KHz on modern radio dials) and have the call letters WFBK, which stood for nothing in particular.
> 2. It could use 100 watts of power, and have a "normal day range, in nautical miles: 50."
> 3. "This station is licensed for broadcasting entertainment and like matter …" with no limit on its hours of operation.[4]

On October 29, 1924, an inconspicuous note in *The Dartmouth* announced that the transmitter was in readiness for the first AM broadcast, the Dartmouth-Brown football game at Memorial Field on Saturday, November 1.

WFBK's start was apparently most auspicious. Brown lost, and the coverage went without a hitch. Horizons widened fast, as horizons commonly do, and soon the program committee of three professors and one graduate student was plotting a schedule of orderly expansion for the students' "broad-casting" station. Despite the liberal provisions of the license, there was no thought of regular programming; few townspeople or students had crystal sets, which were, in fact, banned in dormitories. There would be no Paul Whiteman records or coverage of the 1924 presidential elections on WFBK. Nevertheless, periodic broadcasts of Dartmouth events could reach many alumni and others in the New England area. There were, in 1924, few other AM stations to provide interference, and it was apparently possible to get quite a distance with 100 watts, especially at night and with the radio club's excellent equipment. As for future expansion, the radio club was small but enthusiastic, and given time its station could grow to great things.

"WFBK Station in Wilder Hall Will Send Games and Music Through the Air" reported *The Dartmouth* in mid-December.

> "WFBK broadcasting! The next number on the program will be 'Men of Dartmouth' by the Glee Club." If this announcement should reach you over your radio some night, don't be startled. It will only mean that the College broadcasting station situated in Wilder Laboratory is in tip-top working order and has commenced a program of entertainment for radio fans of New England and the immediate vicinity.[5]

Of course WFBK was not without its birth pains. Equipment troubles forced the club to forgo any broadcasts in December or January. *The Dartmouth* generally took little notice of the venture, and its brief editorial was something less than bubbling over with enthusiasm: "With the College already well known to certain portions of the public through its football team and Outing Club, it is possible that the operations of WFBK will acquaint still larger circles with Dartmouth,"[6] wrote the good, grey "D". Also, the 1170 KHz wave length was unfortunately the same as that of a station owned by a Boston church. The latter had only religion in mind, however, and WFBK was merely required to stay off the air Friday nights and Sundays, when the Tremont Temple Church held its services.

Through the winter and spring of 1925 WFBK was quite active, periodically broadcasting events of interest for those few Hanoverites with radios and to alumni as far away as Pennsylvania and New York – at least to those with sensitive receivers. The efforts of radio club President Robert Weinig '25 and one Frank Appleton, together with the purchase of new microphones and other equipment, greatly improved the station's capabilities. Games, chapel services, talks, recitals, and debates were all carried, with College telephone lines used to bring the sound to the transmitter atop Wilder. It does not appear that any studios were built, for nearly all broadcasts were "remotes." The most ambitious of these was probably the broadcast of the Winter Carnival play *Atmosphere*, in early February, 1925. "Difficulties were encountered during the first scene," noted *The Dartmouth* in passing, "but a new microphone was installed during the intermission, which remedied most of the trouble. The announcements were made by R.C. Saunders '26."[7]

### The Fall of 1925: Great Things to Come?

When radio club members returned in the fall of 1925, they had good reason to expect great things. WFBK, operating mostly with regular club equipment, had put on a remarkably successful series of broadcasts during 1924-25, for which alumni and others had warm praise. Even President Hopkins seemed pleased. The station had thus far been a part-time experiment, but it had a full-power AM license with few restrictions, wide coverage and tremendous potential. The next step would be to renew the license (as had to be done every three months) and begin, perhaps, a more regular program schedule.

Sure enough, on September 28, 1925, a brief note in *The Dartmouth* said that the Class A standard broadcast license had been renewed, this time with the call letters WDCH, which the Commerce Department had suggested as more logical, standing for Dartmouth College, Hanover.

Here, the story really gets interesting. For five days the paper carried no mention of the activities in Wilder. Then, on October 3, an article on the regular meeting of the radio club appeared. Officers had been elected, heelers (trainees) solicited. The last paragraph was somewhat more cryptic: "In reply to numerous inquiries … (the club) wishes to make the following statement: At the present time Dartmouth College has no broadcasting transmitter. It is hoped that in the near future a transmitter will be installed. Until such time, nothing in the way of broadcasting will be attempted. However …" the club would be glad to help you juice up your radio so you could get KDKA or WJZ again.

## A Wonderful Legend

What happened to WDCH? If anything actually had gone wrong with the transmitter – anything technical – it was soon fixed, for within a few weeks the club was again offering to send short wave messages to mom and dad, and tapping out conversations with boats in Barcelona Bay. But not a single mention of student radio broadcasting, other than amateur code transmissions, was to grace the musty pages of *The Dartmouth* for the next 15 years.

More likely the answer was simply unprintable. At the debut of the Dartmouth Broadcasting System in the early 1940s, one alumnus recalled that Dartmouth had tried all this once before. WDCH had been holding its opening ceremonies, he said, and the time had come for President Hopkins' dedicatory remarks. The introduction was made, and the student engineer threw the switch, but unfortunately, the wrong way. Instead of Hopkins the astonished audience got a virulent "Shut that God damn door!" – from someone in the rooftop Wilder control room. Radio at Dartmouth thereupon died a sudden and lasting death.[8]

Other variations have had President Hopkins sitting at home, perhaps with the "Archbishop of New Hampshire," admiring the students' latest activity, when the fatal words came booming forth. Recollections of just what those words were range from the preceding to the limits, but all are epithets in the finest Dartmouth tradition.

Though this makes a wonderful legend, WDCH's demise was perhaps less spectacular in fact. No notices of coming broadcasts had been printed in *The Dartmouth*, although that publication had never been inclined to give much space to the upstarts in Wilder. WDCH may well have failed to rally from an initial setback not because of permanent proscription, but simply because of declining student interest and technical problems. Years later Professor Hull wrote, somewhat vaguely, that "the College telephone system used to bring … broadcasts to the transmitter was not built to accommodate accurate and undisturbed transmission of music. Further, capable personnel for operating the station were limited …" He summed up, "the experiment proved that though members of the radio club might be able to make a transmitting set capable of broadcasting voices and music, the broadcasting of reasonably ambitious programs called for time, energy and technical skill not generally available in a small group of undergraduates ..."[9]

Another account, written in 1936, said that the station "was in operation here in Hanover a number of years ago, but purely as a personal enterprise. Aside from one unfortunate incident which occurred on an untimely occasion, the station proved popular despite the small number of receivers then in operation. However, when the undergraduate who owned the equipment left the College, the station was naturally closed down."[10]

Whatever it was that may have singed the good president's ears in October 1925, and whatever else made WDCH's death so permanent, Hopkins was to hear nothing more of campus radio for a good long time to come. Not, in fact, until the late 1930s.

# Chapter 2

# 1941-1943: The Dartmouth Broadcasting System Is Born

In the early and mid-1920s, at the time of the community radio set in College Hall and the ill-starred Radio Club venture, broadcasting was very much a novelty. Published mentions of WFBK were usually incidental, and invariably took a "here's an interesting curiosity" approach. By the early 1930s, however, radio had become the most pervasive mass medium ever known, even to the point of penetrating the remote Hanover Plain. *The Dartmouth* printed regular program listings for stations that could be heard in Hanover at night, including WGY, WABC, WJZ, and WEAF, as well as NBC and CBS. You could choose from Wayne King, Kate Smith, *Amos 'n' Andy*, "Ben Bernie, the Old Maestro," Ed Wynn, and Abe Lyman, but according to one of the more persistent ads your best bet was "*Kellogg's College Prom*, starring Ruth Etting and the Red Nichols Orchestra: every Friday night on the WJZ Network, NBC."

Radios were first permitted in dormitory rooms – officially – in the fall of 1933. College authorities realized that they were taking a venturesome step, and warned that there would be periodic inspections and a $5 fee for all owners ("for the additional demands on the voltage which the radios will exact"). Sets could not be used after midnight, and dormitories could impose additional "quiet hours" during exams. Undeterred by such restrictions, Dartmouth men began stringing antenna wire in all convenient locations.

They were soon able to pick up a relatively local station, WNBX in Springfield, Vermont; but around 1940 this moved to Keene, New Hampshire, and renamed itself WKNE.[1] In 1936 Dick Dorrance '36 wrote a detailed ten-page proposal for a station to be run by *The Dartmouth*. He proposed a 25-watt AM station operating during the daytime hours, with The "D" selling its advertising time, and claimed that this would cover a 20 to 30 mile area around Hanover, and reach an estimated 5,000 people with radios. The programming, he said, would represent the very best of Dartmouth, confidently asserting that "good program material around Hanover appears to be superabundant." The administration, still smarting from the debacle of the 1920s, appears to have given the proposal little consideration.[2]

There were also occasional other efforts close to home. "WHD," an intra-dormitory station run for the residents of Russell Sage Hall by Hugh Dryfoos '40 during his senior year, made the pages of *Life* magazine in some highly posed pictures just chock-a-block full of collegiate atmosphere.[3] Another, more colorful effort in 1940 was the well-publicized "Illegal Broadcasting Company," which had curious listeners as much as 10 miles away in Vermont until some humorless professor called in the Federal Communications Commission. IBC folded rather abruptly one autumn afternoon when its staff skipped out the back door of its Lebanon Street "studios," just before the feds entered the front.

## Why Not a Dartmouth Station?

In the fall of 1939 a memo from English Professor Stearns Morse arrived on the desk of President Hopkins. It noted that there was a good deal of student interest in radio of late, and suggested that the administration might do well to look into the matter. Although Hopkins was reportedly still somewhat chary of student broadcasting, he agreed, and in January of 1940 appointed a three-man committee to see just how deep student interest ran. Morse would be chairman, with Professor Russell Larmon (who had been on WFBK's program board 15 years earlier) and College Secretary Sidney Hayward as members.

The committee did not have to look far to document "undergraduate interest in broadcasting." Students in the Speech Department, it seemed, had been presenting programs on WNBX for several years. Even as the committee was investigating, WHD and IBC lived their short lives, while an open meeting held in the fall of 1940 by Council on Student Organizations (COSO) Director Robert Lang and newly arrived speech instructor Almon Ives aroused considerable interest. The committee obtained figures: there were 400 students (of about 2,350) with radios, despite a still-standing $2 annual fee; and a poll showed 90 percent of the student body in favor of a campus station.

Most convincing of all were two recent developments. The institution of radio at other elite colleges, beginning with Brown (1937) then spreading to Williams, Swarthmore, Cornell, Princeton, Columbia and most recently Harvard (November, 1940) left little doubt that campus broadcasting was a coming thing. Second, and most important for the success of a Dartmouth station, Richard Krolik '41 and a small group of followers were by the fall of 1940 already studying other stations and working on a proposed plan of operations.

By the end of 1940 Professor Morse and his committee had submitted such a glowing report (albeit one that urged strict control) that President Hopkins could hardly say no. In February 1941 the three-man survey committee was transformed into the Dartmouth Radio Council, adding Lang from COSO, William Mitchel '42 (one of Krolik's co-workers ), radio executive Douglas Storer '21, and subsequently Almon Ives. This brought the Council's membership to seven, three from the faculty, two from the administration and one each from the alumni and the student body. These men were to supervise all radio activities at Dartmouth.

## A Plan for "DBS"

There was little doubt in early 1941 that Dartmouth would get a radio station, but there was considerable controversy over how it would be done. Onetime *Dartmouth* staffer Krolik sought the sponsorship of the newspaper for his project. Six undergraduate radio stations were already owned or operated by college dailies, and besides, he argued at a memorable late-night session with the "*D's*" Directorate, wouldn't it be convenient to own your competitor? *The Dartmouth* agreed wholeheartedly, and under its aegis the first proposal was made to the Radio Council. Not only could it provide the capital outlay and established selling organization to support the station, said the "*D*," but "unless *The Dartmouth* owns such a competing medium, the competing medium will be able to destroy it."[4]

27

Late in February COSO submitted a report of its own, strongly urging that the station not be commercial, not be owned by *The Dartmouth*, and not be under the Radio Council. COSO saw a commercial station as a "tremendous threat" to other non-athletic groups, as well as a poor way to obtain high quality educational programming. Besides, Main Street merchants would never support it – "advertising budgets … are as high as they can go."[5] The report said COSO should operate the station, in an arrangement similar to that of The Dartmouth Players. After some deliberation the Radio Council rejected both a *Dartmouth*-run commercial set-up, and a COSO-run educational one. The student promoters cast about for a way to finance an independent organization.

Complicating their plans were a number of administrative hurdles, including a faculty committee which stood ready to veto campus radio on the grounds that it might create a riot danger in the dormitories. But the College was willing to be persuaded, and after two months of proposals, table-banging and editorial support from *The Dartmouth* (which, despite its own rejection, proclaimed "We're for radio!") Dick Krolik and his followers finally reached their goal. On May 8, 1941, the Radio Council announced its final acceptance of the promoters' new plan for an independently organized, student-run radio station, to be assisted by *The Dartmouth* and under the watchful eye of the council. The College would loan $1,500 to cover the first year's expenses: $550 for wiring the dormitories, $550 for equipment, $250 for soundproofing the studios, and the other $150 for operating expenses. The promoters' own proposal, dated April 10, 1941, and signed by Krolik and four others,[6] would serve as the model for the first "license of operation." It would be the first campus station in the country founded with the official backing of its college administration. Krolik's original designation of WDAR was dropped – the station would be called DBS, the Dartmouth Broadcasting System.

### Goals

DBS was launched with considerable caution, much of it stemming from the Radio Council's fear that the station might become *too* commercially oriented. The original license of operation ran for only one year, and was to be renewed annually thereafter. It outlined in detail the station's organizational and financial arrangements, and provided a clear-cut set of goals. In general, the station was to further the educational purposes which "normally characterize a college of Dartmouth's standing in the educational world." Specifically, DBS would serve three ends:

> 1. To provide a genuine program service to its listeners, "programs more in keeping with the educational objectives of this College and with the interests of the college student than those which are now being produced for general reception by the American radio industry."
> 2. To give undergraduates practical experience in the business of broadcasting.

These two goals have remained Dartmouth radio's *raison d'etre* ever since. The exact wording of the first, in fact, was carried down in subsequent DBS-WDBS-WDCR licenses and constitutions, with the single, significant exception that with the advent of AM, "college student" became "college community."

The third, interestingly enough, disappeared, even though Bill Mitchel – the first station manager and the man who "built" DBS – felt it was the most important of all. In the station's scrapbook, beside an ad which announced this goal, he left the following note to his successors: "This advertisement, which appeared in *The Dartmouth* on June 20, 1941, was DBS's first statement to the College of its primary goal ... It is my sincerest hope that DBS will strive to realize that goal as long as it broadcasts to Dartmouth." It was:

> 3. To better integrate the diverse groups within the College and help make the campus a more cohesive unit; to keep Dartmouth, in Daniel Webster's words, truly "a small college."

### Organization and Finances

Now that all of the seals were finally affixed, the real work could begin. A member of the Columbia station had written, "To begin with, setting up a radio station is no easy matter. One cannot just decide that Old Siwash could use a good radio station on campus, get a couple of fellows together, and have a radio station, just like that."[7] At least Dick Krolik and his friends would not be guilty of that; their organization was carefully designed indeed.

The sage from Columbia had gone on to recommend that the station be rather tightly controlled, especially at the beginning. "To be perfectly frank," he wrote, "you must be careful that your station doesn't walk out from under you ..." General supervision of DBS was to be in the faculty-run Radio Council; beneath the council was a three-man Executive Committee, composed of the station manager, the junior business manager of *The Dartmouth*, and a representative of the council; beneath this was the station manager, the man in day to day control of the station's operations, with all other "directors" subordinate to him. Originally envisioned as a committee of four or five, the early "Directorate" in practice averaged eight to twelve, including the directors of engineering, business, commercials, special events, production, music, sports, etc. No one would receive any pay (unlike the "*D*") and members would be chosen for positions by the station manager, on a competitive basis. Competence, as determined by those already in power, was to be the principal requirement for office, a premise which has served Dartmouth radio well ever since.

Although *The Dartmouth* was denied the opportunity to own DBS, its ties would be close. It was formally agreed that the newspaper would share its well-established news gathering facilities and help sell local advertising for the new operation, at least for the present. This was not wholly an act of charity on the paper's part, since its salesmen would receive commissions for selling radio accounts. The cost of the the "*D's*" Associated Press news machine would be split between the two organizations (this $24 per week item loomed so large in DBS's slender budget that it was agreed to only on the condition that three of the four daily newscasts could be sold to meet the bill).

An even stronger link between Dartmouth's radio station and newspaper in the early days was the similarity of personnel. DBS's first news director and business manager concurrently held similar positions on the paper, while most other station executives and backers (including Krolik and Mitchel) were expatriates from *The*

*Dartmouth*. Such bonds with a going organization were vital, for the College expected DBS to be a sound business venture. Once operations were underway, advertising was to pay not only for current expenses but rental of college facilities and retirement of the original $1,500 loan. Any additional "profits" would be plowed back into station improvements or returned to the College. In late May 1941 Krolik and his followers took the first step toward populating this paper hierarchy by appointing Bill Mitchel to be the first station manager, with hard-working Steve Flynn '44 as his acting technical director. A full Directorate would be chosen by Mitchel in the fall.

Dick Krolik graduated in June of 1941, without ever hearing the station he had worked so long to make possible. He was not to hear it, in fact, until he returned to Hanover 20 years later to address the Third Anniversary Banquet of WDCR-AM. On that night he told his delighted audience, "actually, today was the first time I had heard a sound from this 'brainchild' after 20 years, and it was pretty impressive ... I heard a *magnificent* rock 'n' roll record ..."

### 1941-1942: Building a Radio Station

To Mitchel fell the task of actually building DBS. Krolik's original studies of other campus stations had been hampered by the loss of his technical assistant, Tom Jardine '41, but during the spring of 1941 Mitchel and Flynn, with aid from Thayer School of Engineering, other college stations, and various other quarters, had developed a workable plan, based on that used by Cornell. It would be "controlled wire broadcasting." The signal would be carried from the studios in Robinson Hall over telephone wires to small oscillators, or transmitters, in each of 16 dormitories. These 0.8-watt midget units were also known as phonograph oscillators, because a modified version was sold to people who wanted to "broadcast" from their phonographs on one side of the room to their radios on the other. Each one would broadcast the signal for a radius of about 200 feet, thus covering all dormitories on campus, but no more, and thereby exempting the station from FCC jurisdiction.

In June the long-awaited equipment began to arrive from RCA: three microphones (the best, a Junior Velocity, was still in use at WDCR in the 1960s), a four-input control board, two large turntables and several of the DeLuxe Mystery Transmitters, the latter costing precisely $7.10 each. Approaching final exams notwithstanding, Flynn and his helpers immediately set to work installing these and in mid-June conducted several brief test broadcasts to selected dormitories. They also hosted O.B. Hanson, a helpful NBC engineer who visited Hanover to design DBS' studio acoustics. Hanson's claim to fame was that he was the engineer who gave the signal to put NBC on the air in 1926.

As the spring semester ended there was still much to be done in the way of technical work, advertising arrangements, and program scheduling. Consequently the College agreed to hire Mitchel for the summer, to work exclusively on the station, while Flynn and others pitched in by staying in Hanover through June, carrying on voluminous correspondence during the summer, and returning early in September. Even as Buildings and Grounds workmen hammered and sawed the third floor of Robinson Hall into a reasonable facsimile of a radio station during that summer of 1941, DBS-men toured WNEW in New York to pick up useful production pointers. In a spring poll, students had indicated WNEW was the station DBS ought most to emulate.[8]

## A Castle-in-Spain Becomes a Reality

September found DBS enthusiasts laboring mightily to complete the final technical arrangements and get their station on the air. "DBS, Long a Castle-In-Spain, Goes Into Action" admired *The Dartmouth*, then "Dream Becomes Reality – DBS Approaches Initial Broadcast." The big day – though not the official launch – would be Monday, September 29, 1941, when a week of broadcasting called DBS Testing would begin. On each day DBS planned to send three hours of programming (5:00-6:00 p.m. and 9:00-11:00 p.m.) to a different group of dormitories to test the system and obtain student reaction to the programming.

What College Hall, Fayerweather, Richardson, New Hampshire and Topliff heard on that first night in 1941 was vividly reported in the next morning's *Dartmouth.*

> DBS went through its trial by fire yesterday ... and came through it superbly – came through it as it should, as a well-functioning, snappy, crisp, lively radio station. Sharing an all-day hitch at the control switches of the monitor "panel," three hours of which were supervising a flickering decibel-meter through hellish minutes of actual broadcasting were Stephen Flynn '44, pasty-faced but completely calm and happy at the end of a long day, and Joseph Hirschberg '43, dripping, wild-eyed ...
>
> The day was full of rare and wonderful happenings. Most miraculous of all, perhaps, was the (first) small voice shuttling out unostentatiously, exactly at 5 in the afternoon, like this, no more, no less, "Five pee em by the studio clock, and time for DBS to take to the air for a series of test broadcasts..." Other miracles: the fill-in job on DBS's first program of all time, the 5:00 p.m. news shots, which was comprised yesterday of a reading of portions of a letter from soldier-in-England Charles G. Bolte '41; William R. Davies '44 handling *Jive at Five*, a program of jazz, smoothly and professionally, coming in exactly on the station break as Flynn tossed over one mixer button and slowly twisted another to the right ... Of all the big and little miracles, nicest was the reaction of Hanover telephone operators who called in frequently just to say, "You're doing fine, boys, we can hear you coming in over our earphones." In the one empty second of the day, chief technician Flynn explained this, but we didn't quite get it.
>
> The end of a summer's effort and the beginning of a year's came for William J. Mitchel '42, station director, when at 11:30 he packed the last announcer, technician and kibitzer out of 51 Robinson and sank down to light his 50th cigarette in the last 12 hours ... There are problems up there in 51 Robinson, just like every cynic said there would be. But to the devilish little chap who with a gleam in his eye declared yesterday morning, "Yuh can't t'row voices t'ru de air," we say, stuff it boy, DBS is hot.[9]

The rest of DBS Testing week was no less successful. On Wednesday, Thursday and Friday afternoons the station went on at 1:15 to broadcast running descriptions of the World Series games between the New York Yankees and the Brooklyn Dodgers, permission having been secured through the good offices of network executive Jerry Danzig '34, an alumnus who proved most helpful to the station during its early years. Alex "Babe" Fanelli '42 copied down the information as it came in, and relayed it to Jerry Tallmer '42 (editor of *The Dartmouth*) who read it on the air. It was a thrilling "subway series" (two New York teams), highlighted by Dodger Mickey Owen's fumble in the ninth inning of game four which set the Yankees up to win the series in game five.[10]

Wednesday night brought the premiere of an original radio play, *Dedicatory Remarks*, written by Players' Technical Director Henry Williams. So smooth was this presentation that *The Dartmouth* was moved to gush that "Dartmouth Broadcasting System and the Players crashed the kilocycles last night with a near-professional performance ... technical handling amazing ... strongly reminiscent of a fine Columbia (network) Workshop show ..."[11]

So well received were the first five days of DBS Testing, in fact, that the delighted Directorate decided to stay on the same schedule for another week, October 6-10. Then for two weeks Dartmouth radio was silent as Flynn and his engineers worked to complete the installation of those DeLuxe Mystery Transmitters, and allow simultaneous broadcasting to the entire campus.

### "DBS Salutes the Campus"

The official christening of DBS came on Monday, October 27, 1941, four weeks after DBS Testing had begun its short but successful run and a trifle more than 16 years after WDCH had lived its even briefer career. Programming actually started with an hour of afternoon disc jockey shows, but all ears (at least those historic-first minded) were tuned in at nine that night. Then "nine pee em by the General Electric clock" it was, and M.C. Vic Schneider '41 opened an introductory broadcast entitled, auspiciously enough, *DBS Salutes the Campus*.

It was an ambitious show. For three-quarters of an hour a wide variety of Hanover talent regaled an audience of 200 in the Little Theatre (a small auditorium which until 1963 occupied the western wing of Robinson Hall), as well as hundreds of dorm-dwellers, with music and sketches. There were talks and interviews with Coach McLaughry, Dean Neidlinger and Radio Council Chairman Stearns Morse, all before a huge black velvet backdrop monogrammed "DBS," and all into that gleaming silver Junior Velocity microphone. There were dramatic presentations by the *DBS Workshop* and the Hanover High Footlighters. And there was live music: among other selections, the Barbary Coast Orchestra played Tommy Dorsey's recent hit "Yes Indeed!", the Green Collegians rendered "Jazz Me Blues," and the Glee Club predictably came through with "Twilight Song" (the Collegians having beaten them to "Dartmouth Undying"). The show's introductory remarks ended with this message for future broadcasters: "In a few years DBS will be an old traditional organization with prestige and permanence. No one but elderly members of the faculty will then remember when Dartmouth had no radio station. I hope at that time DBS will still have the same ambitions, the same ideals, and the same spark that has gone into its founding."[12]

Said *The Dartmouth*, "DBS is bound to grow, we think, and this is why: no matter what the handicaps to the men now plugging away enthusiastically in 51 Robinson, they have the enthusiasm – that special, extra quality which is worn by men who usually succeed against obstacles."[13]

The ghosts of the rooftop Wilder control room were apparently absent on October 27, for the show went without a serious hitch. By all visible signs, Dartmouth radio was this time here to stay.

## Programming

Among the most popular records in the nation in the fall of 1941 were Horace Heidt's "I Don't Want to Set the World on Fire," Glenn Miller's "Chattanooga Choo Choo" and Bing Crosby's "You and I." Top-rated network radio shows included *Burns and Allen, Lux Radio Theater, Mr. District Attorney,* and the staccato newscasts of Walter Winchell.[14] This was the radio landscape undergraduates were familiar with, and what they wanted most to emulate.

Through the weeks of November and early December 1941, DBS established regular programming intended to satisfy many quarters: the student body, the education-minded Radio Council, and perhaps even those summertime tutors at WNEW. Students, when polled, had pinpointed their musical preferences as "good music – both popular and classical." This left the DBS programmers a certain amount of leeway, but *Jive at Five* proved so popular that it was moved up to 4:45 p.m. Campus news and more records filled out the afternoon hour-block, while the two hours in the evening brought a 40-minute *Symphonic Hour* (three nights a week) plus a remarkable array of discussions, dramatics, interviews, "specialties" and news reports.

This heavy emphasis on specialty or "production" programming shown by DBS throughout its early years was largely attributable to the Radio Council's insistence that the station be something more than a radio jukebox. The programming provisions of the 1941-42 license of operation were quite detailed, restricting the station to no more than three hours of regular air time per day, and even specifying the approximate hours. Commercials could be no longer than 45 seconds each. Programming was to be divided into education (news, interviews, readings, talks, dramatics, etc.) and entertainment (popular music, sports, variety and quiz shows) and follow, roughly, a 25 percent to 75 percent proportion.

In practice the station did even better than this. An average broadcast day in late 1941 might run as follows:

Afternoon
4:45   *Jive at Five* with Doc Fielding '43 or Vic Schneider '41.
5:15   Campus News
5:20   *The Record Album* (based on Martin Block's famous *Make Believe Ball Room*)
5:45   sign-off
Evening
9:30   *Intramural Roundup*
9:35   *Classics in Jazz* with Bill Zeitung '43
10:00  *Meet the Professor* (interview)
10:15  *DBS Roundtable* with Joe Palamountain '42 (of the "*D*" and DBS) and faculty members.
10:30  Weather Report
10:31  Camel Cigarettes' *Campus Caravan* (South American rumba music)
10:45  "Story by Ross McKenney"
11:00  News Summary by the staff of the "*D*."
11:10  sign-off.

Drama, including some original plays, was presented on *DBS Workshop* and *COSO Presents* (30 minutes), thanks to a close relationship with Warner Bentley's Dartmouth Players. There were readings on *Reading to You*, sports prognostications by *The Dartmouth*'s staff on *How to Pick a Winner*, and commentary on *As We See It* (15 minutes each). The original All-Request Show was *What's Yours*, on which students could hear their favorites by Glenn Miller, Tommy Dorsey, Kay Kyser et al. – or at least as many as could be squeezed into a half hour.[15]

## To England with Love

DBS's most notable special during these first weeks came on November 20. It had been assumed from the beginning that DBS would produce shows for broadcast on outside stations, as well as run its own inter-dormitory hook-up, and for this reason a formal program-exchange agreement had been concluded with Manchester, New Hampshire's brand-new WMUR. This Thursday afternoon saw a unique "Greetings to Dartmouth, England" broadcast, designed to bring a little new world cheer to the blitz-torn isles. The half hour program went, in President Hopkins' words, "from the hills of Dartmouth in Northern New England to the hills of Dartmouth in Southern Old England," and featured talks by College dignitaries and music by the Glee Club (who, with the Green Collegians nowhere in sight, landed "Dartmouth Undying," "Men of Dartmouth" *and* "The Hanover Winter Song"). The program originated in the DBS studios, was piped to WMUR in Manchester, and thence to Boston's WRUL, which sent it to England via short wave. On the same evening WMUR carried to a wide New Hampshire audience DBS' rebroadcast of that Henry Williams play, *Dedicatory Remarks*.

## "That's No Mess ... It's DBS"

Critical reaction to the brand new station was, predictably, mixed. *The Dartmouth* was solidly behind DBS, as were most students. One letter-to-the editor lauded the Robinson Hall broadcasters at length, concluding "I take my hat off to you." Just below it, however, appeared: "To the Editors: We, the poor little freshmen of Dartmouth College, wish to express our deep gratitude to DBS for reading the daily *Dartmouth* to us every afternoon at 5:15 p.m., especially when we paid a lot of dough to read it ourselves. Tra-la, TWO LITTLE FROSHIES. P.S.: Maybe they should go back to experimenting?"[16] Another writer suggested to the producers of *Reading to You*, "Read it to yourself!", while a more poetic malcontent reviewed the entire broadcast day:

> To rest from those books,
> You flip that ole dial,
> To relax with the radio
> And listen awhile.
>
> There's a limit of choice,
> You squirm and you reel.
> Is it D.B.S.
> Or the static and squeal?

A voice from the speaker
Moans in the mike,
As the crew slaps on records
That Dingwall might like.

The boys in the dorms
Are invited to jive,
While Zeitung goes savage
Till quarter past five.

At five fifteen
As a cure for the blues,
There's a sexy ole round-up
Of the "Campus News."

Ole "Sweet Talk" Chief Mitchel
The nasal sensation
Stutters out news
From all over the nation.

Now little fellows
If you're feeling blue
Here's a sure fire sedative
Called "Reading to You."

The stories are killers
Rewritten by Scotty,
They're ever so clever
Without being plotty.

Then "last-minute news"
By "Lebanon Joe"
Who'll scream "buy a DARTMOUTH,"
Before you can go.

Now just a suggestion;
A thing to finesse,
Drop that ole D.
Just say B.S.
                    THE MOLE[17]


## Off Again

The honeymoon ended abruptly in early December. Unfortunately for DBS, December 7, 1941, fell on a Sunday. News of a Japanese attack on Pearl Harbor reached the east coast of the United States in the early afternoon. Engineer Joe Hirschberg '43 later recalled that he had been working at the station, and "I think that we were the first at Dartmouth to receive the news!"[18] As soon as the crisis broke Bill

Mitchel hurriedly gathered his staff and began three days of nearly continuous broadcasting. Nonetheless, a good many students probably first learned the news that would so change their lives from the black headlines of the "D" extra: "JAPS DECLARE WAR ON U.S. – SHOOTING BEGINS."

In an atmosphere of national crisis that Dartmouth radio has rarely had to confront, station members maintained an around the clock listening post, monitoring the BBC, CBC, foreign short wave stations, and all American networks.[19] News flashes were broadcast as they were received, and President Roosevelt's speeches carried live, via the studio radio set. The strain of confused reports and fast-breaking events finally proved too great, however, and on Thursday Mitchel announced that the station could not hope to continue its minute-to-minute coverage "with the degree of responsibility the President (F.D.R.) requests," and would end its flash bulletins.

Regular three-hours-a-day programming, with frequent news summaries, was resumed, but not for long. On December 17, 1941, the station signed off, announcing it would spend the Christmas recess and early January working on its persistent technical problems.

### "DBS – 550, 750, 790, 900 and 1400 On Your Dial"

The studio facilities of DBS were rapidly completed. Two rooms had been rented from the College: 49 Robinson was used as a business office, while across the hall, 51 Robinson, a former Green Key room, had over the preceding summer become studio space. Within the latter was a control room, flanked by a small news studio and a commodious Studio 2. With the mounting of hand-painted but oh-so-professional standby, warning and on-the-air lights during the Christmas recess, these facilities were virtually complete.

Mitchel's principal problem, and that which was to plague every succeeding Directorate as long as the station remained intra-campus, was the transmission system. From the very beginning it was obvious that the multiple-oscillator system would not work. The DeLuxe Mystery Transmitters had to be placed in dormitory basements, with the result that top floors often got no signal at all. Furthermore, those $7.10 wonders insisted on overlapping each other's signals, even when they were set on different frequencies, producing static and/or harmonic echoes all over the radio dial. The upshot was that DBS had to periodically announce the half dozen different frequencies on which it could be heard (depending on what building you were in), while receiving a steady stream of complaints that it was inaudible, unintelligible, or so ubiquitous as to blot out everything else on the nighttime radio dial.

As early as November 1941 Mitchel and Flynn were studying ways to change their awkward multiple-oscillator system to a power line hookup. This would utilize one central transmitter, which would send the station's signal out through the College power lines so that all radios in proximity to electrical wiring, anywhere in the College, could pick it up. This meant both a big new investment and a Pandora's box of new technical problems, but Mitchel went ahead and ordered the necessary equipment at the end of 1941. Defense priorities prevented much of it from arriving, however, so that all through the winter and spring of 1942 Steve Flynn and his engineers had to keep poking, patching and readjusting the existing system while Bill

Mitchel apologized for the "continuing technical difficulties."

## On Again: Into 1942

Dartmouth had been back in session for nearly four weeks before DBS resumed its regular programming, on February 2, 1942, following first semester final exams. As the station returned Mitchel announced a reshuffled Directorate, now including an assistant station manager (John Shaw '44) and sporting several other new faces too. In the Production Department, a junior staff was announced which would be rotated in the positions of "program" director, head announcer, head producer and campus news director.

*The Dartmouth's* ardor for the new station had cooled somewhat by this time. Recalling its "DBS is bound to grow" pronouncements of three months earlier, it now counseled, "DBS should do its utmost to function as a college network and try to avoid the lure of mere simulation of 'big time' broadcasting ... it should try to avoid the fanfare and false glamour of major network radio – rather remain in its niche and direct all its energies toward the service of its college audience and leadership in new forms of radio expression." The paper went on, then concluded its lecture with a fatherly "You're all right, sonny, but don't get too big for your britches."[20] Perhaps more revealing of the newspaper's attitude toward DBS by this time is a letter written by Albert Goldman, business manager of the "*D*," to several college papers that owned radio stations. Goldman wrote, in part:

> The Dartmouth Broadcasting System is now one year old. It has been subsidized by Dartmouth College in spite of the fact that it was originally conceived by *The Dartmouth*. We have made several attempts to take over the advertising function of the radio station. However, we have met with little success.
>
> Within the next few days we intend to submit a plan to the Radio Council whereby *The Dartmouth* will purchase the Broadcasting Company. However, before doing this, I would like to find out (your) arrangement ...

DBS was probably aware of Goldman's scheme, since copies of his letter somehow found their way into the station's technical files. The letters, dated April 17, 1942, were sent to Harvard, Yale and perhaps others.

## DBS Sports

Unfazed by the machinations of its self-appointed godfather, DBS in early February conducted the first of a long history of listenership surveys. There was a redoubled emphasis on sports: January 31, the Saturday before regular programs began, saw the station's first broadcast from outside Robinson Hall, the Army-Dartmouth basketball game from Alumni Gymnasium. By their third "remote" DBS sportscasters felt themselves smooth indeed. It was reportedly the most exciting game yet, with the announcer pouring multitudes of adjectives into the microphone, vividly describing every play. The crew was elated; only afterward did they discover that the engineer had forgotten to plug them in!

37

Despite such setbacks, Dartmouth radio forged on. Away games were either followed as scores came in, or "reconstructed," a process vividly described by Bill Mitchel in the May 1942 *Dartmouth Alumni Magazine*.

> One Saturday night a few weeks ago hundreds gathered around radios in dormitory rooms, a loud-speaker in the Trophy Room of Alumni Gym and a radio in the lobby of the Hanover Inn. Dartmouth played Stanford that night for the NCAA basketball title in Kansas City, and these hundreds in Hanover heard a sports commentator describe the game play-by-play against the background of an excited crowd.
>
> The program originated in the Robinson Hall studios of the Dartmouth Broadcasting System ... A Western Union operator received the play-by-play account of the game in DBS studio one ... a DBS heeler relayed the information to sports commentator Jim Wells '43, who sat before a microphone in studio two ... A freshman radio engineer in the DBS control room sat behind the control board and blended cheering with crowd noise from records after each basket Wells described ... and the hundreds of DBS listeners hung on every word, following the Dartmouth and Stanford players up and down the Kansas City basketball court. Some believed DBS had sent its commentator all the way to Kansas City to cover the game.

### *Bed Pan Alley*

The production and special events directors were no less busy than the sportscasters during the spring of 1942, as the remarkable pace of evening productions continued. Professors frequently lent their talents, as did members of campus organizations (although Professor Bear's *How to Study*, one of the original DBS Testing shows, was unfortunately lost in the shuffle). The intellectual ramblings of *Campus Roundtable* attracted particularly favorable publicity. But since time was precious in a three-hour broadcast day, no regular program except the every-other-evening *Symphonic Hour* got more than 30 minutes, and many had to settle for 15.

One of the first shows given a full hour was *Bed Pan Alley*, an extremely popular disc jockey show originally intended to soothe the inmates of Dick's House infirmary. Other programs broadcast in the spring of 1942 betokened things to come. From 11:05 to 11:25 each night there was code practice for Navy and Civilian Pilot Training students, and "all those who will eventually enter the armed forces"; one of the semester's biggest specials was coverage of Hanover's first blackout; and *Treasury Star Parade* became a regular feature.

March brought a rather interesting letter from alumnus Dick Krolik, now working for the Mutual network in New York and about to enter the Army Air Corps. He had heard that DBS was having its technical and business problems,

> ... but after six months daily contact with network broadcasting, I still think we had the right idea. The colleges need to develop techniques within their own confines – practicing, as it were, on themselves – and then I believe the programs they could produce would fill a real gap in the country's radio picture. I know that Mutual is wide open for special events, such as college programs, and would welcome some good ones. Since I've been here, I can

recall only two or three requests for network time from colleges, and those have been accepted with alacrity …[21]

## 1942

### "This Is DBS – Eastern War Time Is …"

Bill Mitchel completed his tenure with an *Alumni Magazine* cover story on DBS's first year, then handed the reins of management to John Shaw and a new Directorate. Shaw's position of assistant station manager was taken by Jim Wells; Steve Flynn by double-threat Co-Technical Directors Joe Hirschberg and Ted Jones '43; Production Director Pete Geisler '42 by Robert Grant '43. No business manager was announced. Although Shaw and company were appointed in April their term would last only until the fall. The war was in full swing now, and the news from both the European and Pacific theaters was grim. No student could be sure just how much longer he would remain in college before he was called to active duty, or for that matter how much longer the College itself would continue to operate.

Classes continued through the summer of 1942, to allow students to complete their education as quickly as possible. For similar reasons several new courses were taught that summer, one called Radio 20-A. This was run by Stearns Morse and Almon Ives and covered "the history of American radio, microphone techniques, script writing and instruction in the building of radio programs." Since the college was thus never out of session, DBS continued to operate its full schedule of three hours daily throughout the summer months.

DBS had little difficulty obtaining a renewal of its license from the Radio Council on June 1, 1942, but there were two important and two minor changes in its charter. The first had to do with organization. The three-man Executive Committee, which was originally intended to run the station, subject to the Radio Council's general dictates, was abolished. The station manager was put in direct charge, and DBS was one step closer to autonomy. Secondly, the station's divorce from *The Dartmouth* was completed as business relations with the paper were formally abolished. Whereas the "*D*" had played an integral part in the 1941-42 license, it was now nowhere mentioned. Added was "All title to equipment shall rest with Dartmouth College," obvious but previously unsaid, and a formal statement that the faculty committee that had been afraid DBS might create a riot danger in the dormitories might still rescind its approval, if "at any time … the operation of the station in the dormitories becomes objectionable." Other key provisions of the original license were retained, including "the station shall be on the air not more than three hours a day …"

### Personnel Problems … and a New Transmitter

Such were the formal changes. The real-life student organization was still very much in its formative stages under John Shaw. Except for the Radio Council's ultimate (and active) policy and financial control, effective management had been and continued to be almost exclusively in the station manager's hands. The Directorate, a loose collection of other directors, was merely advisory to him. Such a centralized power structure was well suited to the strong, single-handed leadership of Bill Mitchel, as well as to the needs of a fledgling organization, but it inevitably stirred discontent in the ranks. One disgruntled station member wrote, during July, that:

> … the big bone of contention during Mitch's managership was that he took everything into his own hands, and made sure personally that everything went off right. I was at a meeting at which Johnny (Shaw) complained very bitterly about this, and as a result Mitch let his staff members take over. The resulting inefficiency caused him to gradually assume all responsibility again, and this time there were no complaints.
>
> At the time of choosing a new Directorate, near graduation, there was a frantic search for men to fill the top jobs. Since no one had had any previous experience at running the station it was a matter of guess work rather than proven ability that governed the choices. An example of this was the appointment of Bob Grant (as director of programming) after he had only been in the station a few weeks, and had been assigned no major tasks.
>
> When Shaw got in, he immediately tried to make DBS an efficient organization by patterning it after successful established organizations. This meant that the station manager's sole job was to set up the framework of administration, and then act solely as a contact man. I agree entirely with John on this principle – in an established organization. But DBS has not yet gotten its sea legs. In the founding of almost every enterprise there must be some strong hand and fiery spirit to spark the thing – which was lacking after the graduation of Mitchel …[22]

Shaw's problems during the summer of 1942 didn't end with dissatisfied personnel, however. There was the rift with *The Dartmouth*, which by now had blossomed into an open feud; financial problems, born of lagging sales and aggravated by unexpected expenses (studio construction costs, as of April 15, had amounted to $2,545, operating costs to another $225 – all against a projected budget of $1,500); and worst of all, the continuing transmission problem.[23]

Hope sprang brightest for the last-named problem, as the installation of the long-awaited power line system of transmission was finally completed. The new, central transmitter was a surplus Army Signal Corps unit, converted to 640 kc and hooked into the College power lines in the basement of Middle Fayerweather dormitory (two smaller booster units were installed in Dick's House infirmary and the president's home). But no sooner was it in than the FCC dashed off a friendly little note observing that the signal had been heard in Vermont, and that perhaps the boys ought to keep their radiation down to the legal 250 feet from the College power lines.[24] At the same time fraternities and several dormitories still could not pick up the station. Technical Director Ted Jones sent a memo to his engineers in September saying "feel free to experiment and borrow the proper test equipment, always making sure, though, that the next broadcast will not fail to go on the air."[25]

Though the new single-transmitter system failed to resolve DBS's technical problems, at least it put the station on a single frequency. From this time until it went AM in 1958, Dartmouth radio would remain "640 on your radio dial."

**1942-1943**

**"You Can't Do Business with Hitler"**

In October 1942 William Davies took office as station manager, along with a new, smaller Directorate that included William Alpert '45 as technical director and Richard Kanter '44 as production manager (again, no business manager). Davies had worked his way up in programming, under Mitchel and Shaw. As station manager he worked hard to hold off for as long as possible the inevitable wartime demise of the station they had built.

For a while he was remarkably successful. Programming was combined into a single, but longer 7:30-11:05 p.m. nighttime block. *Meet the Professor* and *DBS Workshop* remained, though now joined by the *BBC News From London* and *You Can't Do Business With Hitler*. *Battle of the Dorms* provided a quiz show, Old Gold cigarettes presented the campus news, and *Bed Pan Alley* current big band hits like Glenn Miller's "American Patrol" and Xavier Cugat's "Brazil" (the latter being – probably – the only original DBS record still in the WDCR record files in the 1960s). *The Dartmouth* refused to print any more DBS program notes, so these shows were advertised, during the spring of 1943, in professionally printed weekly program listings.

But the war took its toll. Disc jockey shows and transcriptions gradually became more prevalent as personnel became fewer. As March and April went by, activities and academics were folding fast at Dartmouth, and Davies watched as his staff slowly melted away from under him. Finally, in April 1943 (approximately), after 18 months of nearly continuous broadcasting, DBS announced that it, too, would shut down "for the duration." Bill Davies finished his term as third station manager packing away equipment and chasing around Hanover collecting unpaid advertising accounts.

Dartmouth itself all but closed down after the 1943 spring semester. For the next two-and-one-half years its hallowed halls saw only an emaciated civilian student body of 300 to 500, half of them freshmen, and a somewhat larger number of military recruits being pushed through the wartime V-7 and V-12 Training Programs by a faculty of Navy officers. *The Dartmouth* was replaced by the Navy's weekly *Log*, while 51 Robinson became a recreation room. The microphones in the corner would remain silent until the spring of 1946.

# Chapter 3

# 1946-1951: Bigger and Better

To an alumnus chancing to visit Hanover during 1943-45, the Dartmouth campus must have seemed strange and foreign. During those war years the Navy V-7 and V-12'ers were everywhere, along with all the accoutrements of a military training base – uniforms and commanding officers, reveille and inspections. The small civilian student body, hurrying through accelerated courses and summer sessions, could not support such a time-consuming activity as a campus radio station. Fifty-one Robinson, which had turntables and amplifiers at one end (along with an excellent collection of slightly used records) and newly installed ping-pong tables at the other, was anything but silent. But its periodic recorded jam sessions never left the room. DBS was, for the time being, a memory.

V.E. Day came on May 7, 1945, and V.J. Day on September 2. At the end of 1945 millions of young men were still in uniform overseas, however, and not until early 1946 could the College even begin to rebuild its academic schedule. At that, it was a long time before things were anywhere near "back to normal." All through 1946 former undergraduates were arriving in Hanover to pick up where they had left off, many bringing with them wives and children. Emergency housing was constructed at Wigwam Circle and Sachem Village (near Hanover High), and Fayerweather was converted into a family dormitory.

## Spring, 1946

### "DBS Re-forms"

One of the students returning in early 1946 was Robert Varney '43, who had only one semester to complete before graduation. Varney had most recently been employed by the U.S. Navy as a pilot, but before that he had done production work for the old DBS. Once back in Hanover he set to rounding up others of the 1941-43 staff, and in March arranged with Professor Morse and Al Ives to hold an organizational meeting. That meeting was as enthusiastically received as Dick Krolik's had been five years earlier, and work began immediately to get DBS back on the air before the end of the spring semester.

Varney first outfitted the station with a full staff including himself as station manager, George Barr '45 as technical director, Paul Caravatt '45 as business manager and Dick Kelly '46 as production director. They spent April reinstalling the none-too-ample studio equipment, looking for cheap but new records, and recruiting personnel. Veterans' wives participated as announcers and writers (script girls?), while students were enticed with a notice that read:

DBS is looking for a patter artist ... a Danny Kaye, a mumble-mumble tobacco auctioneer who thinks he can rattle off this front page in jet propelled time. If you think you can manage to make a paragraph sound fairly intelligible, you are requested to drop into 51 Robinson Hall.

At length patter artists were found, and Technical Director George Barr could pronounce the old studios in shape and the old transmitter at least semi-operable, which was all it had ever been. The blessing of the Radio Council (what was left of it) was secured, and Station Manager Varney announced that DBS would emerge from its heap of mothballs on Monday, May 6, 1946, for a month of experimental broadcasting. "When the station goes on the air," he added naively, "the Directorate hopes to start studying again."

### "Lost, One Transmitter"

The best-laid plans of Varney and his men very nearly went awry. Shortly before the initial broadcast was to take place *The Dartmouth* carried an emergency appeal:

> Lost, One Transmitter – Return to DBS, Reward ... will the person or persons (it was pretty big) who borrowed the DBS transmitter out of the Middle Fayerweather basement please contact the studio? The station plans to go on the air this evening, hell, high water, or hangover. It would like its transmitter.

Who filched the transmitter? The "*D*" helpfully speculated that "the postwar status of Middle Fayerweather may have something to do with the transmitter's disappearance. It makes a dandy hanger for washed clothes, or maybe some infant Hercules was intrigued by it and dropped it off into one of those hard-to-find corners were infant Hercules put their playthings ..." The monster was apparently returned in time, for when 7:30 Monday night came, the big moment went without a hitch. With a crescendo from Handel's "Concerto for Orchestra," a roll of drums and a hearty "Good evening, this is DBS, the Dartmouth College Station, 640 on your dial," Dartmouth radio was back, this time to stay.

Among those appearing on the half-hour opening broadcast was Dartmouth's new president, John Sloan Dickey, with his first address to the student body at large. He stressed the station's potential value as a means of informal communication between administration and student body, a medium to bind Dartmouth together and "keep it small." Navy Lieutenant William J. Mitchel must have nodded at that, before going to the stage himself to reminisce with Jerry Tallmer '42 about the trials and tribulations of DBS' earlier days. (Tallmer was 1942 and 1946 Editor of *The Dartmouth*—he wrote the account of DBS' first broadcast—as well as DBS news director.) Bob Varney provided a capsule history of the station, then offered a peek into his crystal ball:

> The future of DBS depends on what the men and women who are here now, and who will be here in the future, make of it. I believe that radio in the liberal college has ever broadening possibilities. DBS, in its present form,

only reaches the dormitories of the College. I sincerely hope that at some time not too far away we will be able to reach the entire town of Hanover, and the neighboring communities. If we can do that, our radio work will cease to be a plaything for a few enthusiasts and become an integral part of both the College and the community…

For the next four weeks of May 1946 it was business at the old stand, two-and-a-half hours a day, five days a week. Good old *Bed Pan Alley* began the schedule at 7:30 p.m. while *The Dartmouth*-AP News brought it to a close at 10:00. In between was an amalgam of old and new. That old standby *Meet the Professor* was back, now shortened to a more collegiate *Meet the Prof* and hosted by an announcer with the enchanting name of Renaldo Fortunato. Dean Neidlinger got his chance to cement student-College relations under the imposing title *The Administration Speaks*. Meanwhile, DBS ground out questionnaires to find out which of the new shows listeners liked best, Dean Neidlinger, *DBS Workshop* or *The Whiskey and Chowder Club*.

DBS closed for the summer on May 29. Shortly thereafter, at a cocktail party at Casque and Gauntlet, Varney revealed that the 1946-47 Directorate would be headed by engineer George Barr; Paul Caravatt would continue as business manager, and Bob MacLeod '46 was production director. The position of assistant station manager was reinstituted with Dick Kelly (who resigned in October), while the news director would be "the as yet unappointed editor-in-chief of *The Dartmouth*. The rapprochement, it would seem, was complete. The technical director? None other than Steve Flynn, who was due back in Hanover in the fall. He would have plenty to do.

### 1946-1947

Although DBS had prodigious transmission problems throughout its intra-campus years, it was never so well equipped to meet them as during the late 1940s. Many station engineers in those days were veterans, men for whom the war had been an extended course in applied electronics. Back on campus they could apply their experience to the obstinate gizmo in the basement of Middle Fayerweather. Under the guidance of George Barr and then Steve Flynn, considerable technical work was done during the summer and fall of 1946, both in the studios and on the transmitter itself. The results were not encouraging: several dormitories and most of fraternity row were still able to pick up DBS only poorly, or not at all.

### Programming: From Sibelius to *The Hot Club*

Behind-the-scenes headaches notwithstanding, DBS returned to its slightly modified "old self" during 1946-47. *The Dartmouth* was suitably impressed with the initial offerings, reporting in mid-October that "the sound-proof studios atop Robinson Hall, silenced by three years of war, was filled last night with newscasters, pianists, announcers, technicians, a pretty secretary and a seeing eye dog … DBS presented everything from Chiquita Banana to Brahms' Second Piano Concerto …"[1]

At first there were the customary three hours of programs each weeknight, but by the spring of 1947 this had increased to four. There were still discussions and interviews, *DBS Workshop* and *The Administration Speaks*, as well as occasional rebroadcasts from the powerful Hallicrafters radio receiver in the control room. A renewed association with The Dartmouth Players aided dramatic productions.[2] But most of the new time was filled with the live and recorded music programs students said they preferred. A typical early 1947 program schedule, as printed in *The Dartmouth*:

7:00 *640 Club* - Music as you request it
7:55 Latest News Headlines
8:00 *Symphonic Hour*, featuring two works by the great Finnish composer, Jean Sibelius.
9:00 *At the Keyboard* - live piano music.
9:15 *The Hot Club*
9:45 *Ski Digest* with Don Hyatt '50
10:00 *These Are the People*, a new DBS dramatic presentation, featuring tonight a transcribed radio play entitled "Conspiracy".
10:30 *Styles in Music*, with the King Cole Trio.
11:00 Up to the Minute World-Wide and Local Associated Press News.

Sports events were regularly covered, and for good reason. During the Dartmouth-Pennsylvania football game, reported a beaming station spokesman, 90 percent of Hanover's radios had been tuned in (no mean feat since about 25 percent of them couldn't get DBS). The ever-active pollsters picked up some other interesting figures during the fall of 1946. By that time 85.7 percent of the men living in dormitories had radios, they reported, and the majority listened between four and ten hours each week (one respondent, who listened 45 hours a week, "was a man in Gile who liked noise most of the time.") Sixty-five percent said that their favorite listening time was 10:00 to 11:00 p.m.

### Chiquita Banana

Reaction to DBS during its first year back was as mixed as it had been five years earlier. *The Administration Speaks,* on which Dean Neidlinger did lively battle with both studio inquisitors and letters-to-the-editor in the morning's *Dartmouth*, received highest praise, but *Styles in Music* got the listeners. In general listeners seemed less provoked by the Dean's Websterian blast at "licentious living" in fraternities than by DBS' commercials. "I left home for two reasons," wrote one, "(1) to return to Dartmouth, (2) to get as far as possible from the incessant, presumptuous 'singing commercial,' that vile and insulting evidence of what radio ad-men think of Americans. Last night I tuned in on DBS, the only station offering reasonable reception in Hanover. To my horror I found myself being urged to use my voting prerogative by an insipid male chorus of croaking crooners, followed by a singularly unmelodious bit of advice relative to the storage of bananas."[3]

Confronted with such jibes the Business Department merely smiled and pointed to the spectacular $2,187 in sales. The Radio Council smiled back and noted the $3,645 in expenses, including $1,400 for technical refurbishing.

One of the first big post-war specials came at 1947's Green Key Weekend (a traditional weekend of parties in May), when station members staged a full-blown variety show in Webster Hall. Featured were the Barbary Coast Orchestra and its torch-singing vocalist (imported from Smith College), a vaudeville team with the unlikely names of Joe Michael and Joaquin Castillo, and a "jive song act" in that brand new language, Voutian. The DBS extravaganza stole the show from the Nugget's Hollywood movie, which followed, but unfortunately it never made the airwaves – because, in producer Bob Shade's words, of "the – uh – nature of the artist's creations…"[4]

### FM in Our Future?

The spring of 1947 also saw a flurry of speculation that there might be FM in Dartmouth's future. Almon Ives made the proposal to his fellow Radio Council members, suggesting that as an alternative (or supplement) to a Dartmouth FM station they might look into low-power AM, too. In any event, something better than the present, poor-coverage power line system was needed. Simultaneously the council heard from Thayer School of Engineering Professor Millett Morgan, who was thinking of setting up a 1000-watt commercial FM station of his own, possibly in conjunction with the College. Steve Flynn excitedly shot off letters to electronics companies asking for price quotations, but interest in FM began to wane as the replies arrived; a 250-watt FM set-up would cost Dartmouth $14,000, while 1000-watts would run upwards of $20,000. Much discussion followed, and President Dickey convened a Committee on Future Radio Policy, which in 1949 issued a report recommending against either an AM or FM broadcasting station at Dartmouth—at least for now.[5]

Before Flynn could return to his familiar job of patching up the balky monster in Middle Fayerweather, however, it was May, and time for the annual changing of the guard. "DBS Appoints Twelve New Heads" announced *The Dartmouth* in its own inimitable style. Then, significantly, just four names were listed as comprising the new Directorate: Station Manager Bob Shade '46, Technical Director Bob Owens '47, Business Manager William Trump '46 and Production Director Emil (Bud) Popke '49.

Almost as soon as DBS resumed regular broadcasting in 1946, these four positions had evolved into the inner circle of station management. They were the key positions: the "SM" was of course paramount; the production director had charge of all programming including scripts, announcing, news, and special events; the technical director controlled studio, remote and maintenance engineering; the business manager advertising, financial management, publicity and personnel activities. Every other position and activity on the station could be subsumed under one of these latter three general operating divisions.

Also, it had become obvious under Barr that a better top decision-making level was needed, neither as concentrated as a single all-powerful station manager (who might be quite strong, like Mitchel, or relatively weak, like Barr) or as unwieldy as a 12-man collection of "directors." The answer was found in a small, tight-knit senior Directorate of upperclassmen, which collectively appointed its successors and other position-holders, and which made all important decisions. The Directorate remained the dominant force in the organization's operation and politics for years to come, effectively in charge of the station. Except for title changes, only two notable alterations were made in this system during the next 20 years: after DBS came under COSO in 1948 the station manager's *formal* seniority over the other three Directorate members was abolished, and in 1960 a fifth Directorate position, that of administrative director, was added. The basic power structure and the SM's acknowledged place as "the head of the station" otherwise remained unchanged.

At the end of May, to the recorded strains of Les Brown's "Leapfrog" (the *640 Club* theme) and the year-end "Dartmouth Hit Parade," DBS completed its first year of post-war broadcasting. In the fall a radically new station was to take shape.

## 1947-1948

The year 1947-48 was in many ways a turning point in station history. Under George Barr DBS had generally reestablished itself on its old footing (no mean accomplishment), albeit with greater reliance on recorded music. Bob Shade's regime marked the beginning of a "dynamic decade"[6] of steady expansion, which culminated with the historic conversion to WDCR-AM in 1958. The progress during 1947-48 was spectacular in all three departments: business, technical and programming. Many station members contributed, of course, but one name stands out: that of the ambitious young junior who took charge of programming, Bud Popke.

"*Jam for Breakfast* Is DBS Menu For Students" headlined *The Dartmouth* when the station returned in early October. That was to be Dartmouth's first morning show, on the air from 7:30-8:30 a.m. with "music, time and temperature." At the same time the evening block was extended to midnight with the most popular and long-running d.j. show in station history, *Music 'til Midnight*. MTM would prove extraordinarily durable, remaining on the air in one form or another for most of the next 33 years; an hour of popular music around 11:00 p.m., right after normal study hours, was perfect for students. Another pattern of many years standing was set when it was announced that both new shows would play request music. In late November the invasion of the weekend began with a two-hour Sunday night program of continuous music. "The show consists of recorded light classics of the Kostelanetz-Block-Rose type," the "*D*" reported, "and requests for numbers on future programs will be honored if sent to Donald B. Hyatt '50, engineer of the show ..."

The first live coverage of an away game in DBS history took place on November 1, 1947 (the Yale game), under sponsorship of the Undergraduate Council. Through the rest of the fall and winter virtually all home football, basketball and hockey games were broadcast as well as those out-of-town contests for which sponsors could be found.

The spring of 1948 brought still more expansion, as *Jam for Breakfast* grew by half an hour and DBS moved further into the weekends. On Saturday afternoons trainees got their chance on *Heelers' Hack Time* (Saturday afternoons presumably being expendable), while the more valuable Saturday evening slot got more recorded music. By the end of the year total regular program time had increased by 75 percent over 1946-47's twenty hours per week.

A typical weekday schedule in the spring of 1948:

Morning
7:30   *Jam for Breakfast* (d.j.)
9:00   sign-off

<u>Evening</u>

7:00    *640 Club* (d.j.)
7:55    Campus and sports news
8:00    *Symphonic Hour*
9:00    Dan Featherston, news commentary
9:15    *Date With Diana*
9:30    *Twing Neely and the White Mountain Ramblers* (live folk music)
9:45    *Music on Record*
10:00  *Styles in Music* (featured artist)
10:25  News
10:30  *Hit Parade*
11:00  *Music 'til Midnight*
12:00  News
12:15  sign-off

There were still a few interviews and *DBS Workshops*, but the general pattern was set when Bob Shade announced that "the regular schedule will include news, music of both classical and popular nature, and as many of the major College events as we can get backing for." Bill Trump more succinctly described DBS as "a station of news, sports and music."

What feature programs were left got better exposure than ever during 1947-48, as an arrangement was made with WLOB-FM in Claremont, New Hampshire, to swap occasional shows. The deal brought DBS the Rochester Symphony, while WLOB listeners heard *DBS Workshop* and *At the Keyboard,* the latter now originating live from the lobby of the Hanover Inn.

### "The Gut Bucket Gurglers"

Such a preponderance of popular music inevitably brought dissent, as from the letter writer who deplored those "monotonous, endless hours of disc jockey chatter and popular tunes."[7] But DBS's most realistic course was to serve, not to reform its listeners, and popular music was what students had always said they wanted. A postcard survey of 500 of them, conducted in February 1948, confirmed this. It also revealed that 92 percent of the 2,820 resident students had radios, 84 percent (2,360) could pick up DBS if they wanted to, and during the preceding semester 82 percent had done so, even though half rated the programs as only "fair." Most of them probably shared the general satisfaction of *The Dartmouth*'s brand-new radio critic, John Sirignano '46. In his column "On the Air" Sirignano gave his impressions of the 1947 fall line-up:

> We had to go to the studio to catch *Jam for Breakfast* (there are four submarginals on my floor in Butterfield who own electric razors) ... Jim Dowaliby does a fine job ... we like especially the regular announcements as to the number of minutes left before the late bell rings for an 8 o'clock class ... Back with us too is Don Burch's *640 Club*, DBS' answer to Martin Block. Burch conducts his show with the same easygoing, good humored style which made the *640 Club* last year's most popular feature.

48

In contrast to Burch's slightly screwball antics, the 8:00 nightly *Symphonic Hour* continues to broadcast some excellent serious music. We wish, however, that the script writers would confine themselves to simple announcements … rather than regaling us with the reading of the blurb jacket of the record album … *Styles in Music* at 10:00 features a half hour of the music of a single popular band, which is fine if you like 30 minutes of the music of a single popular band.

(As for) *Music 'til Midnight* … we've only caught Don Hyatt's version of the show so far, and approve of him heartily. Don's informal delivery, especially his line to the effect that "this is a program of music you like, and music that my wife likes" is quite ingratiating.[8]

On another occasion Sirignano took deadlier aim on *Styles in Music*, which, he said, "is most amusing, although it is doubtful if this is the way the script writers intended it." To prove his point he reproduced a "typical script":

ANNOUNCER: Tonight, *Styles in Music* presents the music of Absalom Swzlstck and his Gut Bucket Gurglers. Absalom first saw the light of day in the little town of Keebird, Kentucky. Absalom's love for music was evident at an early age. He was delighted by the kettledrum effect produced by a baseball bat on the heads of his brothers and sisters. At the age of 16 Absalom was invited to leave Lower Register High School when they discovered him using a test tube rack in the chemistry lab as a xylophone. It was then that Absalom formed his first band, a small combo consisting of a musical saw, a bazooka, two harmonicas, a baseball bat, and Absalom's sole remaining sister. But before we continue, let's hear the Gut Bucket Gurglers in their latest recording, "When Your Hair Has Turned To Silver, I'll Still be Waiting For *Henry V* at the Nugget."[9]

Back like death and taxes were those singing commercials. Chiquita Banana had been replaced by none other than Timetable Mabel. Sirignano dealt her the cruelest blow of all, printing her lyrics.

Soloist: They call me Time Table Mabel / The girl who's in love with a train
Chorus: With a train, with a train
Soloist: It's the Boston and Maine
Chorus: Ever ready, her steady's the all-weather train
Soloist: Yes it is, yes it is, it's my steady / It takes me where I want to be
Through rain or fog I'm worry-free / It goes through storms, it can't be beat
Never leaves me behind because there isn't a seat
Chorus: Her dependable friend is the train
Soloist: I love to travel by train
Chorus: Take the train …
All:     Boston and Maine!

49

### From Robinson Hall to the World

The highlight of the year came in February, when celebrity newscaster Lowell Thomas arrived to do four network broadcasts from the 1948 Winter Carnival. What better place was there on campus to make the CBS crew feel at home than the studios of DBS? And there he was, for 15 golden minutes at each of three closed broadcasts, sitting with President Dickey behind a studio two table, speaking simultaneously into a big, gleaming CBS mike and DBS's proud little Junior Velocity. A fourth broadcast was done from the Little Theatre, with DBS apportioning the limited supply of tickets among eager spectators.

Thomas did not use DBS' microphones, control board, or any other equipment – he had his own remote crew set up in the corner of the room. But at least he used the room, and for three broadcasts DBS Studio Two was on the air from coast to coast. A few days after it was all over, Bob Shade received a brief note, which doubtless stayed on the DBS bulletin board for months:

> Dear Bob,
>
> Many thanks for your cordial hospitality and cooperation. Broadcasting from the studios of DBS seemed just like doing it from CBS or Radio City in New York!
>
> Lowell Thomas[10]

### "It Can't Happen Here ..."

Despite its numerous achievements in programming, the Shade Directorate was fated to be remembered chiefly for one unfortunate broadcast, one which brought DBS possibly the worst publicity in its history. There was a certain amount of irony in the fact that the disaster came on *DBS Workshop*, that one remaining gem of the Production Department, and the special production that was invariably mentioned in interviews as an example of the station's creative programming.

It began simply enough when a *Workshop* producer, lacking inspiration of his own, decided to capitalize on that of Orson Welles. Welles' famous "War of the Worlds" broadcast on the CBS network in 1938 had dramatized an invasion from Mars so realistically that thousands of its more gullible listeners had panicked. But that was in 1938, and with a wide, not always too intelligent, audience. The DBS show would adopt only the general plot line, not the results. And so, on March 24, 1948, at 9:30 p.m., the standard *DBS Workshop* opening boomed out to campus and community. Tonight's show was "It Can't Happen Here."

Cut to a program of Tommy Dorsey music, "from Boston's Totem Pole ..." The relaxing dance music continued for a few minutes, then suddenly was interrupted by a series of urgent news flashes ... an unidentified squadron has been sighted approaching the USA, over Labrador ... before the Air Force can react, Portland, Maine, is leveled in a fiery holocaust, vividly described by an on-the-spot reporter who dodged deafening explosions ... a few nervous minutes later a voice identified as that of the Secretary of the Interior spoke to the nation ... "From all outward appearances the enemy has launched an aircraft attack from somewhere in the circumpolar regions .. the cities of Seattle, Washington; Minneapolis, Minnesota; Chicago, Illinois; Detroit, Michigan; Cleveland, Ohio; Pittsburgh, Pennsylvania; Schenectady, New York; and Portland, Maine have been completely demolished in the first attack …" An appeal goes out to all reservists to report immediately to their bases … World War III has begun.

Then came the moral. Cut to the room of two Dartmouth undergraduates listening to the preceding part of the broadcast:

> (Voice:) I think that dramatic trash we just heard ought to be banned from the air … supposin' someone tuned in after that opening announcement … I tell ya, cheap propaganda just to earn a couple of guys a few bucks oughta be cut out … Ya know, Tom … this time I'm gonna do somethin' … I'm gonna write a letter to *The Dartmouth* and tell 'em what I think of that cheap propaganda … why, with the Army and Navy we've got, and all the atomic research we're doing, it just COULDN'T HAPPEN HERE … (raise popular music background and hold 'til end – then cut all music.)
>
> (Narrator, very solemn from an echo chamber): We are the hollow men, we are the stuffed men, leaning together …

In the words of the next morning's *Dartmouth*, "the T.S. Eliot poem, fast becoming to the college student what William Cullen Bryant was to the nineteenth century Ladies Aid, trails on to the conclusion."

The irony of a title never landed so heavily on its creators as with "It Can't Happen Here," for it soon became apparent that indeed it could. Despite the fact that this was 1948, that the whole idea had been used before (right down to the inclusion of the "Secretary of the Interior," but with the substitution of more believable Russians for Welles' Martians), that the production work was even sloppier than Welles' had been ("We've never put on such a rotten dramatic show," wailed a station official the next day, "even the explosions sounded fake"); despite all this, 1948 Hanover produced a junior version of the panic of 1938. The offices of the radio station and *The Dartmouth* were flooded with distraught students and townsfolk seeking details from the teletype machines. Some reservists scampered off to report for duty, and one worried mother, whose daughter lived in Portland, placed a call to learn of her safety. Downtown Hanover, reported campus police chief Gaudreau, was just a "seething mass."

For the rest of the evening announcements were broadcast every 15 minutes explaining what had happened … but too late. As the truth slowly spread calls began coming in from angry listeners. One harried reservist threatened to punch any station executive he could find.

"FAKE 'WAR' DRAMA TERRORIZES HANOVER" gleefully headlined the next morning's *Dartmouth*, and that was only the beginning. Bigger newspapers quickly picked up the story. *The Manchester Union Leader*, New Hampshire's largest daily, and *The Claremont Eagle* both had front-page reports, the latter amplifying Chief Gaudreau's already exaggerated description into "streets and sidewalks filled with students and anxious townspeople, all awaiting further news …"[11] In fact, reported *The Dartmouth*, there had been "no apprehensive searchers of the 9:50 sky last night, no excited figures scrambling up Balch Hill in the dark. But there was a brief spate of phone calls, excited, irate and annoyed … and many more private complaints."[12]

From DBS the shame-faced apologies flowed thick and fast, with Bob Shade finally announcing that "with our sincere apologies, the Directorate and staff of (DBS) wish to pledge ... that we will not again be guilty of such a breach of good faith." But the fiasco would be remembered for a long time to come. In a lengthy editorial entitled "Tain't Funny" the "*D*" reviewed the script (which it had stolen from the studio during the confusion), then said "(DBS) says it is embarrassed. With material like that, it should be. For propitiation of the ether gods, prescribed the immolation of all copies of the script, accompanied by contrapuntal music – the brittle crack of a dozen Tommy Dorsey records rapidly breaking in the background. For propitiation of an irate audience, recommended: more careful judgment of the sensitivity of listeners in a touchy era to an extremely delicate subject."

## A New Transmitter

Dick Carr's engineers were no less ambitious than Bud Popke's producers in 1947-48. The decision to replace the cranky old Signal Corps transmitter, which had served DBS since 1942, had been made in the spring of 1947. However, the home-made replacement was still being built in the fall. Advance publicity boasted that it would increase DBS's power circle eight times, and at last enable the inhabitants of Wigwam Circle, Sachem Village, and Fraternity Row to hear the station. But when the new equipment finally went into operation, dismayed engineers found that they were still not even covering all dormitories. On that postcard survey of early 1948 only 47 percent said that reception was "good," 26 percent said that it was fair, and a full 21 percent replied that it was poor. Back to the drawing boards. Next year there would be another try.

Improvements made in studio equipment proved more lasting. The old control board was an unimposing little grey box (12" x 18") with a few plain knobs and one lonely toggle switch. It had served since DBS was born in 1941, but it provided only four input channels to handle all microphones, turntables, etc., and gave relatively poor frequency response. Backed by a radio grant of $2,000 from a pitying College, Carr and his staff drew up plans for a much larger board. This new console would be three times as big as the old one, and sport enough rows of buttons, switches and knobs to make any casual visitor wince in amazement that anyone could actually understand how to operate it. When this $850, home-built, eight-input masterpiece went into use in February 1948, DBS's technical quality improved markedly, as did the spirit of the Technical Department (after all, they *could* operate it). Although rebuilt many times afterward, it remained in use as the station's master control board until the fall of 1960, well after the station had gone AM. Another portion of the trustee's grant was used to purchase a much-needed Raytheon remote unit, a small, portable control board which greatly facilitated coverage of home and away sports events, although it still required that lines be leased to the location.

By the end of the year the air of big time radio had even crept into the phone book, with no fewer than three college extensions listed for the studios, production office and business office. Actually, DBS now had five rooms, the original two studios and a control room in 51 Robinson, a writing and recording room across the hall in 49, and a new business office in the only spot available in the building – in the basement.

## COSO, WDBS and the Ivy Network

In February of 1948 the Radio Council, which had exercised jurisdiction over DBS since 1941, was formally dissolved. The station had become a well-established going concern, it was said, meeting the council's first goal of an organization in which students could learn about the business of broadcasting. The obligations and opportunities of better broadcasting, to serve Dartmouth's needs, was now fully in the hands of the student management. For financial purposes the station was, in March, placed under the Council on Student Organizations (COSO).

Simultaneously with the removal of the Radio Council and its commercial restrictions the station made several far-reaching business moves. The Intercollegiate Broadcasting System, a large, loose collection of college stations with which DBS had been associated since 1941, was abandoned, as DBS joined other Ivy League stations in forming a more effective national sales representative. A circular letter from Yale during the fall of 1947 had proposed such a coalition, and DBS had been the first to pick up the idea. With the Radio Council gone and DBS' business dealings in its own hands, the way was clear.

On February 19, 1948, Bill Trump announced that Dartmouth radio would henceforth be known as WDBS, to be in accord with its sister stations. Meetings at New Haven followed, and by early March five Ivy League stations – those of Dartmouth, Yale, Harvard, Princeton, and the University of Pennsylvania – announced the formation of the Ivy Network. Its first chairman was Bob Shade, with the other members rotating to the position annually in alphabetical order of their colleges. The primary purpose of the network was to gain more national advertising for all members, by selling the five prime college markets as a unit. It would also promote the exchange of technical and audience research information, and promote "extracurricular unity in the Ivy League such as now exists on the athletic fields." "However," the reports concluded, "the exchange of programs sill lies in the future."

As another aspect of the new look in business, the rate structure was completely overhauled and made much more complex (and profitable) than had been possible under Radio Council restrictions. There were different rates for prime-time (8:00 p.m.-midnight) and other periods, for local and national advertisers (who paid up to $2.50 per 60-second commercial), and for varying numbers of spots purchased. Recordings of commercials could be made on the station's disc recording machine for $1.50. The business trainee program was also widely expanded in 1947-48, insuring that the work of Bill Trump and his staff would not be lost. In short, there was progress on virtually every business front except sales, which declined by some $900. The foundations had been laid, however, and the sales curve from now to the mid-fifties would be steadily upward.

With the first of May came the annual reshuffling of WDBS' top management. Only half of the four-man Directorate would be new, however. Bob Shade's successor as station manager was former programming chief Bud Popke – as expected – while Dick Carr exchanged his title of technical director for that of business manager. Ken Carpenter '48 would be technical director, and Bob Sisk '50 would be production manager. "The Directorate," announced *The Dartmouth*, "will take over at a gathering scheduled for one this afternoon. 'If it gets too wet, we'll call it off,' said Shade enigmatically."[13]

The station's last major activity of the year traditionally came on Green Key weekend, in mid-May, and in 1948 it met the holiday with expanded broadcasting and several specials. Most special of all was the selection of a Miss Radio of Dartmouth, 1948, the first of a long series of Green Key Queen contests sponsored by WDBS. The winner, chosen from a field of 54, was crowned by bandleader Vaughn Monroe at the Green Key Dance, and presented with an autographed album of his recordings.

## 1948-1949

A future station manager was to write that "it was not until (1948), under the excellent management of Bud Popke and with the enthusiastic members of the first real postwar class – 1950 – in the Directorate positions, that the college station started to become an actual force on campus."[14] Building on the broad advances of the Shade regime, Popke's Directorate produced a second straight year of spectacular progress in programming, technical, and business areas.

### Programming: "If Your Feet Itch To Stamp ..."

Weekly program time, which had jumped by 75 percent during the preceding year, increased another 70 percent under Bob Sisk, to 58 hours a week. Most of this additional time came in the mornings, where the popular *Jam for Breakfast* was now followed by more recorded music, and on weekends. A typical weekday schedule in the fall of 1948:

Morning
7:30   *Jam for Breakfast*
9:00   *Morning Melodies*
10:00  *Swap Shop*
10:25  sign-off
Evening
7:00   *640 Club*
8:00   *Symphonic Hour*
9:00   *Guest Performance:* "Jack English and His Bob-tet" (live)
10:00  *Co-Op Ski Digest*, with Don Hyatt
10:30  *Romance of Song*
11:00  *Music 'til Midnight*
12:05  sign-off

Saturday brought the full morning schedule, an afternoon of *Heelers' Hack Time*, and a versatile evening show entitled *Music to Laugh, Dance, Dream By*. On Sundays there were five hours of music on *Melody Time* (with the Vaughn Monroe recording of the same name as the theme song) and Don Hyatt's *Sunday Serenade*. And throughout the week there were now hourly five minute newscasts, thanks to a brand new United Press teletype machine.

The principal birth during the spring semester was *Candlelight and Silver* at 6:10 p.m., a program of smooth, uninterrupted dinner music (Vincent Youmans, Cole Porter, Jerome Kern) which was to join *Jam for Breakfast* and *MTM* as one of WDBS' longest-running shows. A few weeks later this programming idea was expanded to fill three-quarters of an hour, eliminating the musical catch-all that had opened the evening program block for as long as most could remember. But the *640 Club* (b. 1946), in one form or another, would be back. Listenership for all this radio fare averaged 500 students per night, plus plenty of townspeople (most of whom could get the station), or so the ever-active pollsters reported. As a further indicator of audience size, they pointed to the 1,500 postcard and telephone requests received by the station during the course of the year.

Daily program schedules continued to be printed in *The Dartmouth* as they (almost) always had been, but the newspaper's typesetters got in surreptitious digs by occasionally heading a whole day's programming *Heelers Hack Time*, or listing for 11:00 p.m. *Just a Little Mayhem Til Midnight*. WDBS producer Johnny Gambling '51 parried those low blows by wangling authorship of the "*D's*" radio column, now called "Listening Inn." Never had the critiques been so pointed: "if your feet itch to stamp, and you go for the stuff that jumps, 640 is the bright spot on your radio dial …"[15] (John A. Gambling was the son of one of New York City's most famous radio hosts, John B. Gambling of *Rambling with Gambling*, and would later become a highly successful radio personality himself.[16])

### *WDBS Forum* … and the Magic Wheel

Although the emphasis was more than ever on music, both live and recorded, a fair number of specials continued to be produced. Foremost was the *WDBS Forum*, whose weekly panels of students, faculty and townspeople debated everything from political witch hunting at the University of New Hampshire to world federalism, the atomic bomb, and the meaning of individualism. The resulting intellectual fireworks did not cause audiences to mushroom noticeably, but did bring the station kudos from many important corners. Once in a while, after considerable skull-cracking, the panel would reach singularly basic truths: "WDBS FORUM CONCLUDES," reported *The Dartmouth* one morning in May, "… People Sometimes Think!"

At various other times the college band was carried live from the steps of Dartmouth Hall, the *Workshop* tried to live down its "It Can't Happen Here" infamy with a fine William Saroyan play adapted for radio by John Gambling (but the *Claremont Eagle* took no note), and time was given to class presidential candidates.

An innovation of the 1949 spring term was the long-running *Student-Faculty Quiz*, billed as the station's answer to the network show *Information, Please*. Oddly enough, on the WDBS version the same side (faculty) always seemed to win. Another newcomer in the spring was WDBS' first regular giveaway show, sponsored by Hanover merchant Raymond Gee. This last presentation, though undoubtedly well-intentioned, proved to be a low-rent parody of game shows, as described in the following news story.

> Bud Popke introduces himself as MC of the program, then launches into the first segment of popular records. After five minutes he interrupts the music to announce the evening's first Magic Winning Phrase – one of Mr. Gee's advertising slogans … then, with a properly suspenseful build-up, he spins the "WDBS Magic Wheel." The number it stops on indicates a page in a special combined college-town telephone directory, to which he turns. A second spin reveals how many names to count down from the top.

As an expectant hush falls over the studio, the designated person is called. Is he able to repeat the Magic Winning Phrase? If so, he cracks the jackpot and wins one dollar. If he's never heard of the Magic Winning Phrase, he still receives a handsome consolation prize: one back issue of *The Jacko* (the college humor magazine), or a 50-cent reduction on the yearly subscription rate. Popke thanks him for being on the show, and the music resumes, for five more minutes.[17]

### Carnival, Sports, and Specials

Winter Carnival of 1949 brought the usual extended broadcasting, as well as unusually close cooperation between the station and the Carnival Council. WDBS did announcing, technical, and publicity work for the Council, covered the Outdoor Evening events, and staged disc jockey shows at Thayer Dining Hall to "sell Winter Carnival." The latter presentations were called, of course, *Music While Munching*. An excellent post-Carnival wrap-up "Behind the Scenes" was produced by Don Hyatt, who had spent the gala weekend as only a dedicated WDBS producer could, lugging a wire recorder around, collecting "interesting events."

WDBS continued its traditional coverage of all home football, basketball, and hockey games during 1948-49, in addition to a smattering of baseball, boxing, and Freshman contests. The play by play was provided by juniors Bob Sisk and Dick Hollands '50, among others.

### Technical Department

A historic first occurred in January 1949 when John Gambling and Bob Sisk recorded on-the-spot pre-game interviews and play-by-play for the Princeton basketball game for later broadcast on WDBS using a new technology called "tape recording." The recorder they used was one of the first in Hanover, borrowed from the Dartmouth Co-Op store. By the end of the year the station was making fairly regular use of tape, with its own first small tape recorder, COSO's portable Brush Soundmirror, and several student-owned Brush and Pentron machines. Producers discovered that with scissors and a little splicing tape they could transform their shows into (technically) flawless masterpieces, and demands on the primitive machines were considerable. "Acquisition of a tape recorder has made possible programs which were formerly unthinkable," crowed *The Aegis* (the class yearbook) at year's end. But the station's disc recording machine continued to be used for most commercials and program continuity recordings, and it remained for another year to acquire WDBS' first professional tape recorder.

As a further boon to the sportscasters two RCA 88-A sports microphones were acquired early in 1949. However at the moment the Tech Department was generally less concerned with making life easy for the programmers than with improving the perennially bad broadcast signal. Blanchard Pratt '47, an ex-Navy radio technician, worked all through the fall of 1948 assembling surplus parts into a new, 20-watt central transmitter, the station's third in four years on the air. This one cost about $200, and like the others was to feed the signal into the college high-power lines in the basement of Middle Fayerweather dormitory. It was a prodigious job and in January, 1949, *The Alumni Magazine* told its readers that "at present the black crackle metal chassis, loops of colored wire and shiny new coils, and a dozen empty Coke bottles decorate the maintenance room where Pratt and a helper work late nights fitting parts and soldering up circuits. In this room where radio jargon baffles the layman, they say that the new transmitter 'has been on the redboard' - that is, hitched up temporarily for testing."[18]

Amid a flurry of last-minute crises the unit was installed in time for the station's spring semester return to the air (mid-February). It proved to have considerably more strength and better fidelity than any of its predecessors, performing so well that the delighted engineers didn't even bother to take careful field strength measurements of its coverage. That would prove to be a mistake.

### Business: Neon Sign Prosperity

By the end of 1948 WDBS had about it the air of a thriving enterprise. The station claimed 80 regular student workers who "do something each week," 50 occasional students, 20 occasional faculty contributors, and 10 occasional townspeople. There were weekly station meetings and on December 17 a two-hour Christmas party in 51 Robinson, broadcast on the air of course. At that celebration Bud Popke announced two new Directorate members, John "Red" Whelden '49, to head the Technical Department, and James Gaylord '50, to be business manager.

While Whelden godfathered the new transmitter, Popke and Gaylord continued to give WDBS the most nearly solvent year in its history. The station had traditionally been subsidized by the College, to the tune of about $1,500 per year, plus occasional capital equipment grants. But now sales jumped from $1,250 (1947-48) to almost $2,100 in one year, while expenses increased only $300, to $3,100. The $1,500 subsidy had already been advanced but the next year's station manager was to write ruefully that because of "a most peculiar bookkeeping arrangement" the surplus couldn't be carried over into the next year, and that $400 had been returned to COSO, "rather than purchase equipment ill-advisedly."[19]

The Ivy Network, headed by Bud Popke until the first annual meeting in January 1949, was off to a slow start, landing only two sponsors and $500 in billings in 1948. But WDBS was unquestionably prosperous from local sales. Perhaps the best symbol of that was the brand new neon sign the blazed the letters WDBS from the third floor studio window, for all to see.[20]

### Green Key... and the New Station Manager(s)

Green Key brought the by-now traditional big weekend of extended broadcasting. The Green Key Radio Queen was back too. "All a young aspirant has to do," sighed the envious *Dartmouth*, "is to climb up to the studio between noon and midnight and convince the hierarchy of the station that she looks better than the local microphone."[21] This year's winner, a Colby junior, received an autographed album of recordings by Green Key maestro Claude Thornhill.

When the annual change of Directorates came in May there was plenty of news for the paper to report. For the first and last time in station history there would be two station managers, old sportscasting and announcing buddies Bob Sisk and Dick Hollands. Jim Gaylord remained as business manager and Red Whelden as technical director, while Johnny Gambling assumed the production director's chevrons.

57

A second experimental move was the creation of a junior Directorate, which was supposed to provide wider representation in the station's top decision-making councils. This body only proved that top control must be centralized, however, laying the foundation of the never-too-cohesive executive staff of later years.

After two years of station-building unmatched since the days of Krolik and Mitchel, Emil "Bud" Popke graduated in June 1949. He went straight to a position in commercial radio, at WTOR in Connecticut. But his days in Upper Valley radio were far from over.

### 1949-1950

Building a reputation which even approaches professionalism in any activity on any campus is quite a trick... for station WDBS, officially plunging today into the fourth year of its post-war career, it's a process still going on. For in radio, technical and creative problems run as tough as they ever will. It's a rare electronic technician who steps off the White River bus; Speech 11 turns out few announcers; and as a result, the operating line of the station has been and continues to be, "If you want to work at radio, we need you..."[22]

Thus was the class of 1953 introduced to WDBS, in the freshman issue of *The Dartmouth*. The college station had come a long way in three years, and its horizons showed no signed of contracting. When Bob Varney reactivated DBS in the spring of 1946, there were two-and-a-half hours per day of programming, five days a week. Now there were nine hours daily, including a three hour morning block. The weekend had been so thoroughly invaded that total air time had doubled, then doubled again to 58 hours per week. There were tape recorders, a United Press teletype machine, the Ivy Network, a new transmitter that almost worked, and a budget headed steadily upward toward the deficit-free $5,000 level. If the expansion under Hollands and Sisk was less dramatic than under Shade and Popke, it was no less effective in strengthening the organization that would one day call itself "Dartmouth's most active activity."

### Programming

John Gambling had assumed the production directorship with so many ideas that he could scarcely hold them all until after the summer, so two of the gems of the 1949-50 programming year made their debut during May 1949. *The Collector's Corner,* hosted by Gambling and Bill Brooks '51, featured records of "earlier vintage" (1930-40), stories of artists and "one real collector's item per program." "We want to emphasize that we're not going to play all jazz," reported Brooks. "It'll be about half-and-half, half jazz and half popular. We have some old Russ Columbo records we're going to play."[23] Even more unique was the new *Co-Op Show,* sponsored by the Dartmouth Co-Op store and hosted by senior Don Hyatt with his wife and others as guests. Hyatt, who went on to produce NBC's widely acclaimed *Project Twenty* series, was one of the most talented producers in Dartmouth radio history. He had done much work in his sophomore and junior years, and *The Co-Op Show* was a fitting climax to his student days. This was to be a real variety show he said in May. "The point is that we want each program to be different. We present dramatic skits, all kinds of productions, short stories, musical views of Hollywood, Broadway, and Hanover, and interviews." One of the first shows was a behind-the-scenes view of the 1949 Green Key Weekend, captured on a tape recorder Hyatt lugged around to the Green Key Dance, to bandleader Claude Thornhill, to fraternity houses, etc. Every girl interviewed on that show was told flatly that only 10 percent of Smith seniors intend to get married, and asked what did she think about that? "We got a lot of funny answers... but the boys like to hear women's voices on the air."[24]

The old, disgraced *WDBS Workshop* became *Studio '49* (in January, *Studio '50*), with a renewed emphasis on live drama, but no inspiration from Orson Welles, thank you. The first presentation, in September, was a radio adaptation by sophomore Ronald Marcks '52 of Richard Connell's famous short story, "The Most Dangerous Game." *The Concert Hour* rolled on, despite the complaint of one listener who cried on the "*D's*" shoulder, "Is it necessary for the announcers of WDBS to voice their own personal opinions of musical recordings? I refer to the remark made on *The Symphony Hour*, Sunday, October 16, at 9:35: 'Now we'll go into some ballet music... oh, brother!'"[25]

The chief addition to the musical programming during fall 1949 was a late night show, suavely titled *In the Still of the Night*. Airing seven nights a week, from 12:15 to 1:00 a.m., this was a carefully programmed blend of uninterrupted mood and semi-classical music "specifically designed for those who keep late hours." The blend of Kostelanetz, Paul Weston, Carmen Cavallaro, David Rose and an occasional *Eroica Symphony*, without interruption, proved to be one of the best programming ideas WDBS ever had, filling Dartmouth's late-night needs until the more talkative *Nightwatch* came along in 1956. Otherwise the schedule was largely unchanged in 1949-50:

<u>Morning</u>
7:30   *Jam for Breakfast*
9:00   *Morning Melodies*
10:20  sign-off
<u>Evening</u>
5:50   sign on ("Men of Dartmouth" being played)
6:00   News
6:15   *Candlelight and Silver*
7:00   *Styles in Music*
7:30   Sports News
7:45   *Here's to Veterans: Frankie Carle* (transcribed)
8:00   Various 30-minute shows: *At the Keyboard* (live), *Vestpocket Varieties,*
       *Romance of Song* (semi-classical), *Campus Interview, Broadway Review.*
9:00   *Concert Hour*
10:00  *Club Campion* (personalities on record)
10:15  Various: *Student-Faculty Quiz, Co-Op Show, Singin' Twing Neely* (live
       folk music), etc.
11:00  *Music 'til Midnight*
12:00  News
12:15  *In the Still of the Night*
1:00   sign-off

In addition there were regular news summaries on the hour, and on Saturdays (Fridays during the football season), good old *Heelers' Hack Time.*

## Sports and Specials

Coverage of away games was once again sporadic, dependent on finding sponsors. An early fall meeting of the Undergraduate Council in one breath voted funds for CARE, the Displaced Persons Committee, and WDBS' coverage of the Columbia away game. Then too, the cost of getting there was sometimes only half the problem. Sportscaster Bob Sisk described the Penn game as "sitting almost on one goal line, looking into the blinding sun, and competing with a public address system that was louder than anything I have ever heard. It was like trying to broadcast with someone standing behind me and hollering over my shoulder."[26] It was all worth it however for the station's pollsters reported that during the Columbia game WDBS had captured 92 percent of the student listening audience, and during the Penn game, 95 percent.

Among the programming high points of the year were the 17½ hour all-request show on Saturday of Houseparties weekend, the longest continuous broadcast in the station's history; the hour-long concert from the Hanover Inn by Mrs. Lydia Hoffman-Behrendt; and broadcast of the annual Hums fraternity singing competition. December 1949 saw the beginning of one of WDBS' most enjoyable traditions, the annual swapping of staff with Smith College radio. WCSR had begun arranging swaps with various Ivy League stations almost as soon as it was founded, in the fall of 1948, "for the publicity value." Station Manager Patricia Butler wrote to Bob Sisk in late 1949, saying that although earlier plans had fallen through ("Bud Poopke [sic] was talking to me last year about the idea of Dartmouth coming down here"), the girls were still willing. Probably no sign-up list in WDBS history attracted signatures as fast as the one that Sisk then posted, and in December an enthusiastic crew weathered a snowstorm to bring Smith College an evening of Dartmouth's (radio) finest. Even the station pollsters were there, reporting that "four out of five college houses had several radios tuned to WCSR," while WDBS engineers proudly demonstrated the broadcasting capabilities of their new tape recorder. To further cement this valuable cultural relationship, WCSR on several occasions carried WDBS coverage of Dartmouth away games.

## Enter the WDBS Newsletter

Essential to a station's schedule of specialty programming is adequate publicity, so that interested listeners could know when to tune in. *The Dartmouth* had always cooperated by printing the station's program schedules, except for a period in 1942-43 when the two were feuding. Now the "*D*" suddenly announced that listings would no longer be carried. This caused something of an uproar at WDBS, for listenership to such an irregular, varied schedule could scarcely be maintained without publicity. But after some executive anguish an alternative was found, and in February 1950 Dartmouth was introduced to *The WDBS Newsletter.* Like the *Listener's Log* of later years, the *Newsletter* began as a mimeographed listing of program highlights and other station publicity put out by the WDBS Public Relations Department. At the start only enough copies to post around campus were prepared, but from these small beginnings the *Newsletter* grew to sizeable proportions over the next four years.

Despite inevitable hard feelings an overt break with *The Dartmouth* was avoided, witness the paper's agreement to supply a five-minute campus roundup for each night's *Midnight News*. But the point of the following blurb, from an early *Newsletter*, could hardly be plainer.

> Our special programs represent news when it is news. During the last presidential election the station stayed on the air all through the night, with the reports as they came in. We brought you the name of the 1950 football captain two minutes after the ballots were tabulated, and the winner of the recent interfraternity play contest was announced within ten minutes after the decision was made public.[27]

### A Pollster at Work

The audience researchers were as busy as ever, conducting a continuing survey of when students listened and what they preferred. Results were compiled weekly, thanks largely to the legwork of freshmen trainees. Dick Hollands described "a pollster at work" as follows.

> Here is a scene that is repeated over and over again in every dormitory. There is a knock on the door. A muffled "come in." The WDBS heeler steps into the room, equipped with his list of questions and blanks to be filled in. The room is occupied by two students who have been interrupted from their books. There is not a sound in the room. The heeler only asks his first question, "Are you listening to your radio?"
>
> The occupants look amazed. "Do you hear anything?" one asks. "I guess you're not listening, huh?" says the heeler as he backs out of the door. "Thanks anyway."
>
> The students look annoyed momentarily as the heeler, outside in the hall, fills in the appropriate blanks. He clatters off to his next assigned room, which may be over in another dormitory. End of scene.[28]

In mid-February 1950 News Director Bill Brooks mounted what was probably the most comprehensive listenership survey yet, a printed, 49-question questionnaire that was distributed to the student body at large. Its results had something for every department. The technicians learned that 97 percent of the student body owned or had access to radios, but only half reported their reception of WDBS to be "excellent." Nevertheless only 10 percent now said it was "poor," compared to 21 percent two years earlier. For the programmers the survey revealed that most students thought the station had the right balance of popular and classical music, but there were minor rebellions against bebop and hillbilly programming. News, public service, and sports programming and commercials were all right, but music was preferred. The Business Department got the most disturbing news: 90 percent of those answering admitted that they had never told an advertiser they heard of him on WDBS.

As for program ratings, *Music 'til Midnight*, the all-request jukebox, was far and away the most popular show, with other front runners in terms of listenership as follows.[29]

1. *Music 'til Midnight*          80% (record requests)
2. *Sunday Serenade*          64% (uninterrupted light classical music)
3. *Saturday Night Musical Caravan* 61% (five hours of requests)
4. *Midnight News*          60%
5. *Romance of Song*          58% (semi-classical and popular)
6. *In the Still of the Night*          57% (uninterrupted "mood" music)
7. *Candlelight and Silver*          56% (uninterrupted dinner music)
8. *Morning Melodies*          53% (record requests)
9. *Concert Hour*          52% (classical and opera, with commentary)

All but one of these were musical shows, all using records at that. Hard working Don Hyatt garnered only 37 percent for his innovative *Co-Op Show*, but other produced shows fared worse: 30 percent for *Student-Faculty Quiz*, 22 percent for *The Dartmouth Lecture Series*, and 20 percent for *Studio '50*. *Singin' Twing Neely and His White Mountain Ramblers* brought up the rear with a resounding 14 percent. More clearly than ever, hard work brought kudos and a meaningful contribution by the station but records and a turntable got the listeners.[30]

### Technical

The Technical Department made news of its own in 1949-50, especially under Mike Heyman '51 who succeeded Red Whelden as T.D. during the fall. A "generous financial loan"[31] from the College—nobody would say how much—allowed the purchase of a brand new RCA 77-D microphone, one of the best professional radio-TV mikes available. Then there were the studio turntables, old Fairchild and Rek-o-Cut models in such sad shape as to arouse listener complaints ("free my ears... from their torture" wrote one[32]). After much investigation of the market, Heyman ordered two new RCA 70-D's, turntables whose quality was comparable to the 77-D microphone. They arrived in February, whereupon Heyman rhapsodized as only a technician could:

> They are really beautiful, and the Technical Department up here is slowly going mad in exultation. They arrived today and we had one of them installed for tonight's broadcast schedule. It was rather lucky that they came today because we lost our other Fairchild and the spare Rek-o-Cut was beginning to go... we are absolutely in love with them... hell, they're practically a substitute for women in these barren wastes of New Hampshire.[33]

Some months later the *Newsletter* put it in more practical terms. "Installation of the two new RCA turntables made it possible to present disc shows that feature music and not surface scratches."[34]

## Business, and the New Regime

Revenues continued to climb, setting a new record of almost $3,000. But expenses, two-thirds of them technical, rose even faster, bringing the subsidized station to a rather larger than usual deficit of $1,900. Nevertheless student ad sales was offsetting more than half the cost of running the station.

The new Directorate was named on March 22, 1950, three weeks earlier than it had been in 1949, and more than a month earlier than the customary changeover date of previous years. This was the beginning of a trend to allow the new directors time to settle into their new positions during the relatively peaceful spring semester, while their predecessors were still around to give advice if needed. The new directors would thereby be better prepared to face the battles of the fall, where their year would likely be won or lost. From this time until the advent of the three-term system in 1958 Directorates would be announced in mid-March, instead of April or May, and would take control after spring vacation. In later years the changeover date would move even earlier.

Production Director John Gambling was chosen by his fellow directors to be the new station manager. New Technical Director Albert Warren '52, Business Manager Ted Bailey '51 and Production Director Bill Terry '51 were elevated from the junior executive ranks of their respective departments. In addition to the new junior board, five sophomores were appointed "program directors," each to be in charge of an evening's broadcasts.

As his emeritus project, former Station Manager Dick Hollands wrote a feature article for the May 1950 *Dartmouth Alumni Magazine*. It contained a summary of station operations and history to date, as well as some observations on student radio management in general and what his Directorate had tried to accomplish.

Whenever I've explained the organization of WDBS to businessmen (most of whom know nothing about college radio), they are always aghast when I point out that the top executives change each year. Yet it is this very change that makes possible the ambition mentioned earlier. Each station manager and staff are seeking to make their term of office more outstanding in every respect than that of their predecessors. What about any long-range planning, you say? Well, it would seem that, idealistic as it sounds, a sort of affection for the organization takes hold of its members if they have worked hard for several years and the students in authority take great pains to see that the station can progress even after they have left Dartmouth behind. In that spirit, Bob Sisk '50 and I, as co-managers, recently drew up an equipment plan for the next five years, so that we may buy our equipment on something more than a hit-or-miss basis. This plan can be completely scrapped of course by next year's Directorate, but at least the program has been charted...

Very few men who come out for WDBS are interested in making radio a career. A few more, like myself, find out through working at the station that this is what they want to do in life. The great majority will become businessmen like their fathers, but since radio, even at Dartmouth, is more of a business than an art, the experience they gain can be invaluable. It probably won't help them in getting a job, but the things they learn in working with people should show to good advantage once they start working. Take the station manager's job for instance. The task of maintaining a functioning radio station which broadcasts ten hours a day to the highly critical college audience is not particularly easy in itself, but to do it with staff members who receive no salaries and whose first duty is to their studies gives one some idea of the experience that can be gained. Among other things, one learns that almost all freshmen are idealists who look for the perfection that is never there, who must be nursed through the first few months of disillusion at finding that even seniors can and do make mistakes. If they can be guided through these critical months and still retain their spirit and drive, one finds that he is working with a group whose enthusiasm to learn cannot be equaled anywhere else in the radio field.[35]

Hollands also pointed out that the station's faculty advisor Almon Ives wisely permitted the students to make most of the decisions, but was always there if they needed his advice. He also voiced a familiar refrain that it would help a lot if top management, which put in so many hours, were given some sort of financial reward for their labors, even if were a token $50 at the end of the term.

One of John Gambling's first official acts as station manager was to reverse a precedent set a few months earlier and invite WCSR to take over WDBS for a night. But it was too late in the year, and besides most of the WCSR staff would probably be in town on dates shortly anyway. Green Key Weekend saw the usual extended broadcasting, and once again the WDBS Green Key Sweetheart. This year's winner, having climbed the stairs to the studio at the appointed hours and outshone the nearest microphone, was crowned by Ralph Flanagan at the Green Key Dance, and presented with an autographed copy of one of his albums.

## 1950-1951

### Programming

After three years of rapid expansion under Bud Popke and John Gambling, the WDBS program schedule reached something of a plateau in 1950-51. It was essentially the same 10 hour 7:30 to 10:15 a.m. and 6:00 p.m. to 1:00 a.m schedule. Sleepy men of Dartmouth continued to be roused by *Jam for Breakfast*, skip 9:00 o'clock classes to *Morning Melodies*, and eat illegally in their rooms by *Candlelight and Silver*. On Saturday nights there were five hours of requests on *Musical Caravan* ("Call Hanover 1070!") and on Sunday afternoons the *Opera Hour*.

The station's basic, and listener-demanded, musical orientation was reflected in the fast growing record library, which now numbered some 5,000 popular and 1,000 classical 78 rpm discs. That this library was being kept up to date was reflected in the springtime sale of 78 rpm classical albums ("at a colossal loss") to raise money for the purchase of some of the recently introduced 33-1/3 r.p.m. microgroove LPs.

Chief Announcer Dave Dugan '52 hosted *Newsweek Views the News*, junior John Doty '52, one of WDBS' more glib d.j.'s, reviewed new releases on *What's New* and massacred old ones on *Doty on Discs*, and Sports and Special Events Director Bill Brooks converted the old *Co-Op Show* (b. 1946, as a 15-minute ski report) into a musical museum, spotlighting collector's items. When listeners inquired about Brooks' unusual theme song they were informed it was a 1930 English recording of

"We've Got the Moon and Sixpence," quite unavailable in record stores. However WDBS would gladly whip off some copies on its disc machine for a mere $1.50 each.

The quiz fever spilled over into *Morning Melodies*, where you could win a dollar by identifying the Mystery Melody. Even *SFQ* (*Student-Faculty Quiz*) had that commercial touch. For the second straight year listeners whose questions stumped the panel won a carton of Chesterfield cigarettes.

### "Hi There, Tiger"

Few shows have ever stirred such interest as *Your Lonesome Gal*, which made its debut in January and ran from 11:45 p.m. to midnight every weekday night. She purred and cooed, told you she loved you, then importuned each individual "sugar" listening to go buy some Bondstreet pipe tobacco at the local tobacco shop the very next morning. "You don't have to be in your bedroom slipper to enjoy Bondstreet," she murmured, "you can be standing in your hipboots in the middle of your favorite trout stream..." The effect of those dulcet tones speaking to an all-male audience in the wilds of northern New Hampshire was electric to say the least.[36]

"Your Lonesome Leach!" snarled the envious *Dartmouth,* exposing the Lonesome Gal as a former singer, movie bit player (*Tarzan and the Amazons*) and radio actress named Jean King.[37] At her home in Hollywood she ground out fifteen-minute shows tailored to particular products (usually beer) and areas. Dartmouth got "Bondstreet is just the kind of tobacco for a man a girl likes to have around the house. Like you, honey..." By March she was an established fact at Harvard, Yale, Princeton and Penn, as well as Dartmouth. To readers complaining that hers was "cheap, erotic rhetoric... a flagrant insult to human dignity and intelligence," *The Dartmouth* addressed the following. "We suggest to Dartmouth listeners waiting for the midnight news that they take *Your Lonesome Gal* as a public service test of the maturity of their emotions. The rules are simple. Starting with a score of 100, take off 10 points for each twinge of self-pity or erotic desire. Sixty is not passing—Ed."[38] Perhaps it was a coincidence that Stan Freberg's breathless recording "John and Marsha" proved to be the hit of the 1951 Winter Carnival. In any event Bondstreet canceled after a few months and programming returned to more mundane fare.

On a more prestigious note was a series of *U.N. This Week* forums moderated by one Abdul Sheikh '51, including one edition entitled "How Colby Looks at the U.N." Bill Terry's *Studio '50* (and *'51*) presented live dramas such as Poe's *Telltale Heart, The Crucifixion, Mr. Ginsberg, Alibi Ike* and, once again, "The Most Dangerous Game." The last-named had fortunately been disc-recorded during its original performance. It was one of the few complete shows of the 1940s remaining in the station archives during future decades.

### Listener Criticism

Despite the producers' best efforts the station received persistent complaints about sloppy announcers. "Each fall WDBS seems to try to reach a new depth in low quality announcing and this year it appears to have struck rock bottom" wrote one, who then gave a sample. "(The regular announcer) isn't here tonight. He's taken off but if you guys want to listen that's up to you."[39] Another letter was aghast when the station honored a request to play "It's All Over Now" for the none-too-successful returning football team.[40] But the most interesting reading was contained in the "*D's*" own lengthy critique, published in February.

> Sometime after 10 a.m. yesterday morning a WDBS disc jockey announced pithily, "This is station WDBS broadcasting from the bathroom in Robinson Hall." He was, no doubt, being facetious. At least there was no sound of toilets flushing in the background, and that hoary gag about WDBS broadcasting through the college plumbing system is just an ugly rumor. But the disc jockey's witticism might well but a cue line for an appraisal of WDBS outside its technical excellence.[41]

The article, by one Brock Brower, went on to explain that of WDBS's 65 hours of weekly airtime, 50 was "recorded music for your listening pleasure" and most of the rest news and sports coverage. "Certainly WDBS owes its very existence to Decca, Victor and London recording studios (with an assist from the United Press)." Dugan and Doty were good enough to be bearable, but most d.j.'s talked too much, and as for the current hit tunes, "at times it is almost impossible to tune in WDBS without hearing Phil Harris boom-de-booming 'The Thing' or John making passionate love to Marsha."

Brower admitted that WDBS news was good, and *Studio '51* at least tried, but *Your Lonesome Gal* was "a riotous novelty." He continued, "As long as a disc jockey can arrive at the studio 25 minutes late for his program, as long as the needle can get caught in a groove and stay there for three solid minutes, WDBS hasn't quite grown up."

Fortunately for the station not all listeners agreed. One wrote of the newspaper's critique, "It seemed that I had read most of it several times before. The editorial was, as usual, satirically pointing out the faults of some aspect of life in our times. 'Day by Day' [another column] panned the movie..."

## Specials

Despite this nattering there certainly were highlights this year, among them the broadcasts from 105 Dartmouth Hall of Professor Booth's Shakespearean readings, which were apparently the most popular bit of cultural stimulation ever required of freshmen; in November the first of President Dickey's periodic conversations with the student body at large (called *The President Reports*, these originated by the fireplace in Studio two, and were promptly dubbed "fireside chats"); the premiere of an original sonata by Professor Robin Robinson; the extended coverage during the December 1950 international crisis, when the Chinese entered the Korean War; broadcast of General Douglas MacArthur's address to Congress in April, after his dismissal by President Truman; a Spanish d.j. show staged by the Spanish Club; a swap of Christmas programs with Hawaii's KPOA; coverage of the 1951 Winter Carnival, including a subsequent *Behind the Scenes* special; and the traditional Christmas show, this year featuring "two live plays, a message from President John Dickey, an Edgar Bergen-Charlie McCarthy show, and other assorted items..."[42]

Sports coverage included all home games, but away contests only when special funds could be raised to pay for the necessary line charges. In October John Gambling went straight to the student body, setting up tables in Commons, Thayer

Dining Hall, and at the Hanover Inn corner, soliciting quarters to support a broadcast of the Dartmouth-Michigan game from Ann Arbor. "Worth a quarter" opined *The Dartmouth*, and the game was carried by way of a long distance hook-up with a professional station in Ann Arbor. The World Series was also carried, thanks to the generosity of the Granite State Network and the Mutual Broadcasting System.

## Technical Matters

When Rit Swicker '52 assumed the technical directorship in September he inherited responsibility for the traditional problem child of his department, the transmitter.[43] The current unit had been in service since early 1949 and had seemed to work so well that no comprehensive field strength tests had ever been made. Now, in the fall of 1950 it was apparent that coverage had fallen off considerably so test equipment was obtained and measurements made. The dismayed engineers found "a low modulation percentage, extremely high distortion, poor audio frequency response, and non-symmetrical output waveform."[44] Crisis! Dozens of man-hours would be spent during the next year before the problems were supposedly solved.

As for technical expansion, there was the purchase at last of an RCA Senior Velocity microphone (model 44-BX), to join the Junior Velocity in use since 1941. By the end of the year Swicker could boast of no fewer than eleven microphones, some worth over $100 each. The biggest technical news of the year however was the purchase of the station's first professional tape recorder. Several small home machines had been in use since 1949, but they could not stand up under the hard and continuous use of radio work and the station was forever apologizing about the lack of tape facilities. Tape was clearly the coming technology, so the Directorate felt its purse, carefully checked the market, and in November 1950 ordered one of the finest professional machines available, a $925 Ampex 400. It was the largest single purchase in station history and though the delivery time of "a few days" lengthened into four months, its eventual arrival in February was cause for a station celebration. The *WDBS Newsletter* boasted that "this high fidelity machine is the same type used in motion picture work. It will handle up to two solid hours of continuous recording (on a ten-inch reel)... There are only two other machines of this type in the New England area."[45]

Perhaps most noteworthy about the Ampex 400 was simply that it arrived in good condition and served faithfully for more than 10 years afterwards. This is more unusual than it sounds, for one of the least recognized and time consuming duties of technical directors is to do constant battle with supply houses and repair centers. It would seem that fully half the major equipment ordered from RCA, Radio Shack, Allied Radio, etc., over the years arrived damaged, defective, or late. There was considerable trouble with one of those beautiful RCA turntables, and the purchase of the Senior Velocity Microphone entangled the station in voluminous correspondence with three different sources. Nevertheless Swicker could boast of a large and versatile control board, two high quality RCA turntables (plus others), the Ampex 400, two portable consoles for remotes, the Rek-o-Cut disc recorder, 11 microphones and numerous other pieces of professional-grade equipment.

The student broadcasters had every reason to expect clear sailing for their station in the foreseeable future. Not only was a truly professional physical plant taking shape, but the Upper Valley market, as much of it as they could cover, remained after 10 years theirs alone. There were still no other local radio stations.

This proved to be too good to last.

## Grenades Under the Christmas Tree

When staffers returned from the Christmas holidays they blinked in amazement, and looked again. There is was, sitting insolently in a field on the West Lebanon road, a full power AM radio station smack in their own back yard. It wasn't much to look at to be sure, a small trailer parked beneath a hastily erected tower. But it was 250 watts AM, 16 hours a day, blanketing the entire Upper Valley, Lebanon, Hanover, White River Junction and their environs. Even its call letters proclaimed it to be radio "<u>T</u>win-<u>S</u>tates <u>L</u>ebanon."

It was not a complete surprise to WDBS' leaders. Rumors of a commercial station entering the market began circulating in early 1950, and in May Almon Ives confirmed that a small company that owned stations in Manchester, Claremont and Brattleboro, was indeed planning to do so. By June John Gambling had gathered more details.[46]

Trucked in by the Granite State Network, WTSL burst on to the empty Upper Valley airwaves one fine morning just two days before Christmas 1950, at the un-Dartmouth-like hour of 6:28 a.m. Indeed, very little about it seemed designed to appeal to students. Its programming was typified by that first, 6:28 a.m. program, *The Farm Report*, and by the newscasts from New England's own Yankee Network. But if WTSL was Granite State's Christmas gift to Hanover, it was by that very fact a grenade under WDBS' tree.

Though supposedly campus-limited, the College station in fact covered, entertained, and advertised to most of Hanover as well, and frankly looked toward the day when the lack of any other stations in the market would justify a switch to AM so it could do the same for the whole area. Now, overnight, commercial interests had arrived upon the scene with a station aimed directly at this community market, foreclosing, so it seemed, the students' chance to make hay on a unique situation. WDBS' own survival might not be threatened, but its golden chance to become something more than the ordinary "hi-there-all-you-guys-in-the-dorms" amateur "one-lunger" appeared to be dashed. John Gambling gulped hard and announced that his station was "looking forward to an exchange of programs with the Yankee Network. Rather than suffering by competition, we'll be benefiting from the chance for connections with a commercial set-up."[47] Over and over during years to come WDBS and WDCR would protest that it was not competing with the commercial outfit down the road, that the two stations were aimed at entirely different audiences.

On the surface at least the two stations couldn't have been friendlier. WTSL agreed to supply WDBS with network specials (Yankee got some shows from the Mutual Broadcasting System), especially news and sports events. The college broadcasters reciprocated by sending WTSL coverage of college events, some games, and the weekly *Student-Faculty Quiz*. The WTSL management was even invited to WDBS' annual station banquet.

The real damage was to morale. First of all there was simply the fact of a full power competitor, broadcasting all day long, 365 days a year, and covering all of WDBS' area plus much more besides. If WDBS had any pretensions, it was now put emphatically into its campus-limited place. Professional radio had come to town. Second, there was the double-edged matter of personnel. The first program director and spokesman for WTSL was none other than Emil "Bud" Popke, erstwhile WDBS station manager. Popke had done more, perhaps, than any other single individual to build Dartmouth radio from a shaky, three-hour-a-day club in 1946 to the thriving organization of 1950. Was he now to be the commercial competitor who would put DBS in its place?

Worst of all was the virtual desertion of WDBS by its own current station manager. John Gambling could well have been referring to himself when he made that statement about benefiting from a connection with professionals, for along with disc jockey Jim Rosenfield '52 he joined the staff of WTSL as soon as it opened, agreeing to do all the copywriting, fill 18 hours a week of airtime, and assume the unofficial functions of assistant program manager to Bud Popke.[48] The head of WDBS was at WTSL constantly it seemed, and if that wasn't bad enough he soon began borrowing WDBS records to supplement WTSL's meager library.[49]

Although such shenanigans stirred resentment, the breaking point did not come until someone noticed Gambling and a heeler he had commandeered lugging out the prized new Ampex 400 tape recorder. Technical Director Swicker was furious. As soon as the big machine was back he bolted it into a rack in the control room. For history's sake someone should have kept a record of the ensuing Directorate "conference," for Gambling probably came as close as any station manager to inciting an open revolt. But by this time his term was almost over and he retained his title, at least, until the changeover in early April. Ironically Gambling would in later years become one of the college station's biggest alumni supporters, after he established himself as a major figure in New York radio.

WTSL unquestionably did cut into WDBS' audience somewhat, especially at first. *The Dartmouth* helpfully carried weekly schedules of WDBS and WTSL program highlights side-by-side. They showed that though the college station had great variety, and of course much less bucolic music, WTSL could offer network features including the popular Red Sox baseball and famed news analysts Gabriel Heatter and Fulton Lewis Jr. In March 1951 WDBS' busy pollsters reported their station's share of the college radio audience down to about 72 percent, from 90 percent during 1949-50. There was no doubt that many townspeople who could pick up WDBS' not-so-limited signal would now go with WTSL. The statistics would get better; Bud Popke would be replaced by one Don Tibbetts after a scant three months; and John Gambling would graduate in June. WDBS would learn to live with the commercial competitor on the West Lebanon Road.

### Packed Meetings and Wet Pollsters

Despite the competition, Business Manager Ted Bailey could point to a steadily rising sales curve. His year set another new record, $3,500, and since expenses had leveled off somewhat the deficit was down from the preceding year's high. After three years the Ivy Network finally began to percolate, landing contracts with Lucky Strike and Philip Morris cigarettes, and selling whole shows such as the *Ford Concert Hour* and *Newsweek Views the News*. Ivy brought other benefits too, at least for the station delegation, which in April sallied forth to Princeton to attend the annual Ivy Network Convention. "Meetings, seminars and a cocktail party" highlighted a week's activities.[50]

With about 100 regular station members on the rolls, space was becoming an important problem, as illustrated by Dick Hollands in that *Alumni Magazine* article of a year earlier.

> At times every WDBS room in Robinson Hall (and there are six) overflows with workers. During these periods of feverish activity perhaps some of the Directorate may want to talk privately. This means a retreat to the newsroom, where the UP teletype clatters in the background, to a dormitory room, or even to a Robinson Hall washroom hastily appropriated for a conference. Latecomers to the regular Tuesday station meeting may be obliged to perch on top of the piano or, worse still, stand outside in the hall. WDBS has grown phenomenally in its short life.[51]

The audience researchers continued their program of regular polling, making full use of the free and willing labor pool formed by WDBS' freshman heelers. The figures they produced were useful to program, business, and technical staffers, but in-person polling had its dangers. A March 1951 Newsletter told the sad tale of one freshman heeler. "John Tenca '54, while polling a first floor room in South Mass., was completely (drenched) by a pail of water." The pail, it seems, had been suspended over the door by a mass of wires. The unfortunate pollster didn't even get his question sheet filled out, since the room was empty. His only reported comment was, "Maybe it was meant for the laundry man. I guess I'll go home and get dried off."[52]

### New Faces of 1951

On March 27 the retiring Directorate announced that its successor board would be headed by one of its own. Bill Terry would be the fourth production manager in a row to succeed to the station manager's position. Rit Swicker began a second year as technical director, while former Personnel Director Bud Sawyer '52 became production director and former Record Director Paul Sanderson '52 took over as business manager. They assumed office, as was now the custom, after the March spring recess.

Bill Terry's term began with a number of small victories. There was a large, impressive section about WDBS planted in an April *Christian Science Monitor* story about college radio. WDBS triumphed over the daily *Dartmouth's* "hot-shots" in softball, 14 to 10 (notwithstanding a sports page story which credited the latter with a 329 to 3 victory). The latest chapter in the reciprocal trade program with Smith College was an unqualified success. Bill Terry & co. made the arrangements while attending WCSR's ambitious Intercollegiate Radio Conference in March, and in April a bevy of WCSR announcers and engineers returned the earlier raids by bringing Dartmouth a whole Friday night of "the best radio show ever" (their own description). May brought the many-splendored Green Key Weekend, including the crowing of the fourth annual WDBS Radio Queen, This year's winner, from Mt. Vernon College, didn't even have to climb the Robinson Hall stairs. She was picked by station spotters entrusted with the pleasant job of finding the prettiest girl at Key. She was crowned at the Green Key Dance, receiving from bandleader Ray Anthony an autographed record album and a kiss.

# Chapter 4

# 1951-1955: Into the Fifties

Like a newborn colt that may one day grow into a thoroughbred, but which for the moment must struggle to stand awkwardly on four shaky legs, the early DBS had to devote much of its energy into merely staying alive. Listeners and advertisers would surely support a broadcast day longer than three hours, and the basic goals of the enterprise—to be independent of professional supervision and the campus newspaper, to put itself on a self-sustaining financial basis, and to provide service to and training for the Dartmouth student—all seemed achievable, but they would take time. The solid foundation that Dartmouth broadcasting would one day achieve was not won in a day.

Two major factors held the station back in the 1940s. The Second World War provided the first setback, diverting everyone's energies to a far more important struggle. Then until 1948 an understandably cautious College held a tight grip on the reins, through the Radio Council. Only when full control was passed to the student directors did real growth begin. The new WDBS of Shade, Popke, Gambling and their contemporaries blossomed in program time, technical plant and billings, as well as in the quality that its leaders most earnestly sought, professionalism. By 1951 the station bore little resemblance to its predecessor of 1941. Not only was it bigger and more active, but its student directors enjoyed a degree of autonomy undreamt of by their well-regulated predecessors.

Yet the WDBS of 1951, for all its momentum, was still well short of winning the Derby. Compared to commercial stations, one of which was painfully close by, the broadcast day was strangely short and segmented, the technical plant barely adequate to needs, and the budget embarrassingly small. A visitor to Hanover might enjoy the boys' efforts (if he could hear them), but he would not mistake which was the student operation and which was the local "professional" station.

The 1950s would see Dartmouth's radio experiment mature, as the more or less typical college "one-lunger" grew into a full time business, ready to take on a most unusual challenge. There was no question of the ultimate goal, even in 1951. Bill Terry was building toward the day when WDBS would become the first student-run station in America to gain a full-power AM broadcast license.

## 1951-1952: Programming

The program schedule announced in September 1951 contained few changes. Bright wake-up music set the pace from 7:30 to 10:30 a.m., with music, news and a grab bag of features from 6:00 p.m. to 1:00 a.m. and extended hours of more of the same on Saturdays and Sundays. The station was still off the air weekdays from late morning to late afternoon. The lot of the morning disc jockey was not greatly altered either, to judge by the following story in an October 1951 *Newsletter.*

> "Up in the morning, out on the job, work like the devil—but no pay." Thus sings the morning trio, Solow, Sanderson and Doty, the three who six days a week, every week in the year do the early morning announcing, engineering, record hunting and telephone answering for WDBS.
>
> At 7:00 a.m. every morning Herb Solow crawls grumbling from his Wheeler bed, washes, dresses, and stumbles across the green to Robinson Hall. He turns on the transmitter to warm up the equipment and at 7:28:00 a.m. (straight up) he spins "Men of Dartmouth." At this point he opens his eyes. Until 9:00 o'clock it's *Jam for Breakfast*, music, news and chatter.
>
> At 9:00 on Tuesdays and Thursdays Paul Sanderson begins *Morning Melodies*, featuring the Mystery Melody, which Sandy plays during Chapel Period [a daily 10-10:30 a.m. break between classes, once used for the purpose indicated by its name]. The first person to phone in the name of the Mystery Melody and who's playing it receives a phonograph record. Sandy gets about 20 calls each morning.
>
> On Monday, Wednesday and Friday John Doty wanders in to do *Morning Melodies*. John used to present the Mysterious Refrain in answer to Sanderson's Mystery Melody, but so far this year there has been no sign of John striking back. Steady listeners await eagerly the next weed from Doty's fertile brain.[1]

Many of the fall's programs had a familiar ring. Doty and Len Gochman '53 took over *The Co-Op Show*, continuing music and recorded features like "I Can Hear It Now," but not Bill Brooks' collector's items. *At the Keyboard* continued as a remote from the Hanover Inn lobby.

A Thursday night newcomer, and one that might well tie the Don Hyatt *Co-Op Show* as WDBS's most professional sounding program to date, was *The Hunky Dorey Hour.* Actually a weekly half hour (despite the name) of original comedy, this was "an annihilation of commercial radio, along with several sideswipes at WDBS," according to the 1952 *Aegis.*[2] Like Hyatt's varieties, it depended on the peculiar talents of its hosts, seniors Henry "Hank" Williams '52 and Derek "Deke" Dorey '52, who bantered, talked over each other, and launched into impromptu nonsense. Each episode consisted of skits interspersed with oddball records (bop, Dixieland, novelties). Regular characters included violinist Professor Vladimir Catgut, who dropped semi-tones on the floor, tough-talking author Jay Horton Burg, who wrote nonsensical books, and Cecil, who lived in the radiator. Occasionally a special guest would appear such as producer David O. Bromoseltzernick to recreate his movie epic *Saga of the South*, and Peggy Lee, who Hank discovered was staying at the Hanover Inn. After a long admiring introduction the hosts revealed that the famous songstress had brought her entire orchestra to the studio and was about to sing a song. However listeners never heard her—as the music began she ran screaming from the studio (apparently it was in the wrong key) and down the street as the orchestra kept playing... and playing. The "Hunk" and Dorey managed to sound consistently funny, though they reportedly would dash into the studio each Thursday night one minute before air time, the script "hidden beneath their shirts."[3]

Another creative spirit of the early 1950s was Buck Zuckerman '52, who with his roommate Walker Benning '52 produced *The New Age Hour*, a combination of old jazz records and comedy skits inspired by sardonic humorist Henry Morgan. Buck also hosted *Student-Faculty Quiz*. After graduation he went to Hollywood and, as Buck Henry, had a stellar career as co-creator of *Get Smart*, screenwriter (*The Graduate*), and actor in films including *Catch-22* and *Heaven Can Wait* and TV shows ranging from *The New Steve Allen Show* (1961) to *30 Rock* (2010). He also made frequent appearances on *Saturday Night Live*.[4]

After years of talk the Ivy Network took its first plunge into production. Episodes of *The Ivy Theatre* were produced and tape recorded by member stations at Dartmouth, Cornell, Princeton, Yale, Harvard and Penn, then rotated. Each station thereby had an original drama from a different school each week, but only had to produce one every six weeks. Apparently WDBS had a dearth of decent writers. In March a well-publicized script contest was held. In order to win all one had to do was submit a radio play good enough for production on the *WDBS Prize Playhouse*, or better yet syndication via *The Ivy Theatre*. First prize would be $15, second prize $5, and there would be plenty of Honorable Mentions to go around. But the response was so bad that versatile WDBS staffer Herb Solow '53 had to be recruited to write something worth second prize. First place was filled by the simple announcement, "none worthy."

Sports played a large part in the schedule. In addition to all home games in all major sports, Sports Director Andy Stern '52 and Solow traveled to all away football contests except Princeton (when the College was on vacation) and most basketball games, while Bud Schweich '53 and Paul Sanderson covered as many away hockey games as the budget would allow. (In later years Sanderson was familiar to many graduates as "Weatherbee, the 'BZ Weatherman" on 50,000-watt WBZ in Boston, Mass.) When it was all over WDBS figured it had spent over $500 for installation of long-distance program lines for these remotes, better than 10 percent of the entire station budget. Financial crisis ahead? No, the Ivy Network had come through with a big, gleaming contract from Philip Morris for the whole sports package.

The World Series was carried in the fall, courtesy of WTSL, while the Dartmouth Outing Club program made its debut in January. Appearing on the latter was D.O.C. founder Fred Harris '11, and longtime club advisor Ross McKenney, a fascinating storyteller who had been a feature of the old DBS ten years earlier.

Among the year's specials were periodic fireside chats by President Dickey, in which he discoursed on shoes, ships, sealing wax and the possibility of a rise in tuition. There was the traditional Christmas party in December, and in January the station bravely announced it would carry all of Professor Booth's Shakespearean readings for the term, "regardless of their length."[5]

### "The Old Regime Falls Today"

The pollsters, now under Dave Leunberg '53, were as busy as ever. The results for February were particularly satisfying. WTSL, now a year old, captured only 14 percent of the nighttime student audience, while WDBS got 83 percent (up from 75 percent last year). "We have found that on the average, at any time during the broadcast day, we have an audience of between 400 and 500 listeners," the station optimized. The numerous request shows had no lack of calls either, especially from

Hanover youngsters.[6]

The most striking advances of the year came during the spring of 1952, after the change of Directorates. Even the changeover itself brought significant firsts. Bill Terry made the announcement at the end of March that the new station manager would be Kent Robinson '53, the technical director Bill Gitt '53, the business manager Jim Penney '53, and the newly titled program director, Herb Solow.[7] It was the first Directorate since 1947 with all new blood and no holdovers from the preceding board; and the first in station history in which all members were graduating seniors. This would be the rule, rather than the exception, in years to come. Perhaps equally important was the introduction of a new outlook to the all-important station manager's job. Kent Robinson was the first business person to assume station leadership. All but one of his 10 predecessors were programming men.[8] This subtle reorientation helped steer WDBS toward even more business-mindedness, and also began the badly needed reintegration of the Business Department with the rest of the station.

The Business Department had been suffering from a case of physical separation engendering psychological disunity. Ever since the business office had been located in the basement of Robinson Hall six years earlier, business staffers had become less and less familiar to the programmers and technicians of the third floor, and indeed with the way the station ran. The separation did not greatly hinder the official functioning of WDBS, but it did have decided morale implications, for the two groups seldom mixed socially and each knew rather little of the other. Since programming and technical staff made up by far the larger group, business staffers were to a certain extent strangers in their own station. When Kent Robinson's appointment was announced, in fact, some of the third floor crew admitted that they had never heard of him. The naming of a business manager to head WDBS was an important first step in building a more cohesive, and efficient, station, but it would be several years before the process was in any sense complete.

"The Old Regime Falls Today" proclaimed the *Newsletter*, as the new directors assumed office in mid April, following spring vacation. Robinson's Directorate would preside over the most dramatic surge in station expansion since that of the late 1940s, partly because of the advantages of unity and fresh outlook, and partly because of the foundation its predecessors had laid. A booming business picture made possible considerable technical improvements, which in turn allowed the Program Department to eventually introduce a full-day schedule.[9]

As Advertising Director Robinson had been largely responsible for the revolution in sales. A combination of booming revenues (from $3,500 to $5,700) and falling expenses ($5,300 to $5,100) made the station entirely self-supporting for the first time in its history. Not only was the standard annual subsidy of $1,500 eliminated, but WDBS actually began returning money to the College, and continued doing so, in small amounts, for the next five years. Part of this happy picture was due to the Ivy Network, which not only sold all sports coverage but many individual spots besides. More of it was from local sales, which would allow station revenues to quadruple in the next decade.

## Technical

The object of technical activity during Robinson's regime was nothing short of a whole new studio. The space shortage Dick Hollands had complained about in

1950 did more than just force latecomers to the weekly station meeting to perch on the piano—it effectively limited the broadcast day to its divided 10 hours. Even with this restricted schedule the control room was in constant use, on the air mornings and evenings, and in use for tape recording, rehearsals, training, and maintenance all afternoon. Not until an independent broadcast studio was added would the congestion be relieved and full-day broadcasting be possible.

As soon as the year's financial success became apparent the plans were laid. Backed by the "pleasant bulge" in the coffers and possibly an additional capital grant from the College (again, nobody would say), Rit Swicker sent out the orders: $575 for two professional Rek-o-Cut turntables with Gray tone arms and other accoutrements, $145 for a big RCA 77-D microphone, and more for the parts to build a homemade control board.[10] Swicker and Stuart Fordyce '53 designed and constructed the new studio, which occupied half of the old Tech office at 49 Robinson. Construction and installation of all the technical equipment, including a midget version of the master control board, was done by Bill Gitt with help from sundry others ("everyone on the staff drops by occasionally" said he).[11] When finished, Studio 3X (X for "external control") would be a compact disc jockey studio, completely independent of the main facilities and with its own direct line to the transmitter. Though work began on March 12 under Swicker and continued under Gitt, the studio was not ready for regular use until the fall.

Meanwhile finances looked so good that in April another $500 went out for a Gates Networker remote console and another RCA ("Bantam") microphone. Earlier, a new disc recorder had been purchased "which Maintenance Director William Gitt quickly took under his wing."[12] Unfortunately the engineers could not give new studio 3X their undivided attention. There was the matter of the transmitter. After the revelations of 1950, much time had been spent patching up the old warhorse, and by the fall of 1951 most problems were supposedly remedied. That lasted only until October, when a field representative of the Boston Federal Communications Commission Office drove into town, looked at his meters in amazement, and informed the boys that they were radiating like an AM station, far in excess of carrier current limits. This was especially discouraging since illegal readings were obtained even in areas where reception was poor. Back to the drawing boards. The existing transmitter was retained, but numerous tests were run with the help, as ever, of Physics Professor Willis Rayton, and necessitating occasional interruptions in the nighttime schedule. In addition various other means of transmission were studied.

For the time being the station limped along with partial coverage and illegal power while its directors dreamed of greater things. As early as November 1951 Rit Swicker had written to RCA, "At the present time we have a few of the powers that be of the College administration interested in the possibilities of going 250 watts AM. While the chances are very slim of anything materializing in the near future, we would like to be able to hit them with facts and figures as to the cost..."[13]

### Solow vs. Mr. Emotion

Airtime began to increase once again during the spring of 1952, as if in anticipation of the new disc jockey studio. In March the evening sign-on time was moved back to 5:00 p.m. with the debut of Herb Solow's *Herb at Five*. In May it was moved back again, to 4:00 p.m., with such shows as Ted Hawkins '55's *Broadway*

*Matinee* ("a show that has always been lacking on WDBS... [featuring] for the most part complete musical comedies"), Deke Harrington '54's *Pops on Wax*, Joe Kaplowitz's *Science in the News*, and five others filling the gap. Meanwhile Herb Solow's show was soon truncated to make way for the Ivy Network-sold *General Electric Program*, a lively affair "featuring Fred Waring and over half a hundred Pennsylvanians."[14]

It was Solow who attracted the most attention. Herb featured popular music, but he was no fan of the current number one hit-maker, an emaciated lad who had wailed and sobbed his way to phenomenal success with a series of teary-eyed hit songs including "Cry" and "The Little White Cloud That Cried." Solow simmered while listeners demanded the latest Johnnie Ray records. Then, in April, he had an idea. A few days later the bemused *Dartmouth* ran the following story.

> If you're happy and your eyes are never dry,
> Don't know if it's the thing to do to sob and sigh,
> Singers do it, crowds do it, even Little White Clouds do it...
>
> - from the parody "Try" by Stan Freberg

> But only one singer has parlayed "it" into a million-dollar business. He's America's new swoon king, and he's the object of an "I Can't Stand Johnnie Ray Fan Club" led by Herb Solow of WDBS. Local bobby-soxers will probably cry themselves sick but Solow just doesn't like "Mr. Emotion's" voice. Herb is "unable to see how a person with nothing can draw $4,000 a week at the Copacabana." And a lot of people agree with Herb because applications for club membership have been coming in by mail and phone. Some people have even rushed to WDBS' studio to sign up.
>
> Stan Freberg is the patron saint of the club, mainly on the basis of his take-off on Ray's moist triumph "Cry." Solow plans to inform Freberg shortly of the local movement which has formed to stamp out the "Atomic Ray" menace.[15]

Solow, who knew a good publicity stunt when he saw one, appeared on other WDBS shows to plug the "I Can't Stand Johnnie Ray Fan Club," placed an article in the widely distributed *WDBS Newsletter* ("Send your name to Herb, WDBS, Robinson Hall, Hanover"), and even interviewed callers on the Saturday night request show. Within a week he claimed 160 members, later 250, including "college professors... and professional disc jockeys."

Then he hit the jackpot with a letter he wrote to Barry Kaye, a disc jockey on 50,000-watt WCAU in Herb's home town of Philadelphia, Pennsylvania. Kaye read the letter on his show and Solow was promptly swamped with letters from teenagers across the northeast, most of them less than complimentary.

> PRO:
> "Congratulations to your one-lung college station for its head-on battle with 'Knucklehead Kaye' and his 50,000-watt jukebox." (Delaware)
> "I don't like the jerk either... more power to you." (Pennsylvania)
> CON:
> "I hope you get your microphone wrapped around your neck." (Ohio)

"I hope you're not an example of... college sophistication we're supposed to look to and emulate." (Massachusetts)

"Just who do you think you are... just because you're trying to get some cheap publicity for your broken-down old disc jockey." (Pennsylvania)

"You may think this letter is from a kid, but I am 18 years of age. All I can say is that if I went to the college that they mentioned on the Barry Kaye Show, I'd be ashamed of myself."

"I'm so mad my pen is smoking!"[16]

A formal truce was reached when Kaye called Solow at his dormitory one Saturday night. Kaye admitted that the "Prince of Wails" was a poor singer, but said he was "the greatest entertainer since Al Jolson." Solow just said he was rotten, but agreed to stop sending out membership cards if Kaye would call off his listeners. Kaye promised to read two Dartmouth letters on his show, from John Tenca '54 (who liked Ray) and Don Meltzer '54 (who didn't), and assure his audience that Solow was neither "UnAmerican" nor "anti-intellectual," thus ending the feud. But the letters kept coming. All summer.

## Ashtrays for the Queen

Herb Solow also arranged the annual swap with WCSR in April, packing off a dozen staffers to warm the Smith airwaves. Their five-hour WDBS sampler was reportedly less formalized than Yale's, but infinitely more entertaining. One report read: "'Where's Dorey?' ... the absentees appeared toward the end, waving a document reading Bellows Falls Municipal Court."[17]

Green Key Weekend brought the longest continuous broadcast yet, 41½ hours sprinkled with special programs and 10 straight hours of d.j. Norm Bander '54 (for which he claimed a record). For some obscure reason the choosing of the fifth annual WDBS Radio Queen was delegated to the Green Key Society, but the Mount Holyoke freshman they picked was crowned before the WDBS microphones by bandleader Johnny Long and awarded a handsome pile of loot donated by station advertisers. "A T-shirt, metal tumblers, a scarf, and a few ashtrays" sneered the envious *Dartmouth*.[18]

## Kent Robinson's Status Report

A unique appraisal of WDBS to date was provided at the end of the school year by Kent Robinson. The *Status Report of WDBS* was apparently prepared for the College, since it centered around the persistent transmission problems and how they might be remedied. It also pictured a station that had come a long way from the shoestring days of 1946. In programming WDBS was now broadcasting 12 hours a day, 82 hours a week, and boasted live shows utilizing musical and dramatic groups drawn from both the College and the town, "a United Press Radio News Wire at a cost of $500 per year," and a Sunday night news summary "aimed particularly at the College seniors who are required to follow the news for the Great Issues course." Regarding personnel, "The entire station staff stands at about 125 men, of which around 80 are especially active." In public relations there was a weekly newsletter, transcribed public service shows, periodic talks by President Dickey, and an extensive polling program. In summary, Robinson said, WDBS was fulfilling its avowed purposes by performing a valuable service for college and community.[19]

## 1952-1953

One of the brightest spots of the 1952-53 year, to many staffers, was the station's freshman training program. Training was one of WDBS's fundamental purposes. It was also a necessity to counter the yearly graduation of the station's most experienced staffers. In the spring new Personnel Director Bob Longabaugh '53 had studied other student stations' programs, then laid down the lines of a well-coordinated, and tougher, program for WDBS. During the summer he compiled the 10-page "WDBS Heeler's Manual and Facts to Know—First Edition," outlining the structure and functions of all station departments, as well as the restrictions on and duties of all heelers (trainees).

When the '56s arrived in the fall they were greeted by an organization wonderful to behold. There was the wide-ranging recruiting campaign of freshman week, including daily issues of the *Newsletter* especially designed to introduce them to WDBS; the nicely printed registration form, complete with spaces for a photograph and notation of each individual's four-year progress at WDBS; the training program itself, involving for each heeler individual instruction in his chosen department and familiarization with the whole station through the station manual; and at the end of the term departmental and overall station proficiency tests. The emphasis throughout was on competition. Of the 80 to 100 freshmen who began the program, perhaps a quarter or a third would eventually win "junior staff member" cards and become active producers, announcers, engineers, etc. The frank objective was to weed out those the station would be better off without, then develop the remainder as fully as possible.

The free labor pool provided by the willing and eager freshmen had always been well employed. Under Longabaugh there were a specified number of heeler duties, for which required points were earned. Organized record filing, record pulling for the numerous request shows, legwork for the busy Audience Research Department, and distribution of the weekly *Newsletter* all counted for points.

It was probably the most comprehensive training program in station history, and its momentum carried over for years afterwards. The manual was revised in the spring, and again in 1954 and 1955 (2d, 3d and 4th editions). But in later years the manual and the whole idea of coordinating the various departmental training programs seemed to die out, perhaps for want of another Bob Longabaugh.

### Programming and Publicity Increase

Not to be outdone, Howard Sloane '54's Public Relations Department developed the *WDBS Newsletter* into a smooth-running permanent operation. After March 1952 the *Newsletter* was printed rather than duplicated on the station's Ditto machine; in early October regular full program listings were added on the back; and on October 20 the station began delivering copies to every dormitory room on campus, free of charge. By 1953 the four-man staff, under editor Don Meltzer, had its operation down to a science. The "dummy" was delivered to Hanover printer Roger Burte on Monday morning, 200 copies printed by the photo-offset process were ready by five, then heelers began distribution to assigned dormitories and bulletin boards. Finally copies were mailed to approximately 80 advertisers, college officials and others.

With the completion of Studio 3X over the summer by Bill Gitt and Maintenance Director Peter Roos '54 the long-delayed invasion of the afternoon could at last begin. In September Herb Solow announced that WDBS would now be on air 103 hours per week, up 30 hours from the previous year, with music and news now originating from the new combo studio. ("combo" stood for "combination," meaning that one person could serve as a both announcer and engineer, as was now standard at most stations.) Morning sign-ons would be at 7:30 a.m. and afternoons at 1:30 p.m., resulting in a 15-hour day. But there would still be three hours between the two blocks due to the difficulty of getting announcers and listeners during the late morning class hours. The daily schedule was extended even further to 16 hours in the spring of 1953 with the addition of a morning show cheerily titled *It's 6:30!* (January), and an afternoon sign-on at 1:00 p.m. (March). By the end of the year the weekday schedule looked like this.

Morning
6:30   *It's 6:30 on 640* (d.j.)
7:00   *Musical Clock* (d.j.)
7:30   *Jam for Breakfast* (d.j. with Marty Aronson '55 & Bob Danziger '56)
9:00   *Morning Melodies* (d.j. with Joe Giden '55 & Ken Wash)
10:30  sign-off
Afternoon
1:00   *Cavalcade of Music*
2:00   *Once over Lightly*
3:00   *Masterworks in Music* (classical music)
4:00   *That Light Touch*
4:45   Transcribed public service show (veterans, bonds, etc.), *Science in the News*, or *Strictly Jazz.*
5:00   *Herb at Five* (d.j.)
6:00   *Amidon's News Roundup* (Norm Bander)
6:15   *Candlelight and Silver* (uninterrupted dinner music)
7:00   *Styles in Music* (Dixieland, jazz, bop, western, new releases, etc.)
7:30   *Sports Roundup*
7:45   *Record Scrapbook* (spotlighting an artist)
8:00   *Musical Showcase*
8:15   Various: *At the Keyboard, Best from the West, Variety Time, Studio '53*, etc.
9:00   *Ford Concert Hour* (classical)
10:00  Various: *Campus Hit Parade, Student-Faculty Quiz, Co-Op Show, Deakon's Scratchworks, College Cleaners, Carousel, Waxworks*, etc.
11:00  *Music 'til Midnight* (d.j.)
12:00  *World News Roundup*
12:15  *In the Still of the Night* (uninterrupted semi-classical)
1:00   sign-off

Headlines from United Press were given on the hour, with four five-minute updates spotted throughout the day, and 15 minute roundups at 6:00 p.m. and midnight Weekends had a similar schedule, with more classical music on Sunday and more "pop" on Saturday. Saturday afternoon's *Heelers' Hack Time* was now politely called *Freshman Airtime*. On Saturday nights the all-request *Musical Caravan* ran from 7:00 p.m. to midnight, at which time the newly introduced *Nightwatch* (September 1952) took over with uninterrupted music until 2:00 a.m.

At first glance this all seemed a study in how to present music in as many ways as possible, and to judge by the demands on the record library it was. By the fall of 1952 records from all major labels were being bought by WDBS (few would send free copies to a campus-limited station) and the collection totaled 3,000 popular 78s and 300 classical and semi-classical LPs.

The station maintained a wide variety of shows, however, both in listener-demanded music and in more creative areas.

*At the Keyboard*, sponsored now by Hanover optometrist Ranald C. Hill and produced by Don Meltzer and Peter Robinson '55, continued to be broadcast live from the Hanover Inn each Thursday. College talent was featured.

*Student-Faculty Quiz*, emceed by Norm Bander and produced by two sophomores named Don Wright '55 and Sky Hill '55, continued with the faculty winning regularly and no one getting the free cigarettes offered by the Dartmouth Smoke Shop for panel-stumping questions. The show was rebroadcast over WTSL.

*Deacon's Scratchworks* presented Deke Harrington and old popular records.

*Sandwiches and Milk* had "contests, records, comedy and Bugs Bunny."

*Best from the West* starred western balladeer Steve Weinreb '54.

*The Co-Op Show*, now hosted by workhorse Herb Solow, had the BBC-produced *I Can Hear It Now*, Alan Funt's *Candid Microphone*, and jazz records.

*The Hanover Scene* had Professor Stewart reviewing the College Concert, Lecture and Film Series, plays, books, and "the better motion pictures at the Nugget."

*This World Around Us*, produced by John Moffitt '55, collected the more ludicrous news stories of the week, "anything ranging from the story about the man who was caught nudging a 400-pound safe along with the bumper of his auto... to the fellow who turned on a faucet and saw a trout pour out... and the president of a Fort Worth adhesives firm whose name was Mr. H.B. Stuck."[20]

*The Ivy Theatre* continued with John Varnum '54 as Dartmouth's producer. Varnum's first contribution to the effort: a scratchy transcription of "The Most Dangerous Game." WXPN retaliated with "Two Bottles of Catsup."

The year also brought a number of specials:

In September, there were a rebroadcast of Senator Nixon's news making "Checkers" speech, and coverage of the Walcott-Marciano heavyweight title fight.

In November, presidential election coverage included an all-night broadcast from the WDBS studio. A well organized station staff reported returns while listeners followed on their *Newsletter* scorecards. Half a dozen professors helped analyze the results. During the preceding May WDBS had run a campus-wide poll, and predicted an overwhelming victory for Dwight Eisenhower.

November also offered an interview with Dartmouth alumnus, author and United Nations political advisor Charles Bolte '41, who, although the station apparently didn't realize it, had been the subject of DBS' first program of all time, in September 1941.

In December, there were Robert Frost poetry readings from Webster Hall, and the annual WDBS Christmas Party, featuring two plays, numerous guests, and a rebroadcast of 1951's *Hunky Dorey* Christmas show.

In January, President Dickey, on the first of 1953's Fireside Chats, talked about "the non-academic advantages of Dartmouth." Newly elected President Eisenhower's State of the Union message was carried, and continuous classical music, including classical requests, were broadcast during exam period.

February brought a hilarious interview with adventurer Ivan T. Sanderson (who had landed in Hanover by mistake, after missing his train), broadcast on *This World Around Us,* and April an interview with cartoonist Walt Kelly of "Pogo" fame.

In May, WCSR re-raided Dartmouth, announcing and engineering a full night's program; *Inter-Fraternity Quiz* was carried live; and the crowning of the WDBS Green Key Queen was carried live from Alumni Gym.

In June, once again there was continuous "study music" during final exams.

### A Local News Department

In January the Newsletter announced that "a news department has been organized at WDBS to provide local and college happenings to all of the station's hourly news broadcasts."[21] It was a brave try, but significant local news coverage would have to await the days of AM, years later.

There was no lack of audience participation gimmicks at WDBS. In October Herb Solow, flush with the success of his "I Can't Stand Johnnie Ray Fan Club," tried a favorite bandleader contest, in which Stan Kenton scored a narrow victory over Guy Lombardo. Listeners picked Ralph Flanagan as number three and Sauter-Finegan as number four. Others picked up on Solow's contests. Marty Aronson came up with a "battle of the bands," and Bob Daly '54 conducted a poll of the student body to determine their favorite hits. The first Dartmouth Hit Parade looked a lot like the national hit parade.

1. "Why Don't You Believe Me"
2. "You Belong to Me"
3. "Glow Worm"
4. "Wish You Were Here"
5. "It's in the Book"
6. "Monotonous"
7. "Don't Let the Stars Get in Your Eyes"
8. "High Noon"
9. "Oh Happy Day"
10. "Midnight Sleighride"

Favorite vocalists were Doris Day and Eddie Fisher. Daly wrote a letter to Boston d.j. Bob Clayton and got himself and Aronson invited to appear with their lists on WHDH's *Boston Ballroom*. But Herb had the last laugh. He was probably the only disc jockey in WDBS history to originate his show from Miami (by tape).

The Mystery Melodies continued (Ben Bernie playing "Ain't She Sweet" stumped everybody), cigarettes were occasionally doled out on *Student-Faculty Quiz*, and a contest was even run by the Lee Hat Company, via the Ivy Network, offering $100 for the best 60-second commercial. A Dartmouth listener won first prize and who should cop second but... Herb Solow! Request music was played by almost every show on the air, including the *Ford Concert Hour*.

Sports coverage was as extensive as ever, with all home games and most away contests covered, but this year without the help of Philip Morris or the U.G.C.

## Listenership

On-campus audience research played an important part in the WDBS of 1952-53. The *Newsletter* was used in January as the vehicle for the largest-based poll of students since Bill Brooks' questionnaire of 1950. The questions were included in the January 12 issue, thereby being distributed to all rooms on campus. One-third (319) were completed and picked up a week later. Almost everybody seemed to like the *Newsletter*, reported *Newsletter* editor Don Meltzer, and 61 percent saved it for reference during the week. Fifty-five percent said they listened to WDBS in the morning, but there was no polling for favorite shows. The most frequent comments were: carry still more away games; carry still more request shows; "the same news is read too often"; and airtime should be extended to fill in the late morning and early afternoon. *Music 'til Midnight, In the Still of the Night, Ford Concert Hour, Herb at Five*, and *Styles in Music* got the most frequent favorable mentions, but listeners complained of "too much bop" on *Herb at Five* and "too much prompting" on *Student-Faculty Quiz*.

In mid-May the station announced that it would conduct what by now had become an annual spring poll of student listening habits. It got much the same results.

## Business

WDBS enjoyed another banner year of sales under Business Manager Jim Penney. For the fifth consecutive year income rose, this time to over $6,500, better than five times the 1947-48 figure. With expenses lagging discreetly behind, the station was able to return $700 in "profits" to a pleased COSO. The talk of the Ivy Network during this year was the proposed affiliation of the inter-collegiate organization with the National Broadcasting Company. NBC was interested, and when the annual convention of Ivy station leaders met in Hanover the story leaked to both local and national papers. Under the proposed arrangement NBC would provide the seven Ivy stations (Brown had just joined) with certain major network shows, as well as its on-the-spot coverage of major national news events. WTSL must have quivered in its boots at that, but the matter petered out over the summer when no mutually acceptable agreement could be reached. WDBS was not to be NBC Radio in the Upper Valley, at least for now.

## Technical

The Technical Department took a breather during 1952-53, compared to the rapid expansion of previous years. A new, $300 Hallicrafters multi-band radio receiver was purchased, along with a couple of new RCA microphones. As was customary, it took months to get the latter working properly. And there were the inevitable little tragedies, as on that bright morning in May when *Morning Melodies* was blown off the air by a burned-out transformer in Middle Fayerweather (whose residents thought the place was on fire). Station engineers later admitted that the reason for the trouble was their use of a 15 amp fuse where a one amp fuse was required. "Fuses cost money. If we put in a big enough fuse, it won't blow."[22]

The most headaches were caused by continuing transmission problems. Chief worriers were Stu Fordyce, who had become technical director in September, and his maintenance director, Pete Roos. Chief worry was the fact that the FCC now presumably knew what was going on in Hanover. Basically the problem was that to get the WDBS signal to all parts of the College wiring system, past all the transformers and switches along the way, it was necessary to pump an excessive amount of signal power in at Middle Fayerweather. Leakage in certain odd directions was such that much of Hanover got the station, but fraternity houses, outlying dormitories and top floors of nearby ones often didn't. The College continued to balk at the high cost of AM or FM until all avenues were explored, however, so the patching and planning continued.

The trustees had other things on their minds in 1953. In April 1952, acting on a College request, the FCC had reserved ultra-high frequency (UHF) television channel 21 for Hanover with the provision that it would be for educational use. Eight months later President Dickey appointed COSO Director Warner Bentley to chair a faculty committee to look into the practicality of building such a station. The committee conducted a thorough investigation into programming and technical problems. Its final report in early 1954 concluded that these would present no insurmountable obstacle and that Dartmouth should indeed think in terms of television. Overshadowing all, however, was the projected cost of nearly half a million dollars. The trustees could approve the recommendations only "in principle," not in cash. TV competition for WDBS would have to wait.

## One Hundred Cabinets... and the President's Blotter

Student organizations are never all-business, and this year had its share of intra and extra-station nonsense. Two episodes were particularly notable for their imagination: the Never-Rust Filing Cabinet Hoax, and the Great *Jack-o* Hijack.

"WDBS Peddles Neverrust Filing Cabinets to Dispose of 14,300 Lb. Hoax Delivery" headlined a feature story in a January 1953 *Dartmouth*, which then explained that station officials had received billing papers preliminary to the arrival of 100 aluminum filing cabinets at the White River Junction railroad depot, "as ordered by Radio Station WDBS." What?? As days went by more documents arrived tracing the progress of the seven-ton shipment across the country toward New Hampshire, and causing a certain amount of executive pandemonium at WDBS. Busy "*D*" reporters elicited the following comments from Directorate members: Jim Penney, "no comment," Kent Robinson, "I'm checking," Herb Solow, "Just imagine, we'll have more filing cabinets than anyone on campus!" While Solow helpfully suggested that they'd make dandy Valentine presents, a hasty check was run on the Hood River Aluminum Company. It proved non-existent, and although the $500 freight bill looked quite authentic, Railway Express never did collect.[23]

The other hoax began with the printing of a mysterious treasure map in *The Dartmouth* one Saturday in April. The same night someone called the WDBS request show to say, "Over the running water, which should dispose of a publication we know, several dogged little boys might find clues. If you fall in, just give up and pull the chain..." The entire press run of the soon-to-be-released college humor magazine had been hijacked from the *Jack-o Lantern's* Robinson Hall offices. Many detected a strong scent of fresh fish, but all watched in amusement as new clues sent *Jack-o* staffers scampering around town. There was a note in the Robinson Hall men's room (not to be confused with the nearby *Jack-o* office), another glued to a rock in the Bema (an outdoor amphitheater). The WDBS clue led to another one hidden underneath the Ledyard Bridge. Then, "a Spanish voice, sort of mixed with French" phoned WDBS to say, "*Jack-o, Jack-o*, who's got the *Jack-o's*? President Dickey got the inkling of an idea when he looked under his blotter this morning... hurry, office closes at four." Off went the photographers and reporters to Parkhurst Hall, past a reluctant secretary (President Dickey was out). The offices were always locked except during regular business hours, she protested, and someone was *always* there then. But sure enough, beneath the president's blotter, was a torn sheet of yellow paper with another clue.[24]

Over the next 24 hours more clues appeared in odd places, and more mysterious voices called WDBS, but a tip that the magazines could be found under the B-flat chime of Baker Tower proved false. *Jack-o* editor James Fisher '54 wailed that there was "big Hanover money behind this plot," adding that possibly advertising competitors or counter-revolutionaries were responsible. But he smiled smugly as the 3,000 *Jack-o's* were returned, just in time, and enjoyed an unusually large sale.

Meanwhile, the secretaries in Parkhurst never could explain just how...

## The Directorate Changes

Late in March the customary amount of political speculation was ended by the announcement of the new Directorate. Maintenance Director Peter Roos became the new station manager, sophomore Joseph Giden became technical director, William Robbins '54, business manager, and Norm Bander, program director. Serving under them would be a clearly defined executive staff and other "senior staff officers." The Roos Directorate continued most of the important organizational firsts of Robinson's, and added one of its own. This was the first Directorate in seven years in which all four original members remained in office (i.e. in the academic good graces of the College) for their full term.

## 1953-1954: Business

Peter Roos would later write of his term that "the two major issues... were finances and personnel."[25] The financial difficulties were the result of over optimism. The preceding year had been so successful that the new regime, by Roos' own subsequent admission, went slightly "hog wild" in the fall. The office Ditto duplicating machine was getting somewhat cranky after several years of use, so they would buy a new one. There were a good many letters to be typed, the student office managers were proving none too reliable, and every professional office had office help, so WDBS would hire a secretary. "Nancy (Penny) will be at work from two to four, Monday through Friday," the Directorate proudly announced, "so that anyone can call at that time and be sure of getting someone."[26]

It soon became apparent that sales were not going to be up to last year's snuff, however, and finally in January the sad entry was made in the minutes of a Directorate meeting that "Roos reported that he had spoken to Nancy and she was to leave before finals and for the time being we would try to do without a secretary."[27] Obedient heelers would once again type the daily program logs, and executives could peck out their own letters.

More than office help was cut as the Directorate put into effect stringent economy measures in order to break even at all costs. It was not that the College wouldn't make up any losses, but WDBS had shown a profit for two years running now. With the Directorate trying hard to convince the administration to support a switch to a new mode of transmission, preferably AM, it was vital that the station maintain its image as a sound financial enterprise. There would be little hope for WDBS-AM if the student broadcasters showed themselves subject to financial instability or erratic management. The goal was nothing short of returning $500 to COSO. Though the year fell short of that, an all-important surplus was achieved, $35 to be precise. Total revenue for the year was down about $2,000, but still well above the pre-1952 levels. Business Manager Bill Robbins still had something to smile about.

Roos and Robbins tried some long-range financial planning too, in the form of a "savings fund" to which each Directorate would contribute, and which would be spent every few years on some major equipment purchase. This spreading of costs would allow the long-range equipment planning Dick Hollands and Bob Sisk had dreamed of, but it ran afoul of the same basic problem. Next year's management might either have little enthusiasm for the plans of its predecessor, or might honestly judge the station's needs differently. For such reasons COSO gently said "no" to the

Roos proposals. There would be no saving of money from year to year. Each Directorate would continue to sink or swim on its own. Roos' financial problems also involved the simple matter of knowing how things stood at any moment. COSO's records, though authoritative, were designed for a final accounting, not day-to-day planning. The students' own record-keeping procedures were both antiquated and chaotic, and at year's end Roos urged major reforms to keep up with the new financial waistline of the organization.

The year's biggest little crisis was that afternoon in October when a state tax collector suddenly appeared in the studios, warning ominously against the "advertising" of unstamped cigarettes, because he had heard disc jockey Jim Barker '56 giving away Egyptian cigarettes, on which of course the New Hampshire tax had not been paid.

In April the campus poll takers were put to work again, this time taking an extensive market research survey for the Ivy Network. After long nights of totaling up results, WDBS' bleary-eyed Ivy representative Don Wright reported that the average Dartmouth man spent $370 per year on personals and recreation, and liked Brooks Brothers suits, Ford cars, Gulf gasoline, Budweiser beer, Colgate toothpaste, Lucky Strike cigarettes, and Smith College for road trips. Ivy said thanks.

## A Question of Morale

Personnel relations present a difficult problem for any large volunteer organization, but particularly for one that is growing fast and faced with increasing responsibilities. The WDBS of 1953 was all of that and then some. The larger and more active it got, the more was expected of it as a matter of course. The primary burden of leadership fell on the slightly built shoulders of Station Manager Roos. No top-level strategist in a pine-paneled office, the WDBS station manager had to work in the midst of his organization with almost everyone on the 125-person staff, sometimes down to individual junior staffers or trainees. Formal lines of authority notwithstanding, it was Roos' job to generate an atmosphere of enthusiasm and personally spur station members to individual achievement, while keeping the whole, huge staff working together. He had to maintain the cohesive social aspects of the station, since for its most dedicated workers WDBS was in every sense of the word a fraternity. His job was the definition of leadership, to transform individual potential energy into collective realized effort.

He faced a number of obstacles. The incentives he had were wholly intangible, for no member could receive pay or academic recognition for his work. Instead Roos could only attempt to use a member's love of radio or of the station, his desire for advancement within the organization, and his need for recognition or prestige from his peers to bring about productive activity.

Leadership ability among his lieutenants, through whom he controlled station operations, was also vital. But this was a rare and precious commodity, because they themselves were students just learning the fine art of leadership. Some of Roos' junior (and even senior) managers were simply unreliable. Others did not understand that volunteer workers cannot be directed but rather must be led, using all the subtle techniques of persuasion and motivation. Ironically, unreliability or ineptness were often evident even before a person was appointed, but the Directorate may have had no choice but to appoint them anyway because—and this happened time and time again—they were the only senior individual available. One could only hope they would improve.

Roos wrote to his successor, "I think the major problem that troubled us was the lack of spirit displayed at times during the year." Then he added, "Actually, when viewed from a distance, this was not as bad as we thought it was at the time and I am inclined to think that all Directorates run into it."

Nevertheless it seems clear that personnel problems were a larger concern to the station during the immediate pre-AM period of the 1950s than before. Reasons may have included the fact that the organization was taking on a whole new dimension in size and activity, in programming, business and technical matters. Along with this came a transformation into a "professional atmosphere," with all its impersonal demands and coordination difficulties. In a sense, DBS operated as a small club while WDBS was growing into a sizeable commercial business enterprise. The unequal competition of WTSL was no doubt damaging to morale, serving especially to spur the drive to "go AM." That would be a long, hard battle, and in 1953 victory seemed to be distant if not impossible.

An interesting confirmation of Roos' concerns is a lengthy report titled *WDBS: A Study in Human Relations* written by Advertising Manager Peter Stevens '55 for one of his courses.[28] Stevens cited "the purely subjective observation that at present morale at WDBS is very low," then went on to analyze the problem. There was, he said, "the feeling that a sense of responsibility is lacking to some degree on the part of every station member. The leaders seem to be content with things as they are, and the followers often fail to fulfill their responsibilities... Specifically, most members do not feel that they belong to WDBS as a whole. Thus creditable morale may exist in some departments, but the sentiment that above all the interests of WDBS as a whole come first is lacking." As station esprit had suffered, so had productivity.

Part of the blame, he said, lay with specific personnel. For instance one director, who "ostensibly should be motivated at all times toward broadcasting the best quality of programming... has on occasion (himself) helped to 'break up' an announcer." Others may have been so businesslike that they forgot how to work with people, leading to complaints of "authoritarianism." When the enthusiasm of the dedicated few at the top ceased to be communicated through the ranks, there was trouble.

There were also the physical separation of business (basement office) from the rest of the staff (third floor), the traditional problem of leadership without incentives, different aims of different departments, and the simple fact that some people were just along for a good time.

Roos made a greater effort in the area of morale, formally at least, than anyone in years. There were attempts to make the executive staff a meaningful, functioning body, with regular meetings and the Directorate in attendance. In October Roos inaugurated a steering committee, a semi-formal bull session of interested Directorate, executive staff and others "in the hope that everyone would lay his cards on the table and be frank and in this way we would attempt to correct some of our personnel problems and to achieve better cooperation between the station members." It was a noble idea, and probably did bring into the open some aspects of the discontent in the station that worried Roos. But after a month the meetings were discontinued.

There was talk of paying personnel (avoid it if at all possible) and of a station morale questionnaire (more harm than good), while much emphasis was placed on the Christmas "cider and donut blast" and other station get-togethers. When it was all over the best advice Roos could pass on to his successors was simply to do the best you can to open lines of communication, and the station would muddle through. This was apparently not too helpful for as it turned out, Roos' problems were only a prelude.

## Programming

Norm Bander saw no reason to make any striking changes in the program schedule during 1953-54. WDBS was by this time on the air 109 hours a week, and almost sixteen hours daily, 6:30 to 10:15 a.m., and 1:00 p.m. to 1:00 a.m. Bander's wisest tact was to consolidate the gains already made. The format continued to be recorded music presented in various ways, for most of the day, with productions (many being musical) in the early evening and liberal doses of sports and special events coverage scattered throughout. Sports Director Larry Russell '54, who worked with announcer Jim Rill '54, later recalled landing some notable interviews, including Olympic skating champions Barbara Ann Scott and Dick Button, and Dartmouth basketball captain Pete Geithner '54, the future father of Treasury Secretary Timothy Geithner '83.[29]

One program format originated in 1954 lasted for many years to come. *Night Watch* had begun, in name anyway, as a Saturday night fill-in after the all-request show in the fall of 1952. When Don Cowlbeck '57 and Ray Marks '57 took it over in April 1954 they made it a nightly feature from 1:00 to 2:00 a.m., following but very different from *In the Still of the Night*. As to its music, "instrumentals will be featured leaning toward jazz, progressive and big band rhythm and blues." As to chatter, *Night Watch* would now be very distinctively a personality show, with a five man staff organized to produce it and provide substitute announcers. In early June Cowlbeck put the frosting on the cake with an announcement that in the fall the show would host such guest stars as Martin Block, Paul Whiteman, Skitch Henderson, and Dave Garroway.[30]

One of the few new regular production shows was John Van de Kamp '56's *Episode*, which recreated the happenings of a year in history. "*Episode* shows a good amount of hard work but a dearth of imagination," said *The Dartmouth's* reviewer, who also pointed out that except for a few good NBC news cuts, most of the show consisted of vintage records.[31] *Your Faculty of the Air* made its debut in early 1954, airing each night from 10:00 to 10:15 p.m. On Monday nights Professor Almon Ives hosted *The Hanover Scene,* a preview of local events; Tuesday nights brought Professor Herb West's literary (and related, and no-so-related) ramblings on *Hanover Browsing*; Wednesday and Thursday featured members of the Great Issues and Government Departments tackling national and international events; and on Friday their counterparts in economics discussed recent economic trends.

The Ivy Network's brief flyer into production ended, though much talk continued under Program Coordinator Norm Bander and his successors. With the Ivy Network show killed at the April 1953 convention, *Studio '54* would have to carry WDBS' dramatic banner alone. To keep up audience participation someone came up with "brainbusters" to scatter through the day. Prize? Lucky Strike cigarettes, of course.

Specials for the year included an appearance by Stan Kenton in October, an important address by President Dickey in December, forums and reports preceding the campus-wide referendum on fraternity discrimination, continuous broadcasting during exam periods, an exchange of programs with Radio Brazzaville in French Equatorial Africa in May, and a recording of President Eisenhower's Commencement address at Dartmouth (also used by NBC) in June.

March brought something of a switch on an old theme as "four voluptuous femmes from Mount Holyoke (took over) WDBS this weekend for five hours of 'broad'-casting." Their disc jockey show got no fewer than 130 requests. Green Key weekend had the continuous programming of *Green Key Caravan*, and durable old Vaughn Monroe came back to crown another Radio Queen.[32]

## Training

The freshman recruiting program retained the momentum imparted by Bob Longabaugh a year earlier. Incoming '57s were inundated with special freshman week *Newsletters* which described the station and details of the heeling program. Personnel Director John Moffitt advertised announcing auditions, always the station's most effective lure, with a simple "It can't hurt to try." The auditions were so painless, in fact, that some 97 freshmen took them. After that acute attrition set in. Fifty-six entered the formal training program, and 27 subsequently received their junior staff member cards. Yet at the beginning of the second semester, another 50 signed up.

*Freshman Airtime* continued on Saturday afternoons, and a number of freshman sports contests were carried to give budding sportscasters live practice. For fledgling producers there was something entirely new, the profusely illustrated *WDBS Handbook of Hand Signals* gave trainees a standardized sign language with which to tell engineers behind the control room window to "segue" (interlocked fingers), "fade down" (lowering arm from an upright, extended position) and "turn the mike on" (point at it). For producers in the control room there were appropriate motions for "move closer to the mike" ("arms are extended upright, are dropped to horizontal extended in front of body, and palms are then moved together"), "give a station break" (fists are held together and rotated upward with a breaking motion), "talk" ("fingers are opened and closed in a fluttering motion"), "you're right on time" (finger resting lightly on nose, signifying "on the nose"), and finally "ugh!" (fingers gripping nose tightly).[33]

## Technical

Joe Giden's chief technical problem was the same as that of his predecessors, transmission. With ex-engineer (and first-year Thayer School of Engineering student) Peter Roos as station manager, this became a leading concern of the Directorate as well. The bespectacled Mr. Roos was probably the most report-happy individual in station history. "Roos Reports" abounded, covering meetings of all types, and preserving a detailed record of his attempts to solve the long-standing difficulties (e.g., "Today I tried the signal generator connected through the amp and two .001 mfd condensers to the College 110 in the business office."). For starters he tried carrying a portable radio in and out of Robinson Hall, Massachusetts row and other dormitories. It showed very uneven reception, bearing little relation to the theoretical characteristics of power line transmission. The Ivy Network's cooperatively owned field intensity meter was then obtained (one of the rare examples of technical cooperation between the Ivy stations), and the first definitive coverage map in years drawn up. This revealed excellent reception in Etna Village, but none at the southeast corner of the College green near the studios. However the signal was in many areas far in excess of legal strength.

Roos and Giden had no more success than their predecessors in finding an answer, though not for lack of trying. The best solution, they felt, was to convert to full power AM, presuming (1) a good deal of money would have to be spent in any case, and (2) it might as well buy WDBS the greatest possible coverage. But the time was not yet right. For the present they would limp along with what they had. March 1954 correspondence with the Ivy Network first listed the transmitter strength as "unknown," then later an "estimated 70-90 watts." One Directorate meeting report began with the entry, "Comment made that the transmitter power was up and that there should be some plan of attack if the FCC should come suddenly."[34] But the rumor that WDBS had a switch on its transmitter control rack that could lower power instantly, whenever the need arose, was not true.

The technical picture was otherwise happy enough, although demands on equipment were increasing so fast that new purchases would soon be necessary. There were still only two remote consoles, given constant use by the special events and sports departments, as during one frantic four hour period in which engineers recorded a piano recital from the Hanover Inn and Professor Booth's Shakespearean readings from Dartmouth Hall, ran a *Student-Faculty Quiz* broadcast from the main studio, and broadcast games from Davis Hockey Rink and Alumni Gymnasium.[35]

The lone Ampex 400 tape recorder was holding up remarkably well under constant use, but Giden wrote that "there are many occasions on which we wish we had the use of a second machine. We operate 16 hours a day, and find that many times we either wish to record two programs at the same time or wish to play back a program while also trying to record another. Much of our recording for night broadcasting is done in the afternoon and frequently we have several demands on the same machine at the same time."[36] Giden looked into new Ampexes, but found prices high. By the spring of 1954 the big machine was bordering on nervous exhaustion so it was packed off to the Ampex people in California for a complete overhaul. Unfortunately, it was never quite the same.

## The New Directorate

Early in March the three seniors of the outgoing Directorate chose businessman Peter Stevens as the new station manager. Peter Robinson became technical director, Blake Irons '55, business manager, and Marty Aronson, program director. Shortly after the first meeting of the new directors Aronson was elected president of Pi Lamda Phi fraternity and resigned. His replacement was none other than his predecessor of two years earlier, Bud Schweich, just back from 21 months in the army, who promptly announced that "emphasis will be on live programming in the future, with less attention to disc jockey shows."[37]

Serving under the Directorate would be an executive staff of no fewer than 21 men, but with no more power than its predecessors. The first order of business was the upcoming station banquet, in May. For $2.50 a head station members ate heartily, then watched the retiring directors get Zippo lighters monogrammed "WDBS."

Perhaps the best statement of the job facing Peter Stevens was contained in an *Alumni Magazine* article by retiring newsletter editor Don Meltzer.

> By whatever criteria you choose, WDBS has grown tremendously in the past few years. And it is continuing to grow. In fact, the major problem facing the new Directorate which takes office this month is to keep the station from growing beyond control... when you consider that they must supervise this 16-hour-a-day operation in the time left over after classes and study, using personnel who have no tangible incentives other than the desire for experience, you can appreciate the challenge they face, and the magnitude of their daily accomplishments.[38]

### 1954-1955: Programming

Despite his enthusiasm for live music, Bud Schweich wrought no great changes during his second term as programming chief. Don Cowlbeck's *Night Watch*, which had been off to such an auspicious start in the spring, receded to one night a week, on Saturdays, proving that even a five man crew of red-blooded Dartmouth men was hard pressed to maintain 1:00 to 2:00 a.m. hours for long. The mornings proved somewhat difficult too, and sign-on was soon moved up to a more comfortable 7:30 a.m. A typical schedule in the spring of 1955 was as follows.

Morning
7:30   *Jam for Breakfast*
9:00   *Morning Melodies*
10:15  sign-off
Afternoon
1:30   *Today*
3:00   *The 640 Club*
4:00   *Masterworks of Music*
5:00   *Tell Takes the "A" Train*
6:00   *World News Roundup*
6:15   *Candlelight and Silver*
7:00   *Styles in Music* (folk, western, motion picture music)
7:30   *Jazz at 7:30*
8:00   *Curtain Time*
8:30   *Studio '55*
9:00   *The Concert Hour*
10:00  *Amidon's Sports Show*
10:15  *Your Faculty of the Air*
10:30  *The Co-Op Show*
11:00  *Music 'til Midnight*
12:00  *Graham's World News Roundup*
12:30  *In the Still of the Night*
1:00   sign-off

In addition there were headlines or five-minute news wrap-ups on the hour. Saturdays and Sundays remained the same, for a total of 102 hours per week.

There were not one but two quiz shows now, the venerable *Student-Faculty Quiz* and *Animal, Vegetable and Mineral*. Dramatic presentations included original radio plays by WDBS and the Players, and a recorded BBC dramatic series obtained through the Ivy Network. *Behind the Scenes*, produced by freshman Dave Bowman '58, made its debut in February with a live interview from the Dartmouth Printing Plant on Allen Street, where the daily "*D*" staffers were putting their rag to bed. Later shows starred Chief Gaudreau from the campus police offices and Miss Gill from the Dartmouth Dining Association (from her office, not the kitchens unfortunately). This latter show promised to illuminate such oft-debated subjects as "the process the food goes through before it is put on the counters, the length of preparation, and other questions concerning the food itself."[39]

Important specials included an administration forum dealing with new campus regulations (October), and coverage of the 1954 congressional elections. However there were no more "fireside chats" because President Dickey felt not enough students listened and "the local press coverage of what I had said on the radio was adequate and accurate."[40] Houseparties, Winter Carnival and Green Key Weekends all received extended broadcasting, and there was again 24 hours of classical "music to study by" during exams.

Coverage of away games continued to be a financial problem, and during the basketball season the station announced it could continue coverage only with the help of student donations. As a result $150 worth of quarters rolled in, plus $50 more from business and private donations.

## Listenership

In May 1955 newly appointed Audience Research Director Dave Johns '58 fielded the largest campus listenership study ever, sending out questionnaires to virtually every student. On the basis of 1,086 returns he reported the following: 97 percent owned or had easy access to radios now, though 21 percent considered WDBS poor or not worth listening to. Eighteen percent said they could not receive the station at all. The ratings for regular shows were not unlike those of five years earlier. (As with the 1950 survey, these are the "sometimes listen" and "almost always listen" figures combined.)

1. *Music 'til Midnight*      71% (d.j.)
2. *In the Still of the Night*   55% (classical)
3. *Midnight News*          54%
4. *Nightwatch*             52% (popular music)
5. *Candlelight and Silver*    51% (dinner music)
6. *The Co-Op Show*         48% (d.j.)
7. *Six O'Clock News*        48%
8. *Tell Takes the "A" Train*   42%
9. *Concert Hour*           41% (classical, opera, commentary)
10. *Amidon's Sports Show*    35%

The most popular disc jockey was John Van de Kamp, with Bill Tell '56 second, and Frank Sauter '57 close behind. Students once again complained about hillbilly music and progressive jazz (which had replaced bop), and admitted (94 percent) that they had never told an advertiser they heard about him on WDBS. In addition, 70 percent public-spiritedly thought that Undergraduate Council meetings ought to be broadcast.

*The WDBS Newsletter*, after a four year run and considerable development, failed to return in the fall of 1954, partially because its staff had graduated in June, partially because the Directorate felt the $400 per year expense "not worth it." To fill the gaping hole in publicity *The Dartmouth* agreed to carry WDBS's program listings free, if the station would buy $50 a year worth of advertising. Cheap enough. In fact enough money was thus saved in the public relations budget to allow the purchase of a crate of little glass ashtrays bearing the familiar WDBS monogram (a heavily shaded WDBS atop something resembling an abbreviated lightning bolt), which were distributed to win friends and influence people.

### Technical: A Familiar Subject Looms Large

Peter Robinson's engineering staff occupied itself during the fall of 1954 running the numerous sports remotes and tinkering with the studio turntables, all of which had to be converted to play 45 rpm as well as 33 rpm and 78 rpm records, thanks to the inconsiderate record companies which were engaged in a "war of the speeds." Meanwhile Robinson and his Maintenance Director Jos Demos '56 were deep in transmission studies, making a last, desperate attempt to come up with an intra-campus system that would work and be within the law. To quote a Directorate meeting report from October, "the subject of transmission is looming larger."[41]

The history of WDBS' intra-campus transmission system was one of 14 years of frustration. The original 1941 system of a separate, small transmitter serving each dormitory had been a technical nightmare. So in mid 1942 the conversion was made to a power line system, whereby the College's electrical wiring system was used to carry the DBS signal to all campus buildings. The signal was pumped into the College 2,300-volt high power lines in the basement of Middle Fayerweather dormitory.

It never worked. The principal FCC limitation on such a system was that the signal could not have more than a specified strength (15 uv/m) at 250 feet from the nearest power lines. When this was strictly adhered to, however, both at Middle Fayerweather itself and all along the high power lines, not enough signal got past the transformers and into the dormitories. So the input at Middle Fayerweather was cranked up to as much as 70-80 watts to push the station into more rooms. The result was grossly excessive radiation along the way, especially from the 2,300-volt line.

Complicating all of this, the signal somehow leaked from the college power lines to those of the Granite State Electric Company (which supplied the College), and it was said that as you drove out of town you could pick up WDBS from the roadside power lines clear to the neighboring town of Lebanon. Much of Hanover also got WDBS, but on campus various quirks made the coverage quite spotty.

All through the 1940s and early 1950s station engineers, with help from Professor Willis Rayton and others, had searched for a way to cover the entire campus and still be within the law. Innumerable attempts were made to make the "power line" system work, or to modify it somehow. Meanwhile the staff played a continuing game of hide-and-seek with the FCC. "Whenever the inspectors arrived in town someone would turn the transmitter power down to a level which would comply with the FCC requirements, and when the inspectors left the transmitter would be turned up to its normal power."[42]

During 1953 and 1954 Roos and Stevens kicked around the idea of laying expensive co-axial cable to each dormitory on campus, so that the signal could be fed directly into each building's 110 volt line. Such a system would bypass the 2,300 volt high-power lines altogether, and presumably end the illegal radiation problem. It had worked well at Yale and Harvard, but was finally rejected by the Dartmouth trustees because of the excessive expense, about $15,000. Among other things Yale and Harvard had steam tunnels in which to lay their co-ax cable. At Dartmouth, trenches would have to be dug all over campus.

The last major attempt to find an acceptable campus-limited answer was contained in a January 1955 technical department report. Oddly enough it proposed a return to the multiple transmitter set-up with which DBS had begun in 1941, albeit somewhat modified. Each transmitting unit would this time be located in the attic of its dormitory (a possibility rejected in 1941 because of expense) and equipped with a special radiating antenna running the full length of the building. This system would bring headaches of its own, possibly including those of 1941. For this reason, and because of the increasing hope that the long dreamt-of AM license might be approved, the idea never got beyond the technical department committee stage.

The obvious alternative to unlicensed campus-limited broadcasting was to convert to FM or AM, with an FCC license. FM had been considered many times, most notably in 1947 (q.v.) and during the early 1950s. It had been turned down each time on grounds of excessive expense, insufficient audience (less than two percent of students had FM receivers), and the promise of more coverage problems stemming from Hanover's rugged terrain. AM had also been rejected on grounds of cost and the feeling that "the advantages to be secured by the College from such a station did not justify the cost in money, manpower and headaches inescapably associated with such an undertaking."[43] But as it became apparent that a legal campus-limited system could not be devised, at least not for reasonable cost, AM became a more and more attractive possibility.

## A Historic Decision

Early in 1955 the WDBS Directorate and its friends in the college administration made an all-out attempt to sell the trustees on AM. They presented the long, sad history of wired transmission and the many futile attempts to improve it. WDBS, they said, had probably always operated illegally, and now the problem was coming to a head. The FCC was beginning to crack down on college stations, and had already closed one for lesser offenses than those of WDBS. When the commission got around to WDBS, Dartmouth would undoubtedly lose one of its most valuable and active organizations.

Something had to be done, and it would not be cheap. Each of the three practical alternatives open to the College, a rebuilt wired system (co-ax), FM, or AM, would cost in the neighborhood of $10,000 to $20,000 dollars. Only AM promised a big enough audience to allow the station to pay its own way. Revenues might even increase sufficiently to allow amortization of the entire original investment. Besides,

WDBS-AM would presumably provide a genuine programming service to the whole Upper Valley. If the money must be spent, let it be spent right, once and for all, on a full power AM radio station.

The arguments against AM were imposing. Precedent was solidly on the side of a campus-limited station, such as co-ax cable or very low-power AM or FM (five or 10 watts), as most colleges have. There was already a commercial station in Hanover and it was sure to scream bloody murder at the threat of student competition. And the fact stood: No college or university in the country had ever entrusted undergraduates with the full legal and social responsibility which accompany a commercial AM license.

In March 1955 the trustees reached a historic decision. Dartmouth College would apply for FCC permission to build a 250-watt, commercial AM radio station, and the station, when built, would be entirely student run. Technical and financial considerations, together with unusual trust in the existing student station, had finally carried the day.

The decision of 1955 was tentative. Although $6,500 was immediately appropriated for the station's construction, the project might still be abandoned if the legal or financial barriers to such an unusual undertaking proved too great. Nevertheless the Directorate was jubilant! This was the turning point that station members had been working for ever since 1946, when Bob Varney had brought the old DBS out of its wartime mothballs with a prophetic wish.

> I sincerely hope that at some time not too far away we will be able to reach the entire town of Hanover, and the neighboring communities. If we can do that, our radio work will cease to be a plaything for a few enthusiasts, and become an integral part of both the College and the community.[44]

### Personnel Problems... Again

Even while fighting in private for AM (lest WTSL find out and protest so violently as to torpedo the whole project), the Stevens Directorate had other battles to face on the home front. Personnel difficulties were becoming even more serious than under Peter Roos, as reflected in the remarkable list of complaints and suggestions coming out of the first full meeting of the Production Department in the fall.

1. No prestige in being affiliated as a member of WDBS. Half the campus doesn't get the signal, so we represent no communicative power such as the "*D*."
2. Poor leadership.
3. Elections to reflect the sentiment of entire staff regarding the filling of executive positions.
4. Never see the station brass. No feeling of coordination or closeness.
5. Suggestion box.
6. Heeling programs: screen the new men closer to cut out the undesirables who may in the future scare good men away. Let heelers into the station meetings so that they will more quickly feel closer to the station and not drop out in favor of some other organizations.
7. Poor quality shows. Morning men must be consistent, or habit of tuning on station upon rising will be lost because of frequent occurrence of dead air.

8. More full staff social functions.

9. Staff feels it should have more of a hand in making policy. Be consulted more and be allowed to attend Directorate and executive staff meetings.[45]

Staff resentment soon became so serious that Bud Schweich appointed a 10-man committee to talk out the problems and prepare a formal list of suggestions to the Directorate. The System Revision and Morale Committee was headed by Dave Miller '56. It included many of WDBS' most active members, among them two would be on the next Directorate. Their report was ready by early December and Miller was admitted to a Directorate meeting to present it. As Miller read, Schweich and his fellow directors fell into a stunned silence. The committee, which was supposed to be primarily concerned with the Program Department, had ranged far wider than that. It advocated nothing short of a complete overhaul of the station's management structure. Specifically, outright election of the Directorate, to be supervised by an "active faculty advisor"; elevation of the personnel director to the Directorate, and appointment of a permanent personnel committee composed of Directorate members, to study specific problems; restructuring of and a much more active role for the executive staff; a reorganized, "tougher" training program, including a requirement that all announcing heelers be able to engineer their own shows from 3X or the master control room; periodic opening of Directorate and executive staff meetings, and the airing of all complaints at the general station meeting.

Prefacing all this was the statement that a "crisis" in morale had indeed developed, stemming from:

> The lack of communication between the various departments, and, most important of all, between the Directorate and the remainder of the station members... We would like to stress our concept of the function of WDBS as an extra-curricular organization composed of individuals with a common interest, an interest which is maintained and strengthened by social factors. We are aware of our obligation to our advertisers, but when that obligation has been fulfilled and philosophy directing WDBS' policy should have the promotion of social aspects which breed the much needed esprit de corps as its primary consideration.

Miller's report concluded, audaciously enough, not with a recommendation but with a demand: that his report be presented to the executive staff at a meeting to be held within the next few days.

As the smoke began to clear more experienced minds began to work. Peter Stevens, having done some organizational studies of his own, knew full well that dramatic moves such as electing the Directorate could prove disastrous in the long run, for an organization that depended so very heavily on competent, not just popular, top management. WDBS had grown large and important following its existing principles. One genuinely incompetent station manager could destroy the fragile chances for realization of WDBS-AM, and perhaps might destroy WDBS itself by alienating advertisers or the College administration. He also realized that junior staff members naturally want more power, but never having had to face the problems of running the whole sprawling organization they did not and could not fully understand those problems. They could scarcely be entrusted to make vital long-range decisions, must less restructure the whole station. Stevens had no reason to fear for his own job, but much to fear for the future of Dartmouth radio.

After considerable discussion and explanation of the "facts of life," Miller's committee met again and revised its specific proposals substantially. The new report, which was accepted, laid at least one important guideline for the future WDBS: a preferential poll was to be taken each spring to reveal express staff preferences, and the reasons for them. These would be honestly considered by the outgoing Directorate in choosing its successors, but were in no way binding. In addition a committee was set up composed of the heads of the various departmental training programs, to supervise a redefined station heeling program; several minor changes were made in the composition of the executive staff; and clear-cut job descriptions were to be worked out.

The primary, and best, effect of the personnel problems of 1954-55 was a matter of redefinition of responsibilities, and better understanding by both leaders and staff. The mere existence of Dave Miller's committee proved a helpful morale booster, while Peter Stevens later wrote that since the report,

> The Directorate has merely listened to any and all complaints from personnel. This has had the effect of proving that the Directorate is approachable. We have taken no concrete action except to provide a willing ear, and the results have been amazing! Communications and morale are both improved.[46]

### New Directorate

The preferential poll was held, and in mid-March the new Directorate announced. Production Manager John Van de Kamp became station manager; technical director was Flint Ranney '56, business manager, Henry Jaenicke '56, and program director, William Tell, seniors all.

The new regime promptly decided that "we should so something pretty specific to show that there will be changes made."[47] It then proceeded to render decisions on several weighty matters.

1. "Semantically, the Production Department is now the Program Department."
2. Cider and donut parties were to be held at the station on Saturday nights (they soon petered out).
3. "Controlling, not comptrolling" (nobody understood).
4. The station ought to get Coral and London records (it did).
5. "It was agreed that a special announcement be made at the next station meeting concerning inebriation..." (!).
6. Seniors should be invited to the annual station banquet free (seniors approved).
7. The business office should at last be moved upstairs.

This long-needed move of offices was agreed upon at the very first joint meeting of the new and old Directorates, thus the glory of winning 38 Robinson technically goes to the outgoing directors. Room 38 was occupied by The Dartmouth

Players, and the arguments advanced to get them to swap for the basement business office are of interest. First, WDBS' room four was bigger. Room four had a built-in WDBS program monitor, which, however, could be turned off (perish the thought). "We could supply free of charge at least ten (10) keys to room four." WDBS would move the furniture. WDBS would throw in a free desk, to fill the airy void of The Players' "new and sumptuous quarters." Room four had telephones. "The switch of offices would give the 'behind-the-scenes men' in the downstairs shop more of a feeling of belonging to The Players." "There is no news machine running 24 hours a day next to room four." "The people above room four are very quiet and do not make the ceiling light swing back and forth. (The Dartmouth Players and Professor Henry Williams are located above room four. The latter tenant is very good and seldom has wild parties, the former tenants are somewhat addicted to beer blasts but only infrequently)."

The Players said yes.

## Looking Ahead

The new Directorate learned of its greatest task when it was made privy to the trustee's secret March decision. John Van de Kamp stated it somewhat obliquely to *The Dartmouth.*

> The primary objective of the new Directorate is the improvement of transmission. This has been an extremely painstaking job, but we feel that great strides have been made this year toward the solution of the problem.[48]

Van de Kamp's new Directorate brought to a close what was at least a reasonably successful business year. Sales were almost identical with those of 1954, well below the peak years of 1952 and 1953, but expenses were down enough to produce a good, healthy surplus to return to COSO. Despite growing complaints about the Ivy Network's Yale-bound management, national ads accounted for more than half the station's income. It remained for Henry Jaenicke, though, to show how much WDBS could sell.

At the end of the year physics Professor Willis Rayton, longtime WDBS friend and faculty advisor, announced his retirement from the College due to poor health. After some searching the Directorate chose Bob Allen of the administration as his successor. Rayton had helped Dartmouth radio through its long years of battle with the old wired transmission system; Allen would be of great assistance in the AM wars that lay ahead.

# Chapter 5

# 1955-1958: The Battle For an AM License

What made WDBS grow? For one thing, a series of highly competent and remarkably devoted leaders, who sometimes seemed to put their organization even before their own college careers. Dynamic leadership has a way of building momentum into an organization that can last well after the original source is gone. With periodic renewal, it can continue working almost indefinitely. There was also the strong spur of station autonomy, wisely granted by the College. People can work doggedly on those things which they themselves control and are responsible for, while an activity under the thumb of higher authority is not really theirs to worry about.

Most importantly, the student leadership of WDBS had a compelling goal to aim for. Hanover's radio isolation presented a unique opportunity for them to gain a real, live adult market as their laboratory for learning, and they saw a chance for their station to become something bigger and better than the average campus "one lunger." This would be the real thing in commercial broadcasting, not simulated.

It is interesting to speculate on the history of WDBS had Dartmouth invested its money in an efficient, but permanently campus-limited station. The goal would then have disappeared. The station would undoubtedly have expanded from its first restricted dimensions, but ultimately the students would have been led to think small. It is difficult to believe that such a situation, or the thin pretense of professionalism when only a few dormitories could hear, would have spurred WDBS' leaders to work so hard for so long.

For WDBS the ambitious, long range goal *was* there, so build the students did. The station of 1955 would boast programming, studio equipment, a sales base, and a management organization which, if not already of professional caliber, was close to it. Only the final link was missing.

What made WDBS grow? More than anything, the dream of an AM broadcast license. When the trustees made their historic March 1955 decision, it seemed that the long, quiet struggle had been won at last. But in fact the battle had just begun. Three harrowing years stood between that decision and the day a student engineer could throw the switch putting WDCR-AM on the air.

### 1955-1956

The 1956 *Aegis* had its own thumbnail summary of progress during John Van de Kamp's administration.

> With the replacing of a burned-out transmitter condenser, the new leaders of WDBS increased the station's coverage to include 82 percent of the student body, and most of the dormitory telephones, and thus their efforts were more

widely received than last year. John "J. Wurlitzer" Van de Kamp, as station manager, sent out his pearly tones on the daily *Six O'Clock News*, while "Wild" Bill Tell, program director, entertained cool music fans in the late afternoons from the "A" train. Technical Director H. Flint "Fink" Ranney happily twiddled the dials of the new RCA tape recorder, obtained from funds provided by the fantastic selling abilities of Henry "Babes" Jaenicke as business manager.

Wild Bill Tell's major accomplishment as program director was to at last introduce—and maintain—an unbroken broadcast day, a schedule that was to be followed from 1955-on. Here is a typical December lineup.

| | |
|---|---|
| 6:58 | sign-on |
| 7:00 | *Strictly for the Birds* |
| 7:30 | *Jam for Breakfast* |
| 9:00 | *Morning Melodies* |
| 10:15 | *A.M. Bandstand* |
| 12:00 | *World News Roundup* |
| 12:15 | *George Haines' Today* |
| 1:00 | *The 640 Club* |
| 2:00 | *Masterworks of Music* |
| 4:00 | *Transition* |
| 4:45 | Public Service Show |
| 5:00 | *Tell Takes the "A" Train* |
| 6:00 | *Van de Kamp's News Roundup* |
| 6:15 | *Candlelight and Silver* |
| 7:00 | *Your Faculty of the Air* |
| 7:15 | *Dixieland Bandstand* |
| 7:30 | *Styles in Music* |
| 8:00 | *The Concert Hour* |
| 9:00 | *Rhythm at Random* |
| 9:30 | *Studio '55* |
| 10:00 | *Amidon's Sports Show* |
| 10:15 | *Old Gold Time – Jill Corey* |
| 10:30 | *The Co-Op Show* |
| 11:00 | *Music 'til Midnight* (Frank Sauter) |
| 12:00 | *Lebanon Laundry World News Roundup* |
| 12:15 | *In the Still of the Night* |
| 1:00 | *Night Watch* |
| 2:01 | sign-off |

"Nineteen hours a day is a lot of broadcasting," remarked Ranney, a fact of which Tell and Chief Announcer Frank Sauter were doubtless quite aware as they chased negligent announcers to keep shifts filled. Listeners demanded and got music through most of this long day, performed live on *Variety Time* and *Sultan Swing* ("we emphasize good ensemble work and a swingin' beat"), and recorded elsewhere.[1] The Mystery Melody now won friends for *Music 'til Midnight*. Trainees were told,

Radio at Dartmouth is unique. Relatively untouched by television and by other radio, the Dartmouth community is an air desert broken only at 640 and 1400 on your radio dial. The former by WDBS, the latter by WTS_, which is not our competitor but our complement, aiming its programming not at the College but at the surrounding agrarian area. You thus have a choice of listening to WDBS, hick music, or suffocating from dead air when you turn on your radio in Hanover.[2]

Disc jockey John Kramer '56 tainted this "swingin'" image only slightly when he reported to the music business trade paper *Billboard* that "the biggest record to hit WDBS in the station's 15-year history" was none other than Eddie Arnold's "Cattle Call."[3]

Although WDBS had a song in its heart, Production Manager Richard Harris '58 saw to it that there was something more on its airwaves. John Van de Kamp's own WDBS Players presented on *Studio '55* (and *'56*) such live dramas as *The Red Badge of Courage, Luck,* and a play called *The Large Story*. Said *The Dartmouth* of the latter, "It is the story of Bob Schmetts, a heeler for the daily 'D' as he lived it and wrote it."[4] Station manager and Players director Van de Kamp charitably commented that the WDBS Players,

> have grown into a very reliable and generally high quality outfit. This is the first time in my recollection of station history that we have been able to keep up a deal like this without its eventually dying out. Somehow shows like this put a little more zing in the schedule, and help make the station less of a disc jockey operation.[5]

Other "shows like this" included a brief revival of the *Ivy Theatre*, some BBC transcriptions, and the durable old *Student-Faculty Quiz*, now rebroadcast not only on WTS_ but on several nearby Vermont stations. Dave Bowman's *Behind the Scenes* poked its microphone into Undergraduate Council meetings, while *The Dartmouth* was given its own short-lived forum, *The Editor Speaks*. Perhaps he spoke a little too freely, for in December there was a headline-making rumor that Ike was backing College President John Sloan Dickey for the Republican Vice President nomination (which elicited from Richard Nixon an incredulous, "Ike is backing *who?*"). The rumor was said to have originated "at *The Dartmouth* or perhaps at WDBS itself."[6] Or so the "D" insidiously intimated, despite vehement denials by Van de Kamp.

Some program highlights of the year were a Norman Thomas interview on *Your Faculty of the Air*, coverage of the U.G.C. (Undergraduate Council) debate on whether to adopt an honor system at Dartmouth (it didn't), 24 hour music during January and June final exams, and the crowded WDBS Christmas party of the air. During the first semester's final exams and the immediately following Winter Carnival week there was 280 hours of continuous broadcasting, an all-time record, and sponsorship of what Van de Kamp hoped would be the First Annual WDBS Carnival Dance. Green Key Weekend was blanketed with the *Green Key Carousel*, and the ninth, and last, annual WDBS Green Key Queen crowned by singer Jill Corey of *Old Gold Time* transcribed fame. No doubt the most photogenic show in WDBS history occurred when *Playboy* Playmate Janet Pilgrim appeared on *Variety Time.*

Sports contests were covered by John Kramer and Gary Gilson '57, who traveled to most away games in Flint Ranney's "Heep III," the unofficial WDBS remote truck. Harvard weekend found network sportscaster Bob Neal originating his sportscast to 500 Mutual network stations from WDBS' Studio One.

### Smith's Last Stand

As soon as Van de Kamp took office he revived the traditional staff swap with Smith College's WCSR. In fact he wrote in April 1955 that the idea was so good, why not have two a year instead of one? But the Smithies were busy booking, and plans were postponed until the fall. Eight beautiful WCSR-ites arrived on a Saturday in November. That night they proceeded to take over the 7:00 p.m. to midnight request show with "Where to Find Us—Characteristics of Smith," plus a full hour of Meryl Wilen, WCSR's own "Lonesome Gal" (wonder what she did on WCSR?). "Whenever in Hanover," Van de Kamp wrote afterwards, "you have a standing invitation to drop in." "The arrangements were perfect... you treated us like queens," Smith gushed back. Van de Kamp added that "this kind of thing should be done every year." But it was the last WCSR invasion.

### Listenership

In the spring of 1956 the Ivy Network was back asking for a combined market-research and listenership poll, this time a standardized 76-question monster to be conducted door-to-door. It was carried out by a small army of heelers (trainees) and junior executives under "General" John Long '58, during March and April. Some of the more interesting findings:[7]

1. 89 percent preferred music to other programming.
2. Nobody admitted listening most to "educational" shows, and 37 percent said they never did.
3. Most had at least one friend on the station staff.
4. Heaviest listenership was in the late evening (i.e., *Music 'til Midnight*), next heaviest in the morning.
5. 40 percent sometimes or often had difficulty receiving the station.

### Personnel, Heelers, and Business

Personnel relations were less of a problem for Van de Kamp than for his predecessors. Complaints now found willing Directorate ears; offices and studio space were at last united; more all-station social get-togethers (i.e., "blasts") were held; and perhaps most important, the Directorate showed attention to the little things that build morale, such as sending Christmas cards to all station members. While old recruits were having their morale lifted, new ones got a fourth edition of the *WDBS Heeler's Manual* from Personnel Director Dave Miller. After Miller resigned in February, however, there began a gradual retrenchment from well-coordinated training programs.

Historians and listeners have to be kept happy too, so it was with pride that John Van de Kamp commented in November that,

Public Relations is doing very well, with the 1955-56 scrapbook up to date. The program log in *The Dartmouth* has been changed to include names of announcers in personality shows, and also a listing of classical works to be played on *Masterworks in Music* and *The Concert Hour...* This sort of thing makes public relations mean something. Oliver Witte, Dave Johns and Merv Bagan are to be commended for their work in this field.[8]

Babes Jaenicke guided WDBS to a banner year in sales in 1955-56. Even in September it was apparent that local sponsorship was up substantially, thanks especially to new advertising from Lebanon. Ivy Network national contracts made WDBS resemble a drugstore counter at times (Lucky Strike, Old Gold, Camel and Winston cigarettes, Lanvin perfume, and *The New York Times*), but when the 1956 figures were in, the admen had topped Jim Penney's 1953 all-time sales record by some $300. Once again several hundred dollars was returned to COSO, and WDBS' standing with the College treasurer's office, at least, was as good as (old) gold.

There was evidently progress in the station's own income and expense accounting too, as John Van de Kamp reported in October, "the first financial statement of this year, or any year."[9]

Besides donating the services of his Heep III jeep as a remote truck, complete with a WDBS sign in the window, Flint Ranney accomplished a good many large and small improvements to the physical plant, which was constantly in use. WDBS was using tape recording almost as much as disc recording by this time, making it painfully apparent that some new tape equipment—*any* new tape equipment—would have to be acquired soon. The faithful old Ampex 400 had served long and well over four-and-a-half years of hard use, but despite its overhaul was now beginning to show the effects of age. Among other things, complained Ranney, "it seems to have great speed fluctuations on rainy days."

In June 1955 the Directorate reviewed the prosperous business picture and authorized $125 for an interim machine, whereupon Ranney promptly bought a small (and presumably used) portable RCA. In the fall the market for large professional machines was thoroughly examined. Prices were high but RCA was willing to offer a sizeable educational discount, so in October a check for $900 went out for a big RCA RT-11B (which was still at WDCR ten years later). This purchase gave WDBS two large studio machines and one smaller portable. "This puts us in XLNT shape" wrote Van de Kamp happily, not realizing the maintenance headaches all three would bring.

### For Free or Not for Free

Ranney still had a wealth of projects to address during the 1955-56 broadcast year, such as remodeling the studios and air conditioning the control rooms, which "tend to become extremely hot and stuffy in the spring and early fall." But the College's Buildings and Grounds Department wanted $250 to cool them off, and the Tech budget had become a mite tight after buying the RCAs.

Well, how about donations? WDBS was a strictly non-profit institution and a struggling collegiate one-lunger besides. Encouraged by the gift of some clocks by Bulova the year before, Ranney sent off some letters: to a Massachusetts company for acoustical sound tiles (got them), to the Carrier Company for an air conditioner (no), to Audio Devices for some free recording tape (no), to General Douglas MacArthur, Chairman of the Board of Remington Rand, for some filing cabinets (no). Ah, well, the best things in life could still be done cheaply, at least. With help from Adam Block '57 a brilliant new sign was made for the foot of the third floor stairs proclaiming "WDBS, The Stairway to the Stars... with flashing lights adding to the sexy and schmaltzy effect."[10] A new WDBS banner, 45 rpm and LP record cabinets, new shelves and other necessities were also home-made.

By the spring of 1956 finances were good enough to allow Ranney's successor to purchase another piece of major equipment, a $500 Rek-o-Cut disc recorder to lighten the load on the tape recorders. They also paid for still more repairs on the old, ailing Ampex 400.

### Watch Out for a Black Sedan on the Road to Lebanon...

"That G.D. transmitter of ours is still perking along, but no one understands why or how" wrote Ranney to his predecessor Bill Gitt in December.[11] The Middle Fayerweather monster was in no better shape than ever, but somehow it didn't matter so much anymore, the patching was only for temporary use now. In May 1955 engineers had discovered that for at least a year the thing had been running on a blown-out coupling condenser ("pieces all over the XMTR vault"). When this was replaced signal strength increased 50 percent. Some more repairs in the fall increased coverage still more, and in September Van de Kamp reported happily that "the west side of campus manages to get us quite well, though things are not perfect."[12] A November poll showed that WDBS was then reaching 82 percent of the students, a sizeable increase.

The new coverage was not without its drawbacks of course, as was made clear at the year's first Executive Staff meeting. "Sponsors can hear us this year. Look out!" "Nichols reported seeing a black sedan bearing government plates on the road to Lebanon on October 5, at night..."[13]

### There May Be Delays

Flint Ranney's December 1955 letter to Bill Gitt summed up the progress made towards AM, thus far.

> Last March the trustees approved $6,500 for WDBS's transformation into a commercial AM station, and we got very excited. The problem of whether or not we would then be an unrelated business for which the College would have to pay income tax went to the College lawyers, who did nothing until November, after I had gone to see the College treasurer, John Meck, to ask him what was happening. The lawyers found that it is feasible, and they are now working on the FCC application for a construction permit... (meanwhile) the trustees met again two weeks ago and gave final approval to the plan. It will be at least a year, I'm almost sure, before WDBS is a commercial, 250 watt AM radio station, serving the Tri-Town area, but I am almost sure that by that time we will be that. There may be delays but the change is inevitable. We are keeping this very quiet, because if WTSL heard about it they might try to fight the application, or file one themselves just to delay ours. I really

think, however, that it's almost in the bag. And it'll be wonderful!!!!![14]

"There may be delays" was an understatement. After prodding the lawyers into action in November 1955, with letters darkly hinting that plans were afoot to start a station in White River Junction, Ranney was dismayed to learn that as of February 1956 the WDBS application was still not ready. More complaints to the treasurer's office brought a concise explanation why.

> There remain a number of things to be done which by their nature are bound to be time-consuming. The principal item is the filing of some 24 pages of FCC forms, which require among others things a legal opinion to the effect that the College has the corporate power to operate a commercial radio station, detailed information about each of the trustees and officers of the College, proposed financing arrangements, detailed statement of program service, and several pages of engineering data. The information is coming from various sources and will necessarily take some time to assemble.[15]

While the College filled in forms, WDBS busily collected transmitter cost estimates from RCA, Collins, and Gates representatives (the latter, after seeing the WDBS studios, enthused "You have a nice set-up, and it certainly will be wonderful when you connect it to a new Gates transmitter").[16] Thought was also given to a rebuttal to the objections WTSL would surely raise, but in April 1956, when Ranney and his fellow directors left office, they would still not be needed for some time. The great AM battles, and the most exciting two years in WDBS history, lay after the summer.

The Directorate that would fight the first of those battles was chosen in late March 1956, with guidance from the second annual preferential poll. The new station manager would be former Chief Announcer Frank Sauter; technical director, Adam Block; business manager, Merv Bagan '57; program director and only sophomore, Dick Harris. With them was appointed an 11-man executive staff (including two ex-officio members) and a full complement of senior staff officers.

### 1956-1957

Their year would be an exciting one. Dartmouth radio would come out of 1956-57 bearing remarkably little business or technical resemblance to its old self. This was at least partially due to the ambition of its station manager and program director, who told staffers at their first station meeting that WDBS was now the largest active organization on campus, and they expected to soon become the most influential and dynamic as well.[17]

The first dramatic changes came in Dick Harris' program department. When the station signed on in September, 1956, the 7:00 a.m. to 2:00 a.m. schedule was much the same as it had been previously, but in early October this was scrapped almost in its entirety. Out went six shows that had been WDBS standbys since the original program expansion of the late 1940s, *Jam for Breakfast* (b. 1947), *Styles in Music* (b. 1947), *Morning Melodies* (b. 1948), *Candlelight and Silver* (b. 1949), *The Concert Hour* (b. 1949) and even the popular *In the Still of the Night* (b. 1949). *Concert Hour* had actually existed continuously since DBS's earliest days, under slightly varying names; from 1941-48 it was *The Symphonic Hour*, later it was *Concert Hall*. Out also were the more recent *A.M. Bandstand, Today, Masterworks in Music, Variety Time* and *Strictly for the Birds*.

Out, in fact, went the entire 1941 concept of finely segmented programming, which had limited most shows to thirty minutes or an hour. Although the musical programming itself was not drastically revised, this was far more than a mere name-changing spree. In preparation for AM Harris was replacing the whole patchwork quilt concept of "variety" with an integrated program day, one in which each period flowed into the next and a simplified overall structure prevailed. The new schedule, as it had become established by the spring of 1957, was as follows.[18]

6:58  sign-on
7:00  *Tempo* – bright and bouncy wake-up music, with news headlines or summaries every 15 minutes.
9:00  *Tempo* (cont.) – more music and news, "for the guy who is in his room, whether he is studying or goofing off." Top tunes, including rock 'n' roll, were featured during the 10:00 to 10:30 "Chapel Period," when students were between classes.
12:00  *Serenade* – big band swing and other non-rock popular music.
2:00  *640 Club* – continuation of the preceding, but now with 65 percent current hits (including rock 'n' roll) mixed in.
4:00  *Mike Melvoin's Swinghouse* – 80 percent current hits, with "swing" filling out the rest.
6:00  *World News Roundup* (15 minutes), followed by five minutes of sports, five of weather, and five of editorial commentary.
6:30  Production block – *Student-Faculty Quiz*, dramatics ("including transcriptions and our own attempts"), specialty music shows
7:30  *Evening Serenade* – 30 minutes of "mood" music, followed by 90 minutes of classical, then 30 more of mood, to study by.
10:00  *Everybody Likes Music* – transition to popular music, including old hits, and gradually building up in tempo to...
11:00  *Music 'til Midnight* – the immensely popular all-request juke box of current and old rock 'n' roll hits.
12:00  *Nightwatch*, tapering off quickly to uninterrupted mood music "to study or sleep by."
2:00  sign-off

News and sports reports were scattered throughout, appearing at least once an hour. Most of the music was of the light popular ("easy listening") variety, but as can be seen Dick Harris' Dynamic Radio Concepts did not fail to recognize the huge changes going on in popular music with the explosion of rock 'n' roll on the national scene in 1955-56. This was a period when rock 'n' roll and older styles of ballads and instrumentals co-existed on the popularity charts. However Harris betrayed his own prejudices when he noted "... the undeniable trend from the smooth, progressive sounds of the Brubeck-Baker school to rhythm and blues, at its finest with Fats Domino, and at its most primitive with Elvis Presley and Gene Vincent."[19]

The record library played no favorites, claiming 9,000 discs of all kinds by the end of the year (compared to 500, 10 years earlier). At least a third of these were 45 rpm's, the new medium of current hits.

The production highlight of Harris' year, and a preview of what would become Dartmouth radio's most famous programming achievement in years to come, was the first big election night broadcast. There had already been coverage of the campaigns, with Rob Brown '59 and Frank Sauter conducting interviews at the 1956 Republican National Convention. Then on November 4, 1956, from broadcasting headquarters set up in spacious 104 McNutt Hall, dozens of well-organized WDBS staffers provided geographical coverage of returns, with the public invited to come and watch. A WDBS team even traveled to tiny Hart's Location, New Hampshire, to report the nation's first official balloting, just after midnight. UPI had commandeered the only phone line out of the remote hamlet, so the station borrowed walkie-talkies from Dartmouth's Reserve Officers Training Corps (ROTC), and Rob Brown radioed the results to Al Cameron '60 in the woods below who then phoned them back to Hanover. Bill Cunningham, columnist for *The Boston Herald*, commented on the Dartmouth coverage, "Radio station WDBS did a tremendous job of election reporting... first in the nation from Hart's Location." [20]

New station members, at least those entering the Program Department, had their day in the sun when Dick Harris decided they had been called heelers long enough. "Interns" would be better. Harris also re-wrote the production department manual, originally promulgated by Norm Bander in 1953, and subsequently revised by Schweich and Tell. However the overall station training structure, integrating the individual departments, was by this time dying out. There is no evidence of a station manual or other detailed coordination.

## Going AM

Since it was Dartmouth College that was legally applying for the AM license, the entire matter of preparing the application was in administration hands. Bob Allen kept the Directorate informed on the latest developments, but for Frank Sauter and his directors it must have been a frustrating spring of 1956. Progress seemed painfully slow, and there was virtually nothing they could do but watch.

The last major obstacles to preparation of the application were technical. Keare and Kennedy of Boston, the broadcast engineers hired by the College, finally chose the southeast corner of Chase Field as the most suitable location for the proposed transmitter. Although this was tucked away at the foot of a heavily wooded, signal obstructing hill, K&K blithely reported that "this seems to be eminently satisfactory from a radiation point of view, and also because of its easy access." [21] Meanwhile the Washington firm commissioned to do a frequency search came up with 1490 KC as the station's most desirable location on the radio dial, based on what was available. [22]

There were some nervous moments in August when it was learned that New Hampshire's KBR Network had filed application for a 250 watt station in Keene, N.H., just 52 air miles from Hanover, but Percy Russell, the Washington attorney retained by the College for broadcast matters, did not feel this was close enough to endanger WDBS' chances. The chief threat, said Russell, would come when, and if, WTSL contested the Dartmouth application. Here was something the students could actively contribute to, the preparation of facts to support a rebuttal, and they launched into it earnestly. "Frank, I don't want to see this thing fail because of something on which we muffed," wrote Harris to Sauter.

As Adam (Block) said last month, if it doesn't go through this time it never will. We're carrying the ball for a lot of guys who planned this project before we ever got to college. I'd just like to see it go forward as they intended it, rather than being an eyewitness to the chain just being pulled on the whole scheme.[23]

Later, after an extended period of administration silence, Sauter flew to Washington to find out "just what the heck is going on." But Percy Russell's counsel was the same as the College's: patience. Nothing could be done until the application was filed, and WTSL's reaction became known.

Finally, on September 14, 1956, some 18 months after the trustees' decision, Dartmouth College filed a formal application with the FCC for permission to construct a 250 watt station at 1490 KC. As the news was released *The Dartmouth* quoted a confident Frank Sauter: "We probably won't receive approval or disapproval for a few months, (but) the FCC rarely turns down applications of this sort from educational institutions."[24]

### The Fight with WTSL: First Round

When WDBS' long monopoly of the Hanover airwaves ended with the appearance of WTSL in late 1950, the college station had gulped hard, accepted the fact, and learned to live with it. Now the tables were turned. WTSL, with much more at stake, did not surrender so quietly.

It is understandable that WTSL would contest the Dartmouth application as vigorously as possible, for this was more than a matter of losing an Upper Valley radio monopoly. There was real doubt that such a small market could support two commercial AM stations, and if one was to go under it would almost certainly be WTSL. To WTSL's owners the cards must have seemed stacked against them. First, WDBS, being student-run, would pay no wages and thus have much lower operating costs than WTSL. Second, WDBS was backed by Dartmouth College and could presumably run on a deficit indefinitely if the College felt its activities worthwhile. To a small commercial enterprise like WTSL deficits were a matter of life and death. Perhaps competing stations could co-exist, but that was a big "if" and it was only reasonable for the competitor who stood much to lose and nothing to gain to try to prevent the contest from ever taking place.

The 1956-57 battle with WTSL had three principal stages. The first was an attempt to reach a private agreement with College officials. The Granite State Network had been taken over by the KBR Network, and WTSL's spokesman was KBR Treasurer William F. Rust. Almost as soon as the Dartmouth application was made public Rust met privately with Bob Allen and other College officials. After some discussion he made the following offer: WTSL would give WDBS its evening program time if the application was dropped. This could be done by installing a permanent line from the WDBS studios to the WTSL transmitter. WTSL would end its own regular programming at 8:30 p.m. each evening, after which it would merely simulcast WDBS until the latter's sign-off. The WTSL transmitter would be remote-controlled from Robinson Hall, so that after 8:30 the college station would in effect have possession of a 250 watt, 1400 KC AM transmitter. Agreements could also be reached regarding carrying of network shows from ABC (with which WTSL was affiliated), and WDBS' advertising. In this way, said Rust, WTSL could serve Dartmouth's desire to bring educational programming to the Upper Valley, and avoid the possibility of "serious economic distress" to itself.[25]

When this proposal was turned down, Rust may have made others. *The Dartmouth* later reported rumors that he offered to sell WTSL to the College; however, this would have been quite impractical from the College's point of view, both from the standpoints of expense (building a radio station is always cheaper than buying one) and wasteful duplication of facilities.

The College said no.

### The Fight with WTSL: Second Round

The next step was to formally contest the Dartmouth application before the FCC. This was done in late October 1956, the grounds being that "the grant of a second commercial AM station at Hanover to a tax-free educational institution utilizing student labor must result in unfair competition and economic distress to WTSL."[26] Shortly thereafter WTSL forwarded a copy of its brief to the College trustees, along with a detailed and most interesting (if not always entirely logical) statement of its case.

> Dartmouth College has recently filed an application with the Federal Communications Commission for a new 250 watt commercial broadcast station at Hanover, N.H. Although this action might appear innocuous, it is in effect an attack on our free enterprise system with disregard for private property rights.
>
> There is already a 250 watt fulltime commercial broadcast station at Hanover. This WTSL, an ABC Network affiliate, serving the people of Hanover, Lebanon and White River Junction since 1951, and regularly paying taxes and supporting the families of seven full-time employees living in the community...
>
> Hanover has a population of only 5,000 and the combined population of Hanover, Lebanon and White River Junction is less than 12,000.[27] Manchester, with a population of 82,700, is the only New Hampshire city with more than one broadcast station. It is obvious that two commercial stations should not be built in Hanover as both cannot survive.
>
> A Dartmouth officer recently stated to us that WTSL is "doing such a poor job that it would be of no great loss" if Dartmouth should force WTSL out of business. The fact is that WTSL is an ABC Network affiliate and is as well programmed as any station in a small town... We also deplore the public taste in music, literature, art, automobiles and such, but do not think that this is a matter to be resolved by a tax free educational institution using unpaid labor and donated capital to parallel and compete with a struggling small privately owned radio station in a town that is very small for one station and impossible for two.
>
> The record shows that in nearly 40 years of radio broadcasting in the United States this is the first time any educational institution has gotten itself in the unfortunate position of attempting to obtain a commercial radio station where the grant of such a station would cause economic distress to an

existing broadcast station.

There are only about seven commercial AM stations licensed to schools. Practically all of these were started by the 1920s, were the first stations in town, and are now network stations operated for profit by professionals with no specialized programming aimed at a student body or faculty...

We have a substantial investment in WTSL both in time and money, and we naturally do not want this investment destroyed capriciously. We ask that you kindly investigate and give us your support in seeing that the Dartmouth application is withdrawn.

> Very truly yours,
> WTSL, Inc.
> W.F. Rust, Treasurer[28]

The FCC rejected the WTSL protest with scarcely a nod, on the grounds that competitive conditions played no part in licensing decisions. Entry into broadcasting is free to anyone legally, technically, and financially competent, providing "airspace" is available and that the public interest will be served.

WTSL's protest did not become public until January 1957, when it suddenly hit *The Dartmouth* in large black headlines, along with complete reprints of Rust's letter and the FCC's reply. The "*D*" itself did not rally to the side of the college broadcasters as it had in 1941, however. Obviously relying on a partial knowledge of the facts, it first printed a long and ambiguous editorial which generally sided with WTSL. WDBS-AM offered "exciting" possibilities, true, but it might also create problems. Maybe it would be better to avoid them altogether by buying WTSL, going FM, or remaining campus-limited. When Bob Allen and Frank Sauter patiently explained the infeasibility of such schemes, the paper became even more confused, suggesting weakly that there were still many legal problems to overcome, and that perhaps more adequate preparations ought to be made. Besides,

> Confusion between the dual purposes of serving both the College and adjacent rural areas seems likely. It is doubtful that the station can at the same time remain an outstanding student-run activity, adequately serve both the College and the surrounding area, and not drive WTSL out of business.[29]

By the end of the week, after a U.G.C. meeting had been held to clarify the plans for AM, the paper finally found its range. In an editorial entitled "Ends and Means" it approved of the ends wholeheartedly. Dartmouth radio surely needed better (and legal) coverage, and might also provide a genuine educational programming service to the entire Upper Valley. But the means it could not condone. If WTSL stayed in business there would be no problem. "But if by some miscalculation, WDBS, in the process of doubling its income, does happen to make commercial operation unprofitable for WTSL, the responsibility for community service, not merely education, reverts to the College." *The Dartmouth* frankly doubted that WDBS could ever bear such a dual responsibility.

> This may be possible but we wish to be spared the necessity of waking up each morning to a quotation of the previous day's livestock and grain market

prices, just as we are sure our neighbors will not be especially interested in College "private" business, such as a discussion of the campus car and parking problem by a member of the administration...

*If* WTSL remains in business, *if* the College does not have to pay WDBS staffers, *if* the station is not required to be broadcast 365 days a year, and *if* those responsible for the station are willing to serve the needs of the community not only in "uplife" but in information and entertainment, then this experiment will be a noble one, worthy of praise and imitation. But things would be much easier, the ends would be more easily achieved, and the means more acceptable, if this station could be undertaken on the same basis as most college stations, noncommercial, and therefore unimpeachable.[30]

No one could have proven it in 1957, but every one of those "if's" would come true.

In any event the College stood squarely behind the project, rejecting both the advice of the campus newspaper and the objections of WTSL. The trustees had weighed the problem carefully two years earlier and concluded that AM was the only financially and technically sound solution, the market was ample for the students' augmented sales efforts, a real programming service (not duplication) would be provided, and an excellent opportunity for practical student training would result. Their decision was not now likely to be reversed.

WTSL did not help its case when the voluble Howard Chase, station manager of WTSL and a Dartmouth graduate, paid a visit to President John Sloan Dickey in January 1957. Chase opened the meeting by making thinly veiled threats to the effect that he might use Dartmouth's pursuit of an AM license to attack the College's fund-raising activities, obtain negative publicity in *The Manchester Union Leader*, and even call for a congressional investigation into any favorable FCC decision. Dickey let him go on for 15 minutes before replying that he was greatly offended by Chase's diatribe, which sounded very much like blackmail. After sputtering about being "misunderstood," Chase eventually slunk out of the office, leaving behind an incensed adversary who was no doubt more resolved than ever to see the matter through.[31]

### The Fight with WTSL: Third Round

At the end of January 1957 word was received that approval was imminent (causing the "*D*" to repeat that it was all a mistake, then add caustically "Things might have been so much easier... just last week Amherst applied for its educational FM channel").[32] But this proved a mirage. Unable to sway either the FCC or the College with its protests of economic distress, William Rust's "small, struggling, privately owned network" tried one more legal ploy to derail AM radio at Dartmouth.

The vehicle was the KBR Network's application for a 250 watt station in Laconia, N.H., just 45 miles away—and strangely enough, on a frequency of 1490 KC. By FCC regulations two parties competing for the same frequency allocation within a range of 50 miles (for 250 watt applications) have their applications joined and studied as one problem. Dartmouth, which had been so near to approval, now incurred all the delays of the KBR application as its own, and also had to meet William Rust's new objections, made on the grounds of likely signal overlapping on

1490 KC, and the doubt on his part that Dartmouth could secure a waiver on minimum wage legislation. Doubtless the strategy was to delay the awarding of the construction permit for as long as possible while trying to see that the waiver was not granted.

The complications arising from provisions of the federal minimum wage law, that commercial radio stations must pay the federal minimum wage to all employees, were the most serious threat of all. It was here that the arguments of unfair competition could properly be used. If the Labor Department's Wage and Hour Bureau ruled that WDBS-AM would have to pay every staff member $1.25 per hour, Dartmouth AM radio would indeed be doomed. It took Percy Russell months to iron out this complex problem, as well as the snags at the FCC.

### Spring of 1957: A New Directorate Takes Charge

There had been considerable optimism in January 1957 that the license was almost won, but as of March, when the new Directorate took office, the entire AM question was again in doubt. Named to succeed Frank Sauter was his program director, Dick Harris. Harris was the first station head to adopt the title of "general" manager and the last, for many years to come, to serve more than one year on the Directorate. The new program director would be John Long, business manager, Dave Johns '58, and technical director, Al Pulsifer '58.

Dick Harris acknowledged the obvious by stating that his regime's prime objective would be the conversion to AM, then set about preparing the station as he had the Program Department. A series of Ditto-duplicated letters to station members kept the staff informed on the tortuous progress of the lawyers in Washington, and also on changes taking place within the station.

### Programming and Business...and Tech

Long's program department instituted seminars for announcers, a new emphasis on local news, and a logical order to the schedule of newscasts (which had previously tended to come on quarter hours, half hours, and five-minutes-after-the-hour in a pattern that no one could understand). Some minor changes were made in Harris' program lineup, and more news-oriented production shows, including one called *Conversation,* were under development. Finally, as a sure way to perk up the early morning shows, a coffee maker was installed in the main studios.

Business Manager Dave Johns would have one of the most vital roles in the new WDBS, as expenses were sure to rise considerably with AM. The 1956-57 year had been a disappointing one financially, with sales down sharply from the previous year's all time high. They were around the $5,000 level, however, and most important of all, at least for the sake of appearances, for the sixth straight year the station had a surplus... of exactly one dollar.

In preparation for the great year to come in business, Johns and his staff devised a better servicing policy for downtown merchants, introduced such on-the-air novelties as musical backgrounds for commercials, and began a study of the advertising market with an eye to moving onward and upward.

The greatest changes would of course be in Al Pulsifer's technical department. The Tech workshop, which had long occupied the space outside Studio

3X, was now moved to the second floor news room (room 37), and the news machine moved to a much more convenient location next to the studios. This switch would allow the rebuilding and expansion of Studio 3X. Plans were also laid for the major rebuilding of the main studios and the installation of new equipment that would come with AM.

Work on the old Middle Fayerweather transmitter produced the best intra-campus coverage yet, ironically, and of course there was the continuous work needed to keep in operation the three obstreperous tape recorders, the tired old Ampex 400, the relatively new but decrepit big RCA, and the hopeless RCA portable.

### Death of an S.O.P.

The "new look" took its toll among the established standard operating procedures of WDBS. One of the first to come under attack was the traditional practice of assigning an engineer to each disc jockey show. In the early days of the station this had been a physical necessity, because of the separation of control room and studio. After the construction of the disc jockey "combo" studio 3X in 1952 it remained a practical one, because so few announcers had (or desired) any engineering proficiency.

As daily broadcasting increased from 10 hours in 1951 to 19 in 1955, however, the engineering staff was spread thin indeed, and announcers argued that they would do less harm behind the board themselves than the pea-green freshmen being assigned to them. In the spring of 1957 the whole system of d.j.-plus-engineer came under a blistering attack from John Long and his Chief Announcer Rob Brown. For the sake of decent program quality, the deadwood engineers had to go ("What would the program be without them? Better!"[33]). The missed cues, the records played at the wrong speed, the forgetting to turn on the announcer's microphone, all sounded bad enough on intra-campus WDBS. On AM they would be intolerable. Besides, an announcer-engineer could coordinate talk and records himself, on the spot, thus be able to run a much tighter show than when he had to arrange everything in advance with the engineer.

No, protested the programmers, they were not mad at Tech, nor were they trying to destroy the department. Pulsifer would still be able to recruit good engineers for remote broadcasts, production shows, maintenance, and other work without the lure of endless disc jockey shifts. In fact, they said, his department would likely become smaller in numbers but better in proficiency and usefulness.

Overthrowing such a basic and well-entrenched system naturally stirred resentment and opposition, but the announcers had a point. By 1960 it was a rare disc jockey who didn't "combo" his own show.

### Harris Exhorts

For the station at large during the spring of 1957 there were station meetings, regular Saturday night bull sessions (both suffered from attendance problems), the annual May station banquet, and pep talks in those mimeographed station letters from Dick Harris. From April, 1957:

These are the more noticeable changes appearing at WDBS, but there is far more under the surface. On all levels of the station a new approach and a new spirit is evident. This is WDBS *in action*...

Our new training program, our long-range plan, our new esprit de corps aims at building WDBS into the finest college station in the country. This, gentlemen, is not misplaced idealism. Nor is it beyond our scope to bring the highest broadcasting standards to WDBS. We have all the advantages and few of the disadvantages of the radio industry, and we have every opportunity to bring performance of higher calibre to the listener. We are on this threshold of professional-sounding radio. It takes cooperation, interest, and hard work to make the step, but we must not sell WDBS or ourselves short...

Without top-notch radio, increased range is meaningless... Our programming policy is radio aimed at the Dartmouth student with the balance necessary to make it listenable for all those within the new range of WDBS. Our overall policy is, in all departments, to develop compact, competent and cooperative activity. In short, our business for the coming year is to make WDBS *hot!*[34]

The legal hassle over a minimum wage waiver and overlapping signals with the Laconia station had kept Percy Russell and the other Washington lawyers tied up since January. In April 1957, though, the legal logjam finally began to break when the Labor Department ruled WDBS-AM exempt from the minimum wage law, provided that the station made no profit for either the College or itself, did not engage in competitive behavior that might be detrimental to the life of any existing station in the area (i.e., WTSL), and remained a purely student-run extra-curricular activity.

Once this crucial decision had been handed down, approval was a matter of time. In early May the KBR network dropped its formal objections when Dartmouth found another available frequency, 1340 KC. This left the problem of 365 days-per-year broadcasting, required by a standard broadcast license. So sure were the lawyers of securing FCC permission for summer "silent periods" however, that this was put off until the following spring. If the station was somehow constructed before Thanksgiving, 1957, it could stay on over Thanksgiving and Christmas vacations.

Frank Sauter and the graduating seniors just missed the big moment for which they had worked so long. On June 28, 1957, the FCC issued to Dartmouth College a C.P. (construction permit) for a 250 watt commercial AM station, at 1340 KC.

### "W" — What?

After issuance of the C.P., obtaining an operating license was merely an administrative formality. The license would, however, specify the hours of permissible operation (automatically full time for WDBS' frequency) and the call letters. The latter proved something of a problem because "WDBS" had been foreclosed by the Duke Broadcasting System (which ran a professionally staffed AM operation). Dartmouth's second choice, WDRB, was also in use so the Directorate decided on WDRT, and used this in its promotional material during the late spring and summer of 1957 as the "station to come."

During the summer it was learned that a prior application had gotten to WDRT too (in addition someone noticed that it might be pronounced "dirt"), so Harris and his directors started looking for yet another combination that was euphonious, meaningful, and unused. WDRC would be good because it matched Harris' slogan of Dynamic Radio Concepts, but a big station in Connecticut already had that. Finally they decided on the call letters that would become so familiar to the Dartmouth of the future. When the station returned in the fall, no matter what the state of AM preparations, it would be WDCR, Dartmouth College Radio.[35]

### 1957-1958: The Era of Committees

The year just past had certainly brought exciting developments, but they had taken place mostly in Washington, Parkhurst Hall, and the unhelpful columns of *The Dartmouth*. For the student staff at WDBS it had been a year of watching, waiting, and helping in little ways where they could. Now, at last, the students were no longer in the wings. Now it was up to them to actually build Dartmouth's AM radio station. This was a year of action and dramatic change, and it was an exciting year for everyone from Dick Harris down to the lowliest freshman trainee. Everything seemed to center around one all-consuming purpose, preparation for the historic December or January day (latest estimate) when WDCR would become WDCR-AM.

The spirit of enthusiasm and change was spread by the *WDCR Newsletter*, resurrected in the fall by Public Relations Director Roger Schulz '60. This Ditto-duplicated intra-station newssheet, billed as "The Oldest College Radio Station Weekly," served to keep everyone informed, toss bouquets to especially hard-working station members, and generally provide much needed unity for the station as a whole. It survived, on and off, for many years thereafter.

Dick Harris' principal attack on the problems at hand was more formal, however. If his regime was to receive one short, oversimplified label, it would have to be the Era of Committees. During the fall of 1957 ad hoc committees and reports evaluated virtually every aspect of station operations, from program theory to ad writing. Although these did not of themselves wreak cataclysmic changes in the way the station operated, they did stimulate thought and discussion among their executive authors, verbalizing the myriad procedures and problems that WDCR-AM would inherit. They were an important force in constituting the new WDCR, at least among its leaders. Among them were the following.

> Dave Lazar '61's Committee on the Writing of Ads, With Regard to the General Station Evaluation echoed problems which business managers eternally face: not enough rotation of spots ("there is nothing worse than hearing the same ad over and over again"), not enough pre-reading by d.j.'s (or better, not enough pre-recording of ads by businessmen), and not enough common sense in writing the spots in the first place.
>
> Fred Lockyear '59 and Bill Cogswell '61's Committee on the Status, Current and Future, of the Continuity Department called its subject "a rather nebulous entity" consisting of one person who typed the daily program logs. A bigger staff and control of all NCSAs (Non Commercial Spot Announcements, for charities, community events, etc.) and promotional announcements was recommended.

Carl Bahn '60's *Scope* Committee reviewed the all-weekend show that was intended to be "a *Monitor* on the College level," concluded that it tried too hard and ought to be dumped ("Who are we trying to kid?").

Ron Kehoe '59's Committee on Public Issues Programming investigated how WDCR-AM could meet the FCC's religious, agricultural, news, and special events programming minimum hours per week, and concluded that it would not be hard. Also, the station should avoid editorializing, but offer a willing and eager stage for others "who will stick their necks out for us."

Chuck Brower '60's personal General Philosophy of Programming was just that.

John Allbee '59's Committee on NCSA's and Promos thought they were a good idea, but ought to be limited to items of particular local interest.

Jon Cohen '60's Committee on the Reevaluation of the Production Trainee Program concluded that the revisions already made in the 10 week program by Jon Cohen were just what was needed.

Jon Cohen's Committee on the First AM Broadcast began, "it is essential that the first broadcast on WDCR-AM be something spectacular," explained how to do it, and got Cohen put in charge of the affair.

Jon Cohen's further Committee on the Reassessment of the Block System (of presenting production shows) felt the system ought to be dropped.

## The Kehoe Report

Ron Kehoe's Committee on General Programming submitted the most interesting report of all, in retrospect, coming as it did from the man who would be the first general manager of WDCR-AM. Kehoe was one of the station's most authoritative newsmen, possessed of "magnificent pipes, and a cadence that was a dead ringer for Edward R. Murrow's delivery."[36] In 17 single-spaced pages he expressed bluntly and intelligently the programming challenges WDCR-AM would face, and how he thought it ought to meet them. Kehoe reaffirmed the traditional philosophy that WDCR was in business to program to students, not to townspeople, high schoolers, farmers or anybody else who might listen in. But with AM more outsiders than insiders would be listening. The Lebanon housewife's wants, though never paramount, should at least be taken into consideration. The ideal answer would be a format designed to meet student needs, but not in such a way as to alienate others (as would rock 'n' roll in the morning, for instance). Regarding WDCR and public service he said,

Some of our listeners... will appreciate any intelligent effort to meet their needs; others, probably the majority, will be indifferent; still others will be implacably hostile to any pretensions on our part to "higher concepts." Nevertheless we think that radio has a definite, profound responsibility to its patrons... our service function must be realized and emphasized more than it has been heretofore..

WDCR has a threefold function of entertainment, information and education. The listener should be made consciously aware only of entertainment and information, with education disguised as one of these (or

116

both) wherever possible. The more keen-minded, who are seeking higher-level broadcasting, will still recognize and appreciate education for what it is.

Kehoe went on to demonstrate that a basic music-news-special events format was the best vehicle with which to accomplish these functions. It would also best fit what student and other listeners wanted, and what WDCR could practically maintain. There were no illusions about the need to sound "intellectual," or of the taste of the Dartmouth man. "He is not nearly so sophisticated, cultured or discriminating as an outsider might suspect." In fact, claimed Kehoe, he was on the whole rather boorish and vulgar, "cynical and hypercritical of anything that dares to be unusual or original..." The best service to such an audience would be to provide the relaxation it wants, keep it informed, and for those who will listen, emphasize quality, not quantity, in production work.

The "Kehoe Report" is much too long, too caustic, and too specific to reproduce here. But for anyone interested in the fundamental outlook on which WDCR's early program policy was founded, it is recommended reading.

## Programming

The format established by Dick Harris in 1956 was not altered greatly, for it had been designed with AM in mind. Though program names varied somewhat between 10:00 a.m. and 4:00 p.m. (*Strictly Instrumental, Easy Listening* and *640 Club* being used in various combinations) the musical sequence remained unchanged. There was light popular music in the morning, blending into upbeat top tunes between four and six in the afternoon, news at six, followed by the production block until 7:30 p.m., then serious and quiet mood music until sign-off (now) at 1:00 a.m., except for an hour's break for top tunes during *Music 'til Midnight*. Saturdays had popular music all day (*Scope – A Weekend on Dartmouth Radio*), and Sundays mostly classical music. Daily programming was down slightly to 18 hours, but this amply fulfilled the FCC's minimum AM time requirement of 12 hours per day, eight before six o'clock, and four after.

So much music and so many neophyte announcers produced the danger of rock 'n' roll popping up where it wasn't supposed to, keeping Harris and John Long busy enforcing the format they had carefully worked out. There seemed to be a particular danger that *Tempo*, with its format of "all kinds of music," would drift off the deep end, but Dick Harris protested that WDCR was not about to become a "radio juke box."

## "Congratulations on Your Smash Hit, (Blank)"

The record library was having its own little renaissance under Don Knapp '60, who reported at the end of the first semester a total of 11,000 discs in his files: 5,000 popular 45 rpm's, 5,000 of the old 78 rpm's (which were rarely played), and 1,000 popular and classical LP albums. To supplement these the station regularly borrowed records from the local record store, Music and Recording Studio, in exchange for on-the-air plugs. (Did customers at M&R know that they were getting used records?) The WDCR "Hit Parade" was based on the national listings in *Cashbox*, while Kehoe got his own personal top 10 printed in a weekly d.j. feature of

117

that magazine.[37]

Up to this time the station had always purchased most of its discs from wholesalers, and Knapp's budget showed expenditures of $400 for the first term alone. Few record companies would send free samples to a campus-limited college station, but AM would be a microphone of a different color. Once WDCR became a standard commercial station free 45s, at least, should be easy to come by. In anticipation Knapp mimeographed form letters with which to pester the record companies. "We find that your hit record _____, is not in our record files. In view of the fact that we have already received numerous listener requests for _____, we ask that you forward it..."

### SFQ Meets IFQ

The most notable addition to the production block in late 1957 came as the direct result of a suggestion by a freshman trainee. In early 1956 Joe Goldberg '59 suggested a quiz show matching fraternities, with successive rounds to determine a champion for the year, and to be called *Inter-Fraternity Quiz*. This would not only capture some of the competitive flavor lacking in *Student-Faculty Quiz*, he said, but would be great public relations with both fraternities and the student body at large. Dick Harris had agreed from the start, but plans to get *IFQ* rolling during the fall of 1956 came to naught, so it made its debut in the fall 1957 lineup, as a counterbalance to *Student-Faculty Quiz*. It later replaced that venerable production and itself became a WDCR standby.

John Long also introduced a number of transcribed shows from the BBC and the National Association of Educational Broadcasters (e.g., *People Under Communism*) on the theory that WDCR should concentrate its own meager capabilities on fewer and better productions. Faculty members were also used to advantage during the year. The English Department's *Supplement* presented, among other things, "a discussion of the 'San Francisco poets,' using records of their poetry read to a jazz background."[38] Registrar Robin Robinson appeared in November to explain the radical new three-term system, which was to replace the traditional semesters in the fall of 1958. With unheard-of Saturday classes and three-and-a-half days (only) for examination periods in store for Dartmouth, the new system certainly needed explaining. In February a long-distance line allowed rebroadcast of the big New York dinner held to honor President Emeritus Ernest Martin Hopkins' 80th birthday. The principal speaker of the affair, President Eisenhower's chief of staff Sherman Adams '20, would be back on WDCR's newscasts a few months later in connection with a scandal involving a vicuna coat that forced him from office.

The budget began to vibrate a bit when no advertiser was willing to sponsor WDCR's traditional home and a way sports coverage, but arrangements were made to sell individual ads during the games. In addition WTSL agreed to pick up half the tab for program lines (necessary for all remote broadcasts) in return for the right to rebroadcast all games. During the Princeton game in November, WDCR coverage was piped to no fewer than six stations in New Hampshire and Vermont, as well as to the Dartmouth club in Chicago.

## Business: Out of the Frying Pan and Into the Fire

Dave Johns' business department was also proceeding with AM in mind. For 10 years now the station's national advertising representative had been the Ivy Network, that loose union of Ivy League stations founded chiefly by dedicated souls from Dartmouth and Yale. But even in the words of Ivy's own president, its history had been checkered. "The first few years Ivy meandered along a primrose path, surrounded by the River Styx. Actually Ivy could not do anything but progress, just as a person who begins walking has no other choice but to set himself in motion..."[39] The first goal was reached and Ivy was established, but then, "during the mid 1950s... Ivy went into a critical state of decline. A good many factors caused this, including poor management and collusion within Ivy itself, a lack of real leadership, and retrenchment in some of the stations, and problems in the radio industry as a whole" (i.e., television).[40]

One major irritant was Yale's built-in dominance of the network. Ivy headquarters was in New Haven and operating personnel were always Yale men. In 1956 Ivy released a 25 minute professionally produced film called *This Is College Radio*, promoting the medium. However virtually the entire film was about a day at WYBC (the Yale station), with scarcely a mention of the other five Ivy stations.[41]

More important was a simple matter of finances. WDCR would be the only AM station in a collection of campus operations, and Harris felt it could do better on its own. Even at this low point in Ivy history the network accounted for fully 40 percent of WDCR's advertising revenue. Nevertheless WDCR quit as of January 1958 to look for greener pastures. No longer would its announcers proclaim, "this is the Ivy Network." Foster and Creed, a professional agency with offices in Boston and New York, was engaged as WDCR's national representative. Though Dick Harris could not have known it in 1958, the station's income from national ads would thereupon disappear almost entirely.

It was unlikely that enough new local advertisers would immediately be signed to cover the increased expenses of AM, and so another duty of Johns and Harris was to formulate, and explain, new, higher rates. "We are not in the radio business, as such, to make a hatful of money" went the large ad run in *The Hanover Gazette* and *The Valley News,* which then explained that this was the first rate increase in eight years. "It will cost a little more to be at 1340 on your radio dial, because it will cost us more to obtain our news, records, and other services that enable us to bring you radio of the highest caliber."[42]

## Technical

The most striking changes during the fall of 1957 were those in WDCR's technical plant. Pulsifer's staff completely rebuilt 3X, the disc jockey studio, enlarging it and installing three new Gates turntables and a big, gleaming Gatesway control board, the first professionally built console in the station's history. After an all-out weekend's work in December (for which the *Newsletter* tossed bouquets to Messrs. Jim Picken '59, Don Caress '60, Don Knapp, George Whitehead '61, and Al Cameron '60), the new 3X was ready for on-the-air use.

That done, the even bigger changes planned for the main studios could get underway. The extensive carpentry work was too much for fumble-thumbed students to undertake, so it was college workmen who over Christmas vacation dismantled the control room-studio one-studio two complex, which they had built in 1941, and constructed the new arrangement. There was an enlarged master control room ("M.C."), eliminating the old, small "news studio"; two approximately equal-sized sound studios, dividing what had been the huge studio two; and a connecting corridor. All were separated by double thicknesses of soundproof glass. The new studio one would be the main production studio (with engineering done as before from master control), while the new studio two was auxiliary, normally serving as home for the expanding record library. This construction was finished by January.

Most of the control room's old equipment was retained, including the big, student-built (1948) console. Tape recorders were once again proving a problem, however, leading to the purchase of a new, portable RCA SRT-2, for $350.

### The New Transmitter

"With the tap of their little hammers, the discreet whir of their little saws, and the muffled 'squnch' of their little shovels digging into mud,"[43] College Buildings and Grounds workers began construction of the small, cinder block transmitter building at Chase Field, in early November, 1957. The 15 by 15 foot structure was completed approximately a month later, with last minute help from a huge marquee tent to keep out the snow and a charcoal stove to keep the wet cement from freezing. Beside it was erected a 150-foot orange and white antenna tower, guyed by steel cables. One hundred and twenty underground "radials," extending out 150 feet from the base of the tower like the spokes of a wheel, were buried beneath it, to strengthen the signal. (These would cause endless problems in later years when careless grounds workers inadvertently dug them up or damaged them, compromising the signal.) Finally trenches were dug across the field for the cables that would connect the transmitter with the main studios, from which it could be operated by remote control. Everything was in readiness but the transmitter itself.

And there was the rub. The $5,000 RCA transmitter was supposed to arrive early in December 1957, and on that basis Harris had all fall been promising AM by the second week in January. But somehow it was "delayed at the factory" until the first of the year. That date proved a month too early too, and actual installation did not begin until February 1958, by three WDCR engineers and Thayer School Professor Huntington Curtis ("a real pain, but he knew what he was doing"). All were holders of FCC First Class Radio Engineer's licenses. The big moment, they said, could come during the first week in March.[44]

### March 4, 1958

That was the cue for the final phase of the AM publicity campaign. Readers of *The Valley News, The Hanover Gazette*, and *The Dartmouth*, and of course station listeners had since September been treated to a series of display ads proclaiming the coming of WDCR-AM, its operation and its goals. "We've been asked about the operation of WDCR...," began one newspaper ad, which then hammered home the familiar message. "After our bills are paid, there is nothing left for owners or staff. We can't and wouldn't have it any other way." Finally, as the debut of WDCR-AM drew nigh, imaginative, modernistic ads blared "New Power—High Tower...

Tuesday night at nine." On March 2, WDCR left the air for two days of final technical preparations.

March 4, 1958. First for station members was a celebratory cocktail party at the Dartmouth Outing Club building, followed by the traditional station banquet. Then, at 8:58 p.m., their radio station once again went booming out to dormitory radios—this time to all of them—and to all of the rest of the Upper Valley as well. The first sound was the same sound that would be repeated at the beginning of each broadcast day that followed (and had been on most before), "Men of Dartmouth" by the Glee Club. At nine o'clock sharp there was precisely two seconds of time tone, and Dick Harris: "The time is 9:00 p.m. You are tuned to Dartmouth radio, WDCR, 1340 on your dial... from this moment on serving not only the Dartmouth community but the entire Upper Valley..."

For the next hour the College Hall ballroom, and 1340 KC, resounded to a potpourri of music and talks, tied together by Master of Ceremonies Carl Bahn. There had to be speakers of course. President Dickey was on tape, but Paleopitus chairman Ron Snow (for the student body), NBC's Jerry Danzig (for the radio industry, and alumni), Almon Ives (faculty), Westinghouse's Donald Edgeman (another radio big shot), and Justice Amos Blandin of the New Hampshire Supreme Court (government) all were there live. The Barbary Coast Orchestra gave forth sundry swing tunes, the Injunaires did "Standing on the Corner" from the Broadway show *The Most Happy Fella* (lately a favorite of theirs), and a Dartmouth junior named Chip Fisher, who was billed as RCA Victor's newest record star, sang his "big hit," "I Love Your Pony Tail." Outgoing General Manager Dick Harris and his successor, Ron Kehoe, were the ghosts of Christmas past and present, and a well-written 10 minute presentation of station history from 1941 to 1958 provided the backdrop. [45]

The whole affair, produced by Jon Cohen and Al Cameron, was certainly well prepared. Each speaker was allotted precisely five seconds of applause before and after his talk, and Carl Bahn's opening words were to be, "Thank you Dick... we got quite a crowd here in College Hall..." If none too imaginative, it was big, colorful, and well attended by VIPs, the way an inaugural ought to be. It was historic not so much for what it contained as for what it signified. For the first time the federal government and a college administration had entrusted the entire operation of an AM radio station to a student organization.

Reaction to WDCR-AM was mostly of the good-luck-and-hope-you'll-have-lots-of-educational-shows variety, both in newspapers and letters from listeners. "We'll be listening," said *The Valley News*, which added that henceforth it would carry the station's program schedule each day. Sure enough, next week there were the listings for both Upper Valley AM stations, "WHSL, 1400 KC" and "WDRC, 1340" (*sic*).

### New Directorate

The 1959 Directorate had been named early in February, well in advance of the AM launch. The first general manager of WDCR-AM, Ron Kehoe, would have as his business manager Ariel Halpern '59, as technical director, Robert Johnson '59, and as program director, Jon Cohen. How would Kehoe tackle the job of making something of the AM station his predecessors had so laboriously built? "Public issues programming will highlight the new Directorate's efforts," said he. "We don't believe in creating issues, but we do want to explore them and bring them to light." [46]

Indeed, the brightest feather in Kehoe's public service cap was the Public Information Program (PIP) series. These carefully prepared hour-long specials were intended to delve into major problems of the Dartmouth community, including religion on campus, military conscription, fraternity problems, atomic fallout, conformism, and safe driving. The last-named program, titled *The Milk Run*, was perhaps the finest and certainly the most dramatic program of the year. "IN FOUR YEARS OF MILK RUNS NINE DARTMOUTH MEN DEAD" read the printed posters advertising it, above a gory photograph of one student who had just wrapped himself around a tree at 90 miles per hour.

Did you drink with him in the last few hours of his life..?
How did you feel the next morning when you heard he was dead?
Thursday night at 10 WDCR wants you to listen to the story of *THE MILK RUN*. Anything else you have to do isn't as important.

In May a grant of $1,500 from the H.V. Kaltenborn Foundation provided the series with a tremendous boost, and WDCR with considerable prestige. The series continued through 1959 and 1960 with its own executive staff member in charge, called, of course, the "PIP director."

With local signal coverage came the station's first real venture into local news gathering. The local news department idea of some years earlier was dusted off and renamed Information Central. The goal was "to get out and cover news of interest to Dartmouth students."[47] The rest of the broadcast day was filled with the light musical entertainment listeners wanted. Two changes were made in Dick Harris' original schedule. In a small move back toward the old segmented approach, the production block was now separated from the six o'clock news by a period of music. Putting all of WDCR's non-musical programming together into one big block, it was felt, was offering too much of a good thing at once. In addition there was a much expanded emphasis on "personality" disc jockeys on shows featuring current hits. Saturdays could no longer be wasted on trainees, so a 6:30 to 7:00 a.m. *Farm Show* was introduced to give them very-early morning practice, where they could do little harm. The spring 1958 schedule was as follows.

6:28   sign-on
6:30   *Farm Show* (trainees)
7:00   *Tempo*
10:20  *Easy Listening*
1:00   *Newsreel*
1:10   *Easy Listening*
2:00   *The Johnny Haynes Show*
4:00   *The Bob Johnson Show*
6:00   *Newsreel* and *Sportsreel*, followed by *Hanover Browsing, U.N. Report* or analysis.
6:30   *Everybody Likes Music* (light popular)
7:30   Production: *Faculty Favorites, English Supplement, BBC World Theatre*
8:30   *Concert Hall*
10:30  Production: *Student-Faculty Quiz, Paris Star Time, Music from the Spanish World*, or *Inter-Fraternity Quiz*.

11:00 *Newsreel*
11:10 *Music 'til Midnight*
12:00 *Nightwatch*
1:05  sign-off

Friday nights were occupied by the three-hour *John Haynes All-Request Show* and *CB's* (Carl Bahn's) *Nightwatch*, while Saturday afternoon and evening listeners were treated to the *Jock McNair, Fred Lockyear, Rick Guilford, "CB,"* and *Ron Kehoe* shows.

### Shall We Rock?

Despite its plug on the WDCR inaugural show, Chip Fisher's smash-hit-to-be "I Love Your Pony Tail" had not taken off in sales, so one fine weekend in April WDCR d.j.'s undertook a full scale promotion of the record on the Friday and Saturday night request shows. Both sides of the record and Fisher's RCA Victor LP, *Chipper at the Sugar Bowl*, were played incessantly, and a half hour feature on his "rise to stardom" aired. In a subsequent press release Jon Cohen crowed that WBZ's 50,000 watt disc jockey Norm Prescott (doubtless a regular WDCR listener) had called to add his commendations and that sales of Fisher's record had "boomed." Most of those who received the press release presumably deposited it in the same place they had put the record, however, and that was the last that was heard of Chip Fisher.[48]

Such efforts notwithstanding, it seemed unlikely that WDCR-AM would become the big rocking sound of the Upper Valley any time soon. Most students liked rock 'n' roll (witness the tremendous listenership of *Music 'til Midnight*), and it was given its place in the late afternoons, on *MTM*, and on Friday and Saturday nights. That was all. Dick Harris and Ron Kehoe shared a nagging fear that popular music coupled with AM might push WDCR off the commercial deep end. Again and again, in interviews and ads, in staff meetings and formats, they reiterated that WDCR would not become a "juke box of the air." Kehoe, who bore a heavy responsibility for shaping the future of the station, expressed the extreme position when he wrote to his program director in July, 1958: "Some of our listeners we're better off without, and this means specifically the teen-age set from the Tri-Town area. I'm through with catering to that bunch to the detriment of the college students, faculty and (town) in that order. When we play for the teeners we get nothing for our efforts, whether in dollars or prestige, but a public notion of *us* as greasy headed, immature little hipsters too. That's the ultimate degradation."[49] For publication there was a somewhat less hot-under-the-collar position. "Although it is impossible to measure the Dartmouth taste, the variety of students makes it conform pretty well to the average audience. We try to give a balanced program, not going whole-hog on the extremes of classical or rock 'n' roll music."[50]

Thus a compromise was reached, although one of WDCR's closest friends, College Chaplain George Kalbfleisch, was moved to write in April, "I think I shall remain forever intrigued by Mr. Kehoe's defense (in *The Dartmouth*) of Dartmouth College Radio's fulfillment of its 'obligation to the college community' by its 'policy to broadcast NO rock and roll... before 3:00 p.m., *with the single exception of the Chapel Period...*'"[51]

## Publicity, Personnel, and Paleopitus

Kehoe continued Harris' AM publicity campaign. Listeners presumably now knew that WDCR-AM was there, at 1340. Now was the time to explain the programs available to them, and get them to listen. In addition to regular program listings in *The Dartmouth* and *The Valley News*, folders and information sheets were printed containing WDCR Program Profiles, showing at a glance the full week's programming. The most popular shows were described and the what, why, how, who, where, and when of Dartmouth College Radio briefly summarized. On the front of the folder, beneath the station's new monogram ("WDCR" in modern block letters) was the slogan of the day: "A new tower of power for the radio voice of the Big Green..."

Kehoe and Personnel Director Carl Bahn did not neglect the matter of personnel relations, so important in the new, bigger, ever more businesslike WDCR. The Saturday night cider and donut parties had been a little off target, but the annual spring beer blast was a smashing success. More novel was a mimeographed WDCR Certificate of Achievement, to be given to new station members on completion of their initial training and their showing of "genuine interest in WDCR while in the training program." Other awards were to go to "the senior staff announcer who has shown the most improvement lately, and the junior staffer who has likewise shaped up most."[52] The awards were short lived. As ever, an open ear to complaints and suggestions and periodic get-togethers proved the best leadership tools for WDCR's managers.

Another of the station's perennial problems was the work load on its general manager, which was growing even larger with the coming of AM. The old Directorate position of assistant station manager had proven unworkable over the long haul, so Kehoe decided to establish an assistant to the general manager, rotating monthly among non-executive staff personnel. In Kehoe's own words, "it will carry no authority of its own... (but) it gives us the chance to reward our men and observe them under the pressure of responsibility."[53] The first "A to the GM" was to be appointed in the fall, but like so many other good ideas its practical success depended on the personalities involved, in this case on the availability of good up-and-comers and the ability of the general manager to make their job meaningful, but not too. Apparently neither Kehoe nor his successors could turn this neat trick and the position disappeared, though the problem remained.

No more successful were Kehoe's persistent attempts to get the general manager into the student governing body, Paleopitus. He did, however, locate a replacement for faculty advisor Bob Allen, who left Dartmouth in June 1958 after seeing the station through its three year transition to AM. To help during the occasionally painful adjustments of the next years would be longtime friend, sometime advisor, and the man who in 1941, as a newly arrived speech instructor, had helped to get the whole thing started, Professor Almon Ives.

Dartmouth College Radio emerged from the three years between March 1955, when the decision to seek an AM license was made, and March 1958, when AM was realized, a station very much unlike the WDBS of old. Following are some pertinent facts about the status of the three major areas of operation, as of June 1958.

## Technical: Legal Responsibility

Besides the addition of the transmitter complex at Chase Field, WDCR's studios had been remodeled so completely as to be unrecognizable to a graduate of 1955. The conversion to AM had also provided the opportunity (and College money) to buy new technical equipment, and thousands of dollars had been invested in the new 3X console, tape recorders, turntables, and so on. With the exception of the master control board and the Ampex 400, the major equipment with which the engineers and announcers of 1958 worked was almost wholly new since 1955.

The place of Tech in the organization was changing too. In one respect, studio engineering, it was less. As more and more announcers learned to "combo" their own d.j. shows, engineers were required only for the more complex sports and news remotes, production shows and off-the-air taping sessions. There were plenty of those, and as the programmers had predicted the main effect on the Technical Department was simply a weeding out of marginal members.

In another respect, that of maintenance, the responsibility of Tech was vastly greater, and not only because of the increased inventory of studio equipment. Overnight WDCR had changed from a typical college inter-dormitory hookup, so limited it did not even need to be licensed, to a full power AM broadcast station, subject to federal licensing with all its detailed standards and restrictions. The control that the FCC so studiously avoids in programming and business, it fully makes up for in technical specifications. Among other things every AM station had to have on call at least one holder of a First Class Radiotelephone Operator's License. That little document permitted its holder to tear apart and put together any transmitter, including 50,000-watters, and was obtained by passing a five hour examination on theoretical and applied electronics administered by the FCC.

Where would WDCR get such a highly (and legally) qualified technician? For the first year of operation WDCR's legal "First Phone" was a Thayer School of Engineering professor, even though three student license holders did most actual maintenance of the transmitter. After the professor left in 1959 the College permitted a student First Phone to take his place. Thereafter a student physics wizard was recruited each year to take the test, and assume legal responsibility for WDCR's transmitter, until the requirement was dropped in the 1980s.

## Programming: Two Audiences to Woo

Ever since its return to the air in 1946 Dartmouth radio had been simultaneously expanding its program day and building a pervasive music-news-special events format. The process was virtually completed with Bill Tell's unbroken 19-hour day in 1955, and Dick Harris' completely revamped seamless schedule in 1956. With both student and community audiences to woo, WDCR blended the following into an integrated program day.

|  |  |
|---|---|
| Mornings | - light, popular music |
| Afternoons | - same, but increasing the tempo to popular and rock 'n' roll hits |
| Evenings | - news in depth, production shows, serious music; and an hour set aside for "rock 'n' roll after booking" between 11:00 |

p.m. and midnight.
Early morning  - quiet mood music

Dartmouth sports were thoroughly covered, but now there were fewer other College events such as speeches, concerts, dramatics, etc. In the prestigious area of production work WDCR was working on the principle of less quantity and higher quality, which sometimes worked (as with the PIP series) and sometimes didn't. There was probably as much good creative programming on WDCR in 1958, however, as at any time in the preceding half dozen years. Nevertheless it was inescapable that elaborate productions and particularly dramatic presentations were disappearing from radio generally at this time, as television usurped that function.

A pre-1955 alumnus would have found the station's 1958 broadcast day unfamiliar, for only *MTM* and a few odd production programs survived from the old WDBS. But that did not mean there were no constants to rely on. Ninety percent of freshman recruits still wanted to be disc jockeys. Ten percent of them made it, and began by sounding horrible on the air, although now at 6:30 a.m. instead of on Saturday afternoons. Decent producers were still hard to come by, d.j.'s talked too much, and the one regular show that had survived, *Music 'til Midnight*, was still far and away the most popular juke box on campus.

### Business: Staggering Costs to Bear

The budget too faced a prodigious dual burden. The approximate cost of AM electronic equipment (transmitter, tower, control equipment) appears to have been around $10,000, while studio reconstruction, new studio equipment, the Chase Field transmitter building and legal costs brought the total cost of "going AM" to slightly under $30,000. This constituted a classic case of how estimates grow. In 1955 the trustees had appropriated $6,500, far less than the projected $15,000-plus needed to fix the intra-campus system. A year later the AM estimate had grown by a couple thousand, and by early 1957 it was being given as $12,500. In January 1957 *The Dartmouth* discreetly stated that cost estimates varied from $8,000 to $30,000, thereby managing to hit the true figure—but just barely. Nevertheless the true cost of alternatives would probably have grown as well, and the trustees were certainly right about one thing. Only AM held the potential to generate enough revenue to recoup its costs.

The station was supposed to be self-supporting, so it would pay all of these costs, $5,000 out of the current budget, and $25,000 by means of a long-term capital loan from the College, to be amortized over the next 15 or 20 years.

WDCR also had to support the much higher operating and maintenance costs of AM, a total that by the early 1960s was expected to reach a level of about $16,000 per year. This would require an income three times that of the early and mid 1950s, so Dave Johns, Ariel Halpern and the rest of the small sales staff set out to sell for all they were worth. With the help of increased rates, the lure of AM, and their own unique interpretation of the new call letters ("We Deliver Cash Results") they managed to bring in over $8,000 for 1957-58, easily breaking all previous WDBS records. Unfortunately expenses topped even that, producing a moderate sized deficit for the first time in seven years. And the disastrous effects of leaving the Ivy Network had not yet been felt. Another big drag on sales was the refusal of the

126

College to allow beer advertising. Dick Harris later recalled making a passionate plea to allow such ads, only to be told by President Dickey that he was loathe to face any parents who had heard a beer commercial on the College station on their drive up to Hanover. The salesmen did have the new selling point of AM coverage, but despite that sales remained heavily concentrated in Hanover and ads heavily student-oriented.[54]

The Business Department itself remained much the same as it had been at WDBS. With the consolidation of offices on the second floor, the department finally got to know the rest of the staff, but it was perennially understaffed and dependent largely on the dynamism of its business manager. If he didn't do his job well, as was too often the case, the general manager and/or his up-and-coming advertising director had to fill the void as best they could.

### What They Said

It was as obvious then as it is now that 1958 marked a basic turning point in station history, and much was said and written about the station's state and its likely future. It is interesting to note, with the advantages of hindsight, exactly "what they said." Regarding WDCR-AM itself, the boasts were more than generous.

A Ron Kehoe letter of December, 1958: "The straight music-and-news format cannot satisfy WDCR's aspirations and conscience to serve its public well... Since March 4, WDCR has enjoyed undreamt-of success in programming and sales. Community reaction has been one of acclaim, and sales revenue has climbed steadily as buyers see for themselves a unique opportunity to reach the rich Ivy league market and the Dartmouth College community..."[55]

A Bob Johnson letter of February, 1959: "With 250 watts in this country we can usually count on covering 12 to 15 miles to the north, 12 to 15 to the east, 20 to 25 west and 25-30 miles south. Late at night we have been up in Seymour, Connecticut, Newark, New Jersey, and Northhampton, Mass. ... There are 50,000 listeners within the range of our signal, most of whom listen to us..."[56] (Note: For only mild exaggeration, halve each of the preceding figures.)

And they were scornful of the past. Said the 1957 *Aegis*: "Just 10 short years ago, WDBS was on the air only four hours a day, and its 12 man staff and 500 record library could well have earned it the title of Smallest Station in the Nation... By comparison, the year 1956 looked in upon a smooth-running, highly efficient organization... the once tiny record library had grown to an astonishing total of over 9,000 recordings. The latest in transmitting and recording equipment had replaced the handmade, second-hand antiques of earlier years. Truly, this was the progress of a Dynamic Decade in collegiate broadcasting."[57]

The future would be rosy and non-competitive. *The Hanover Gazette* in February, 1958: "Programming will emphasize the educational aspects of Dartmouth for both the college audience and the surrounding communities, Kehoe said. Lectures by members of the faculty, quizzes, panel discussions, drama, documentaries, and news analysis will be featured as well expanded local news coverage. 'We hope to be more than a juke box,' he explained."[58]

*The Dartmouth* in February, 1958: "'We are by no means competing with the outfit down the road,' asserts Program Director Long, 'Each station has its own particular appeal. You might call it a town and gown situation'."[59]

127

The same issue of *The Dartmouth*: "The program director relaxed in one of the new studios and told us that the new WDCR's programs 'will still be pure Dartmouth, beamed at the students. If the townspeople want to sort of peep at us, they're welcome to... We may have to be a little more careful,' he added."[60]

Some other quotes were honest reflections on where WDCR stood, and fascinating glimpses into the kind of devotion that had put it there.

Ron Kehoe in July, 1958: "My biggest job between now and the end of my term, as I see it, is to build an image of WDCR in the public mind. We have been too careless about this in the past. Image-building is at once one of the most difficult, exciting, and rewarding phases of radio management and publicity... The image I want to construct is one of the utmost sophistication, friendliness, and hard-headed intelligence. We will represent the epitome of good taste, a willingness to serve the public at all times, and a lot of good common sense. Programming is of course the place to start, and Public Relations will do the rest."[61]

Bob Johnson, having explained to the manager of the University of Connecticut station, which was dreaming of AM, how WDCR had done it, February, 1959: "So there it is in all its complexities. I assume that UConn is interested in an AM station. Well, although we are the *only* entirely student-run commercial AM station in the country, we are looking for company, and we wish you luck. If your time schedule runs like ours did, it will take two years to convince your trustees, two years to convince the government, and another year to build it. I was lucky. I got in on WDCR during the last three years. But without some ambitious thinking back in 1953-54, I could never have reaped someone else's results. Although you will never see your AM station before you graduate, I wholeheartedly advise your going ahead."[62]

# Chapter 6

# 1958-1964: "Top 40, News, Weather and Sports"

Six student general managers headed WDCR-AM during the years 1958-64: Ron Kehoe '59, Al Cameron '60, George Whitehead '61, Ted Mascott '62, Sturges Dorrance '63, and Al McKee '64. They proved that Dartmouth's unique radio experiment was workable, and helped it make the difficult transition from campus-limited operation to licensed commercial broadcasting.

### An Anniversary

In March 1961, at WDCR's third annual station banquet, the guest of honor was a special one. Dick Krolik, the man who began it all two decades earlier, returned to Hanover to recall, in an entertaining talk, the months of struggle in which Dartmouth radio was born. Krolik was the echo of an era long past, and several months later that echo was amplified when an even more significant anniversary rolled around.

> If you're surprised tomorrow night at 9:00 p.m. when the fellow next to you in the Nugget [a local theater] suddenly leaps to his feet and turns slowly to face Robinson Hall, you shouldn't be. After all, that fellow's only performing his homage as he sees it. In fact you ought to know too that tomorrow night at 9:00 marks the twentieth anniversary of the first official radio broadcast at Dartmouth College.[1]

Twenty years in which the shaky DBS became the ambitious WDBS, which in turn became WDCR-AM. The anniversary was celebrated with a full week of promotional activity, masterminded by Sturges Dorrance. It included an illustrated feature article in *The Dartmouth*, an hour-long program called *Twenty Years Behind the Mike*, a rebroadcast of the durable old *DBS Workshop* favorite "The Most Dangerous Game," and some other historic shows (*Hunky Dorey* showed up on *The Comedy Spot*).[2] Of course there was a contest for listeners: guess how many hours Dartmouth radio had been on the air since that first official broadcast in 1941? With remarkable precision, the judges determined the correct answer to be exactly 50,894 hours. With equally remarkable foresight the organizers gave as prizes cheap transistor radios so small they could pick up only nearby WDCR. That was not so unreasonable they thought, for as the 20th anniversary article in *The Dartmouth* concluded,

> Programs are improving and there's promise of excellent things to come; concerts by well-known symphony orchestras, stimulating discussions, a rebirth of radio plays, and more live music on the air. There have been a lot

of improvements in WDCR's first 20 years and there are more to come.[3]

## An Insidious Decline Begins: Sagging Grades

That was the word for publication. What never made *The Dartmouth* was the story of the station's sometimes painful adjustments to its new, more demanding, AM status. With the departure of those rock 'n' roll watchdogs Harris and Kehoe, WDCR's programming began to slip perceptibly. Not only did the wrong music begin to pop up in the wrong places, but the whole level of program continuity and production quality edged gradually down. More than that, the station's sense of "drive" seems to have sagged. Why? To be sure there was a shortage of strong staff, but that had always been the case. More likely it was a lessening of control and leadership. The great goal of AM had been won. What would take its place?

It was not a precipitous decline, but it was unmistakable and insidious. The station's year of truth came in 1960, when several unhappy developments brought the inevitable rude awakening. First, during the spring, came academic disaster, a combination of flunk-outs among key staffers and an unusually low academic average among those who remained. Raised eyebrows in the College administration surveyed the enormous total of hours WDCR's most devoted members were spending on their station, then put its leaders on notice. Dartmouth would not permit any extracurricular activity to undermine its members' college careers, and if the radio bugs could not keep theirs in proper perspective the station's activities might have to be forcibly curtailed. As President Dickey never failed to remind students in each year's Convocation address, "Your business here... is learning."

## Tired Ears

The second shock wave hit in the fall of 1960. That program quality had been slipping since WDCR went AM was to no one more apparent than newly appointed faculty advisor Almon Ives. But the station was in almost every respect the students' own, and only they, not he, could be expected to correct it. How to get them to do so was the eternal problem of college-station relations.

Most importantly, Ives had to document his case. Certain faculty members with little understanding and less genuine interest in student radio had been firing off "disgrace to Dartmouth" generalities for years. Generalities and the narrow academic view made little impression on the young men faced with the practical problems of running a radio station. To give them advice they could use, and to see if he himself had a case, Ives did something unprecedented.

> On Tuesday, October 25, 1960, I listened continuously from 6:00 a.m. to 9:00 p.m. ... I tape recorded a sample of each announcer during that time and made tape recorded comments about his delivery and general impression. I secured program logs for that week which indicated that what I heard on Tuesday was typical of the other four days of the Monday-Friday schedule.[4]

What followed was the most stinging official critique in memory. Ives' well-documented (but impressionistic) conclusions were as follows.

1. "12 to 13 hours of off-the-cuff disc jockey programming misrepresents the quality of Dartmouth educational tastes and standards." (One lone hour in the afternoon, d.j.'d by Peter Drowne '62, was "thoughtfully prepared.")

2. "Two hours of canned, purchased, ticker-tape news does not serve the needs of the Dartmouth community. WTSL and WWRJ both offer this service and sometimes read the news better at that. Dartmouth could offer background, interpretation, and comment on the news."

3. "Only 18 to 20 hours of music is played each week of which the Music Department need not be ashamed—less than 15 percent of the program schedule. 80 percent of the music offered is tasteless."

4. "Usually no more than one hour of live production per day is offered." (On that Tuesday there was but 30 minutes, *Interfraternity Quiz*. "It was good but seemed lonely.")

5. "Little imagination or creativity is exhibited in getting the staff and students of Dartmouth College to engage in comment, opinion, response or reaction to world or domestic events." Of course they did not flock to the station's doors; but why were they not even sought? Even easily obtained classes and lectures, Ives said, were seldom broadcast.

6. "Positive damage is being done to the character of many students who are not being required to do their best when they produce a show under the aegis of Dartmouth College. The pursuit of the trivial, the tawdry, the commercially inane and vacuous, as exemplified by 10-12 hours of disc jockey shows per day, fosters a destructive narcissism inimical to the goals of education generally, and subversive of Dartmouth's goals in particular."

7. "Dartmouth's reputation is being damaged in our own community among those few discriminating listeners whose opinions matter."

Seeking to help by hurting, Professor Ives did not mince words. Read today some of the charges smack of academic elitism, railing against "debased" rock 'n' roll, advocating fine classical music all day (i.e., music by dead white Europeans), and virtually ignoring the major news production that had just occurred on election day. Nevertheless these were serious charges that could not be answered by simply citing personnel problems or a lack of money. In particular, "it's what the students want" was considered no excuse at all. A meeting with the Directorate was set for November 11.

> Perhaps on Armistice Day the Directorate and a group known as Friends of Dartmouth Radio can come to some agreements and plan a course of action which is genuinely in the public interest. Hopefully the Directorate will decide that to lead student taste is a challenge as well as a duty.

Substantial problems are not solved in a day, especially not by committees. However Professor Ives' detailed reports of the Armistice Day conference and a December faculty poll show that a fascinating and occasionally penetrating dialogue was begun on the station's place and potential. Yet one more blow was needed to halt the station's decline, and that one was perhaps the most telling of all.

131

## ... And Financial Disaster

The year 1960-61 was, to put it mildly, a year of financial disaster. Among other setbacks, the station's business manager had to resign early in his term due to academic problems. Problems were becoming apparent by the end of 1960, and when the final figures were in six months later there was red ink everywhere. WDCR lost $6,500 that year, more than the station had cost Dartmouth in the past dozen years combined. The one argument that had won the day for commercial student radio in the first place, that it would at least be self-supporting, was cast into doubt.

Surviving documentation indicates that there was considerable discussion within the administration during early 1961 about how to address the station's problems. Among the proposals were to cut back the hours of broadcasting (so that students could concentrate on "the best"), postpone plans to increase the station's power, eliminate commercials, or explore low-power FM. All were rejected.

Three sledgehammer blows in six months, one at staffers' neglect of academics, one at the quality of daily programming, and one at the station's solvency, had the desired effect. Extreme devotion still characterized the inner circle of station members, but there were fewer academic excesses. More important, new recruits were constantly warned about the dangers of getting in over their heads. This author can remember the most frequently heard advice of his own first days at WDCR, as a freshman in the fall of 1960: "Don't you have any booking to do? Well, do it! *Then* come in to the station."

General Manager George Whitehead calmly took charge and began program reforms. His successor, Ted Mascott, convinced that he had inherited WDCR in its year of truth, launched a full scale, do-or-die administration. In March 1961, days after he assumed control, he issued an ambitious outline of planned programming improvements. During the following year he succeeded in jarring the business, program and technical departments to the point where his successor could consider himself heir to both financial surplus and faculty goodwill.

## Business

How that trick was turned is a classic story of the right people in the right places at a critical time. Mascott and his business manager, lanky Tom Hall '62, inherited a sales staff that was at best disheartened. Expenses had risen sharply and steadily after 1958, as expected—$8,500, $11,500, $14,000, $16,000—but income had been unexpectedly erratic. Fiscal 1959 (July 1958-June 1959) had seen substantial losses. Fiscal 1960, under Cameron and Frank Greenberg '61, was a year of comeback with $1,500 in profit (applied to the debt). In a large presentation graph Cameron confidently projected that by 1963 expenses would level off at about $16,000 while income soared gloriously to $20,000 or more. What he didn't count on was the widely varying abilities of business managers and the inherent tendency for spending to follow, or surpass, income upward to the skies, but to virtually never go down. In 1961, while expenses chugged right on up, the bottom fell out of sales.

There were serious questions about WDCR's basic financial stability. Would it forever depend on the performance of the current business manager? Could it even survive two disastrous years in a row? That question never had to be answered. Hall and his super-dynamo successor, Hal Deane '62 (who took over when Hall left for

Tuck School in the fall) turned defeat into an unprecedented boom by a complete reorganization of their department. Deficit became surplus in 1962 on a record-breaking $18,600 gross, nearly twice that of the previous year. It is not an exaggeration to say this was the golden age of sales, at least to this point.

Deane and his understudy, and successor, Stu Mahlin '63 fairly revolutionized the station's selling procedures. Stylishly printed radio fact sheets and rate cards, personalized ad plans and other sales aids lent a touch of Madison Avenue to the station. Merchants were assailed with figures, clearly emphasizing community over campus: *59,000* people in the broadcast radius, spending $106 million each year, compared to 3,000 students who spend $1.6 million. Regular servicing of accounts and updating of commercial copy, under the business manager's personal scrutiny, began to mean something. Accounts were to be held as well as won.[5]

Revenue from national advertising, which had almost disappeared after the 1958 inspiration to quit the Ivy Network, returned once pride was swallowed and Ivy was rejoined in December 1960. (Earlier, Al Cameron, disgusted with Ivy's Yale-mindedness and slowness in paying, had set stringent conditions for rejoining. When these were accepted he had decided to stay out anyway.[6])

There was new income stability. Though renewed national sales (Nucoa, Ford, various cigarettes) were a welcome boost, their total did not much exceed the $2,000-$3,000 of earlier years. In the enormously enlarged sales figures of the 1960s, they therefore constituted a much smaller proportion—perhaps 10 percent vs. the earlier 50 percent—thus protecting WDCR from dependence on a few uncertain national ads. This strength was dramatized on that black day in 1963 when the tobacco industry suddenly decided, en masse, to cancel all campus advertising. The heavily dependent *Dartmouth* was severely hit, and many other college newspapers and stations were financially wiped out. WDCR, with its wider sales base, weathered the gale with little more than disappointed hopes.

The local sales base was broadened. WDBS had found it difficult to sell Lebanon and White River Junction merchants spots that they could not hear, even if the idea of bringing them Hanover customers was valid. Now, armed with greater power and the same basic pitch ("We deliver the Dartmouth community, *plus!*"), and some aggressive salesmanship, Deane and his successors broadened WDCR's clientele by 20 miles. A larger number of advertisers meant greater financial stability. A few of the new contracts ran to four figures, something unheard of in the 1950s. That of Lebanon discounter Rockdale's (what Dartmouth man of the '60s could forget, "Take the Ride to Rockdale's, where bargains *is* our business!") alone exceeded the entire station budget of DBS's earliest years.

Hall, Deane, Mahlin and those who followed generated considerable momentum, which lasted for years. The year 1963 set a stunning all-time record of $23,000, and 1964 almost $20,000. The station hoped this level would become as dependable as the $5,000 average of the middle 1950s.

Although the 1960s saw many business innovations, much remained constant. The student salesman's basic pitch did not change. The Sales Department continued to be driven by two or three key staffers, one of them the general manager, and continued to be one of the smallest in the station (five or six members), constantly in need of talent. Most consistent of all, so much so it could almost be called a law, expenditures never failed to keep ample pace with booming revenues. Even with the elimination of debt payments to the College, ambitious plant expansion and rising operating costs made increased revenues necessary as well as desirable.

Money to spend would have no meaning if the programming it supported was not improving also. Whitehead and his successors had another job to do

## Programming of the Early Sixties

WDCR's academic and financial difficulties, though not publicized, were a crucial test. The third attack, on programming, would have less immediate but no less critical consequences. Dartmouth radio was unique as a student-run broadcast and management laboratory, and the College had always shown considerable permissiveness in allowing it to set its own standards, scattered faculty gripes notwithstanding. But a periodic kick in the shins helps the best of people, not to mention a campus station that is starting to slip.

So they said the announcers were bad, music inane, news and production shoddy, and programming in general "offensive to the educated mind." Ted Mascott and Program Director Jim Varnum '62 set to work designing what appeared to be momentous changes but were in reality a simple tightening of control and reapplication of the sound music-news-production format laid down by Dick Harris in 1956. They knew well that WDCR could not muster the resources for long hours of elaborate production work, and contrary to what some critics proclaimed, most students and townsfolk would listen only to up-to-date news and music anyway. To foist on them something else, especially if it could not be done well, would hardly be a public service.

The early morning got *Contact* (7:00-9:00 a.m.), originally an elaborately produced imitation of Dave Garroway's *Today Show* (tightly formatted information or interest features every five minutes, two announcers, news machines clattering behind everything). Later this relaxed into an easygoing blend of non-raucous morning music and newscasts.

Later in the morning Sturges Dorrance first experimented with rebroadcasts of the station's taped production shows, but finding that he couldn't get engineers up that early to put them on he then turned to the light classical music of *Carousel* (9:00-11:00 a.m.) and show tunes of *Best of Broadway* (11:00-12:00 noon). Though popular, these proved so difficult to program (just what *is* "light classical" music?) that a music programmer was assigned, when one was available, and log sheets pasted on the front of LPs to prevent *The Grand Canyon Suite* from being played every day. (The *Suite*, available in several recorded versions, was apparently everyone's idea of what light classical music is, and was so overplayed that it was eventually banned altogether.) Since only trainee announcers were available during the morning class hours, talk was kept to a minimum.

Afternoons remained much the same, although 12:15-3:00 p.m. was now *Swingalong*, and futile attempts were made to carefully regulate its format. The idea was to gradually increase the musical tempo from easy to upbeat, to flow into *Swinghouse* at 3:00 p.m. This was trickier than it sounds. *Swinghouse* itself remained the Upper Valley's number one hit parade emporium, contrasting sharply with the succeeding soft jazz of the *Suppertime Show* at 5:00 p.m. Note that *Swingalong* and *Swinghouse* contained no "swing" (i.e., big band) music. They were both devoted to current pop songs, mainly rock 'n' roll.

Six to seven p.m. was the News Department's hour in the sun (see below), while 7:00 to 9:00 p.m. provided relief for Professor Ives' sore ears with classical music. This area of programming received a substantial boost in 1962 when Dorrance found a spot in the budget for several hundred dollars worth of new classical LPs. Prior to that happy day the station had frequently been reduced to borrowing from the Baker Library record collection which, if well stocked, was far too scratchy for airplay. At 9:00 p.m. came the production block, followed by news at 11:00 p.m. and then the indestructible *Music 'til Midnight* (rock) and *Nightwatch* (calmer music) until 1:00 a.m.

Top d.j.'s of the late 1950s included Mike Melvoin '59 (who specialized in jazz), Carl Bahn '60, and Kevin O'Sullivan '60. Those in the early 1960s included Bill Woolley '63, Guy "Rock" MacMillin '64, and Fred Hill '65. Despite Hanover's remote location, the "rock jocks" were on top of the latest hits. MacMillin was credited with "breaking" several hits, and he came back from France in late 1963 with an armful of 45s including some by a little-known group named the Beatles whom he promptly introduced to Upper Valley listeners.[7]

Most people who were alive in 1963 recall where they were when they heard the news that President Kennedy had been shot. November 22, 1963, was a day this writer will always remember. I was on the air, hosting the *Swingalong* program, whose format called for gradually increasing the tempo from softer to louder rock 'n' roll, to lead into *Swinghouse*. Suddenly, at approximately 1:40 p.m., the UPI teletype started ringing with the first bulletin that shots had been fired at the presidential motorcade in Dallas, Texas. A newsman rushed in to read the bulletin, then said "back to you" as he ran out to find News Director Jeff Panitt '65, who was in class. We immediately started interrupting the show with bulletins as they came in, but during the next hour there was considerable confusion about the president's condition. We all instinctively knew that, until we found out what was going on, it would better to keep the music toned down. WDCR was one of the most listened-to stations in the area, and there was little television reception, so thousands would be tuning in to find out what was happening. By the time the dreaded bulletin came across the wire at approximately 2:35 p.m. that the president was dead, the News Department had mobilized. Someone found an LP of Beethoven's doleful *Missa Solemnis* to put on the turntable in place of Lesley Gore and Rick Nelson, and all regular programming was suspended.

All of this occurred with no involvement by administrators, professors or "professionals." The students were in charge, knew they had a serious responsibility in a time of national crisis, and rose to the challenge. Young men grew up that day.

During the next few days the Dartmouth campus, like most of the country, was in shock. WDCR provided continuous coverage.

### Don't Call Us...

Saturdays contained mostly popular music and Sundays mostly classical and production shows. The ever-popular Saturday night *All-Request Show* drew more phone calls than it could handle, but mostly from local high schoolers. Requests from dormitories, where only 10 cent pay phones were available (there were no private lines, and cell phones hadn't been invented yet), were understandably rare. For a while the station tried calling the dormitories on an announced schedule to collect requests. It worked, but the jibes (*"The Don't-Call-Us, We'll-Call-You Request Show"*) were overpowering.

A more enduring tradition involved WDCR's sign-off. Jock McNair '60 habitually closed his *Nightwatch* show by reading the station's closing announcement over his theme, Jackie Gleason's mellow "Unforgettable," then blending into the equally sentimental "Dartmouth Undying." So popular was this smooth combination of words and music that just before his graduation in 1960 McNair spent a whole night recording it, in all possible variations; "we return at 6:30 tomorrow morning," "... at 9:00 a.m.," "broadcasting with one thousand watts power" (in case it was ever granted), etc., so that WDCR would always be able to close its broadcast day with the dulcet tones of McNair, Gleason and the Dartmouth Glee Club.

Alas, it was not to be. Next fall WDCR did the impossible and moved its sign-on to *6:00* a.m. But his idea, the musical combination of "Unforgettable" and "Dartmouth Undying," lived on for many years as the station's sign-off.

The quest for better sound and bigger audiences did not stop with the sign-off. Station breaks, which had once begun "This is the Ivy Network...", then "This is Dartmouth College Radio...", morphed once again. The old student (hence amateur) image should be played down during the day, reasoned businessman Stu Mahlin, since potential out-of-town listenership was then highest. So the dictum went out, "This is TRI-TOWN RADIO..." with nary a mention of Dartmouth while the sun shone.

However at night, when more prestigious programming was scheduled, coverage reduced and audiences smaller anyway, the station reverted to "Dartmouth College Radio." It was a subtle psychological move, though there was bound to be confusion behind the mikes as dismayed disc jockeys looked up at the studio wall and read the sign, "MAINTAIN WDCR'S SCHIZOPHRENIA!"

## A Kaleidoscope of Varied Programming

Meanwhile the producers of the early 1960s created quite a few series to interest the more attentive listener. Produced shows are highly personal, usually held together by the interest and special knowledge of a single individual, and few outlive their creator's college career. The roster of WDCR's better efforts is, accordingly, a kaleidoscope of producers' varied interests and specialties.

Jazz shows under many and varied names have been perennial favorites. Since they are seldom scripted, and depend wholly on their producer's talents, the best were absorbing studies of the jazz world, the worst merely bad d.j. shows. Among the jazz shows were *Scope of Jazz, Jazz Unlimited, Opus de Jazz, Jazz Party, Modern Jazz Showcase, Basin Street Beat,* and *Dixieland Jazz Party* (the latter two were short lived, due to the curious shortage of Dixieland enthusiasts on campus).

*The Ed and Charley Show* was a real feather in the station's cap, the first original comedy series of note since 1952's *Hunky-Dorey Hour.* A series of "offbeat conversations," its title was a take-off on the frequent joint appearances of Republican leaders Senator Everett Dirksen and Representative Charlie Halleck, dubbed by the media "The Ev and Charlie Show." But like *Hunky-Dorey,* it depended entirely on the creativity of its two producers, Michael (Ed) Hobbs '62 and Geoffrey (Charley) Murphy '63. After a brief run it died a lasting death at Hobbs' graduation in 1962.

*Shubert Alley,* the brainchild of Bob Cohn '66, brought weekly ramblings about the musical lore of Broadway.

*Pick of the Past*, this writer's eccentric indulgence from 1961-64 (engineered for most of its run by Bob Gitt '63), resurrected popular records of varying degrees of antiquity from 1901 to the 1950s, some loaned by Upper Valley listeners, organized into various themes ("World War I Hits," etc.). One notable episode in 1964 consisted of a long distance telephone interview with Ulysses "Jim" Walsh, a nationally published writer who had known some of the recording artists of the early 1900s. Gitt and I left behind an carefully annotated 45-tape 460-track library of hits of the 20th century, so that the station would always have a readily accessible library of historic music. It apparently did not survive very long.[8]

*Comedy Spot*, produced by such mysterious entities as "Seymour" and "Pasba" (Seymour Herzog '64 and Paul Balgley '66, respectively), sampled the world of comedy on record.

*Front Row Center* broadcast a full Broadway cast album with brief commentary straight from the liner notes. A thoroughly enjoyable hour with many fans, it proved that simplicity is sometimes the best policy.

*Interfraternity Quiz* proved that good ideas don't fade away.

*Forum, Focus* (which once ambitiously aired *every* night at 6:30) and *Issues* were some of the more successful "adventures of the intellect," as guided by discussions or talks.

*Folkways*, WDCR's standard folk music showcase, was joined at times by *Folkforms* and *Hootenanny Hall* (Sunbeam Razor's brief 1963 flier into the folk world). These were usually made of the same stuff as the jazz shows, one talkative devotee playing his record collection, but sometimes featured live performances by collegiate minstrels, direct from studio one.

*Quest* was popular Hanover Reverend Jay Buell's offbeat look at life through music and discussion.

*Kaleidoscope* was just that, filling two hours on Sunday nights with "comedy, drama, jazz, interviews, discussions of important issues... something for every interest."[9] Two of the most popular regular features were Professor Herb West's weekly iconoclastic musings on life and literature, and Professor (emeritus) Lew Stillwell's memorable "Battle Nights" accounts of great military campaigns.

In a similar vein was *Festival*, "a showcase of the spoken and musical arts" whose heady offerings ranged from "Ernst Krenek's 12-tone musical compositions to the humor of S.J. Perelman, from a consideration of George Gershwin as a serious musician to samples of modern poetry, from a survey of modern jazz to this week's dramatization of a Joseph Conrad short story." It was perhaps best known among station members for its bombastic opening, with stately music and intoned promises to "Educate, elucidate, explore, enlighten, and *perhaps*... to entertain."[10]

*Communiqué* was Fred Eidlin '64's series of taped interviews with ambassadors to the United States, gathered during his summers and vacations. A rather good way to meet ambassadors, one would think.

*The Short Story* was Production Director Dorrance's brief experiment with literature read by students.

*Foreign Student Speaks* made use of the exchange students who came from all over the world to study at Dartmouth.

*Reader's Roundtable* had General Reading Program Director Professor John Stewart discussing G.R.P. books with students.

Classical music appeared regularly on *Concert Hall*, the successor to the Concert and Symphony Hours of old, and also on Professor Robin Robinson's *A Little Night Music* and *Opera Showcase*, on *The United States Steel Hour*, *Modern Showcase*, Mike Delizia '64's *Art of Music*, and the taped *Boston Symphony Concert* (the latter supported for a time by a special College fund).

*WDCR Workshop*, possibly the most avant-garde show on the air, toyed with drama, readings and offbeat effects. Lacking a suitable offbeat (and dedicated) producer to maintain it week after week, it gradually faded from the schedule.

*Spotlight*, a brief but well-made series of early 1963, featured interviews with up-and-comers in popular music, gathered by producers Ted Gerbracht '64 and Walt Huss '65 during their vacations. Working with record label publicists, Gerbracht landed interviews in New York during the summer of 1962 with, among others, 20 year-old Barbra Streisand and 21 year-old Bob Dylan, both then on the cusps of their fabulous careers. Unfortunately the tapes apparently do not survive.[11]

Among other home-grown production ideas that graced WDCR's schedule for one or two terms were *Major League Baseball Quiz* (1960), *Mind Over Matter* (research students describing their projects, 1962), *Wonderful World of Women* (in literature, that is, 1962), *The Reader's Voice* (1962), *Wide World of Music* (1962) and the similar *Passport to Music* (1960), *Recently Released* (record albums, 1963), and *The Student Author* (reading and discussing, 1963).

Transcribed (or "canned") shows were generally avoided in these years although being professionally produced they were often quite good. Among those broadcast on a regular basis were *Image Russia* (NBC, 1960), *Paris Star Time* (1961), *Century of Song* (1961), *Democracy in America* (based on Alex de Toqueville's writings, 1962), *The Educated Imagination* (CBC, 1963), *The Creative Mind* (BBC, 1962), *The Eternal Light* (eternal) and, never to be forgotten by Dartmouth men of 1962, *Stand By for Crime* and *The Shadow*. Heh, heh.

Perhaps the most famous of all production series in the early 1960s, and one of the most innovative and professional in station history, was *Tales for the Midnight Hour*, produced by Paul Jones '65 and aired Sunday nights at midnight from 1962 to 1965. Originally a horror anthology, it quickly turned into a hilarious parody of the genre, with scripts written primarily by Jones and Guy MacMillin. Each story was introduced by host Franklyn Gordon (Jones) in deep, sepulchral tones, in a heavy echo chamber, against the throbbing strains of Mussorgsky's *Night on Bald Mountain*. The stories, generally 15 to 30 minutes in length, were imaginative, among them tales of ghost walkers, oriental rituals, giant grasshoppers, a malevolent dentist, a cocktail party in a mortuary, and a little girl who said "rain, rain, go away" once too often. Most had surprise endings. Over time the show developed continuing characters. Franklyn lived in a crypt in Norwich, Vermont, and ran a repertory playhouse in nearby Ezekiel Corners. Also heard was his equally creepy brother Ben, their boozy Aunt Sarah Gordon, hapless Professor Rudolph Humbert, and suicidal sleuth Eric Starnes and his idiot assistant Bruno. Franklyn always spoke in a deep echo chamber, even when the person he was talking to did not, and broke into loud cackles at inappropriate times.

There was a good deal of improvisation by the talented cast of student actors, which most frequently included Jones, MacMillin, Fred Hill, and Jack Weinstein '67. Many other station members made occasional appearances. Elaborate sound effects were added by engineers Sidney Marshall '65, Kerry Citrin '66, Michael Busch '66, and others. *Tales* was so well crafted that it continued to be rerun on WDCR for at least five years after Jones graduated in 1965. Three dozen episodes survive, and they deserve to be heard.[12]

## News

News had long been one of Dartmouth radio's weakest areas, despite frequent attempts to energize it. One of Ron Kehoe's first actions in 1958 had been announce that the station would begin editorializing on campus issues. This brought a swift rebuke from the administration, which said that the trustees had explicitly forbid any editorializing on the new AM station because of potential legal liability. Kehoe called a station meeting at which the staff urged defiance ("they can't tell us what to do!"), then fired off a strongly worded protest. *The Dartmouth* joined in with an editorial backing the station, and urging others to protest this "unjustified" censorship. President Dickey subsequently met with Kehoe and told him the ban must stand, but if the station wanted to speak out on current issues it should call it "commentary" not an "editorial." Considering the actions he could have taken, it was another example of how supportive Dickey was of the student broadcasters.[13]

By 1960, due to the energetic Hal Levenson '61, WDCR's news coverage had begun to expand. One memorable report in early 1960 was broadcast from the scene of a major demonstration outside the Merrimack County Jail, about 50 miles from Hanover. This was during the "red scare," and liberal activist Willard Uphaus had been incarcerated there for refusing to turn over the names of his followers. Levenson recalls that some of the station's reporters were sympathetic to Uphaus on free-speech grounds, but they remained impartial on air.[14]

Chasing, writing, analyzing, editing and reporting the news is a full time job, and extreme dedication and long hours are required of any part-time amateur staff that pretends to professionalism. News gathering is easy to talk about, hard to put into practice, and almost impossible to maintain over long periods. These prodigious hurdles are the measure of the success of News Directors Geoff Murphy, Henry Clay '64, and Jeff Panitt, in their 1962-64 overhaul of WDCR's news operation. Money bought some things, first a subscription to Radio Pulsebeat News. Murphy signed the contract with this colorful outfit, which was WDCR's first audio service. It ran for about a year until Murphy and Mike Hobbs tried to visit its headquarters during one vacation, and after considerable searching found it in a slum section of New York. Shortly thereafter service abruptly ended; the place reportedly burned down and its manager fled the country. The station then signed with UPI Audio, which provided on-the-scene audio reports ("actualities") from reporters around the world.[15]

The dedicated staff mounted an elaborate news training program, sent student reporters to municipal offices, town meetings and news in-the-making all over the Upper Valley, and made possible the most remarkable monument to WDCR News of all, *The Six O'Clock Report*. While there were other newscasts—15 minutes at 8:00 a.m., noon, and 11:00 p.m.—and periodic special projects, most of the department's energies, day in and day out, focused on this one nightly hour. Ten minutes consisted of national news from the UPI wire service. Produced "new" each night were sports, business, and weather reports, station-gathered local news, and two home-grown analysis features. "Dateline" sometimes analyzed and sometimes watched. One memorable segment on Dartmouth's ROTC program found Jeff Panitt with his heavy tape recorder charging up an enemy hill alongside warring ROTC cadets, trying to get a puffing cadet colonel to give his "reactions." "Commentary" was Dick Horner '66's well-written daily commentary on the news.

## Election Night and Other Specials of the Early AM Years

There were many specials of the early AM era of which any station could be proud, but probably the most spectacular was the coverage of the November 1960 and 1962 election nights. These built on the 1956 initiation of enhanced, out-of-studio coverage of elections, and spread it to both presidential and midterm election years. Dartmouth Broadcasting's big "election night" broadcasts have been perhaps the crowning achievement of its entire programming history.

The News Department had covered elections before, of course, but usually from the safe confines of the studio and using regular News Department resources. In the fall of 1960 General Manager George Whitehead and News Director Hal Levenson decided to expand on Dick Harris' 1956 coverage and do something even bigger. Why not get the whole station involved? Planning began weeks in advance, and dozens of staffers from all departments took part. The College Hall ballroom was reserved and wired for broadcasting by the Technical Department, with elaborate (temporary) microphone, signaling and intercom systems. Tables were arranged around the hall, one each for Northeast, South, Midwest and West, national, and local. Returns were collected from stringers strategically located at polling places for miles around. As the night progressed experts around each table reported and interpreted the returns from their regions, while a quick-witted moderator in the center of the hall tied the whole production together.

In a particularly prescient move, Professor John Kemeny, chair of the Math Department, and his colleague Professor Tom Kurtz were enlisted to write an election results prediction program for Grafton and Coos counties and run it on the College's first general purpose computer. This was a Royal McBee LGP-30, one of the earliest "desk computers," located in the basement of College Hall. Whitehead and Dick Wright '61 read the computer-generated predictions as part of their New Hampshire coverage.[16] Early in the evening the computer projected Nixon over Kennedy as the winner in those counties, and Wesley Powell as winner in the gubernatorial race, both of which proved accurate. In the years to follow Dartmouth would become one of the leading institutions in the country in the advancement of computer sciences, and of course computer voting models would become standard.[17] Spectators were encouraged to watch this multi-ring circus from a roped off area, and were provided with coffee, an auxiliary news ticker to watch, and large chalkboards on which staff members posted results as they came in. The entire production was supervised by Levenson and Harry Ungar '62.

Buoyed by its success, the station mounted a similarly elaborate production for the midterm election in November 1962, this time staged in the Robinson Hall Little Theater and adding phone reports from station friends in Boston, New York, Philadelphia and Chicago. Principal anchors were Guy MacMillin, Bill Subin '63 and Sturges Dorrance, and the producer was Paul Jones. An estimated 1,200 onlookers stopped by to gawk. The broadcast aired until 3:30 a.m. and reportedly consumed 42 dozen donuts, 20 gallons of coffee, 200 sandwiches, and nine cases of Coca-Cola.[18]

These election nights earned much credit for the station and demonstrated the results that could be achieved when resources were concentrated on a single production. One of the most imaginative documentary productions was Dorrance's *Directions in Broadcasting* week in the spring of 1963. This was an entire week of provocative features, long and short, scattered throughout the daily schedule and focusing on the future of broadcasting in America from many angles. Quick on-the-street interviews ("What do you think about..."), gathered with a portable tape recorder and lasting 30 seconds to a minute, were sprinkled through the daytime disc jockey shows to catch the attention of the casual listener. One minute essays on the services and statistics of broadcasting were similarly programmed toward the same end, while attention-getting promos heralded the longer nighttime productions. The latter included Paul Jones' *Voices Through the Air*, an hour-long audio history of radio featuring excerpts from famed network shows of the past. On another night Dorrance led a panel discussion on radio's future, hosting industry figures from Boston and New York and broadcast live from the new Hopkins Center. The entire production culminated with the 15th anniversary convention of the Ivy Network, in Hanover. The principal address, by NBC-TV producer (*Project Twenty*) and WDBS alumnus Don Hyatt '50, was rebroadcast to cap the week.

Each year from 1959 to 1964 produced its share of individual specials. Nineteen-sixty's *Dartmouth in Portrait*, assembled by Tad Cantril '62, was carried three times on the Voice of America then deposited in the Library of Congress. A Carlos Montoya feature in February, 1961 brought five pages of raves from a Cornish Flat listener ("finest radio program I have heard on 'standard band' USA in more than 20 years... a major contribution to cultural development").[19] The four-part *This Summer in Hanover* series introduced listeners to Dartmouth's first summer term, and Hopkins Center activities, during the spring of 1963, while Peter Cleaves '66's *Separatism in Quebec* (1964) was rebroadcast over an educational station in Boston. Numerous visiting notables provided a rich source of programming for WDCR. A 1959 interview with a visiting British rugby team was aired by the BBC. One conducted in 1961 with a short, balding little man named Homer Tomlinson, the self-proclaimed (in all seriousness) "King of the World," who was on a triumphal visit to his Dartmouth subjects, was not as widely heard but certainly attracted attention at the time.

The 1959 *Aegis* included an impressive list of recent WDCR interviewees including Clement Atlee, Arctic explorer Vilhjalmur Stefansson (later aired by the CBC), Dave Garroway, West Point star cadet Peter Dawkings, H.V. Kaltenborn, and Commander James Calvert of the atomic submarine *Skate*. A year later a *Dartmouth Alumni Magazine* article boasted of Governor Nelson Rockefeller, Vice President Richard Nixon (by an intrepid reporter who, microphone in hand, trotted alongside Nixon's moving car), Senators William Proxmire (on a train at the White River Junction station), John F. Kennedy, Albert Gore, Styles Bridges and Norris Cotton, Governor Robert Stafford of Vermont, Pierre Mendes-France, Madame Pandit, J. Robert Oppenheimer, and Panama's President de la Guardia, plus entertainers Hal Holbrook, Duke Ellington, Josh White, Pete Seeger, the Weavers, the Kingston Trio, the Brothers Four, and Louis Armstrong. A classic and much-used publicity photo shows Armstrong behind a well-identified WDCR microphone, being interviewed by Mike Melvoin. My own 1964 backstage interview with Johnny Cash can be found online.[20]

## The Record Library

The heart of a largely music-oriented station is its record library, and in the 1960s WDCR's blossomed as never before. The AM on the letterhead made it possible to obtain promotional copies of records, and a much enlarged budget brought subscriptions to the major labels for their new LPs. Several hundred dollars were spent rebuilding the classical, Broadway show and spoken-word libraries, and hundreds of staff hours went into rebuilding the huge, cross-referenced card files, which had fallen into disrepair during the late 1950s. The library's physical plant grew to keep pace. When this writer ended two years as record librarian in 1963, the station's collection stood at 12,000 discs. Fortunately my predecessor Bill Woolley had introduced a color-coding system in 1961, making it possible to find something in this mountain of sound.

Even the station hit parade, published by the librarian, burgeoned. Dubbed the Tri-Town Top 25 in line with current doctrine, it was mimeographed weekly and distributed through record stores in Hanover, Lebanon and White River Junction. Record hops by station d.j.'s also brought WDCR to the Upper Valley's younger set. Did they respond? Ask Fred Hill, who once wondered aloud on *Swinghouse* whether the Beatles were really all *that* popular. More than 100 phone calls in 30 minutes almost got the station's phone disconnected.

## Training

The splintered training programs hobbled along during the 1960s much as before. Announcing, production and news each offered their own, with little all-station coordination. No great things were expected of trainees (which seems a shame since station members are never again so eager to follow directions and work as when they first join the station), although some were used for occasional record-filing parties and staffing the *All-Request Show*.

During 1958-59 however production trainees were required to write critiques of WDCR's program schedule. The results were enough to gladden the heart of any training director, five-to-ten page carefully typed "term papers," the kind of thing no old hand at the station would think of spending time on. It was advice from novices, and sometimes showed it. "*Music 'til Midnight* [the station's most popular show] is poorly designed to supply what the audience wants," wrote one. But sometimes from the mouths of babes came more constructive comments.[21]

"Why not invite students and members of the faculty who are active in something of current interest... for interviews, for example Professor Williams or John Colenback on *Romeo and Juliet*, or [coach] Doggie Julian on this weekend's two games..."

"Mike Melvoin is probably one of the best announcers and disc jockeys... At times he changes his voice, attempting to be funny. It would be better if he would stay himself..."

"*Comment* should go on more frequently. This could follow the six o'clock news and could be culled from editorials in *The New York Times* and *Herald Tribune*, *Time*, *U.S. News and World Report*, etc."

142

Dramatic presentations, instead of being weekly and bad, should be once every three or four weeks and be better prepared.

On *The Hanover Scene*: "This is an excellent reading of the College bulletin for all those who cannot read. Especially enjoyable was the time the program opened with that pleasant ditty, "Yes! We Have No Bananas," because the banana tree was blooming in the greenhouse..."

On *Interfraternity Quiz*: "The question difficulty is to be questioned... the questions are not diverse enough."

On *Kaleidoscope*: "The intent of the show is excellent. The very fact that a show of this kind has no particular focus demonstrates the difficulty of presentation. The listener gets the feeling that there is no purpose connected to the show. It is very difficult to sustain interest in such a show for two hours."

Suggestions for shows? *Faculty Bullsession*, to be countered later in the week by *Student Bullsession*.

## Sports

Sports coverage continued to be extensive, with Bob Hager '60 serving as sports director in 1958-60. He recalls doing play-by-play for football, basketball, and hockey, along with Mike Hollern '60, Bob Colyer '60, Tom Green '62 and "Del" Lucas '61. Highlights included the 21-12 football win at Princeton in 1958 that clinched Dartmouth's first outright Ivy League Championship; two first round NCAA playoff games from Madison Square Garden; and two remotes from Charlotte, North Carolina, when the basketball team made the "Sweet Sixteen" (Eastern regionals). Some important games were fed, on request, to alumni clubs around the country.[22]

Football got even hotter in 1962, as the Dartmouth team, under legendary coach Bob Blackman (1955-1970), scored its first perfect season since 1925. It would have two more by the end of the decade, and win four more Ivy League titles. Blackman's overall 16-year record was an enviable 104 wins, 37 losses, and three ties.

New remote broadcast equipment made possible the "Dual Sports Network." During the winter, when basketball and hockey games overlapped by a period or two, the earlier was broadcast live and the latter delayed (on tape) until just after the first ended. A less successful experiment was *Sports Bandstand*, a quasi-d.j. show on Sunday nights that combined the weekend scores and sports stories with Dixieland music. Original, at least.

## Programming Flops and Father MacDonald

Of course the Program Department of 1958-64 had its setbacks, of which four were particularly notable. First was the attempt in 1960 to revive the WDCR Green Key Queen. The association with Green Key Weekend had provided much valuable publicity in the early 1950s, and it is not altogether clear what killed the station's attempt to revive it.

Then there was much talk, planning and inquiry during late 1961 into the possibility of affiliating with a national network, primarily for newscasts. Al Cameron's 1959-60 Directorate had been so adverse to the idea that it attempted to write a prohibition into the WDCR constitution ("Such an arrangement would establish a detrimental relationship of dependence on outside sources of programming...").[23] Its successors thought otherwise. The chief possibility this time was ABC, but as with NBC before, the idea was eventually scrapped because of expense.

A more inventive proposal in the spring of 1961 was that WDCR unite with WTSL for occasional stereo broadcasting, one channel to be carried by WDCR and one by WTSL. Stereo was at this time quite new to the public, having been introduced on records in the late 1950s. The idea finally bogged down because of probable FCC disapproval (two competing stations concluding an agreement to regulate their programming, even in this sense, could be construed as collusion), and because WTSL showed little enthusiasm.

The most colorful, and by far the most public, of WDCR's programming disasters during this period surrounded the "Hums" broadcast of May 1962. The Interfraternity Hums (singing) competition was held each spring outdoors on the steps of Dartmouth Hall, and was among the College's most ivy-covered traditions. Music lovers and friends of the College came from miles around to watch the 40 and 50-man choruses do their popular and comedy numbers, through a week of eliminations leading up to the Friday night finals. The college station's broadcast of the event was just as traditional, being both good programming and excellent public relations.

Of course when this many red-blooded fraternity men are brought together to sing, some refrains of a lascivious nature may reasonably be expected, at least on occasion. Indeed, it is not unreasonable to assume that over the years a few such outbursts had found their way through the station's live microphones to the radios of the Upper Valley, although the station took great pains to avoid this happening. All participants were notified in advance, in writing, when they would be carried live, and announcers on the spot had prepared "background" scripts with which to drown out embarrassing lyrics, if necessary.

That didn't change the headline of the Monday morning *Dartmouth*, "WEST LEB. PRIEST OBJECTS TO HUMS' LYRIC ON WDCR."[24] Psi Upsilon had just finished its act during the Friday night finals, it seems, and while marching off stage had given forth with a few lusty lines. So enraged at this infamy was the Reverend Edward J. MacDonald that he promptly took pen to hand to file a protest with the Federal Communications Commission.

Again, as in the 1948 "It Can't Happen Here" debacle, *The Dartmouth's* item was picked up by other papers, including the big *Manchester Union Leader,* which almost daily ran rather virulent front-page editorials by conservative publisher William Loeb. This time the *Union Leader* chose to view the incident not as a novelty but as a touchstone for a moral crusade. "DARTMOUTH STUDENT RADIO ERRS GRAVELY" headlined the front page editorial, which congratulated Father MacDonald for chastising the station.[25] "Freedom of speech does not include using the name of God in vain or being sacrilegious—ONE WOULD THINK THAT ONE OF THE BASIC BUSINESSES OF EDUCATION IS TO TEACH GOOD TASTE AND REVERENCE," roared the *Union Leader* in alternating regular, medium and bold-face type. "We sincerely hope that neither Father MacDonald nor Dean Seymour will let the matter drop until the guilty have been punished. THERE SHOULD BE CLEAR INDICATION THAT THIS OFFENSE AGAINST GOD AND MAN WILL NOT BE REPEATED."

Well. *The Union Leader* neglected to say that Dean Seymour, while "shocked" at the incident, categorically declined to blame WDCR. "There is no doubt in my mind," he told *The Dartmouth* in its original story, "that in this situation the radio station was performing a public service and this was just one of those accidents which have occurred before in the annals of radio." Besides, WDCR had "gone beyond the line of duty" by notifying fraternities by letter that they would be on the air live.

What about that standby copy? Program Director Bill Woolley, who had been the red-faced announcer on the spot, explained lamely that it was all a terrible coincidence. He usually read commercial copy while each fraternity marched off, but in this case, just as Psi U. began to depart, "the wind blew Woolley's copy of the commercial out of reach. Because his only aide had left temporarily to sing with his own fraternity, Woolley continued to broadcast Psi U. while he recovered the copy." "I recovered my copy just as the lyrics in question were sung and went on the air just after they were concluded," Woolley said.

The president of Psi U. chimed in with an even more remarkable story. His men always hummed or changed the lyrics when marching *on* to the steps, he said, and in marching off did not sing them "until the group was around the corner of Dartmouth Hall and beyond the hearing of most of the crowd." Alas, on Friday they started too soon.

WDCR, Psi U. and the College apologized profusely to everyone who would listen, but the *Union Leader's* ears were closed. In a follow-up editorial it grumbled, "we have no desire to prolong this controversy, but we do believe that there is need for improvement in the *attitude* of some of the students at WDCR..."[26]

Feeling that the best defense against this kind of nonsense was simply to ignore it, WDCR displayed prodigious self-control and let the matter drop. The *Union Leader* soon found other unsuspected enemies of God and Man to pounce upon, and the FCC chose to ignore the whole affair.

## Technical Department

Even while the business and program departments were undergoing their painful crisis and comeback in the early 1960s, the Technical Department was steadily moving forward. Through a process of expansion and modernization, made possible by the new, higher levels of income, the "re-equipment" of the station begun in 1955-58 was virtually completed. A major landmark was the power boost to 1,000 watts in early 1961. The FCC was at this time giving automatic approval to 250-watt stations wishing to boost their daytime power to 1,000 watts, and few missed the chance. Prodded by a desire to remain competitive (WTSL had applied for the increase) as well as the opportunity to strengthen the erratic signal outside Hanover, the Directorate in early 1960 persuaded the College to apply to the FCC and finance a new transmitter. Approval was in hand by fall, and a shiny new 1000/250 watt Gates transmitter arrived soon after. It was designed so that power could be reduced at night; in theory 250 watts at night carried as far as 1,000 watts during the daytime, although practical experience left some room for doubt.

"The target date," exulted the *Newsletter*, "is still January 3rd... and Bob 'printed circuit' Hargraves says that we have a good chance of being 1,000 watts as the Winter term broadcasting begins. A fine Christmas present that would be. Now, those of us unassociated with WDBS who are tired of hearing the old timers refer to 'the good old days' will have something to look back on. 'Well, son, I remember when old 'DCR was only 250 watts. Yes, son, those were the good old days'."[27]

But technical problems prevailed, as always, and it was not until after "many shenanigans, several all-nighters, and much sweat (and perhaps an occasional unkind word or two)" that the big day finally arrived in April.[28] First there was an enthusiastic "1000 watt bumper sticker" contest heralding the news. (Every party has its pooper, in this case an irate listener who complained that the sticker had torn the chromium off her bumper and demanded a new bumper. After test-tearing stickers off several bumpers with no visible damage, the station politely declined.) President Dickey and other luminaries then crowded around the control panel in Studio 3X and performed the official switch-flipping.

The same college grant that financed the new transmitter also made possible the acquisition of a big new Gates master control panel in 1960. Replacing the station's 12 year-old homemade model, which had served well but too long, this multi-purpose control board made taping and live production work a pleasure. Simultaneously the station faced a problem familiar to all modern broadcasters, namely replacing tape recorders. Under the hard, continuous use of radio work the most expensive models wear out fast, and some in use at WDCR clearly needed retirement. Among the machines bought were a $600 Ampex 601, a professional portable in regular use for years afterwards. A used Revere, bought at the same time (fall 1959), was placed in d.j. studio 3X as a temporary replacement. There it stayed for the next year despite emitting periodic whirrs, pops and shrieks while announcer's microphones were on, and occasionally devouring whole the tapes fed into it. It was later retired in disgrace to become the News Department's editing and tape-eating machine.

Ted Mascott's 1961-62 regime added a huge, rack-mounted, $1,475 Ampex 351, the industry standard; another Ampex 601; and a handy portable Sony 200 which proved extremely useful to salesmen demonstrating commercials to potential advertisers.

Not only did these purchases relieve the strain on the old equipment, they gave WDCR on-the-air versatility undreamt of five years earlier. Production kept pace. *Six O'Clock News* producers quickly claimed that they could not work with fewer than four machines arrayed around them in Master Control. Still, the logical next step of cartridge machines, adopted by so many stations, was investigated and rejected by succeeding Directorates.

The possibility of television at Dartmouth had been a continuing subject of discussion within the administration, if not at the radio station. A 1962 memo by Provost John Masland observed that "no single issue in the last decade has received as much attention and produced as much material for the files, including numerous recommendations, with as little action as television." Aside from Dartmouth Film Society director Blair Watson's involvement with the New Hampshire Educational Broadcasting Council, the College had done little. A new review by Professor Clark Horton (who confessed he did not own a TV set) recommended that at least Dartmouth should import the signal of the University of New Hampshire station, and perhaps contribute some programming to its small educational network. But as with the early 1950s review, no action was taken.[29]

## Mobility — Plus

The most far-reaching purchase of all during the early 1960s came in 1962, a small package with a big voice indeed. The $1,000 FM remote unit, manufactured by Marti, allowed live, on the spot (or moving) coverage from anywhere in the Hanover area. A 15-watt FM transmitter sent the signal back to the studios on a special FCC-assigned frequency (101.73 MHz) for broadcast. This was the biggest boon to mobile programming since the first small portable console of the 1940s. The latter had made it possible to leave the studio for the first time, but the process was expensive and difficult. Telephone lines had to be leased in advance and a fixed location found near telephone company facilities, so except for well-sponsored sportscasts and major campus events, remotes were understandably rare. The Marti made remotes as easy as going out, aiming the little transmitter at a special Robinson Hall antenna, and plugging it in, or hooking up a battery. Besides saving money, this made possible fast on-the-spot news reports, remote d.j. shows from advertisers' stores, regular Sunday morning broadcasts of church services from Hanover, Lebanon, Norwich and environs (a different church each week), and even coverage of the 1963 Spring crew races from an "EDCR Launch" cruising down the Connecticut River behind the athletes.

Other imaginative applications were explored on Saturday afternoon's *Program PM,* which spiced its six hours with brief live features from roving reporters. Once such interview, which became a classic of its genre, originated from the kitchen of a rural Vermont church amid the clatter and conversation of preparations for a church supper. Later the unit was mounted in a car, for an experimental all-night d.j. show (the d.j. was in the moving auto, roaming the Tri-Town area), while another year's crew races were described by an incognito Dean Seymour ("our announcer, Mr. X") hanging from the side of a sports car cruising down the highway beside the river. Not all ideas came to fruition, however. The college "bell lady" refused to grant an interview from atop Baker Tower just before its hourly chimes were to sound; and the suggestion that *Tales for the Midnight Hour* originate from a local graveyard was quietly buried.

Bob Gitt, chief engineer and then technical director during 1961-63 waged a particularly ruthless campaign of painting, paneling, and Coca-Cola bottle cleanups, giving WDCR a professional appearance which undeniably helped student morale and pride in the station. The money spent on a good-looking as well as good-sounding station, especially one run by a large volunteer staff, was by no means wasted.

Station pride was similarly boosted by the acquisition of new second floor offices in the fall of 1963. The traditional, crowded WDCR Office became general purpose workspace, as administrators and businessmen moved across the hall into a plush, carpeted private Directorate office and a bright, modern business office replete with desks, tile floor and fluorescent lights. Even before this, the station crowed that it was "the best-dressed, entirely student-operated, college-owned, commercial AM station in the country. We are unique!"[30] But it was still WDCR. There were empty Coke bottles everywhere.

Although the general trend of training programs at this time was toward less structure and coordination, the Technical Department stood out with a well-organized schedule for its trainees. Partially this was due to the easily definable nature of the material, as opposed to the less tangible skills needed for production and announcing. But equally important was the prodigious effort of the engineers. Bob Gitt devoted the entire summer of 1961 to constructing the definitive *Tech Manual*, 100 single-spaced pages, profusely illustrated (in color!) and covering virtually every aspect of the department as it then existed, right down to how to thread the Ampex 351. It is not known if a single trainee ever weathered the entire tome, but it long served as the basis of the training program and a valuable reference, besides striking a certain amount of awe into the hearts of those viewing the Tech Department from the outside.

### "Weird Music and Frequency Oscillations"

Always of interest to station members was how far away they could be heard, even under freak conditions. One of Don Knapp '60's first projects in early 1959 was to stage a special "DX" broadcast in cooperation with the National Radio Club. This is a group whose hobby it is to pick up the most distant radio stations possible, usually in the wee hours of the morning when radio signals carry furthest. Working with sensitive receivers and headphones they ferret out likely candidates from the background "garble" of the radio dial, log as much of their programming as possible, then write the station concerned for confirmation that this was actually broadcast when they heard it. Since 250-watt WDCR normally couldn't be heard much further than just outside of town, even at midnight and with a strong tailwind, Knapp arranged a 1:00 to 5:00 a.m. broadcast when other stations on 1340 KHz would be off the air, to consist of "weird music and frequency oscillations."

The DX Special got advance publicity in the NRC newsletter and plenty of dial-searchers were waiting on the appointed evening of April 13, 1959. Unfortunately that was the night chosen by one WIRY in Plattsburgh, New York (1340 KHz) to begin all-night programming, and for many the WDCR show was "QRM'ed" (drowned out by interference). About half a dozen letters were received, including one from Proctorville, Ohio, some 700 miles away, and probably the most distant point yet reached by WDCR.

### New Position on the Directorate

Nineteen-sixty brought the first major organizational change since the four-man Directorate evolved in the late 1940s. The problem was to find a way to handle the growing organizational aspects of WDCR, including personnel, publicity, public relations and office management. These had been almost incidental in the fledgling DBS of old, but as the station's size and activity mushroomed its front office operation began to demand full time attention, time which the overburdened general manager did not have. The assistant to the general manager had not attracted talent, nor had junior staff positions grouped in a general manager's department. In fact, the only positions that seemed to consistently attract reliable upperclassmen were those at the top, on the Directorate itself.

The answer was an independent department headed by an administrative director. Reporting to him were the comptroller, guardian of the station's financial records, the publicity (later promotion) director, the public relations director (public service announcements), and the personnel director. The latter was responsible for recruiting, the newsletter, and the "D.O.S." or daily operations supervisor, a sort of duty officer who manned the office for a full day taking calls and coordinating (each station member was required to pull D.O.S. duty two or three times a term). The administrative director also undertook special projects. Bill Matthews '61, first to hold the position, set an example by writing a feature story on WDCR for the June 1960 *Dartmouth Alumni Magazine.*

Another change in 1960 involved the technical director. Although this department head was expected to have a working knowledge of electronics, he was an administrator first, a technician second. But by law, the FCC held the station's chief engineer (the "first phone" license holder) legally responsible in all technical matters. Shouldn't this individual therefore be in charge of the Technical Department, even though his knowledge was more of electronic circuitry than people planning? So in 1960, the chief engineer became head of the department.

Two years later the retiring Mascott Directorate felt it had its answer. Better to head Tech with the best administrator eligible, whether or not he had an FCC first class license. If he didn't, which was usually the case, the chief engineer would be his assistant, not the boss.

Perhaps the most significant staff change occurred in 1960 when Business Manager Henry Goldsmith '62 hired the station's first permanent secretary, Mrs. Evelyn Hutchins. "Mrs. H.", as she was known to all, was the 42 year-old sister of Warner Bentley's secretary, married to Richard "Hutch" Hutchins (who ran Tanzi's store), and the mother of three boys. A friendly, outgoing woman, she ran the office and became a mother figure to the boys (and later girls) of WDCR. She stayed with the station for nearly 20 years.[31]

### Administrative Department

One of the chief goals of early AM management was to generate publicity that strengthened the image of WDCR as a professional operation. One vehicle with which to do this was *The Listener's Log*, instituted by General Manager Dorrance, Production Director Dan Matyola '63, and the new Administrative Department in the fall of 1962. In some ways it echoed the *Newsletter* of the early 1950s. There had long been talk of reviving the latter, but plans had always foundered on the old bugaboos, too much work and expense. Now the time and people were finally right. Dorrance convinced the Directorate that the expense was worth it, and then himself provided the drive to get it off the ground. Wisely, he started small; the first *Log* was modest and mimeographed. Later it was printed under a regular contract with Roger Burte Printers. A special two-tone heading was prepared, and both sides of the page were used yielding three to four pages. By 1964 the *Log* had become a small listener's magazine, headed by a feature article or two and listing the next week's sports and production programming in detail.

The mailing list, which at first contained only a few hard-core friends of the station, gradually expanded by word-of-mouth and then by on-air promotion to close to 500 listeners around the Upper Valley. The volume made possible economical third-class mailing (in those days relatively reliable) and the purchase of an inexpensive addressing machine to speed the flow. A special issue, in April 1963, was mailed to several thousand potential listeners.

The *Log* brought the station prestige and interested listeners, usually the more attentive type since its focus was on production and specials. It also served to mollify faculty critics who complained of rock 'n' roll all day. Some were taken aback to see just how much "better" programming there actually was each week. Through the hard work of Matyola and his successor editor Bob Cohn it became an established feature of WDCR.

Although the *Listener's Log* was the outstanding publicity achievement of the early 1960s, there were several other projects. After Bill Matthews produced his article for the *Alumni Magazine* in 1960, Sturges Dorrance reached a much different audience with an illustrated article published in *Broadcasting*, the industry's leading business publication.[32] Reprints of this were flashed in front of potential advertisers for years afterwards. Printed schedules were distributed in the late 1950s, and in 1961-62 similar schedules were prepared in handy card form, for each term. No one would have to wonder what was on this station!

WDCR was basically not a contest-driven station at this time, but successful promotions were held at special times, for example on the transition to 1,000 watts of power, and on the 20th anniversary.

### Those Old Payola Roll Blues

There is no record that any record promoter bothered to try to bribe WDCR (the most this writer ever got was a Zero candy bar intended to promote an obscure Lawrence Welk record of the same name). Nevertheless the black shadow of the 1960 payola scandal, generated when the FCC discovered the mercenary record plugging of some metropolitan d.j.'s, fell even on the north country. For several months during the spring students were compelled to guiltily read a long "records donated by..." list at the end of each music show, since virtually all 45 RPM's were promotional copies. The FCC later ruled this precaution a bit farfetched.

An even more painful legal storm clouded the disc jockeys' usually sunny skies in 1962. WDCR, like all other users of copyrighted music, paid royalties to the three big composer collection agencies, BMI, ASCAP, and SESAC. These organizations periodically audit stations to determine whose songs were being played most, and thus who should get the royalties collected. "A complete log of all music aired by you during April," the neat letter on Program Director Bill Woolley's desk almost offhandedly requested. With 40 individualistic d.j.'s, 18 hours a day, and no full time employees? But popular songs, classical passages, background themes, even little snatches used in commercials all were written down as they went on, complete with label, record number, composer, etc. Listeners never knew, but few WDCR alumni who lived through that month of April 1962 will ever forget it.

### The Fondest Dream

Year-round broadcasting had long been one of the station's fondest dreams, and while it was not realized in the early 1960s substantial strides were made to reduce the silent periods that once came automatically with all vacations. One singularly heroic example was the schedule maintained during Commencement and the subsequent Alumni Week in June 1962. Final exams were over and most undergraduates had left town, but a hardy band of broadcasters dug in to carry WDCR into the summer. Besides regular programming, local residents were treated to a live broadcast of Commencement, plus on-the-spot coverage of space hero Alan

Shepherd's triumphant return to his New Hampshire home town. Later, as several hundred alumni arrived for their week of festivities, shows were aired especially for them, including music of their college days and an introduction to the new (to them) WDCR-AM.

## Two Surveys

An area that always needed work was audience measurement. How many people were listening? Where did they live? What kind of consumers were they? Both for sales and management purposes any station needs a report card once in a while, but getting it, especially for a small station with limited funds, can be difficult. For WDCR, which reached a potential 45,000 listeners in the surrounding communities but only 3,000 students on campus, the old dormitory checks would obviously not be too meaningful. There were no commercial measurement services in the market, so two major surveys were taken by the station itself in the early AM era. The first was by Tuck Business School student Ariel Halpern '59 in 1958, and the second by this author as administrative director in 1963.[33] Each survey measured the student and community audiences separately, then combined the results for an overall picture of WDCR's audience vs. that of the competition.

Business Manager Halpern conducted his survey as a project for a class during November and December of 1958. It was the largest station survey to date, and the first to sample WDCR's new Upper Valley audience. A squad of station members was organized to man the telephones for 14 continuous hours on one "average" radio day asking people what they were listening to when called, and then prepare and distribute survey questionnaires to every room on campus.[34] Two Tuck School professors acted as advisors, but it was Halpern's job to organize, supervise and compile.

The results were in by January. The two sets of figures were based on 810 phone calls to local residents and 442 postcards returned by students (about 11 percent of local, six-town, homes and 14.8 percent of the student body, respectively). They showed WDCR ahead of WTSL in nine of the 14 hours in the broadcast day sampled. Hour-to-hour figures were suspiciously erratic, but radio listenership was greatest in the late afternoon and evening, with the morning second and the early afternoon a poor third. WTSL led in this latter time period, and was behind most of the rest of the day.

The survey received some newspaper publicity, which brought an angry response from Howard Chase of WTSL, who called it inaccurate and biased. He threatened to "take action," although nothing seems to have transpired.[35]

Halpern's efforts, though laudable, were rendered obsolete sooner than anyone could have imagined. Out of nowhere appeared the Upper Valley's third broadcaster, WWRJ, just across the river in White River Junction, Vermont. The curiously run 1,000-watt daytimer, founded on a shoestring in 1959, was proudly billed as White River's *own* radio station. For three years it struggled to stay above water, its disc jockeys sometimes trying country music, sometimes rock 'n' roll, until the station finally went bankrupt in June 1962. Several months later, in early 1963, it resurfaced, refinanced and refurbished, as WVTR, "The Voice of the Green Mountains." This time there were more experienced professionals at the helm and the station carved for itself a viable foothold, mostly among WTSL's former White River listeners.

Besides the emergence of a White River station, there were other reasons for a new survey. The 1958 survey gave no indication where WDCR's listeners lived (it is questionable whether many calls were even made outside of Hanover), of favorite shows, of preferred programming, or of overall station vs. station standing. And although size made the survey look impressive at first glance, a close look offered serious questions as to its accuracy. There were erratic hour-by-hour figures, a strange boom in listenership at night, when radio listenership is normally low, no real analysis of probable accuracy or distorting influences, and the very results themselves, which flew in the face of WTSL's generally accepted Upper Valley supremacy. If WDCR had indeed overturned WTSL's well-entrenched seven-year lead in AM, the station made little of it at the time.

The introduction to the 1963 study described progress after Halpern.

Further surveys were taken under the Mascott (1961-62) and Dorrance (1962-63) Directorates, and for that matter probably under Whitehead's (1960-61) too. Unfortunately in each case rather little was kept of permanent records or final reports, and it is difficult to reconstruct either their scopes or their findings. It appears that none approached the size and prestige of the Halpern study however. This was doubtless no fault of the individuals involved, but rather was due to limitations of money and, especially, time. General managers cannot run listenership surveys.[36]

### The 1963 Brooks Study

*Radio Listenership in the Upper Valley: 1963* was intended to fill what had become by that time a gaping hole in WDCR's knowledge of its own audience. Halpern's sample size was doubled; 980 questionnaires were returned by students and 1,966 calls made to Upper Valley residents (32.6 percent of the student body and 25.5 percent of local homes). Calls were spread over a week to insure a more accurate average. Instead of reporting individual hours, there were four listening periods of the day, corresponding to programming. This made possible detailed audience breakdown by town within each time period, showing for the first time WDCR's strength in "enemy territory" outside Hanover.

In addition the survey was designed to double check results (actual listening when called and general preferences) and show students' favorite programs, differences between college classes, and allow general comments. The 22-page final report carefully defined and analyzed all results, as well as the survey methods used and projected accuracy. It was hoped that this document, which was deposited in the College library, would be a useful reference for future Nielsens.

The execution of the survey, in May 1963, was one of those colorful "everybody pitch in" affairs which characterized WDCR's greatest successes. Sociology Department and Tuck School of Business professors offered advice, but the week of continuous phone calls, and the mimeographing, folding and addressing of 2,300 student questionnaires was strictly a student affair. So bountiful was the resulting harvest of data that the final compilation was not finished until August.

Among the findings for the non-campus community was that WDCR was the number one station in greater Hanover by a substantial margin, both in stated preference and actual audience; WDCR's strongest time period was in the afternoon, with popular music, while WTSL's was in the morning and early evening. WVTR, two months after its launch, had not yet gained a particularly large audience outside White River Junction, and even there it split the market rather evenly with WTSL.

WTSL was as expected well entrenched in the Upper Valley as a whole, due to its long head start and year-round programming. Nevertheless the student station was number one by a wide margin in their common home town of Hanover, close behind in the towns to the north and west, and with a significant (about 12 percent of total audience) foothold in poorer but populous Lebanon, West Lebanon, and White River Junction to the south. Overall the student broadcasters could regularly expect between 2,000 and 3,000 community listeners during the peak hours of the morning, shattering forever the image of WDCR as a strictly student affair.

On campus the audience was as solid as ever, with WDCR preferred 20-to-one over WTSL and WVTR combined. The roster of most listened-to shows was likewise familiar:

|  | % of student body (3,000) that "usually" listened |
|---|---|
| 1. *Music 'til Midnight* | 60% |
| 2. *Swinghouse* | 38% |
| 3. *Night Watch* | 30% |
| 4. *Eleven PM News* | 25% |
| 5. *Contact* | 23% |
| 6. *Swingalong* (12-3 p.m.) | 17% |
| 7. *Suppertime Show* | 14% |
| 8. Production Block (evenings) | 13% |
| 9. *Six O'Clock Report* | 13% |
| 10. *Concert Hall* | 12% |

The top two programs were rock 'n' roll deejay shows. However while rock music seemed the preferred kind, it was markedly less so among seniors than among freshmen. Upperclassmen appeared to prefer classical music and jazz more than their younger classmates. The favorite production show was Paul Jones' sometimes mysterious, sometimes hilarious *Tales for the Midnight Hour*, followed by folk and jazz shows, *Interfraternity Quiz, Comedy Spot, Pick of the Past* (yaaay!) and *Shubert Alley*. Half the returns included comments, but on most bones-of-contention (should WDCR have more or less rock 'n' roll, jazz, classics, educational shows, etc.) about the same number were for as against. The only thing everyone could agree on was that the announcers ought to announce better.

As soon as the results were in General Manager Al McKee set out to make sure they were used. The rather detailed and technical 22-page report, which showed both the strengths and weaknesses of WDCR, was reduced to four concise, favorable pages suitable for flashing at advertisers. Bar graphs dramatized the results and special inserts were prepared for Hanover-oriented businesses (WDCR is No. 1!) and for those aiming at Lebanon and White River Junction (WDCR is a force to be reckoned with and, at current rates, delivers the most audience for the dollar). In addition McKee drew up a special salesman's guide on how to use the survey to advantage.

Although the materials were there, the Business Department unfortunately made little use of them. In this respect, the importance of follow-up action to exploit such surveys can hardly be overemphasized. WDCR was stronger than many of its advertisers realized.

## A College and Community Station

Even before 1958 Dartmouth radio had been popular with townspeople, some of whom could pick it up through system leakage. With the advent of AM the era of strictly campus broadcasting was left behind, as the surveys dramatically showed. WDCR now had two distinct audiences to serve, students and a substantial part of the regional community, probably the area's upper socioeconomic groups at that, to judge by the concentration of listeners in relatively well-off, college-oriented Hanover and Norwich.

The dire prognostications of *The Dartmouth* notwithstanding, it did that job remarkably well. It was both a training ground and a thriving, $20,000 per year business; an outlet for college news, sports and cultural events, and the preferred entertainment of thousands of college and community listeners. WTSL weathered its first competition quite well, as the Upper Valley proved adequate to support not two but three AM stations, while listeners were richer by the choice now available to them.

The community image of WDCR as "the students' station" nevertheless persisted, for better (on this basis most sales were made) or worse. But it was proven, for the first time in America, that students could be entrusted not only with a full power commercial broadcast station but could advance their own practical education and provide genuine community service at the same time.

"Red" Whelden (standing) and the original DBS control board (1946)

WDCR's proud new Gates master control board (1962)

1960 Election Night broadcast

1960 Election Night, Prof. John Kemeny at right

Lowell Thomas broadcasting nationwide from WDBS (1948)

Mike Melvoin interviews Louis "Satchmo" Armstrong (1959)

Presidential candidate Nelson Rockefeller faces the WDCR microphone and an appreciative crowd (1960)

Robinson Hall, longtime home of Dartmouth Broadcasting

# Chapter 7

# 1964-1970: Years of Social Turmoil

The 1960s had begun quietly enough. Vietnam was a distant land that few had heard of, the civil rights disturbances in the American South were far removed from the Hanover plain, and, perhaps most significantly, the adult establishment was very much in charge. Freshmen arriving in 1960 were told to gather at Baker Library, wearing suits and ties. There they were ushered one at a time into a huge, ornate room where they were greeted individually by President John Sloan Dickey. He was an imposing, gracious man, and it was a little like being presented to royalty. By 1969 there were sit-ins and protests, and ultimately protesters occupied the administration building and forcibly evicted Dickey from his own office. What a difference a decade made.

In the late 1960s Dartmouth entered a period of turmoil, beginning with quiet protests which escalated to bitter confrontations, a full scale riot when George Wallace appeared on campus, a defiant valedictory speech calling for U.S. defeat in war, and finally the storming of the administration building and the arrival on campus of state police and National Guard troops to put down the student rebellion.

Dartmouth radio was tested during these tumultuous times. How would it react? What part would it play in the nationwide assault on authority? It was, after all, a completely student-run enterprise, and one with a very prominent voice in the community. It was heard everywhere on campus and throughout the surrounding region. It was in many ways the "voice" of Dartmouth.

To the dismay of activists it proved to be a centrist force, not taking sides. It did however give voice to many. Its deeply embedded guiding philosophy, developed and handed down over the years by its student leaders, and encouraged by the light-handed control of the College, was one of professionalism. Recruits were told "we do not want to sound like a bunch of college students. It's our station and we should act and sound like professional broadcasters."

General managers during this period were Robert Hartford '65, Allan Ryan '66, Owen Leach '67, John Hopke '68, Jeff Kelley '69, and Paul Gambaccini '70 (with Stu Zuckerman '70 sharing leadership responsibilities as station president in 1969-70).

## News Coverage

WDCR's greatest contribution to the region during this period was its exceptional news coverage, and the crown jewels of news were the election night extravaganzas. For the 1964 presidential election the News Department produced seven one-hour *Election Countdown* specials that were syndicated to other Ivy Network stations during the fall. On election night, November 3, 1964, WDCR was a key player in Ivy Network coverage that originated live from Radio City in New York and was syndicated to 30 to 40 college stations across the country. Forty minutes of each hour consisted of network coverage, co-anchored by WDCR Program Director Jeff Panitt '65, and 20 minutes originated locally from each station. News Director Paul Klee '66 orchestrated a station-wide effort in support. *Sponsor,* a national advertising magazine, published a major article about the production, marveling that the entire tab had been picked up by sponsor Western Electric.[1]

The 1966 midterm election was also an Ivy Network production, with national coverage live from New York City and local coverage from Alumni Hall in Hopkins Center, produced by Program Director Bob Buck '67, anchored by Owen Leach, and complete with statisticians, regional desks, and a gallery for onlookers. The national team in New York included WDCR's Dave Houston '67. Local reporters fanned out to campaign headquarters and polling stations around the region, with political junkie (and future U.S. Secretary of Labor) Bob Reich '68 moving from precinct to precinct with a remote unit. Newsman Arthur Fergenson '69 recalled covering the campaign headquarters of General Harrison Thyng (R), who was running for senator against incumbent Tom McIntyre (D), and getting a concession statement from Thyng just before the candidate disappeared, giving WDCR an exclusive which it shared with other stations.[2]

The 1968 presidential election, held at the height of the Vietnam War, was one of the most turbulent in U.S. history. WDCR reporters conducted many interviews during late 1967 and early 1968, in the run-up to the all-important, first-in-the-nation New Hampshire Primary. Paul Gambaccini recalled having to maintain his professionalism while interviewing Republican candidate Richard Nixon, who he disliked intensely, while Dave Prentice '69 and Stephen Zrike '71 have commented on the "rock star" status of Democratic challenger Eugene McCarthy.[3]

On primary night, March 12, 1968, the whole country was watching New Hampshire. WDCR coverage originated from its studios with student reporters phoning in reports from around the state. It was one of the most dramatic primaries in U.S. political history. McCarthy nearly beat deeply unpopular President Lyndon Johnson, leading to the latter's withdrawal from the race. Zrike recalled being the only reporter at the headquarters of also-ran Harold Stassen (R), who got 0.71 percent of the vote, and conning him into making an early concession statement so that he could rush over to Nixon headquarters "where the action was." (Zrike lined up some dead microphones alongside WDCR's and told Stassen that his words would be fed to the rest of the press corps.) The station covered the fall election (Nixon vs. Hubert Humphrey) in-studio, with reports again phoned in. Mark Willen '68 was the producer and Jeff Kelley anchorman, with political analysis by Win Rockwell '70 and government professor Edward Gude. The station received a United Press International award for excellence for this coverage.[4]

Among the News Department's other finest moments was coverage of the tragic Moose Mountain airplane crash in October 1968, which occurred in the midst of a WDCR charity marathon broadcast. A commuter airliner crashed into the mountain while approaching Lebanon airport. Program Director Dave Prentice and newsman Arthur Fergenson rushed off to the remote location in a car loaned by a faculty member, while General Manager Jeff Kelley calmly read reports on the air as they came in. Calm professionalism was exactly what was needed. For a time no one knew whether anyone had been killed and wire services were calling WDCR for information, since no one else was on the scene. Gradually as information became available the names of the dead were read by Kelley; among them were Music

Department Chairman Milton Gill and several others associated with the College. In all, 32 people had died. Paul Gambaccini, in his book about his days at Dartmouth, recalled a touching scene when a well dressed middle-aged gentleman walked into the station and approached Kelley, calmly asking if the young man had any information on the fate of his wife, then his brother, and then his friend. Looking down at his clipboard, Kelley had to confirm, one by one, that they were all dead. The gentleman quietly said "thank you," and slowly walked away. Not too many students have had to deal with a tragedy this large, this publicly, but WDCR was widely praised for its steady professionalism.[5]

Although WDCR did not editorialize or take positions on the issues of the day, it did air a considerable number of news and discussion programs. In January 1966 *Issues* followed controversies swirling around campus. Also that month newly appointed Local News Director Jeff Kelley stepped up local coverage, which previously had been shortchanged. It had always been difficult to get Dartmouth students interested in covering the local events of a small, semi-rural New England community—but that's what professionals did. Their work was heard on *WDCR Reports*, a full hour of news nightly at 6:00 p.m. produced by Chris Kern '69. It was an ambitious production, consisting of 20 minutes of national and local news with Kelley, Jim Flynn '67 and Bob Reich, five minutes of weather, five minutes of commentary, 10 minutes of sports, stock market and business, and features such as reports from Chuck Adams '68 who was taking part in a foreign study program in West Africa. It was certainly a remarkable production for a local station. The community appreciated the attention, and it was "heavily sponsored." In the fall newsbreaks were added throughout the day, local news at 15 minutes past the hour, and national at 45 minutes past the hour.[6]

In October 1967 energetic Bob Reich, a campus leader since his freshman year, and then chair of the senior student leadership council (called Palaeopitus), launched a series on current issues and conflicts called *Dartmouth Inquiry*. In 1969 David Graves '70 originated *Tri-Town Talk Back*, billed as WDCR's first phone-in talk show. Another long-lived series introduced in the late 1960s was *Noon Hour*, an eclectic mix of news and interviews both serious and light. Guests included visiting dignitaries and campus figures such as coach Bob Blackman. There was also Sam Brylawski, the teenage brother of a Tuck School graduate student, whose specialty was playing the "William Tell Overture" on his head by knocking on his skull, while altering the shape of his mouth. He also took phone requests.[7]

**Turmoil on Campus**

Protests against America's growing involvement in Vietnam were gradually spreading across the country, but in the fall of 1965, 77 percent of Dartmouth students and 68 percent of faculty still supported U.S. policy regarding the war. In April 1966 a student survey showed 70 percent in support of the war and 25 percent opposed, with general opposition to draft card burning. In November 1966, after a flood of anti-war stories in the media, support had begun to erode but a majority (53 percent) still favored continuing military action. Less than 10 percent advocated getting out, while the rest wanted negotiations.[8]

The strife in American society came to Dartmouth in many forms, and was thoroughly covered by WDCR's news and public affairs programs. In February 1965 two Dartmouth students working for the Student Non-Violent Coordinating Committee (SNCC) were arrested during civil rights protests in Selma, Alabama. Also that month Malcolm X spoke on campus, just two weeks before he was assassinated in New York City. Stokely Carmichael spoke at Dartmouth in November 1966, but the speaker who caused a riot was segregationist Governor George Wallace in May 1967. WDCR was in the thick of it. Wallace had been on campus four years earlier, in 1963, and had received a generally polite reception when he addressed 4,000 students in the Field House, although there were silent pickets outside. But times were different in 1967. His speech in Webster Hall was interrupted by shouts and heckling, and midway through the talk a group of unidentified protesters began marching toward the stage. Jeff Kelley and Paul Gambaccini were broadcasting the event, and Gambaccini jumped up and confronted the angry leader with a microphone and the simple question, "Excuse me, but who are you?" "My name is Joe Topping, I teach at Colby," the man calmly replied, before resuming his fist-waving. Eventually Wallace escaped to a waiting car, which was swarmed by a crowd estimated at 500 students, shouting and banging on the car. Surveying the scene newsman Owen Leach remarked, "George Wallace's car is outside, but he isn't going anywhere." The Hanover chief of police called it the worst riot in 22 years.[9]

In the days that followed there were profuse apologies for the seeming show of intolerance toward Wallace (*Time* magazine compared the students' actions to "the venom of a Southern mob barring a school door to a Negro child"), but Wallace seemed to enjoy it all, and his standing among some in the country was burnished by the image of Northern liberals denying free speech to someone with whom they disagreed. A similar incident occurred in October 1969 when Dr. William Shockley, a Nobel Prize-winning physicist (as co-inventor of the transistor), came to campus to speak at a meeting of the National Academy of Sciences. Shockley promoted eugenics, the view that high birth rates among the less intelligent (including poor blacks) were having a deleterious effect on the human species and should be discouraged, a view that understandably infuriated civil rights advocates. As he attempted to begin his address he was drowned out by a group of black students who clapped continuously, and he subsequently left without speaking at all. WDCR newsmen Zrike and Graves taped an interview with Shockley but, in a rare instance of censorship, the station declined to air it.[10]

Meanwhile drug use had begun to spread on campus, particularly after the "Beatles Summer" of 1967 (the group's landmark album *Sgt. Pepper's Lonely Hearts Club Band*, widely seen as an invitation to "turn on," was at the height of its popularity).[11] As one student put it, it changed "campus consumption from booze to weed" virtually overnight. This did not go unnoticed and in September 1967 newsman Arthur Fergenson caused an uproar with a broadcast commentary asserting that there were drugs and drug pushers on campus. The story was picked up by the statewide *Manchester Union Leader*, and Fergenson later claimed that he was blamed by fellow students for causing the destruction of more drugs than any other individual in Hanover. The administration did not deny the charge, and in January launched its first sweeping drug probe.[12]

Arthur Friend Fergenson—nicknamed "Friendly" Fergenson—was one of the colorful characters who inhabited the station in this period, a campus gadfly and proud conservative who delighted in tweaking the liberals then dominating campus debates. He delivered a regular commentary on the 6:00 p.m. news from 1966 to 1969.

He says that there were few attempts to rein him in, once exception being when he announced the formation of COGRA ("The Committee on George Romney's Appearance"), mocking the handsome, square-jawed, centrist 1968 presidential candidate who was ultimately driven out of the race due to his repeated gaffes in interviews. At various times Fergenson played a Jewish Santa Claus, hosted a call-in talk show, and co-anchored the evening news with the very liberal Bob Reich. He was frequently at odds with Martha Luehrmann, a faculty wife and self-described "flaming liberal" who often appeared on the station. Nevertheless, Fergenson, Reich, and Luehrmann were all good friends.[13]

Meanwhile opposition to the war was growing louder and more vociferous. By early 1968 lines of protesters were standing silently in front of a flag on the College green every Wednesday at noon, visible from WDCR's windows in Robinson Hall. Fergenson organized a line of war supporters to face them. In the spring one-third of seniors said in a survey that they wouldn't serve in Vietnam if drafted. Then during June graduation ceremonies, James Newton '68 gave a fiery anti-war valedictory address, hoping for a U.S. defeat and urging students to refuse to serve. On the hugely publicized "Moratorium to End the War" day, October 15, 1969, as millions marched across the country, Program Director David Graves devoted an entire day to listener calls and discussions. This was followed a month later by a massive march on Washington. Gambaccini, Graves and filmmaker Bill Aydelott ("Eye-de-lot") '72 piled into the station's own station wagon and drove to Washington to cover the event. While there they relayed audio reports back to Hanover. In true collegiate fashion they bunked with somebody's girlfriend, got tear gassed at DuPont Circle, and witnessed anti-war music stars Pete Seeger and Ritchie Havens singing "Give Peace a Chance" to a vast crowd—accompanied by none other than the squarest conductor on the planet, Mitch Miller. To listeners back in Hanover, New Hampshire, this was exciting stuff![14]

Not all was mobs and tear gas, however. Gambaccini also recalls interviewing The Peace Pilgrim (Mildred Ryder), a 60-ish lady in a blue track suit and sneakers who had been walking back and forth across the country for peace since the 1950s, as she walked through Hanover.[15]

One of the most memorable events of these years for many students was WDCR's live broadcast of the first national draft lottery on December 1, 1969. It had a very personal meaning for most Dartmouth students (still all males), as the numbered birthdates being drawn in a nationally televised lottery determined who would be first to be drafted—and in all likelihood, sent to fight in Vietnam. Large posters were placed on the walls of the station, with the dates posted as they were announced, and a crowd gathered. Everywhere on campus radios were tuned to the station. Young men who drew a high numbered date (unlikely to be drafted) pumped their fists in the air and cheered while some who drew low numbers (first to go) were literally in tears. Staffer Tim McKeever '72 recalled, "you could hear outbursts from the dorms and frat houses, some cheering, some swearing." It drew quite possibly the largest audience in station history.[16]

## The Occupation of Parkhurst Hall

All of these events were but supporting acts, however, to the dramatic moment that will be burned into Dartmouth's history for as long as the College stands. As might be expected, it came about as the culmination of a long series of developments. Anti-war campus organizations had begun to coalesce in 1966, and by 1968 were given a major boost by screaming headlines of riots and student uprisings across the country and in Europe. Student occupation of buildings at Columbia University in the spring of 1968, and their violent expulsion by New York City police, received national attention. In early April 1969 students at Harvard occupied Harvard Hall to protest the presence of the Reserve Officer Training Corps (ROTC) on that campus, before being expelled by baton swinging, mace-wielding police. The times were ripe for action at Dartmouth.

In 1968 members of the Dartmouth Students for a Democratic Society (SDS) had blocked army recruiters, and during early 1969 there were public debates and forums about both U.S. involvement in Vietnam and the future of ROTC at Dartmouth. In February 1969 the faculty voted to recommend phasing out ROTC. On April 22 nearly 300 students and faculty members staged a peaceful sit-in in Parkhurst Hall, the administration building, to demand the immediate end of the program.[17] This led to two referendums, among students (April 28) and faculty (May 5), which showed a split between those who wanted ROTC phased out gradually (to accommodate those students still enrolled in it) or ended immediately. The SDS, led by David H. Green '71, had had enough.

Just after 3:00 p.m. on Tuesday, May 6, 1969, about 50 SDS members and supporters gathered on the Green and marched in a phalanx into Parkhurst, systematically evicting the inhabitants.[18] Some, including Dean Thaddeus Seymour, were forcibly carried out. President John Sloan Dickey left peacefully, after arguing with students outside his office. The protestors then nailed shut the huge oak doors of the building, hung anti-war banners from the windows, and draped a scarlet flag emblazoned with a picture of Che Guevara from the president's office window. There was no violence and students (and a few supportive faculty) continued to come and go from the building while the students chanted and sang Beatles and Bob Dylan songs.

Even before the occupation word had spread that it was about to take place, and WDCR newsmen rushed to the scene, which was only a few hundred yards from their studios. Gambaccini was the first to arrive, even before the protestors (busy secretaries looked at him curiously, wondering why he was there with a tape recorder), then began taping comments from alarmed administrators as they were being hustled out ("Don't you have any *manners*?" said one to an underclassman who was pulling him by the arm). The tapes were quickly edited and played on the 5:00 p.m. news for the whole region to hear.

A crowd estimated at between 800 and 1,300 gathered outside the building. Or rather, several crowds gathered. Some were supporters, some were unsympathetic faculty and conservative students. Students Behind Dartmouth (SBD) staged a counterdemonstration by dressing in suits and ties, singing Dartmouth songs and practicing football cheers. Another group, Students Against Pineapple Pancakes (SAPP), was apparently a satire. Reporting on all this from the Parkhurst steps was Dave Graves, who by now had a live link back to the station.

Meanwhile the administration moved swiftly, obtaining an injunction against the protestors from a local court by around 5:30 p.m. This was read to the protestors, accompanied by several moving deadlines, but the protestors refused to leave. New Hampshire Governor Walter Peterson arrived on the scene, and state police and National Guard troops began assembling at the Lebanon armory. Finally, at around

3:00 a.m. the following morning, they arrived in a convoy of busses. It was a dramatic, almost cinematic scene with lights and bullhorns as the students were given one last chance to vacate. When they did not, the police broke down the door and carried out 56 people, one by one, through a long cordoned-off line to the waiting busses. Unlike the situation at other campuses there was no violence, which obviously disappointed some of the protestors, one of whom cried into a WDCR microphone, "I've been maced" (no mace was used, nor did the police use weapons or clubs).

All of this was broadcast on WDCR, which subsequently was flooded with requests from the national media for information and audio clips. Bill Aydelott had shot film of the event and was involved in an auto accident while rushing the footage to White River Junction for immediate shipment to Boston and the major media. Unhurt but resourceful, and knowing that he was responsible for the accident, he crawled out of the wrecked car and filmed the scene. Later, when he was charged with reckless driving, he convinced the judge to suspend the sentence on condition that he donate the film of the wreck for use in a public service announcement.

The following night a large crowd marched on President Dickey's home, and finding him not there proceeded to the home of Dean Seymour. The popular dean emerged in pajamas to talk to the crowd, and asked them not to wake his children. The crowd wound up cheering him.

In the aftermath of the occupation 54 students were arrested and those convicted were given 30-day sentences which they served in jails around the state. Only a few were suspended from the College, and one—David Green—was expelled.[19] Two junior faculty members also left. ROTC also left campus, not to return until the 1980s.

### Music Programming: Rock 'n' Roll Is Here to Stay

Although it had a robust news department, WDCR was by this time a top 40 station with music filling most of its schedule. By 1966 *Swinghouse* had been replaced weekday afternoons from 3:00-5:00 p.m. by the more appropriately named *Sounds for the Tri-Town*, playing hit songs from the station's weekly top 25 list. Judging from a description given by chart compiler Gambaccini, who had been given the job as a freshman because of his intense fascination with the music business and record charts, its compilation had apparently become more art than science.[20] "Gambo" did check with local record stores (whose sales of individual titles were usually in the single digits), notably Modern Music in Lebanon, but his rankings were equally determined by what was moving up the national charts as reported in *Billboard* and *Cashbox* and on his own intuition about what would be "the next big hit." The goal was for WDCR to be ahead of what was popular, not just reflect it. If he couldn't rationalize putting a great new record on the chart, it might become Pick Hit of the Week or Sleeper of the Week, and thus be exposed on *Sounds for the Tri-Town* or the even more popular *Music 'til Midnight*.

Although their shows had prescribed formats, d.j.'s did have some latitude in what they played. One record familiar to all was the Beatles' "Hey Jude," which was the station "bathroom record." It was so named because at seven minutes and 20 seconds in length, it allowed a d.j. with an urgent need to relieve himself time to run down to the second floor bathroom and back before it ended.[21] Apparently

Dartmouth men of the late '60s had weaker bladders than their predecessors. The "bathroom record" of the early 1960s was Marty Robbins' "El Paso," which clocked in at only four minutes 40 seconds (I recall that this disc was hung on a nail in the studio wall, to be grabbed quickly in case of emergencies). Whenever either of these records was played, insiders knew where the disc jockey was.

Among the top d.j.'s of this era were Gary Erickson '67, Scott McQueen '68 and Tom Draper '68. (After graduation McQueen and fellow d.j.'s Randy Odeneal '68 and Ted Nixon '68 would form Sconnix Broadcasting, which became a highly successful radio group that owned stations in large and small markets.[22]) Draper was responsible for a show called *The Rhythm and Blues Hall of Fame*. Gambaccini took it over in 1967 and, inspired, produced his own *Ten Years of Motown* special. However when black activist and d.j. Wally Ford '70 expressed an interest in doing a similar show, Gambaccini had a self-described "crisis of conscience." Perhaps a rhythm and blues show *should* be hosted by an African-American. Ford got his show, despite concerns that he might use it as a racial soapbox (which he did not). In April 1968 he did deliver an impassioned editorial on the night of the Martin Luther King assassination, but the entire station suspended regular programming to broadcast tributes to the fallen civil rights leader that day. The only time Ford says he got into trouble was when he played the Beatles' "Why Don't We Do It in the Road?"[23]

Then Ford created a show that would serve as the template for a black-hosted programming block that would endure on WDCR for the next 15 years. In early 1969 he asked for and was given a slot four nights a week at 1:00 a.m., when the station normally signed off, so that he could stay on for as long as he wished, and play whatever he wished—a free form mix of jazz, soul, comedy, and artists little heard on the station of that day, such as Roberta Flack and Jimi Hendrix. Ford was well known on campus and the show, called *What's Happening?* (how '70s!), got a good reaction. Once he said he'd end the show unless he got 20 calls, and the switchboard was flooded by calls from students and professors. The name of the show came from a chance remark. Ford almost missed the first broadcast, running to the station and into the studio. As he was getting ready to sit down the engineer asked "What's the name of this show?" Ford didn't hear the question and blurted out "What's happening?"[24] And so it became, called that for years to come.

By September 1969 WDCR expanded to all-night broadcasting, with *What's Happening?* from 1:00 to about 2:30 a.m., a mix of music (some nights underground rock, some nights "underground classical") from 2:30 to 5:30, then *Dawn Patrol*.[25]

WDCR did more for music on campus than just play records. In January 1966 it co-sponsored and broadcast a highly successful concert in the Hopkins Center, with folk singers, rock bands, and the Dartmouth chorus the Injunaires. Four to five hundred students and their dates attended. The station also interviewed the many "name acts" who performed on campus, including the Lovin' Spoonful, Ray Charles, and radical poet Allen Ginsburg (who cursed at skeptical students, "Fuck you in the mouth!"—which promptly became a dormitory catch phrase).[26]

Few visiting celebrities made as great an impression as legendary singer Judy Garland, who visited the campus in January 1967 along with Tom Green '60, who was working with her on her autobiography (and was also, reportedly, her lover). She stayed for four days and shot pool with the studly brothers of Alpha Theta, of which Green had once been president. "I'd love to live in Hanover" she cooed, but she never came back.[27]

WDCR had at least one rock star on its own staff. Disc jockey Wayne Wadhams '68 had organized a garage band ("The D-Men") before he came to Dartmouth. They got a recording contract and in the summer of 1967 scored a national hit under the name the Fifth Estate with a rock version of "Ding Dong! The Witch Is Dead." Ironically this old chestnut, from *The Wizard of Oz*, was intended as a sarcastic protest song, but most took it as a catchy novelty and it reached number 11 on the national charts. Wadhams took the 1967-68 year off to tour with his band, ultimately graduating in 1969. He went on to a long career in music, producing and teaching.[28]

### Sports and Other Programming

Sports remained a key component of the WDCR schedule, especially during football season. This was the era of coach Bob Blackman, which some consider Dartmouth's golden age, and sponsors lined up to be on broadcasts of the powerhouse team that was winning repeated Ivy League championships. Among the play-by-play announcers was Richard "Sandy" Alderson '69, who would later become general manager of the Oakland Athletics and the New York Mets. In 1963 a professional Dartmouth Football Network had been organized by WVTR, but it collapsed. In 1965 WDCR formed its own Dartmouth Football Network, which got off to a shaky start when sponsors held out, but stations in Laconia, Keene, Newport, and Claremont soon joined and the venture became profitable. WDCR's success led to some friction with the Dartmouth College Athletic Council (DCAC), which dreamed of syndicating coverage, perhaps with professional announcers, and making a bundle for itself. DCAC threatened to revoke the station's rights to the games, but the College backed the station. This pattern would be repeated in the future, as the DCAC periodically sought to either extract more revenue or cancel the coverage rights, while the station argued that football was essential to its finances and image.[29]

Other notable programs of the late 1960s included *Pooh Corner* (c.1967), a charming Sunday morning children's show featuring faculty wife and actress Martha Luehrmann reading stories and talking with children from the Hanover community. It would run for nearly 18 years, hosted by Luehrmann and others.[30]

In an unusual episode, WDCR and *The Dartmouth* joined forces in late 1967 to co-sponsor a Dartmouth team on *GE College Bowl*, an erudite NBC-TV quiz show (they had such things then). A Dartmouth team had appeared on the show in 1960, coached by WDCR advisor Almon Ives, and won three weeks in a row before losing to New York University. This time there was a big build-up during the winter, with try-outs, practice sessions and coaching by faculty members. The administration fretted, but concluded that it would be good publicity because the nationwide telecast would include a short film about the College. The team was top-notch, beating all local comers, but when it appeared on the network on March 31, 1968, it lost in its first match-up, to the University of Southern California, in a hotly contested game.[31]

### *Let's Help* Is Born

One of the most notable charity initiatives in the history of Dartmouth Broadcasting was born in 1967. *Let's Help* was an elaborately orchestrated two-month charity drive held in the fall, focusing on a single beneficiary, and consisting of numerous elements including remote broadcasts and a fund-raising dance on December 9. The first beneficiary was the Save the Children Federation and raised money for a clinic in the Vietnamese village of Ngoc Thanh. According to participant Larry Barnet '68 it was inspired by those pro and anti-war protests taking place on campus. He recalled that "[At least] we could all agree on helping the children affected by the war." Director Bill Moyes '70 commented at the time "Our opinion of the war is irrelevant, the purpose is to help the people." It touched a chord with idealistic students and townspeople and was a striking success, raising $3,000 and winning a public service award from competitor WNHV.[32] For the next several years *Let's Help* was an annual WDCR event.

The second annual *Let's Help* was launched in October 1968 to benefit A Better Chance, a program to help educate minority kids in local area schools.[33] This one was highlighted by a 39-hour marathon on the weekend of the Dartmouth-Harvard football game, hosted by d.j. Paul Gambaccini and newsman Jeff Kelley, who took pledges with record requests and attempted to stay awake all weekend. The station was teeming with volunteers, manning the phones and taking pledges, pulling record requests to be played, and bringing in food from the Red Door delicatessen. It got off to a good start but after a short time was violently interrupted by the news story of the year (at least in Hanover), the horrific Moose Mountain airplane crash. Staffers were pulled away to cover the breaking story, calls were coming in from wire services seeking the latest information—it was chaos! One more catastrophe then hit; that food from the Red Door turned out to be tainted, causing mass food poisoning, including weary d.j. Gambaccini. Miraculously, though, the unfolding tragedy only encouraged donations, and the campaign ultimately topped its goal, raising over $4,500.

The third *Let's Help*, in November 1969, benefited the Lebanon Regional Vocational Training Center. Events included a 37-hour marathon, trick or treating on Halloween, a day on which students could forgo dinner in return for a donation by the dining hall to the campaign, and a November 24 Celebrity Day on which college and local notables hosted or appeared on many WDCR programs. One of those appearing was WNHV owner Rex Marshall. Shows with special hosts or guests included *Daybreak, Tri-Town Talk Back, Noon Hour* (with President Dickey), *Sounds for the Tri-Town,* and *Music 'til Midnight*. Directing the campaign were Randall Davis '70, James Coakley '72, and Peter Walkley '71. Nearly $6,000 was raised, which was used as matching funds to obtain an even larger federal grant. Center Director Roger Allen said, "WDCR has helped in many ways other than money. In a community project of this nature money isn't everything—the publicity really sold it to the community."[34]

### Things of Beauty

Like most commercial stations WDCR staged periodic promotions, among them an annual Frisbee giveaway starting in the spring of 1968. The "professional model" Wham-o Frisbees were awarded to those who submitted the most innovative "Things of Beauty." Hundreds of listeners sent in all sorts of unusual objects that they considered a thing of beauty. Some even came from schools that made it a class project. The submissions, some personally delivered to the station, included collages, murals, pictures of loved ones, a tape loop of a man's heartbeat, a South American butterfly, a porcupine, a picture of a $10,000 bill, a delicious blueberry pie, a piece of a woman's wedding veil, and even a live baby. One young lady submitted herself, and won instantly. Many of these objects (presumably excluding the baby and the young lady) were displayed in the rotunda of the Hopkins Center. The station said "WDCR would like to thank all those who spent time and energy to prove that beauty still exists in this desolate world."[35]

In another promotion the grand prize was a Kawasaki motorcycle, a prize so totally cool that staffers of course had to test drive it. One almost crashed it, but the bike survived and was duly awarded to a lucky listener.[36]

## Summer Broadcasting

The long-held dream of year-round broadcasting was finally realized in 1965. Summer broadcasting had been an urgent priority since the introduction of a regular Dartmouth summer school in 1963, in which students and adults (including women) arrived on campus to take not-for-credit courses. General Manager Ryan, Sean Hennessey '67 and Dave Houston kept the station on the air during the summer of 1965 under an agreement worked out with the College by which they enrolled in and received credit for a summer course, which was offset by a reduced course load during the regular school year. The course enrollment was necessary due to the Department of Labor requirement that station staff be enrolled students. They were also provided with free room and board. They were augmented by female summer exchange students Frederika Moxon and Kathy Hilgenderoff from Vassar, Mark Blanchard '66, Art Lewis '66, Steve Dalphin '69, Bob Cohn '66, Bob Sauer '66, Dick Roth, and Hanover High student Dian Lewis as station secretary/newsperson (a few years later local student Meg Colton served as a summer newsreader). The station initially operated from noon to midnight.[37]

Unfortunately a similar agreement could not be reached in 1966 (the College wanted too much of the station's advertising revenue to make it feasible), so there was no summer broadcasting that year. However in 1967 a new agreement was reached. Six staffers received free room and board, took one summer course each without charge, and had a reduced course load (and tuition) in the spring and fall.[38] Among those keeping the lights on in summer 1967 were future GMs Kelley and Gambaccini, along with Scott McQueen, Henry Allen '69, Chris Kern '69, Fred Ochs '69, and Lyle Nyberg '69. From this point on WDCR stayed on the air year-round.[39]

## The Station Prospers

The community responded to WDCR's strong programming, and the station prospered financially. Advertising revenues, which hovered in the $20,000-$25,000 range during fiscal years 1965, 1966 and 1967, rose to $30,000 in 1969 and approximately $45,000 in 1970.[40] Powering this surge was a group of enthusiastic student salesmen led by Sales Directors Bob Throndsen '69 and Ken Jones '70 and station President Stu Zuckerman. Stu brought in Harold H. Segal of Boston to be the station's regional sales representative, and arranged remotes from store openings and promotions for area advertisers such as the Killington Skiway. Among the sponsors most familiar to listeners were Ward Amidon Jewelers, Miller Auto, Purity Supreme supermarkets, and the Super Duper food store (famous for its jingly time tones). In addition a rejuvenated Ivy Network was feeding national ads to the station. WDCR played an important role in the new success of the multi-school sales network. The network's May 1965 convention was held in Hanover, presided over by network president John Catlett (Tuck '66) and with Metromedia radio head John V.B. Sullivan '36 as the featured speaker. Three years later, in 1968, WDCR Business Manager E. Doane Grinnell '69 was elected chairman of the network.[41]

There was new competition. White River Junction's WWRJ, founded in 1959, had struggled, then morphed into WVTR in 1963. In the summer of 1966 it was sold by Frederick Daley to nationally known actor and pitchman Rex Marshall, the "voice" of such products as Reynolds Aluminum, Auto-Lite Spark Plugs and Maxwell House Coffee. A dynamic competitor, he hosted a classy interview show called *Breakfast at the Hanover Inn* right down the street from Robinson Hall. He changed the call letters from WVTR to WNHV and the programming to country music (which was popular in the region).[42] Listeners could now choose between top 40 on WDCR, country hits on WNHV, or soft Mantovani-type music on traditional market leader WTSL. The latter presented what one WDCR staffer called "terrible" news ("One announcer insists on calling the Chinese Communist Party leader Mao Te-Sung"[43]).

Television was coming to the Upper Valley as well, if haltingly. Residents with well-placed antennas could pull in a few distant stations, while others signed up for limited cable service from Twin States Television, Inc., which had begun operation in the mid 1950s. By the early 1960s Twin States was offering five stations (from Boston, Burlington, Vermont, and Poland Spring, Maine), for $4.95 per month. It had about 1,800 subscribers in 1963, rising to 3,000 by 1966.

September 1966 saw the launch of WRLH-TV in Lebanon, owned by local TV dealer Nelson Crawford and affiliated with NBC. This was the area's first and, as it would turn out, only local commercial TV station. It was a low power UHF station on channel 31, and was perhaps the smallest NBC affiliate in the nation. Broadcasting in black and white (already out of date in 1966), with a staff of about eight people, it nevertheless produced some local news programming. In April 1968 the University of New Hampshire's educational station WENH-TV in faraway Durham, set up a local relay station on channel 15.[44]

Radio was the dominant medium in the market however, and the student station was a powerful competitor to the two local commercial stations. A preference survey conducted in the spring of 1965 showed that WDCR was strong and largely unchanged from the 1963 Brooks study, but that WVTR had become the number one station in the market at the expense of WTSL. A telephone listenership survey conducted in December 1967 by a class at the Tuck School of Business showed WDCR to be overwhelmingly dominant in Hanover in the morning, and also competitive in the tri-town area as a whole (41 percent share of audience, vs. WNHV's 47 percent and WTSL's 12 percent). By early 1967 WNHV was proposing to bring in the Pulse radio survey company to field a professional (and expensive) listenership survey, the first in the market since 1954, to show how far they'd come.[45] There is no indication that this actually took place however.

## Technical

WDCR's Technical Department showed its mettle on November 9, 1965, when a massive power blackout hit the eastern United States and Canada, plunging approximately 30 million people into the dark. Staffers scrambled to find a generator and got the station back on the air within about an hour and a quarter, after which News Director Owen Leach and Chief Announcer Bob Buck broadcast continuous reports to worried residents of the Upper Valley. WDCR was for a time the only area station that was on the air. It received kudos for its timely reporting, including from President Dickey and members of the college administration who said that "they were once again convinced that WDCR was indispensable to the Dartmouth community."[46]

In early 1966 WDCR was named the official Emergency Broadcast System station for the region (EBS had replaced the earlier Conelrad notification system). Reflecting the cold war mentality of the day, a special bomb shelter studio with backup power and a line to the White House was constructed beneath the Hopkins Center for use in case of a national emergency. Fortunately it never had to be used.[47]

The EBS designation was an honor, but not without its scary moments. A few years later on a Saturday morning in February 1971 the teletype machine went berserk, continuously ringing its bells with an Emergency Action Notification from the government, meaning that WDCR was supposed to go into attack mode immediately and all other stations in the area were going off the air. The senior staffer checked the security codes on file and found that the message was authentic. As one last check he decided to see if WBZ, the 50,000 watt EBS station in Boston was broadcasting alerts, but "it was still rocking and rolling" (even though at least one of its competitors had gone off the air). It turned out that a low-level operator at the federal command center in Colorado had put up the wrong tape and sent out an alert instead of a test to stations across the country! Hanover listeners never knew.[48]

Of more immediate import to on-air personnel was the installation, at last, of three Spotmaster cartridge machines in September 1966, for playback of commercials and interstitials. These replaced bulky Ampex reel-to-reel tape decks that had used tiny three-inch reels of tape which were constantly getting tangled or lost. Other new equipment was also installed. In 1969 WDCR acquired its first news vehicle, a large and somewhat unwieldy Ford station wagon without power steering, obtained as a trade-out with a local auto dealer. After a few years the beast was replaced with a smaller, more manageable Chevy Nova wagon.[49]

The busy disc jockey studio was upgraded in 1967, at a cost of $5,000.[50] The studio, which had been located at the back of the building overlooking the college dining hall (an unappetizing site!), was moved to the front with a sweeping view of the always-active College Green and in view of passing motorists, who would sometimes honk their horns. This placed it adjacent to master control, facilitating switching between studios when necessary. The media played were vinyl 45s and LPs, with jingles and advertisements on the recently acquired cartridge machines.

### Station Management

The Directorate, which ran the station, continued to evolve as student leaders grappled with how best to manage the rapidly growing organization. In 1967 the position of administrative director was replaced with an assistant general manager (Laurence Barnet), but this lasted for only a year. Finding a student willing to focus on management of the unglamorous "back office" continued to prove difficult. In 1968 the Directorate was enlarged to six members, adding the sales and news directors, both of whom had taken on increased responsibility in the new WDCR. In

1969 there were two very strong candidates for general manager. So as not to lose either, a unique structure was created in which Paul Gambaccini was named chairman and general manager (responsible for air product) and Stu Zuckerman became president (responsible for sales and finances). It worked because the two worked well together, but shared leadership would be the exception in subsequent years.[51]

As one of the most visible and influential organizations on campus the station attracted a large number of recruits, with staff numbering 100 to 150 during most terms. WDCR was widely perceived as a place where the best could rise irrespective of their personal characteristics or connections. Even as minority rights tensions were beginning to surface on campus (principally involving African Americans and Native Americans), no one accused the radio station of being anything other than a true meritocracy. Black activist and d.j. Wally Ford, who was also president of the Afro-American Society, commented that he simply had to prove himself and work his way up. Later black staffers would have a different attitude, however.[52]

WDCR certainly looked hip and cool in an unusual recruiting film produced for the station by Bill Aydelott in 1968-69. *WDCR Mission Impossible* was a six-minute epic modeled on the then-popular TV series *Mission: Impossible*, consisting of fast cuts of existing clips and staged sequences. There were glimpses of national political candidates being interviewed by student newsmen, a Hanover police car racing down the road with WDCR's news cruiser (the station wagon emblazoned with a station logo and emergency lights) seemingly in close pursuit, an interview in progress with President Dickey, announcers and engineers in the studios, at sports events, and in the record library, and even some comic bits (a newsman first interviewing a dog, then an apparently unconscious athlete). All of this was set to Lalo Shifrin's throbbing music from the TV series. Among those making their acting debuts in the film were Mark "Loon" Stitham '72, Paul Gambaccini, Win Rockwell, Bill Moyes, Chris Brewster '72, Stu Zuckerman, John Marshall '71, John Lippman '71, Curt Welling '71, and Aydelott himself.[53] The clever film was used as a recruiting tool for years to come. Aydelott shot other films of station hi-jinx, and—not surprisingly—went on to become a professional filmmaker.

Despite student enthusiasm for the station the time commitment it demanded, particularly of its senior leaders, continued to be a problem. There were many discussions about this with the administration, and in 1965 the College experimented with granting the top five managers of WDCR (and also the top five staffers at *The Dartmouth*) a reduced course load.[54]

### The Board of Overseers Is Established

A significant organizational move, and one that would become highly consequential in the future, was the formation of the WDCR Board of Overseers in March 1966. It consisted of four administration or faculty representatives and the student Directorate, and was intended to be an oversight body, replacing the Council on Student Organizations (COSO), but dedicated exclusively to the station. It would not run the station, but rather serve as an advocate within the administration, act as a sounding board for the students, and approve major decisions such as those involving financial commitments. According to Assistant College Treasurer John Bryant, one of the founding members, it was formed not because of any crisis but rather because the station had become "a business" and he wanted to give the students "a better experience." Another founding member, longtime station advisor Professor Almon Ives, recalled that "consideration was given to proposals that would have limited the autonomy of the student directors," but "President Dickey apparently felt that student control was important."[55]

Joining Bryant and Ives on the original board were George O'Connell from the College News Service (soon replaced by public relations man Bob Graham) and Dean Thaddeus Seymour, although the latter was never really involved.[56] The chairman was the student general manager. One meeting was normally held per term, and there was an annual dress-up dinner at an overseer's home to provide an opportunity to socialize.

In years to come the overseers would exert increasing—though never total—control over the station. For now, however, the students were still very much in charge.

### What About the Alumni?

Up to this point the station had had little organized contact with its growing body of alumni, other than to periodically invite a notable alumnus to address a meeting or dinner. Among those so invited were NBC president Pat Weaver '30 and Metromedia broadcasting executive John V.B. Sullivan '36, at the WDCR 10th anniversary banquet in March 1968.[57]

In January 1966 the station launched the *WDCR Alumni Newsflash*, a chatty eight page newsletter edited by Public Relations Director Mike Ryan '68 and sent to several hundred station alumni. It did not request donations, or anything else, but simply shared news of the station with alumni who had walked its corridors and who remembered those days fondly. It was apparently the first widely circulated alumni mailing, and was worth saving for a reason no one could have known at the time. The clever cartoon adorning the front page was drawn by none other than sophomore Robert Reich, who would later become internationally known (albeit not for his artistic skills).

Another *Alumni Newsflash* was published c.February 1967, edited by Doane Grinnell, and claimed a circulation "nearing 500." However no more would be issued for the next 10 years. Thereafter they would appear sporadically.

### Dean Seymour's Traveling Road Show

Alumni also heard about the booming campus station via a unique road show headed by the popular Dean Seymour ("a dean, a magician, a barker, a talent scout, and no mean shot with a snowball"). "Dartmouth on the Road," organized and ring-led by Seymour, traveled up and down the East Coast introducing "alumni, high school students and others to some of the diversity of Dartmouth students' interests." It was first fielded in 1967, and the 1969 edition consisted of Seymour and 30 students including an engineering major who had developed a foam-type fire extinguisher, a computer geek (a novelty then) demonstrating Dartmouth's pioneering time-sharing system, foreign studies students, and the Dartmouth Five, a Dixieland band that entertained. WDCR's busy Bill Aydelott contributed two films, one about the radio station and the other illustrating "the facilities of the College with a *Laugh-In* type format." Popular disc jockey "Wild Bill" Moyes co-produced both the show and a promotional spot called "Reggie Wrinkle's Floating Opera" that was used to promote it. He said the spot "confounds the adults and delights the youngsters."[58]

## A Capsule Lost in Time?

One mystery of the late 1960s is the 200-year time capsule allegedly buried under the College Green by the class of 1969, containing campus artifacts including tapes of programming from WDCR. Two long stories about the project appeared in *The Dartmouth*, with extensive details on the organizers and their plans. However when I interviewed those gentlemen 40 years later they claimed to know nothing about it. Neither did the general manager or program director of WDCR at the time.[59] Was it a hoax, or is there a time capsule lurking beneath the Hanover soil, waiting to unleash the raucous sounds of 1960s Dartmouth radio? If so, the memories of all associated with the project must have been buried with it.

## FM Discussions Begin

The seed that would grow into the next great chapter in Dartmouth Broadcasting history was planted in the spring of 1969. FM radio was broadcasting's stepchild, and little thought had been given to seeking an FM frequency for Dartmouth. The AM station was thriving. However newly appointed General Manager Paul Gambaccini thought that an FM station might be a good way to obtain more air slots to accommodate the legions of students who wanted to be broadcasters. So he raised the possibility of applying for an FM license at a Board of Overseers meeting. "The station was hot," he later recalled, and "the motion passed easily."[60]

He put together a proposal and sent it to Alex Fanelli, special assistant to President Dickey, for comment. In it he emphasized that the present organization was strong and could handle the added responsibility; that FM, while still small, was growing rapidly; that his burgeoning staff needed more air slots; and that it could and should be commercial. He noted how well Dartmouth's original $30,000 investment in AM had paid off, with the station now estimated to be worth $200,000. "FM may very well become more listened-to and more respected than AM," he wrote. "This is not the way it is today, but it may very well be the situation tomorrow."

Finally, there was a need to act, as there was only one FM frequency available in the area. "The need for action is urgent. If we are to act, we must act now, before someone else seals off our FM chances."[61]

There were three key decision makers in the administration to whom the president looked for advice on such matters: the dean of the College, the provost, and the treasurer. Treasurer's representative Bryant, who was also an overseer, recalled pitching the idea to Dickey, saying somewhat dramatically (but presciently) that AM would eventually die out and they might have to shut the AM station down. FM, he said, was the future. Meanwhile station advisor Almon Ives helped drum up faculty support.[62]

In September Treasurer John Meck wrote that the trustees' Executive Committee had approved filing for the FM frequency, although they deferred a final decision on the $28,000 loan needed to pursue the matter. Another problem arose when the lawyers discovered that the Federal Communications Commission had placed a temporary freeze on multiple station ownership in a single market (as would be the case if Dartmouth owned both an AM and an FM station). At the same time a fall survey of community leaders and residents revealed that WDCR was highly appreciated in Hanover and that there was public support for an FM sibling.[63]

Gambaccini had optimistically projected that it might take a couple of years to get an FM station on the air. In fact it took more than three times that long, with many battles, many setbacks, and a lengthy campaign against formidable odds that recalled the battle for AM in the 1950s. It would occupy much of the time and energy of the next six Directorates, but ultimately it would secure the future of Dartmouth Broadcasting.

### The End of One Era, the Beginning of Another

For 25 years President John Sloan Dickey had been a friend and supporter of (and occasionally a stern parent to) independent, student-run radio at Dartmouth. It is doubtful that "the only commercial, full-power AM station in the nation run completely by students" would have existed without him. Now, in 1969, he announced that he would retire the following spring. He was succeeded on March 1, 1970, by the brilliant mathematics professor and computer pioneer John Kemeny, who had once written computerized vote projection programs for WDCR's election coverage. Kemeny would prove to be an equally strong supporter of station independence, even though he would ruefully remark of the station the College had created, "you aren't anyone until you have been misquoted by WDCR."[64]

# Chapter 8

# 1970-1976: The Struggle to Launch FM

The 1960s bequeathed to the 1970s a strong, independent WDCR, one that by all accounts had handled the turmoil of the late 1960s exceptionally well, with its reputation not only intact but burnished. So far, at least, Dartmouth's experiment with student-run commercial broadcasting was proving to be a striking success. The Directorates of the early 1970s continued the station's momentum, with strong programming and service to the community. They faced two new major challenges, however: the unexpectedly long and torturous battle to launch an FM station, and what would become perhaps the greatest financial crisis in the station's history. In addition they had to deal with the delicate issues of integrating women into the previously all-male staff as Dartmouth went co-ed, demands from African-American staffers, and the most concerted attack on the station's independence in its history.

General managers during this stormy period were John Marshall '71, William Downall '72, Fred Frawley '73, Carter Yates '74 (who used the title Chairman of the Board), David Hunt '75, and Chris Davidson '76.

## Sales: Going Off a Cliff

As the decade began everything was rosy in sales. The momentum of the late 1960s continued into the new decade, and the station's case to advertisers was bolstered by the results of professional Mediastat listenership surveys commissioned by the station in 1970, 1971, 1972 and 1974. These surveys were cheaper than those conducted by Pulse or Arbitron, but were still nationally recognized. Although the numbers fluctuated, they showed WDCR highly competitive with WTSL and WNHV in the Hanover-Lebanon area. For example in the Spring 1971 Mediastat WDCR had a daily cumulative audience of 7,500 listeners, vs. 6,100 for WTSL and 5,600 for WNHV.[1]

The relatively young composition of WDCR's audience was desirable to some advertisers, a barrier to others. According to the early 1970s Mediastats approximately half the audience consisted of adults 18-34 and another quarter were teenagers, with the reminder split evenly between adults 35-49 and 50-plus. The gender breakdown was approximately 50 percent male and 50 percent female. Individual shows varied.[2]

Armed with these numbers Sales Director John Shapleigh '71 and his hustling staff (including Charlie Smith '73 and Dave Simpson '74) rang up nearly $58,000 in sales in 1970-71, a new record. With expenses at about $50,000, this produced a surplus of $8,000 to use toward future FM expenses. A system evolved that separated the initial sale from ongoing service of that account. Shapleigh and his men would land the accounts, but then a large pool of staffers, including d.j.'s, managers and even directorate members, would service them on an ongoing basis, each one hopefully building a relationship with his assigned merchants. This work was not optional; if a d.j. wanted a prime shift, he was expected to service at least three accounts. Once he ascertained the client's priorities, however, he could turn to the Production Department under John Rockwell '72 to produce the spots. Thus the work was spread around, and almost everyone at the station got involved to one degree or another. Among the prominent advertisers in the early 1970s were the Hanover Co-Op, Campion's men's clothing store, the Dartmouth Travel Agency, Gateway Motors, Michael's Radio & TV, Killington Skiway, Omer and Bob's Bike & Tennis Shop, Tallulah's Restaurant, and Smith Auto. The Ivy Network was beginning to struggle but did bring in national clients including Coca-Cola, Dunkin' Donuts and McDonald's.[3]

The 1970 boom was only a prelude, however. In early 1971 the sales director's position was taken over by energetic economics major Charlie Smith, who pushed the sales effort to the limits. Through a variety of hard-driving tactics, he propelled sales in 1971-72 to an astonishing $75,000, more than three times what it had been just five years earlier. Among other things he organized sales efforts by the calendar (e.g. Christmas packages went on the street around Labor Day, when budgets were being set); produced demonstration spots for potential advertisers; joined the Radio Advertising Bureau so that senior staffers could take their sales courses; placed emphasis on the Mediastat surveys to sell against the competition, which rarely used audience data; and hired and pushed new regional representatives (Campus Media, Inc., and Radio Time Sales, in addition to Harold Segal of Boston) to include the station in regional packages. A highly complimentary *Boston Globe* article about WDCR's extraordinary news department was widely distributed. Smith even showed prospects some of Bill Aydelott '72's films about the station. Some tactics were opportunistic. A year earlier Smith had gone on sales calls with Ken Jones '70 in which the two would announce themselves to receptionists as "Mr. Smith and Mr. Jones." The boss would come out just to see who "Smith and Jones" were. Other circumstances were simply good luck. There was a flood of political advertising in 1971-72 (Nixon, Muskie, McGovern), especially from Senator McGovern who "raised money in the morning and cut checks for ads in the afternoon"; and the College lifted its ban on beer advertising, a major product category at Dartmouth. Mrs. Hutchins (who did the logs and billing) was swamped.[4]

Expenses rose as well, but by the end of the fiscal year the station had a $20,000 surplus to use for future expenses, an all time record and more than the entire budget a few years earlier. The station was in awe, and the College was pleased. Overseer John Bryant reportedly told Smith, at graduation, "you're either going to make money or go to jail." Fortunately, it was the former.

The station's revenue problems slipped in quietly through the back door, as problems often do. Unfortunately Smith's stellar performance was a demonstration not only of the station's potential, but of its dependence on specific individuals. Smith graduated in 1972 (a year early) and was succeeded by managers who worked hard but could not keep up his pace. His immediate successor, Len Schulte '74, quit after a few weeks to work for WRLH-TV. Revenues dropped to $56,000, while expenses soared to $67,000, producing a significant loss that ate up half the surplus of the previous year. Then it got worse. According to some accounts, in 1973-74 revenues dropped below $50,000, while expenditures stayed at approximately $66,000, producing a cavernous deficit. Why? One later post mortem said that there was insufficient effort to "eliminate bad bookkeeping practices and increase profits." Another said that "the management was not in top form and all control of expenses was lost while next to no sales were made." Smith himself, who continued to work for stations in the area for a few years, felt the students of the 1970s just weren't "committed."[5]

That may have been a bit of an exaggeration, but in early 1974 incoming Sales Director Royce Yudkoff '77 complained that in recent months there had been no official head of the department, and no functioning members other than himself. The spread-the-work program, which required a good deal of coordination, had fallen apart. Staffers were driven off by an impossible workload; salesmen were now expected to make the sale, fill out contracts, write the commercials, and schedule them on the logs. Clients were not serviced, outdated copy was being run, appointments with new clients were made but no one showed up. Efforts to recruit new members for the department had failed. "The job of selling did not—and does not—appeal to most students," Yudkoff said. "The WDCR Sales Department is in critical condition."[6]

The test of an organization is not whether it runs into trouble, however. Virtually every organization, and certainly every business, does. What's important is whether it develops leadership that can meet those challenges. Arguably the most valuable lessons Dartmouth broadcasting can teach its student leaders come when there is adversity, not when the money is pouring in. The constant turnover of WDCR's leadership, which might seem like a weakness, can in some cases be a strength if "new blood," having learned the ropes during its first three years, is determined to do better than its predecessors during "its year."

Incoming General Manager David Hunt knew he faced a crisis. The College was having second thoughts about FM. With deficits this large there were serious questions about the ability of the students to run even one station. As one alumnus recalled, "David really confronted the financial woes of 'DCR very transparently and dramatically in a station meeting in Robinson that was unforgettable. He had a chart that showed us sinking into financial oblivion."[7] Expenditures were slashed. Staff was exhorted. Package plans (rather than just simple rotations) were introduced. A second-year Tuck Business School student was brought in to advise on marketing. A new national representative, Market 4 Radio in New York, was engaged (apparently displacing the Ivy Network). Station overseers were even asked to meet with important clients and try to mollify those who were angry about their mistreatment in recent months.

By November 1974 Hunt was able to report to the overseers that "sales right now... seem to be on the upswing. A capable staff consisting of Royce Yudkoff (sales director), Rich Zimmerman, and Dave Wood, with some help from others, is now turning the tide of ill-will created by the previous failures." Meanwhile Business Manager Al Goldin '76 went to work on billing and accounts receivable.[8]

There were intense discussions during 1974-75 about more fundamental changes in sales procedures. The first idea was to start paying student salesmen modest commissions, as did some other campus organizations such as *The Dartmouth*. The outgoing Carter Yates Directorate voted unanimously in favor of this, but the College lawyers shot it down on the grounds that it would violate the Labor Department rule that in order to avoid paying minimum wage to *all* staffers, the station had to remain an extracurricular activity in which *no* staffers were paid.[9] Another idea, to reward salesmen with some type of contest, also gained little traction.

## We'd Better Hire a Professional Salesman

By early 1975 talk had turned to the possibility of hiring a professional sales manager. This would represent a major change for a previously all student-run station, but the lawyers felt it was allowable if the individual was an independent contractor rather than a station employee. By mid year the station was ready to move forward. To soften the organizational blow, students would work with the newly hired professional, and hopefully learn from him or her. New General Manager Chris Davidson, a born diplomat, was given the unenviable job of approaching General Manager Jim Canto of WTSL (no friend of WDCR) and Rex Marshall of WNHV to notify them in advance and head off possible challenges when they found out that the student station was going to be sold locally by a professional salesman. They grumbled, but went along.[10]

It seemed like a good idea, but the first attempt at professional sales was a disaster. Following a series of interviews the station hired 38 year-old Alexander "Sandy" MacDonald, formerly with WTSN in Dover, New Hampshire, and WEEI in Boston, to begin on August 1, 1975.[11] He crashed and burned almost immediately. By September potential replacements were already being interviewed and in early October Davidson wrote that MacDonald "will be leaving us shortly."

What happened was not entirely clear, even at the time. MacDonald has been described as a rather rough-edged individual, with some personal problems, who had difficulty dealing with inexperienced students. One overseer later commented that the job was just too much for him. Few even remember him today.[12]

By November 1, 1975, a successor was in place. Lynn Mann was formerly with WCNL in Newport, New Hampshire, and WTSV in Claremont, New Hampshire, and operated as Lincoln Consultants. Smart, authoritative, and deep-voiced, she was well liked. She did not immediately turn sales around but did lay the foundation for eventual growth. She remained with the station for about two years, until mid 1977.[13]

While these efforts mended frayed relationships with advertisers, and gave the College some confidence that the student leadership was capable of dealing with problems, the financial results were mixed. The nation had tumbled into an economic recession that lasted from 1973-75, driven by a Mideast oil crisis, "stagflation" (inflation accompanied by a stagnant economy), and high unemployment. Hunt's administration was able to bring revenues up to about $53,000 and expenses down to $56,000, resulting in a modest loss. This was despite approximately $5,000 in capital expenses for FM equipment that year. However in 1975-76, with the leadership focused on other issues including getting FM on the air, income plummeted again, to $43,000. At the same time expenses soared to almost $70,000, creating an eye-popping deficit of $27,000. Even before the final numbers were in, overseers chairman Professor Jordan Baruch ("bah-roosh") commented that "in fact, the station has had a disastrous year financially."[14]

Things would get better. But it would take time.

## WDCR News Heard 'Round the World

The station was in decidedly better shape on the programming front. The WDCR News Department in particular outdid itself.

Elections were given far more extensive coverage than one would expect from a local station. The 1970 midterm elections were covered with numerous interviews leading up to election day in November. News Director Stephen Zrike '71 recalled covering President Nixon when he came to Montpelier, Vermont, to support a candidate, and meeting Nixon's press secretary Ron Ziegler. He told Ziegler that if the administration wanted to relate to young Americans it should reach out to the college press. A few months later Zrike got a surprise invitation to a presidential press conference in Washington, D.C., which he duly covered for WDCR listeners. On election night the station used a computerized prediction program developed by staffer Bic Jayne '73 and Professor Thomas Kurtz, and running on the pioneering Dartmouth Time Sharing System. It worked well except for one race, in which the loser was predicted to win by the winner's actual margin. It turned out the that the historical tables on which the projections were based had been reversed.[15]

In the run-up to the first-in-the-nation 1972 New Hampshire presidential primary newsman Bill Sigward '74 recalls covering an early 1971 press conference in Manchester held by George McGovern to promote his long-shot candidacy. A small group of local and regional reporters showed up then immediately left, leaving Sigward to conduct what was possibly the first in-depth interview with the appreciative candidate after he had entered the race. The primary itself was covered in-studio with reporters calling in reports from campaign headquarters across the state. Bill Downall and Bill Aydelott anchored, and Tim McKeever '72 was producer. There was a live remote from the Manchester headquarters of the leading Democratic candidate, Edmund Muskie, who won the primary by a small margin but would ultimately lose the nomination to anti-war candidate McGovern. On the Republican side newsman Jack Beeler '73 recalled the spirited campaign of anti-war Representative Pete McCloskey against President Nixon. WDCR's aggressive coverage won an award for "Best Election Coverage of the Year" from United Press International.[16]

The November 1972 election was thoroughly covered as well, with election night anchored by Sigward and produced by John D'Auria '74. The Nixon landslide was no surprise, but perhaps the friendliest candidate was arch-conservative Mel Thomson, who was running for (and won) the New Hampshire governorship. Although hardly in sync with the liberal voices at Dartmouth, "he always had time for a WDCR microphone" and was on-air with station reporters on election night.[17]

The 1974 midterm elections were also thoroughly covered. Freshman newsman Rick Beyer '78 remembers covering one of the most fascinating races, for the open senate seat from New Hampshire, which turned into the most contested election in U.S. Senate history. Republican Louis Wyman initially defeated Democrat John Durkin, but by only 355 votes, then lost in a recount, then won in another recount, by two votes! The Senate took up the case and spent nearly two months wrangling over the issue without coming to a conclusion, even though the Democratic majority repeatedly tried to seat Durkin through procedural maneuvers. Finally a new election was scheduled, in September, 1975, which Durkin won. Some commentators feel that the battle, in which Republicans became increasingly united as they fought an overwhelming Democratic majority, helped pave the way to the eventual Republican takeover of the Senate in 1980. WDCR received a special citation from UPI for its coverage of the saga.[18]

In the weeks leading up to the 1976 presidential primary WDCR carried live a series of forums with candidates who passed through Hanover, among them

Ronald Reagan, Jimmy Carter, Mo Udall and Elliot Richardson. Four or five student leaders met with each candidate and asked questions; WDCR's Chris Davidson was the moderator. Davidson recalls that the Reagan appearance was particularly controversial, as the candidate's advance team tried to stage manage the event, and pro and anti-Reagan students gave the candidate "his most strenuous grilling of the day" — which Reagan handled adroitly.[19]

Primary night itself was extremely ambitious. This was the year WDCR launched the Dartmouth Election Network (DEN), aggressively syndicating its coverage to other stations. There was considerable risk in the plan. A few years earlier the University of New Hampshire station had tried something similar (albeit on a smaller scale), and failed. Station advisor Jordan Baruch said that the station was "putting its neck on the golden chopping block" and if it failed "it will be a magnificent screw-up" heard by a million people. But he "admired the level of guts" shown by the students.

Planning for the broadcast began in November 1975, with upwards of 80 station members participating in various aspects. News Director Jeff Sudikoff '77 was the overall producer, Personnel Director Bob Baum '77 coordinated the big staff, engineers Ted Bardusch '76 and Jordan Roderick '78 wired up special studios, and Mark Tomizawa '78 coordinated incoming calls from reporters. Hanover High School students and even staff writers from *The Dartmouth* pitched in.

The February 24, 1976, broadcast originated from Thayer Dining Hall, and was anchored by Sudikoff. Reporters called in from campaign headquarters, the Dartmouth computer center ran projections, and professors opined. Rick Beyer reported from Gerald Ford's headquarters, while Chris Davidson covered Ronald Reagan's. Other highlights included commentary from none other than William Loeb, the outspoken owner of the *Manchester Union Leader*, interviewed at his home by Peter Hirshberg '78.

The entire production went without a hitch, and the results of the syndication effort were spectacular. Twenty-nine stations in a four-state area signed up, carrying the voices of Dartmouth reporters from northern New Hampshire to Massachusetts in the south, and from Portland, Maine, in the east to Burlington, Vermont, in the west. WINS in New York and WEEI in Boston carried some segments as well. In addition the Voice of America picked up the feed, making Dartmouth's reach international. Stations could carry from five to 55 minutes per hour, and the feed was free in return for carriage of WDCR's embedded commercials (stations also got local time to sell). About one-third agreed to broadcast the entire four hours of coverage.

UPI was so impressed it awarded the station its Outstanding Achievement Award for 1976. The College was impressed as well. Not everyone was pleased, however. The station received an angry letter from the National Election Service, which had made a business of gathering and distributing local poll results and didn't appreciate the competition. Nevertheless this was one of the two most widely heard election nights in station history (the other was 1980), with more than one million listeners. Whatever the station's transitory financial problems, it was excellent public relations for Dartmouth.[20]

## Campus Turmoil Subsides

As the decade began, anger over the Vietnam war and social injustice was still boiling over, and the station covered it all. On April 30, 1970, President Nixon announced that U.S. and South Vietnamese troops had invaded eastern Cambodia to root out the Viet Cong who had taken sanctuary there. The Cambodian incursion, coming at a time when many wanted the U.S. out of Vietnam entirely, set off demonstrations on campuses across the country. On May 4 Ohio national guardsmen shot and killed four unarmed students during a standoff at Kent State University, leading to widespread strikes. In an unprecedented move, President Kemeny suspended classes at Dartmouth for "a week of reflection" on the policies of the United States.

WDCR responded swiftly. News Director Stephen Zrike said "the Directorate of WDCR does not think that the station should take a political stand on the controversy over the Indochina war. This would affect our position as broadcasters of objective news and information." Instead the station said that during the week it would broadcast a special report every hour announcing workshops, meetings and other functions taking place on campus, devote discussion shows such as *Noon Hour* and *Tri-Town Talkback* exclusively to the war issues, and present feature reports on the issues. It also sent a team to Washington, D.C., to cover the protests there. Zrike later recalled that the station maintained a policy of rigorous impartiality, forbidding staff from signing petitions or participating in causes.[21]

This did not satisfy campus protesters. In a mass meeting held on May 13 strikers lodged specific complaints against WDCR. They claimed that recent coverage of a protestor's speech had not included his call for support of the Black Panthers; that Martha Luehrmann had been admonished for raising war issues with children in her program; that there was too much coverage of demonstrations elsewhere and not enough of local protests; and that WDCR and wire service stories contained "biased coverage of strike issues and... 'racist' overtones in many stories." Some suggested that the station should subscribe to the Liberation News Service in order to "balance" its coverage. General Manager John Marshall deflected the criticisms, but agreed to meet with the protestors.[22]

The station certainly gave coverage to all viewpoints. In January 1971 University of New Hampshire student activist Mark Wefers, who had attracted attention by traveling to North Vietnam and broadcasting on Radio Hanoi, where he said that American troops should turn their guns on their officers, appeared on *Noon Hour* and *Tri-Town Talkback*. Zrike invited conservative publisher William Loeb to debate Wefers on the air. Loeb replied by calling Wefers "a no good little bastard" and saying "the only way I'd talk to him is at the end of a gun and I'd shoot him on the spot."[23]

As U.S. troops left Vietnam over the next two years, campus protests quickly dissipated. By the time of the Paris Peace Accords (January 1973) and the resignation of President Nixon (August 1974), they were barely a memory. An alumnus who arrived on campus in the fall of 1973 remarked to me, "Campus turmoil? At Dartmouth? By our time... that had all died down."[24]

There were some hangovers from the 1960s. The station reported on a campus drug raid in 1974, in which nine were arrested.[25] Other legacies were more positive. The station won a public service award from UPI for its April 22, 1970, coverage of Earth Day, during which it devoted an entire day to interviews and discussions of environmental problems, broadcast short "eco-facts," and had staffers manning pickup trucks collecting roadside debris and hauling off junked autos.[26]

In June 1973 newsmen covered extensive local flooding, including one live report from a canoe. To cover the building of a towering bonfire structure on the Green, the News Department commandeered a cherry picker and interviewed builders 50 feet up in the air. A photo of this mid-air interview, with a WDCR banner draped from the bucket, was much used in later years. To get to more conventional news stories the station in early 1974 acquired a brand new Chevy station wagon, replacing its first (and now very worn) mobile unit from the 1960s.[27]

Among continuing programs, *Noon Hour* blossomed in the 1970s into a premiere showcase for important and interesting people passing through town. Chris Davidson, who began doing interviews on the show as a freshman, recalls the heady experience of interviewing such luminaries as Judith Crist, King Vidor, Dr. Benjamin Spock, conductor Nicholas Harnencourt, Jimmy Carter, Fred Friendly, Richard Salant, Senator Jim Jeffords, and Erich Segal. Helen Gahagan Douglas, the former California congresswoman who lost a bitter race for a senate seat to Richard Nixon in 1950, and who happened to live nearby with her husband actor Melvyn Douglas, came in for a notable (and gloating) interview around the time of Nixon's fall in 1974. Indian sitar-player Ravi Shankar sat on the studio floor for his interview. Among the others conducting interviews on *Noon Hour* were John Donvan '77.[28]

*Week in Review* aired on Friday nights with Professor Jeffrey Hart and *The Dartmouth's* Paul Gigot '77 (who would later become editor of *The Wall Street Journal* editorial page). As part of its 13th anniversary celebration in early 1971 WDCR sponsored a high-profile panel discussion on the media, with guest panelists Bill Beutel '53 of WABC-TV, Robert Dickey of WINS radio, Herb McCord '64 of WCBS-FM, Professor Hart, and advertising executives Thomas Schwartz '57 and Harold Segal.[29]

Perhaps the most ambitious news special of these years was a spring 1974 series called *Retrospect*. This was an eight (or nine?) week series of three-hour specials, airing Saturdays from 9:00 a.m. to noon, with each episode profiling the events of a single year in the past decade through music and audio news clips. It was produced by John D'Auria, with Aaron Schindel '75, Bill Sigward (archival music), and Music Department Professor Jonathan Appleton on the Moog synthesizer. Later Chris Davidson and announcer Doug White '75 were involved. The station was quite proud of this massive production, and there were attempts to update it after D'Auria graduated, but that did not come to pass.[30]

## A Creative Boutique

There was a flowering of scripted programming in the mid 1970s. A similar phenomenon seemed to occur every decade or so when a group of particularly creative students came together and used the broadcast platform to bring the region the kind of innovative entertainment that was almost entirely absent elsewhere on the dial. Best remembered from the 1970s was *Midnight Mulch*, a kind of free-form sketch comedy show that aired from 1975 to 1977, usually at midnight on Friday or Saturday. Generally 20-22 minutes in length, it consisted of short, nonsensical sketches, built loosely around a theme that was also the sponsor of that night's show ("brought to you by money...", "by time...", "by the bicentennial...", etc.). According to one participant the script for each show was usually sketched out over dinner, after which "we would write like mad, hunt frantically for sound effects, fly into the studio a couple of seconds before midnight still trying to pre-record the bits that were supposed to have re-verb or something... very much 'on the fly'."

A few episodes survive. They are introduced as coming from "The Teatop Room at the Hotel McAllister," and sample bits include riffs on arch-conservative New Hampshire Governor Meldrim Thomson (always described as en route but never showing up), and interviews with world leaders (each asked the same uncomfortable question, "How's your love life?"). Another bit was "The Steve and Idi Show," a parody of popular singers Steve Lawrence and Eydie Gorme, with the latter replaced by African dictator Idi Amin.

> Steve: "Hi, I'm Steve Lawrence..."
> Idi: "And I'm Idi Amin."
> Steve: "Hey, you're not the right Eydie..."
> Idi: "You're not the right Steve!" (sound of machine gun fire)

There was no producer or indeed any formal structure to the team, although Jeff Sudikoff, Mark Tomizawa, and inveterate practical joker Peter Hirshberg were ringleaders. Other frequent participants were Kevin Koloff '77, Richard Mark '77, Maura Harway '77, Tom Mayer '77, John Donvan, Kristy Weinschreider '79, Roger Klorese '77, Scott Thayer '77, and Peter Threadgill '77. Koloff, who played guitar and banjo, contributed some hilarious original songs including "Thank God I'm a City Boy!" and "Mutilated Baby." Many of these '77s and '78s remained friends after their Dartmouth days, and get together annually in the Hanover area.[31]

Another comedy series was *Dry Clean Only*, which aired in the early evening around 1975-76, produced by Donvan and Neal McCarthy '78. Still another was *The One AM Report* (1976-77), live, improvised, comedy bits originating from nearby towns in the middle of the night, using the remote unit. Mark and Sudikoff were the perpetrators of that one, with Bruce McDowell '79 as the home base engineer. In one episode they visited the control tower at Lebanon Airport ("What do you do all night?"), in another they intercepted a night owl attempting to use the first all-night Automatic Teller Machine (ATM) in Hanover—which of course promptly ate his card. In still another, they knocked on the door of U.S. Senator Norris Cotton at 1:00 a.m.[32]

The WDCR "creative boutique" also created innovative commercials which were appreciated by local merchants. John Donvan recalls producing one for Tallulah's, an elegant restaurant, in which two characters raced through a blizzard to get to the fine establishment. For Omer and Bob's sports shop, Chris Davidson created a jingle which was sung by Margaret Busch '76 to the tune of "A Bicycle Built for Two":[33]

> Omer, Bo-ob, tennis is your stead,
> You sell big names,
> Like Bancroft, Yamaha and Head,
> When I have a Dunlop racquet,
> I'm proud to make the scene,
> [uncertain words...] how very helpful you have beeen!

## Other Programming

Of course music continued to be the station's bread and butter, with *Daybreak* in the morning, *Sounds for the Tri-Town* in the afternoon, and *Music 'til Midnight* at night the top shows. A typical schedule (from 1974) was:

6:00    *Daybreak* - easy listening and "soft top 40" music, with news updates
9:00    *Carousel* - light classical music
11:00   *Top of the Morning* - folk, Broadway, light jazz music
12:00   *Noon Hour* - showcase news and interview program
1:00    *Sounds for the Tri-Town (I)* - softer top 40 hits and oldies
3:00    *Sounds for the Tri-Town (II)* - current top hits, some progressive rock
5:00    *The Suppertime Show* - jazz and easy listening, mostly instrumental
6:00    *WDCR Reports* - the day's major newscast with local and national news, sports, special reports, commentary, etc.
7:00    *Concert Hall* on Monday/Wednesday/Friday, alternating with *A Little Night Music/Opera Showcase* on Tuesday/Thursday - the station's classical showcase, conducted three nights by students and two by the popular Professor Robin Robinson, who brought context to his presentations.
10:00   News and sports.
10:15   *Music 'til Midnight* - progressive rock, "longer, louder, and faster than the variety played during the afternoon."
12:00   *What's Happening?* - soul and black music; "the d.j. will conduct his show at times almost like a rap session."
2:00    *The All-Night Show* - experimental and open formats, chosen by the d.j.

Five minute newscasts were scattered throughout the day. Weekends were home to the popular *All Request Show*, the syndicated *American Top 40* countdown show with Casey Kasem, *The Hall of Fame Show* (oldies), *Sportsline* (call-in), jazz, religious programming, and children's show *Pooh Corner*.

*Pooh Corner* was one of the little gems of Dartmouth radio, a Sunday morning tradition for nearly 20 years. In 1975 it won a public service award from the New Hampshire Federation of Women's Clubs for best children's program. In fact WDCR won three of the Federation's four state-wide awards that year, the others being for a League of Women's Voters program and for *Noon Hour*. A few months later faculty wife Martha Luehrmann left *Pooh Corner* to enroll in Tuck Business School, and it was taken over by Diane Walker.[34]

The station continued to issue a weekly top tunes chart, which grew to become "The Big 34" but was, according to compiler Kevin Koloff, "nothing scientific." Top d.j.'s included Mark Stitham '72 (aka Mark Dillen), Steve Kepes '72 (aka Steve Drake), and Warren Hashagen '73. There was room for specialty shows as well, including a late night show hosted by Native American Howard Bad Hand '73, and another of Hawaiian music (plus player pianos, music boxes and calliopes) with Allan "Bic" Jayne. The weekly oldies show, *Hall of Fame,* was hosted by among others Tom Spilotis '73 and Dave Marston '74. WDCR d.j.'s did not limit their musical activities to the station. Spilotis was a blind student who was in a campus revival band called Bobby & The Corsairs, while Marston ran a jukebox business in town.[35]

WDCR may have sounded very commercial but it was also hip enough to attract rock star Steve Miller, who was in town for a concert, to sit in as guest d.j. for an oldies hour in 1971. He arrived a bit late, he said, because the Hanover Inn wouldn't serve him dinner without a tie.[36]

## Sports

Of course there was regular coverage of Dartmouth sports. In the fall of 1970 football coach Bob Blackman resigned after a stellar 16-year career. He later coached for the University of Illinois and then Cornell. He was succeeded by Jake Crouthamel (1971-77), who at first continued Blackman's winning ways but later began to falter. In the fall of 1975 WDCR had another run-in with the Dartmouth College Athletic Council, which had placed paid advertising on WTSL and WTSV but not on the College's own station. Six months later the DCAC's Jack DeGange recommended to the administration that WDCR be stripped of local football exclusivity so that the DCAC could sell it to competitor WTSL. This, he said, would result in more professional coverage and rejuvenation of the failing Dartmouth Football Network with feeds to stations in New Hampshire and Vermont. Overseer Jordan Baruch politely declined, saying that WDCR could not afford to lose the revenue.[37]

## "WDCR Smiles on the Aged"

*Let's Help* continued to be the chief vehicle for WDCR's public service efforts. The fall 1970 edition extended over more than two months, benefitted the Upper Valley Association for Retarded Children, and was coordinated by Mark Woodward '72. Among the events were features on *Noon Hour* and *Tri-Town Talkback*, trick or treating on Halloween, a barbequed chicken sale, another Celebrity Day on WDCR, and a music-talk marathon with Bill Aydelott. Ticket sales for a January fund-raising concert featuring the James Gang with Joe Walsh was a bit disappointing however.[38]

The fifth annual edition was launched in October 1971 on behalf of the Grafton County Home for the Aged ("WDCR Smiles on the Aged" *The Dartmouth* snarkily observed). Directed by Warren Hashagen, it included the usual trick-or-treat fundraiser, charity basketball games, and an "Adopt-a-Grandparent" program in which local families visited a resident of the home. However the capstone was a marathon broadcast by Aydelott, in which he promised to stay on the air continuously for at least 72 hours taking pledges and record requests, in return for which area merchants agreed to contribute $1,200, plus $35 for each additional three-hour block that he could stay awake. Many stratagems were used to keep him going, including dunking his head in water, bringing in his high school drum kit ("about ten minutes with the trap set would get me going for another hour"), doing a phone interview with WBZ personality Larry Glick (which brought in donations from outside the market), and traveling outside the studio for remotes. He was checked each day by a physician from the Dartmouth Medical School, and listeners were assured that "no drugs were used." In the end he lasted an incredible 129 hours—nearly a full week—setting an all-time station record and collecting more than $3,000. The entire *Let's Help* campaign that year raised a record $7,555.[39]

In fact Aydelott probably held the world record for longest single-d.j. marathon in radio history for many years, although nobody was keeping track of such things then. Not until 2007 was a longer one reported, when a North Carolina student d.j. claimed to have lasted for 175 hours.[40]

Unfortunately this would be the last *Let's Help* for more than two years. In January 1974 the Carter Yates administration mounted a somewhat scaled down version on behalf of the Lebanon Opera House, taking donations during a *History of the Beatles* special and sponsoring a ski day at Whaleback Mountain Ski Resort. The campaign was orchestrated by Director of Development Tom VanBenschoten '74.[41]

Summer broadcasting continued in 1970 (expanding to 24 hours a day) and 1971, with student management again granted room and board and course accommodations by the College. But special summer arrangements would soon become unnecessary.

### Women Enter Dartmouth — and WDCR

For more than 200 years Dartmouth had been an all-male institution. Wah-hoo-wah, "animal house," and road trips to women's colleges were deep-seated College traditions. But times were changing. In the 1960s many all-male colleges (including Georgetown, Princeton, and Yale) began admitting women, and although many now remember Dartmouth as abruptly "going co-ed" in 1972 this was in fact the culmination of a process that stretched back for nearly a decade.

In 1963 the College launched its first summer term, with non degree courses and programs for 291 women and men of all ages. By 1965 there were 438 enrolled in 70 courses taught by 42 teachers. About half of those enrolled were women. Discussions were also beginning on campus about whether the College should admit women during the regular school year, although most were opposed. In May 1965 a special live edition of WDCR's *Tales for the Midnight Hour* featured an interview with two hooded members of the LOTF ("Lest the Old Traditions Fail") Society, which had stolen the clapper from the bell in Dartmouth Hall to protest "creeping weenie-ism" at Dartmouth, including the possibility of admitting women.[42]

In early 1968 the College staged its first Co-Ed Week, in which women from numerous colleges exchanged rooms with Dartmouth men (who went to their campuses) and attended classes, discussions and social events. In 1969 1,000 women from 18 colleges made the trade. Also in the 1968-69 academic year the Drama Department admitted nine female exchange students for a full year's study (ostensibly to "advance educational opportunities in theater for the male students"); the following year the exchange program grew to 70 females in all departments.[43] None of this benefited the radio station very much, however. Although some women were on staff during the summer sessions, most were not at Dartmouth long enough to work their way up through the ranks at WDCR. There was an occasional faculty wife such as Joanna Sternick, who co-hosted *Noon Hour*. In 1971-72 General Manager Bill Downall made a concerted effort to recruit more women, but none of the six who signed up for training in the fall were still with the station by winter.[44]

There were debates, protests, and aborted attempts to forge an alliance with a nearby women's college. President Kemeny used WDCR as a principal vehicle for discussions of the issue (as one staffer put it, "at that point, before the Internet and computers, [radio] was the best way to communicate rapidly with the students and staff"). Finally in November 1971 the trustees voted to enroll women as full undergraduate degree candidates the following fall. Kemeny made the announcement at a press conference broadcast live from the WDCR studios, further evidence of the importance the College placed on the station as the vehicle for communicating its most important decisions.[45]

One of the problems the College faced in admitting women was simply how to accommodate them within its limited physical plant, without sharply reducing the number of men accepted. While this may not have been an issue at a larger institution, it would have considerable impact on one of Dartmouth's small size. The solution was the simultaneous introduction of the Dartmouth Plan (or "D-Plan"), under which the College would operate year-round, but students would be required to take staggered terms off during their junior and senior years. This would free up classroom and dormitory space and accommodate a larger student body. Some feared that the plan would create problems for student activities because a single group of student leaders would no longer be in residence together for a full year. Individual members might be off-campus for a term. However WDCR adapted well, appointing acting Directorate members where necessary, and the D-Plan did not become a serious issue for many years.

Meanwhile the first class of women arrived in the fall of 1972 and several signed up for the popular radio station. Among them were Margaret Busch, Pam Gile, and Kathy DeGioia ("de-joya"), all members of the class of '76. Others, like Lonna Slaby '74, had transferred to Dartmouth. Given the professional atmosphere at the station they were welcomed like any other new recruits, and trained by senior staffers including Program Director Jack Beeler, News Director Bill Sigward, and newsman Al Shepard '73.[46]

A common theme runs through the comments of the Dartmouth women of this era that I interviewed. They felt welcomed at WDCR. Unlike some other institutions on campus, it was not sexist, and certainly not a "boys club." Some upperclassmen on campus were clearly resentful about the arrival of women. They had enrolled in an all-male college and felt that the women were now encroaching on their space. There were stories of wolf whistles on the street, insulting banners hung out of dormitory windows, and men in the dining hall ostentatiously rating the women who walked by. At first the women were few in number, and one told a rather touching story about how hard it had been for her during her first term. She said she would have not returned to Dartmouth had it not been for the radio station and how welcome the staff there made her feel. Said another, "The station was great to women."

Many of these women had thick skins (two of them hung a banner in their dorm room reading "When better men are made, Dartmouth women will make them"). They quickly began to make their mark at the station. Gile was one of the first women to read news on the high-profile *Daybreak* show, and Slaby one of the first female d.j.'s (her brother, Jeffrey Slaby '80, was a d.j. some years later, making them probably the station's first brother/sister d.j. act). DeGioia started in news then switched to engineering. Later waves of women were also important staffers. Maura Harway was an engineer, newsletter editor, and all-round station "social director." Nancy Levin and Ginger Crowley (both from Smith College), and newswomen Carolyn Salafia '77, Leslie Embs '77, and Barbara Reinertsen '77 were also well known.

It took time for women to work their way up through the management ranks. An early role was that of station ombudsman, a newly created position designed to help ease tensions and facilitate communication in the rapidly growing organization. Pam Gile held the position in 1974-75, and Maura Harway and Nancy Levin did so in 1975-76. Harway also served as production director in 1975-76. It would be the late 1970s before women were appointed to the Directorate, however.

There were, of course, bumps along the way. Harway describes an encounter with the college athletic department, which wouldn't allow females to travel to away games on the team bus—meaning that she and DeGioia (as WDCR technicians) couldn't cover the game at all. The women fought the rule, but lost. A more serious incident occurred in 1974, when General Manager David Hunt co-signed a letter in *The Dartmouth* expressing strong opposition to the admission of women to Dartmouth. This caused a minor storm at the station. Hunt quickly wrote a statement for the station newsletter saying that his personal opinions would never affect how he ran the station, its opportunities would be open to all, and that if anyone *ever* felt unfairly treated they should let him know immediately. It was just what was needed. Far from being antagonized, female staffers appreciated his honesty. "He got it," said one.[47]

### Black Protests: "An Unlocked But Closed Door"

Black/white relations were more problematic, and despite the best of intentions no one seemed to know what to do about it. African-American enrollment at Dartmouth had historically been low, probably more because of its remote location than due to any overt racism.[48] That began to change in the late 1960s, as did black activism. The late night soul music show *What's Happening?*, begun in 1969, became the home base for black on-air talent at WDCR. Unfortunately its d.j.'s never really integrated into the station at large. A system evolved in which the (white) program director appointed a black director for the show, and he in turn would assign other blacks to the nightly shifts. According to some station members the black d.j.'s weren't even seen around the station during the day, and did not mix with station regulars. In January 1972 a visiting Colby student wrote an overview of the station in which she described *What's Happening?* as "fascinating listening and perhaps even a little frightening because of the wide difference in musical taste and choice by the black disc jockeys..."[49]

In 1974 a widely distributed broadside by three black students, popularly known as "The Redding Report," attacked many campus institutions, including WDCR. It demanded that a seat be reserved for blacks on both the station Directorate and Board of Overseers. Around the same time *What's Happening* was given a new name, the potentially more divisive *Blackside*, while the Directorate discussed ways to improve black-white communication at the station.[50]

Discussion and debate continued through 1975, while *Blackside* became a popular and well-known program on WDCR. Its unofficial leader was Cruz Russell '75, a gregarious personality who recruited new d.j.'s from within the African-American community and assigned shifts. They saw themselves as a "station within a station," an underground operation that called itself Boogie Down Productions (complete with T-shirts bearing the name). There was close coordination with the Afro-American Society. Among the show's personalities in this era were Ben Bridges '74, Phil Omohundro '76, Wally Gonzalez '75, Glenn Wright '77, and Jim "Wash" Washington '77. One popular black d.j. was Walt Callender '78, who promoted his show with a much-repeated jingle sung by Robin Smith '79 ("All day and all night, I run around with nothing on but the Walter Callender Show"). His show proved so popular he was eventually given a daytime shift.[51]

Finally in early 1976 long-simmering resentments blew up as three black staffers went public with their grievances. "Racism Charged, Denied at WDCR" screamed the front-page headline in *The Dartmouth* (which embarrassingly had to later admit it switched the photos of two of the black students). The blacks charged that WDCR was run by a self-perpetuating, all-white clique that excluded blacks, and that they were not encouraged to move beyond the late-night *Blackside*. If an announcer sounded too "black," they said, he was excluded from high-profile time periods for fear of alienating the community.[52]

Accusations of racism were incendiary in these racially charged times, and General Manager Chris Davidson, who would later say he was blindsided by the blast, responded as calmly and diplomatically as he could. Pointing out that there were three black members on the Board of Overseers, he said "there is black input at the absolute highest level of Dartmouth Broadcasting." AM Operations Supervisor Mark Tomizawa added that d.j. assignments were strictly on the basis of ability, including technical capability and delivery, and none of those in question were excluded from high profile time periods because of an accent. In shift assignments as well as in management positions, anyone who was willing to work hard and learn the ropes could advance at the station.

But this was not the point. Black d.j. and newsman Bert Ifill '76 perhaps put it best, and coined a memorable phrase, when he called WDCR "an unlocked, but closed, door." "To someone who is used to a closed door being locked," he said, "there is no incentive to try to go through that door."[53]

A professor writing in *The Dartmouth* pointed out that the situation was the inevitable result of WDCR's prized professional neutrality. It did not see itself as a proactive promoter of social change (especially when change was demanded by one group against the wishes of another). Rather its goal was to operate like a business, serve the wishes of the majority, and thus attract the largest possible audience. Black d.j. Ben Bridges *had* been removed from the top 40 afternoon show *Sounds for the Tri-Town*, he said, because Bridges tried to import his smooth black style, thus breaking the show's format.[54]

In the wake of this embarrassing and highly public dispute station management and the overseers went into overdrive trying to improve communications. Overseers Chair Jordan Baruch mediated, urging everyone "not to get too excited." Minority Affairs Director James Washington was given new responsibility, and was quoted in *The Dartmouth* as saying that if he couldn't resolve problems internally he had a direct line to Baruch. However even Washington's appointment showed how raw emotions were. When he was inadvertently not invited to an overseers meeting that had previously been scheduled for the weekend after his appointment, he fired off an angry and widely distributed letter accusing the Directorate of bad faith.[55]

Meetings were held, everyone talked, *Blackside* was moved into an earlier, better time period, and eventually things calmed down. The Afro-American Society published an article encouraging its members to get involved with the station. In later years Washington recalled that there were "bumps and bruises" along the way, but that by the time he graduated people were at least better able to communicate. It would not, however, be the end of Dartmouth Broadcasting's racial problems.[56]

### Vah Hoo Vah!

Another flashpoint in the 1970s involved Dartmouth's Native American heritage. Dartmouth was founded in 1769 ostensibly for the education and instruction of Native Americans, and evidences of that heritage were everywhere, from the football team (the Dartmouth Indians) to the campus cheer, "Wah-Hoo-Wah!" In the 1970s there were complaints that this was demeaning and campus institutions, including *The Dartmouth* in early 1972 and the DCAC in the fall of that year, began phasing out Indian symbols. Others fought back, saying that this was a violation of free speech and was stripping away tradition in the name of political correctness. In 1974 the College officially declared "use of the [Indian] symbol in any form to be inconsistent with present institutional and academic objectives of the College"—although it did not actually ban it.

WDCR had never been particularly associated with Indian symbols, but it was not immune from the controversy. In the wake of the College's pronouncement General Manager David Hunt posted a memo on the station bulletin board asking staffers not to use the term Indians or related terms like "scalped" or "wah-hoo-wah" on the air, in order not to offend anyone, especially "Native Americans in the Hanover area." Underneath someone scribbled "all six of them," and "vah-hoo-vah!" (apparently referring to a recent promotional spot in which a Henry Kissinger-like character had uttered that). A year later GM Chris Davidson had to direct his sports director not to permit an intramural game to be played between "The WDCR Savages" and "*The Dartmouth* Tomahawks."[57]

The "ban the Indian" movement remains controversial to this day.

## Staff and Administration

The station actively recruited from incoming classes, boasting that it served 50,000 people, had $100,000 worth of equipment, 20,000 records, and the largest budget of any organization on campus. Staff members networked among dormitory friends and fraternity buddies. One prospect who filled out a questionnaire in 1973 wryly said he applied because he was curious—and because "Cater and Ifill threatened me with bodily harm" if he didn't.[58]

There was no shortage of recruits. In 1972 Bill Downall estimated that the station had an active staff of 110 to 120, with about 30 of those devoting 10 or more hours per week, and directors putting in 50 to 60 hours (on top of their school careers!). There was some fretting about the effects of the D-Plan, but by and large it was a committed and satisfied staff. A 1974 survey revealed that 75 percent felt satisfied with what they got out of working for the station, and 75 percent felt great or very great loyalty to WDCR.[59]

Reliable staff was always at a premium, however, and "crumping" (missing an air shift) was an issue. Above all the station wanted recruits who would adopt its professional work ethic. "Rip Read Is Dead" read one freshman recruiting ad. "There's no room at WDCR for the newsman who thinks radio journalism means ripping copy off of a teletype and reading it. Today's WDCR newsman must understand what he is reporting and why. There is room at WDCR for the newsman who can think."[60]

One of the station's biggest fans was Mrs. Lucy P. Gregg, an elderly widow from a prominent Washington, D.C. family who had moved to Hanover in the 1960s and worked in the chaplain's office at Mary Hitchcock Hospital. She adopted the station, wrote letters to local newspapers praising its activities, called in to encourage new announcers when they debuted, baked pies for the staff, and even invited them to her home on School Street. She became known as WDCR's "fairy godmother." In

December 1975, at a reception at the Hanover Inn, the students presented her with a pewter bowl engraved with the words "From the women and men of WDCR—we are richer for knowing you."[61]

Managing such a sprawling station remained a challenge. In 1971 the position of ombudsman was created to facilitate communication between staff and management. Also added was a director of development (later the director of development and legal affairs, or "DODALA") to handle the many complicated phases of the FM station application. There were also regular staff meetings and a chatty newsletter published each week by the ombudsman. Discontent with the way in which the Directorate was chosen (i.e., by their predecessors) led in early 1975 to the establishment of a planning council, consisting of the general manager, program director, business manager and two others from the station at large, one of whom was evidently understood to be a black staffer. The Planning Council chose the Directorate, sat on the Board of Overseers, and was "the highest link in the station's chain of command" even though the Directorate continued to run the station day-to-day.[62]

Although it may have seemed like a good idea at the time, the Planning Council ran into trouble almost immediately, as have other schemes over the years to democratize what is more appropriately a business-based, top-down management structure. Everyone likes the idea of having power, but organizations usually work best when power is earned, and the best judges of who should have it are generally those who are already managers. The first uproar came around August 1975 when a seldom seen black staffer was chosen to fill a vacancy on the Planning Council over a hard working white favorite. By 1977 the council had been dissolved.

A more long-lasting change was the expansion of the Board of Overseers in 1975, brought about largely in response to the station's financial difficulties. Originally it had consisted of nine members—one faculty, three administration, and the five-person student Directorate. Now there would be 12: three faculty, two administration, two community leaders, and the five-person student planning council. The faculty advisor replaced the student general manager as chairman, and for the first time some meetings would be open to the public.

The first faculty chair was Professor Jordan Baruch, an eminent engineer who had recently joined the faculties of the Tuck School of Business and Thayer School of Engineering from Harvard and M.I.T. Although he was only at Dartmouth for two more years (before leaving to become assistant secretary of commerce in the Carter administration), he guided WDCR's student management through some of its most difficult challenges, including the launch of an FM station, the black protests, and a faculty attack on station independence. His calm, steady hand was much appreciated by the students of the time, as was his ability to provide guidance and support without infringing on the Directorate's own sense of independence. When I asked Baruch why he chose to become involved with the student radio station, he said he was impressed by how "self organized" and determined to be professional it was. "That was strange for students."[63]

Baruch set a template for the overseers that would last for many years: help the students, but don't preempt them. Although the overseers were the representatives of the College (the license holder) and could literally dictate station operations if they chose to, the custom instead was to provide a forum for debate, press for financial stability, and lobby for faculty and administration support when necessary. They interacted only with top station management; to the rest of the staff they were practically invisible. Yet every station manager I spoke to from the 1970s to the 1990s, when asked "who really ran the station?", answered emphatically, "*We did!*" (meaning the students).

The last link to the earliest days of Dartmouth Broadcasting was severed in 1974 with the retirement of Professor Almon Ives, a longtime supporter who had helped launch the station in 1941. Ives, who had left the overseers in 1970 and most recently served as interim dean, was feted at a March 1975 banquet where he was presented with a bound volume of letters, from station founder Richard Krolik '41 (on White House stationery!) and more than two dozen former general managers thanking him for his immense contributions over the years. Ives responded graciously to each writer. "The important thing for WDCR," he said, "was that your response strengthened their sense of continuity with the past... reassured the outgoing Directorate that their hard work had been worthwhile... and encouraged the incoming directors to tackle the tough tasks [ahead]." As always, his focus was on the students.[64]

### The Sices/Luehrmann Attack on Station Independence

Not all faculty shared his view. Physics Professor Arthur Luehrmann, who served on the overseers from 1972-74, and French Professor David Sices envisioned a very different kind of station. During 1973-76 they orchestrated a long assault on WDCR's programming, and that planned for the new FM station, which they felt should dump popular music and emphasize classical fare and intellectually stimulating panels and lectures. Unlike Professor Ives, who 13 years earlier had worked behind the scenes to bring the student leaders on board, Sices and Luehrmann were very public, even confrontational, in their criticisms. In early 1974 Luehrmann submitted five letters from faculty members sharply criticizing the current programming. General Manager David Hunt responded with a detailed defense of the station, but Sices shot back with an excoriating critique of Hunt's position, saying "I do not find it convincing."[65]

The board resolved that Luehrmann and Program Director Wally Gonzalez should work on a survey of students, faculty and administration. But Luehrmann drafted a loaded introduction that suggested the goal of the questionnaire was "changes in the basic premise upon which the station has been operating," followed by similarly slanted questions. Hunt and Gonzalez argued for a more balanced questionnaire, and provided a detailed breakdown of current programming with the presumed audience for each show. Sices laid out what *he* wanted: 35 hours per week of classical music, 20 hours of news and public affairs, 10 hours of folk music, 10 hours of plays, and seven hours of rock music (with "commentary and discussion").[66]

The results of the survey, if any, are unknown, but Sices and Luehrmann renewed their attack in 1975, circulating a petition to the faculty in the fall asking for their support in establishing a committee that would investigate replacing the student management with a professional manager and enforcing a program policy they felt would be more worthy of Dartmouth. They even handed out leaflets at a classical concert which read, "if you believe that a steady stream of rock music is far from the best way that a leading American university can serve the cultural and entertainment needs of the public in its region... [write to] President Kemeny."

Kemeny, in a meeting with GM Chris Davidson, said as far as he was concerned the station should remain student-run and "shouldn't budge an inch" in responding to these faculty demands. Letters flew back and forth in *The Dartmouth*, and on November 24 there was a four hour meeting on the subject attended by Sices, Luehrmann, senior administration and student management members, and even retired station advisor and elder statesman Almon Ives. Deftly moderated by Jordan Baruch, it allowed everybody to air their opinions ("the meeting was impressive both in the honesty and openness displayed"). It concluded that (1) everybody was in favor of "quality programming," (2) everyone should continue to talk, (3) a faculty/student study committee should look at station programming, (4) for now, at least, the students would remain in charge.[67]

Undeterred, Sices and Luehrmann brought the matter to a head by introducing a resolution before a meeting of the full Arts & Sciences faculty on January 19, 1976, advocating a station restructuring. This generated more than an hour of debate, during which Sices, Luehrmann and Music Professor Jon Appleton (an overseer) argued for passage, while administration Vice President Frank Smallwood, History Professor Gordon Wood, and Baruch opposed. Chris Davidson, who was in the audience as a reporter, was surprised to be called on to speak by President Kemeny (students did not normally address such meetings), and improvised his own defense of the station. In the end the resolution—which would have started a process to profoundly change the character of Dartmouth radio—was defeated, although not by an overwhelming margin. The vote was 29 in favor, 38 opposed.[68]

In the aftermath there were lengthy interviews in *The Dartmouth* (which was no doubt looking over its shoulder at what the faculty had tried to do to its sister medium), in which each side restated its case. Luehrmann took one more swipe at the station in a February letter alluding to its "naive commercial model." However he also sent a congratulatory telegram to the station on the night of the FM launch. For his part Davidson studiously avoided gloating, and made nothing but conciliatory statements regarding student-faculty cooperation going forward.[69]

The 1973-76 attempted coup was perhaps the most public airing of differing views of the purposes of Dartmouth radio in the station's history. A station filled with classical music and intellectual programming might sound attractive, but would probably have been impossible to execute with an all-student (or even mostly student) staff, would have had few listeners, and would have required a large, ongoing subsidy from the College. It also would have destroyed the independence that students prized, and learned so much from, over the years. As staffer Kevin Koloff put it in a letter to *The Dartmouth*, most of the volunteer staff would probably walk out if dictated to in that manner. On the other hand a strictly commercial operation that made no use of the College's enormous intellectual resources made no sense either. In the end the faculty was distracted by many other pressing issues (ROTC, the Indian symbol, integrating women into the student body), and the administration cast its lot with the students. Overseer John Bryant, a longtime station observer, felt that President Kemeny would never have approved of a professionally managed station. It would be up to future generations of student leaders, not a faculty committee, to find the right balance between service to the community, professional experience, and financial stability.[70]

## Television at Dartmouth?

AM. FM. What about television?

There had been talk about the possibility of television at Dartmouth since the 1950s. In 1954 a television committee chaired by Warner Bentley had submitted a "carefully prepared report" on the subject, but despite various proposals, nothing was done. After the University of New Hampshire launched station WENH-TV in 1959 there were suggestions that Dartmouth should contribute programming to that educational station and rebroadcast its signal in the Hanover area. Finally in 1968 WENH itself set up a translator on channel 15, which brought its signal to the market.

Low-power UHF station WRLH-TV had launched in 1966, and operated on a shoestring. The first news director recalled that he was hired when he mentioned that in addition to writing and reporting he knew how to operate a bulldozer. Owner Nelson Crawford had him grade the road to the transmitter.[71] WDCR staffers played a major role in operating the station. Several took part time jobs there, including Bill Aydelott, Bill Sigward, and Len Schulte, and stories abounded about mishaps (as when Sigward's nose began to bleed during a newscast, and when an unmanned camera began to slip and slowly panned down to the announcer's bare feet). There was turmoil behind the scenes as well. The station went off the air in 1968, was sold to new owners, who sold it in 1971 to a consortium including none other than Sconnix Radio Enterprises, founded by recent WDCR alumni Scott McQueen and Ted Nixon. They put it back on the air, but it only lasted until 1974 before going dark for good.[72]

Then the story gets a little unclear. At some point during the 1970s or 1980s (nobody remembers exactly when) WDCR alumni received a flyer soliciting their support for a plan to obtain a television license for Dartmouth. It may well have been the dormant license for WRLH's channel 31. The plan did not originate at WDCR, but may have been the work of film society director Blair Watson, who had been involved in the television discussions of the 1950s and '60s. Nothing came of this, and instead Taft Broadcasting hired Chris Davidson (who had just graduated) to scout the area for potential staff, physical plant, and economic possibilities. Taft applied for and got the license, but NBC decided that the small market wasn't worth its time and almost sunk the deal. Eventually the network relented and channel 31 went back on the air as an NBC affiliate, this time in color, on September 27, 1978. The new call letters were WNNE-TV. In later years the station continued to employ Dartmouth students part time, until it abandoned local programming and began rebroadcasting WPTZ from Plattsburgh, New York in the 1990s.[73]

So why not television at Dartmouth? The answer seems to be that the market simply isn't big enough to sustain it, at least on a commercial basis. Today Hanover and Lebanon are served by cable systems that import network affiliates from Boston and Burlington, Vermont, along with a collection of regional stations from various locations in New Hampshire and Vermont. There has been no local television in the market since the 1990s.

## The FM Wars

Paul Gambaccini recalled that the original proposal to the overseers to seek an FM license "passed easily." That was the only thing that happened easily in the quest for FM. What followed was a long and frustrating battle reminiscent of the AM wars in the 1950s. FM almost didn't happen.

John Marshall's Directorate picked up where its predecessor had left off and spent much of 1970 working on a detailed plan for the trustees, researching equipment, discussing potential programming, and drafting a budget. By the end of the year this had been submitted to the College. The total price tag: $133,000. Realizing how much work still remained, and the singular focus it would require, they did one more thing for their successors. They created the new Directorate position of director of development, specifically to work on FM.

In January 1971 the trustees approved the plan and new DOD Tim McKeever was off and running. During the summer he supervised a Community Needs Survey of 150 community leaders, who wanted FM programming to be roughly equally divided between classical music, rock, and "other" (religious, folk, sports, jazz), with approximately 10 percent reserved for news. Meanwhile the College lawyers, led by Erwin Krasnow of Kirkland, Ellis, and Rowe in Washington, D.C., worked on the legal aspects of an application.[74]

In January 1972 the trustees voted to finance the project with an appropriation of $15,000 for legal fees. Construction costs were to be paid for with $42,000 from WDCR's reserves and the remainder from a loan by the College, to be paid back over five years with eight percent interest. The station was doing well, and the College was treating this as a financial investment. The cost estimate for FM had been brought down to $95,835 through careful pruning, so the amount of the loan would be about $54,000.[75]

By early April 1972 rumors were flying of an imminent filing, and *The Dartmouth* ran a front page story about them. It was well known that WTSL also wanted the sole open FM frequency in the market, and newly appointed WDCR General Manager Fred Frawley was forced to evade questions about when Dartmouth might apply, to avoid giving the competition too much information. *The Dartmouth* also interviewed WTSL General Manager Jim Canto, and he was equally cagey about his plans even while complaining bitterly about the "unfairness" of having to compete against a student-run, College-supported station. Like his WTSL predecessors Canto was a rather nasty competitor who never missed an opportunity to bad-mouth the college kids. When über salesman Charlie Smith ran into him in 1971 Canto forcefully asserted that he was losing money because of unfair competition from WDCR, which he said was College subsidized (it was not), "mercilessly" undercut rate card (it did not), and used a "cheap, slanted" survey (Mediastat) to take business from him. However when Canto was asked to pick another survey company and share the cost of having *it* survey the market, he refused.[76]

Rex Marshall of WNHV, on the other hand, showed no such animus toward the students. Of course he already had an FM companion station (launched in 1969).[77]

In late April Dartmouth finally filed its application for FM frequency 99.3 MHz with the Federal Communications Commission. The 150-page document was compiled primarily by former DOD Tim McKeever and GM Bill Downall (plus the lawyers), and included interviews with community leaders and examples of WDCR's service to the community. WTSL filed shortly thereafter. Tellingly, according to the applications Dartmouth's FM station would be programmed almost entirely independently of its AM sibling, while "due to financial restrictions" WTSL's would simply simulcast its AM cousin.

What followed was a long, agonizing period of waiting. The FCC typically took a least a year to review applications, longer if they were contested (as this one was). The legal bills mounted and finally in August 1973 Canto agreed to drop his competing application if Dartmouth would pay his legal bills to that point. WDCR also agreed to turn over to him an engineering study that could help him identify another frequency to apply for. Miraculously, relations with Canto improved markedly after the buy-out. Canto intimated that WTSL was for sale (it did change ownership in 1974, although he remained general manager), and it did eventually get its own FM license, but not until 1986.

With WTSL out of the way the FCC quickly approved Dartmouth's application, on September 19, 1973. Then, in a stunning reversal, just a few hours later it withdrew the approval. A surprise competing application had come in postmarked one day before the deadline, consisting of "hardly more than a name and an address." Although it did not meet the legal requirements for filing, the FCC was legally obliged to give the sender 30 to 90 days to complete it. The new applicant was Robert Powell of Powell Communications, owner of WMOU in Berlin, New Hampshire, and several small newspapers. Powell claimed that he had "long been interested" in opening a station in the Hanover area, although why he waited until the last possible minute was unexplained. *The Dartmouth* editorialized, weakly, that WDCR ought to get the license but everything was on hold again.[78]

There were hopes that Powell might not follow through with a full application, but he did, and it looked like there might be years of further delays. New estimates put potential legal expenses as high as $40,000. In addition WDCR was in what appeared to be financial freefall, piling up big deficits in 1972-73 and 1973-74 and wiping out the earlier surplus. The College began to have second thoughts about FM. It was going to cost more than expected, and the station reserves meant to pay for it were melting away.

There were discussions about applying for an educational FM license instead, or dropping FM altogether. Privately the administration even discussed the possibility of selling the AM station to make way for FM; however it felt the students would never go along. In February 1974 the overseers asked the newly installed Hunt Directorate to "review the station's goals as they pertained to FM" and make its recommendation. New Director of Development and Legal Affairs Carey Heckman '76 was designated to compile and write the report.[79]

Heckman was an interesting choice. He was one of the few staff members who had been vocally opposed to FM, and had been selected for the Directorate despite that stand. Now the fate of FM was largely in his hands. He plunged into his assignment with fervor, laying out in a 23-page report the entire history of the station, based in part on this writer's history written in 1964, and on interviews with past managers including Dick Harris '58 and Ron Kehoe '59, who had launched AM. He wanted to know not only what happened, but why and how. To his surprise he ended up reversing his stand. "Coming to the conclusion to continue seeking an FM license was extremely difficult for me to make," he wrote. "My complete reversal is the result of somewhat intensive research and thought over the past two weeks."[80]

The report made several recommendations, most notably to "repair" the current AM programming, to repair AM management, and to pursue FM. Dartmouth radio's entire history and culture of student entrepreneurialism called for it. "The Board of Overseers of WDCR should continue the fight for the sake of the College community, the WDCR staff, and posterity," he said.

With this rallying cry, and Hunt's firm moves to bring the station's financial problems under control, College doubts were put to rest. There was still the problem of Robert Powell, however. Things dragged on into the summer until he suddenly withdrew his application. Depending on which source you read, either the College bought him out, or Powell went bankrupt. On August 14, 1974, the FCC abruptly granted the long-sought construction permit for FM. Program Director Wally Gonzalez is said to have choked on his Thayer soup when he heard the news.[81]

Technical Director Bill Taylor '75 immediately began ordering equipment, and in the fall members of the Directorate visited WBCN in Boston for advice on building an FM station. However when the next Directorate took over in March 1975 things were still moving slowly. Essential equipment had not yet arrived and construction of new studios in Robinson had not yet begun. Under FCC rules a permittee had one year to put a station on the air, so a five month extension was obtained, giving Dartmouth until early February 1976. It would be tight.

In anticipation of FM WDCR began realigning and tightening its format. Around this time a system of color coding records was introduced, red, green, or yellow, to manage music by time period.

By early 1975 the financing of the station was being formalized. Instead of growing, estimates for the construction of FM had actually come down, due to relentless paring and economizing. What had been a $133,000 estimate in John Marshall's day had been reduced to $96,000 in 1972 and now to about $74,000. A second studio would be postponed, and students would do much of the construction. In February 1975 President Kemeny approved a $56,000 loan (now 10 years at eight percent), while saying "it is essential for WDCR to strengthen the financial end of its operation and to provide initiative and continuity in its sales force." This would be augmented by $18,000 from the station's reserve fund. The College expected to be paid back, and the students promised to do so, pointing out that "earlier loans from Dartmouth... have been paid in full."[82]

Clearly the students were learning valuable lessons in running a business and in financial accountability. This is undoubtedly what Kemeny had in mind when he added, "in addition to the very valuable experience WDCR provides [in] programming, the station can also serve as a training ground for students who are interested in acquiring business experience."

Several more pieces of the puzzle needed to fall into place. To determine the programming mix more surveys were conducted and listener input received. The internal debates were hot and heavy; "virtually everyone had their own ideas." Eventually the overseers accepted a plan worked out by Program Director Jack Fidler '76 and AM Operations Supervisor Mark Tomizawa calling for both stations to have mixed schedules. FM would have a considerable amount of classical music (6:00 a.m. to 2:00 p.m. and 7:00 to 9:00 p.m. daily), to take advantage of the stereo signal, with folk and "light rock" in the afternoon (when AM was broadcasting top 40) and progressive rock later at night. At least at the start, FM would basically feature niche musics while AM would be the mainstream station emphasizing top 40 and middle-of-the-road music and news.[83]

Call letters had to be finalized. According to Chris Davidson preferred choices WDFM and WFMD were taken. WFRD was the fourth or fifth choice. Making the best of the situation the station said it stood for "FM Radio at Dartmouth," but some folks called it "Fred."[84]

Work proceeded furiously on facilities. This included a new FM interview studio (studio 6) and FM master control (studio 7) on the third floor of Robinson, along with storage space that would be turned into another studio (studio 5) once funds became available. The expansion space included the takeover of the German Club's "Schlossmacher Lounge," named after a German professor of the 1950s who fiercely resisted any station encroachment on club space. Visiting alumnus Rich Swicker recalled that when students teased him that radio would eventually take over the lounge he'd roar, "over my dead body!" Swicker added, "I guess he was right."

Technical Director Ted Bardusch and Chief Engineer Jordan Roderick led a team of students installing the stereo FM equipment as soon as it began to arrive in the spring of 1975. Bardusch and Roderick did most of the studio wiring themselves, including building the entire control board from scratch (which saved much money over a pre-built unit). As the deadline drew closer they worked almost continuously, including Christmas break, becoming legendary in station annals for their fierce dedication to the project. Richard Mark called them "nocturnal animals." The installation of the transmitter (a 3.0 kw Collins 831 D-2 unit) was accomplished by Bardusch and engineering consultant Ted Churchill. The station would broadcast from a 165 foot shared tower atop Craft's Hill in Lebanon.[85]

Bardusch may well hold the distinction of being the only student to literally "die" for the station. While working on the AM transmitter in the spring of 1975 it shorted out and electrocuted him, stopping his heart. Fortunately he had imposed a rule that said "two minimum go to the tranny shack," and trained everyone in CPR, and his companion that day, Bill Taylor, was able to revive him.[86]

In September 1975 *The Dartmouth* optimistically headlined "WFRD Is Almost Here," with promises of "sometime in November." A feature story was also arranged for the December 1975 *Dartmouth Alumni Magazine*, which would appear at about the same time. But there were glitches, especially with that hand-made control board. Bardusch and Roderick redoubled their efforts and in January final tests were being run. It was, in the end, one of the most advanced radio facilities north of Boston, and remarkable for a small market.[87]

Wrapping up one other detail, the overseers in January 1976, after considering several names for the new combined AM/FM entity, settled on "Dartmouth Broadcasting."

### The Big Night Arrives

Finally on February 19, 1976, at 8:00 p.m., WFRD, 99.3 on the dial, officially went on the air with a lighthearted hour-long inaugural broadcast hosted by Richard Mark. Entertainment included The Dartmouth Aires and The Dartmouth Distractions vocal groups, The Dartmouth Players in an excerpt from *Kiss Me, Kate*, a classical piano duet to show off the stereo sound, a student rock band called Push, and the Barbary Coast dance band, which had appeared on the WDCR inaugural 18 years earlier (Mark: "They haven't aged a bit"). Woven through the broadcast was a multi-part history of Dartmouth radio, presented by Kristy Weinschreider and d.j. Steve Meili '78. Steve began with the 1874 birth of Marconi, whereupon Kristy interjected "Skip ahead, Steve." Steve said, "Right away, ma'am!" There were short speeches by notables including President Kemeny, Jordan Baruch, and station legend Almon Ives (who predicted "a Dartmouth communications satellite linking us with universities everywhere," and observed that "just as the locusts come every 17 years, something new will happen at the radio station every 17 years"). Following the inaugural special Rick Beyer delivered the first newscast on WFRD, which he almost referred to as "WDCR." According to early estimates the new station could reach a potential audience of about 45,000 people, vs. 35,000 for WDCR.[88]

In the afterglow of the stellar evening two of the people who made it possible were not forgotten. A photo in *The Dartmouth* showed gangly Jordan Roderick and bespectacled Ted Bardusch receiving a giant award citation (on a plywood board) from President Kemeny for their exceptional effort. As staffer Peter Hirshberg described their work, "it was a matter of thousands of hours, hundreds of feet of wire, ten thousand solder joints." Why would two students, ostensibly at Dartmouth to gain an education and earn a diploma, put so much sweat and toil into a student activity they would soon leave behind, all for no pay and no academic credit? The answer may shed a little light on why this particular student activity has engendered such intense loyalty over the years. Roderick commented, "This station represents an idea, an ideal idea. No one would have bothered to do all that work if this were just a radio station." Later he would add, "Dartmouth Broadcasting is one of the few organizations on campus which is made up entirely of dreams and hope and creative energy run amok."[89]

# Chapter 9

# 1976-1984: The Early Years of FM

The late 1970s and early 1980s may not have seen as much tumult on campus as the late 1960s, but they were hardly quiet years. Students of the 1970s had good reason to worry about the adult world they would be entering as America deteriorated into a morass of economic woes, rampant inflation, a severe energy crisis, and setbacks for the U.S. overseas including the Iran hostage crisis. The early 1980s saw a dramatic confrontation between liberalism and conservatism, both nationally and locally, with Ronald Reagan in the White House, conservative governors in New Hampshire, and the founding in 1980 of *The Dartmouth Review*, a feisty and influential off-campus newspaper whose escapades brought Dartmouth some of the most intense national media scrutiny it has ever received.[1]

Locally, WDCR and WFRD remained principal players in the Upper Valley media world. FM was rapidly gaining ascendancy over AM in the radio industry at large, but in Hanover, which was a step behind national trends, WDCR only gradually ceded its dominance to its new FM sibling. The guiding philosophy of the stations remained professionalism and independence.

General managers of the combined stations during this transitional period were Richard Mark '77, Jordan Roderick '78, John Bussey '79, Joseph Mannes '80, Jeff Zimmerman '81, Mark Belmonte '82, Jeff Shapiro '83, Dan Daniels '84, and Katie Mulligan '85.

## FM Takes Root

As the launch of WFRD approached it became clear that it needed some designated staff, even though most of the launch work was being done by WDCR's senior management. Early in 1975 Roberto "Bert" Ifill '76 was appointed as the first FM operations supervisor, reporting to WDCR Program Director Rick Zimmerman '76. Ifill was quickly succeeded by Kevin Koloff '77 during the summer and Ronald Fleischer '77 in the fall and winter, when the station finally went on the air. Not until the following year's Directorate was announced in February 1977 did WFRD gain its own Directorate-level program director. That position was filled for the first half of the year by Chris Carstens '79 and for the second half by David Corey '78.

At this point WFRD was clearly WDCR's "little sister." Soon after its launch *The Dartmouth* ran a story headlined "Local Stations Unhurt by WFRD," which appeared to be an understatement as neither WTSL nor WNHV expressed the slightest concern. WTSL's Jim Canto said that the new student FM in no way competed with his station, and boasted that "our business is better than at any other time in our 25 years." WNHV-AM-FM owner Rex Marshall saw "no present or future friction" between his FM station and Dartmouth's. Both pointed out the differences in programming. WFRD's mix of classical, jazz, and progressive rock was expected to draw a predominantly young, college-oriented audience, while WTSL's easy listening and WNHV's mix of easy listening and country music would draw a broader, more adult audience. Critical to all were of course advertisers, and Canto got in a typically sly dig by saying "local advertisers know what stations their customers listen to because they are listeners themselves" (i.e., to *his* station).[2]

The sales figures confirmed WFRD's meek start. In the fall of 1976 the College was forced to extend the stations an additional $80,000 loan, to cover both cost overruns in launching FM and very soft sales revenues. "Apparently [the previous Directorate] figured that the FM would bring in full revenue from day one," lamented General Manager Richard Mark. "No radio station does that. It was an unreasonable assumption." There were few if any advertisements on WFRD at the start, and by time they began to appear in 1978 they were so novel that Dave Corey had to admonish his freewheeling disc jockeys to please treat them with respect. "If you have commercials scheduled during your show, play them," he cajoled. "Do not badmouth the ads or the sponsors." "If you cannot find [the ad], look around."[3]

### News: A Primary Night to Remember

The News Department continued its extraordinary record, providing the region with the kind of news coverage normally heard in only the largest U.S. radio markets. In the summer of 1976 the station obtained press credentials to both the Democratic and Republican National Conventions. Rick Beyer '78, Mark Tomizawa '78, and Bob Baum '77 reported from the Democratic gathering in New York City in July, but when it came time to book travel to the Republican convention in Kansas City in August the station had run out of money. Beyer went to see President Kemeny during Kemeny's regular open office hours, and asked if he could help. Beyer later recalled that "he heard me out, then gave me a list of different places in the College to go for money. In each case he would add, 'Tell them I sent you.' He said after I had done that I should come back to him and he would give us the rest. Which he did."[4]

Beyer, Tomizawa, Kevin Koloff and Nancy Levin (an exchange student from Smith College) then covered the Republicans, staying at Levin's home in Kansas City to save money. It was a livelier than the Democratic meeting (Jimmy Carter had sewed up the Democratic nomination before the delegates arrived). Incumbent President Gerald Ford faced a stiff and well-organized challenge from former California Governor Ronald Reagan. The students also planned to produce a documentary about press coverage of conventions, and Beyer was looking for an opportunity to score an interview with one of the celebrity newsmen there. Finally, on the last day of the convention, at 2:30 in the morning, he spotted an exhausted David Brinkley leaving the NBC booth and making his way toward an escalator. Beyer ran up, microphone in hand, peppering the weary Brinkley with sweeping questions about the nature of political coverage. At first Brinkley reluctantly indulged the young reporter, but when Beyer hit him with one question he stormed off in a huff, making the interview something of a station classic.

Beyer: "People often say that the people who work in network coverage are more showmen than newsmen, especially the floor people and the anchor people too.

Do you have a comment on that?"

Brinkley (clearly irritated): "I do. That is such a stupid remark I won't really respond to it. I don't want to talk to you anymore." (walks away)

Beyer: "Thank you very much, sir..."[5]

The documentary was never made.

Coverage on election night in November 1976 was another major production, live from Thayer Hall, with regional desks and returns posted for onlookers. Thirty to 40 staffers were involved, and John Donvan '77 (who later became an ABC network newsman) was the anchor. Among those organizing the event were Beyer, Jordan Roderick, Chip Behal '79, Gerry Cox '79, Barbara Reinertsen '77, and Barbara "Binky" Moses '78.[6]

During the next four years the station's continuing political coverage included a live broadcast of President Carter's February 1978 "town hall" meeting in Nashua, New Hampshire, and coverage of the midterm elections in November 1978.

The best was yet to come. In 1980 there were ferocious battles within both parties for their nominations. On the Democratic side, unpopular President Jimmy Carter faced stiff challenges from Senator Edward Kennedy and California Governor Jerry Brown, and on the Republican, Ronald Reagan was duking it out with George H.W. Bush. New Hampshire's looming first-in-the-nation primary took on enormous importance, and as early as September 1979 Dartmouth radio began planning primary night coverage that would equal or surpass its 1976 triumph. When the big day came, February 26, 1980, more than 100 staffers were deployed in a carefully planned series of broadcasts carried on both WDCR and WFRD. The first report was from Dixville Notch, New Hampshire, where the first balloting took place at 12:01 a.m. That evening there was six hours of continuous coverage live from Collis Center as results came in from the rest of the state. Student reporters called in from nine campaign headquarters across the state (using "newsie boxes," or mixers, built specially for the event by the Tech Department), pre-election poll results from the Government Department were read as were the latest computer vote projections from the computer center, all accompanied by commentary from Professors Robert Nakamura and Jeffrey Hart. There was even a special "cool" Dartmouth Election Network theme, mastered at the Electronic Music Studio. At the center of all this hubbub were co-anchors Tom Farmer '81 and Phil Weber '82, with Farmer also serving as executive producer of the broadcast. Behind the scenes everyone from General Manager Jeff Zimmerman on down pitched in.[7]

As one later report put it, "The noise of some 50 data gatherers and computers and recap writers and editors and rewrite staff made for just the right level of commotion behind the anchors—and a spectacle that had to be seen to be appreciated."[8]

Carter won the Democratic primary (narrowly) and Reagan the Republican, but the big winner on radio that night was Dartmouth Broadcasting, and Dartmouth itself. The student newsmen were heard in 39 states via feeds to 20 radio stations (plus one TV station), including 50,000 watt powerhouse WBZ in Boston. Many of these carried the five-minute recap segments, five minutes before every hour. An estimated eight to 10 million listeners heard Dartmouth that night, on a pivotal day in American political history. It was without a doubt one of the proudest moments in Dartmouth radio history.

Coverage on election night in November was not quite as extensive, but the stations still managed to carry live reports from 15 campaign headquarters and host a panel discussion among five professors (Colin Campbell, Gene Garthwaite, Jeffrey Hart, Lynn Mather, and Charles McLane). Six stations carried Dartmouth's feed, generally for longer periods than in February.[9]

The November 1982 midterm election night coverage was anchored by incoming News Director John Landrigan '84, who said that as soon as the 1982 winners took office he began planning the 1984 coverage. The 1982 coverage won an award from the Associated Press for Best News Feature by a College Station.[10]

Landrigan was back in 1984 as producer of the WDCR/WFRD New Hampshire primary night broadcast, which while not as widely carried outside of Hanover as the 1976 and 1980 editions (two stations carried the Dartmouth feed this time) was certainly impressive. It consisted of a six hour broadcast co-anchored by Katie Mulligan and John May '85, the first election night male-female anchor team, and originated from the newly opened Rockefeller Center. (Dartmouth's Rockefeller Center, not to be confused with the New York City landmark of the same name, opened in September 1983, was dedicated to public policy studies, and was named in honor of alumnus Nelson A. Rockefeller '30.) Once again station reporters called in from campaign headquarters, and there was commentary from Professors Robert Arseneau, Richard Winters, and Frank Smallwood. May called it "a technical nightmare and dream."[11]

The amount of work that went into these productions, by an all-student staff, should not be underestimated. May later recalled that "there were quite a few candidates to cover and in retrospect it seems like a huge logistical undertaking to get everyone to the right place and get their phone lines installed and get their live feeds working, but there was enough institutional knowledge built up that we managed it without any great drama." He also noted that "Everyone, even those in the studio or control room, dressed professionally. The guys wore coat and tie, and the women, as I remember instructing them in a newsletter, wore 'whatever you wear then the guys have to wear ties'."[12]

During the summer General Manager Mulligan sent reports back from the Democratic convention in San Francisco, using the NBC satellite. November election night coverage was live from Rockefeller Forum with anchors Bill Furlong '86 and Russell Kemp '87, reporters calling in reports from candidate headquarters in New Hampshire and Vermont, and Professors Arseneau and Smallwood providing perspective. "We would love it" if students came to watch the broadcast, said Mulligan.[13]

### News, Public Affairs, and *The Dartmouth Review*

News and public affairs also offered a steady diet of worthwhile regular programs. In early 1978 Public Affairs Director Steve Renick '78 listed the then-current lineup: *At Dartmouth* (campus issues, Monday), *Something's Happening* (interviews, Tuesday), *It's Your Health* (alternating with minority affairs, Wednesday), *Environmental Insight* (Thursday), *Upper Valley* (community issues, Friday), *Podium* (visiting scholars, Sunday), *Week in Review,* and *Scan.* Later public affairs programs included *Open Line* (1981) and *Dial Dartmouth* (1983), the latter a call-in/interview show which took out a full-page advertisement urging listeners to "Air Your

Views!"[14]

The Montgomery Fellowships (established in 1978) brought a steady stream of notables to teach on campus during the late 1970s and early 1980s, some of whom were interviewed, including author Kurt Vonnegut. There was a program on environmental issues hosted by Professor Bob Norman, and one on politics coordinated by the League of Women Voters.[15]

There were also plenty of campus issues to talk about. During the late 1970s debate raged about what to call the Dartmouth teams, now that the term "Indians" was verboten. For a while Dartmouth Woodsmen seem to lead (1976-77), then Mad Dogs placed first in a poll (1978). Later Timberwolves was proposed (1984). Eventually the College settled on Big Green, which hopefully offended no one. Another flashpoint was the college alma mater, written in 1894, titled "Men of Dartmouth." That did not sit well with many when Dartmouth became co-educational in 1972, and various proposals were made to change the lyrics or scrap the song altogether. In 1980 the Cobra Senior Society proposed replacing the opening words "Men of Dartmouth give a rouse, for the college on the hill" with a new verse starting "Men and women sing as one, for the college we all love." This produced considerable resistance, particularly among alumni. Finally, in 1988, the song was re-titled simply "Alma Mater" and various lyrics changed, including the opening which became "Dear old Dartmouth give a rouse..." A later line, "Stand as brother stands by brother" became "Stand as sister stands by brother..." Fortunately nobody altered the most memorable lines,[16]

> They have the still North in their hearts, the hill-winds in their veins,
> And the granite of New Hampshire, in their muscles... and their brains!

WDCR/WFRD stayed studiously neutral in these heated debates, which have never really died down. As late as 2010 I attended a performance by an alumni chorus in which certain parts of the song sounded garbled. Afterwards I mentioned this to the director, and he sighed, "we let each member sing it the way he wants to."

The battles over team names and the school song garnered some national attention, but nothing attracted the national media to Dartmouth as much as the exploits of *The Dartmouth Review*, a conservative off-campus newspaper founded by disaffected staffers from *The Dartmouth* in 1980. It was distributed free on campus, as well as mailed to many alumni. Among *Review* staffers over the next few years were students who would later become nationally prominent, including author Dinesh D'Souza '83 and TV commentator Laura Ingraham '85. The paper's backers included English Professor (and onetime Nixon-Reagan speechwriter) Jeffrey Hart and national conservative leader William F. Buckley Jr.[17]

Whereas WDCR/WFRD gave exposure to all sides while staying relentlessly neutral, the *Review* knew no such bounds. Needless to say the *Review* continued to call the College teams the Indians and the alma matter "Men of Dartmouth" (the paper distributed copies of the original lyrics to incoming freshmen each year). But it also attacked what it considered to be liberal excess and political correctness on campus, often with brio, greatly annoying the administration. One of the first flare-ups occurred in 1983 with the publication of an expose of a black music professor's rather loosely run class, titled "Professor Bill Cole's Song and Dance Routine." Cole was outraged, excoriating the publication, going to reporter Laura Ingraham's dormitory and banging on her door, demanding the *Review's* subscription list, and ultimately suing for $2.4 million. A year later the paper stirred up another hornet's nest when a reporter secretly taped a gay rights meeting and published the transcript. It also described an associate college chaplain as a supporter of the North American Man Boy Love Association, which led to another lawsuit.[18]

National media, including *The New York Times, The Wall Street Journal* and *60 Minutes,* began to run features on the ideological furor at Dartmouth and the College agonized over what to do. It railed, to no avail. One suggestion was to sue the paper over the use of the name "Dartmouth," since the paper was not officially associated with the College, but that would be seen as an attack on free speech. *The Dartmouth,* after a period of bemusement over the *Review's* antics, eventually turned against it, attacking its funding and trying to discourage advertisers from supporting it. But the *Review* rolled on, creating even more angst for campus liberals in years to come. It won most of the lawsuits aimed at it, and inspired similar publications to start up on other campuses.[19]

Perhaps the most insightful comment about the *Review* came years later from eminent Judge Laurence Silberman '57, himself a conservative, who said "I thought its writers were in some respects sophomoric but after all, they were sophomores. They were sometimes cruel, but I think *The Washington Post* is often cruel."[20]

Where was the college radio station in the midst of these nationally publicized political disputes in its backyard? The controversies that captured the attention of major media received very little coverage on WDCR/WFRD. It is true that a radio station is federally licensed and cannot take sides in the same way that a newspaper can. It is also true that Dartmouth radio had a long history of distancing itself from campus news in order to sound like a community station. Most of the staffers I spoke to from this era simply shrugged off *The Dartmouth Review* as not on their radar. Some claimed it was published chiefly for alumni, and a few intimated that it was actively disliked by station staffers who felt it was anti-diversity (ironic since the *Review's* own staff was rather diverse). The majority, however, agreed with News Director John May who said it was simply that station news coverage focused mainly on the Upper Valley, and stayed away from "internal College politics."[21]

May later said "we did cover a story about a confrontation between someone delivering copies of *The Review* [on campus] and another person who bit the *Review* staffer. We also ran a public affairs discussion about College funding for the Gay Students Association, which *The Review,* of course, opposed. (In protest, they tried to get College funding for a Bestiality Society.) The on-air discussion was lively but not especially acrimonious. After the show, as people were leaving Studio One, Dinesh D'Souza made a surprisingly conciliatory remark... to the effect that he didn't intend any offense, he was just trying to make the show interesting."[22]

Whether WDCR and WFRD were simply trying to remain above the fray, or "missing in action" during one of the biggest national Dartmouth stories of the 1980s, is open to debate. Perhaps, as one news director later remarked, "we fell short."[23]

## Music Programming

Stereo WFRD programmed plenty of classical music, which must have warmed the hearts of Professors Sices and Luehrmann, but its early schedule was best exemplified by an afternoon show called, appropriately, *Mixed Bag.* Unlike top

40 station WDCR, its focus was on the College community.

WFRD Monday-Friday Schedule (1977)

6:00   *Prelude* - short classical compositions, news on the half hour
9:00   *News*
9:10   *Carousel* - one major classical work
11:00  *Feature* - classical themes (e.g. vocal, Baroque, new releases)
12:00  *Noon Hour* - news and interview program
1:00   *Mixed Bag* - folk and soft rock (non top 40), with news updates
5:30   *Evening Summary* - newscast simulcast with WDCR
6:00   *Jazz Horizons* - soft jazz
7:00   *Concert Hall* - one or two major classical works
9:00   *Music Thru Midnight* - progressive rock
1:00   sign-off

To the extent that WFRD had an identity with listeners it was one of quirky variety, with an early station slogan being "You Won't Hear It Anywhere Else." Early tag lines for the station were "FM 99" (1977), "99FRD" (1980) and "99FM" (1981).

The WFRD schedule saw few changes until early 1981, when pressure from the College to increase revenues resulted in the station cutting back on classical music in the morning. This produced howls from classical fans, to which Promotion and Public Relations Director Harry Jeffcoat '83 frankly replied that "classical was not making it as an advertising medium." He added that classical fans could turn to WVPR, the recently launched (1977) Vermont Public Radio station in Windsor, Vermont.[24]

The change left the schedule even more muddled however, alternating from classical (6:00-9:00 a.m.) to rock (9:00 a.m.-6:00 p.m.), back to classical (6:00-8:00 p.m.), then to jazz (9:00-11:00 p.m.), and finally back to rock (11:00 p.m.-2:00 a.m.). So in January 1982 FM Program Director Tracy Weatherby '83 streamlined it into three long blocks, with rock in daytime (6:00 a.m. to 6:00 p.m.), classical in the evening (6:00 to 11:00 p.m.), and *Jazzbeat* in late night (11:00 p.m. to 2:00 a.m.). That brought complaints from late night rock fans as well as from some staffers who felt they hadn't been consulted, but Weatherby replied that "because people didn't know what they'd hear when they tuned to WFRD we lost a lot of listeners... on the whole I think this will be a great improvement to the station."[25]

Although classical music was relegated to the evening hours when audiences were smaller, it remained an important part of WFRD. In 1983 FM Program Director Robb Cutler '84 announced the launch of *Prelude*, a sponsored classical program guide that helped mollify listeners. In November 1983 one of the station's most stalwart faculty supporters, Professor Robin Robinson (affectionately known as "Rob-Rob"), the genteel host of *Opera Showcase* and *A Little Night Music*, was honored for his 25 years playing classical music on the station (actually he began in 1955). An endowment was created in his honor to purchase classical records for the station. He would continue to host his programs for nearly 20 more years.[26]

The loose, experimental atmosphere that characterized WFRD in its early days was beginning to change as well, as management pushed the station toward a smoother, more professional sound. In early 1983 FM Program Director Gary "Boot"

Seem '84 and Music Director Brian Goldner '85 tightened the rock format with explicit restrictions on record choices (to lessen repetition), greater consistency between d.j.'s, and even standardized catch phrases that d.j.'s were urged to use. One d.j. (Rich Wesley '84) quit, saying that canned phrases were "an insult to the intelligence of the jock and the listener," and others grumbled that the changes had been made without consulting them. But the changes stuck, and WFRD steadily edged toward the professional model of its parent.[27]

Meanwhile WDCR dominated its young offspring in sheer size of audience with its proven formula of middle-of-the-road and top 40 music. Once its classical programming and one of its signature newscasts (*Noon Hour*) had moved to FM, AM became even more oriented toward popular music.

WDCR Monday-Friday Schedule (1977)

6:00    *Daybreak* - easy listening and soft top 40 music, with frequent news updates

9:00    *Top of the Morning* - easy listening and older top 40; news updates

11:00  *Midday* - easy listening, Broadway, light top 40, comedy

12:00  *News*

12:15  *Midday* (continued)

1:00    *Sounds for the Tri-Town* - current top 40 hits and oldies

5:30    *Evening Summary* - comprehensive news wrap-up

6:00    *Jazz Horizons* - soft jazz

7:00    *Contemporary Rock* - Album-oriented rock and top 40

9:00    *News*

9:15    *Night-line* - public affairs show

10:00  *Blackside* - soul, disco and soft jazz

1:00    sign-off

This schedule remained relatively stable into the early 1980s. *Jazz Horizons* was removed from the schedule in 1978 and replaced with a rebroadcast of WFRD's prestigious noontime public affairs show. *Blackside* was renamed *Nightflight* and moved to an earlier, 9:00 p.m. start time (eventually, in the early 1980s, it became *Blackside* again).

Weekends brought a potpourri of programs on AM, many of them longtime station traditions, including a call-in request show (which for a time ran on both Friday and Saturday nights), Casey Kasem's extremely popular syndicated *American Top 40* countdown show, *Sportsline* sports quiz, *Morningstar* religious programming on Sunday morning, the charming *Pooh Corner* children's program, and Professor Robin Robinson's seemingly eternal *Opera Showcase*. In the late 1970s d.j. Mike Sullivan '80 channeled the popular Mr. Kasem with his own *Top 30 Countdown* on Monday nights, featuring the top 30 hits in the Hanover area.

The AM music staff (normally three to five people) was a key component of the Program Department. The station's weekly top tunes chart, compiled by the AM music director, helped guide much of the programming and was more a way to shape the sound of the station than a statistical compilation. Jason Klein '82 later recalled using the national *Billboard* charts and a "sense of what would work" on the station, plus perhaps some local feedback, when he compiled the chart. The music staff also maintained the library of color-coded LPs and 45 rpm's, with those in heavy rotation being recorded on cartridges for easy access.

By 1984 the pop music format was set at five songs per hour from the top 30 (including two or three with green labels, designating "power rotation"), one or two recent extras (orange labels), one or two oldies (purple), and the rest chosen by the d.j. from the library. AM Program Director Greg Beasley '85 characterized WDCR as a CHR (contemporary hit radio) station, with a strong mix of AC (adult contemporary) and oldies.[28]

In an interesting 1984 document called *The Official WDCR Format Book* Beasley emphasized that while d.j.'s were expected to follow the station's format, they were deliberately given latitude ("the actual songs to be played are up to the individual jock") and should inject personality into their shows. He continued,

> What I would like to emphasize is that our format is relatively distinctive compared to the other area stations. We've decided on this format after 26 years because it is a good compromise between getting great ratings and being fun to do. Remarkably, we do both. If we were on one extreme (complete format) then all songs would be selected in advance for the jock and jocks would do nothing but read cards and push buttons. If we were on the other extreme (no format) where people would just come in and play anything at all, then we would become a "typical" college station with only a weirdo fringe listenership. We would lose our advertisers and our ratings. My guess is that neither of these alternatives is an attractive goal.

Beasley had other advice for his d.j.'s as well. He wanted them to sound "smooth" (i.e., professional), conversational, and always speak as if the listener was a friend to whom they were talking. Inject a little humor if you can, he said, but don't be sarcastic and *never* mock advertisers. Pre-read your copy, and feel free to adapt it to your own language (except for ads). Without overdoing the chatter, WDCR should have a little more personality and be less of a jukebox than some of its competitors. "Don't underestimate the capacity you have to lift people up or change their lives a little."

A majority of the announcing staff wanted to play popular music. Staff lists from early 1982 categorized d.j.'s and found that 60 percent specialized in rock, 32 percent in classical, and 24 percent in jazz (some had multiple specialties).

The stations enhanced their professional sound further when they began carrying the NBC Radio Network in May 1981. There had been a running debate over the years about the advisability of signing with a network. Would it ruin the student experience, or make the station sound more generic? The chief advantages were the hourly NBC newscasts, which were of course solidly professional and covered the nation and the world, so that Dartmouth's own student newsmen could concentrate on the community. NBC also brought top notch features such as *Meet the Press*, film critic Gene Shalit, Dr. Joyce Brothers and political humorist Mark Russell. It was also an attractive deal, as NBC (which did not have an affiliate in the market) offered its feed for free if the station bought a satellite dish to download the signal. General Manager Mark Belmonte called it the station's "biggest step forward since signing on in 1958." That was perhaps a bit of hyperbole, but as an addition to, rather than a replacement for, student air product it obviously worked well, and WDCR remained an NBC affiliate for the next 15 years.[29]

Initially NBC was carried on both WDCR and WFRD, but problems arose when the popular *American Top 40* program was purchased by ABC, threatening its continued appearance on the stations. To solve this WFRD affiliated with ABC Contemporary Radio in 1983, although that affiliation only lasted for a few years.[30]

The Associated Press wire service and CompuWeather service also gave the students tools to sound professional. Also helpful to local coverage was the station's well-worn 1974 Chevy wagon, which was replaced in 1983 with a shiny new GMC Jimmy. Students called the mobile unit the MU - or "moo."[31]

### A Ticket to Paradise

Both stations staged regular promotions during the late 1970s and early '80s. Among the notable examples were an AM "Sounds of Summer" contest with posters, T-shirts, and bumper stickers (1978); an FM "Summer Celebration" featuring a week of specials including a night of international music and a look back at music of the '60s (as well as a nine-week, nine-show Beethoven celebration with commentators from the Music Department), also in 1978; an Upper Valley Dance Extravaganza co-sponsored by both stations and staged by Business Manager/entrepreneur Fran L'Esperance '79 (1978); "Sounds of Summer II" with a canoe and moped as grand prizes (1979); "Great Moments in Radio" (1979); "99 FM Rock in Spring," in which listeners had to guess the serial number of the station, with a $3,000 stereo system as grand prize (1981); a "Cliffhangers" mystery contest in which listeners guessed the flaws in alibis and detective work (1981); "Labatt's 50s 6-Pack," sponsored by Labatt's Ale, in which listeners had to identify songs from the 1950s from medleys of six brief snippets (1982); "Rock 'n' Spring Giveaway" (1982); "Two Ways to Win" (1984); and "Musicard" (1984).

Not all promotions worked out as planned. In 1984 FM Program Director Ray Wagner '85 managed to book the Clash to play Thompson Arena, anticipating a big haul, only to discover that the band got 85 percent of the gate. This so frustrated station staffers, who had promoted the show endlessly on the air, that at the concert they held up a big sign in the audience reading simply "85%." Of course no one knew what that meant, and the amused lead singer shouted from the stage that it was one of life's many mysteries.[32]

One of the biggest promotions was the annual "Ticket to Paradise" contest. In the 1982 edition more than $10,000 in prizes from local merchants was given away over an eight-week period, including a waterbed. The grand prize, a Windjammer Cruise for two from Garber Travel, was won by a woman from Norwich. According to WDCR Promotion Director Peter Herzig '84, it was "the most successful contest we've had yet; we collected an incredible number of entry slips."[33]

### Sports

Sports remained an integral part of the WDCR/WFRD schedules. During the 1977-78 season the stations covered nine football games, 26 hockey games, 24 basketball games and most of the baseball season. Many of these were away games, and some were quite exciting. In February 1978 sportscaster Dave Title '79 flew to South Bend, Indiana, to cover the Dartmouth-Notre Dame basketball game. Dartmouth was having a terrible year (3 wins, 9 losses), and it was widely assumed that the Big Green would be utterly demolished by the powerhouse Midwestern team, which Dartmouth rarely played, on the latter's home court. But it turned out to be an unexpectedly close contest, causing Title to exclaim on the air, "Holy shit! I can't believe this!"[34]

Plans for the 1979-80 season included play-by-play of games in 11 different sports, including all football, all men's hockey, all men's basketball, and all home baseball games. Other sports covered at least partially were men's and women's soccer, women's field hockey, women's hockey, women's basketball, men's lacrosse, and men's crew. Men's hockey had an stellar season (19 wins, 11 losses), culminating at the NCAA championships in Providence, Rhode Island, where Dartmouth made it to the semi-finals. Terry Large '79 did the play-by-play for the Dartmouth stations.[35]

The announcing team for football in the fall of 1980 was Alan Eagle '83 and Kevin Connolly '83 on play-by-play, and Peter "Shetty" Frechette '82 doing color. A typical broadcast began with a 10 minute pre-taped interview with Coach Joe Yukica, included a half-time interview with a knowledgeable pro such as famed *Boston Globe* sports columnist Ernie Roberts, and culminated with a post-game show wrapping up the game. Among the top Dartmouth players at the time was Jeff Kemp '81, son of congressman Jack Kemp. Jeff went on to an 11-year career in the NFL.[36]

Nevertheless WDCR/WFRD had to again contend with a Dartmouth College Athletic Council (DCAC) that threatened to revoke its rights to top Dartmouth sports. In the summer of 1979 WTSL made "a very attractive proposal" for football, basketball and hockey, forcing the station into an intense round of negotiations with the DCAC. DCAC Information Director Art Petrosemolo said "I think this is the first time we've actually put the rights out for bidding. We simply wanted to see what it was worth. Of course you're going to ruffle some feathers any time you do this." General Manager Joe Mannes, Sports Director Bob Oliver '82, and some sportscasters grumbled ("I think they were basically using 'TSL to get something out of us," said one), but Mannes and Oliver were professional about it and an agreement was eventually reached.[37]

One of the chief complaints of the DCAC over the years has been the sometimes less-than-professional quality of the student sportscasters. Some were quite good, but others weren't, and all were of course learning their craft. The DCAC didn't care about training, they just wanted the games to *sound good*. In 1980 the problem arose anew according to a report by station management, which said that "The Beacon Sports Network [which syndicated Dartmouth games outside the immediate area] has duplicated our broadcasts of Dartmouth sports events using its own staff, objecting that the quality of our announcers and technical crew was unfit for networking on non-student run stations." The suggestion was made that WDCR/WFRD hire a professional announcer, "but this suggestion was very unpopular with station members." Another problem was that one of the stations to which Beacon sold its coverage overlapped with part of the WDCR/WFRD coverage area, and the station was advertising locally to draw listeners away from the Dartmouth stations.[38]

This was an instance in which two of Dartmouth radio's most fundamental goals were in conflict. Which should take priority: to provide a real-world training ground for student broadcasters, or to sound thoroughly professional? For the time being, at least, Dartmouth chose to retain the unique character of its broadcasting experiment, and let the students be heard.

## Dracula and a Mountain of Coke

There was little scripted drama or comedy on radio by this time. In 1976 WFRD broadcast an entire night of special programming on Halloween consisting of a "Wife of Bath" debate between Professors Gaylord and Travis, a pre-recorded adaptation of Wilde's humorous tale *The Canterville Ghost*, and live coverage of Professor A.B. Paulsen reading an H.P. Lovecraft story. Boo![39]

The *Canterville Ghost* radio play was produced by Maura Harway '77, directed by Peter Threadgill '77 and starred deep-voiced Gerry Cox as the hapless ghost. There were a few other dramas broadcast in this period, including a production of Isaac Asimov's *Nightfall* by Harway and Dave Reed '79.[40]

In the fall of 1981 Lucretia Grindle '83 proposed a series of radio plays, produced by non-station personnel including Grindle and Professor Laurence Davies of the English Department. Their first production was an adaptation of *Dracula*, based on an Orson Welles script found in the library's Special Collections. Grindle also needed sound effects and ended up "running around and finding a vet somewhere near White River Junction who had huskies who howled nightly as the Montrealer [train] went through, and standing in zero degrees one night with a tape recorder waiting for them do 'do their thing' so we could use the tape for Dracula's wolves." Her second production was John Millington Synge's dark *Riders to the Sea* in early 1982. There may have been one more radio play in early 1983, but hopes for a regular bi-weekly production did not materialize. Grindle went on to become a successful novelist after graduation from Dartmouth.[41]

The main focus, however, was on music, news, sports, and public service campaigns. In the summer of 1977 one last *Let's Help* campaign was fielded. More modest than earlier efforts, it included a live broadcast of two bands on a Saturday afternoon and proceeds from two film showings at the Nugget Theater. The goal was to raise capital funds for the purchase of a building in Lebanon for the Upper Valley Senior Citizen Council, a campaign with an overall goal of $100,000. Due to limited summer staff and other factors, only $288 was raised by the station. A later report stated that "It was a credit to the organization that this was attempted at all and even more so because it was summer term. Kudos on this program go to Joyce Blankenbaker ['80] who organized and ran the entire program." It would be the last *Let's Help*.[42]

The demise of the big, sprawling *Let's Help* initiatives may have been due to several factors. Some suggested that the growing local United Way campaigns were crowding out individual efforts such as those of WDCR/WFRD. Or it may have been that the idealism of the '60s had waned somewhat, and the stations were simply becoming more and more commercially focused. This did not mean the end of public service on Dartmouth radio, however. In the late 1970s the station staged fundraisers for the newly opened Montshire Science Museum, including a May 1976 "kite day" organized by Peter Hirshberg '78 with contests for kite design and highest flyer and a demonstration of "fighting kites." The event raised money as well as visibility for the struggling Museum.[43]

In November 1980 the stations joined other campus organizations to promote the United Way campaign. One of the station's more colorful charity stunts was the Thanksgiving 1981 "Mountain of Coke" campaign, in which WDCR broadcast live from atop a huge mountain of donated cases of Coca-Cola stacked in the parking lot of the K-Mart Store in West Lebanon, selling cases to benefit the United Way. More than $2,000 was raised.[44]

## Competition

For the time being, at least, the Upper Valley remained a small, competitive, radio market with few outlets. The three AM stations (WDCR, WTSL, and WNHV) had been joined by two FMs (WFRD and WNHV-FM), but the former was just getting started and the latter merely simulcast its AM parent. On August 13, 1977 Vermont Public Radio launched its first station with WVPR-FM, 89.5, in Windsor, Vermont, about 17 miles south of Hanover. Its programming was mostly classical music and NPR programs, which took some of the heat off WFRD to serve that audience. It also provided internships for Dartmouth student broadcasters.[45]

Nibbling on the fringes of the market were easy listening station WTSV-AM and WECM-FM (106.1), which simulcast WTSV, in Claremont, New Hampshire, about 25 miles to the south. Right now it was not much of a threat, but in years to come that would change.

One minor blip on the Upper Valley media horizon was new television station WNNE, channel 31, which had arisen from the ashes of the old WRLH in September 1978, this time broadcasting in color! Although there were fears it might take money out of the market it did not prove to be much of a threat to the dominant radio stations. It did, like its predecessor, provide some internships. Even less of a factor was Dartmouth closed circuit television, which debuted in 1977 and was used mostly for instruction.[46]

Faced with this media concentration some enterprising students apparently tried to take matters into their own hands. In March 1977 *The Dartmouth* ran a story headlined "Maverick FM Station Airs Rock" claiming that a one-half watt FM station calling itself WSKI was broadcasting rock music in the evenings on 104 MHz, from an undisclosed location on campus. Its phone number was a pay phone in the Hopkins Center. "I don't consider them a big threat to WDCR" said WDCR/WFRD Chief Engineer Jim Ancona '78. Of course the whole thing may have existed only in the mind of the writer for *The Dartmouth*, which was known to occasionally print "gag" articles.[47]

In terms of audience, surveys showed varying rankings in the late 1970s and early 1980s, with either WTSL or WNHV generally number one in the Upper Valley as a whole but with WDCR leading in Hanover (campus and community), and strongly competitive in the rest of the region. At first WFRD trailed far behind its AM cousin, but by the early 1980s it had made considerable headway.

Different surveys showed different parts of the picture. Two 1977 Hanover surveys supervised by Mark Tomizawa showed 50 percent of students listening most to WDCR and 30 percent to WFRD, with no more than six percent for any other station. In town he found 42 percent listening most to WDCR, 25 percent to WTSL, 17 percent to WFRD, and 10 percent to WNHV. Interestingly he found that 90 percent of residents had an FM radio either in their home or car. He also estimated that 85 percent of Dartmouth students, 50 percent of Hanoverites, and 20 percent of the rest of the region were regular listeners of either WDCR or WFRD. Tomizawa immediately assembled a student sales force to hit the streets with these results.[48]

By the early 1980s Dartmouth Broadcasting was again hiring professional survey firms to document its position in the market for advertisers. Arbitron (the industry standard) was too expensive, Pulse was out of business and Mediastat was getting mixed reviews, so the stations first hired Radio Index (1981) and later Birch (1983). These surveys generally showed WNHV leading in total audience, with the WDCR-WFRD combo tied at number two, although individual surveys could vary. One May 1981 Radio Index telephone survey showed WNHV (AM plus FM) leading in the Upper Valley among all listeners aged 12-plus with a 25 percent share, followed closely by WDCR (21 percent), WTSL (16 percent), WECM (10 percent), and WFRD (8 percent). Demographically WDCR attracted younger listeners aged 12-34, while WNHV dominated among older adults, and WTSL was somewhere in the middle.[49]

WNHV and WTSL sold mostly on the basis of long-standing relationships with advertisers, not surveys. But WTSL in particular didn't like these numbers one bit, and in 1978 commissioned its own survey—conducted by Dartmouth's Tuck School of Business, no less!—which showed that *it* was the most popular station in the market, with 33 percent of the audience. However even that survey showed WDCR to be a strong competitor, ranking number two with a 23 percent share, followed closely by WNHV AM/FM (22 percent), with WECM (7 percent) and WFRD (4 percent) bringing up the rear.[50]

### Following the Money

In 1976 the *Broadcasting Yearbook* began publishing the advertising rates for many individual radio stations, which gives us an interesting insight into what the Upper Valley stations charged advertisers. The following numbers are "rate card," which is higher than advertisers actually paid since they usually got discounts for packages of ads, but they provide a rough idea of the relative value the market placed on each station.

During the late 1970s WDCR's morning drive-time rate was about $7.00 for a 30-second spot, compared to approximately $8.00 on WTSL and $10.00 on WNHV (AM plus FM). WFRD trailed at $4.00 per spot. WTSL and WNHV began raising their rates in 1978, followed a year later by the Dartmouth stations, and by the early 1980s the rate comparison was $9.00 for a spot on WDCR, $16.00 on WTSL and $14.00 on WNHV. Clearly, competing against well-entrenched local business interests, which had deep roots in the community, was not easy. However it was excellent training for student entrepreneurs who would have to face similar challenges when they graduated into the real world of business.[51]

The student management was up to the challenge and attacked the station's sales and revenue problems forcefully in the late 1970s and early 1980s. The first step was to replace the regional sales representative (New England Spot Sales), which was not performing satisfactorily. After a series of interviews Sales Director Mark Tomizawa hired the Kettell-Carter firm in Boston in the spring of 1977. Jack Kettell and Tomizawa immediately set to work designing a new (and higher) rate structure and going after new clients. General Manager Jordan Roderick proudly reported to the overseers that "there has been something of a revolution" in the Sales Department. Kettell-Carter would remain the stations' regional representative for the next dozen years.[52]

Tomizawa's next job was to fix the local sales problem. Following the Sandy MacDonald debacle, Lynn Mann had stabilized the local selling effort during 1975-77.

However by 1977 there was dissatisfaction with her performance, and during the summer she was let go. Jeff Lyon '77, a recent graduate who wanted to go professional, started selling for the station during the summer and became its acting sales manager during the fall and winter. Lyon began to turn the situation around but left in early 1978.[53]

Meanwhile there was turmoil on the student management side. Although the College was pressing the station to improve revenues, some of its departments undercut that goal. In June 1977 the Dean's Office told hotshot sales manager Tomizawa on short notice that he would be leaving campus for the fall term to study in Mexico (part of "The D-Plan," in which students were expected to study off-campus for at least two terms). He was replaced by Keith Quinton '80 until Jim Ancona took office early in 1978. Ancona came in with a great deal of energy, but almost immediately had a run-in with the college disciplinary committee over a seemingly minor matter and was told that as punishment he could not participate in any extracurricular activity, including WDCR. General Manager John Bussey protested bitterly about this to the College, calling the committee's decision shortsighted and cavalier, but to no avail. To the Directorate it was another in a series of clashes with College departments that seemed to undercut their best efforts to turn the station around (another was an episode in which the Athletic Department dug up part of the station's transmitter ground system, which abutted an athletic field, then seemed reluctant to fix the problem). Fortunately the Board of Overseers, which included representatives from the college administration, was often able to intervene and work things out.[54]

On the professional front Jeff Lyon was replaced in May 1978 by Bob Furman (aka Wildcat Productions), who continued the sales recovery. A report to the overseers in August said Furman "is the big story in the Sales Department. Bob has done a commendable job. He has boosted our sales to record highs and has expended much energy toward improving operations at the stations." However there were complaints about student production follow-up and enough salesmen on the streets. In August 1979 Furman quit.[55]

He was replaced in November by Will Stanley (aka Willpower Productions), who stayed for five years and was one of the most successful professional salesmen in station history. He too had problems getting students to follow through on some of his sales, and did some of the production work himself, bringing in Peter Skinner to help out. He also employed sales representatives Scott Curtis and Heidi Dietschi-Cooper for a time to sell the station. (The station's professional sales representative operated as a consultant, and hired his own support staff.) Stanley took sales to spectacular heights, and it was a blow when he tendered his resignation in 1984, in order to invest in and help run alumnus Jeff Shapiro's venture to buy sleepy WTSV and WECM-FM. He was replaced by Laura Canada.[56]

The final breakthrough in the sales logjam came in November 1977 when College attorney Cary Clark announced that he had researched the issue of paying commissions to student salesmen and determined that it *would* be legal to do so. This came like a thunderclap at the overseers meeting. Paying commissions had been brought up repeatedly in prior years as an obvious way to incentivize students to do one of the hardest jobs at the station, but had always been dismissed as not legally possible. Now that it was, the overseers immediately approved a one-year trial, which was successful. Eventually a scale was arrived at whereby sales to Class "A" accounts (the station's most loyal advertisers) earned a five percent commission, those to general accounts seven percent, and those to new accounts more than seven percent. As in earlier years everyone was urged to get involved in servicing accounts, including Directorate members.[57]

The combination of a determined management, hard working sales managers, the right professional salesmen and commissioning students had the desired effect. The financial trauma of the mid 1970s began to heal. Revenues, which at their nadir had dropped below $50,000, rose to the $60,000 level in fiscal year 1977, and $80,000 in 1978. Then, under Will Stanley, they really took off. By 1981 they reached approximately $150,000, and by 1984, $300,000. The station was paying off its College loans and building up a reserve fund. Money was coming in. The main problems now were collections (sometimes the station had to go to small claims court to collect), and fulfillment. The College even suggested that with all this money coming in perhaps the profits should be distributed to support other campus clubs, a suggestion station leaders roundly rejected.[58]

Although professionals were now helping the station, student salesmen continued to be extremely important to the sales effort, at least for a while. In 1978 it was estimated that the professional sales representative was bringing in approximately $40,000, the student salesmen ("house accounts") about $30,000, and the regional rep about $10,000. Eventually, though, the professionals phased the students out. In terms of programming that brought in advertising dollars, popular music ruled. In the early 1980s the syndicated *American Top 40* alone was said to bring in $26,000 per year.[59]

WFRD was also beginning to contribute financially. Tracking its exact contribution was difficult because many sales were for both stations together, but in 1979 Business Manager Jean Scarrow '80 noted that it had grown from 10 to 16 percent of gross revenues, due mostly to its rock programming. In 1983 Business Manager Bennett Zimmerman '85 estimated FM's contribution at 40 percent, and by early 1984 Katie Mulligan was putting it at "nearly 50 percent."[60]

### Technical

Getting FM on the air was a huge triumph for the Technical Department. Broadcast engineer Dan Churchill had consulted on that; later Lindsey Collins and Dick Schellens of the Medical School consulted for the station. However most of the work was done by the students themselves.

The first major challenge came in mid 1978, with the replacement of the "radials" buried underground around the WDCR tower, necessitated by the accidental damage caused by college maintenance personnel. This work was necessary before the station could get its regular license renewal. It was a $5,000 job and the station hoped to save money by enlisting station members to help with the physical labor, but few of them showed up so the work fell largely on the engineers, led by Technical Director Chip Behal. A few years later, with money pouring in, Technical Director Ned Roos '83 oversaw the purchase of a new $14,000 AM transmitter and a $6,000 emergency power generator, "due to the spontaneous combustion of the old one" (1982). His successor Joel Margolese '85 worked on installing a large satellite dish to receive the NBC and ABC network feeds (1983). Both of them had to fight off a DCAC scheme to force WDCR to move its transmitter tower, a move that would have cost between $40,000 and $200,000, so that the teams could use the space as a playing field.[61]

Two major studio construction projects, planned but deferred due to cost when WFRD was launched, were finally completed in the early 1980s. In 1982 AM studio 5X became a reality. Designed by Brad Carpenter '82, the $28,000 facility included a 12-channel solid state stereo control board from Broadcast Audio, two Technics turntables, four tape cartridge players, two digital transmitter controllers and a plethora of supporting equipment. Peter Harris '83, Richard Wesley, Wally Broadbent '83, John McNeill '83 and Ned Roos completed all work except for carpentry. The major project of 1984 was the construction of FM studio 3X, a state-of-the-art facility that promised to improve air product and make maintenance easier. Built at a cost of $50,000, it was also wired entirely by students, under the supervision of Technical Directors George Bourozikas '86 and Janice Sakowicz '85 and consulting engineer Lindsey Collins. In November it was dedicated by President David McLaughlin, who seemed most impressed by the fact that the students had paid for the whole thing themselves. General Manager Mulligan said that the new studios were part of a five year plan to bring all eight of its studios up to current standards. Given how quickly technology changes, she said, by the time that plan was completed it would be time to start all over again.[62]

There were also "routine" crises which regularly tested the students' ingenuity. John May recalled one summer morning, between terms, when WDCR suddenly went off the air. This was not especially unusual, but none of the usual fixes, like trying to restart the transmitter remotely, worked. "The problem felt different from a normal tranny crash," he recalled. May drove to the transmitter shack and found nothing wrong; there simply was no signal coming in from the station. There were few staffers around to help (it was between terms), but it was finally determined that the buried telephone company cable carrying the signal from Robinson Hall to the transmitter had been cut by a construction crew. Frantic calls to New England Telephone brought little help (they thought the station's phone was out), and May couldn't broadcast from inside the transmitter shack itself because of interference. So he hauled a cartridge machine and an armload of music and ads, plus the longest audio cable he could find, to the transmitter site, set up a folding table in a nearby field and broadcast from there until the phone company got its act together.[63]

There was a long debate during 1984 about the desirability of converting WDCR to AM stereo, at a cost of about $20,000. AM Program Director Greg Beasley promoted the idea, saying that it represented the future and WDCR would be the first such station in New Hampshire. But Technical Directors Margolese and Bourozikas resisted, saying that it would put undue pressure on the Tech Department at a time when so much else was going on. In December Beasley's successor David Wachen '87 wrote a 10-page memo laying out all of the arguments and endorsing the idea, but it never came to pass. It turned out that AM stereo was not the next "big thing," although it is possible that the future of AM broadcasting would have been different if it had been widely adopted.[64]

## Staff and Administration

As one of the best known activities on campus, Dartmouth radio continued to attract a large and enthusiastic staff. Some joined on freshman activities night, but many were recruited by personal contact from current station members. Future General Manager Jeff Shapiro recalled being invited to the station as a freshman by a dormitory friend, then lured into a business department meeting with the promise of free pizza. (They promptly made him comptroller.) Several of the station's top leaders came from the Tri-Kap fraternity, where older brothers networked with new arrivals. These included Joe Mannes, Bill Goddard '81, Mark Belmonte, Greg Beasley, and Shapiro.[65]

At any given time there were about 100 to 125 students on staff. There was a lot of camaraderie, and many recall going on "license runs" to Boston to take the (easy) FCC exam for a third-class radiotelephone operator's license, which was required of all d.j.'s. The station had training programs, and when there was a shortage of strong candidates one year, AM Program Director Sally Nutt '80 came up with a "big jock/little jock" mentoring program.[66]

Although student salesmen now got commissions, virtually everyone else worked for free. It was possible to pick up a little pocket money by staying on campus and working shifts during the semester breaks, when d.j.'s were paid. Another incentive, in 1984, came in the form of a $1,500 grant made to one student per term who had applied for and received a non-paying internship at a radio station. General Manager Mulligan hoped that students participating in the program would bring their experience back to the station and "help make it a better organization."[67]

Among the nagging staff problems was that of "crumping" (missing an air shift). A "Proposed 99FM Crump Policy" from the early 1980s dealt with this humorously. Sickness was "no excuse," it read ("If you can go to the doctor you can come to work"); neither was the death of someone you knew ("There is nothing you can do for them..."); nor was an operation ("We believe that as long as you are an employee here you will need all of whatever you have, and should not consider having anything removed"). As for the d.j.'s own death, "This will be accepted as an excuse but we shall require two weeks' notice."

### Women Advance

Dartmouth became co-educational in 1972, and by 1981 40 percent of the student body was female. Dartmouth broadcasting never reached that percentage, although the reasons are not entirely clear. Hardly anyone interviewed for this book, male or female, saw the station as exclusionary in any way. It may simply be that the radio profession, and the heavy diet of rock music featured by WDCR/WFRD, were not as appealing to young women as to men.

However women did sign up for the station. A departmental tally in 1977 revealed that while only 17 percent of the entire station staff was female, approximately half of the News Department was female. News was one of the first areas to attract women, and it was also the first area in which women moved into management positions. Barbara Reinertsen appears to have been the first female news director, in the spring of 1977, followed by Harriet Schwartz '78 (briefly) in 1978, Linda Button '79 in 1978-79 and Margaret Smith '82 in 1979. The first women on the station Directorate were Business Manager Kristy Weinschreider '79 and Director of Development and Legal Affairs (DODALA) Barbara "Binky" Moses, both appointed in February 1977. Other early female executives included Jean Scarrow '80 (classical director, business manager), Sally Nutt '80 (AM program director), Janice Scott '80 (minority affairs director), Patricia Walsh '81 (ombudsman), Kim Smith '82 (technical director), Patricia Lippoczy '83 (legal affairs), and Tracy Weatherby '83 (FM program director). Finally, in 1984, the station had its first female general manager, Katie Mulligan. As Mulligan ended her term a year later she reflected back on running a large volunteer organization that was "almost ridiculously committed." From it, she said, she had learned a great deal about "management, leadership, and friendship."[68]

## The Minority Conundrum

While women were assimilated relatively smoothly into the station, African-Americans were not. There were no public blow-ups on the scale of the 1976 protests, but friction continued. The Directorate and overseers talked constantly about the problem during 1976-78, and in 1978 summarized the issue this way.

> At the April 9-10, 1976 meeting of the overseers, the Planning Council reported that minority involvement at the stations was satisfactory. While this was certainly true, it is just as certain that satisfactory was not the whole story. There was a definite tension then between black and white.
>
> Today the story is much the same. Minorities are involved in every part of the staff and management in numbers larger than ever before. The tension, however, remains. There are those who think promotion and opportunity should be doled out on the basis of professional merit. On the other side of this issue are those who believe minorities have a right to express themselves on radio without regard to formats, professional codes and laws which they see as racially biased.[69]

An attached letter from an unhappy black station member provided a personal perspective on the issue. He said that while he enjoyed his work at the station, he was "discouraged" by statements he heard that, while not blatantly racist, suggested that some felt blacks "are, as a group, inferior." He did feel that the station showed more respect for minorities than some other campus organizations, but that it needed to improve. "The sad part of it is that these people don't even realize their own prejudices."

The station's leaders worked hard to ameliorate tensions. They coordinated with the Afro-American Society on recruiting, and effectively turned over the entire *Blackside* programming block to that group. They strove to keep the minority affairs director position filled and urged that individual to talk regularly with them. A major point of discussion during 1977-78 was whether the minority affairs director should be seated on the Directorate. There were numerous discussions about this, including a public meeting in July 1978 at which many points of view were aired. In the end this was not done, in the belief that minority managers would have greater legitimacy if they earned positions of authority. This is essentially what happened in the next few years, as African-Americans appeared on the Directorate as sales manager and AM program director.[70] Meanwhile the minority affairs position was reconstituted to emphasize minority recruiting as well as follow-up with recruits who did join the station, to make sure they did not feel "abandoned."

Clearly these difficult issues were not unique to Dartmouth Broadcasting. To some degree they were reflected throughout society—and still are.

Much of the African-American involvement with the stations revolved around WDCR's *Blackside*. The name was changed to *Nightflight* for a time, but then changed back. By the early 1980s there were problems staffing the 17 hours per week devoted to the show, and one (white) general manager said he had to d.j. it himself ("I learned to appreciate rap"). In 1982, amid complaints of "stagnation" and complacent d.j.'s, AM Program Director Bob Gray '83 attempted to limit its hours in order to broaden the number of d.j.'s on air, but this met with fierce resistance from black staffers who considered the entire block "theirs." The show was in effect untouchable. Finally its name was changed to *PM Dimensions*, and WDCR's black programming block seems to have ended not long after.[71]

### "An Unstable Situation"

One problem which has dogged the station throughout its history has been the incredible amount of time required of students to maintain this marvelous machine. Successive managements have somehow managed to deal with it, but at times it erupted into a full blown crisis. One such time was 1977, shortly after the launch of FM. General Manager Jordan Roderick recounted to the overseers some of the impressive achievements of his organization in recent months, but then said, "There are storm clouds on the horizon." He continued, "Surveys we have taken show that the average station member spends about five to ten hours in the station per week. Needless to say, none of the achievements I have mentioned above is the work of five hour a week workers." Then he listed the Directorate's weekly workload:[72]

| | |
|---|---|
| General manager | 40 hours |
| Sales manager | 40 hours |
| AM program director | 45 hours |
| FM program director | 30 hours |
| Business manager | 26 hours |
| Development/legal affairs | 22 hours |
| Technical director | 19 hours |

"This," he said, "is an extremely unstable situation." It was of course on top of their full student course loads. The previous year several senior managers had resigned, at least in part because of the time commitment required. Occasionally a student even flunked out of Dartmouth because of overcommitment to the station, although this appears to have been rare.[73]

No one had a good answer for this, although it was perhaps a warning to the overseers not to squeeze the student management too hard for increased revenue or unnecessary initiatives.

One change made in 1980 to lessen the burden on seniors was to start and end Directorate terms somewhat earlier. For many years the custom was that a new Directorate would be chosen in the winter and take control in the spring. For most Directorate members, this meant serving from the spring term of their junior year through the winter term of their senior year. This left only one term before graduation, and also meant they had little time to advise their successors. Starting with the 1980 Directorate the new team was announced in November (at the station banquet) and served from January until December.

At the time FM was launched the governing overseers asked the Directorate to think about the fundamental goals of the new, enlarged organization. In March 1976 Richard Mark delivered a 18-page essay outlining the new management's thinking. It largely mirrored the twin traditional goals of Dartmouth Broadcasting: to provide a unique programming service to campus and community, and to serve as a training ground for students. Interestingly, it emphasized that "Programming should be a showcase of those things which Dartmouth students do well rather than be a mirror of commercial radio. In producing such programs, the station member should strive for professionalism, not to be a professional."[74]

The overseers (and later the trustees) endorsed these recommendations, with one significant addition. The final document was prefaced with the statement that these goals were to be pursued "within the constraint that Dartmouth Broadcasting be financially sustained by its own operation." It was the first explicit statement that Dartmouth College was as interested in having campus radio pay for itself, as in what the station actually did. This would have profound consequences in years to come. But for now, at least, the students continued to operate pretty much as they had.[75]

Discussions between the Directorate and the overseers on how to make the new and larger operation more manageable, and fiscally stable, continued into 1977. In October 1977 the station held a "think tank" to discuss the station's problems and brainstorm possible solutions. Directorate member Binky Moses commented, "We are considering asking the trustees to provide us with institutional support, which we have not had so far." At its next meeting the overseers listened to the students and agreed that while the stations were running well, it was not fair to finance such an intense level of activity "out of the management's hide." They rejected draconian solutions such as selling one of the licenses, or bringing in professional management, and instead asked the management to draw up a realistic five-year financial plan showing what capital and operating expenses would likely be over that period. If advertising revenues fell short, the College would make up the difference, assuming the trustees agreed with the plan.[76]

General Manager Roderick and his senior managers then set to work drawing up the plan, which involved a multitude of assumptions and unknowns. It predicted that the next five years would see a financial crunch. Under "moderate" assumptions expenses would fluctuate between $105,000 to $127,000 per year (including College loan repayments, and payments into a reserve fund), while revenue would grow slowly from $67,000 to $81,000. Capital expenses, such as replacement of worn-out equipment, would begin to abate in the mid-to-late 1980s, with the next big replacement cycle beginning in the early 1990s.[77]

One suggestion repeatedly made by student managements over the years was that hard working senior managers should be paid at least token compensation. The suggestion now was $200 per term for each Directorate member. This opened a real can of worms, however (Why only the Directorate? What happens in "down" years? Is it even legal?), and was not approved.

The rest of the five-year plan, with its promise of support if revenues fell short, appears to have been accepted in 1978. It was a useful exercise but was almost immediately outdated, as such plans often are. As noted earlier, revenues over the next few years rose faster than anyone anticipated, largely eliminating the station's financial woes.

221

## The WRKO Report

Still looking for a way to lessen the burden on student management, the overseers next discussed hiring a management consultant to address three big areas of concern: how could the heavy demands on student management be lessened, how could the stations achieve a steadier stream of income (as opposed to the wild swings of recent years), and was it really possible to meet all three trustee goals—quality programming, student training, and financial self-sufficiency? Would the station have to reduce its level of activity, or could it accomplish its goals by reorganizing its management structure?[78]

At first Rick Devlin, the aggressive young manager of WOR radio in New York, showed interest in the project, but in the end it went to a team from WRKO radio in Boston led by General Manager Jack Hobbs. Unfortunately their 19-page report landed with a thud. After spending a day at the station (much of it looking for documents in the chaotic files), the team recommended, among other things, (1) hire a broadcast professional to provide ongoing advice and guidance, (2) establish separate managements for the two stations, (3) write lots of manuals, (4) do lots of market research, and (5) pay people. They also recommended a rather rigid bureaucracy, with top-down management like their own. Scribbled on a copy of the report in the files are notes like "no!", "why?", and "totally false." The report was quietly filed.[79]

### Committee on the Future of the Stations: "Money is Irrelevant to Morale"

Several smaller changes were made in the late 1970s to lessen the load on station management. The number of station members serving on the Board of Overseers was cut from five to one (the general manager), in order to give students more time to actually run the station. "We're trying to free the students as much as possible," said board chair Jordan Baruch. At about the same time the first station alumnus, one with real-world broadcasting credentials, was appointed to the board, making it no longer the exclusive province of administrators and faculty. The first alumni appointee was none other than John A. Gambling '51, onetime WDBS general manager and now one of the top radio personalities in New York. He served from 1975-79 and proved to be extremely helpful and a great friend of the station. Succeeding him in the alumni seat was Jim Varnum '62, onetime program director who had returned to Hanover to become president of Mary Hitchcock Hospital. Other alumni would follow in the 1980s, including James Rosenfield '52 of CBS and newspaperman Guy MacMillin '64.[80]

In 1982 formal guidelines were approved for the overseers, which added an executive committee to deal more quickly with issues that arose between regular quarterly meetings.[81]

In 1983 low morale at the station led General Manager Dan Daniels to convene a Committee on the Future of the Stations (COFS), which addressed "the directionlessness that has prevailed in the last two years." The stations were making money, but staffers were frustrated and dissatisfied. It was a thoughtful and far reaching document which could serve as valuable reading today. Addressing the problem of management style in the preliminary discussions, this exchange took place (names have been omitted here).[82]

222

As a reason for ineffective management, [one member] pointed out that we are all students with no prior experience. Some had high school experience, which [another member] said was nothing compared to the management problems we face here. [The first member] continued that some have talent, others simply do not. But none have real experience, we are here to get that experience.

Among the recommendations were a formal program of mentoring by current leaders, and encouraging leaders to delegate more responsibility so that those on their way up learn about leadership and responsibility as well as the technical aspects of station operation. Other recommendations were greater transparency on the part of the Directorate, more interaction between a retiring Directorate and its successor, a more clear-cut statement of station purpose that was frequently repeated at meetings, updated manuals, and surveys of station members ("How are we doing?"). "Money is irrelevant to morale," the report said. "What we need are goals and well-defined ways of meeting them, and incentives to work here. We also need some way to pursue *controlled* growth."

Another suggestion, presented almost as an afterthought, would have major ramifications in the next few years: "Make the formats of the two stations more distinct from one another." More on that in the next chapter.

The station still made relatively little use of its growing body of alumni. DODALA "Binky" Moses mailed out the first *Alumni Newsflash* in 10 years in August 1977, with a cover greeting by Overseer John Gambling and articles about the launch of FM and a diagram of the new office and studio layout. It brought "enthusiastic responses" and led to another in winter 1978. But there would be no more until 1982.[83]

Moses also sent letters to some 250 alumni in the field of communications asking about the possibilities of internships and jobs at their companies.

## Landmarks

Dartmouth radio was now moving through its fourth and fifth decades, and several landmarks were observed. Perhaps the most poignant for those who toiled there in the 1960s and 1970s was the retirement in 1979 of Evelyn Hutchins, the beloved "Mrs. H," after 19 years with the station. She had served as secretary, traffic coordinator, symbol of continuity, and mother hen to successive waves of eager young men and women who passed through. Years later, in 2008, she was feted at WDCR's 50th anniversary celebration and the affection in the room was palpable. She passed away on July 12, 2011, at the age of 93.[84]

Mrs. H was succeeded in the fall by Winona "Winnie" Lacoss, who would remain at the station even longer and become equally beloved.

The College itself saw a major transition in June 1981 with the retirement of President Kemeny and the induction of businessman David T. McLaughlin, former CEO of the Toro Company, as Dartmouth's 14th president. Kemeny had strongly supported the independence of Dartmouth Broadcasting, and so did McLaughlin, although he was seen as a somewhat distant figure. His tenure at Dartmouth turned out to be rather short (1981-1987), marked by battles with the faculty as well as with students protesting the College's South African investments and reinstatement of ROTC.[85]

WDCR celebrated its 20th anniversary in March 1978 with a front page feature story in *The Dartmouth*, in which General Manager John Bussey talked about the enormous achievements of the station over the years. In September 1981 it marked the 40th anniversary of the first DBS broadcast.[86]

The biggest celebration, however, was WDCR's silver anniversary in May 1983. This was a major event, with a full weekend of events designed to "honor the people who founded WDCR and those who made it grow." Approximately 900 alumni were contacted and more than 100 came to Hanover including such luminaries as John Gambling, former CNN chief Maurice Schonfeld '53, CBS executive James Rosenfield '52, ABC reporter Bill Beutel '53, and NBC Washington Correspondent Bob Hager '60. There was a series of seminars and panels on subjects such as "Ethics in the Media," "Broadcasting Careers," and "Swaying Voter Opinion," all open to the public and some broadcast, and of course a banquet. A pocket history of the station, edited by General Manager Dan Daniels, was distributed. There was much coverage of these events in *The Dartmouth* and a feature story in the alumni magazine. Daniels predicted there could be a TV station at Dartmouth in the next five years, and, as for radio, "we hope we will be doing this well in another 25 years."[87]

One possibly unintended consequence of the celebration was that it exposed young staffers to alumni of earlier generations, some of whom were dismayed by the heavily commercial direction the stations had taken. That got at least some current managers thinking about the basic purposes of Dartmouth broadcasting. More recent alumni thought commercial was just fine, however, so it was a mixed message, and there was no doubt about the College's primary interest: revenue.[88]

Congratulations poured in, including a letter on White House stationery signed by Ronald Reagan ("I have many happy memories of my years in radio and I know what an exciting and rewarding experience it can be"). Downstairs in Robinson Hall *The Dartmouth* published its own slightly snarky congratulations in an editorial headlined "Congratulations, kids." It repeated its earlier praise of the station for its "singular achievement in redefining the concept of responsibility," then added, "Like WDCR, *The Dartmouth* held a gala celebration to mark its 25th anniversary. But that was back in 1824."[89]

The radio station and *The Dartmouth*, as the two main campus media outlets, periodically ribbed each other, although they were not really in competition. There was perhaps a hint of envy in a 1976 joke article headlined "WDCR Gets Loan, TV, Copter" which explained that the hyper-active station upstairs was reported to be getting a $3 million loan from the College to build a TV station (to be dedicated by Walter Cronkite), was getting a helicopter for "Guy in the Sky" rush hour traffic reports, and might sublease the chopper as a gunship to reduce Hanover's stray dog population. The first three programs to be produced on the new TV station would be *Maura Hartmann, Maura Hartmann*, about a mature woman at Dartmouth, *Lost in Space*, featuring lectures on modern sculpture by Professor McGrath, and *Wild Kingdom*, about the College fraternity system.[90]

# Chapter 10

# 1985-1990: The Birth of 99Rock

The year 1985 marked a major turning point for Dartmouth Broadcasting, as well as the beginning of a tumultuous period for Dartmouth College. In radio it was the year in which the formats of WDCR and WFRD were essentially flipped, setting a template that would endure for the next quarter century at least. FM became a thoroughly commercial station designed principally to make money, and AM the outlet for student creativity. This was done abruptly, and imposed top-down, causing great turmoil in the station ranks.

As for the campus, the year led into what has been called Dartmouth's "Winter of Discontent" (1985-86).[1] Although the very public conflict was ostensibly over the College's investments in the apartheid-driven South African regime, it was really about much larger issues of intellectual freedom, dissent, and tolerance (or intolerance) of unpopular viewpoints. Like the Vietnam conflicts of the 1960s it put a national media spotlight on Dartmouth, to the delight of some and the dismay of others.

General managers during this period were William Furlong '86, David Wachen ("walk-en") '87, Andy Shapiro '88, Seth Skolnik '89, Seth Rosenblatt '89, and Tim Reynolds '91. In addition a custom of "acting" or temporary general mangers began around this time, with the temporary GM replacing the regular GM during terms in which the latter was off campus. These included George Bingham '87, Robert Striker '88 and Tom Stone '90.

## A Major Programming Overhaul

During 1983 Dan Daniels' Committee on the Future of the Stations had addressed the manageability of such a large operation by students, as well as how to insure a steadier revenue stream. Treasurer's representative John Bryant hammered this last point home repeatedly at overseers' meeting—the College wanted the stations to be financially self sustaining, if not a profit center for the College. Daniels' successor Katie Mulligan made developing a strategic plan for the future of the stations the centerpiece of her administration. Driving these discussions, she would later say, were two principal factors. First, the radio industry was changing. Nationally FM listenership had surpassed that of AM 10 years earlier, and while the insulated Upper Valley lagged behind, it was inevitable that change would come here as well. Better to get ahead of the curve than be left in the dust as was happening to AM stations in many markets. Second, the FM signal simply had wider reach than that of AM. Dartmouth needed that reach to remain competitive. Behind everything lurked the matter of finances.[2]

The discussions took on sudden urgency in October when Sales Manager Will Stanley abruptly resigned, taking with him some of the stations' prized clients.

His replacement Laura Canada faced a difficult challenge selling the Dartmouth stations with their mish-mash of programming against Stanley's new station, a much more focused FM competitor. The student leaders knew they needed to do something, and quickly. At the end of the year Mulligan's Directorate recommended a truly radical move to the overseers: reverse the roles of the AM and FM stations. For WFRD the new goal would be "to give students the experience of running a fully commercial, formatted FM radio station, whose goal will be to provide a consistent, sellable air product competing for the largest possible market share." For WDCR, it would be "to give students the opportunity to create varied and diverse programming with an emphasis on quality and originality... it will become the 'college' radio station, offering alternatives that we have no room for now."[3]

Several advantages were advanced for the plan. It would provide more options for students, who could choose to "do their own thing" on WDCR or join WFRD and learn to run a thoroughly commercial operation; it would decrease staffing needs, especially between terms, because WFRD could be simulcast on WDCR whenever the latter did not have enough staff; by making the programming more distinct it would presumably satisfy the needs of both the campus (AM) and Upper Valley (FM); and by giving FM a singular focus, it would hopefully make more money.

To grab the attention of both audiences and advertisers, the changes would have to be quick, and dramatic. WFRD would have to dump its classical, jazz and other programming overnight, and go exclusively with tightly formatted rock music. Changes at "hit radio" WDCR could be more leisurely, since it was envisioned as free form, but it would have to take on a new, more college-oriented personality.

The overseers worried about elements of the plan. Would WDCR have any real future? Yes, said retiring GM Mulligan, it would still have a format and not become a hodge-podge, but it would offer a place for alternatives. Would it simply simulcast FM? No, that would be done only when absolutely necessary. What would happen to FM's classical listeners? They would be fully informed in advance, and "the feeling is that the listeners will not mind." Interestingly there was apparently no discussion of what the student staff thought of the change.[4]

That last omission was a mistake. When the changes were announced internally on January 10, 1985, they set off a firestorm. This seems to have been not because of the changes themselves, but the unilateral way in which they were made. Dartmouth radio staffers were an enthusiastic and hard working group, and they thought of the facility as their station, a sort of club or fraternity into which they put a lot of work, in return for which they expected to have some input. Staff revolts in prior years had been dealt with largely by having the student leaders make an effort to simply listen, giving junior staffers the feeling that their opinions counted too. Polls, all-station meetings, and committees had all been used as ways to bring everyone in. But in this case, apparently, one of the biggest decisions in station history was made behind closed doors, and simply imposed. The result was predictable. An emergency meeting of the full Directorate at 10:00 p.m. on the night of January 10 was raucous, with charges and counter-charges, and at least two members walked out, one in tears. An open station meeting was quickly called for the next afternoon, which not everyone heard about, so a second station meeting was convened that night at 7:00 p.m. That one was even louder, with insults and a near fist-fight between two senior staffers. Others had to pull them apart.[5]

On the following day, January 12, the overseers held a special meeting at which the changes were quickly approved. Most of the Directorate was present, but no mention was made of the staff furor during the previous two days.

The changes were announced to the campus ten days later by General Manager Furlong, in a front page story in *The Dartmouth*. He recited all the reasons for the change, including more opportunity for student creativity on WDCR and for rock-loving d.j.s to pursue their passion on WFRD. WFRD, he said, "is tentatively scheduled to begin eighteen hours of rock music a day on February 4."[6]

The community learned about the changes in February through stories in the *Valley News* ("Goodbye Basie and Bach, Dartmouth's FM Station Goes All Rock and Roll") and *New Hampshire Times* ("WFRD Turns Its Bach"). These set off a flurry of complaints from area classical listeners. Wrote one, exaggerating somewhat, "It's certainly pitiful when an institution of higher learning with two radio stations devotes all time on both of them to the 'granite in their brains,' hard rock. Is it really impossible to provide the least bit of classical, jazz, or folk music, news, documentary or any other programming of general interest?" Old critic Professor David Sices was even more cutting, declaring that WFRD no longer deserved its license, and no longer deserved to represent Dartmouth College.[7]

Publicly Furlong lamented, "All I can say to [critics] is, look, I enjoy listening to classical music too, but I can't afford the time to go and play it while managing a radio station." Privately, to Sices, he wrote a remarkably blunt and angry response.

FM Program Director Margo Jacobs '86 began to implement the changes, but not fast enough for some on the Directorate or overseers. During the summer, while she was off campus, acting General Manager David Wachen and acting FM Program Director Bill Spencer '88 tightened the station's format considerably, exerting more centralized control over the music mix and the scheduling of news and weather updates. According to some the sound also began to shift from the intended AOR (album-oriented rock) toward more hit-oriented CHR (contemporary hit rock).[8]

When Jacobs and others returned in September they were furious. Charges and countercharges flew back and forth about alleged secret meetings, feuding enemy camps, who was told what and when, and authority undermined. The feud was published for all to see in the pages of *The Dartmouth*. A dramatic station meeting was held on September 21—moderated, appropriately, by drama Professor James Steffensen—at which five staff members resigned. Among them were two members of the Directorate, Jacobs and Technical Director George Bourozikas '86. They emphasized that they were not doing so because of the format change, but because of the way they had been treated, and the "deep factionalism at the station." "It reached the point where I couldn't take it anymore," said Jacobs, "and I had to get out." Rivalry between staffers affiliated with the Tri-Kap and Phi Tau fraternities was also said to play a role. For public consumption, at least, Wachen responded that the new more "professional" sound had received "good feedback from advertisers" and that "some advertisers that left us are coming back now." Nevertheless, during its first, tumultuous year the new WFRD had four program directors: Jacobs, Spencer, Rick Rosson '88, and Mike O'Connor '86.

The turmoil at the station gradually subsided, but some listeners were still mad. In April 1986 a petition was circulated on campus decrying WFRD's new "slick, commercial" format and asking it to challenge listeners by playing a wider variety of new and different types of music—not just "current hits and 'old music from the mid-

'70s'." It attracted 120 signatures. Acting General Manager George Bingham defended the station, saying that it offered valuable training for students, and needed to attract listeners throughout the region in order to pay its bills. He pointed to WDCR as the place for alternative programming.[9]

A year later an opinion piece in *The Dartmouth* attacked WFRD, under the colorful headline "All We Hear Is Radio Gaga." It complained about the FM playlist ("if I had a dime for every time I've heard Billy Joel's 'Italian Cafe'... or David Bowie's 'Changes,' I'd be a millionaire"), about its d.j.'s ("those kids pretending they're big-city radio personalities [are] plain ridiculous"), and about the poor quality of WDCR's signal.[10]

## Q106 Becomes an Upper Valley Powerhouse

However management was committed to the new direction, and there were signs it was working, which was important because there was a powerful, new competitor in town.

Almost as soon as he graduated in 1983 former General Manager Jeff Shapiro and his friends began putting together a plan to buy their own station. With Mark Belmonte (his predecessor as GM) and Belmonte's roommate Bill Goddard '81 (a former business manager) he looked at small-market stations in New England, and learned that WTSV/WECM-FM in Claremont was for sale. This led to a long series of negotiations. Their first challenge, as cheeky fresh-faced kids just out of college, was simply to be taken seriously by the hard-bitten entrepreneurs who ran local radio. To raise capital they brought in former WFRD Program Director Ken Elias '82 and current Sales Manager Will Stanley as investors, and made an offer to WTSV owner Chris Dante, which he rejected out of hand. But they kept at it and eventually, in August 1984, reached a deal to buy the Claremont stations for $600,000, half of what Dante had originally asked.[11]

Shapiro, Belmonte and Goddard took over in November and immediately began remaking WECM, 106.1 KHz, into a hard-rocking FM powerhouse. (WTSV remained a country music station.) They fired staff and retooled the format. During the winter it became "Moose 106" ("The Moose on the Mountain") and by the summer of 1985 they had changed its call letters to WHDQ—"Q106"—and launched major promotional campaigns including a Q-Cash contest and a "Ticket to Paradise" giveaway. Will Stanley came aboard as sales manager, bringing with him his deep connections to Upper Valley advertisers. Shapiro also repositioned the station's tower for wider coverage, and over the next few years set up three translators to bring its signal to even more communities, including Hanover.[12]

With a high-energy staff, and three times the power of WFRD (9.8 kw vs. WFRD's 3.0 kw), Q106 became the leading station in the Upper Valley virtually overnight. A professional Birch Radio Survey in early 1986 showed Q106 reaching nearly 40 percent of adults in the "Hanover Trading Area" each week, with WFRD and WTSL in a close race for number two and WDCR far behind.[13]

Birch Radio Survey (1986)
(Weekly reach among adults 18+)

| | | | Format |
|---|---|---|---|
| 1. WHDQ-FM | | 39.6% | Top 40 |
| 2. WFRD-FM | | 25.3 | Album Oriented Rock |
| 3. WTSL-AM | | 24.8 | Adult contemporary |
| 4. WKXE-FM | * | 16.9 | Middle of the road |
| 5. WCVR-FM | ** | 13.9 | Country music |
| 6. WNHV-AM | | 11.4 | Middle of the road |
| 7. WDCR-AM | | 3.8 | Top 40, various |

*Formerly WNHV-FM. Duplicated WNHV-AM for 65% of its schedule.
**A country music station in Randolph, Vermont.

Note that four of the top five stations in the market were now FM. The stations had different strengths, however. WFRD led in men 18-34, while WHDQ's biggest lead was among women 18-34. WTSL led among older listeners.

Occasionally there was some sniping between the stations. When Q106 banned Guns N' Roses from its air because of the rebellious band's drunken cursing on the 1989 *American Music Awards* telecast, WFRD d.j. Tom McArdle '91 called the ban the "height of stupidity in today's age." John "Jags" Aguilar '90 added that while he didn't condone the band's behavior, "being loud, raunchy and rude is what rock 'n' roll is all about and we're not into music censorship [at WFRD]."[14]

The rivalry between WFRD and Q106 was generally friendly, however. They were, after all, all Dartmouth men. (For a time in 1987, in fact, Jeff Shapiro's younger brother Andy was General Manager of WFRD and thus Jeff's direct competitor.) In a 1989 interview Jeff refused to trash his competition, saying it played somewhat different music and "[they are] carving out their niche." He then got in a little dig, however, saying that he did not think WFRD posed any threat to his station, which he claimed reached 60,000 weekly listeners to WFRD's 17,000.[15]

There were few other changes in the market. After years of trying WTSL finally won an FM license and launched WTSL-FM, "Lite 92.3," in January 1987. Programming adult contemporary ("soft pop music") and targeting adults 25-54, it posed little threat to the market's two major rock stations, WFRD and Q106.[16]

Nor was the area's only local television station, WNNE-TV/channel 31, much of a factor. Despite a 1988 article celebrating its 10th anniversary and claiming great success, it proved difficult to sustain news or other local programming in such a small market. Beginning in 1990 WNNE became a semi-satellite of WPTZ-TV in Plattsburgh, New York, and over the next 10 years gradually phased out its local programming. By the 2000s it was simply rebroadcasting WPTZ. While it was still broadcasting local news, however, it provided internships to many Dartmouth students, among them WFRD/WDCR News Director Russell Kemp '87 and ace sportscaster Brett Haber '91.[17]

### The Birth of "99Rock"

Despite occasional brickbats, Dartmouth radio was committed to its new direction. Upon taking office as general manager in mid 1987 Seth Skolnik said his goal was "making programming on both stations the best it can be." He added that FM was dedicated to album-oriented rock, while AM was eclectic, "including jazz and urban contemporary music designed to appeal to the College community."[18]

One issue was deciding on a consistent slogan for the station. Increasingly radio stations were known by short catch phrases, and "Q106" had captured the imagination of the market. At first the "new" WFRD was known as 99RockFM, but during 1986 there were debates about changing this, or even the call letters themselves (which some still called "Fred"). Finally in the Spring of 1987 FM Program Director Abdhish Bhavsar '87 introduced the simple "99Rock" as part of a Phrase That Pays contest in which people on the street could win prizes by repeating the slogan, "No one plays more rock music than 99Rock." Although one staffer later remarked "We didn't give out much" (in terms of prizes), at least the slogan stuck.[19]

The new 99Rock was strictly commercial. Dartmouth was hardly ever mentioned on the air. FM Program Director Bhavsar recalled culling the CHR (pop hits) albums out of the active library in 1986 in favor of AOR (album rock) fare; the less favored material went into the back library or the dumpster. "For once in the history of the station you could turn your radio dial to [WFRD] and hear the same type of music at any time of the day." His successor Mark Wachen '89 (younger brother of GM David Wachen '87) described the carefully planned music rotation practices of the late 1980s. Pie charts were used to map out the types of music to be played. Five to eight songs were deemed "heavy rotation" and played every four hours, while certain others were "medium rotation." Perhaps 40 percent of an FM d.j.'s music was thus predetermined. He could chose the other 60 percent, but from carefully defined, color-coded categories. Oldies were controlled so that a given title was played no more than once in five days. To build a sense of camaraderie and excitement among the staff a lounge was built with cable TV and pizza runs, and a new logo with flames and jagged lettering was emblazoned on a free bumper sticker.[20]

Staffing was not a problem, even when WFRD went to 24 hour broadcasting in 1989. Reportedly 80 to 90 students showed interest in doing the overnight shift, just to get on the FM station. Future GM Beth Krakower '93 remembered getting her start that way. On Friday nights "it was actually pretty busy, with lots of calls coming in," she said. "Everybody was out partying." During interims manpower was more of a problem and locals such as "Little Wolf" (Peter Skinner) and Will Putnam were sometimes brought in. Hanover High student Greg Anderson did the morning drive show for a time.[21]

By 1990 it was time to fine-tune the sound, which had "kind-of been stagnating" according to Program Director Eric Wellman '91. Downplayed were some of the progressive, heavy metal and "glam" rock acts such as Skid Row and Warrant (of *Dirty Rotten Filthy Stinking Rich* fame) in favor of longer established, broader based bands such as AC/DC, Led Zeppelin, Deep Purple and Bon Jovi. "In terms of radio," said GM Tim Reynolds, "this area is about 15 years behind the rest of the country... We're back in the '70s." Added Wellman, "there's a cry for classics [in this region]." They also expressed concern that older men and women in general were turned off by too much heavy metal.[22]

Some d.j.'s objected to the change, and at least one shifted to WDCR where he could play what he wanted. But Tina "Roxie Yoxie" Yoxtheimer '91 summed up the feelings of most when she said "some of the changes may be painful to me, but I support [Wellman] because I think he has sound theories based on research."

If excitement was building around 99Rock, it was fading fast at WDCR, the onetime top 40 AM flagship. Students did not want to listen to music on AM; they were either listening to FM or to a Walkman or boombox. The widely distributed weekly top 30 list was discontinued around 1985, since WDCR was no longer a top hits station (although there were still internal playlists). In the opinion of one veteran of the period, the AM d.j.'s played for themselves. During 1985-86 simulcasting FM became so prevalent to fill in the holes in the AM schedule that AM Program Director Seth Rosenblatt had to work to cut it back in 1987.[23]

### "Sound at the Speed of Light"

One change that affected both stations was the switch to CDs. Compact discs were introduced in the U.S. in 1983, and despite the fact that early players cost as much as $2,000, sales grew steadily during the rest of the 1980s. CDs began to turn up in Hanover, and some record companies began sending them to radio stations. Although it was not yet using them on-air, WDCR/WFRD established a CD library in 1986 in anticipation of doing so, and also began giving away CDs obtained on trade-out from Hanover Audio in spring contests.[24]

The story of how WFRD obtained its first on-air CD player is often told by station veterans. According to Seth Rosenblatt, a local arcade was running a promotion, "one of those arcade games where you collect the tickets, and once you get thousands of tickets you can turn them in for something. We had dozens of people playing games and keeping their tickets for months." Rosenblatt, Mark Wachen, Priscilla Huff '91, and Carolyne Allen '89 were among those collecting tickets and eventually Rosenblatt accumulated enough to trade them in for a new CD player, which was promptly installed in the studio. Memories differ as to exactly when this took place, but the best estimate seems to be the spring or summer of 1987.[25]

Disc jockeys were still primarily using LPs and 45s, so when they hit the button to play a CD on the shiny new toy it was introduced with fanfare, such as "Sound at the Speed of Light!" This did not always go well. Sometimes the CD would "hang," producing a ringing sound, and once a d.j. left the studio with the player running only to have it stop after the first track waiting for a play command to continue. The station was bombarded with calls from listeners. Eventually professional units were purchased, but it would be many years before vinyl was completely replaced by CDs.[26]

### *Breakthrough* Fails, *Pooh Corner* Departs

Early in 1986 Mark Greenstein '86 and a dozen staffers began producing a weekly two-hour show on WDCR called *Breakthrough,* which counted down the top alternative music tracks on college campuses, based on national publications such as *The Gavin Report* and *College Music Journal*. With its mix of music not heard on normal pop-oriented countdown shows, commentary on the music, and college humor, it attracted an audience and Greenstein and his cohorts began hatching an ambitious scheme to syndicate it nationally. They obtained estimates for duplication and distribution, and wrote up a plan to solicit sponsors and affiliates. Their production company would be called "The Dartmouth Radio Network."[27]

They brought their plan to the Board of Overseers. They proposed that Dartmouth Broadcasting provide $4,800 in start-up funds, the use of its studios, and permission to use the name "Dartmouth." In return, the station and College would receive the use of a professionally produced show, an estimated revenue cut of $7,800 per year, and favorable nationwide publicity for Dartmouth College.

Apparently the plan was a little too risky, or entrepreneurial, for the overseers, as nothing seems to have come of it. However, as in the cases of Scott McQueen and Jeff Shapiro (who became station owners shortly after graduation), it showed how the experience of working at WDCR/WFRD could inspire budding entrepreneurs. Greenstein later earned a law degree and founded several educational companies, including **www.ivybound.net**.

A much longer running WDCR program that came to an abrupt end was *Pooh Corner*, the charming Sunday morning show on which an adult from the community brought children into the studio to talk and read stories. It was begun in the late 1960s by faculty wife Martha Luehrmann, and by 1985 was being hosted by Rick Fayen and sponsored by the Dartmouth Bookshop. Unfortunately Mr. Fayen and station management fell to squabbling, and as of August 1985 he moved the show to WNHV. It is not known how long it lasted there.

### Promotions

Consistent with its mandate to be thoroughly commercial WFRD, like most local radio stations, held a steady stream of contests and promotions. The goal was to stage at least one large-scale promotion each quarter. In the summer of 1986 the station fielded a bumper sticker contest with the grand prize being a car stereo; unfortunately this was topped by a simultaneous Q106 contest in which the grand prize was a *car*. Later several CD players were given away in a "Heat Up Your Winter" contest, two area residents won a trip to the U.K. to attend a U2 concert in "U2 in the U.K.", the station and the Student Assembly worked together to promote concerts by George Carlin and Hooters (1987-88), and other contests featured tickets to Bon Jovi and Ziggy Marley concerts. There was a popular "Rock & Roll Election" contest in 1988, and a "Show Us Your Rock" contest the following year, in which contestants sent in appropriate objects. One man submitted a model of the Old Man of the Mountains (New Hampshire's state symbol) with "99Rock" carved into it, which sat in the offices in Robinson Hall for years afterwards. In other contests staffers drove a beat-up car on to the College Green and let contestants smash it with hammers, and ran a "Mud Bowl" tournament in which ten teams competed to win an all-terrain mini-jeep.[28]

Probably the most successful promotion of the era was 1989's "Be Part of the Rock," in which 100 listeners won pieces of a giant 128 square-foot jigsaw puzzle, then converged on the Powerhouse Arcade in West Lebanon on a Sunday afternoon to piece them all together and determine who had the one piece that did not fit. That person won an all expense-paid ski trip to Colorado. This drew considerable press attention. "We had probably 300 or 400 people at the arcade," said FM Program Director Mark Wachen. "It was nuts."[29]

### Election Coverage

By now major biennial election coverage was a Dartmouth radio tradition, part of the station's DNA so to speak, and it continued to be one of the station's proudest achievements. Election nights during the late 1980s were not as widely syndicated as those of peak years 1976 and 1980, but they were substantial.

On congressional election night in November 1986 the Dartmouth Election Network (DEN) positioned student reporters at 24 campaign headquarters in Manchester, Nashua, and Concord, New Hampshire, and Burlington and Montpelier, Vermont, to phone in reports and interviews with the candidates. Broadcast headquarters was at the Hinman Forum at Dartmouth's Rockefeller Center, where anchor duties were shared by David Wachen and Raffiq Nathoo '87 (local) and Jack Steinberg '88 (national). Professors Robert Arseneau and Richard Winters provided analysis. News Director Sherri Burkholder '88 was in overall charge of the production, assisted by Tech Director Bob Striker, Chief Engineer Jeff Gershengorn '88 and about three dozen others. Burkholder was quoted as saying that WDCR and WFRD were the only stations in the state with the necessary staff to cover so large an event. The coverage, or portions of it, were offered to other stations, but apparently only one (WKNE in Keene) took the feed.[30]

The 1988 New Hampshire primary was a bigger event. Major battles were shaping up within both parties, with Republican Vice President George H.W. Bush facing a stiff challenge from Senator Bob Dole, and Massachusetts Governor Michael Dukakis facing off against Congressman Dick Gephardt and Senator Paul Simon. The Republican candidates staged a nationally televised debate at Dartmouth on January 16 while the Democrats debated a week later at the University of New Hampshire. Teams of DEN reporters followed the candidates around the state all fall and winter, using the station's mobile unit.

One story that has become part of station lore is that News Director Jennifer Avellino '89 asked former Senator Gary Hart the question about marital infidelity that brought down his candidacy. This is what actually happened. Hart announced his candidacy for the Democratic nomination in April 1987, declaring that he would bring to government "the very highest standards of integrity and ethics." On May 3 the *Miami Herald* broke a story claiming that he was in fact having an extramarital affair. Although politicians' private lives were at this time generally considered "out of bounds," the story spread like wildfire, and reporters hounded him for a comment. On May 6 he was scheduled to deliver a foreign policy speech at Dartmouth's Hopkins Center, followed by a press conference in the Hayward Lounge of the Hanover Inn. WDCR provided a live feed of the event to NBC. According to Avellino the big room was packed with reporters from the national media, and she had secured a seat in the front row. Sitting next to her was Paul Taylor of *The Washington Post.* It was Taylor who asked the explosive question, "Have you ever committed adultery?", to which Hart, taken aback, responded weakly, "I do not think that's a fair question." That response sealed his fate, and two days later his campaign collapsed.[31]

Although she did not ask the question, the photo that flashed across the nation showed a flustered Hart facing the reporters with Avellino (one of the few women in the room) in the front row watching him intently as he attempted to answer.

On primary night in February the student reporters who had been following each candidate were stationed at their headquarters in Manchester, Nashua and Concord. Back at the station Avellino and Russell Kemp co-anchored, while a team directed by Seth Rosenblatt made calls to more than 250 precincts across the state to gather results. Professors Arseneau and Frank Smallwood did the analysis. The executive director was Bob Striker. (Overlap of personnel from one election to the next helped keep this massive operation on track.) In all, more than 50 staffers were involved. "The kind of people we're competing with really says a lot about what we're doing," said Kemp. "We know of no other college station in the country that even comes close to this." Six New Hampshire stations took the Dartmouth feed.[32]

DEN took to the air again in November 1988 to report the results of the midterm election, this time focusing on gubernatorial and congressional races in New Hampshire and Vermont, with national results taken from the AP wire as they came in. Avellino and Brett Haber co-anchored, with Professor Arseneau on hand for analysis. Three to six stations were expected to take the stations' feed, although the actual number that did so is not known.[33]

## Campus Strife: Shanties and More

Controversies and protests continued to roil the campus, causing some to describe Dartmouth of the mid 1980s as "Berkeley East." The 1985-86 academic year began with the reinstatement of the Reserve Officers Training Corps (ROTC), the object of such fury in the 1960s.[34] Twenty-seven cadets enrolled. Then the biggest story of the decade began to unfold, literally on the radio station's doorstep.

It began on November 15 when students protesting the College's investments in companies doing business in South Africa started erecting shanties in the center of the Green to dramatize their cause. Dean Shanahan told them to stop, they ignored him, and the College did nothing. Eventually four shanties were erected, festooned with anti-apartheid and other slogans. On January 9, 29 activists staged a sit-in in President McLaughlin's office, demanding divestment. Again the College took no action. By this time some were saying the point had been made, and the unsightly (and illegal) shanties should be removed before the College's major annual winter event, Winter Carnival, was held. Then the spit hit the fan.

At 2:45 a.m. on the morning of January 21, 12 students, nine of them associated with *The Dartmouth Review*, arrived with sledgehammers and began systematically dismantling three empty shanties (avoiding the fourth, when they realized two women were inside). They called themselves "The Dartmouth Committee to Beautify the Green Before Winter Carnival" (DCBGBWC). Police arrived within a few minutes and before much damage was done, took them away, and then released them. The following afternoon 200 pro-shanty students rallied on the Green to protest the attack, and on January 22 more than 200 occupied the administration building, also in protest. *The Dartmouth* (which had earlier called for the removal of the shanties) editorialized that the 12 students should be expelled. On January 24 President McLaughlin cancelled classes for a day of forums and discussions. This was not enough for the faculty, however, which adopted a resolution denouncing McLaughlin and narrowly defeated a vote of no confidence in him. There were further sit-ins, vandalism (spray painting slogans on dorms), and occupation of the Baker Library bell tower from which pro-shanty protesters hung banners.[35]

The 12 DCBGBWC students were brought before the Committee on Standards (COS) and charged with "malicious damage to property, disorderly conduct and violence." Two who agreed to renounce *The Review* were given little or no punishment, but the other 10 were hit with harsh penalties ranging from two-term to indefinite suspension from the College. Meanwhile those who had erected the shanties in the first place, as well as the pro-shanty and sit-in demonstrators and anti-apartheid vandals were given mild reprimands, or no punishment at all.

The obviously unequal treatment of the two groups of students brought a deluge of national media attention. Dartmouth was once again in the national spotlight, portrayed as a hotbed of "liberal fascism" by going easy on left-leaning protestors while severely punishing those who disagreed with them.[36] The conservative students were not about to go quietly, however. *The Review* had powerful backers, and the threat of lawsuits was raised. The College realized that this could become a public relations nightmare, and eventually retreated. By April the sentences had been reduced to probation or single-term suspensions. All of the students involved appear to have ultimately graduated.

This time Dartmouth Broadcasting did not look the other way. Here was a very big story, taking place in front of Robinson Hall and even visible from the station's windows. According to News Director Avellino the story received extensive coverage on the college stations, including two-to-three minute reports as events unfolded. In May, *Great Issues,* an hour long Sunday discussion show simulcast on WFRD and WDCR, featured Chris Baldwin '89 of *The Dartmouth Review* debating Scott Nova '87, one of the leaders of the anti-apartheid protests. Although many in the student body (and presumably at the station) disliked *The Review's* tactics, the News Department covered what was obviously a very big story in a professional manner.

*The Review* continued to provoke in the following years. A series of articles beginning in 1987 mocked the College's sex education program, which included skits and "condom races." A bigger story began with the publication of another article on Professor Cole's Music 2 class, in February 1988, this one including a transcript of one of his colorful lectures. Following publication of the article four *Review* staffers approached Cole after one of his classes, politely offering him a chance to respond either in an interview or in writing. Cole erupted into a string of obscenities and broke the camera of one of the students. Cole was later complimented by the administration, while the students were charged with harassment. Three were suspended from the College and the fourth placed on probation for a year. This did lead to a lawsuit, which ended when a Superior Court judge ordered the students' immediate reinstatement.[37]

Without taking sides the station reported on these controversies, primarily on WDCR (the campus station) rather than on WFRD (the commercial half). It also dealt with continuing controversy over the "Men of Dartmouth" alma mater, and the fact that during the height of the shanty controversy 100 Dartmouth women signed up for a *Playboy* "Women of the Ivy League" photo shoot. Not everyone was consumed with politics. Besides news reports, the main vehicles on the stations for exploring issues were *Great Issues* and WDCR's in-depth interview show, *One on One,* hosted by Avellino.[38]

## Sports

Dartmouth football was having a terrible run in the mid 1980s, leading to the firing of Head Coach Joe Yukica in November 1985. He sued and was reinstated, but then resigned after another poor season. The team's record gradually improved under successor Buddy Teevens, reaching seven wins-two losses and a tie for the Ivy

League title in 1990. Dartmouth Broadcasting's coverage improved too, under pressure from the athletic department. Around 1986 Rick Adams, who had recently joined the College as coordinator of publications, and who formerly worked for WTSL, was hired to become the lead sports announcer for the stations. Students gained experience working with him. In 1990 Adams joined the Board of Overseers and in 1991 became its chair.[39]

## Public Service

Public service campaigns, especially those on the scale of the *Let's Help* campaigns, dried up in the 1980s. The focus now was commercial, and alumni of the period seem surprised when asked about charity efforts, being unaware that Dartmouth radio had ever done such things. There were a few small scale initiatives. In 1988 WDCR staged a "Treats without Tricks" campaign, promoting the safety of children on Halloween, but even this had commercial overtones. "New accounts were started because of this promotion," said AM Program Director Carolyne Allen, "and greater ties with the community in general were formed."[40]

A new station tradition began in December 1989 with the first end-of-year 99-hour (four day) marathon aired between Christmas and New Year's to collect food and clothing for The Listen Center, a local food kitchen. Eric Wellman was the tireless d.j. He recalled playing entire box sets of CDs (a new format at the time) from Eric Clapton, the Allman Brothers, and others so that he could take catnaps while the CDs were on continuous play. Following his example, annual 99-hour charity marathons would continue to be broadcast each December for the next several years.[41]

## Business

Revenues during the late 1980s were generally in the $250,000-$300,000 range, although there were some bumps along the way. In fiscal year 1985 they dropped 25 percent from the prior year (the last full year of Will Stanley's tenure), leading to fears of a huge deficit in 1986. That did not occur. New professional sales representative Laura Canada began to build sales up again, although not as fast as some overseers wanted. Lingering questions about Canada's performance led College treasurer's representative John Bryant to bring in Clayton "Clay" Ashworth as the top sales honcho, over Canada, in the fall of 1987. The idea was to bring major market sales techniques to the station, but it didn't work. The set-up created friction and in mid 1988 Canada left, followed by Ashworth in the fall.[42]

That began a revolving door of professional sales representatives, including Arthur Shannon (fall 1988-August 1989) and Dorian Jaye (August 1989 to 1991), with Alan Fahner, David Higley, and Melanie Edson as supporting salespersons.

Another problem was "trade-outs," in which the station accepted goods (used as contest prizes) in place of cash. Trade-outs generally averaged about 10 percent of revenue, but in 1990 jumped to 23 percent, an unusually high level.

The stations continued to charge less than their competitors for advertising time. According to rate card figures published in *Broadcasting Yearbook* in the late 1980s, WDCR was charging $19 for a morning drive time spot and WFRD the same, while WTSL charged $29 and WNHV, $22. Q106 didn't publish its rates, but seems to have charged substantially more than any of these. As for WFRD vs. WDCR, sales now tilted at least 2:1 or 3:1 in favor of FM.[43]

### "I'll blitz you!"

Things were relatively quiet on the technical front in the late 1980s. Careless College construction workers once again damaged the underground radials surrounding WDCR's tower in 1988, necessitating expensive repairs. Around the same time the tower was upgraded with the installation of a folded unipole system to improve the signal.[44]

Tech Director Mark Dattar '90 compiled a useful manual for his department called "The Technical Director How-To," covering everything from use of the mobile unit to emergency procedures when the power went out. As for keeping things organized he ruefully admitted "The tech closet has traditionally been a rat's nest," a statement with which technical directors of all eras can agree.

The student technical staff was by this time assisted by a professional consulting engineer, who was on-call and came in as needed. Gary Savoie assumed this position in 1986, replacing Dick Schellens, and remained with the station for the next 10 years. Often these professionals serviced other stations in the market as well.

The fall of 1984 brought an early harbinger of the coming digital revolution when for the first time the College "strongly recommended" that all incoming freshmen acquire a personal computer. A special discount was offered on the just-introduced Apple Macintosh, with financial aid available for those who needed it. (PC ownership was made mandatory in 1991). At the same time the campus was being networked and eventually every dorm room, classroom, office and laboratory was wired to the network. At first students could communicate, awkwardly, by using the Dartmouth College Time Sharing System (DCTS), which had been developed in the mid 1960s. To do this they had to log on to the College mainframe using a program called DarTerminal, scroll through all the messages that had been posted, then answer the one intended for them.

In late 1987 a computer center team including Rich E. Brown, David Gelhar, and Jim Matthews began working on a simpler program which they dubbed BlitzMail— because it was developed in a frantic "blitz" of activity. It resembled modern e-mail, long before most Americans had heard of such a thing. The user typed in the name of a student or faculty member, even an approximation, the name directory determined a match, and on command delivered the message to that person, instantly. The team spent the first nine months of 1988 refining the program with the help of beta testers, and it was officially rolled out to freshmen in the fall of 1988. They embraced it so enthusiastically that it promptly crashed the servers. BlitzMail became wildly popular and to blitz someone quickly became a campus verb. The term is still in use today.[45]

Standalone PC's began showing up at the radio station in the mid 1980s and BlitzMail became central to staff communication. However logs were still done on terminals connected to the Kiewit Computer Center via the DCTS.[46]

### Staff & Administration

Women continued to play a leadership role at the station during the late 1980s, even though they constituted only about 20 percent of the staff. There were several women on the Directorate, including Business Managers Joy Turnheim '86, Sherri Burkholder, and Sarah Freitas '92, and Program Directors Carolyne Allen and Ashley Zeiler '90. The well-remembered Jennifer Avellino was a pillar of the News Department for most of her time at Dartmouth. She first joined *The Dartmouth*, but then "wandered upstairs" to the radio station one day and stayed. Like many regulars, she says she "lived at the station."[47]

That kind of extreme dedication is what fueled the station, although management continued to look for ways to reduce the time burden. In 1987 the month in which a new Directorate took over was changed again, from January 1 of the junior year to February or March of that year. Although there was some variation from year to year, most future Directorates served from February or March of their junior year to the same point at the end of their senior year. This seemed to be the right balance between allowing seniors enough time before graduation, and providing overlap with (and the opportunity to give advice to) their successors.

In August 1985 the turmoil at the stations led Dean Edward Shanahan to appoint an Ad Hoc Committee on Dartmouth Broadcasting, comprised of faculty and administrators (but no students) from the Board of Overseers, to consider the future of the stations and make recommendations. Among the options Shanahan wanted considered were hiring professional management, and/or selling one of the stations. Former advisor Professor Bruce Pipes set the stage by recalling that both the 1978 WRKO report and a 1983 evaluation by GM Dan Daniels raised the same issues: "Both speak of consistency problems; both speak of the lack of coherent, long range goals for the stations; both speak of overworked staff; and both speak of morale problems and the fact that many staff members do not enjoy working at the stations."[48]

The task force report, issued in May 1986, rejected such drastic moves in favor of more incremental changes, including a clear statement of goals and a reorganization of the overseers to include more professional expertise. To bolster continuity it recommended that candidates for the Directorate be required to serve at least three out of the four terms in their year. Regarding a professional general manager, it felt that "Such a move would sacrifice the student management experience in favor or revenue maximization." It did recommend a more hierarchical structure in which members of the Directorate would formally report to the general manager, rather than being his or her equals. In practice future Directorates would continue to work as a governing committee, however, rather than having the general manager be solely responsible for station operation.[49]

The chairman of the Board of Overseers in the early 1980s was physics Professor Pipes (1981-84), succeeded by James Steffensen from the Drama Department (1985-88) and then Peter Travis from the English Department (1989-90). The latter frankly considered himself a "figurehead." The most influential member of the board was probably treasurer's representative John Bryant, who continually pushed for financial accountability. Indeed, many of the students I spoke to from this era considered the overseers to be primarily concerned with finances, and little else. Programming decisions were left almost entirely to the students. Except for the senior leadership, most station members had virtually no exposure to the board, and in some cases barely knew it existed.[50]

Bryant had been one of the original founders of the Board of Overseers in 1966, and when he stepped down in 1988 the last link with the 1960s was severed.

(Dean Seymour had left Dartmouth in 1969, Almon Ives retired in 1974, and Bob Graham left the board around 1974.) Bryant was replaced by Matt McMannis, but newly appointed Dean of Student Life Holly Sateia essentially assumed the role of "leader" of the board. She would remain deeply involved with Dartmouth Broadcasting for the next dozen years.[51]

The tumultuous tenure of David McLaughlin as Dartmouth's president came to an end as well. In 1987, after six years of battling with students, alumni, and the faculty (75 percent of whom had voted no confidence in him in 1985, accusing him of a lack of "intellectual leadership"), he said he was not ready to devote the next 10 years to a major fund-raising campaign and stepped down.[52]

His successor, James O. Freedman, was a liberal intellectual and *very* popular with the faculty. An owlish-looking man with large round glasses, his view was that Dartmouth should be a haven for intellectuals and more like a university (some called it the "Harvardization of Dartmouth"). That was controversial, but he also garnered praise as a staunch advocate of diversity, expanding the College's Latino, Jewish, women's, and African-American studies programs. He seems to have paid little attention to the campus radio station, or indeed to any student activities. For them his tenure (1987-98) was a period of benign neglect.[53]

### Remembering Its Roots

Although there were no major anniversary celebrations during the late 1980s on the scale of the 1983 WDCR silver anniversary, there were reminders to each new class of the station's long and eventful history. One was unassuming Professor Robin Robinson, who continued to present erudite comments on classical music on whichever station, and in whatever time slot, the students chose to give him. In October 1987, as he approached his 30th anniversary on WDCR, the station dedicated Studio One as "Robin Robinson Studio."

Another stalwart was John A. Gambling '51, a one-time (and somewhat controversial) general manager who in later days became the station's first alumni overseer, a willing advisor to the students, and a supporter of many of the station's activities. In October 1989 *The Dartmouth* published a major profile of the folksy New York radio star, who was one of the station's most illustrious alumni.[54]

# Chapter 11

# 1990-2000: Can WDCR Be Saved?

By 1990 it was apparent that AM radio was in trouble. FM was sweeping the industry and monopolizing the audience for music. Yet some AM stations continued to prosper by carving out alternative niches for themselves, for example in news radio, talk radio and specialty formats such as ethnic and public radio. Could Dartmouth's unique attempt to provide an AM broadcast outlet for student creativity find its niche?

There were at least two major attempts in the 1990s to create a new programming model for WDCR. Both failed, for different reasons. Meanwhile its FM sibling WFRD thrived, at least commercially. And for the time being, the College continued the tradition established decades earlier by President Dickey of exerting a fairly light measure of control. The students still felt very much in charge of the stations.

In addition there was agitation on behalf of women at Dartmouth Broadcasting, a major renovation of the studios, and the first hints that student control might not last.

The ten general managers during this decade were I. Neel Chatterjee '91, Beth Krakower '93, Sally Huntoon (Vitali) '93, Amy Ertel '94, Philip Augur '95, April Whitescarver '96, Vivian Lee '97, Brent Laffoon '98, Jonathan Flynn '00, and Sean Byrnes '00. Those filling in as acting GM during terms in which the regular GM was off-campus included Eric Peterson '91. Barry Cole '93, Brian Sward '95, John Strayer '96, Henry Broaddus '97, Mike Henry '98, Chadd Kline '99, Dhruv Prasad '99, and Abbey Nova '01.

### 99Rock Soars

This was a golden decade for 99Rock, WFRD-FM. The vision promoted by student leaders of the 1980s, of a commercial FM powerhouse in a market with still-limited (though real) competition, was essentially realized. Aided by a strong professional sales staff, and rarely mentioning Dartmouth on-air, the station made money.

Of course not everyone agreed with this vision. A thoughtful letter in *The Dartmouth* in 1990 conceded that the "classic rock" format was OK, but wanted the station to stop ignoring Dartmouth. "It seems as if the station is ashamed of their college... The FM station is just as much a part of Dartmouth [as AM]; it shouldn't have to slight its own school in the pursuit of higher ratings and profits. It should carry more announcements on the Dartmouth community, and cater to the needs of students." Disc jockeys should have more latitude to play what they wished, and the station should be piped into the Thayer Dining Hall (which it currently wasn't).[1]

A few days later WFRD Program Director Eric Wellman '91 responded that Dartmouth Broadcasting clearly served the College with WDCR. The whole idea was for FM to be a formatted, community-oriented station, providing both revenue and real-world business experience for the staff. This required "disassociation" from Dartmouth on-air. As for d.j. choice, "The majority of songs are selected by the individual d.j. from a library of approximately 10,000 sides" (he failed to mention the color-coding system, which restricted d.j. choice to certain genres of music). This push-and-pull between students who expected both stations to serve them, and management's realization that it had to appeal to the broader community to remain financially viable, would continue for years to come.[2]

WFRD's on-air disassociation from Dartmouth was so strong that one student of the early 1990s told me that he initially thought it was a professional station, not a student activity, and did not realize it was run by students until the spring of his freshman year when someone suggested he stop by Robinson Hall. He was quickly welcomed, and two years later became general manager.[3]

Despite Wellman's protestations, WFRD was tightly formatted and became more so as the 1990s progressed. A weekly playlist from 1994, compiled by Program Director Andrew Kersey '94 and Music Directors Peter Jastreboff '96 and Keith Miles '96, consisted of just 35 cuts, each assigned a specific number of plays (from six to 17) during the week. The top four tracks were Soundgarden's "Black Hole Sun," Pink Floyd's "Take It Back," Collective Soul's "Shine," and Traffic's "Here Comes a Man." The top phone request was for the Allman Brothers' "No One to Run With." Plenty of other 1970s-80s acts were also on the list, including the Smithereens, the Pretenders, Mötley Crüe, Aerosmith, Rush, Cheap Trick, John Mellencamp, and ZZ Top, along with newer bands such as Counting Crows and Pearl Jam. Programmers used a color-coded pie chart to map out what kinds of music d.j.'s could play, with very little latitude allowed in morning and afternoon drive time, a little more at other times of the day. Disc jockeys might be able to augment assigned cuts with certain CDs from the library, including older tracks, but they "couldn't just bring in a record they liked. There was no Herman's Hermits heard on WFRD."[4]

WFRD was categorized in the early 1990s as an AOR (album-oriented rock) station, but within that broad descriptor featured about 70 percent classic rock and 30 percent contemporary acts. In 1994 summer General Manager John Strayer, pictured long-haired and slouched in his chair like a prototypical teen rocker, told a reporter from *The Valley News*, "At Dartmouth, students listen to classic rock. I don't know whether to be proud or disgusted, but every time I walk by Psi U (a fraternity), they're blasting our station. You know, it's the Rolling Stones. And while I love the station, sometimes I want to say, 'Hey kids, you know, people are recording new music every day'... It's something about Dartmouth. It's kind of hard to put your finger on. Change comes very slow here... There is a definite culture that still loves classic rock."[5]

In time the area's fascination with older bands did begin to wane. As early as 1990 Tim Reynolds had predicted that "In about five years the format's going to flip. WFRD will start to be the alternative music format. We can't listen to classic rock forever." The change came gradually, however. In 1995-96 new FM Program Director Keith Miles, in an attempt to "wake up" the format, shifted the balance to 50 percent classic rock and 50 percent hard-edged contemporary, with more new bands like punk rockers Green Day. The Rolling Stones and the Beatles made a comeback of sorts under his successor, Mike Henry, who shifted the mix back to something more like 70/30, but then the station faced a crisis when competitor Q106 suddenly shifted to classic rock, largely overlapping with WFRD's format.[6]

In order to address this as well as other station issues, in 1997 Dean Lee Pelton asked the student leadership and the overseers to form a task force on the future of WFRD. The Tuck School collaborated on a market research study of area music preferences, and over the next few years the station shifted to a strong emphasis on modern rock as represented by contemporary bands such as Nirvana, Linkin Park, Blink 182, and the Foo Fighters. Bye, bye, Pink Floyd.[7]

Other steps were taken in 1995-96 to project a more polished (some would say "slick") station image. A new station logo was introduced with the words 99Rock WFRD in jagged-edged black and white type over a bright red background, replacing the previous more traditional lettering. It fairly screamed ROCK 'N' ROLL and was still in use in the 2010s. More apparent to listeners, perhaps, was a new, authoritative "voice" for station identifications and interstitials, one that would not change as students came and went. Production Director Mike Henry recalled spending months listening to tapes from professional announcers and negotiating with their agents, before settling on the commanding tones of Paul Turner, a Chicago actor who sold his voice to selected stations across the country. Turner was also the announcer on *The Howard Stern Show*.[8]

Despite its strict formatting, there was some room for personalities on 99Rock. *Get the Led Out* was a well known show devoted exclusively to Led Zeppelin. Disc jockey Brent Laffoon attracted attention in the mid 1990s, along with a lengthy 1997 profile in *The Dartmouth*. Tall, laid-back, and universally described as a "surfer dude" (although there is no surf in Hanover), he was known on air as Coco Jones. He also served as general manager. FM Program Director Kendra Kosko '99, who described herself as "high strung," called Laffoon the calmest guy at the station, quite a contrast with often-driven Dartmouth students. "It's good," she said, "we balance each other out." In later years he settled by the beach in Venice, California, and became (among other things) a yoga instructor.[9]

Sometimes 99Rock d.j.'s attracted more attention than they wanted. Another newspaper item told the story of a depressed, broken-hearted woman whose spirits were lifted when late night d.j. Jim Donnelly '97 agreed to play her song request. She was so grateful she decided to pay him a 2:00 a.m. visit at the studio. "I had a friend up there with me, luckily," he remarked. "When you are on late at night, you play bartender."[10]

On rare occasions the station would even put a live band on the air, as when the indie band Fool's Progress (aka Acoustic Junction) played live in the studio in 1997.[11]

Music media was changing as well. At the beginning of the decade 25 percent of the music played was still from LPs. By the time of the studio reconstruction in 1995-96 the use of vinyl on WFRD was non-existent, although some LPs were still played on WDCR. There were still turntables, but the equipment was considered so specialized that styli were sometimes stolen by students for use in their rooms.[12]

### Stunts, Bigger Stunts, and the Goo Goo Dolls

Like many professional rock stations WFRD staged a steady parade of contests and promotions. As the decade unfolded these became bigger, in part in response to the over-the-top contests staged by Jeff Shapiro's Q106 which included giving away a house and Porsche automobiles. 99Rock promotions in 1990 included live broadcast of the Hanover Streetfest, a Concert Caravan for Paul McCartney, a Venus Swimwear Pageant (at which General Manager Eric Peterson had the pleasant task of serving as a judge), and the 99Rock Snapple Summer Cruise giveaway. The following few years brought two well-remembered hearse giveaways, expense-paid trips to Rolling Stones, U2 and Pink Floyd concerts, and "Who Is the 99 Rocker?" That last one was particularly innovative. The 99 Rocker was someone in the Upper Valley, and the listener who guessed their identity would win a two-carat diamond ring. Clues were given out ("They hang with the in-crowd," "They work at a river," "They're called boss," etc.), gradually becoming more specific, until the subject was revealed. It turned out to be the manager of the Holiday Inn in White River Junction, which was ironic because he was definitely beyond the target age of the station. Mostly it was his young employees who listened to 99Rock.[13]

There was another diamond ring giveaway, trips to Scotland and Hawaii, and a Million Dollar Getaway dream vacation contest in December (not a bad time to get out of frigid Hanover). In 1994 listeners were treated to a bumper sticker contest, in which Phil Augur cruised the region in the station mobile unit looking for 99Rock bumper stickers and handing out prizes when he found one. He was surprised to find them at the very edge of the station's coverage area, far from Hanover.[14]

Perhaps the biggest ongoing promotion of the 1990s was Rocktober, which began in the fall of 1992 and consisted of a full month of Halloween-themed contests and giveaways of CDs, T-shirts, concert tickets and other prizes. In 1993 the station scored an endorsement by gregarious Vermont Governor Howard Dean (1991-2003), who issued an official proclamation naming the month Rocktober in recognition of the college station's "commitment to better broadcasting." He repeated this official action in 1994 and 1995, even posing with station representatives wearing a 99Rock T-shirt while grinning broadly and raising both arms in a kind of double fist-pump. "It was a lot of fun. Governor Dean's a great guy, friendly and down-to-earth" said General Manager Augur. Meanwhile the Rocktober grand prize escalated to a trip for two to Germany for Oktoberfest.[15]

The station also considered contacting conservative New Hampshire Governor Stephen Merrill, but decided "It was not worth Merrill's time." (According to one source Merrill eventually capitulated and endorsed Rocktober after being tweaked by Dean in a promotional spot.)[16]

WFRD celebrated its 10th anniversary as 99Rock in the summer of 1996, with a "Rock Solid Summertime" promotion and a contest to guess the one-millionth song played on the station, as "painstakingly calculated by the station's research department." The prizes included pit parties, giveaways, and a chance to win a $100,000 lottery (the station was insured in case someone did win). The grand prize winner in fact got $1,000 in cash and a "valuable prize package." And what was the one-millionth song? Neil Young's protest anthem "Rockin' in the Free World."[17]

More promotions followed in the late 1990s including "Metallica May" with a trip for two to Palm Beach, Florida, to see Metallica in concert, a "Peppers in Paris" promotion with an expense-paid trip to Paris to see the Red Hot Chili Peppers, and "Listener Appreciation Days" on which CDs were given out to "thank our listeners." Reaching ever higher, a "Million Dollar Mountain" promotion was planned for a group of ski resorts which would sport a potential grand prize of *$1 million*, said to be the largest prize ever offered in an Upper Valley promotion. However not enough resorts signed on to make the mega-promotion possible.[18]

Generally the College had no problem with these very commercial promotions, since the station did not associate itself with Dartmouth on the air, although there was some push-back over the slogan used for a contest to give away tickets to a Rolling Stones concert ("99Rock Wants You to Get Stoned!"). A bigger issue arose over the promotion that became the most spectacular, and profitable, venture of the entire decade, 99Rockfest. This was a full-blown summer rock concert to be held in August 1998, at the fair grounds in North Haverhill, New Hampshire, about 30 miles north of Hanover, featuring six bands. It was organized by Sales Manager Tim Hoehn to address revenue problems and involved almost the entire staff in planning and logistics. The bands were not top-liners but in a stroke of luck the station signed an up-and-coming band called the Goo Goo Dolls. Shortly thereafter, and before the concert was held, the Dolls suddenly catapulted to stardom with the number one hit, "Iris" (from the movie *City of Angels*). Although they were now red-hot, they said they would honor their contract with the station, which attracted other strong acts including Marcy Playground and Fuel. Rockfest turned out to be hugely successful, attracting around 5,000 people and making a reported $70,000, completely erasing the station's deficit that year. It was the biggest music festival ever held in the Upper Valley to that time.[19]

The day before the concert, however, a story about it appeared on the front page of the *Valley News* and College administrators went ballistic. Worried about potential liability issues, they railed, "Dartmouth is *not* in the rock concert business!"[20] It turned out that the dean who had OK'd the concert, Lee Pelton, had left the College and his successors claimed they knew nothing about it. It was too late to cancel the 1998 event, but the following year when discussions were initiated about an encore, nervous administrators shot it down. Rock concerts were a high-risk business, and Dartmouth would not allow them in the future, no matter what the financial and promotional payoff might be.[21] It was one of the earlier examples of the College undercutting an entrepreneurial student management. It would not be the last.

### Dartmouth Radio Tip-Toes Into the Internet Age

Another form of promotion that was launched in the mid 1990s with little fanfare would become hugely important in years to come. In fact, it was such a minor event at the time that it has been hard to document exactly how it began.

The World Wide Web, which facilitated communication between computers connected to the Internet, rolled out gradually in the early 1990s. A turning point was the introduction of the Mosaic web browser in 1993. Dartmouth, a pioneer in all things computer-related, had its own site on the web by early 1994 (**www.dartmouth.edu**) and offered students the opportunity to set up pages on this site. The station's leaders were not quite sure how to do this, but some of the younger staffers were and in fact were already setting up their own personal pages. When a station web presence was proposed the reaction of the leadership was an offhanded, "sure, let's have a web page."[22]

WDCR's first web page (**www.dartmouth.edu/community/broadcast/wdcr**) was apparently launched in the spring of 1995, by Phil Cheung '97. That fall FM Program Director Keith Miles and staffer James Muiter '98 constructed a similar page for WFRD. They said they were pursuing acquisition of **www.wfrd.com** as a dedicated address for the station (this apparently launched in 1996).[23] These early pages were aimed primarily at the student body and contained air schedules, new music being added to the on-air rotation, station contact information, d.j. pages, and promotion of upcoming events. Keeping them up to date was a problem from the start, and eventually a formal "webmaster" position was established.

As early as 1996 there was discussion about streaming WDCR on the Internet, but the technology was not yet ready. When the subject was raised in a 1999 overseers meeting as a way to address WDCR's signal problems "the idea was briefly discussed with the [decision being to] keep the status quo until webcasting has been around longer." By 2000, however, WDCR was being streamed online, at least to students on campus, using Quicktime software.[24]

### On the AM Band

As the student half of the Dartmouth Broadcasting duopoly, WDCR delivered a wide variety of programming during the 1990s. The music was mostly progressive/alternative, on individualistic shows like *Club Beat* (house music), *Dusky Discs* ("with a Dr. Demento-type personality named Spam") and *Homegrown Showcase*. The latter, which began in 1990, consisted of music by local bands and interviews with their members, often taped in the station's studios. It was produced by musician/promoter Pete Skinner and spun-off a now-collectable cassette and CD featuring some of the bands (*99Rock Homegrown, Volume 1*). The show would continue on AM and later FM for more than 20 years. On *Vic's Picks* Victoria Haliburton ("a survivor of the sixties") tackled themes including rock protest music, playing 20 such songs in a row at the time of the 1992 Rodney King riots in Los Angeles. Meanwhile late-night d.j.'s played bartender to night-owl listeners, and accumulated stories. Derek Pollard '95 reported getting repeated requests for Guns N' Roses' "Paradise City" from the same caller, who kept changing his voice; Betsy Cowles '92 got "weird calls" from "a mixed kind of crowd"; and Kahaganu Kai '95 heard from a drunk who needed a ride home. Kai kept him on the phone until he could arrange for a listener to pick him up.

A 1996 summary described the AM schedule as consisting of 16 hours per week of rock, six hours of ska, four hours of jazz, four hours of opera, three hours of classical, and two hours of gospel, along with the two-hour sports program *From the Bullpen*, the weekly 30-minute news program *Inside Focus*, a nightly newscast, and the 20-year old *Environmental Insight*. A sampling of the many d.j. shows broadcast in this era includes *Future Shock* (alternative rock), *The Battery* (heavy metal), *Jazz Beat*, *Quiet Storm* (R&B/soul), *PMD* (rap/hip-hop), *Techno*, *Spam* (1980s), *Reggae Uprising*, *Ska*, Latino music, and Korean music. The station was judged to have "no unifying theme."[25]

In the late 1990s WDCR was practically the home of rap and R&B in the area, with shows like John McWilliams' *Namor's Crib* (named after a comic book) and d.j.'s Jasson "DJ Dash" Walker '98, Reginald "Reggy" Belhomme '00, " Candy Andy" Warner '99, and Shaunda "L'il Shaun" Miles '99.[26] Like its FM sibling, WDCR on rare occasions broadcast a live band, such as the Boogymen in 1997.[27]

On another musical planet genteel Professor Robin Robinson was still presenting his weekly *Opera Showcase* and *A Little Night Music*. Even though he was now on AM (with a lower signal quality), and Vermont Public Radio had taken many classical listeners away from WDCR, he continued to devote up to six hour a week researching selections and preparing his scripts. In 1996, at age 93, he was the subject of a detailed profile in *The Dartmouth* which pointed out that as a member of the class of 1924 he had been associated with the college for more than 70 years.[28]

Comedy shows continued to be a rare commodity, dependent on the availability of students with very special talents. But just as the station had produced *The Hunky Dorey Hour* in the 1950s, *The Ed and Charley Show* in the 1960s, and *Midnight Mulch* in the 1970s, it now had *The Steve and Doug Show* with the comic duo of Steve Zrike '98 and Doug Young '98. The show, which ran for two full hours every Tuesday night, consisted of commentary on campus and local events, call-ins, in-studio guests and skits. Regular characters included "Phil Mancuso" who brought them cheese from Philadelphia, Englishman "Billoughby", and "Worldclass Pepe" who swam the Connecticut River looking for the New Hampshire-Vermont state line. There were stories of horrible dates, awkward shower situations (Dartmouth now had co-ed bathrooms), a "massive kissing spree," and unfortunate instances of personal hygiene gone awry. The pair was likened to "a bickering old couple," continually interrupting each other, with Zrike often playing the straight man to Young.[29]

As the official campus station WDCR promoted and covered many campus events. In 1998 these included Dartmouth Up All Night, a big spring Friday night mixer at the Collis Center that drew more than a thousand students for singing, dancing, movies, pool, Nintendo games, and a myriad of other activities; DarCorps, a day of community service in which students fanned out across the Upper Valley to work at schools, retirement homes, museums and other service agencies; and The Dartmouth Pow-Wow, a weekend of events celebrating native American culture with dances and crafts.[30]

Although WDCR offered a lot of diversity, its programming day was decidedly uneven and unpredictable and the station struggled to be noticed. This was no longer the top 40 powerhouse of the 1960s and '70s, blaring from every window on campus on a warm spring day. Disc jockeys were urged to promote their own shows with BlitzMail "blasts" to everyone they knew, and stories were planted in *The Dartmouth* as often as the newspaper would print them (which wasn't often). WDCR did not run commercial contests like its FM sibling, although in 1998 Program Director Brian Sleet '00 did stage a 99Rock-like promotion with Virgin Records in which the station gave away new CDs by the Verve and Massive Attack, and tickets to a summer concert featuring those artists.

### News: Bolt the Doors, Here Comes Bill Clinton!

The Dartmouth Election Network (DEN), whose massive coverage of primaries and general elections had attracted so much attention to Dartmouth during the 1960s, '70s and '80s, became more uneven in the '90s. Station "newsies" covered the 1990 congressional elections from the studios and on AM only, but the broadcast did involve a large staff, reports from the field, and analysis by government professors Robert Arseneau and Richard Winters. General Manager Neel Chatterjee called the 1990 coverage one of the station's "most important activities" and "a feat to organize."[31]

Money and staff was lacking to give full coverage to the 1992 New Hampshire Primary, so the station instead participated in an MTV Rock the Vote campaign to sign up young voters at Dartmouth. It sponsored a Rock the Vote concert headlined by Drivin' N' Cryin' with supporting bands Cliffs of Dooneen and O+, and a rally to register GM Beth Krakower. By the end of the campaign 600 students had registered to vote.[32]

Perhaps the most memorable moment came shortly before the primary, however. Sales Manager Tim Hoehn received a call saying that candidate Bill Clinton was next door at Collis and was willing to come over and appear on the station. Hoehn protested that the station was "tightly formatted" and asked if he could be scheduled at another time, but Clinton was not to be denied. He showed up anyway with his entourage in tow, bounded up the stairs of Robinson Hall to the third-floor studios, and talked his way on to the air for 20 minutes of impromptu discussion in the middle of afternoon drive time.[33]

The fall 1992 general election coverage was a little more organized, with Rob Simmelkjaer '93 serving as anchor and a 12-station hookup.

Coverage of the 1994 congressional election was "not a big deal," but for the 1996 New Hampshire primary the stations were back in fine form, mounting their most extensive coverage since 1988. Under the leadership of News Director Vivian Lee campaign events were covered during the months leading up to the primary, including a Dartmouth visit by GOP candidate Bob Dole and New Hampshire appearances by President Clinton, Elizabeth Dole, and candidate Pat Buchanan. Primary night itself originated from Morrison Commons in Rockefeller Center and was produced by former News Director Sabrina Serrantino '95 and co-anchored by Rory McGee '97 (who was fresh from an internship at CNN). Scores of staffers participated, phoning in reports from 10 major campaign centers across the state. The broadcast was carried on both AM and FM and syndicated to 10 to 15 other stations, including some in the Midwest.[34]

The November 1996 election night was another "massive production," with field reports, political commentary and sound bites from the candidates themselves. Ms. McGee headed up the production as DEN director.

The 1998 congressional elections were relatively low-key, despite the Monica Lewinsky scandal and the looming impeachment of President Clinton. Under News Director Tim Wright '01 the AM station provided continuous coverage from Dartmouth's Rockefeller Center, with commentary from a panel of professors.[35]

DEN geared up again for the 2000 New Hampshire primary, providing interviews with candidates visiting the area, and live coverage of a two-night CNN Candidates Town Hall at Dartmouth in October 1999. Primary night in February 2000 was a major production live from Rockefeller Center, produced by News Director Todd Piro '00 and Brian Maloney '01 and co-anchored by Piro and Mike Bayer '01. Reporters phoned in results from the field, and Prof. Dean Spiliotis provided commentary. The broadcast was carried on both WDCR and WFRD, and, in recognition of changing technology, instead being syndicated to other stations the coverage was streamed on the Internet on **www.voter.com**. This would be, unfortunately, one of the last hurrahs for large-scale DEN election coverage.[36]

## A New MU... And Other News

The busy News Department covered many stories besides elections. At the beginning of the decade, under T. "Fin" Repczynski '91, there were about 20 people in the department, half of them women, and it was one of the most active and prestigious activities at the station. Later news directors included Sally Huntoon, Ann Koppel '94, Adrienne Kim '95, Phil Augur, Sabrina Serrantino, April Whitescarver, Vivian Lee, Cheryl Chua '97, Kathy Healy '97, Ted Huang '98, Jon Flynn, Lisa Kahn '00, Todd Piro, Timothy Wright, and Marni Zelnick '01. Several of these went on to become the station general manager.

Coverage of breaking news was greatly aided by the station's mobile unit, or "MU." Emblazoned with WFRD and WDCR logos, and used by all departments, the 1983 GMC Jimmy got a lot of use and was finally replaced with a 1993 Chevy Blazer. This too was used pedal-to-the-metal, and was finally replaced around the end of 1999.

NBC News inserts kept AM listeners up to date on world events, such as the Gulf War of early 1991. There were hourly *Gulfwatch* updates (with Andy Rotenberg '92), and *Great Issues* was back on the air with Gretchen Almy '92. April Whitescarver orchestrated extensive live coverage of President Clinton's visit to Dartmouth in June 1995 to deliver the commencement address. Clinton was introduced to sales honcho Tim Hoehn who began "you probably don't remember me but...", to which the president, remembering his impromptu 1992 appearance as a candidate, immediately shot back, "Sure, you're the guy from the radio station!"[37]

*The Dartmouth Review* continued to foment controversy on campus, and public affairs show *On Target* attempted to illuminate left-right issues by convening a panel representing both sides.  This proved easier said than done. In 1993 a conservative guest accused the station of censorship, complaining that an episode had been canceled after it was taped in order to stifle his opinions (the "left wing" participants had not shown up). In 1994 the series was canceled "because it was unable to meet its goal of including a diverse group of people and views."[38]

Controversial issues got a sustained airing in the mid 1990s in part through the efforts of Hank Broaddus. In 1995 he produced and hosted *Dartmouth Dialectic*, a lively *Crossfire*-style roundtable featuring representatives of *The Dartmouth Review* and *The Beacon* (conservative), *The Bug* (liberal), and *Spare Rib* (women's issues). It tackled issues ranging from the Dartmouth fraternity system to U.S. military involvement abroad. "Although things have remained civil," Broaddus commented, "we've maintained a tension that's needed." Added Sean Donahue of *The Bug*, "I think it's interesting to see what's in other people's heads."[39]

Two years later Broaddus launched *Talking Heads*, on which members of the Conservative Union and the Young Democrats sparred on issues ranging from abortion to affirmative action. In 1998 notable visitors to the Dartmouth campus were interviewed on *Rocky on the Radio*, produced in cooperation with the Nelson A. Rockefeller Center for Public Policy. Among those facing the WDCR microphone were conservative activist Ralph Reed, presidential candidate Lamar Alexander, National Security Advisor Anthony Lake and playwright August Wilson.[40]

### A Christmas Tradition

The annual 99-hour Christmas charity marathon begun in 1989 was repeated on WFRD most years during the 1990s, collecting food and clothing donations for the Listen Center in Lebanon, which provided services to the underprivileged. The 1991 edition, for example, was reported to have brought in "hundreds of pounds of food" for the center. Records are incomplete, but Eric Wellman manned the microphone in

1989 and 1990, Beth Krakower took over in 1991, Sean Quinn '93 was the dauntless d.j. for the 1992 edition, and Andrew Kersey spun the discs (and stayed awake) for 99 hours in 1993. Phil Augur did the honors in 1994, and Keith Miles was the sleepless wonder in 1995. Quinn told a reporter "it's one of the most important things I've ever done, certainly at Dartmouth... I've played every song that exists." GM April Whitescarver recalled, "I took [Keith] food occasionally or checked to make sure he was awake. He was nutty by the end of it." Brent Laffoon was the 99-hour man in 1997. He fell asleep while broadcasting from a bed in a store in Lebanon.[41]

## Sports

The stations continued their extensive coverage of Dartmouth sports. *Sportsline* offered highlights on Sunday nights, and Sports Director Robert Simmelkjaer launched *Sportsnight* on WDCR in 1991. (Simmelkjaer would later become a vice president at ESPN.)

Dartmouth football was on fire in the early 1990s, winning three straight Ivy League championships. The star quarterback was Jay Fiedler '94, who would later go on to a long career in the NFL. This created great interest in Dartmouth radio's broadcasts of the games, and discussions were held as early as 1991 about ways to bring that coverage to alumni and others across the country. In the fall of 1992 the station signed with TRZ Sports Services which had recently launched a unique telephone distribution system called Teamline, enabling fans anywhere to listen to live coverage of games over the telephone (or on a speaker phone), for a modest fee. Many top sports were offered, including NFL football, NBA and NIT basketball, NHL hockey, and major league baseball. Dartmouth received a commission for this, albeit a modest one. By December 1996 Big Green games had logged 2,000 calls on the service, netting the athletic department $3,266.[42]

The station's football coverage was highly regarded, due to professional lead announcer Rick Adams and some strong student colleagues, notably Sports Director Dean Maragos '96. However there was a drumbeat of complaints from athletic department Sports Information Director Kathy Slattery during 1993 and again during 1995-97 about student coverage of other sports. This included unprofessional behavior, no-shows and "too much enthusiasm" in the press box (to which the students said, "What?"). Sometimes a feed from the opposing team's coverage was substituted. The athletic department once again threatened to take the games to a non-Dartmouth station (WTSL or more likely WNTK). Harried General Manager Vivian Lee, Sports Director Chris Emond '99 and Overseer Rick Adams dealt with the problems as best they could, but staffing such a large operation with top-notch talent was a continuing problem.

As for Dartmouth football, it was too hot not to cool down. Beginning in 1998 it began to falter. During the next 14 seasons the Big Green posted a .259 overall average (36 wins, 103 losses), exceeding .500 in only one season. Even the return of coach Buddy Teevens in 2005 did not help.

## Sales

Gross sales were generally strong in the 1990s, averaging in the $300,000-$500,000 range. The catch was that one-third or more of this was typically received as trade-outs, meaning the station received goods rather than cash (used for contests, etc.), so the station was sometimes cash-strapped. Another problem was that the College's Department of Student Life, to which the station reported, was itself short of funds and had come to regard WFRD (in good years) as an ATM from which it could take money to pay for its other activities. Thus rather than building up a reserve against bad times the stations were "zero-ed out" at the end of each year, forced to turn any profits over to the College, giving them no margin when a bad year came along. No business operates this way. In the view of many it was another example of the College chipping away at the stations' traditional independence.

In 1990, a soft year, the overseers pushed hard to increase revenues. There was talk within the administration of possibly selling the station (as well as the College's money-losing skiway). As one overseer told me, "there are always factions [in the administration] looking for an excuse to do that." The station had not had a stable sales staff since Laura Canada and Clay Ashworth left in 1988, and collections from advertisers who failed to pay were becoming a major problem. At the urging of Dean Holly Sateia (and over the objections of some Directorate members) the overseers appointed a committee of four overseers to look into ways to increase revenues, and deal directly with the professional sales staff. At the same time, Laura Canada—now known as Laura Daniels—rejoined the staff.[43]

The sales staff—Dorian Jaye, Daniels, and sales associate Marcia Aldrich—struggled to raise revenues in a weak economy. During 1991 Jaye was fired, Aldrich left, and former General Manager Seth Rosenblatt '89 filled in as a temporary salesman. Finally in October 1991 Tim Hoehn, an experienced sales executive who had been in radio in the region for about 10 years, came aboard and began one of the longest and most successful runs of any general sales manager in station history. Within six months the dire financial picture had begun to turn around. Hoehn attributes this to three things: (1) a program of ambitious sales promotions, (2) taking full advantage of an improving economy, aided by the fact that 1992 was an election year filled with political advertising, and (3) adding older bands to the musical rotation, which broadened the station's demographic appeal. It also didn't hurt that more national money was coming into the market, in part because of Q106's spectacular promotions.[44]

During the next few years Hoehn and Daniels were joined by sales associate Kenan Guarino, who was succeeded late in the decade by Julie Kaye. Longtime secretary Winnie Lacoss was promoted to "station manager" (at least in the national sales listings), which meant she supervised the commercial logs. This tight-knit team of professionals remained in place for most of the decade. They were employees of the College, rather than independent contractors as in previous years, and there was no question to whom they reported. When Dean Sateia met Hoehn she said, "you report to me." The sales staff's interaction with the student Directorate varied by administration, but was clearly less than in previous years. The student leaders didn't mind. In fact, most of the students I talked to regarded the divorce of sales from the rest of station operation as natural, freeing them to concentrate on programming, which they enjoyed more anyway. Although technically the general manager also reported to Dean Sateia (the trustees' representative), the students still felt very much in charge.[45]

This separation of sales and programming could only work if WFRD (which accounted for nearly all sales) maintained a strong, commercial air product, so there were continual efforts at building a sense of professionalism. In 1993 the station acquired a new production library with which to produce professional-sounding commercials, and also mid-decade a practice began of sending the general manager and two or three members of the sales staff each year to the annual National Association of Broadcasters (NAB) convention, for exposure to developments in the larger world of commercial radio. Students rarely went on sales calls, however.

By the latter part of the 1990s Hoehn began to feel that the virtual abandonment of sales by students had gone too far, and looked for ways to make them more aware of this essential aspect of broadcasting. He brought in David Pearlman, a top executive at CBS-Infinity Broadcasting, to give a talk about careers in radio sales, and filled an auditorium in Dartmouth Hall with eager listeners. However there was little follow-up.

## The Competition

The combination of constant promotions and a tight, commercial sound led to strong audience ratings for 99Rock. The station now subscribed to Arbitron ratings, the (expensive) industry standard, which Hoehn maintained he needed for sales purposes. In 1992 WFRD boasted that it had the highest cumulative audience of any local station, and in 1993 it placed second in average quarter hour share in both Windsor Country, Vermont (11.8 share) and Grafton County, New Hampshire (5.8 share). Since different stations were number one in each county, this made WFRD number one overall in the two-county combined area.[46]

In 1994 WFRD claimed to be the "number one rock station" in the region, "solidly ahead of our nearest competitor" (presumably Q106). In addition, the station reported, "When the Arbitron ratings arrived, it came as a very pleasant surprise to find WDCR showing up in the survey for the first time in a long while, with 2,400 listeners per week. Since the Arbitron survey does not include college students, who make up the bulk of 1340's audience, this shows WDCR has appeal outside the Dartmouth community." WFRD averaged 17,000 listeners per week off-campus.[47]

WFRD repeated its number one ranking in the 1995 Arbitron report, with an average of 10,600 listeners. (This does not imply a decline; Arbitron survey numbers were notoriously variable.) By 1997 the station's strongest direct competitor was WGXL ("XL92"). This was the former WTSL-FM, at 92.3, which had converted to format known in the industry as "Hot AC" (hot adult contemporary hits). Ironically top WFRD d.j. and Program Director Mike Henry did a shift on XL92 during his senior year, under the name Tom Cougar, in order to gain experience. On 99Rock he was known as Mike Chapman. Wonder if listeners noticed the similarity?[48]

WHDQ ("Q106") continued to be a competitor as well, especially when its format overlapped with 99Rock's classic rock component. A new rock station at 101.7, WVRR ("V101"), had little impact. Talk stations in the market sometimes got the largest audiences overall, albeit older ones (as Phil Augur later commented, "Rush Limbaugh ruled!"), but 99Rock tended to be at or near the top of the heap among music stations.

All of this began to change at the end of the 1990s when the federal government relaxed its rules on multiple station ownership. First local entrepreneurs such as Bob Frisch (WTSL) and Jeff Shapiro (Q106) began to buy up additional stations, then national goliath Clear Channel Communications moved in, buying up multiple stations, bundling and selling them as packages and often programming them as remote-controlled jukeboxes. The era of independent, locally owned stations competing with each other was coming to an end. This would greatly affect standalone station WFRD in the 2000s.

Meanwhile a local broadcaster named Robert Vinikoor hatched a bizarre plan that could, if realized, have shaken up the entire market. In 1997 he secured an FCC construction permit for a *50,000* watt AM station licensed to Hanover, with the call letters WQTH. He even trucked in a transmitter from Canada. Although the station would have to reduce power at night (to avoid interfering with a station in Iceland!), during the day it would be heard all over the Northeast.

A station this powerful would require an antenna farm of four 266-foot towers on Etna Road in Lebanon. The Lebanon town fathers were furious, demanding that the project be scaled back or abandoned. They declared that the highest tower they would permit in town was 42 feet. Vinikoor went to court, and the case (with appeals) made it all the way to the New Hampshire Supreme Court, which ruled in his favor in 2002. The town then fought him using other tactics, such as requiring that a huge fence be built around the property, which would have cost millions. In 2006 Vinikoor moved his proposed location to Claremont, but it appears that the idea eventually died.[49]

The idea of television at Dartmouth still percolated in the background. In early 1991 *The Dartmouth* reported that cable TV would be available in all dormitory commons by February, and shortly thereafter a group of students led by Troy Seitz '93 launched DTV!, which aimed to use the intra-campus system to distribute student-produced programs. Seitz said they were beginning with a half hour news and comedy show, but hoped to expand to three hours per day, five days per week. Dartmouth radio was explicitly cited to show that "students can handle this kind of programming responsibility." Despite grand plans, however, television proved far more time-consuming and expensive to produce than radio, and DTV! never took off. It is still around in 2013, but with only occasional telecasts.[50]

## Does WDCR Have a Future?

Despite occasional flashes of brilliance, such as the now-intermittent election night broadcasts, WDCR was becoming more and more an afterthought, even for the students it was supposed to serve. For music programming, the industry and the Upper Valley were moving to FM or to non-radio music sources like MTV, portable media devices, and later the Internet. Compounding WDCR's woes were nagging signal problems. It couldn't even be heard in many dormitory rooms.

There were two major attempts in the 1990s to reshape WDCR, much as WFRD had been reshaped into the highly commercial 99Rock.

The first involved branding WDCR as the market's leading news station through a signature newscast. In January 1994, under News Directors Phil Augur and Adrienne Kim, WDCR launched *Dartmouth Nightly News*, an ambitious program of news and features broadcast five-nights-a-week at 5:30 p.m. Anchored by Grant Bosse '94 and Alyse Kornfeld '95, it was an elaborate production combining national, international and regional news with features including interviews and coverage of campus events. A newly installed Associated Press computerized newsfeed facilitated editing of national news. "It's a wonderful opportunity for any student interested in broadcast journalism to get involved because there are so many aspects to the program," said Kim. A large and dedicated staff was required to keep such a labor-intensive program going, and while subsequent news directors made it a continuing priority, staffing issues at times forced a cut-back to three-nights-a-week with Tuesdays and Thursdays filled by news from the entertainment world on *Entertainment Blitz.*[51] *Dartmouth Nightly News* continued at least until 1998, but eventually succumbed to staffing issues.

An even more ambitious scheme was hatched later in 1994 by Augur. Newly appointed as general manager, he returned from the National Association of Broadcasters convention impressed with the success of AM stations around the country that had turned to a news and information format. It seemed to be an answer to the "AM dilemma." Moreover Dartmouth was uniquely positioned to serve as a source of such audio content, with its lectures, debates, visiting notables, etc. In addition he heard stories of the big election night extravaganzas of the past, and the recently launched *Dartmouth Nightly News* seemed to provide the basis for a reenergized news department. It would be called "Smart Radio." He discussed the idea with sales chief Tim Hoehn and the professional staff, who agreed—but unfortunately he did not recruit others to support the proposal. On December 14 he announced to the Board of Overseers that by the Spring of 1995 he intended to convert WDCR to a news/talk station. "AP and CNN both offer news services that we can run all day long, breaking in with local news, student talk shows, Dartmouth sports, etc." Station finances were currently strong, a local talk station (WNTK) had recently vacated the market, and "there is hardly a better time" for Dartmouth Broadcasting to make such a move. He promised to work out the details, almost offhandedly suggesting that Dartmouth apply for an educational FM license to provide a home for student musical programs. In the interim WDCR would simulcast WFRD to prepare for the changeover. A few days later he circulated a letter to the station outlining his plans.[52]

The response was swift, and overwhelmingly negative. Overseers Chairman Rick Adams responded with a stiff letter saying that no format changes would be made without overseers approval, and discussion by the full Directorate. He wanted "a detailed plan for phasing out the current format, including a timetable for changeover, cost analysis and budget impact documentation, revenue projections, as well as a report on station membership and Directorate response to the proposal and any available listener response information." Augur was specifically forbidden to make any changes to the WDCR format in the meantime.[53]

If Adams was stern, WDCR Program Director Pamm Quinn '95 was outraged. She said she had not been consulted, and had returned to campus after the holidays to find Augur dismantling the AM music library and effectively "firing" her entire d.j. staff. She also claimed gender and racial discrimination for good measure.

The conflict raged into January. Quinn quit, and on January 26 the battle spilled into the pages of *The Dartmouth* under the headline "Turmoil at WDCR." Quinn's replacement was Keith Miles, which stirred up further antagonism because he was identified as an "FM guy," and was not the favored candidate of WDCR d.j.'s, at least one of whom quit over the matter. Quinn then wrote a fiery letter to the newspaper denouncing the plan, and much else about the station that she didn't like.[54]

Dean Sateia wanted Augur to conduct a survey to see what kind of audience support there was on campus for a news/talk station. Accordingly, toward the end of the winter term a questionnaire was sent to a random sample of 200 undergraduates. Response to the survey was low (17.5 percent), but of those who did respond 94 percent wanted "more music" from their campus radio station, vs. only 17 percent who wanted "more news." Of course any survey conducted over the prior 40 years would have probably shown the same thing, which hadn't stopped the station from mounting major news and election coverage, discussion programs and other socially important programming. But, Augur admitted, if the goal of WDCR was to give students what they wanted and finances were not an issue, then rock music was the way to go. Other interesting survey results were that 34 percent of students listened to 99Rock, 28.5 percent to WDCR, and 15 percent or less to other area stations; that a major complaint about WDCR was its poor sound quality; and that 13 percent of the students who had never listened to WDCR had never heard of the station.[55]

Unfortunately most of the debate was not about the merits of Augur's plan, but rather the way it had been unilaterally announced. Since he had not recruited allies, or even sold his idea to the Directorate, he was left essentially alone to defend the plan. "I didn't handle it right," he later admitted. In his senior year, facing furious opposition, and about to leave office anyway, he simply let it go.[56]

He had raised serious issues about the future viability of Dartmouth's AM station, however, and overseers Sateia and Adams put together a task force consisting of administrators and students to discuss the matter. There were meetings in March and April but without anyone with Augur's passion for change (he was not on the task force) it sputtered and died. Asked about the task force years later, participants I spoke with (including Adams) didn't even remember it.

There can be endless debate about whether a news/talk WDCR would have ever worked. There were obviously many obstacles, most notably a high-maintenance programming model at the very time student participation in radio was declining. Some think not, believing that WDCR-AM was essentially doomed, and nothing could save it. On the other hand, new ideas can be contagious, and some AM stations that took programming risks survived and even thrived. If you take no risks, you are guaranteed to fail. Perhaps the most thoughtful post mortem on Augur's proposal came years later from a philosophical Tim Hoehn, who commented, "Who knows? Maybe if he'd succeeded WDCR would still be on the air today."

### Rebuilding Robinson Hall

The major event of the 1990s affecting the technical plant—in fact the biggest construction event in station history—was the complete renovation of Robinson Hall in 1995-96. The multi-million dollar renovation had long been planned by the College to bring the historic building (built in 1913-14[57]) into compliance with the Americans with Disabilities Act, as well as to add safety exits and an elevator, upgrade the electric, heating, plumbing and internet infrastructure, and reclaim the large dead space occupied by the Little Theater, which had been closed off in the 1960s. Several of the student organizations occupying the three-story building were forced to relocate, but due to cost considerations the radio stations continued to operate from the building while construction went on around them. Planning for the huge project was done during 1994-95, and occupied much time by the Augur Directorate, working with station engineer Gary Savoie and Tech-Net, Inc. They took the opportunity to modernize the studios and upgrade much of the equipment, at an estimated cost of $150,000.[58]

Once construction began in August 1995 there were constant problems with noise, dust in equipment, and cordoned off areas of the building to work around. At one point a wall was torn down and workmen found a time capsule left there by Scott McQueen and his colleagues in 1968 during the *last* renovation; it said "if you're finding this you must be starting your own renovation—here's a dollar to help!" The Whitescarver Directorate monitored the progress of the multi-stage project, culminating in the consolidation of all studios and offices on the third floor of the building in early 1996. The entire project was not completed until August 1996, by which time the Lee Directorate was halfway through its tenure, and Savoie had been succeeded (in June) by a new station engineer, Ned Roos '82.[59]

The shiny new studios were certainly welcome, although there were inevitable glitches. The studio floors were so springy they caused CDs to skip, and listeners began calling in about some strange sounding records. It turned out that some of the new CD players had been wired out of phase so that no vocals were being heard. On the other hand the three new Auditronics control boards were a joy to use, as was the new digital editing equipment which greatly facilitated news editing. No more razors and splicing tape.[60]

## Staff Issues

The large number of hours necessary to run such an elaborate operation continued to be an issue. Cara Abercrombie '97, an AM program director, wrote eloquently about this dilemma in *The Dartmouth* in 1996.

> Imagine working 20-50 hours per week without pay in addition to taking a normal Dartmouth course load while trying to maintain some semblance of a normal student life. Seems impossible, but Dartmouth's radio stations WDCR-WFRD require that students in their leadership positions make the organization their number one priority.[61]

She went on to say that she loved the station, but found her job in management to be "thankless and stressful." "Current Dartmouth students," she said, "don't seem to have as much time to devote to any one organization. Our generation of Dartmouth students are more academically oriented than previous years. More of us are writing theses and doing independent research projects and do not have the time to devote our lives to one activity." She cited the fact that the recent studio reconstruction was supervised by a hired engineer, whereas the construction of the 1980s (and '70s) had been accomplished almost entirely by students. Nor was the student time crunch only affecting radio. Students no longer wanted to build the big Winter Carnival snow sculpture either, although they still wanted to have one.

However in talking to alumni and administrators of the 1990s I heard differing opinions about these issues. While some thought the commitment required by the stations was overwhelming, others said that at the end of the day shifts were filled, positions filled, and what needed to get done did get done. While there is lore about students flunking out due to overcommitment to the stations, I have found very few that actually did so. (Students would occasionally resign from the station to deal with academic pressures, or would take a term off.) General managers and program directors of the '90s said that while it was always hard to find good people, and there were occasional hiccups, attracting enough dedicated staff was not a major problem. Todd Piro recalled the third floor of Robinson as a "bustling place" in the late '90s, and longtime Sales Manager Tim Hoehn commented that even in his final year, 1999, Dartmouth Broadcasting was one of the two biggest extracurricular activities on campus, a "beehive of activity," in sharp contrast to the situation a decade later. Dean Sateia confirmed that the time commitment required of students by the stations, while sometimes heavy, was similar to that required by other campus activities.[62] Overall staff size remained in the 150-200 range, with perhaps 20 to 40 constituting the "core" team.

Some staffers even managed to be active in other campus activities as well. John Strayer, a summer general manager, wrote for *The Dartmouth*, was on several student committees, and was president of Amarna, a Greek-like undergraduate society and residence. David Grelotti '96, an AM program director, ran for Student Assembly president.[63]

A bigger issue was factionalism within the station. AM and FM were often seen as opposing camps, and, as we have seen, when an "FM person" was chosen as WDCR program director over an "AM guy" in early 1995 it caused an uproar. The following year the AM program director wrote an impassioned report for the overseers complaining that AM was getting second-class treatment by the sales, promotion and production departments, and urging that WDCR have its own separate directorate.[64]

General managers of the 1990s dealt with these problems in various ways. Beth "Bobo" Krakower (1991-92), the first female GM in six years, took over at a time when the station had developed something of a "frat house" atmosphere. No shrinking violet, she went toe-to-toe with the guys and won their respect; at one point she had a panther tattooed on her ankle while on-air doing the morning show. There was an increase in diversity and inclusiveness in the station staff. Krakower's successor, Sally Huntoon (1992-93), a smart and well-liked pre-med student, continued this policy and worked to bring the AM and FM staffs together largely through the news department they shared (she was a former news director). The biggest challenge for Sally's friend Amy Ertel (1993-94), oddly enough, was dealing wisely with the flood of money by then coming in. As Tim Hoehn later astutely observed, "it's easier to deal with no money than with lots of money."[65]

Phil Augur (1994-95) was a "take charge" kind of GM with a bold vision for the stations, which sometimes worked (*Dartmouth Nightly News*) and sometimes didn't (the WDCR reformatting). In the wake of the latter, April Whitescarver (1995-96) was a self-described "surprise choice" for GM. She had spent her first two-and-a-half years at Dartmouth involved in other campus activities, and did not arrive at the radio stations until January 1995, plunging in enthusiastically under the tutelage of News Director Sabrina Serrantino. Just a couple of months later she was appointed general manager over a widely favored internal candidate. She was met with suspicion by the polarized staff, especially that of WDCR ("Who are you?" "Do you plan to get rid of AM?").

In addition the campus was rocked that year by three student suicides, including that of a star athlete, leading the administration to urge highly involving student activities to "throttle back" and not put too much pressure on students.[66] That was especially difficult for Dartmouth Broadcasting, which was at the moment surging in so many ways (listenership, revenues, reconstruction activities). But Whitescarver was smart, skillful, and attractive — some of the guys, it was said, were smitten with her. She saw her assignment as calming the waters, and she did so with aplomb. It probably didn't hurt that she was previously best known, according to a story in *The Dartmouth*, for an impromptu Valentine's day dating plan she started in her sophomore year, whereby guys and girls who submitted their names were randomly matched on blind dates. "Some dates worked out, some were disasters!" she laughed, but by her senior year she was matching up 50 to 60 people. Who would not be charmed by that?[67]

Her successor Vivian Lee (1996-97) was a soft spoken but savvy leader who adroitly managed a number of strong egos on the Directorate that year. A "newsie," she maintained news as an important part of the station's culture. Brent Laffoon (1997-98), a tall, laid-back, friendly guy, was well liked by all, and was even held over for an additional term in the spring of his senior year. Jon Flynn (1998-99), faced with some major financial challenges, helped Tim Hoehn pull together the wildly successful summer 1998 Rockfest concert, one of those rare big all-station projects in which everyone pulled together to stage a major event, one that also boosted morale. Sean Byrnes (1999-2000), a tech wizard who had been technical director for the prior two years, kept things on an even keel.

No matter how much time it required, and whatever the internal rivalries, the station remained a central part of the Dartmouth experience for many of its members. Kendra Kosko, an FM program director, wrote an especially lyrical piece about her love affair with the station in a 1997 article titled "Love and Passion, Robinson Style."[68]

> For me, my affair with 99Rock started as somewhat of a joke. I had always told my parents that if I couldn't get into law school, I was going to be a disc jockey. It was a joke, and also somewhat of a far-fetched fantasy. Well, not entirely, but hey, the idea of conquering all media is quite an attraction. So now, I have this thing with the station. I don't want to call it a relationship — that might mean commitment or something, so I'll say the station is my "special" friend... Well, this innocent little affair of sorts grew on me and I began to spend more and more time there. I even went so far as to take the big leap and pretty much marry the damn thing... that's right, I applied for the Directorate... a position that turns into a time suck, sometimes greatly rewarding, mostly thankless, [but] looks GREAT on the resume.

The payoff? She gave countless hours and in return got experience that went far beyond what she learned in Greek and Roman studies classes. No professor would assign an interview with Slash, or force her to see concerts or mingle with other radio people, she said. "This wouldn't be such a great school if all you took away was what you learned in class. Robinson Hall is a great place to start diverting your attention from those books. Forget all the relationship problems you've had in the past and fall in love — it will change your life and possibly your future."

### Minorities and Women

One staffer of the 1990s commented to me that there were no black-white tensions at the station in these years because there were hardly any blacks on staff.

That might have been a bit of an exaggeration, but not much. Since the demise of the *Blackside* station-within-a-station of the 1970s and '80s, African-American participation in Dartmouth Broadcasting had been limited. However other minorities, particularly Asian-Americans, were becoming decidedly more prominent in station management. So were minorities such as the one represented by Sports Director Casey Sixkiller '00, who would go on to become a Washington lobbyist for Native Americans and an expert in tribal law.

The issue of gender representation was complex. Views on it depend on who you talk to. Clearly this was the decade in which women rose to the most senior leadership positions at the station. Five out of ten general managers during the 1990s were women, along with numerous program directors, business/finance directors, news directors, and even an occasional technical director. But some felt it was still a "boys club." Priscilla Huff '91, an active member of the news and d.j. staffs, felt she was blocked from leadership positions. In 1992 GM Sally Huntoon drew up a three-year plan to recruit more women to the station. Her successor Amy Ertel founded Women in Broadcasting, an initiative "that hopes to give women a supportive niche at the predominantly male College radio stations."[69]

About a third of the staff was female, Ertel said, but most of them worked behind the scenes and not in high-profile positions such as disc jockeys. It was hard for some women to feel comfortable because of the male to female ratio. "It can be intimidating when you're in a room full of men and they're swapping the bull," she added. "You can be absorbed into the walls or you have to be able to dish it out." News Director Sabrina Serrantino commented that "The women who come in are pretty gutsy to begin with." One goal of the Women in Broadcasting project was to develop a mentoring system for women, and help them find positions in broadcasting after they graduated as well as while they were at Dartmouth. The initiative was strongly supported by incoming GM Augur, FM Program Director Andrew Kersey, and other men in management. It was publicly endorsed by Dean Holly Sateia, a leading member of the Board of Overseers.[70]

This was not enough for some. Pammela Quinn, who had been appointed AM Program Director in early 1994, was clearly upset about gender issues on campus generally. In November 1994, in reaction to the resignation of Student Assembly President Danielle Moore '95, Quinn wrote a scathing opinion piece in *The Dartmouth* in which she asserted that, "I have encountered both subtle and overt sexism and complete disrespect since the day I arrived on campus. Making the problem worse are the men (most of the male students at Dartmouth I would say) who react violently to such a claim and refuse to listen... I demand that each and every man on this campus examine his behavior and ask himself whether he really has treated every woman with whom he has come into contact with the respect she deserves." She then took aim at Dartmouth Broadcasting. "Often I have considered resigning my position and quitting altogether because the atmosphere at the radio station is blatantly sexist and abusive to me and to the other women working there. [But] I have been advised by Dean of Student Life Holly Sateia to 'stick with it,' to provide an example for other women at the station."[71]

Two months later, after Phil Augur rolled out his plan for the transformation of WDCR, she blasted the station in print again. "Women and people of color have traditionally been excluded from Dartmouth Broadcasting and positions of management," she said. "The issue of diversity and the need to increase it has been constantly neglected, leading to what is presently the least diverse group of directors in recent memory."[72]

But others, including many women, felt that this was overstating the situation. Serrantino, one of the leading contributors to the station's success in news, was quoted as saying she was skeptical that sexism was prevalent on campus. "I think this is a rather liberal institution and I do think there is ample opportunity to thrive in any environment and any sector here." If an organization was sexist, she added, it was much more effective to seek to change it from within rather than from without. Other women leaders at the station conveyed similar attitudes. April Whitescarver called gender discrimination a "non-issue" during her term, and Vivian Lee was not even aware of Quinn's criticisms. Nevertheless the initiatives of Huntoon and Ertel suggest that Quinn was not alone in her concern about the situation.[73]

Most staffers I spoke to from this era, male and female, felt that the imbalance in gender representation at Dartmouth Broadcasting (roughly 70 percent male/30 percent female) was due primarily to the fact that women simply weren't as interested in broadcasting, and not attracted to the hard rock music that WFRD played. This of course was an issue not only at Dartmouth radio, but in the industry nationwide. On-air, women were much more likely to be d.j.'s on WDCR (where programming was very individualistic) than on tightly formatted rock station WFRD. When women did enter the management ranks, it was often in news or business affairs rather than as programmers or "techies." But there were always exceptions. In an organization dependent on volunteer talent, the doors were always open.

Sadly, the initiatives begun by Huntoon and Ertel to increase female participation at the station were quickly forgotten. General managers of the late 1990s were not aware of them, and hardly anyone remembers them today. No documents relating to them could be found in the station's files.

### Alumni

A more successful venture was the re-start of the Alumni Relations Department under Sally Huntoon, which led to a new series of alumni newsletters and outreach to the station's by-now large body of successful alumni. In March 1993 Alumni Relations Director Diem-Trang Do '94 sent a letter and a bumper sticker to several hundred alumni inviting them to join the newly established Friends of Dartmouth Broadcasting and to send the station comments and contacts. This was followed in the summer by the first alumni newsletter in four years, full of information about developments at the station. Approximately six more newsletters would be issued over the next five years. It was a productive venture, resulting in donations and professional contacts for current and graduating staffers. During 1996-97 alumni provided the funding and contacts that allowed three staffers to have valuable off-campus internships—Mike Henry at WNEW-FM, New York, Robert Ristagno '00 with the *Geraldo Rivera Show*, and Jon Flynn with WNBC news. The station also announced an alumni homepage on the Internet to facilitate contact between students and alumni. The initiative petered out around 1998, but showed what a valuable resource the station's alumni could be.[74]

## Looking Toward the Future

The 1990s began with a story in *The Dartmouth* boldly titled, "Dartmouth Radio: The Students Are in Control." However there were soon signs that student control might not last. From the shifting of responsibility for sales from the students to College administrators (to whom the professional staff now reported), to the diversion of station profits to support other student activities, the tepid response to new directions for the AM station in 1995, and the squelching of the student-initiated Rockfest in 1999, there were repeated instances in which the overseers, or the College itself, simply stepped in and handed down orders. Of course as the legal license holder for WFRD and WDCR, the College had every right to operate the stations as it wished. However it is hard to believe that this pattern of control would have been exercised during the days of Presidents Dickey or Kemeny, when the principle of student autonomy was strongly supported.[75]

That said, these were individual incidents and ongoing overseers control of the stations was by no means heavy-handed. Most of the time the overseers acted as a sounding board and deferred to the students if the students seemed to have a reasonably well thought-out plan of action. During most of the decade there were quarterly meetings (and often dinners) attended by the overseers and the student Directorate, at which issues were discussed. These were chaired by Rick Adams until 1996, and by alumnus and former GM Tim Reynolds after that, with Dean Sateia and her deputy Brenda Goupee playing a major role in board decisions. Reynolds was an active chair, frequently trading emails with student leaders between meetings. The overseers also initiated a program of awards named after past station leaders to recognize exceptional student achievement. These included The Robin Robinson Award, the Almon Ives Award, the John D. Bryant Creative Production Award, the Ronald Kehoe '59 Award, and the Al Shepard Memorial Award, the latter named after a well-liked '73 who was a mentor to many younger students, and who died tragically a few years after his own graduation.

While some student leaders got the clear impression that certain board members believed the stations should be managed by professionals, the board took no action to make such a change. Students still felt in control, and in effect they were, especially when it came to programming. "Students run the station, but any of the money we make goes back to the College," said GM Neel Chatterjee in 1990. Program Director Eric Wellman added that students at Dartmouth were better off than in a communications program such as that at Syracuse University, because "If Dartmouth had a broadcasting program, students would have no control. Professors would be running the whole thing. Also [students trained at broadcasting schools] would be well trained in broadcasting but could never run a station." Looking forward to his own career, Wellman said "I have to believe I'll be better off having had so much experience." (Wellman went on to become program director at radio stations in the New York market.)[76]

Virtually every senior leader I spoke with from the 1990s echoed the belief that the students were still very much in charge.

Dartmouth presidents were not as involved with the station as they had been in the past. There were no more fireside chats (as with Dickey), or press conferences at the station (as with Kemeny). President Freedman was succeeded in 1998 by history professor James Wright, who became preoccupied with an ambitious and controversial Student Life Initiative designed to reshape campus life. The goals were noble (address drinking and other excesses at fraternities, create a friendlier campus for minorities) but the clumsy, top-down implementation infuriated many with its apparent attack on the Greek system and implication of a speech code. It led to an outright revolt among alumni who elected three successive write-in candidates to the Board of Trustees, defeating the administration-approved candidates. The battle raged on for the next decade, overshadowing Wright's strengthening of the College's finances and physical plant. The campus radio station seemed to be the last thing on his mind.

In December 1999, after nine successful years as the station's sales chief, Tim Hoehn resigned. Frustrated with the College's slow-moving bureaucracy and its unwillingness to consider bold moves such as the 1995 AM talk radio proposal or the 1999 rock concert initiative, he moved on to become co-owner of WMXR in Woodstock, Vermont, and later ran a yellow pages business and published a pet lover's magazine (*4 Legs & a Tail*) in Lebanon. Hoehn's frustrations would foreshadow significant changes in Dartmouth radio in the decade to come.

# Chapter 12

## 2000-2006: "Basically, It Was a Disaster"

The early 2000s represented a major turning point in the history of Dartmouth radio. Declining student involvement, increasing competition, and administration encroachment on student independence had been building slowly in the 1990s. In the early 2000s these combined with sudden and dramatic changes in the media landscape to create a kind of perfect storm.

Distribution of music via the Internet exploded virtually overnight with the launch of Napster (1999) and other illegal file-swapping sites, which were followed by a wave of legal music sites including iTunes (2003) and YouTube (2005). At the same time the iPod (2001) and other portable digital media players were introduced, allowing the user to create a personal music library of thousands of songs and carry it around anywhere. None of this seriously diminished the overall audience for radio (adults listening in cars, etc.) but it did siphon off younger listeners. More importantly, it made college students, from whom the station recruited its staff, much less interested in radio.

Both WFRD and WDCR struggled through some pretty choppy seas during this media upheaval, and the air product suffered. The staffing problems were compounded by a grand experiment to stabilize revenues that seemed like a good idea at the time, but turned into a disaster. This was the Joint Sales Agreement, or JSA, which outsourced sales for the stations entirely.

Station general managers during this tumultuous period were Dan King '02, Michael F. O'Donnell '02, Eric McDonald '04, Kerrin Egalka '04, Noah Kekane Yuen '05, and Nikhil V. Gore '06.

### The Launch of the JSA

The early 2000s brought profound changes to the Upper Valley radio market. Texas-based Clear Channel Communications (owner of 830 stations nationwide) entered the market in 2000, buying multiple stations and packaging them together for sales purposes using a well-honed, professional sales force and industry-standard Arbitron ratings. In order to compete radio entrepreneur Jeff Shapiro had expanded the local holdings of his Vox Radio Group as well, to four stations.

As a standalone station, often tarred by competitors as run by "a bunch of college kids," 99Rock had a difficult time competing. By putting together combinations of stations Clear Channel and Vox could offer advertisers whatever demographics they desired, and larger audiences as well. With its modern rock format 99Rock was a one-trick pony, offering only a young, dominantly male audience.

The possibility of turning over WFRD's time sales to one of the local multiple-station owners, presumably Jeff Shapiro's Vox, had been discussed in the late 1990s but hadn't gone far. By 2001, however, station finances were in dire shape, the result of competitive changes compounded by a deep national economic recession. Losses were approaching six figures and there was real fear that the College would seriously consider selling the station. The possibility of a JSA with Vox was raised again, but it was very controversial. Some board members questioned the College's financial accounting regarding the station, which had grown so complex hardly anyone understood it. They feared that the College was draining off profits when times were good, but penalizing the station when they were bad. There was also fear that a JSA would take away one of the fundamental pillars of the student experience—running a real business—and thus undermine a basic purpose of a student-run station. The general manager, Dan King, was strongly opposed to such a move.[1]

Others argued that the very existence of the station was threatened if finances could not be brought under control. It was better to sacrifice the sales side, which students had never been very good at, to save the programming experience, at which, arguably, they were much better. Sales had been semi-autonomous for the past 25 years anyway, ever since a professional sales staff had been introduced in 1975.

The debate raged on, creating tensions between the student leadership and the overseers. Dan King's term as general manager (2000-01) came to an end in early 2001, but to the surprise (and some think, dismay) of the overseers he was reelected for a second term by the student leadership. However at the end of the Spring 2001 term he resigned, due to medical issues and "other factors." He was succeeded as general manager by Michael O'Donnell who was much more agreeable to the idea of a JSA.

What happened next was perhaps unprecedented in the history of Dartmouth Broadcasting. The idea of outsourcing sales was still unpopular among the student staff, and of course was a direct threat to the livelihood of the station's current professional salespeople. So the overseers convened a small executive committee, which excluded the students (except the general manager) and met behind closed doors to decide the issue. Around Thanksgiving 2001 they made the decision to sign the JSA and give Jeff Shapiro's Vox Radio Group exclusive responsibility for selling WFRD air time, which he could package with that of his other stations. The decision was made at a time when most students were out of town. The student leaders were not even given a copy of the contract; if they needed clarification of one of its provisions, they had to ask the chairman of the Board of Overseers.

The board did try to make the deal as student-friendly as possible. It included a provision for Vox to provide internships and conduct workshops for the students. The exact terms were kept secret but according to published reports the station would receive a guaranteed $13,000 per month from Vox, regardless of sales. Of that, $2,000 had to be paid to the College for overhead. In addition, although this is less clear, the station may have received a percentage of sales revenue above this amount.[2]

The board also tried to take care of the professional staff. Both salespeople were offered positions with Vox. Julie Kaye accepted, but Laura Canada (formerly Daniels) did not, and left the station to work first for a local bank, and then for WNNE-TV. The position held by Winnie Lacoss, the much-loved station secretary since 1979, was eliminated too. She was given a position in Dean Joe Cassidy's office, from which she retired at the end of 2003.[3]

By early 2002 the JSA was in place. Vox kept in close contact with the Board of Overseers, and Jeff Shapiro even had a non-voting seat on that body. The students now had a steady, guaranteed income stream to work with, and the College was receiving a steady (if modest) income as well. Any thought that the station might be sold or closed down was eliminated, since the College was fully invested in the deal. The wolf was no longer at the door. However for the first time in decades there was no sales presence, or even a secretary, on the third floor of Robinson Hall.

Although the JSA made sense financially, the way in which it was unilaterally imposed dealt a body blow to the concept of student independence that had for so long been at the heart of Dartmouth radio. There was lingering resentment for years to come. Interviewed a couple of years later one Directorate member said of the decision, "It was shady." Another called it "highly abnormal," and said she'd never heard of such a momentous decision simply being handed down by the board. Other staffers of the period to whom I spoke expressed their resentment in terms that were even more blunt.[4]

Although subsequent student administrations came to accept the new reality as "the way things are," it clearly changed the dynamic between the administration (firmly in charge) and the students. The fierce dedication of so many Dartmouth radio staffers in prior decades, fueled by a genuine sense of ownership, seems to have waned noticeably in the 2000s. While many reasons are commonly given for this, the willingness of the administration and overseers to effectively shut the students out on one of the most important decisions in station history appears to have been a tipping point.

### 99Rock Rocks On

In the short term, at least, the burden of financial worries was lifted and the students could concentrate on WFRD and WDCR programming. WFRD was now consistently modern rock, and the on-air slogan or "positioner" was changed in 2003 from "the Upper Valley's solid rock station" to simply "the modern rock station." At the same time Heath Cole from Vox Radio conducted a seminar for the student d.j.'s in which he explained how "during the music sweeps the music never stops, how you open talk-ups [d.j. chatter] with the positioner, you backsell only one song, you tease only one upcoming band," and other tricks of the trade. "The jocks' talk-ups have been shortening but getting more to the point," said Program Director Eric McDonald. "According to our sales team, station recognition is improving." To insure consistency McDonald and Training Director Sebastian Miller '02 used a "skimmer," which recorded air product only when the d.j.'s microphone was on, allowing them to efficiently review jock performance throughout the 18-hour broadcast day.[5]

Besides regular d.j. shifts there were still some specialty shows on 99Rock. One of the more popular was the long-running *Homegrown*, which presented interviews and performances by rock bands from the local area and New England. There was a lot of local musical talent. Among the hosts were Derek Herro and Chris Johnson. Another popular entry was *Night of the Living Dead*, dedicated to the Grateful Dead.

The station promoted itself via its website, which at times of maximum on-air promotion could average as many as 3,500 "hits" per day. Web Director Alex

"Spyder" Middleton '06 updated the busy site to include on-air schedules, profiles of d.j.'s, and a FanMail system. It also offered Club 99 for station fans, which provided special content and gathered demographic information about listeners that the station could use in its sales efforts. In 2005 the station promoted its all-night programming online with the tagline, "Sleep with Us!"[6]

Of course you can't please all the people all the time, and campus complaints that WFRD was *too* commercial continued to surface from time to time. In 2003 *The Dartmouth* published a long opinion piece under the headline "Change the Channel" in which William Meland '03 argued that WFRD should abandon its "misguided attempt to compete in the dark world of corporate radio" and become a free form station on which students could play their favorite songs "in crystal clear FM stereo, without being told what to play and when to play it." Calling the current station "a sad artistic wastrel," he said "Instead of running WFRD as a pseudo-commercial enterprise with poor quality music and 30-second ads for laundry detergent, we should tailor the station's content to the real market it should serve: ourselves." He listed several colleges that had such stations, not mentioning that all of them were heavily subsidized.[7]

There were immediate rebuttals to this piece, including one by former GM Dan King which pointed out that the "free form" station Meland wanted already existed in the form of WDCR. In an era of acute cut-backs, the College was not about to start subsidizing campus radio so that Mr. Meland could play his favorite bands in stereo rather than mono. His column, King said, "insult[ed] the dedicated students of Dartmouth Broadcasting."[8]

In 2005 *The Dartmouth* published an article on both the stations and the struggling DTV (a closed circuit television operation), suggesting that while 99Rock made money it was "merely filling a position for its sponsors rather than broadcasting music that it values." WDCR, said d.j. Mat Brown '05, "is really free form radio and you can do whatever the hell you want." FM Program Director Deb Wassel '07 took immediate offense at the article, firing back the next day that her station was not a corporate sellout but rather a place where students could experience what it's like to work at a real station. Meanwhile WDCR provided a place for student expression. "Before I stumbled on 99Rock during my freshman winter," she said, "I felt lost and out of place; finding the radio station was a blessing for me, and has been an amazingly positive experience as well as a huge part of my Dartmouth career."[9]

## Sales Promotions

99Rock continued to stage promotions, although not at the pace of the 1990s. The annual Rocktober promotion continued each fall, giving away CDs and concert and movie tickets. The 2003 edition was introduced with the line, "Why go sober in Rocktober? We'll quench your thirst with new rock six-packs and concert tickets all month long!" However an unamused professor objected, so it was changed to "The only thing clear about our channel is... the music."

Another popular promotion of the early 2000s was Battle of the Bands, staged both on-campus and in local clubs such as the Fuel Rocket Club in Hanover and Electra in West Lebanon. A "battle" at the latter featured the up-and-coming indie band Paranoid Social Club. A 2003 Winter Carnival charity battle at Collis Student

Center featured three main bands and three solo acts, with the winner getting 10 hours of live studio time. It was a big success: "Three hundred people were brought in, and lines were nuts [even] with an $8 cover charge," reported Eric McDonald. Dan King noted that by sponsoring and featuring entities besides the station's own personalities, like local rock bands, the station could attract a lot more people, and also raise its credibility on campus.[10]

There were also numerous remotes for major advertisers such as Benning Street Bar & Grill, Upper Valley Lanes, and Miller Auto.

## WDCR Programming

Over on the AM side the strength of the schedule varied from year to year, depending on the effectiveness of each year's staff recruiting campaign. There were also seasonal swings, typically with a burst of activity in the fall, then fall-off in the spring and summer. The station needed 30 to 60 active d.j.'s for its checkerboard of programming, vs. half that many on 99Rock. Recruiting was essential. Students were not naturally drawn to (or sometimes even aware of) Dartmouth's AM radio station, and had to be sold on joining it. Once they were engaged, however, the freedom to program their own time slots as they liked (either music or talk) proved to be a strong draw. The AM and FM staffs were separate. Sometimes an FM d.j. would "defect" to AM for the greater programming freedom. No one went the other way.[11]

WDCR saw a surge in interest in 2003 under AM program directors Drew Van Ness '05 and Pedro Hernandez '04, aided by a raft of news and public affairs shows drummed up by hard-working News Director Nikhil Gore. D.J.'s began to branch out beyond their own programs and make appearances on other shows, and even arrange trips to concerts in Boston, Manchester, and Concord, New Hampshire. Almost every key time slot was filled and Hernandez kept in touch with d.j.'s who had dropped out due to time constraints to encourage them to rejoin the station at a later date.[12]

New CD players were installed, which allowed for "live scratching, chopping, and five more digital effects." The units also had beat counters and speed controls to allow d.j.'s to indulge their creativity. Some young d.j.'s were intrigued by the presence of *turntables* in the studios! By now this type of equipment was uncommon, identified mostly with clubs and considered itself a creative musical instrument. The d.j.'s were "curious to try them out." Unfortunately they were unaware of the fragile nature of the styli which suffered from abuse and even theft. Eventually the station was forced to obtain a locked cabinet in which to keep the small but expensive styli.[13]

Many shows were built around various types of rock music, but there were specialty shows as well. One was an audio story project produced by the students of Thetford Academy. "North Country Weekend" brought inner-city kids to Hanover for a weekend, during which they were given the opportunity to record their own radio show in the WDCR studios. Afterwards they were given a CD of their show by Technical Director Lynn Lee '05. *Environmental Insight* with Robert Norman continued. Perhaps the raciest show was *In Your Pants*, a sex-education program hosted by Jennifer Kosty '06 and Sheila Hicks '04, which asked (and presumably answered) such questions as "Is it safe to have sex in the water (or the river)?", "Where can I get sex toys in Hanover?", "Are there any STD's you can get while using a condom?", "How 'deep' is the average vagina?", and "Does the G-spot actually exist?"[14]

News and sports-related programs were generally scheduled between 4:00 and 6:00 p.m. (afternoon drive time), and six out of seven days a week were solidly booked.

All of this activity showed that it was possible to program an AM station full time even in an era when students had supposedly abandoned the medium, and when there were few listeners. However this did depend on active recruiting and hard work by the station leadership. By early 2005 WDCR had fallen into a kind of funk, with only 17 shows on the air and a dispirited leadership. But another upsurge occurred in 2006, under Program Directors Pam Cortland '06 and Julio Gil '08, with 47 shows and the largest number of d.j.'s in four years. Shows ranged from "political and sport talk, to metal, country, and even Christian rock." Among the highlights were Alex Middleton and Andrew Argeski '06's *NRO Radio* on which faculty members shared their musical tastes while discussing their lives and work. Leah Prescott and Alysondra Duke of Dartmouth's Sexual Abuse Awareness Program presented *Eyes and Ears: Seeing Violence... Hearing Silence*, a significant public service program each Tuesday, which "put together hip hop, underground and poetry music, as a forum for students to learn about sexual relationship violence and also for anonymous callers to break their silence on their experiences." Clearly, Dartmouth's AM station added a different, and important, voice to the community.[15]

The programming was often laudable, but attracting listeners was a challenge. There was no money for paid promotion, students weren't accustomed to listening to AM radio, and the programming wasn't commercial enough for the larger community. So d.j.'s and hosts were constantly urged to promote their own shows, at least on campus, which many did via flyers and BlitzMail blasts. The aforementioned *In Your Pants* was promoted by provocative postings on the web and flyers in Collis Student Center. The station held "a workshop of sorts where the d.j.'s brought supplies and worked for a few hours designing posters to put up in their dorms." Caught up in the spirit of the initiative, "the always-original Lance Kramer ['06] decided to walk around campus for a day wearing a large sign advertising his show."[16]

The WDCR website was used for promotion, but unfortunately its location (**www.dartmouth.edu/~brdcast**) was not exactly self-evident. Why didn't the station use **www.wdcr.com**? Apparently the station didn't pursue it in the 1990s, and by the early 2000s it had been scooped up by a "cybersquatter," a company that buys thousands of domain names cheaply before legitimate users can get to them, then tries to resell them for exorbitant prices. Eventually it was purchased by Wind Dancer Consultants in San Diego.

### Robin Robinson: The End of an Era

One of the most remarkable chapters in Dartmouth radio history came to a quiet end in 2002. Professor Robin Robinson, a dignified gentleman known affectionately as "Rob-Rob," had been a fixture at the station for nearly half a century. His programs, *Opera Showcase* and *A Little Night Music*, were programmed from his own vast record collection, and were carefully researched and scripted each week. They began in 1955 on WDBS and continued in later years on WDCR, WFRD, and finally on WDCR again when FM became a full-time rock station. (He also had a program on WTSL in the 1950s). The station, in appreciation for his long and loyal service, named an endowment after him in 1983, a studio in 1987, and a student prize in the late 1990s.[17]

Although serious about his music, he also had a twinkle in his eye. I recall an incident in the early 1960s when his program had to be truncated for some reason one week. The following week he returned to the air with the sly comment, "And now, *A Little ... more... Night Music*." As he passed through his 80s and into his 90s staffers recalled that he sometimes dozed off during his shows. His engineer would wake him 30 seconds before the end of the selection, to resume his narration.

Born in 1903, Robinson had attended Dartmouth majoring in mathematics and Greek, graduating with honors in 1924. He earned his PhD in mathematics at Harvard in 1929, and began teaching at Dartmouth in 1928. He eventually served as chairman of the mathematics department, director of the Great Issues course, and registrar, in which capacity he organized the academic schedule and introduced computerization to course scheduling and registration procedures. He retired in 1968 but returned in 1970 and served another 10 years until retiring again in January, 1981. He wrote a number of books, including one with John Kemeny.[18]

He hardly ever missed a show, and showed up like clockwork for the broadcast of February 25, 2002. A few days later he died suddenly, two months short of his 99th birthday, and a day after driving to the Hopkins Center to attend an event. The following week's program was delivered by his grandson, Andrew Walkling. Robinson left behind two children, five grandchildren, and generations of appreciative members of the Dartmouth Broadcasting family. Scripts for many of his programs are now at the College's Rauner Archives.[19]

## News

Election coverage, once the pride of Dartmouth radio, receded in the 2000s. On the night of the nail-biting 2000 Presidential election (Bush vs. Gore) the Dartmouth Election Network (DEN) presented relatively comprehensive coverage live from Rockefeller Center, broadcast on both WFRD and WDCR, starting at 6:30 p.m. Included was commentary, live interviews, and prepared features by news staffers. However the competition the broadcast had to face was illustrated by a story in *The Dartmouth* headlined "Media Competes for Your Vote." It listed all the choices available to students that night, including coverage on ABC, CBS, MSNBC, CNN (which would be on all night at Rockefeller Center), Fox News, C-Span, PBS, and four major websites. At the very end of the article, almost as an afterthought, the story mentioned that, oh yes, the Dartmouth radio station would be covering the election too.[20]

The November 2002 midterm election coverage was a flop. News Director Lynn Lee described it as follows: "Started a bit late. Manpower was a big problem, no writers. All reporters backed out. Just conducted phone interviews with press heads. Political groups were no help at all." The suggestion was made that perhaps a government class should be recruited to run the next one.[21]

Coverage of the January 2004 New Hampshire primary was hobbled by the resignation of the news director the previous fall. Replacement co-News Directors Vikash Reddy '05 and Scott Glabe '06 (a curious pair; Reddy was president of the

Young Democrats, and Glabe a staffer at *The Dartmouth Review*) pulled together coverage of a number of campaign events during the fall. These included speeches by Senator John Edwards, General Wesley Clark, Governor Howard Dean, Chrissy Gephardt, former Labor Secretary (and WDCR alumnus) Robert Reich, and the White House representative for Faith-Based Initiatives. Records are skimpy, but it appears that coverage on primary night was subdued. Coverage of election night itself in November (Bush vs. Kerry) was non-existent, due to a lack of staff. One staffer felt that a contributing reason was the College's Student Life Initiative crackdown which discouraged an after-coverage party to reward the staffers.[22]

Although election night coverage was disappointing, the News Department did contribute news and public affairs series to the AM schedule. In a 2003 report News Director Nikhil Gore reported that there were five on the air: old standby *Environmental Insight* plus *The Political Roundtable, The Conservative Hour, Dartmouth Democrats*, and *Sports Hour*. Some of these were the product of collaboration with campus publications. *The Dartmouth Review* contributed to *The Conservative Hour*, while *Dartmouth Free Press* Editor-in-Chief Clint Hendler regularly appeared on *Dartmouth Democrats*. The department was also working on a special African affairs show.[23]

### Sports

The Sports Department did not have the luxury of "off" periods as there was a constant stream of games to cover. Often it was a scramble to cover them all. Sports Director Keith Burdette '03 recalled one Saturday when there were three broadcasts in three cities in one day, and only two sets of broadcast equipment. JT Mohr '03, who happened to be returning from Alaska, flew into Boston and jumped in a cab to Harvard, where he met Alex Taylor '04 who had driven the mobile unit down from Hanover. Together they covered the Harvard-Dartmouth basketball game at 2:00 p.m. then high-tailed it back to Hanover to cover another game there at 7:00 p.m. Meanwhile, Burdette broadcast men's hockey from Burlington, Vermont, also at 7:00 p.m. According to Burdette, "all of it went off without a hitch!"[24]

Fortunately Mohr and Taylor did not have to contend with anything like the March 14, 2003, ECAC quarterfinals game (Dartmouth vs. Colgate), a four-overtime thriller that was the third-longest game in college men's hockey history. Burdette reported that as of May that year, the Sports Department had covered 10 hockey games in four states.

Staff to cover all these games was recruited wherever it could be found, including non-student ranks. An early 2005 report by Sports Director Tim Katz '05 listed the play-by-play and color teams for men's and women's hockey, and men's and women's basketball. They included five current students and two alumni, Keith Burdette and Gino Beniamino '04, both of whom had remained in Hanover after their graduations and volunteered at the station. Burdette later commented, "I knew that my help could probably be used if I stuck around." Both students and non-students were reimbursed for travel expenses to away games, but otherwise received no compensation.[25]

The College Athletic Department generally expressed satisfaction with the station's coverage, although in 2006 women's basketball coverage was moved to WUVR, an AM station in Lebanon.[26]

## Technical

Following the major studio reconstruction and upgrades of 1995-96 the technical plant was relatively stable during the early 2000s. By 2005, however, problems began to emerge with the station's technical quality, particularly the on-air signal. These concerns would escalate rapidly over the next few years. The 10 year cycle of equipment replacement common in broadcasting was beginning to be felt.[27]

The College had decided to apply for an increase in FM transmitter power from 3.0 to 6.0 kw around 2002, in order to be competitive with other stations in the market. However the progress of the application was painfully slow, first within the College bureaucracy and then at the FCC. The increase was finally authorized in late 2006.[28]

Another technical improvement that was badly needed, but painfully long in coming, was Internet streaming, so that the stations could be heard live around the world on the Internet. Use of the Internet was spreading like wildfire, especially among the younger listeners to whom the Dartmouth stations appealed. In the late 1990s the overseers discussed the possibility of streaming the AM signal, but deferred action.[29] There were several issues. Live audio streaming uses a significant amount of bandwidth, and nobody knew how widely it would be used. It might be possible to stream within Dartmouth's on-campus "intranet" system, but feeding the signal(s) out over the College's connections to the worldwide Internet could potentially choke those connection points. There were also legal issues. The Digital Performance Right in Sound Recordings Act of 1995 and the Digital Millennium Copyright Act of 1998 had granted record labels the right to collect royalties when their recordings were streamed over the Internet (a right they did not have for over-the-air station play). AFTRA, the radio performers' union, also demanded payment to announcers when commercials were streamed. There was a major battle going on in the early 2000s over how much Internet stations would have to pay, and how the royalties would be collected. Everybody wanted a piece of the pie (or the whole pie, if they could get it).

Although exact dates are difficult to verify the first live on-campus streaming of WDCR appears to have taken place in early 2000 using QuickTime software. In February the station's website proudly proclaimed, "Now you can listen to WDCR over the web!" However this lasted for only about a year, and from 2002-05 streaming seems to have been limited to occasional special events, such as the 2004 and 2005 Convocations, the 2004 Democratic National Convention, and sports coverage. The latter was streamed not only on campus but to the wider world by a professional service (SurferNetwork) paid for by the Athletic Department.[30]

In early 2005 WFRD began on-campus streaming for the first time. According to the website the user needed only "Winamp, Windows Media Player, iTunes, XMMS... any mp3 player with a brain!" Later in the year WDCR resumed campus streaming as well. But off-campus streaming, the 21st century solution that would bring the Dartmouth stations to alumni and to the rest of the world, remained blocked. Finally in mid 2006 a new Directorate, under GMs Deborah Wassel and Susannah Thompson '08, decided to take the bull by the horns. Thompson wrote in August, 2006,

> It has been the hope of Dartmouth Broadcasting for the last five or so years
> that we will finally get in place a good quality, clear, world-wide Internet

stream. The previous Directorate met with many obstacles, mostly from the administration and various departments, when they tried to implement the stream, and they eventually became discouraged from trying any longer. But with a new group of people on board and a fresh perspective (as well as a perceptible demand from the Board of Overseers) we decided to try again.[31]

With the help of overseer Gordon Taylor, Thompson secured the cooperation of the College IT department, and worked with Heath Cole and former tech director and webmaster Alex "Spyder" Middleton to get the streams up and running. A dozen friends across the country who had cable or DSL connections were recruited to log in and check the quality of the feed. When the results were satisfactory, and without waiting for all approvals to be in, the station simply "flipped the switch." (Middleton reportedly wanted to be able to hear the station after he graduated.) Since then, Dartmouth radio has been broadcasting to the world.[32]

## A New Era of Recruiting

Dartmouth radio had always recruited incoming freshmen by participating in activities night, placing articles in the freshman issue of *The Dartmouth*, and at various on-campus events. In the station's heyday, it was not a hard sell. Radio broadcasting was glamorous, and students sought out the station. But in the 2000s this changed. Both the AM and FM stations had limited visibility on campus, and there was hardly ever a mention of them in *The Dartmouth*. Active, aggressive recruiting became a necessity. In fact, it became necessary to sell radio itself.

The Battle of the Bands events proved to be a good recruiting tool, giving Dartmouth Broadcasting "an excellent image as being an organization that can throw a great party!" The station also held outdoor barbeques, and free pizza at the station open house really drew 'em in. As GM Kerrin Egalka observed in 2003, "Free consumables really seem to have worked for us this term." Station veteran Jeff Shapiro put it even more succinctly. "Students want three things—pizza, beer, and sex. You can't give them the last two, so give them pizza!"[33]

Other recruiting tools included remotes from the food court and background ("wallpaper") ads on the public access computers scattered around campus.

It was especially important to get to freshmen early. In the fall of 2003 Marketing Director Lavinia Weizel '04 reported that with the '07s arriving "Dartmouth Broadcasting directed all of its energies toward a single goal: recruitment." Packed into orientation week were multiple high-profile remotes, a party at Fuel, barbeques, participation in the activities fair and a new media-specific fair, sports department T-shirts, and raffles for free CDs. The result was 13 new FM d.j. candidates, 10 new AM d.j.'s, 10 new "newsies," nine new members of the Sports Department, and four new members of the Production Department—almost 50 recruits in total.[34]

Getting them in was one thing, holding on to them another. Many recruits of the 2000s seemed to treat radio as something to dabble in, rather than commit to. 99Rock in particular, with its tightly controlled format and need for consistent voices (meaning five-day-a-week shifts for many d.j.'s), seemed at times to be all business and no pleasure. A canceled trade deal whereby staffers who agreed to come in at 6:00 a.m. to do the morning show could at least get a free breakfast from the Hanover

Inn was much missed. Lack of dedication by lower level staffers increased the pressure on senior managers who had to cover for them simply to keep the station on the air, and there was burn-out. This resulted in increasing turnover on the Directorate from term to term. During 2003-04 at least 24 students cycled through the eleven Directorate positions, including four news directors, four sports directors, and three finance directors. Most of the resignations were due to lack of time. News was for a time split between two directors, one (Vikash Reddy) for day-to-day operations and one (Scott Glabe) for the Dartmouth Election Network.

Reddy later became FM program director and urged that the station be made more conducive to social interaction, a kind of clubhouse where staffers could hang out, eat lunch, and even study. The station could add amenities such as a TV and a PlayStation, he said, and stock drinks and snack food. Earlier, GM Kerrin Egalka had launched a crusade to simply clean the place up, saying "It has been an embarrassment to bring people into our station due to the mess," which also contributed to poor treatment of the equipment and a general sense of unprofessionalism. In her "Giant Station Clean-Up (aka Queer Eye for the Straight Radio)" new furniture was purchased, walls painted, and new carpeting laid. Unfortunately these efforts, while laudable, tended to be transient and failed to change the increasingly lackadaisical culture of the staff.[35]

### The Grand Experiment

The most significant development of the early 2000s, however, was the rise and fall of the Joint Sales Agreement, or JSA. When it began, in 2002, it seemed to represent the answer to one of the station's most fundamental problems, the wide swings in sales revenues. In the new competitive environment, some doubted that Dartmouth Broadcasting would ever break even again. In addition, maybe, just maybe, a JSA would make the station a better training ground for future businesspeople by bringing in a professional organization with whom they could work (although one suspects this was a secondary goal).

At first, things went well. In late 2002 Vox projected that sales for the year would be up nine percent over the prior year, nearing or exceeding the $300,000 mark. Wally Caswell and Julie Kaye were handling Vox sales for the station. "Combo sales" (with other Vox stations) were paying off. While sales was always a struggle the sales team thought it was "a winnable battle." Even WDCR brought in some dollars, primarily for sports.[36]

With its new, steady income, the outlook for the station was even rosier. In May 2003, as fiscal year 2003 neared its end, General Manager Egalka reported that "Good things are definitely happening for us in the money department. We will most likely end the year on a very high surplus... and we've already begun ordering some necessary things for the station, such as new CD players for AM and FM, a mixer for AM, and a computer for the GM office. As well, we finish paying off our loan from the College this year..." Relations with Vox, she said, were "going great."[37]

Despite this early optimism, there were problems almost from the start. The first major issue was the lack of a station secretary, the position previously filled by the beloved Winnie. The decision makers seem to have underestimated the degree to which the station secretary was the glue that held the station together, a consistent (and friendly) physical presence on the third floor of Robinson who knew everybody and everybody knew. In addition, the position filled some very practical functions, such as reliably answering the phones, taking care of visitors (such as listeners who came in to pick up their prizes), and routing questions to the right staffer. There was much board discussion during 2002 and 2003 about how to deal with this. Suggestions were made to use voicemail messages, mail out prizes, hire an intern, or find someone else in the building (some other organization) to fill this function. No satisfactory solution was found.

An even more serious issue that began to emerge was the unreliability of the d.j. staff, and therefore of the air product itself, especially on the tightly formatted WFRD. It was increasingly difficult to find competent students willing to devote five or 10 hours a week to a Monday through Friday time slot, and consistency of voices each day was vital for a commercial station. The all-important morning drive time slot (starting at 6:00 a.m.), when listenership was highest, was particularly hard to fill. In earlier decades, when the station had major listenership both on campus and off, the morning show was the prestige slot and sought after despite the grueling hours. Now, with listenership almost entirely off-campus and with little d.j. leeway due to the rigid formatting, it was less so.

There were continuous recruiting efforts, and local non-Dartmouth volunteers were pressed into service. Senior staff had to pick up much of the slack, however, and in early 2003 WFRD Program Director Sebastian Miller reported having often personally been on the air 40 hours a week, and sometimes as much as 60 hours (as a consequence of which, he said, "I was 'strongly urged' by one of my professors to withdraw from a course because of lack of attendance"). Miller went on to say, "Staffing problems, which have been significant hindrances over the past several terms, were only exacerbated by the D-Plan and Hanover winter doldrums. The over-extension of many Dartmouth Broadcasting members has yielded a malaise that was, at times, crippling." He urged that some type of automation, allowing shows to be pre-recorded, be investigated.[38]

In the fall his frustrated successor, Eric McDonald, reported that "New d.j.'s are not likely to take anything before 11:00 a.m. or after 6:00 p.m.; asking them to do so will result in a look of disgust and revulsion. Three new d.j.'s who signed a contract (a formal commitment) quit before their first shift, and since the term has started one more has stopped. All gave 'lack of time' as the reason for leaving. When I asked 'You can't even swing three hours a week?', they said 'Nope'." Fortunately, a dedicated core group filled in, but the problem was growing. McDonald finally persuaded friendly competitor Chris Garrett (morning show host on WSSH/WZSH) to check 99Rock at 6:10 a.m. each morning, and call the d.j. and McDonald if the station was not on the air.[39]

Staffing problems affected sports coverage as well. Sports Director Keith Burdette reported that it was a "big problem" that required "constant juggling." Upperclassmen he approached "all seemed scared about the time commitment and having to travel with the team on weekends." He and JT Mohr covered many of the games.[40]

It got worse in 2004. Shifts were not covered, spots were not read, and at times 99Rock signed on as late as 10:00 a.m. This created enormous tension with Vox, which had to have a reliable product to sell. Advertisers were angry too, and some dropped the station. A major blow came when Miller Auto, owner of four dealerships in the area, cancelled its contract in late 2003. "The client wants nothing to do with us," said Shapiro. Vox reported that station sales were down $30,000 from the prior year, while other stations in the market were up.[41]

## Broadcast Automation

As the situation reached crisis proportions, the overseers were forced to confront the possibility of installing a broadcast automation system. Disc jockeys had been using some limited-capability programs such as CoolEdit and WaveCart to load portions of their programs on a computer hard disc (where many song files now resided). Full broadcast automation is a computer-driven system that allows d.j.'s to prerecord their "talk-ups," or comments between records, and then combines those pre-recorded bits with recordings and commercials stored on a hard disc in the exact order specified by the station log (which is also stored on the computer). The procedure is also called "voice tracking." An announcer could pre-record his two-hour program in a few minutes this way, and then leave the station. The computer would run everything (music, commercials, talk-ups) in the proper order in the designated time slot, which might even be the next morning.[42]

Broadcast automation was sweeping the industry in the early 2000s, especially on smaller stations. The reason, quite simply, was to save money. If it was done right listeners didn't know the difference, and a station could be run with only a handful of employees. When the station was on full automation, for example after business hours, no one even needed to be on the premises.

In the case of Dartmouth radio, automation was highly controversial. There was a long and lively debate about it at the November, 2003, overseers meeting. On one hand there was fear that it would undercut the educational purpose of student radio if the station became an "automated jukebox." Staff problems in the past (and there had been many) had been resolved by a determined management that rose to the challenge, did effective recruiting, and inspired loyalty and a sense of ownership among the staff. Automation would obviate the need for any of that, and take the easy way out. There were fears that the air product simply wouldn't be as good. And as much as proponents believed that it could be used sparingly, and only in extreme cases (missed shifts, etc.), it was so seductive that it could eventually take over the entire station. Overseer Ned Roos sagely observed that although he was against automation, "It will come in. For the time being we will use it as planned, but... we will end up voice tracking more and more. There has been declining enrollment in Dartmouth Broadcasting for many years. Automation will get around this problem now—but it will also make it easier to run the radio station with fewer and fewer people. It will change Dartmouth Broadcasting."

Proponents argued that automation was necessary, inevitable, and urgently needed. If students wanted a real experience in running a radio station in 2003, this was how it was done. The commercial viability of the station, and therefore the viability of the JSA, was in real jeopardy due to unreliable air product. Automation did not have to take over the station, they argued, it could be used only when needed to ensure spots ran reliably and dead air was avoided. It could also be evaluated after a period and continued or discontinued. Moreover there was an underlying feeling that what had worked in the past to correct these sorts of problems (i.e. leadership) would not work anymore; times had changed.

Board chairman Tim Reynolds made it clear that this decision would ultimately be up to the students. There were several strong student proponents, including Eric McDonald and Deb Wassel, each of whom served at various times as FM program director and as general manager. It took most of 2004 to reach a decision, but by the fall the Directorate had decided to install an automation software package made by Simian. The target date was Thanksgiving 2004, which was achieved with the help of McDonald (now a non-student volunteer at the station). Its first real test was during the 2004 Christmas break, when most students were off campus. McDonald, current FM Program Director Vikash Reddy and salesperson Julie Kaye kept an eye on it and, fortunately, it operated without a hitch.[43]

It the early months there was a genuine effort to restrict the use of voice tracking, and to keep as much of the air product as possible live and local. Voice tracking was used only to cover missed shifts, rather than to allow d.j.'s to skip shifts whenever they wanted or to pre-record shifts during the highest listening periods (e.g., the morning). The voice tracking equipment was kept in a locked studio and d.j.'s were required to contact the program director and obtain permission before using it. However Ned Roos' observations were prescient. Eventually, voice tracking (and a largely absent staff) would become the norm.

Another, related problem then loomed. Everyone agreed that voice tracking was not desirable for the all-important morning drive time shift, and it was still proving impossible to get students into the studio reliably at 6:00 a.m. every day to do it. In response, in early 2005 the station hired Eric McDonald to be the regular "morning man." Hiring a professional to do a key d.j. shift was a huge break from past practice and there was dissent by some students and overseers. However GM Kekane Yuen strongly defended the move as a "temporary, stop-gap solution" and pointed out that McDonald was not an anonymous non-student but rather a recent general manager and volunteer at the station who knew its operation and culture intimately. Yuen freely admitted that the move did not solve WFRD's larger staffing problems, but at least it would get the station through the present crisis. Concurrently, the morning shift was renamed *The Rock 'n' Go Morning Show*, while afternoon drive time (which also had high listenership) became *99 Point 3 Stooges*.

Several less controversial steps were also taken in 2004-05 to address the deteriorating air product crisis. A new production music library from Brown Bag Productions helped the station generate fresh, format-appropriate ads for clients. A new station voice (said to "sound younger") was obtained for station slogans and identifications. And Jeff Shapiro stepped in with in-station contests to incentivize d.j.'s and management to perform. For example, if the station could stay on the air reliably for three months without dead air, key leaders would get free Rolex watches! (They failed.) Shapiro had a very good reason to try to get WFRD air product back on track. In September 2004 he had sold his four local stations and Vox to Nassau Broadcasting, and transferred the JSA contract to sell 99Rock to another of his companies, Great Eastern Radio. So he was now selling 99Rock alone. He couldn't hide its flaws in a package with other, better run stations.[44]

The changes mollified advertisers, at least for a time. Sales Manager Kathy Whedon found it "easier to sell the station to advertisers, who have all noticed the changes." Miller Auto even came back.

After a short period of euphoria, however, old problems began to reassert themselves. Eric McDonald left Hanover in the fall of 2005, and the morning show was back in student hands. D.J.'s were reluctant to come into the station on short notice to cover emergency situations, or to do remotes, which were important to many advertisers. Even with automation, there simply wasn't enough FM staff to keep WFRD on 18 hours a day, much less 24 hours. "To be frank," said GM Nikhil Gore, "the station would not be on the air from 10:00 a.m to 4:00 p.m. if not for automation."[45]

The problems, interestingly, did not include listenership. In the fall 2005 Arbitron ratings report (which WFRD did not buy, but was shown by others), 99Rock tied KISS for number one in the key sales demographic, as well as taking number one from 10:00 a.m. to 3:00 p.m. and number two in afternoon drive time.[46] Ratings-wise, it was a strong showing. Nevertheless tension with Great Eastern continued, and Kathy Whedon virtually stopped selling the station. The student management struggled to keep long term clients, such as Miller Auto, happy. The assumption in early 2006 was that despite the rough patch, 99Rock had got its air product back on track (mostly), and ratings were good, so Great Eastern would renew the JSA when it expired on April 1, 2006.

Then Jeff Shapiro dropped a bombshell. There would be no renewal. Four years of broken promises, a constant need to incentivize a staff that was supposed to be his partner, swings in student responsibility as managements constantly changed, efforts at coaching that went nowhere, and often angry advertisers as well, all took their toll. There was, he later said, a kind of "malaise" at the station. It was very different from the station he had known in the 1980s, or the professional stations he now operated. The JSA, he later said, was the only business deal in his career on which he lost money. "Basically, it was a disaster."

So suddenly, Dartmouth radio was again on its own. No guaranteed monthly income, and no sales partner to provide a safety net, a net that had been, perhaps, a little *too* comfortable. What would the students do?

# Chapter 13

## 2006 to Date: The Professionalization of Dartmouth Broadcasting

The transformation of Dartmouth Broadcasting from a student-driven organization to one in which professionals played key roles both in management and on-air was rapid following the collapse of the JSA in 2006. Some lament the loss of the student experience that characterized the station for most of its history, while others say the change was inevitable if the station was to survive in the vastly different world of 21st century radio. However one views it, there is no doubt that these years brought a much more stable and professional-sounding WFRD, one that could compete effectively in the Upper Valley market. This was largely due to operations manager and jack-of-all-trades Heath Cole, who according to many not only rescued the station from near-collapse in 2006 but shaped it into a modern, commercial operation, while involving students where he could. WFRD's sibling, WDCR, continued to serve as an outlet for student creativity, although its programming has been much more uneven from year to year.

The years since 2006 also brought other changes. Probably the biggest was the demise of WDCR-AM, just months after its 50th anniversary celebration. It now exists solely as an Internet radio station. Both it and WFRD now broadcast to the world via this new transmission medium. Other changes included a considerable increase in recruiting activities, newly necessary to draw students into the unfamiliar (to them) world of radio, a period of involvement by station alumni, who intervened to rebuild the deteriorating studio infrastructure in 2009-10, and an upsurge in public service activities.

General managers during this transitional period were Deborah Wassel '07, Susannah Thompson '08, Pavel Sotskov '09, Schuyler Evans '10, Madison Rezaei '12, Shirine Sajjadi '11, Charles "Tony" Quincy '11, Ryan Zehner '12, Christopher Zhao '13, and Shane O'Neal '14.

### Picking Up the Pieces

The overseers moved quickly once Jeff Shapiro announced the non-renewal of the Joint Sales Agreement, which officially ended on April 1, 2006. Dean Holly Sateia pulled together a committee of students, faculty and administrators who determined that the best course of action was to hire a professional operations manager and sales manager, both of whom would report to the overseers with a "dotted line" to the student Directorate. Almost simultaneously it was learned that Heath Cole, who had worked for Vox Radio during the early days of the JSA, then switched to Nassau Broadcasting when the latter bought out Vox, had just been laid off in a corporate downsizing. Cole was already familiar with the Dartmouth station, having been in the market for many years and having trained Dartmouth's d.j.'s when Vox represented the station. A month of intense negotiations ensued between Cole and overseers Joe Cassidy and Gordon Taylor (representing the College), ending with Cole being hired as operations manager around the first of May. Julie Kaye, who had been selling 99Rock since 1999 under various arrangements, was hired from Great Eastern to be sales manager, and both took up residence in Robinson Hall.[1]

Cole's responsibilities were described by General Manager Susannah Thompson as being to direct the sales efforts, help with financial operations and "assist the student staff with day-to-day operations such as recruitment, production, and particularly training." He had started listening to the station again after he was approached for the job, and was appalled by what he heard. The all-important morning show was being voice tracked, and weather reports were sometimes introduced by a pre-recorded voice followed by background music but no announcer (because the live announcer hadn't shown up that morning). Sometimes the station was off the air entirely. To the ears of a professional, it was a mess![2]

Cole and Kaye sat down with Thompson and the staff and told them what they already knew—that they *had* to get their act together, immediately, or there would be nothing to sell. The students rose to the challenge, and the two professionals hit the streets in a heavy sales push, keeping one ear on the station to make sure the air product stayed on track.

The new arrangement began with an enthusiasm and optimism absent from the station for some time, and with GM Thompson and FM Program Directors Jake Schindel '09 (spring) and Debbie Wassel (summer) as chief cheerleaders. But it hadn't addressed the fundamental problem of finding students willing to reliably take on tough challenges like a high profile morning show starting at 6:00 a.m. (later 5:00 a.m.), five days a week. Wassel, backed by Cole and former GM Nikhil Gore, argued hard to hire a professional morning d.j. She even found money in the budget to pay for a part-timer, through savings elsewhere. Unlike former General Manager Kekane Yuen (who had hired an ex-student to be the morning man in 2005) they made no claims that this would be a "temporary" solution.[3]

The overseers were very concerned about such a move. The professionalization of sales was supposed to relieve students of that burden so that they could concentrate on programming; was that to be taken over by professionals too? What would be left of the student experience of independently running a broadcasting station? But Wassel and Cole (and others) argued that the model simply hadn't worked in recent years, and that it was more important now to have a professional-*sounding*, financially viable station with as much student involvement as students were willing to put into it, but no more.

In the end they won the argument, mostly because those opposed couldn't offer a viable alternative. Cole approached his old friend Chris Garrett, who had been in the market since the 1990s on various stations, and who said he could start in late September. Garrett, a somewhat gruff-voiced individual but a thorough professional, took over *The Rock 'n' Go Morning Show* after a suitable promotional build-up and immediately turned it into a reliable, consistent destination for listeners who wanted hard rock music in the morning.

By fall Wassel (who had taken over as general manager) and Cole were brimming with enthusiasm. Wassel told the overseers, " The FM station is sounding better than ever... We've come such a long way, and I think that we finally have the capacity to start doing some really professional projects on the FM side." Cole added that sales, which had been anemic, "continue to improve, which is very exciting. We see an increase in not only listenership but in client interest as well." Although both acknowledged that the station had a long way to go, it was at least headed in the right direction.[4]

### "The World Famous 99Rock!"

Professionalizing the morning show was one thing, but the key to a strong, commercially successful station with this format was a tight, disciplined playlist that defined precisely what would be played throughout the day. For better or worse (and there are some on both sides of *that* argument), personality disc jockeys and individual music choices are a thing of the past in modern commercial radio. As Heath Cole commented in an early report, "[We] need to stop trying to be A&R executives at record companies. Based on research, our ratings, and our listeners in the market, we need to play the hits, and play them often. That's not to say that we can't be ahead of the curve on new music. Properly dayparted, and surrounded by the right songs, WFRD can still deliver the perception of being the place for new music."[5]

An example of how this works can be seen in a 99Rock playlist issued in 2011. It was credited to the "FM-Music Directors panel" consisting of three students (Chris Zhao, Dave Lumbert '12, David "Hoagie" Kastner '12) and two professionals (Chris Garrett, Heath Cole), but in fact was compiled each week mainly by Cole. It contained about 80 alternative rock tracks designated to be played during the week, and the number of plays each would receive. The top five (with 35 plays each) were by AWOLNATION, Blink 182, Red Hot Chili Peppers, Foo Fighters, and Foster the People. A computer program called Selector scheduled each play, with proper separation, according to a set of rules, and added in cuts from the station's 400-plus selection library (which was also stored on hard disc). Thus the music to be played that week was almost completely mapped out by the computer program. Disc jockeys in most time periods had almost no latitude, although they could suggest additions to the list to Cole.[6]

The core music library was downloaded each week from a professional music service. Ironically boxes of promotional CDs continued to arrive in the mail, from smaller labels and aspiring artists hoping to get played, but they were mostly ignored.

The tempo could vary somewhat by the time of day, as plotted out and controlled by the computer program, certain programming blocks were given distinctive names or themes, and of course d.j. voices varied (to the extent they were heard; tracks were sometimes played back-to-back, and "talk-ups" tended to be brief). Chris Garrett was the familiar voice in the morning, sometimes joined by Heath Cole (who also appeared in the afternoon) or a student. Among the student d.j.'s most familiar to listeners during this period were Deb Wassel, Chris "Chubbs" Symeonides '07, Jake "Shindig" Schindel, Pavel Sotskov, Schuyler "Sketch" Evans, British-accented Ellie Stoltzfus '10, Steve "Steve-O" Elliot '11, Shirine Sajjadi, Lucinda LaCour '12, Madison Rezaei, Tony Quincy, Jeff Ledolter '13, and Anneliesse Duncan '13. Students missing shifts was still an occasional issue, and beginning in 2010 d.j.'s were required to sign "contracts" making explicit what was expected of them. The approved way to refer to the station on-air was "The World Famous 99Rock!"[7]

An essential element in making this all work was voice tracking, which, as Ned Roos had predicted, virtually took over the station. Except for a couple of key shows (morning and afternoon drive times), students and even professionals would come in, record the short talk-ups for their show in a few minutes, load them into the computer and then leave. This meant that there were far fewer missed shifts and everything ran like clockwork, but it also meant d.j.'s were usually brief and extremely generic in what they said. They could also re-record mistakes. According to one later program director, by his term only about five hours per day (20 percent of the schedule) was live, with the rest pre-recorded and computer-driven. He claimed new d.j.'s did not even know how to broadcast live anymore, and if confronted with a live microphone they would "freeze up."[8]

Thematic blocks included *The 3 O'Clock Rock Block, Cage Match, Furious 5 at 9,* and *99 Minute Nightmare,* the latter a late night heavy metal show. Some older shows that didn't quite fit with the format were either cancelled or moved to WDCR, including *Night of the Living Dead* (a Grateful Dead show, hosted by Jer Bear), *School of Rock* (older tracks) and *Uplink* (indie bands). Occasional syndicated shows were carried, including, starting in 2011, the weeknight *Loveline,* hosted by Dr. Drew Pinsky. Others were mostly on the weekend, including *Out of Order* (Jed the Fish), *House of Hair* (Dee Snider), *Hard Drive with Lou Brutus,* and *Racing Rocks* (former MTV VJ Riki Ratchtman).[9]

One very distinctive show on 99Rock that survived the move to 24/7 uniformity was a revival of the popular series of the 1990s and early 2000s called *Homegrown.* It returned to the air in 2007 under the title *Home Brew* (the earlier title was thought to evoke drug associations!), featuring local bands either in studio or on location playing five of their songs and chatting with the host. The 99Rock web site solicited bands to appear, carefully specifying that the show only wanted "local bands who don't suck." The Sunday night program was an immediate favorite, bringing in listeners across the country and attracting more than 600 "friends" on its myspace.com page. Hosts have included Jake Schindel, Pavel Sotskov, Phil "Cheesesteak" Aubart '10, Maia Pfeffer '11, Mayuki Shimizu '12 and David Lumbert.

Each year ended with a Top 99 Tracks of the Year countdown in December. The year 2011 brought a special feature, "Happy Birthday 99Rock," as the station celebrated its 35th anniversary. Hits of the 1980s and '90s (which now qualified as oldies) were played at 35 minutes past the hour, which, Assistant GM David Lumbert observed, was popular with the station's d.j.'s "who are being introduced to AC/DC and Ram Jam for the first time."[10]

99Rock was established now as an alternative rock station and, at the persistent urging of Cole, its playlist began to be reported in national publications *Radio & Records, Billboard, Tek Report* and Nielsen's BDSRadio.com. To be listed there a station had to meet certain programming and ratings requirements, and 99Rock's acceptance gave the station recognition in the music industry.[11]

Part of 99Rock's success rested on an ongoing connection with its listeners, and this was pursued though social media such as Facebook and MySpace, Internet messages to fans, and its own website. The latter was redesigned in 2011 by Mike Urbach '14 to include individual bio pages for each d.j., a provision for blog posts, rotating banners, and music news.

## Sales Promotions

Soon after his arrival Heath Cole began launching sales promotions, another pillar of local radio. These included remotes, such as the weekly Friday night remotes from the Benning Bar & Grill in Lebanon in 2007. There were also daily giveaways of tickets, CDs and other smaller items for the "ninth caller" or the person who could answer a particular question. Soon phones at the station were ringing constantly as listeners called in to *The Rock 'n' Go Morning Show* and other programs to bag some swag.

Cole also brought back the big contests that were so familiar in the 1990s. The grand prize in 2006's "99 Rocks Vegas" was a trip to Las Vegas. This was followed in May 2007 by "Survive It & Drive It," a car giveaway modeled on the TV show *Survivor*. Five 20-something finalists crammed into a Saturn Ion at a dealership in White River Junction to see who could outlast the others and win the car, while a webcam watched their every move and 99Rock d.j.'s broadcast live reports on the action. The contestants competed in periodic challenges to win benefits (such as a shower in the motel across the street), but then it was back into the car where they squirmed, tried to catch naps, and once a day voted somebody out. "It's a Machiavellian snakepit in here," said one. The colorful stunt drew a lot of attention, including a feature story in the *Valley News* and coverage on several television stations.[12]

Other contests in 2007 featured tickets to Cracker, Wolfmother, and Third Eye Blind concerts, a Florida getaway for two, and trips to the Six Flags theme park. The station hosted concerts at the Whalestock dirt bike racing event at Whaleback Mountain (July), and at Field of Rock 2007 in Ludlow, Vermont (August). In September 99Rock broadcast from the Vermonster 4x4 mud racing event in Bradford, Vermont, where Chris Garrett and Sketch Evans rode in a off-road vehicle during the competition. Then there was the New England Punk, Goth & Metal Festival in Worcester, Massachussetts, on Halloween. The winner of that contest not only got tickets to the spooky event but was driven there in a black limousine.[13]

The big spring contest in 2008 was "The Off Road Prize Load," in which 99Rock and Lucky's Motor Sports gave away a brand new Yamaha ATV. Other events in 2008 included live coverage of the Home Life Show at Leverone field house (where Ryan Wilson '09, Zach Mason '10 and Sketch Evans gave away prizes and played Guitar Hero 3 with seemingly each of the 10,000 people who passed through). The station was back at Vermonster 4x4 in May, and staged a special celebration on Cinco De Mayo, with the *Rock 'n' Go Morning Show* live from Margaritas in Lebanon and the afternoon show live at Gusanoz Mexican Restaurant. The latter broadcast included a special "Sink O De Mayo" where audience members bobbed for prizes in a kitchen sink full of mayonnaise.[14]

The year continued with the third annual Summer of Six Flags promotion and ended with the "12 Hogs of Christmas."[15]

During 2009 the station utilized its increasingly close ties with record labels not only to get concert tickets for up-and-coming alternative rockers like Silversun Pickups and Cage the Elephant, but also to score backstage passes so that winners could hang out with the band members.[16]

In 2010 the station featured a mix of contests, including a "best tattoo contest" at a local Harley-Davidson dealership (January) and a blarney stone promotion celebrating St. Patrick's Day. The latter involved painting 99 small polished stones green, numbering them, and depositing them around the listening area. Clues to their locations were given on air, and listeners who found them won CDs, DVDs, tickets, and apparel. Not all property owners were appreciative ("Hey, did you hide something here, I have people ripping my place apart!"), but about half were found. The year also saw the revival of the annual month-long promotion known as Rocktober (retitled Rocktober Fest), 31 days of rock, haunts, and prizes, which had been a staple in the 1990s.[17]

October 2011 also saw the first-ever College Radio Day. WFRD and WDCR joined more than 350 other college radio stations around North America online and on the air to celebrate the important contributions of college radio to America's airwaves.

## Rivals & Ratings

99Rock carved out a distinctive niche for itself in the now crowded Upper Valley radio market, namely hard-driving modern rock, while perennial competitor Q106 (WHDQ, Claremont) focused on classic rock of the 1970s-80s-90s and carried the popular syndicated show *Imus in the Morning*, Z97 (WZRT, Rutland) emphasized contemporary pop, KIXX (WXXK, Lebanon) owned the country market, and XL92 (WGXL, Hanover) was home for adult contemporary, including the syndicated John Tesh show. Others that sometimes penetrated the top ten included Mix 98.1 (WJJR, adult contemporary), New Country the Wolf (WXLF, country), V102 (WCVR, classic rock), and WWOD (oldies). All were FM. These and most of the 40 stations with some audience in the market were corporate group-owned, although by who changed constantly. The rate at which local radio stations have been bought, sold, and traded in the Upper Valley in recent years is dizzying.

WFRD did not subscribe to the Arbitron ratings service, which regularly measured listenership in the market, because of the cost (about $25,000 per year). Many other smaller stations did not do so either, because larger advertisers that bought time in the market already had them and local advertisers were not as concerned with ratings, only whether their advertising seemed to bring in business.

Nevertheless ratings did provide an objective picture of the station's actual audience, and station personnel often got a peek at them from others, even though they couldn't use them in their own sales efforts. 99Rock did well in "the Arbitrons" throughout this period, a reflection of the musical niche it had carved out as well as its increased professionalism. In the fall of 2007 it ranked number one in the market in its primary demographic of 18-34, number six overall (listeners 12+), and number four in the key sales demographic of 25-54. Leading the market in adults 25-54 were #1, Z97, #2, KIXX, #3, Q106, and #4, 99Rock, tied with XL92 and WWOD. Chris Garrett's *Rock 'n' Go Morning Show*, Heath Cole at midday, and Sketch Evans in the afternoon drive time were all number one in their time periods in 18-34's.[18]

In the fall of 2008 99Rock moved down to number nine overall, but in fall 2009 it was back up to seventh (fourth locally). Spring 2010 was even stronger. 99Rock was now number two in 25-54, trailing only Q106 and ahead of corporate-owned powerhouses KIXX, XL92, and "New Country the Wolf."[19]

In the years after 2006 the sound of 99Rock "settled down," according to Heath Cole. Both music and announcers were more reliable and predictable, day-today, as well as less "college raunchy," which appealed to women. The audience shifted from a predominance of men 18-34 to a more even balance of men and women, and a stronger appeal to the adult 18-49 and 25-54 categories that advertisers love. Still, this was no warm and fuzzy station. At seemingly every break the deep-voiced announcer growled, "New rock first on 99Rock!", followed by the thundering crash of drums and electric guitars.[20]

## WDCR Programming

While WFRD got its act together, WDCR was a different story. Its schedule and staff fluctuated wildly from one term to the next. The basic schedule was supposed to be a checkerboard representing the many different interests of Dartmouth students. However the shows were often very much alike, being varying shades of rock music. Sometimes there were simply not many checkers on the board. WDCR's fortunes at any point in time depended largely on the effectiveness of that year's recruiting drives, and on leadership. According to managers of the period, the station needed 30 to 60 d.j.'s and a full schedule (at least in the afternoons and evenings) to operate effectively.[21]

In early 2006 WDCR Program Director Julio Gil '08 reported that the station was doing "very well," with close to 40 d.j.'s, ranging from freshmen to grad students. Most time slots from 10:00 a.m. to 2:00 a.m. were filled, with programming ranging "from video game shows, to music shows, even (sic) to political talk shows." Political talk was evidently considered an outlier.[22]

During the summer of 2006 the number of d.j.'s dropped to 13 doing only seven shows, and campus listenership was also low, with Gil pleading for worldwide streaming to help boost the station's reach. In the fall the staff rebounded to between 30 and 40, who got weekly two-hour slots to program however they wished. Shows ranged from classic rock to rap, reggae, opera, and talk shows, and filled 4:00 p.m. to midnight most days of the week. However according to a story in *The Dartmouth* the station still remained largely invisible on campus. Even the reporter couldn't remember the call letters, repeatedly calling it "WDRC." A d.j. was quoted as saying, "AM radio is amazing here and no one listens. It is too bad."[23]

Things fell apart in early 2007. There was no program director, and according to GM Wassel the station "has become disorganized and more unprofessional." She added that essentially the station was "a disaster with technical problems and jocks who are disrespectful of the equipment and station." A d.j. "contract" was used to try to make clear what was expected of them, but without real leadership the station floundered. There was considerable simulcasting of WFRD simply to stay on the air. In the spring new WDCR Program Director Rob Demick '10 removed several problem students from the staff and worked on recruitment.[24]

There was some improvement in the fall of 2007 with student shows from 6:00 p.m to midnight each day. The rest of the day (18 hours) was filled with classic rock from the mid '60s through the late '80s, automatically selected by a Winamp computer program. This included such artists as the Beatles, Rolling Stones, Led Zeppelin, the Who, AC/DC, Aerosmith, and Van Halen, in a kind of giant iPod shuffle play. By February 2008 there were 31 d.j.'s (27 of them freshmen or sophomores), maintaining the same 6:00 p.m. to midnight schedule, but Demick was proud to boast that in a year "WDCR has gone from a station with no working equipment, no leadership, no identity, no program director, no music directors, and no money to a station that just now has no money, and that is actually a lot more positive of a statement than it sounds." In May 2008 new Program Director Zach Mason reported that the station was considered fully staffed with 33 d.j.'s.[25]

A major event of the spring on WDCR was the live broadcast, on March 6, 2008, of the finale of the first-ever *Dartmouth Idol* talent competition. The winner was Liz Vaughan '08, a confidant young woman who belted out a powerful rendition of Aretha Franklin's "Think," backed by a full band and chorus. WDCR had a major presence at the show, raising its campus image. Although *Dartmouth Idol* became an annual event, including a surprise appearance in 2010 by Dartmouth President Jim Kim doing a Michael Jackson impersonation, 2008 was the only year broadcast by the station.[26]

The next major upswing occurred in the fall of 2009, with a record 60 students on the air (including 20 returning upperclassmen). Program Director Shirine Sajjadi reported that many were actively advertising their own shows, which built larger audiences than in the past. The winter term was highly successful as well, with about 50 on staff. Sajjadi raised the possibility of podcasts as a way to spread WDCR programming by allowing listeners to download whole shows, but this could not be done legally for music programs because the record companies demanded payment for distribution of their music in this manner.

The renaissance continued in the spring of 2010 with about 50 on-air staffers plus more from the news and sports departments, and regular original programming between 4:00 and 11:00 p.m. most days. Program subjects ranged from Asian Pop to talk (*All Things Dartmouth*), and a sports call-in show and roundup produced by David Jiang '12. News programming began to make a comeback as well, with *Views from the Valley*. "DCR's programming definitely has a certain eclectic quality to it," commented Program Director Pierre Guo '12. "This quality reflects the diversity of the student body and the organization's ability to function successfully." Building listenership remained a challenge. The station was now exclusively on the Internet and, although data was scanty, it appeared that the number of Internet listeners maxed out at about 15 at any given time.[27]

The momentum continued in fall 2010 with 22 original shows on the air (including half a dozen new hosts), ranging from a half hour special on sustainable living to an hour of heavy metal rock. Many publicity efforts were undertaken, using BlitzMail show reminders, postings on social media, and campus posters and bake sales. Program Director Hannah Iaccarino '12 brought new continuity to the schedule, with top of the hour time checks as well as weather and news updates at the 13th and 40th minutes of the hour. "This formatting," she said, "organizes the station and provides continuity between shows."[28]

Participation fell off somewhat during 2011-12 with less than 20 d.j.'s, and a somewhat curtailed schedule. There was a move to record and archive shows so that there would be student-created programming for most of the time during the late afternoon and evening, even if it had to be repeats. Most of it was music, along with a few oddities such as *Lexical Gaps* (language), *The H.P. Lovecraft Channel,* and *Big Green Gossip Live*. There was little interest in news or talk, however ("people wouldn't listen" according to one staffer). Program Director Gregg Fox '13 worked to rebuild the schedule, in the spring reporting about 25 d.j.'s and 15 different shows. This number remained relatively stable through 2012-13. It was a small but loyal crew.

Approximately one half to three-quarters of the hosts carried over from one term to the next.[29]

There seemed to be little effort during these years to make anything coherent out of this feast-or-famine mish-mash, however. Most shows were simply students playing their favorite records.

## News

The news operation was more uneven than in earlier years, also varying according to the effectiveness of leadership and recruiting. This is a little puzzling. While there are easy generalities given such as "Students aren't interested in politics," in fact on a campus such as Dartmouth there are always plenty of politically and socially involved subgroups who want to talk about their causes. It should not be hard to invite the Young Republicans and the Young Democrats to debate, to tap into the resources of *The Dartmouth Free Press* (liberal) or *Dartmouth Review* (conservative), or for that matter any number of professors. There are also groups advocating women's issues, conservation, health, and numerous other issues. There was little room for this kind of low rated programming on tightly formatted WFRD, but even on WDCR, which was free of commercial constraints, the attitude of management (with some exceptions) seemed to be "It's just a place to play your favorite records." If someone brought them a different kind of program they would probably put it on, but there was little outreach.

The News Department, which is where this type of programming would logically originate, was in a funk. In the fall of 2006 News Director Chris Symeonides gave a particularly pessimistic report, stating "The News Department for WFRD-WDCR has fallen short of the promise that was displayed in previous terms... To my knowledge, there is no news presence on WDCR." He then asked a fundamental question.

> The question is what to do in the future. Are we committed to having a News Department in the future? With automation and the many strides that FM has made, this seems less and less likely to be the case. AM is such a crapshoot every term that it is impossible to predict what path it can form there. Right now we are at a crossroads—should we recruit more students to help out and commit ourselves to perhaps upgrading our systems or are we going to junk the whole thing? At this point, I cannot answer this.[30]

By early 2007 Symeonides had made some small progress in reconstituting news breaks on 99Rock, but "As for WDCR, it is such a mess that we have no idea who is doing what, so I have been unable to oversee any news coverage there."[31]

His successors echoed the despair. During 2007-08 and 2008-09 there was no separate news director, instead the duties were combined with numerous others handled by energetic Schuyler "Sketch" Evans (in one report he was listed as interim FM program director, music director, production director, and news director). In early 2008 Evans reported that "the battle continues in this department for students willing to do what it takes to put out a consistent news report on 99Rock... It is extremely difficult to find students dedicated to putting in the time and working with us five days a week, especially if that means waking up early in the morning [to report news on the morning show]." WDCR Program Director Zach Mason was reported to be trying to put together a couple of weekly political shows.[32]

From time to time there were glimmers of hope. Alex Belser '08, a former staff writer for *The Dartmouth*, wandered upstairs to the radio station in the fall of 2006 and for a brief period plunged head-long into radio news, dazzling everyone with his energy. He *was* willing to get up every morning to do news reports on the *Rock 'n' Go Morning Show*, adding an important dimension to that key program.

The real revival of the News Department had to wait for the appointment of freshman Madison Rezaei as news director in early 2009. Like Belser, Rezaei was willing to be in the studio reliably at 5:00 a.m. every morning to do the news, and she soon developed (with Heath Cole and Schuyler Evans) the concept of the "news whip," a short, punchy, once-an-hour 30-second report on a single story designed to capture the listener's attention. The goal was six news whips per day. Hourly newscasts were instituted on 99Rock, and there was regular news and weather on WDCR as well. She also launched and hosted a Sunday morning public affairs program on 99Rock called *Views from the Valley*, the most ambitious News Department project in several years. Debuting on October 18, 2009, it covered news from Hanover, Lebanon, and White River Junction with an approximately 20-minute lead story/interview, followed by a six-minute segment on local and national headlines, a 10-minute community segment promoting station-sponsored events (e.g. Toys for Tots), and another, 15-minute closing interview.[33]

Rezaei supported all this activity with an energetic recruiting campaign, largely among her own freshman classmates. After getting names at a Dartmouth Broadcasting orientation and open house, she followed up individually with each one and set up training immediately. A major draw was the fact that the short news whips drafted by the recruits were on the air the next day. She then continued to give them individual feedback, positive and negative, every few weeks. All of this yielded a news department staff of about 20 people, the largest in years. To keep the machine running Rezaei appointed several sub-managers, in charge of contacts (with local sources), news whips, and recruitment. At the end of one report to the overseers, she boldly declared, "We have the potential to bring the News Department back to its former glory, and I think we're off to a great start."[34]

Rezaei's successor Catherine Treyz '13 (who also became news director as a freshman) kept the momentum going in 2010-11. Her *Views from the Valley* included Olympic-themed episodes containing interviews with former luger Cameron Myler '92, ice hockey silver medalist Sarah Parsons '10, and 2010 bronze medalist Andrew Weibrecht '09. Another episode highlighted TEDxDartmouth, a high-profile event that presented "big thinkers" in short, intimate idea exchanges. Banking interviews became an important tactic, as did occasional repeats of "timeless" items, to keep the program filled. In 2011-12 news activity began to flag a bit, although *Views from the Valley* (renamed *Valley Voices*) continued with Elizabeth Faiella '12 as host. She added coverage of the arts along with public affairs. "An amazing number of people come through campus that we can talk to," she said. "I think that it's really important that that people have the opportunity to hear these stories and engage with these people."[35]

## R.I.P. Dartmouth Election Network

If the News Department was a shadow of the vibrant operation of the 1960s-90s, the Dartmouth Election Network (DEN) was like a ghost stalking the station corridors, its glories in the past. The last major DEN election night production, with stringers calling in from across the region to update listeners on the results, had been in 2000. With the proliferation of instant news sources available to students and community (cable, Internet, etc.), such an elaborate production no longer made sense. Nothing was planned for the November 2006 midterm election night, but at the last minute wunderkind Alex Belser pulled together a two-man live broadcast with commentary from young government Professor Joseph Bafumi.

In the spring of 2007 the station approached *The Dartmouth* about cooperating on 2008 election coverage, but "The D" wasn't interested. By the fall the station had built up a DEN team of approximately 20 people, and at a September 26th Democratic candidates' debate held at Dartmouth interviews were conducted with John Edwards, Bill Richardson, Mike Gravel, and Dennis Kucinich, as well as the wives of Edwards and Kucinich and a host of campaign officials. Later there were interviews with Barack Obama (by remote hook-up) and Republicans John McCain and Mike Huckabee. Unfortunately on primary night, January 8, 2008, there were few volunteers for a live broadcast and some of the interviews were of such poor quality they could not be aired. According to Schuyler Evans, who was then running the News Department, "Everybody got results instantly from the Internet, there was no place for radio."[36]

Despite campus interest in the historic November 2008 election (Obama vs. McCain), there was no DEN coverage, nor was there any for the hotly contested November 2010 midterm election. The next major political event covered by DEN was the Republican candidates' debate held at Dartmouth on October 11, 2011. WFRD and WDCR carried live cut-ins around Hanover during the day leading up to the big, nationally televised debate from Spaulding Auditorium at Hopkins Center. Following coverage of the debate itself, live coverage alternated between the studios, Hopkins Center, the Green, and the 99Minute Spin Room, where the candidates and their representatives gathered after the debate. Special guests appearing on the station included Ron Paul, John Huntsman, Michelle Bachman, Newt Gingrich, and even Dartmouth President Kim, who teamed up with station anchors Chris Zhao and Larry Anfo-White '13 during the first 10 minute segment of the night. The ever-loquacious Ron Paul was live in the studios the next day. This immensely successful coverage led GM Ryan Zehner to declare, "I want to expand the role of our news department, which has fallen off in the past few terms. Our phenomenal experience covering the Republican presidential debate has convinced me that Dartmouth Broadcasting can cover news very well, and that it can be the most fun aspect of radio."[37]

There was no coverage of primary night itself, January 10, 2012, due both to overwhelming competition and the fact that it fell at the very beginning of the term. DEN's strong suit was emerging to be not the election nights themselves, as in the past, but rather coverage of events (such as debates) in the lead-up to the elections.

## Sports

High profile sports coverage was the last major area to be handed over to professionals. There had long been a tense relationship between the station and the Dartmouth College Athletic Department (DCAD), which had zero interest in having its games used as a training ground for Dartmouth broadcasters. It wanted professional coverage, the widest possible distribution, and if possible a stream of income from any broadcasts. In the past when the DCAD had threatened to take its games away from the station and assign them to commercial interests, the administration had intervened on behalf of the students. After half a century, however, the athletic department finally got what it wanted. As of 2007, due to student sportscasters "causing problems," all games would have play-by-play coverage by professionals, hired by the DCAD. Students could provide color commentary, do interviews, and "learn from" the professionals. Of course student sportscasters varied widely in ability (some had gone on to notable careers in sportscasting), but even if they happened to be as good as or better than the professionals, from this point on hired sportscasters were in charge.[38]

There was a long and somewhat contentious discussion about this change at the next meeting of the station overseers. When asked point-blank if the athletic department had "put their foot down," GM Debbie Wassel said it was a "mutual decision." However Wassel, Cole, and College representative Gordon Taylor, all advocates of station professionalization, strongly defended the move, saying that the DCAD was a "customer" and had to be satisfied. In any event it was a done deal, written into the contract with the DCAD.

Among the professionals providing play-by-play were Dave Collins (football, basketball, baseball, hockey), Bob Lipman (football), morning d.j. Chris Garrett (football, hockey), Wayne Young (football, baseball), and Dick Lutsk (who replaced Lipman in 2011 as "the voice of Dartmouth football"). Numerous students contributed color and interviews, as promised. Regular sports directors during this period included Dylan Higgins '09, Schuyler Evans, Jeremy Seidling '09, David Jiang, Gil Whelan '14, and Shane O'Neal.[39]

Most games were carried on either WFRD or WDCR, although WUVR-AM frequently carried basketball using Dartmouth's announcers. A 2009-10 arrangement with WTSL for basketball carriage was short-lived.

With student sportscasters reduced to a supporting role on game coverage (still a major endeavor), the department turned its attention to launching a sports talk show. *The Big Green Scene*, organized by Sports Director David Jiang in cooperation with the DCAD, was broadcast on WDCR with a Sunday morning repeat on WFRD, beginning in the spring of 2010. It was a major production, bringing in athletes, coaches and students for a half hour filled with informative and sometimes light-hearted interviews, recaps, and highlights. Recurring segments included "What You Missed," "Behind Enemy Lines," "Coach Talk," and "Alumni Connection." The show even attracted the attention of *The Dartmouth*, which ran a feature story on it in February 2011. In it Jiang admitted that the show was listened to more in the community than on campus, which he attributed to the fact that "radio is such an old technology to most students." However the show was streamed on the web, and the Dartmouth Sports Network (DSN) maintained an active site (**www.dartmouth-sportsnetwork.com**) containing information and sometimes podcasts of the shows.[40]

In 2011 *The Big Green Scene* was nominated as one of four national finalists for "Best Sports Reporting by a College Station" by College Broadcasters Inc.[41]

### Staffing

Beginning in 2006 Heath Cole and Julie Kaye were a welcome "constant presence at the station," something much missed since the departure of Winnie Lacoss four years earlier. Cole in particular worked well with the students, who gave him high marks for keeping operations running smoothly while maintaining a sense of continuity and experience from year to year.

That said, the third floor of Robinson Hall was not the beehive of activity that many alumni remember from the 1990s and before. In fact there were often very few students around. They came in, voice tracked their show, and left, the music having been pre-programmed for them (at least on FM). The station sometimes seemed like a ghost town. Lights were blinking, and computers were in control, but there were no people in sight. Efforts were made from time to time to encourage a greater sense of community among the staff, including in 2007 establishment of a blog about station activities (**www.dartmouthbroadcasting.blogspot.com/**). It was certainly engaging, with snapshots of students at various station activities, but except for a period during the Schuyler Evans administration (2009-10) it was not kept up to date.

Management turnover continued to be a problem. One of the more bizarre episodes in station history took place in 2007. Alex Belser, a junior, was a new recruit to the station who had distinguished himself by his energy and enthusiasm. He had done wonders for the News Department during the last quarter of 2006, and after only a few months at the station was named general manager for 2007-08. A few days later he announced on the air that he was leaving, and disappeared—from the station and from Dartmouth. He was not heard from again. (Former GM Susannah Thompson returned to serve out his term.) According to reports at the time, he was one of three newly recruited Directorate members who abruptly left Dartmouth.[42]

Other Directorate positions turned over with alarming rapidity, or were filled by new recruits with little experience. The year 2010 set some sort of record with four general managers in a single calendar year: Schuyler Evans (winter, graduated), Madison Rezaei (spring, resigned), Shirine Sajjadi (summer, temporary replacement), and Tony Quincy (fall). The fact that the stations ran as well as they did is a testament to the dedicated students who remained, as well as to Heath Cole and the professional staff.

Amid the staff turmoil the overseers made efforts to focus the students on long-term planning and leadership issues. In the spring of 2009 marketing and strategic planning executives Carl Strathmeyer '70 and Bob Kirkpatrick '72 led a retreat for the station staff on "Planning for the Future of Dartmouth Broadcasting in The Era of iPods and Internet Streaming," while Grant Bosse '94, a professional political analyst, led a session on rebuilding the News Department. In 2010 General Managers Rezaei and Quincy both laid out ambitious goals for each department. In some cases turnover meant that attendees at these sessions might be gone before they could implement what they'd learned, but the exercises were nevertheless useful. Both the News Department and WDCR experienced something of a renaissance following the spring 2009 "think" sessions.[43]

Efforts to involve alumni seem to occur about once a decade, and a new series of alumni newsletters was issued beginning in early 2007, after a nine-year hiatus. Five were published between 2007 and Fall 2009. Then they stopped again.

Most of all, the key to a successful operation was constant and pro-active recruiting. In the past recruits had flocked to the station, but now they needed to be convinced to try the (to them) largely unfamiliar medium of radio. Because *they* weren't listening, they assumed no one was and that radio was a "dying" medium, which could not be further from the truth. Once they tried it, and realized how many people in the community it reached, they sometimes became fascinated with the business of broadcasting. But it was a struggle to reach students. Even always-optimistic GM Thompson wrote, "We are still lacking in overall student involvement. That is, the station is still not very visible on campus and I truly believe, like many others, that if we could only get students through the door they would immediately be attracted to the station and would see what a great place it is."[44]

Numerous recruiting techniques were used, and the whole Directorate pitched in. In fact, it was something of a bonding experience for them. In order to introduce the station to freshmen *before* they were freshmen, a barbeque was held during Dimensions weekend, a weekend in the spring when prospective students are invited to visit the campus. Events were also staged during freshmen orientation week and at the start of each term, with station members handing out 99Rock cups, key chains and condoms (!). Well, know your audience. Weenie roasts in front of Robinson Hall, under the Dartmouth Broadcasting awning, were also popular (students who visited the station got a ticket, redeemable for free food outside). Not only were d.j. positions promoted, but also those in business and news, to make clear that there was a lot more to a radio station than what's on the air. BlitzMail messages were sent to the entire student body pointing out that experience at the station could lead to internships in business, and including testimonials from alumni about how the station had helped them in their careers. In 2008 Marketing Director Andy Sloan '09 staged WFRD fraternity dance parties, followed by an after-the-party mix show on WDCR, to promote the stations on campus.

Effective recruiting campaigns required that leaders be on campus at inconvenient times (e.g., before a term began), a lot of planning, a lot of time, and good person-to-person selling skills for individualized follow-up. The enthusiasm with which recruiting activities were pursued varied from year to year. In November 2009 GM Schuyler Evans reported that due to a concentrated campaign that year the total station staff had ballooned to more than 140 people, nearly triple the number a year earlier. Reaching prospects early, and reaching them often, was key, he said.[45]

The second "R" was of course retention, keeping newbies involved once they had signed up. Because of the way the stations now operated, with heavy reliance on technology, is was difficult to generate the "club" feeling of earlier days. A social director was appointed (when possible) to work on this. An idea promoted by Social Director Philip Aubart was to hold a station dinner ("Everyone has to eat!"). Since there was no money in the budget to pay for this, it was held at the student food court, where each person's individual meal plan covered the cost of the event.

A different kind of recruiting took place in 2007. Jeff Shapiro began managing the Clear Channel stations in Lebanon and approached both Cole and Garrett to leave Dartmouth Broadcasting and come to work for him. Both declined.[46]

## Public Service

One station activity that saw a considerable upswing in these years was public service. This was driven largely by Heath Cole and the professional staff, although students also participated.

In 2006 99Rock staged a series of remotes supporting the Marine Corps Reserves' Toys for Tots Campaign. This became an annual tradition in November or December of each year.[47]

The major event of 2007 was "Polly's Think-Pink Radiothon," staged on November 8 to honor Pauline Robbins-Loyd, a radio personality who was known and loved by broadcasters throughout the area. Only 30 years old, she had been fighting breast cancer for two years, and when Cole learned that the disease was terminal and she was going into the hospital, he immediately started calling other stations in the region to organize a fund-raising marathon in her honor. The 13-hour marathon was broadcast live from the Norris Cotton Cancer Center at Dartmouth-Hitchcock Hospital, originating with WFRD and simulcast on a hastily assembled network of 20 stations in a four-state area. More than $41,000 was raised for cancer research as Polly listened from her hospital bed. There was considerable coverage of the event on local television and in newspapers.[48]

Polly passed away on January 12, 2008, and there were hopes that the marathon could be continued as an annual event in her memory. A second marathon was indeed held, on October 20, 2008, but thereafter it became too difficult to get stations to agree to carry it.

Other efforts in 2007 included an October remote supporting the construction of a community playground in West Lebanon, with 99Rock joining volunteers and the mayor. Another Toys for Tots brought in 4,000 toys for 2,500 children. Campaigns in 2008 included Relay for Life benefiting the American Cancer Society (which won the station a Public Service Campaign of the Year award), the Suicide Prevention Walk, and Red Cross blood drive remotes. Public service in 2009 included remotes for the March of Dimes, Prouty 2009 (a bicycle-thon and challenge walk for cancer research), the Quechee Balloon Fest, three days for the Haven Food Bank (filling a trailer at the Harley-Davidson dealership), the New Hampshire/Vermont's Got Talent contest in White River Junction benefitting Friends of Vets, and many more. Cole estimated that the value of the airtime donated by the station to charitable causes in 2008-09 was approximately $90,000.

The strong commitment to public service continued in 2010-12. The station mounted a Relief for Haiti effort within 48 hours of the devastating earthquake there in January 2010, and major time was dedicated (usually through remotes) to the Red Cross, the Prouty, Toys for Tots (7,000 toys collected in 2010), the Tri-Kap Easter Egg Hunt, Earth Day, ACS Relay for Life, and Hurricane Irene relief. One of the station's most distinctive efforts was "Tornado Relief 2011" in May of that year. Cole arranged for a large truck to be parked in the Wal-Mart parking lot for a week, filling it with donated food, bottled water and other supplies. Cole and Chris Garrett then drove the truck across the country to the hard-hit city of Joplin, Missouri, broadcasting from stops along the way. For their efforts the station won the First Place Public Service Award for 2011 from the New Hampshire Association of Broadcasters, which was presented by Governor John Lynch at a ceremony in October.[49]

## Sales

These were difficult years financially for Dartmouth Broadcasting. From a low point in 2005-06 (when Kathy Whedon virtually stopped selling the station), revenues gradually improved. Following the end of the Joint Sales Agreement in early 2006 Julie Kaye and Heath Cole worked hard to rebuild relationships with local advertisers. They had to fight entrenched perceptions—"college kids don't buy our products," or (from a Toyota dealer) "18-34 year olds don't buy Toyotas"—by showing them that 99Rock's audience was much broader than that.[50]

Whatever harm it did to the student experience, automation and professional announcers did make 99Rock more saleable in the marketplace. Exact financials for this most recent period are (and should be) confidential; however, it is clear that Dartmouth Broadcasting was deep in the red at the start of the period, gradually rising to something closer to though not quite break-even by 2008. Then, the Great Recession hit the U.S. economy like a sledgehammer. Radio, like everybody else, was hard hit. According to one sales report in late 2009, many advertisers had cut their buys in half. "Sales, like everything else, is battling the economy." "Local businesses are floundering... [there is] uncertainty everywhere," lamented a worn-down Julie Kaye, shortly before her retirement in May 2010. She was not replaced and Heath Cole assumed her responsibilities. Morning man Chris Garrett also now did some sales work.

Despite the dark talk, things slowly got better. The second half of 2010 and early 2011, in particular, showed a healthy recovery. Costs were kept under control and although there was still red ink, it was gradually moderating, and was far less than in some other areas of College operations.

One side effect of Kaye's departure was that it opened the door to some student involvement in sales, which she had always opposed. 99Rock could not afford the high price of Arbitron ratings, so in the summer of 2010, as a Tuck School project, Tony Quincy and Ryan Zehner scraped together an assortment of listener data for the station such as demographics of contest winners, and of the station's Facebook fans. They compiled this into a presentation which they took on sales calls with Cole. As a supplement to traditional selling methods it was surprisingly effective, especially with local advertisers who were less interested in buying strictly by the numbers than their national brethren. It also gave both students, who were future general managers, insight into the real world of station sales.

### Sic Semper Video

The possibility of television at Dartmouth had been talked about since the 1950s, but did not get very far. Costs were high, and the student infrastructure required would be even greater than that for radio. In 1991 DTV was organized to distribute student-produced programs on the intra-campus instructional system. Despite equipment and a modest amount of seed money from the College, it never amounted to much.

By 2007 the TV club was moribund. No one was even sure who was in charge. Its equipment was stored in a room within the Dartmouth radio office suite, and Dean Cassidy offered DTV to the radio station to run. Some Directorate members, particularly FM Program Director Pavel Sotskov, were intrigued. The idea would be to fill most of the day with on-screen scrolling announcements of campus events along with programs and contests on 99Rock, with the audio track consisting of the station's regular signal. It sounded like a great way to promote 99Rock, as well as to provide a campus service.

Sotskov, Cole, and others spent almost a year trying to pull the project together. However the equipment in storage turned out to be mostly unusable, and no one from the former staff could be located to show the radio staffers how to get the system up and running. At one point it was estimated that it would cost the station $25,000 to restart DTV. With many other priorities, the radio station finally gave up on the idea. Most of the equipment was thrown out.[51]

Around 2010 DTV did start operating again, with a new staff and from a different location. However few programs were produced, mostly reviews and short newscasts. Some are now on the Internet. There were new discussions involving GM Madison Rezaei about a possible "merger of sorts" of DTV and Dartmouth Radio, but again nothing came of it. *Sic semper video.*[52]

## Technical: Streaming to the World

Worldwide streaming of WFRD and WDCR had finally begun in 2006, with both streams originating from somewhat dated computers at the station. WFRD could be accessed through **www.wfrd.com**. In 2007 the web portion of WDCR was rebranded WebDCR, accessible through a site by that name.[53]

In 2010 Cole and GM Tony Quincy became concerned that due to all the legal requirements that had grown up around streaming a commercial radio station like 99Rock, this jury-rigged system "was going to bite us." After some research they farmed out the streaming of 99Rock to Liquid Compass, a commercial service in Denver, to which they sent the signal and which then put it on the Internet, keeping track of royalty payments for records played and blocking commercials for which AFTRA payments might be required. In January 2012 Cole learned that iHeart Radio, a new, free Internet distribution service run by Clear Channel Broadcasting, was about to launch its first group of college stations, joining the more than 800 commercial stations it carried. A few phone calls later WFRD was added to the list as the first Ivy League station distributed by iHeart. 99Rock was featured in Clear Channel's national press release.

Streaming was still in its infancy. Only an estimated five percent of total radio listening was via the Internet, although that figure was growing, especially among younger listeners. In addition streaming meant that WFRD and WDCR could be heard anywhere, even hundreds of miles away on a iPhone, making them easily accessible to far-flung alumni and others. In time streaming could increase the visibility of the stations enormously. The iHeart app has been downloaded to more than 47 million iPhone and android devices, and the stations could also be accessed through a few other free radio apps such as tunein.com. The main barriers to Internet distribution, from the station's point of view, were the hefty royalties demanded by record companies, and the lack of offsetting revenue.

## Alumni to the Rescue!

Another problem was the steady deterioration of the studio equipment, most of which dated from the 1995-96 rebuilding. After more than a decade of constant and not-always-gentle use, it needed repair or replacement. In financially stressed times maintenance had been a secondary priority, but it could no longer be postponed. There were major problems with the WDCR control board, and headphones in the WDCR studio simply didn't work. Student engineers, not as knowledgeable as their predecessors, simply didn't know how to fix them. (One Technical Director commented," I have had absolutely no experience with tech or with radio stations; despite this, I am enjoying very much learning new things about the station.") The station's on-call professional engineer generally dealt only with emergencies.[54]

By 2008 the situation was becoming alarming. Cole reported to the overseers that "The current quality of transmission of WFRD and WDCR are beginning show signs of decay and neglect." The FM program director called the quality of the 99Rock signal "subpar." Its deteriorating quality was beginning to affect sales.[55]

Relief came from an unlikely source. Station alumni had traditionally not been involved in the day-to-day operation of the station, serving instead as advisors on the Board of Overseers (which met three or four times a year) and occasionally offering help through seminars or internships. Oddly, Dartmouth did not make it easy to donate money to the station either, preferring that donations go to the College. This was resolved and Friends of Dartmouth Broadcasting fund drives were held in 2007 and 2008. Overseers co-chairs Bob Kirkpatrick '72 and Stu Zuckerman '70 reported contributions of $4,200 and $4,600 from 40-odd alumni in those two years. Then in 2009 onetime General Manager Paul Gambaccini '70 made a significant contribution, increasing overall donations in that year to nearly $40,000. His gift was dubbed the "Paul and Pavel Project," after the general manager that year, Pavel Sotskov. Together with other donations it provided funding for important equipment upgrades, including a new Millennium Digital production board.[56]

At the same time several alumni, hearing of the station's technical difficulties, offered hands-on help. Eric McDonald '04 secured the donation of a new control board from Cox Radio, and George Whitehead '61 arranged the donation of another board. Whitehead, an experienced engineer and advisor to New Hampshire Public Radio, spent countless hours at the station, and with electrical engineer Dwight Macomber '70 and technologist Carl Strathmeyer '70 worked on installing new equipment and fixing the old. In 2009 Whitehead, Macomber and Strathmeyer formed a Technical Advisory Committee. With the assistance of broadcast engineers Chip Behal '79 and Tom Eckels '72, broadcast equipment manufacturer Gerrett Conover '87, and engineer/scientist Dr. Eric Kintner '67, they rolled up their sleeves, examined the entire technical plant including studios and transmitters, and produced a detailed, eight-page report on the state of the station's equipment, They then refurbished the plant while serving as mentors to the students. With talent like that helping them, the student leadership was deeply grateful.

The goal of the Paul and Pavel Project was to have the stations back in shape technically by the time Gambaccini arrived in Hanover in summer 2010, for his 40th anniversary reunion. This was accomplished.

Despite this rather striking demonstration of the willingness of alumni to help, no fund drives were held in 2010 or 2011, no alumni newsletters sent out, and the Technical Advisory Committee was disbanded. While alumni, if approached correctly, offer a potentially deep well of support for the station, the students seemed reluctant to ask.

In 2012 a major construction project was ordered by the College, in order to reclaim the station offices at the front of Robinson Hall for other purposes. This resulted in a considerable reduction in the space allotted to the station. Since there were few students physically at the station anymore, it probably did less harm than it would have a dozen years earlier. The positive side of the reconstruction was that the College simultaneously invested a considerable amount in upgrading the studio equipment, facilitating digital recording, archiving, editing, and streaming.[57]

## The Death of WDCR

The 50th anniversary of WDCR was marked by a weeklong celebration. March 3-9, 2008, was designated "retro week," with each day dedicated to a different founder of the station (some now deceased) and including music from his era.[58]

Monday: Dedicated to Richard "Dick" Harris '58, general manager in the year leading up to the launch, and the first voice heard on WDCR.
Tuesday: John Long '58, Harris' program director, who established the format.
Wednesday: Ronald "Ron" Kehoe '59, WDCR's first general manager.
Thursday: Jonathan "Jon" Cohen '60, the first program director, and co-director of the opening broadcast.
Friday: Robert "Bob" Johnson '59, the first technical director.
Saturday: Ariel Halpern '59, the first business manager.
Sunday: John Sloan Dickey, president of Dartmouth from 1945-70, who encouraged the station's unique independence.

Thursday night happened to be the night of the *Dartmouth Idol* finale, which WDCR and WFRD carried live. During the event Rob Demick, Zach Mason, and Phil Fazio '10, clad in tuxedos, cut a cake celebrating WDCR's 50th anniversary. There was also a special exhibit on the station website displaying still pictures from each decade of its history (and that of WDBS). It was hoped that alumni could gather in Hanover for the celebration, but due to scheduling considerations the reunion banquet took place on June 12, in order to coincide with class reunions. It was a gala evening. The star of the show was lively, 89-year-old Evelyn Hutchins, "Mrs. H.," who as secretary from 1960-79 was a "second mom" to generations of students. Others attending included Paul Gambaccini '70 from London, Mark Stitham '72 from Hawaii, filmmaker Bill Aydelott '72, and longtime advisor John Bryant.[59]

Ironically discussions regarding shutting down WDCR had already begun. There was a long discussion of the subject at the overseers meeting in February, 2007, with many drawbacks to AM enumerated: students don't listen to AM radio (or any radio) anymore, there are few listeners in the community, there is no advertising on the station, the signal is deteriorating (which would require a lot of money to fix), and it costs money to operate. The general feeling seemed to be that AM's time was past, and it was time to move the station exclusively to the Internet. "A college radio station should keep [up] with technological trends."

Still, a decision had not been made when the College's hand was forced in late August 2008. The AM signal went off the air due to technical difficulties at the transmitter site, and according to some accounts *nobody noticed* for several days. There were no calls from listeners, not even from station staffers. Consulting engineer Gary Savoie visited the transmitter site and thought that the guy wires and radials might be damaged; the College's Joe Cassidy and Gordon Taylor then circulated a memo saying it would cost $63,000 to restore the station, and recommending that it be permanently shut down. Both reports were incorrect. George Whitehead and his son-in-law (also an engineer) visited the site in early October and determined that in fact a switch was defective. Once that was fixed, the station was back on the air. However by this time there was little enthusiasm for continuing AM broadcasting, and the signal was shut off again.[60]

According to FCC regulations a station could remain off the air for no more than 12 months before forfeiting its license. A final decision had still not been made in August 2009, so Whitehead and others worked to get WDCR-AM back on the air at least briefly, to retain the license. They found that power to the site had been cut and the telephone link from studio to transmitter was broken, so they rigged up the Marti remote unit to get the signal to the transmitter, and borrowed a small portable gasoline generator (which had to be refilled three times a day) to provide power. Chug-chug-chug and WDCR-AM was back on the air. (The first program broadcast this time, on August 20, was the 1961 documentary, *Twenty Years Behind the Mike,* followed by hits of the 1950s and '60s; it was like a broadcast from another era.) The jury-rig system worked well enough for the station to stay on the air for 35 days, before being shut down for good in late September. No one knows if anyone was listening. The station's signal continued to stream on the web throughout all of this, of course.[61]

Finally a vote was taken at the November 2009 overseers meeting to sell the broadcast license and equipment, and operate WDCR solely as a web station. There was little discussion. President Kim's recent call for College-wide austerity in light of the terrible economy militated against any attempt to keep it going. No legitimate buyers could be found, and a year later the license was simply turned in to the FCC. As of 2012 the call letters WDCR were apparently in use only by a low power Catholic FM station in Decatur, Illinois ("Decatur Catholic Radio").

The AM transmitters were disposed of in early 2011. The principal transmitter, a 1982 Nautel Ampfet-1, turned out to be the first one ever built. Nautel bought it back as a historical artifact. Two back-up Gates transmitters were sold to ham radio operators.[62]

The sturdy Chase Field tower, erected in 1958, was taken down on August 24, 2011. It was still strong, and with normal maintenance could probably have lasted for another 50 years. It fell proudly, all in one piece, when its guy wires were cut. Once it was hauled away, the Athletic Department at last got the playing field it had coveted for years.[63]

WDCR was now officially WebDCR, although WDCR, DCR, and even "AM" continued to be cited in various places for years afterwards. The old frequency, 1340, even remained on the station's logo. At first student managers complained that the lack of AM broadcasting was a roadblock to recruiting, and wanted the signal restored. But within two or three years new students coming in felt otherwise, telling me that they didn't mind that there was no broadcast component to the station. Said one, "who listens to the radio, anyway?"[64]

## The Professionalization of Dartmouth Radio

There is no doubt that after six decades of relative stability, the culture of Dartmouth Broadcasting changed dramatically in the 2000s. This came about as fundamental aspects of station operation, beginning with ad sales and spreading to operations, key air shifts, sports coverage, and technical maintenance were turned over to professionals. One question that I asked every station alumnus I interviewed, from classes of the 1940s to those of the 2000s, is "When you think about it, who *really* ran the station?" The answer from classes up to the 1990s was always the same, a proud and emphatic "*We* did!" Their sense of independence, even defiance at times, of the administration was palpable.

The answer from classes of the 2000s was different, at least in tone. There is still a student general manager and Directorate, of course, and they are justifiably proud of their station, but they are much more likely to tell you that they work together with or learn from the professionals. No one today would seriously call WFRD "the only completely student operated commercial broadcast station in the nation" (the stock descriptor of the 1960s and '70s). One general manager described the administration's private conversations with the station's professionals, to which he was not privy, and felt that his own relationship to the administration was "vague." Another student described the general manager as the "people person," managing staff, while the professionals ran the station day-to-day. A long-time overseer agreed that that the Board of Overseers had taken on more responsibility for the station over the years, while the students had less.

The change came about in stages, and in most cases with the backing of the student leadership of the time. It wasn't imposed. Some feel it was the inevitable consequence of declining student interest in the medium of radio. Then too, Dartmouth Presidents John Sloan Dickey (1945-70) and John Kemeny (1970-81) were staunch advocates of station independence, feeling that it was an excellent real-world learning experience for students. Presidents after Kemeny were more distant and remote, as layers of deans and administrators were added to the College staff.

Whatever the reasons, Dartmouth radio is not the vibrant club it once was. Disc jockeys often voice track their shows and leave. There's not much activity on the third floor of Robinson Hall, and even the d.j. lounge is mostly empty. GM Ryan Zehner observed in 2011, "Although the station is doing very well internally, we could always have a better culture. One worry is that we might have become too business-like, and that not enough students know each other on a more friendly level. I want to have more station social events, so that everyone can have a rewarding time as a member of DB."[65]

On the other hand WFRD is an exceptionally well run 21st century radio station. Much of the credit for that goes to Heath Cole, the operations manager, who has not only helped the students fashion a tight, commercial sound that would work well in any market, and mounted a steady stream of public service initiatives that make Dartmouth proud, but is also personable and extremely popular with the student staff. If the goal is to have a well-run commercial station where students can learn how it's done, it could hardly have a better person at the center of the operation.

Several people close to the situation told me that if a group of students wanted to take more forceful control of the stations, with a clearly thought-out and credible plan of action, the College would probably not stand in their way. But this has not happened.

Despite periodic grumbling the College has continued to support the station, financially and otherwise, through thick and thin. In 2012 it invested in a major upgrade of the facilities, with modern, digital equipment for both WFRD and WebDCR. In recent years the stations have been in the red. Over the long haul, however, they have not only paid for themselves (unusual for a student organization), but have been a remarkably effective training ground for future leaders, as shown by the fervent testimonials of hundreds of alumni. According to many of them, it was one of the best parts of their Dartmouth education.

At this writing Dartmouth has recently appointed a new president, mathematics professor Philip J. Hanlon '77, succeeding Jim Yong Kim, who left in 2012 to head the World Bank. Dartmouth Broadcasting is under the capable control of Heath Cole and Assistant Dean of the College for Campus Life Kate Burke, who says that her goal is "to provide the best possible student experience."[66] The new administration may well determine the long-term future of the unique and productive institution known as Dartmouth Broadcasting.

1979 bonfire, with coverage by WDCR news (lower right)

Pres. McLaughlin, dedicating the new AM studio (1982)

Gov. Howard Dean (VT) proclaims "Rocktober"! (1994)

The 99Rock mobile unit ("MU"), with the gang (1995)

General Manager Deborah Wassel (2007)

L-R: Liz Faiella, Cooper Thomas, Heath Cole, Ryan Zehner (2012)

The 99Rock staff and tent at work (2009)

Geanette Foster, Eileen Chen, and Bukola Badipe-Hart with the mobile unit (2013)

# Appendix 1

# The Leadership of Dartmouth College Radio

The station's senior leadership—"The Directorate"—was not formally defined as the station manager plus three general department heads until after World War II. Before that, the equivalent of the modern Directorate and Executive Staff were lumped into one big "Directorate" with the station manager as its head. Listed below for 1941-47 are the senior members of that group, those in overall charge of programming, business and technical areas. In recent years the distinction between Directorate and junior management has again become somewhat vague. A horizontal line in each year's listing separates the Directorate (first group) from non-Directorate positions.

The listing also includes, where available, a brief indication of members' later careers, including earned advanced degrees and professions. It is interesting to see how few went into broadcasting. However nearly all will tell you that the experience they gained at Dartmouth radio, running a real business, was very valuable to them in later life no matter what their career path.

Amazingly, neither the station nor Dartmouth has any detailed files on past station leaders, so the names shown here were laboriously reconstructed from mentions in station publications, reports in the campus newspaper, and in some cases asking those who were there. For career information the starting point was the online alumni directory (at **www.dartmouth.edu**), however this is often vague, frequently incomplete, and reflects only current activities. Supplementary research was done online, in class reunion books, and in publicly available biographical sources such as Linkedin. In deference to privacy, addresses and other personal information are not shown. They are available to alumni in the online directory.

I would love to locate staff lists for additional years, so that more junior staff members can be credited. Please contact the author with these and for any errors or omissions, preferably *with documentation*. Check my website (**www.timbrooks.net**) for updates, which will also appear in future editions of this book.

Several thousand other men and women worked long and hard for Dartmouth radio (there are generally 100-200 students working at the station in some capacity every year), and some of them are mentioned in the text. All deserve appreciation and acknowledgment. While it is not possible to list (or even identify) them all, station alumni are encouraged to keep in touch with each other through the online alumni directory.

In the following list, an asterisk (*) indicates that the person served previously or subsequently, and that full information on them can be found nearby in an earlier or later entry. A "d." and date indicates that the person is deceased. Italicized initials in the "state" position indicate a foreign country: Britain (*GB*), Canada (*CA*), Germany (*DE*), Hong Kong (*HK*), Singapore (*SG*), Sweden (*SE*), Switzerland (*CH*).

Format: Title, Name, Advanced Degrees; State - Principal profession

Station founder           Richard Krolik '41 (d. 11/6/11); DC - Publishing; broadcasting (Time-Life)

**1. 1941-1942** (announced: September 20, 1941, by Mitchel)

| | |
|---|---|
| Station Manager | William J. Mitchel Jr. '42 (d. 6/12/03) - Public relations (Ford) |
| Asst. Station Mgr. (Feb. 1942) | John Shaw '43 (d.3/14/92), MBA '56 - Sales, textile industry |
| Production Dir. | Peter Geisler '42 (d. 5/5/91) - Advertising (J. Walter Thompson, others) |
| Business Mgr. | Frederick "Buzz" Cassidy Jr. '42 (d.1/28/03) - Chemical industry, management |
| Technical Dir. | Stephen Flynn '44 (d. 8/1/02) - Network TV; sales admin. (NBC) |

**2. 1942** (annc'd: Apr. 6, 1942; to change again in fall)

| | |
|---|---|
| Station Mgr. | *John Shaw '43 |
| Asst. Station Mgr. | James Wells '43 (d. 7/6/03), MCS '47 - Food industry, CEO (Wm. Underwood Co.) |
| Production Dir. | Robert L. Grant '43; FL - Sales management, contracts (Mobil Oil) |
| Co-Tech. Dir. | Joseph G. Hirschberg '43, MS '50, PhD '52; FL - Physicist; professor (Univ. of Miami) |
| Co-Tech. Dir. | Edward "Ted" Jones '43 (d.1/26/93), BS '44 - Engineer (Baldwin piano co.) |

**3. 1942-1943** (annc'd: Oct. 16, 1942)

| | |
|---|---|
| Station Mgr. | William R. Davies '44 (d. 2/9/10) - Radio/TV broadcaster, non--profit fundraising |
| Production Dir. | Richard T. Kanter '44; FL - Computer industry, electric motors (Ajax Corp.) |
| Tech. Dir. | William Alpert '45, LLB '48; NY - Law; real estate attorney |

**4. 1946** (annc'd: Apr. 11, 1946, by Varney)

| | |
|---|---|
| Station Mgr. | Robert Varney '43 (d. 5/19/82) - Public relations (Sperry Rand, Honeywell) |
| Production Dir. | Richard A. "Rick" Kelly '46; NY - Network television; production exec.(NBC) |
| Business Mgr. | Paul J. Caravatt Jr. '45 (d. 4/3/09), MCS '47 - Marketing; advertising, video production, CEO (Caravatt Communications) |
| Tech. Dir. | George Barr '45 (d. 12/26/98) - Publishing, marketing |

**5. 1946-1947** (annc'd: Jun. 10, 1946)

| | |
|---|---|
| Station Mgr. | *George Barr '45 |
| Asst. Station Mgr. (rsg Oct.) | *Richard Kelly '46 |
| Production Dir. | Robert MacLeod '46 (d. 5/2/79), MA '55 - Education, writer |
| Business Mgr. | *Paul Caravatt '45 |
| Tech. Dir. | *Stephen Flynn '44  - (see 1941-42) |

**6. 1947-1948** (annc'd: May 8, 1947)

| | |
|---|---|
| Station Mgr. | Robert L. Shade '46 (d. 2/13/75) - Insurance executive |
| Production Dir. | Emil J. "Bud" Popke Jr. '49 (d. 5/24/12); MI - Radio station owner , sales |
| Business Mgr. | William Trump '46 (d. 7/4/82), MCS '48 - Radio station sales, management, real estate |
| Tech. Dir. | Robert Owens '47 (d. 6/2/92) - Data processing, computer sales |
| Tech. Dir. | Richard S. Carr Jr. '49; CT - Sales, marketing |

**7. 1948-1949** (annc'd: May 1, 1948; took control same day)

| | |
|---|---|
| Station Mgr. | *Emil "Bud" Popke '49 |
| Production Dir. | Robert Sisk '50 (d. 8/8/04), LLB '56 - Law, chairman law firm |
| Business Mgr. | *Richard Carr '49 |
| Business Mgr. (Dec.) | James F. Gaylord '50 (d. 1/8/11), MCS '51; ME - Human resources (Scott Paper, Federal Reserve) |
| Tech. Dir. | Kenneth W. Carpenter '48, MBA '50, MS '50; CA - Software engineer (Lockheed) |
| Tech. Dir. (Dec.) | John W. "Red" Whelden '49, MS '51; MA - Engineer (Raytheon) |

**8. 1949-1950** (annc'd: Apr. 13, 1949)

| | |
|---|---|
| Co-Station Mgr. | Dick T. Hollands '50, LLB '59; VA - Finance, broadcasting (NBC, NAB) |
| Co-Station Mgr. | *Robert Sisk '50 |
| Production Dir. | John A. Gambling '51 (d. 1/8/04) - NY radio personality (WOR) |
| Business Mgr. | *James Gaylord '50 |
| Tech. Dir. | *John "Red" Whelden '49 |
| Tech. Dir. (Oct.?) | Ira Michael "Mike" Heyman '51 (d. 11/19/11), JD '56; CA - Education; law professor, chancellor (UC-Berkeley) |
| News Dir. | Bill Brooks '51 (d. 4/14/05); CT - Marketing (Texaco), real estate |

**9. 1950-1951** (annc'd: Mar. 22, 1950; took control Apr. 18)

| | |
|---|---|
| Station Mgr. | *John A. Gambling '51 |
| Production Dir. | William H. Terry '51; MD - Movie production (Warner Bros.), prod. mgr. |
| Business Mgr. | Theodore W. Bailey '51; CO - Manufacturing; administration |
| Tech. Dir. | Albert S. Warren '52, BS '56; NC |
| Tech. Dir. (Sep.) | Richard K. "Swick" Swicker '52 (d. 1/28/10) - Television producer, director (NBC, freelance) |
| Chief Announcer | Dave Dugan '52, MA '55; KS - Radio-TV newsman (CBS), journalism professor. |
| Spec. Events Dir. | *Bill Brooks '51 |

**10. 1951-1952** (annc'd: Mar. 21, 1951; took control after spring recess)

| | |
|---|---|
| Station Mgr. | *William H. Terry '51 |
| Production Dir. | Sewall C. "Bud" Sawyer II '52, MA '80; MI - Advertising |
| Production Dir. (Oct.) | Arthur B. "Bud" Schweich '53; MO - Stage manager (theater, TV), medical technician |
| Business Mgr. | Paul "Sandy" Sanderson, Jr. '52 (d. 6/21/86), MALS - Education, headmaster Suffield (CT) Academy |
| Tech. Dir. | *Richard K. "Swick" Swicker '52 |
| Chief Announcer | *Dave Dugan '52 |
| Sports Dir. | Andrew A. Stern '52, M.Phil. '51; CA - Radio-TV producer, photographer, educator (UC-Berkeley) |

**11. 1952-1953** (annc'd: Mar. 26, 1952; took control after spring vacation)

| | |
|---|---|
| Station Mgr. | Kent C. Robinson '53 (d. 6/30/03), MBA '54 - Apparel industry (chairman, Buster Brown) |
| Program Dir. | Herbert F. Solow '53; CA - Television; writer, produced or supervised many hit shows incl. *Star Trek, Mission Impossible* (NBC, Desilu, MGM)) |
| Business Mgr. | James Penney '53 (d. 1/11/00), MBA '54 - Advertising, marketing |
| Tech. Dir. | William C. Gitt '53; MA - Engineer; computers, film, audio recording |
| Tech. Dir. (Sep.) | J. Stuart Fordyce '53, PhD '59; OH - Research scientist (NASA) |
| Production Mgr. | *Norman R. Bander '54 |
| Record Dir. | William White '54; NJ - Book publishing, health care administration |
| Public Relations Dir. | Howard Sloane '54 (d. 10/2/10), MS '58, PhD '59 - Education; psychology professor |
| Classical Music Dir. | David Sices '54, PhD '62; NC - Education; French professor (Dartmouth) |

**12. 1953-1954** (annc'd: Mar. 25, 1953; took control Apr. 14)

| | |
|---|---|
| Station Mgr. | Peter E. Roos '54, MS '55, MBA '60; MA - Manufacturing (H.K. Porter), management consulting |
| Program Dir. | Norman R. Bander '54 (d. 2/17/93) - Marketing, advertising |
| Business Mgr. | William T. Robbins Jr. '54, MBA '56; FL - Investment banking (Kidder-Peabody) |
| Tech. Dir. | Joseph M. Giden '55, LLB '58; CA - Law, business law; partner |
| Sports Dir. | Larry B. Russell '54, BS '60; GA - Hotel executive |
| Classical Music Dir. | *David Sices '54 |

**13. 1954-1955** (annc'd: Mar. 10, 1954; control after spring vacation)

| | |
|---|---|
| Station Mgr. | Peter von S. Stevens '55, MBA '56; NV - Financial analyst, money manager, trader, writer |

| Program Dir. | Martin L. Aronson '55, JD '58; MA - Law; trial lawyer (criminal, injury) |
| Program Dir. (Apr.) | *Arthur "Bud" Schweich '53 - (see 1951-52) |
| Business Mgr. | Blake W. Irons '55 (d. 12/18/10), MBA '56; CT - Insurance (Aetna) |
| Tech. Dir. | Peter G. Robinson '55 (d. 1/9/05) - Personnel exec. (Richardson-Vicks) |
| Sports Dir. | Dave J. Steinberg '55, LLB '58, LLM '59; PA - Law; performing arts (recording industry) |
| Chief Announcer | James M. Barker '56; MN - Media production, broadcasting, airline pilot |
| Production Mgr. | *John K. Van de Kamp '56 |
| Dir. Of Dramatic Pgms | Arnold Kroll '56 (d. 9/27/11), LLB '59; FL - Finance; investment banker (Lehman Bros.) |
| Advertising Dir. | Robert Horton '55 (d. 12/7/07), MBA '57 - Banking, telemarketing |
| Comptroller | *Henry R. "Hank" Jaenicke '56 |
| Ivy Representative | Donald A. Wright '55, MBA '57, CPA '69 ; IL - Marketing, accounting |
| Chief Studio Engineer | *H. Flint Ranney '56 |
| Maintenance Engineer | Greg Knowles '55, MS '60; NY - Producer-director, film & TV |
| Maintenance Dir. | Joslyn "Jos" Demos '56, PhD '70; MD |
| Personnel Dir. | John C. Moffitt '55;   CA - Television producer-director, ATAS |
| Record Dir. | Wesley "Wes" Smith '56, MDiv '59, MS '74; NM |
| Audience Research Dir. | Marvin "Mickey" Baten '56, MBA '57; NY - Finance administration, investment advisor |
| Public Relations Dir. | Robert J. Bransten '56, MBA '58; CA - Food marketing (Western Can), real estate |

**14. 1955-1956** (annc'd: Mar. 18, 1955; took control immediately)

| Station Mgr. | John K. Van de Kamp '56, JD '59; CA - Law; CA Attorney General, candidate for Governor |
| Program Dir. | William K. Tell Jr. '56 (d. 10/10/12), JD '59; CT - Law; Chief Counsel (Texaco) |
| Business Mgr. | Henry R. "Hank" Jaenicke '56 (d. 5/30/11), MBA '58, PhD '63; TX - Education; accounting professor |
| Tech. Dir. | H. Flint Ranney '56 (d. 12/21/12); MA - Recording executive; broker, real estate |
| Chief Announcer | Robert Peyton '57; CA |
| Chief Announcer (eff. Sep. '55) | *Frank A. Sauter '57 |
| News Chief | William Hildick '58; OR - Sales (Norton Co.) |
| Sports Dir. | John E. Kramer '56, MA '61,'63, PhD '65; FL - Education, professor of sociology (SUNY) |
| Controller | Andrew L. Nichols '58, LLB '61; MA - Law; attorney, Pres. Appalachian Mountain Club |
| Advertising Dir. | Jay Trepp '57, MBA '58; MA - Administration |
| Ivy Network Representative | *Marvin "Mickey" Baten '56 |
| Chief Studio Engineer | Wendell M. Smith '57, MS '58; NH - Engineer, administration |
| Co-Maintenance Dir. | *Joslyn "Jos" Demos '56 |
| Co-Maintenance Dir. | Alden Purrington '53; CT - Computers, database/systems engineer |
| Production Mgr. | Donald Cowlbeck '57 (d. 1/30/76); MA - Advertising (Foote, Cone, Belding) |
| Recording Chief | Merritt Clark '56, MS '57; CT - Engineering (N.E. Telephone) |
| Personnel Dir. | Dave P. Miller '55, MBA '62 ; NC - Finance, accounting (Cyanamid, Formica) |
| Public Relations Dir. | *Robert Brantsen '56 |
| Audience Research Dir. | *David H. Johns '58 |
| Record Dir. | Richard J. Wallace '56 (d. 3/20/79) - U.S. Navy captain, pilot |
| Dir. of Engineering Heelers | James Groebe '56, MBA '58; CO - Marketing, sales |
| Dir. of Announcing Heelers | *Frank A. Sauter '57 |
| Dir. of Production Heelers | Addison "Addie" Bowman '57, LLB '63, LLM '64; HI - Education; law professor |
| Green Key | *Frank A. Sauter '57 |

**15. 1956-1957** (annc'd: Mar. 21, 1956)

| Station Mgr. | Frank A. Sauter '57 (d. 12/6/94) - Advertising writer |
| Program Dir. | Richard M. Harris '58, MBA '59; CT - Marketing, sales (P&G, General Mills) |
| Business Mgr. | Merwyn Bagan '57, MD '62, MPUB '95; NH - Physician; neurosurgeon |

| Tech. Dir. | Adam T. Block '57, MBA '58; VA - Visual arts/design; administration |
|---|---|
| Chief Announcer | George H. Haines '58; VA - U.S. Foreign Service, counselor |
| News & Spec. Events Dir. | Robinson B. Brown '59; MN - Radio promotion, management (WCCO) |
| Sports Dir. | Richard Bareuther '59; PA - Sales (Scott Paper, Avon) |
| Comptroller | *Andrew Nichols '58 |
| Advertising Dir. | *John H. Long '58 |
| Ivy Representative | Paul D. Robinson '58; MD '62, MHS '65; FL - Physician; pediatrician |
| Chief Studio Engineer | *Allen H. Pulsifer '58 |
| Maintenance Dir. | Jack R. Turnbull '57, MS '58 ; VA - Information technology |
| Production Mgr. | *Addie Bowman '57 |
| Personnel Dir. | *David H. Johns '58 |
| Dir. of Production Heelers | Jules F. Rose '57; FL - Marketing, consulting |

### 16. 1957-1958 (annc'd Mar. 20, 1957)

| General Mgr. | *Richard M. Harris '58 |
|---|---|
| Program Dir. | John H. Long '58 (d. 8/20/06) - Advertising; founded marketing firm |
| Business Mgr. | David H. Johns '58, MA '60, PhD '66; CA - Professor of political science (San Diego State U.) |
| Tech. Dir. | Allen H. Pulsifer '58, MS '60, PhD '65; MD - Education; professor chemical engineering |
| Chief Announcer | *Robinson B. Brown '59 |
| Sports Dir. | *Richard Bareuther '59 |
| Broadcast supervisor | *Ronald F. Kehoe '59 |

### 17. 1958-1959 (annc'd: Feb. 12, 1958)

| General Mgr. | Ronald F. Kehoe '59, LLB '62; MA - Law; Asst. Attorney General (Mass.) |
|---|---|
| Program Dir. | Jonathan L. Cohen '60, MBA '61; NY - Human resources, finance (Goldman Sachs) |
| Business Mgr. | Ariel Halpern '59 (d. 12/29/85), MBA '60, MBA - Finance, investment analyst (Goldman Sachs) |
| Tech. Dir. | Robert A. Johnson '59 (d. 5/2/12), MAT '64, MA '70; CT - Education; high school French teacher |
| Broadcast Supervisor | Richard Guilford '60, JD '63; MI - Law; attorney, real estate, trust, estate |
| Chief Announcer | John Haynes '59 (d. 2/21/07); MS - U.S. Marines: pilot, public affairs; consultant |
| Production Mgr. | J. Stuart Sandberg '60; NY - Priest |
| News & Sports Dir. | Robert Hager '60; VT - NBC news reporter |
| Local Advertising Mgr. | Robert D. Clark '60 (d. 6/29/06), LLB '65; - Law; attorney, trusts, estates |
| National Advertising Mgr. | C. Daniel Johnson '59 (d. 3/5/98), MBA '60, MS '60 - Engineer, product development (Kodak) |
| Chief Engineer | James S. Picken '59 (d. 11/23/96), MSEE '60 - Electronics engineer (NSA) |
| Chief Studio Engineer | Donald L. Caress '60, BS '61, MD '63; FL - Physician |
| Chief Remote Engineer | *Don B. Knapp II '60 |
| Personnel Dir. | Carl R. Bahn '60; NC - Marketing |
| Promotion Mgr. (rsg. June) | *Robinson B. Brown '59 |

### 18. 1959-1960 (annc'd: Mar. 5, 1959)

| General Mgr. | Allan W. Cameron '60 (d. 6/10/11), MALD '65, PhD '79; MD - Information technology; strategy management |
|---|---|
| Program Dir. | Roger J. Schulz '60; *CA* |
| Business Mgr. | Frank R. Greenberg '61, LLB '64; CA - Law; attorney |
| Tech. Dir. | Don B. Knapp II '60, MD '64; FL |
| News & Sports Dir. | *Robert Hager '60 |
| News & Spec. Events Dir. | Harold Levenson '61; VA - TV news director |

### 19. 1960-1961 (annc'd: Mar. 5, 1960)

| General Mgr. | George R. Whitehead '61, BE '62, MBA '79; NH - Engineering, financial planning; management |
|---|---|
| Program Dir. | William R. Cogswell '61, MAT '63, MA '76; NY - Education; high school educator |

| | |
|---|---|
| Business Mgr. | Henry Goldsmith '62; NJ - Finance (Playboy Enterprises) |
| Acting Business Mgr. (spr 60) | George F. Meyer '62 (d. 10/3/05), MBA '63; OH - Manufacturing (Schlegel Corp.), marketing |
| Chief Engineer | Robert F. Hargraves Jr. '61, PhD '67; NH - Information technology; professor, CIO |
| Administrative Dir. | William J. Matthews III '61, MD '65; CA - Physician; anesthesiology |
| News Dir. | *Harold Levenson '61 |
| News Dir. | Frederick M. Asher '63, PhD '77; MN - Education, professor art history (U. of Minnesota) |
| Chief Announcer | *Jim Varnum '62 |

**20. 1961-1962** (annc'd: Feb. 1, 1961; control at March banquet)

| | |
|---|---|
| General Mgr. | George T. "Ted" Mascott '62, MBA '66; NY - Marketing executive (Merck), environmentalism |
| Program Dir. | James W. Varnum '62, MHA '64; NH - Hospital administration; president (Mary Hitchcock) |
| Business Mgr. | Thomas P. Hall '62, MBA '63; NH - Marketing, strategic planning (Ford), investment management |
| Business Mgr. (June) | H.A. "Hal" Deane Jr. '62; SC - Marketing (General Motors) |
| Chief Engineer | James M. Knappenberger '63, MBA '66, MS '84; CA |
| Chief Engineer (later) | Donald A. Steen '62, MS '64; NY - Engineering (North American Philips) |
| Administrative Dir. | J. Philip Smith '62, MS '64, PhD; CT - Education; teaching, admin., college president (Southern CT State University) |
| Chief Announcer | Tim Dodd '63, LLB '66; IN - Law; attorney |
| Broadcast Supervisor | Jim S. Dial '63, MBA '66; CA |
| News Director | Geoff Murphy '63, MBA '64; IL - Finance; CFO (Beatrice Foods) |
| Special Events Director | Michael Hobbs '62, JD '65; VA - Information technology, public television |
| Production Director | *Sturges Dorrance '63 |
| Sports Director | Tom Green '62, LLB '65; DC - Law; attorney |
| Advertising Director | Hal Trefethen '63 (rsg 8/61) (d. 6/7/88), MBA '64 - Finance, investment advisor |
| Comptroller | Jeff Plancey '63, DMD '66; NJ - Dentist |
| Chief Studio Engineer | *Bob Gitt '63 |
| Head Remote Engineer | Dave Schwartz '63, MD '67; FL - Physician, radiologist |
| Maintenance Engineer | *Don Steen '62 |
| Public Relations Director | *Pete Stern '63 |
| Personnel Director | Peter P. Drowne '62, MA '65; MT - TV/film production |
| Record Director | *Tim Brooks '64 |

**21. 1962-1963** (annc'd: Feb.20, 1962; control Mar. 4)

| | |
|---|---|
| General Mgr. | Sturges D. Dorrance '63; WA - Television station management; consultant |
| Program Dir. | William H. Woolley '63, MS '64; NJ - Retailer, men's clothing |
| Business Mgr. | Stuart J. Mahlin '63, MGA '65; OH - Human resources; administration, consultant |
| Tech. Dir. | Robert R. Gitt '63, MBA '65; CA - Film preservation expert (UCLA) |
| Administrative Dir. | Peter M. Stern '63 (d. 5/14/99), LLD '66 - Law; attorney |
| Administrative Dir. (later) | Brent R. Cromley '63, JD '68; MT - Law; litigation, politics, magician |
| Chief Announcer | *David K. Shipler '64 |
| Broadcast Supervisor | *Michael Delizia '64 |
| News Director | William Subin '63, JD '66; NJ - Law; attorney, criminal, civil |
| Special Events Dir. | *Jeffrey Panitt '65 |
| Co-Sports Dir. | Edwin A. McCabe '63, JD '66; MA - Finance, treasurer (ABS Industries) |
| Co-Sports Dir. | Harry R. Zlokower '63, MA '66, MBA '78; NY - Public relations |
| Production Dir. | Dan Matyola '63, JD '71; NJ - Law; attorney, real estate, litigation |
| Record Director | *Tim Brooks '64 |
| Advertising Dir. | *William E. Craig '64 |
| Dir. of National Accounts | Douglas G. Montgomery '64, MPA '66, PhD '69; OR - Professor, corporate management (power co.) |
| Chief Engineer | *Dave Schwartz '63 |
| Head Studio Engineer | Joel L. Granick '65, MD '72; IL - Physician |

| | |
|---|---|
| Head Remote Engineer | Cole D. Letteney '63 (d. 6/3/11), PhD '67; TX |
| Maintenance Director | Ronald S. Rosenfeld '63, MD '67; ME - Physician |
| Comptroller | Stephen J. Garland '63, PhD '67; PA - Computer sciences (Dartmouth, MIT) |
| Public Relations Dir. | *Robert L. Hartford '65 |
| Personnel Dir. | Richard E. Danziger '63, PhD '68, MD '76; CA - Physician, U.S. Navy, private practice |
| Publicity Dir. | *Brent R. Cromley '63 |

**22. 1963-1964** (annc'd: Feb. 28, 1963, control April 1)

| | |
|---|---|
| General Mgr. | Alan R. McKee '64, MA '68, MALD '69; MD - U.S. foreign service; ambassador (Swaziland) |
| Program Dir. | David K. Shipler '64; MD - Journalist (*New York Times*), author |
| Business Mgr. | William E. Craig '64, LLB '67; GA - Law; real estate, environmental law |
| Tech. Dir. | Frederick "Ted" Gerbracht Jr. '64, MA '71, MA '76, PhD '93; NY - Information services; chief security officer |
| Admin. Dir. | Timothy "Tim" Brooks '64, MS '69; CT - TV network research executive (NBC, USA/Sci-Fi, Lifetime), author, consultant |
| News Director (Apr) | Henry E. Clay '64, LLB '67; VA - Law; attorney, staff counsel |
| News Director (fall) | *Jeffrey Panitt '65 |
| Special Events Dir. | *Jim Dial '63 |
| Chief Announcer | Alfred "Fred" Hill '65; VT - Broadcaster, fundraiser |
| Record Director | Allan Hislop '65, MA '72; NH - Education; Spanish professor |
| Production Dir. | Paul M. Jones, Jr. '65; PA - Sales, marketing |
| Broadcast Supervisor | Park L. Price '64; ID - Sales, administration (GM), auto dealer |
| Sports Director | George Wittreich '65, MBA '71; MA - Finance; CFO |
| Maintenance Dir. | Michael D. Busch '66; CA - Software; publishing/writing on aviation |
| Head Remote Engineer | *Mike Lewis '65 |
| Head Studio Engineer | Forrest R. Martin '65 (d. 11/12/76) - Real estate |
| Regional Adv. Dir. | *Mark Blanchard '66 |
| Local Adv. Dir. | *Rob Hartford '65 |
| National Adv. Dir. | *Bob Sauer '66 |
| Comptroller | Michael A. Delizia '64; MI - Insurance industry |
| Comptroller | *James S. Frank '65 |
| Public Relations Dir. | John Haskins '65, JD '70, MA '70 & '02; LA - Education; professor |
| Promotion Dir. | Walter J. Huss '65 (d. 5/25/05) - Radio announcer, photography |
| Personnel Dir. | Paul Balgley '66 (d. 11/26/96) - Recording studio co-owner |

**23. 1964-1965** (annc'd: Mar. 2, 1964)

| | |
|---|---|
| General Mgr. | Robert L. Hartford Jr. '65, MBA '74; OH - Manufacturing; president |
| Program Dir. | Jeffrey Panitt '65, MIA '67, DIP '90; VA - Government intelligence officer; telecommunications |
| Business Mgr. | Allan R. Boyce '65, MBA '69; WA - Marketing, human resources (Burlington Railroad) |
| Tech. Dir. | Michael K. Lewis '65, JD '75; DC - Law; mediator, arbitrator |
| Admin. Dir. | James S. Frank '65, MBA '67; IL - Administration; president; fleet management |
| News Dir. | Paul Klee '66, BA '69; NH |
| Promotion Mgr. | Greg Eden '66, JD '75; TX - Finance; investment management; CEO |

**24. 1965-1966** (annc'd: Mar. 1, 1965; control Mar. 9 banquet)

| | |
|---|---|
| General Mgr. | Allan A. Ryan Jr. '66, JD '70; MA - Law; intellectual property officer (Harvard) |
| Program Dir. | Robert M. Cohn '66, MBA '69; NY - Publishing; marketing |
| Business Mgr. | Mark W. Blanchard '66, MBA '72; NH - Administration; small business entrepreneur |
| Tech. Dir. | Christopher B. Kilgour '66 |
| Admin. Dir. | Robert B. Sauer '66, MBA '68; MA - Marketing/market research |
| Chief Announcer | *Robert B. Buck '67 |
| News Dir. | *Owen G. Leach '67 |
| Production Mgr. | *Michael "Sean" Hennessey '67 |

Head Remote Engineer       *Eric C. Kintner '67

**25. 1966-1967** (annc'd: Feb. 15, 1966; control in two weeks)
| | |
|---|---|
| General Mgr. | Owen G. Leach III '67; NJ - Broadcasting; research consultant |
| Program Dir. | Robert B. Buck '67, JD '70; CA - Transportation; consumer services |
| Business Mgr. | Michael A. "Sean" Hennessey '67; *CA* - Video production, farming |
| Business Mgr. | Malcolm A. "Mac" Cross Jr. '68; OR - Broadcasting, director |
| Tech. Dir. | Eric C. Kintner '67, MA '69, PhD '76; MA - Scientist, optical physicist |
| Admin. Dir. | Patrick G. Maddox '67 (d. 9/6/91), MA '69, PhD '77 - Social science research, China trade studies |
| Chief Announcer | *Scott R. McQueen '68 |
| Chief Announcer | Andrew C. Barrie '67; *CA* |
| Production Dir. | Steven M. Friedman '68, PhD '78; OH - Administration, mental health |
| Production Dir. | *Laurence G. Barnet '68 |
| News Dir. | James T. Flynn '67, JD '74; CO - Law; attorney, mediation |
| Sports Dir. | David D. Sicher '67, MBA '69; NY - Finance; investment management |
| Special Events Dir. | Christopher O. Kern '69; MD - Computer sciences; government |
| Record Dir. | James Jay Brady '68 |
| Classical Music Dir. | William L. Paschke '68, MA '69, PhD '72; KS - Education; mathematics professor |
| Dir. Announcing Trainees | *Scott R. McQueen '68 |
| Local Adv. Dir. | John F. "Jack" Bolger, Jr. '69 (d. 5/21/93); MN - Publisher, catalogs, magazines (Bolger Publications) |
| Acting Sales Mgr. | *John R. Hopke Jr. '68 |
| Comptroller | Michael J. Zavelle '68, MBA '71; NM - Finance; education |
| Chief Engineer | James A. Brodsky (Jane Fleming) '68; CA - Computer programmer |
| Head Studio Engineer | *H. Lawrence Henchey Jr. '68 |
| Head Remote Engineer | David H. Barrett '67, MD; AK - Physician |
| Maintenance Dir. | Andrew J. Longacre '67, MS '68, PhD '73; VT - Product engineering (Welch Allyn Inc.) |
| Dir. Engineering Trainees | *Christopher B. Kilgour '66 |
| Public Relations Dir. | Michael F. Ryan '68, MBA '69; NC - Finance; bank president |

**26. 1967-1968** (annc'd: Jan. 31, 1967; control Feb. 16 banquet)
| | |
|---|---|
| General Mgr. | John R. Hopke Jr. '68; LA - Radio, music marketing (record industry) |
| Asst. General Mgr. | Laurence G. Barnet '68; NY - Radio station owner, hospital administration |
| Program Dir. (first) | Scott R. McQueen '68; FL - Radio station group owner |
| Program Dir. (second) | Ted Nixon '68, MED '01; NY - Radio station group owner; French teacher |
| Business Mgr. | David L. Walden '68, JD '76, LLM '79; GA - Law; international, corporate, immigration |
| Tech. Dir. (part year) | H. Laurence Henchey Jr. '68, MBA '74; MA |
| Tech. Dir. | Henry V. Allen '69, BE '70, MS '71, PhD '77; CA - Scientist; electronic/electrical manufacturing |
| News Dir. | *Jeffrey S. Kelley '69 |
| Sports Dir. | David S. Jeffery '68, JD; VA - Law; attorney |
| Chief Announcer | *Ted Nixon '68 |
| Dir. News Production | *Mark W. Willen '69 |
| Record Dir. | *David L. Prentice '69 |
| Classical Music Dir. | Philip P. Youngholm '69, AM '74; CA - Information services, systems support |
| Production Dir. | *Christopher O. Kern '69 |
| Dir. Announcing Trainees | Robert D. Shellard '69, MBA '71; VA - Television, planning & administration (CBS-TV) |
| Local Adv. Dir. | *John F. Bolger '69 |
| Comptroller | *E. Doane Grinnell III '69 |
| Head Remote Engineer | Dirk Hughes-Hartogs '68, MS '71, PhD '75; CA - Information technology, intellectual property law |
| Maintenance Dir. | Frederick W. Ochs Jr. '69, MS '72, PhD '74; CA - Consulting |
| Dir. Emergency Planning | *Henry V. Allen '69 |

Public Relations Dir.          Samuel P. Swisher '68, MBA '70; MA - City government; community planning (Mass.)

**27. 1968-1969** (annc'd: Feb. 12, 1968; control at March banquet)

| | |
|---|---|
| General Mgr. | Jeffrey S. Kelley '69, MS '70; DC - Public relations (DuPont, U.S. government) |
| Program Dir. | David L. Prentice '69, MBA '71; *CA* - Advertising, marketing, publishing (yearbooks) |
| News Dir. | Mark W. Willen '69; MD - Publishing, politics; sr. editor |
| Business Mgr. | E. Doane Grinnell III '69 (d. 3/17/94) - Marketing, railroad industry |
| Sales Dir. | Robert S. Throndsen '69; WA - Public relations; TV news reporter |
| Tech. Dir. | Frederick J. Klein '69, MBA '71; VA - Consulting, transportation/ distribution; president |
| Chief Announcer | William C. Moyes '70, MBA '72; CO - Radio station owner |
| Local News Dir. | John Lippman '71; DC - TV reporter, news executive, government analyst |
| News Production Dir. | Alan F. Gordon '69, MPH '91; MA - Administration, publishing |
| Dir. News Announcers | Brent G. Petty '70, BA '70, MD '74; MD - Education; professor pharmacology |
| Sports Dir. | William H. Greenwood '69, MA '73, PhD '77; MI - Consultant (Greenwood Consulting Services) |
| Production Dir. | William D. Sewall '70, JD '77; CA - Information services, security anagement |
| Dir. Announcing Trainees | *David A. Graves '70 |
| Music Dir. | Lyle F. Nyberg '69, JD '73; MA - Law; corporate attorney |
| Classical Music Dir. | *Philip P. Youngholm '69 |
| Comptroller | *Donald R. Balcom '70 |
| Credit Manager | Douglas J. Nichols '69, PhD '80; MA - International public health |
| Dir. Advertising Development | *Stuart G. Zuckerman '70 |
| Public Relations Dir. | *Paul M. Gambaccini '70 |
| Chief Engineer | *Carl R. Strathmeyer '70 |
| Maintenance Dir. | Robert B. Garman '69, BE '70, SM '77; NJ - Research administration, computing (Exxon) |
| Head Studio Engineer | Larry E. Parkhurst '69; CO |
| Head Remote Engineer | John T. Russell '69, MALS '77; NH - Industrial administration; quality engineer |
| Dir. Engineering Trainees | *John C. Shapleigh '71 |

**28. 1969-1970** (annc'd: Feb. 10, 1969; control Feb. 22 banquet)

| | |
|---|---|
| Chairman/GM | Paul M. Gambaccini '70, MA '74; *GB* - Radio/TV personality (BBC) |
| President | Stuart G. Zuckerman '70; NY - Sales and marketing (PBS) |
| Program Dir. (spring 69) | Winthrop A. "Win" Rockwell '70, JD '75; MN - Law; partner |
| Program Dir. (1969-70) | David A. Graves '70; MA - Broadcasting (Gen. Mgr.), Internet |
| Comptroller | Donald R. Balcom '70, MRP '72; IL - Fund raising; capital campaign director |
| Sales Dir. | Kenneth M. Jones Jr. '70, MBA '72; CA - Health care administration |
| Tech. Dir. | Carl R. Strathmeyer '70; MA - Consulting; strategy management |
| Production Dir. | John S. Rockwell '72, MS '76; NY - Recording studio owner (Rockwell Audio Media) |
| Record librarian | Peter D. McClanathan '71, JD; IL - Law; attorney |

**29. 1970-1971** (annc'd: Feb. 1970)

| | |
|---|---|
| General Mgr. | John H. Marshall '71, MA '76, JD '77; VT - Law; managing partner |
| Program Dir. | Mark D. "Loon" Stitham '72, MD '75; HI - Psychiatrist |
| News Dir. | Stephen K. Zrike Sr. '71, MBA '73, MS '73; MA - Consulting; marketing/ market research |
| Business Mgr. | Allen M. "Mac" Barrett Jr. '71, MED '83; MD - Public relations |
| Sales Dir. | John C. Shapleigh '71, JD '76; MO - Hospital administration |
| Tech Dir. | Dwight F. Macomber '70, BE '77, ME '90, PhD '01; PA - Electrical engineering |
| Production Dir. | *John S. Rockwell '72 |

**30. 1971-1972** (annc'd: Feb. 5, 1971)

| | |
|---|---|
| General Mgr. | William D. Downall '72, MS '82; IN - Journalist, information systems consultant, author |
| Program Dir. | Stephen D. Kepes '72; GA - Sales; administration, investment advisor |

| | |
|---|---|
| Business Mgr. | Robert G. Kirkpatrick '72, MBA '74; NY - Advertising; global media director |
| Sales Dir. | J. Charles "Charlie" Smith '73; MD - Software (Microsoft) |
| Tech. Dir. | Michael L. Rieger '72, BE '73, MSEE '74; WA - Research & development; group director |
| Dir. of Development. | Timothy A. McKeever '72, JD '75; WA - Politics, law; commercial litigation |
| News Dir. | *John C. "Jack" Beeler '73 |
| Ombudsman | Mark J. Woodward '72; VT - Writer, editor, administrator (Thayer School) |
| Production Dir. | *John S. Rockwell '72 |

**31. 1972-1973** (annc'd: Jan. 31, 1972; control Mar. 4)

| | |
|---|---|
| General Mgr. | Alfred "Fred" Frawley III '73, JD '76, LLM '80; ME - Law; corporate, intellectual property |
| Program Dir. | John C. "Jack" Beeler '73, JD '76; OH - Law; corporate, real estate, international |
| Business Mgr. | William Hatch '73; NH - Finance; banking |
| Sales Dir. | Leonard E. Schulte '74 (rsg spr 72), JD '77; FL - Law; government; public affairs director |
| Tech Dir. | Bruce H. Curran '73 ME '82, MS '93; RI - Biotechnology; biomedical, medical physicist |
| Operations Mgr. | Stephen D. Chakwin Jr. '73, JD '78; CT - Law; attorney, product liability, employment |
| News Dir. | William Sigward '74, MBA '76; NY |
| Ombudsman | Warren Hashagen Jr. '73 (d. 4/2/09), MBA '85 - Finance; CFO (The Gap) |

**32. 1973-1974** (annc'd: Feb. 6, 1973; control at Mar. 3 banquet)

| | |
|---|---|
| Chairman of Board/Tech. Dir. | Carter H. Yates '74, ME '76; SC - Marketing |
| Program Dir. | John D'Auria '74, MD '80; FL - Medicine; anesthesiologist |
| Business Mgr. | Thomas S. Lord '74, JD; NH - Education (primary/secondary) |
| Sales Dir. | David D. Simpson '74; TX |
| Operations Supervisor | John E. Huisman Jr. '74, MBA '79 ; NC - Information Technology |
| Dir. Of Development | Thomas VanBenschoten '74; CO - Broadcast sales, investment |
| News Dir. | *Aaron J. Schindel '75 |
| Music Dir. | Douglas E. White '75; NY - Charitable fundraising; consultant |

**33. 1974-1975** (annc'd: Feb. 6, 1974; control Feb. 20). Six person Board of Directors (Production Dir. replaced by Technical Dir. in fall).

| | |
|---|---|
| General Mgr. | David E. Hunt '75, JD '78; ME - Law; attorney, estate planning |
| Program Dir. | Wallace M. "Wally" Gonzalez '75, MBA '85; PR - Financial consultant |
| News Dir. (rsg 1/75) | Aaron J. Schindel '75, JD '78; NY - Law; partner |
| Production Dir. (rsg 5/74) | Gregg E. Fairbrothers '76, MS '77, MBA '83; VT - Investing, education; professor (Tuck) |
| Production Dir. | Ross E. McKinney, Jr. '75, MD '79; NC - Physician, professor |
| Dir. Development & Legal Affairs | Carey E. Heckman '76, JD '79; NH - Law, computer sciences; professor (Dartmouth) |
| Sports Dir. | William P. Guider '75; CT - Retailing (Caldor), real estate |
| Tech Dir. | William A. Taylor '75, ME '78; MA - Design engineer |
| Business Mgr. | Alan L. Goldin '76, MD '83, PhD '83; CA - Medical research; microbiology, professor |
| Sales Dir. | *Royce G. Yudkoff '77 |
| Ombudsman | Pamela Gile '76; NH - Human resources manager |
| Chief Announcer | F. John Potts '75, MBA '90; IL - Government relations, pres. Illinois Strategies |
| Minority Prog. Dir. | Cruz C. Russell '75, MPA '83; NJ - Government; administration (Port Authority, NY-NJ) |

**34. 1975-1976** (annc'd: Mar. 1, 1975 banquet)

| | |
|---|---|
| General Mgr. | Christopher C. Davidson '76; CA - Network television; program executive (CBS) |
| Program Dir. (spr, sum 75) | Richard "Rick" Zimmerman '76, MBA '80; OH - Marketing; food/beverages (P&G, SunnyD) |
| Program Dir. (fall 75, win 76) | John F. "Jack" Fidler '76; MA - Finance, banking; information technology |

| | |
|---|---|
| Business Mgr. | J. Randall "Randy" White '76, MBA '78; IL - Food industry; corporate affairs |
| Business Mgr. (sum 75) | H. Arthur Heafer '77, MD; TX - Physician, family practice |
| Sales Dir. | Royce G. Yudkoff '77, MBA '80; MA - Finance; investment (media/communications) |
| Tech Dir. | Edward E. "Ted" Bardusch '76; WA - Software development |
| Dir. Devel./Legal Affairs (spr 75) | Martin S. Karl '76, MBA '77; PA - Consulting, educational materials (High Touch/High Tech of N.E.) |
| Dir. Devel./Legal Affairs (sum 75) | Peter Threadgill '77; MD - Computer scientist |
| Dir. Devel./Legal Affairs (fall 75, win 76) | Richard W. Mark '77, JD '80; NY - Law; business, litigation |
| News Dir. | *Jeff Sudikoff '77 |
| Acting News Dir. (Jan 76) | Stephen Saglio '77, MD '85; CA - Physician, family medicine |
| Sports Dir. | *John F. "Jack" Fidler '76 |
| Sports Dir. (second) | Dave Cutler '77, MD '81; CA - Physician, family practice, medical director |
| Production Dir. | Maura Harway '77, MBA '79; NY - Finance; administration (Sesame Workshop) |
| Music Dir. | Charles D. Peos '77, MBA '79;NJ - Financial services |
| AM Operations Supv. | *Mark Tomizawa '78 |
| FM Operations Supv. (first) | Roberto N. "Bert" Ifill '76, MA '79, PhD '92; MD - Education; asst. professor |
| FM Operations Supv. (sum 75) | Kevin Koloff '77, JD '80; CA - Law; entertainment law |
| FM Operations Supv. (fall 75) | Ronald P. Fleischer '77, MM '81; IL - Law; attorney |
| Chief Engineer | *Jordan M. Roderick '78 |
| Chief Engineer | William D. Sinclair '76, MSEE '78; CA - Product engineering; president (Data Spectrum) |
| Ombudsman (spr, sum 75) | Nancy Levin (exchange student from Smith) |
| Ombudsman (fall 75, win 76) | *Maura Harway '77 |
| Public Affairs Dir. (Jan 76) | *Gerard R. "Gerry" Cox '79 |
| Personnel Dir. | Robert L. Baum '77, JD '81; MD - Law; attorney, mediator, arbitrator |

**35. 1976-1977** (annc'd: Feb. 28, 1976 banquet)

| | |
|---|---|
| General Mgr. | *Richard W. Mark '77 |
| Program Dir. | Mark S. Tomizawa '78; MA - Advertising; agency founder (Smash) |
| Business Mgr. | Alan L. Folz Jr. '77; TX - Finance; investment management |
| Business Mgr. (fall 76) | David C. Corey '78; MN - Finance, insurance |
| Sales Dir. (Feb-Aug) | David D. Borland '77, MBA '80; IL - Sports/recreation club consulting; owner |
| Sales Dir. (fall 76) | Jeffrey P. Sudikoff '77; CA - Telecommunications (founded IDB WorldCom), finance, investment, philanthropist |
| Acting Sales Dir. (win 77) | *Peter Threadgill '77 |
| Tech Dir. | Jordan M. Roderick '78, MBA '80; WA - Wireless executive, president (AT&T, Cingular) |
| Dir. Devel./Legal Affairs | Christopher S. Carstens '79, MBA '89; NY - Human resources; administration |
| News Dir. (spr 76) | Rick J. Beyer '78; MA - Writer, filmmaker |
| News Dir. (sum 76) | Steve Levitan '78, MBA '81; NJ - Finance; hedge fund |
| News Dir. (fall 76, win 77) | John Donvan '77, ME '80; DC - News correspondent (ABC) |
| Sports Dir. (rsg 7/76) | *Dave Cutler '77 |
| Sports Dir. (eff 8/76) | John J. LeBlanc '77; NH - Software engineer |
| Production Dir. | Bruce McDowell '79; NH - Software engineer |
| Production Dir. (eff fall 76) | *Dave Title '79 |
| AM Opns Supv. | *James Ancona '78 |
| FM Opns Supv. (rsg 10/76) | Greg Rinehart '77, MD '81; MO - Physician; plastic surgery |
| FM Opns Supv. (spr, sum) | *Ronald Fleischer '77 |
| Chief Engineer | *James Ancona '78 |
| Planning Council | *John Donvan '77 |
| Planning Council | Thomas Mayer '77, JD '81; NY - Law; corporate, partner |
| Minority Affairs Dir. | James H. Washington '77, MPA '78; MD - Government; administration (FAA); consulting |
| Ombudsman | *Maura Harway '77 |
| Public Affairs Dir. | *Gerard R. "Gerry" Cox '79 |

**36. 1977-1978** (annc'd: Feb. 26, 1977 banquet)

| | |
|---|---|
| General Mgr. | *Jordan M. Roderick '78 |
| PD-WDCR | David G. Title '79, MED '83, '88, DED '90; CT - Education; superintendent of schools |
| Co-PD-WFRD (spr, sum 77) | *Christopher S. Carstens '79 |
| Co-PD-WFRD (fall 77, win 78) | *David C. Corey '78 |
| Business Mgr. | Kristy Weinschreider (Rudel) '79, MBA '81; NY - Finance; hedge fund; chief admin. officer |
| Business Mgr. (winter '78) | Rich vonRiesen '80, MBA '80; WA - Finance; CFO; medical systems |
| Sales Dir. | *Mark S. Tomizawa '78 |
| Sales Dir. (fall 77) | Keith Quinton '80, MBA '82; NH - Finance; portfolio manager |
| Tech. Dir. (spr, sum 77) | Timothy A. Andrews '78, MS '80; MA - Health care, medicine; principal |
| Tech. Dir. (fall 77, win 78) | Arthur B. "Chip" Behal Jr. '79, MBA '88; NY - Broadcast engineering; finance |
| Dir. Devel./Legal Affairs | Barbara C. "Binky" Moses '78, JD '82; NY - Law; business, securities litigation |
| News Dir. | *Rick Beyer '78 |
| News Dir. (spr 77) | Barbara L. Reinertsen '77; ME - Non-profit administration (United Way) |
| Sports Dir. | Paul Elmlinger '80, JD '84; NY - Law; finance, international |
| AM Chief Announcer | *Kevin Koloff '77 |
| Minority Affairs Dir. | Lloyd E. May '78, JD '84; MS - Law; financial services |
| Ombudsman | *Keith Quinton '80 |
| Ombudsman (winter '78) | *John C. Bussey '79 |
| Public Affairs Dir. | Steve J. Renick '78, JD '81; CA - Law; attorney |

**37. 1978-1979** (annc'd: Feb. 24, 1978 banquet; control Mar. 14)

| | |
|---|---|
| General Mgr. | John C. Bussey '79; DC - Writer, author (Wall Street Journal) |
| PD-WDCR | James M. Gifford '80; MD - Administration, writing; president |
| PD-WDCR (winter 79) | Joseph R. Mannes '80, MBA '82; TX - Corporate finance, investment management; director |
| PD-WFRD | William N. Isaacs '80, MS, MPH, DPH; MA - Leadership training; writer; academic |
| PD-WFRD (spr 78) | William Toman '78, JD '82; WI - Law; partner |
| Business Mgr. | Francis A. "Fran" L'Esperance III '79, MBA '83; NY - Finance; private equity, venture capital; president |
| Sales Mgr. (rsg 4/78) | James P. Ancona '78, MS '95; MA - Software |
| Sales Mgr. (second) | Donald S. Hofmann '79; CT - Water treatment company; president |
| Sales Mgr. (winter 79) | Robert G. Ponce '80; NY - Finance; private equity, venture capital |
| Tech. Dir. (first) | *Arthur B. "Chip" Behal '79 |
| Tech. Dir. (second) | Paul Albrecht '79, MS '83, PhD '86; MA - Administration; VP |
| Dir. Devel./Legal Affairs | Stephen P. Storfer '80, MD '86; CT - Pharmaceutical; associate director |
| Dir. Devel./Legal Affairs (spr 78) | Gerard R. "Gerry" Cox '79 , MD '83, MHA '97; NC - Health care administration; military |
| News Dir. (spring 78) | Harriet Schwartz '78, MA '80; MA - Information systems, marketing |
| News Dir. | Thomas Farmer '81; WA - TV producer (CNN), marketing executive |
| News Dir. (summer 78) | Linda Button '79; MA - Marketing |
| Sports Dir. | *Paul Elmlinger '80 |
| Minority Affairs Dir. | Janice V. Scott '80, MBA '88; TX - Real estate; acquisition and leasing (BP) |
| Ombudsman | Patricia Walsh '81, MD '87; MA - Physician; geriatric psychiatry |
| Classical Dir. | *Jean Scarrow '80 |
| AM Music Dir. | Michael M. Sullivan '80, MBA '83; MD - Finance; CFO |
| FM Music Dir. | T. Scott Bucey '81, JD '85; CA - Law; real estate |

**38. 1979** (annc'd: Feb.24, 1979 banquet; control spring term)

| | |
|---|---|
| General Mgr. | *Joseph R. Mannes '80 |
| PD-WDCR | Sarah "Sally" Nutt (Van Leeuwen) '80, MBA '84; CT - Home manager, caregiver |
| PD-WFRD | Kenji Hayao '80, PhD '90; MA - Education; political science, professor (Boston College) |
| PD-WFRD (summer '79) | Jeffrey M. Zimmerman '81, JD '84; NY - Law, radio-TV; deputy gen'l counsel (Time-Warner) |

| | |
|---|---|
| Business Mgr. | Jean M. Scarrow '80, MBA '85; MA - Administration; insurance (Liberty Mutual) |
| Business Mgr. (spring '79) | Peter Ley '81, MBA '85; NY - Finance, communications industry; CFO |
| Sales Dir. | *Robert G. Ponce '80 |
| Sales Dir. (summer, fall '79) | *Stephen P. Storfer '80 |
| Tech. Dir. | Jonathan F. Panek '81, BE '84, ME '84; MA - Software engineer; chmn Mass Audubon society |
| Dir. Devel./Legal Affairs | *William N. Isaacs '80 |
| Dir. Devel./Legal Affairs (sum, fall '79) | *Peter Ley '81 |
| News Dir. | Margaret A. Smith '82, MBA '84, JD '89; MD - Law; government (SEC) |
| Sports Dir. | Robert W. Oliver Jr. '82 |
| AM Music Dir. | *Jason E. Klein '82 |

**39. 1980** (annc'd: Nov. 1979; control Jan. 1980)

| | |
|---|---|
| General Mgr. | *Jeffrey M. Zimmerman '81 |
| PD-WDCR | Mark J. Belmonte '82; FL - Government; system network analyst |
| PD-WFRD | Merrill J. Baumann Jr. '81, JD '85; OR - Law, corporate; intellectual property |
| PD-WFRD (summer 80) | Kenneth A. Elias '82, MS '88; AZ - Auto industry consultant |
| Business Mgr. | William D. Goddard '81, MBA '83, JD; CT - Finance; insurance, risk management |
| Sales Mgr. | William G. Dorman '81, MS '82; HI - Journalism; radio-TV (Toyko correspondent) |
| Tech. Dir. | Kimberly F. Smith (Quirk) '82, BE '83, ME '83; NH - Software; renewable energy |
| Tech. Dir. | Bradford D. Carpenter '82, MAR '86; CA - Architecture/planning |
| Dir. Devel./Legal Affairs | Jason E. Klein '82, MBA '86; NY - Publishing; CEO (Newspaper National Network), consultant |
| News Dir. | Philip H. Weber '82, MBA '86; PA - Administration; CEO, consultant |
| Sports Dir. (first) | *Robert W. Oliver Jr. '82 |
| Sports Dir. (second) | Alan R. Eagle Jr. '83, MBA '88; CA - Telecommunications, software, corp. communications (Google) |

**40. 1981** (annc'd: Nov. 17, 1980; control Jan. 1981)

| | |
|---|---|
| General Mgr. | *Mark J. Belmonte '82 |
| PD-WDCR | *Philip H. Weber '82 |
| PD-WDCR (summer) | Robert E. Dinan '83, MS '84, MMGT '88; MI - Education, primary/secondary; math teacher |
| PD-WFRD | *Kenneth A. Elias '82 |
| PD-WFRD (summer) | Peter R. Barry '83, MBA '90; NC - Finance; investment management |
| Co-Business Mgr. | Jeffrey D. Shapiro '83; NH - Radio station group owner |
| Co-Business Mgr. | Joseph M. Kirby '83; NY - Sales; division manager |
| Tech. Dir. | Peter O. Harris '83; MA - Software |
| Legal Affairs Dir. | *Margaret A. Smith '82 |
| Legal Affairs Dir. (summer) | Patricia J.D. Lippoczy (Hedley) '83, MBA '87; CT - Marketing, finance (General Atlantic) |
| Public Affairs Dir. (first) | Kevin P. Lane '83, MA '88, PhD '92; *CH* - Prof. political science; consultant (McKinsey) |
| News/Sports/Public Affairs Dir. (second) | Paul L. McGorrian '83 (d. 8/25/89) - Newspaper reporter, foreign correspondent |
| News Dir. | *Kevin P. Lane '83 |
| Ombudsman | *Thomas Farmer '81 (see 1978-79) |
| Training Dir. | *Tracy D. Weatherby '83 |
| Promotions Dir. | Peter Herzig '84, MBA '89; NY - Finance; investment management |
| Blackside | Cathy Bagley '82, MD '86; SC - Physician (OBGYN) |
| AM Music Director | *Robert R. Gray '83 |
| AM Music Dir. (summer 81) | Daniel C. Goldin '82; WI - Publishing; buyer |
| Chief Engineer | *Edwin G. "Ned" Roos '83 |
| FM Promotion & P.R. | Harry Jeffcoat '83, BA '85, MIA '87; SC - Administration, finance |

315

**41. 1982** (annc'd: Nov. 14, 1981 banquet)

| | |
|---|---|
| General Mgr. | *Jeffrey D. Shapiro '83 |
| PD-WDCR | Robert R. Gray '83; MA - Home manager |
| PD-WFRD (first) | Tracy D. Weatherby '83, MBA '87; CA - Marketing co. (technology, healthcare); founder |
| PD-WFRD (summer, fall) | Gary S. "Boot" Seem '84; VT - Marketing; in-store radio |
| Business Mgr. | Stuart J. Birdt '83, MBA '87; NY - Finance; investment banking |
| Tech. Dir. | Edwin G. "Ned" Roos '83; MA - Consulting engineer |
| News Dir. | Daniel L. Daniels '84, JD '87; CT - Finance; tax, trust, estate planning |
| Chief Announcer | Frances Jones '84, JD '87; KY - Corporate General Counsel |
| Training Dir. | Adam Burck '84, MMGT '90; IL - Finance; venture capital |
| FM Music Dir. | Brian Goldner '85; RI - CEO (Hasbro) |
| Blackside Dir. (winter) | Alan B. Bond '83, MBA '87; NJ - Finance |
| Blackside Dir. (fall) | Michelle Duster '85, MFA '90, MA '97; IL - Freelance writer, writing instructor |

**42. 1983** (annc'd:     )

| | |
|---|---|
| General Mgr. | *Daniel L. Daniels '84 |
| PD-WDCR. | Lenwood K. Ivey Jr. '84; CA - Student |
| PD-WDCR (fall '83) | Lonnie E. Staley '85; NY - Advertising; media director |
| PD-WFRD | Robert S. "Robb" Cutler '84, MS '11; CA - Software; computer sciences, education |
| News Dir. | John W. Landrigan '84, MA '01; NH - Administration; fund raising |
| Business Mgr. | Bennett L. Zimmerman '85, MBA '89; CA - Finance; investment management |
| Acting Bus. Mgr. (winter '83) | Anita L. Butler (Allen) '84, JD '87; CT - Law; attorney |
| Tech. Dir. | Joel H. Margolese '85, MBA '90; MA - Software engineer, marketing, app developer |
| AM Music Dir. | Robert D. Blum '83; OH - Advertising; president |
| Training Dir. | *Michael R. O'Connor '86 |

**43. 1984** (annc'd: Nov. 12, 1983 banquet)

| | |
|---|---|
| General Mgr. | Kathleen "Katie" Mulligan '85, MED '90; HI - Education (primary/secondary); head of school |
| PD-WDCR | Gregory W. Beasley '85, MBA '89; CA - Information technology, consultant |
| PD-WFRD | Raymond R. Wagner Jr. '85, MS '87, PhD '93; TN - Consulting, strategy; VP |
| PD-WFRD (summer '84) | Thomas Connolly '85; TX - Government relations; lobbyist |
| Business Mgr. | William B. Furlong Jr. '86, MBA '91; WA - Information technology, software; CEO |
| Tech. Dir. | Janice S. Sakowicz '85 - Financial services |
| Tech. Dir. (winter '84) | *Joel H. Margolese '85 |
| Tech. Dir. (summer '84) | George Bourozikas '86; NY - Information technology, consultant |
| News Dir. | John M. May '85, PhD '94; CA - Computer scientist; R&D |

**44. 1985** (annc'd: Nov. 10, 1984 banquet, control Jan 1985)

| | |
|---|---|
| General Mgr. | *William B. Furlong Jr. '86 |
| Acting GM (fall '85) | David S. Wachen '87, JD '92; MD - Law; commercial, media litigation |
| PD-WDCR (winter '85) | *David S. Wachen '87 |
| PD-WDCR (spring '85) | Gerrett H.A. Conover '87; NJ - Radio equipment; EVP (Radio Systems, Inc) |
| PD-WDCR (fall '85) | Mark S. Greenstein '86, JD '92; CT - Education; teaching, president |
| PD-WFRD (rsg 9/85) | Margot K. Jacobs '86, MA '89; SE - Finance; international banking |
| PD-WFRD (summer '85) | William D. Spencer '88; CO - Software |
| PD-WFRD (eff 9/85) | Richard D. "Rick" Rosson '88, SM '94; MA - Engineer; materials manager |
| PD-WFRD (fall '85) | Michael R. O'Connor '86; IL - Radio programming (Clear Channel), marketing |
| Business Mgr. | George E. Bingham '87, MBA '99; NY - Finance; banking, real estate |
| Business Mgr. (winter '85) | Joy Turnheim (Smith) '86, JD '88, MBA '93, MPH '97; NC - Education; professor; business |
| Tech. Dir. (rsg 9/85) | *George Bourozikas '86 |
| Acting TD (spring, sum '85) | Eric Overton '87, BE '89, ME '89; TX - Information technology, CEO |
| News Dir. | Russell W. Kemp '87, JD '98; CO - Law; corporate, partner |

| | |
|---|---|
| News Dir. (winter '85) | Manus J. Clancy '85; NY - Finance; commercial real estate |
| AM Music Dir. | Christian Terfloth '88, MBA '93; *DE* - Management consulting; technology |

**45. 1986** (annc'd: Nov. 1985, control Jan. 1986)

| | |
|---|---|
| General Mgr. | *David S. Wachen '87 |
| GM (spring '86) | *George E. Bingham '87 |
| PD-WDCR | Richard M. Lerner '87; NJ - Administration; director |
| PD-WDCR (summer '86) | Jeff Gershengorn '88; FL - TV sports producer (Golf Channel) |
| PD-WFRD (winter '86) | Raffiq A. Nathoo '87, MBA '91; NY - Finance; investment/merchant banking |
| PD-WFRD (spring, sum '86) | *Richard Rosson '88 |
| PD-WFRD (fall '86) | Abdhish R. Bhavsar '87, MD '91; MN - Physician; opthalmologist |
| Business Mgr. | Andrew J. Shapiro '88, MBA; CA - Communications, mobile media |
| Business Mgr. (summer '86) | Seth M. Skolnik '89, MBA '94; CA - Digital media/technology; admin., marketing |
| Tech. Dir. | Robert L. Striker '88, JD '94; MN - Law; real estate |
| Tech. Dir. (spring '86) | *Jeff Gershengorn '88 |
| News Dir. (first) | *Russell W. Kemp '87 |
| News Dir. (second) | Sherri L. Burkholder (Fosdick) '88; VA - Public relations; consultant |
| FM Music Dir. | *John F. Natalie '88 |

**46. 1987** (annc'd: Nov. 21, 1986; served Jan.-Jun. 1987)

| | |
|---|---|
| General Mgr. | *Andrew J. Shapiro '88 |
| PD-WDCR | Seth A. Rosenblatt '89, MBA '93; CA - Marketing; technology industry |
| PD-WFRD | *Abdhish R. Bhavsar '87 |
| Business Mgr. | Gregory C. Dinges '89; OR - Finance; CFO (Nike) |
| Tech. Dir. (winter) | *Gerrett H.A. Conover '87 |
| Tech. Dir. (spring) | *Robert L. Striker '88 |
| News Dir. | Jennifer Avellino '89; MD - Journalism; radio-tv; producer (Reliable Resources) |
| Sports Dir. | Wayne S. Johnson '89, JD '92; FL - Law; litigation, worker's compensation; partner |
| FM Music Dir. | *Mark E. Wachen '89 |

**47. 1987-1988** (annc'd: Jul. 1987; control Jul. 1987)

| | |
|---|---|
| General Mgr. | *Seth M. Skolnik '89 |
| PD-WDCR | *Seth A. Rosenblatt '89 |
| PD-WFRD | Mark E. Wachen '89, MBA '94; NY - E-Commerce; CEO |
| Business Mgr. | *Sherri L. Burkholder (Fosdick) '88 |
| Business Mgr. (summer '87) | Ashley J. Zeiler (Hager) '90, JD '94; GA - Law; partner |
| Tech. Dir. | Jeffrey S. Kuskin '89, BE '90, MSEE '92, PhD '97; NY - Electrical engineer |
| News Dir. | *Jennifer Avellino '89 |
| Sports Dir. | John F. Natalie '88; VA - Education; social studies teacher |
| FM Music Dir. | Peter D. Delano '89 MBA '98; MA - Finance; investment management |

**48. 1988-1989** (annc'd:    ; control winter 1988)

| | |
|---|---|
| General Mgr. | *Seth A. Rosenblatt '89 |
| General Mgr. (spring '88) | *Robert L. Striker '88 |
| General Mgr. (summer '88) | Thomas Stone '90, MD '95; KY - Physician; ophthalmologist |
| PD-WFRD | *Mark E. Wachen '89 |
| PD-WFRD (summer '88) | *Ashley J. Zeiler (Hager) '90 |
| PD-WDCR | Carolyne G. Allen '89, JD '00; NY - Law; intellectual property, other |
| PD-WDCR (spring '88) | *Seth A. Rosenblatt '89 |
| PD-WDCR (summer '88) | Brian R. Davis '89; CA - Voice actor |
| News Dir. | *Jennifer Avellino '89 |
| News Dir. (summer '88) | Paul C. Zimmerman '90; *GB* - E-commerce |
| News Dir. (winter '89) | *Brett Haber '91 |
| Sports Dir. | David H. Kramer '89, JD '93; CA - Law; intellectual property, litigation |
| Sports Dir. (spring '88) | *John F. Natalie '88 |
| Sports Dir. (summer '88) | Abdul K. Kallon '90, JD '93; AL - Law; judge |

| | |
|---|---|
| Business Mgr. | Sarah E. Freitas (Waldman) '92, JD; VA - Law; attorney, U.S. Government (Justice Dept.) |
| Business Mgr. (spring '88) | *Sherri L. Burkholder (Fosdick) '88 |
| Business Mgr. (sum, fall '88) | Pryce T. Boeye '90; IL - Food industry |
| Tech Dir. (fall '88) | Marc O. Baptiste '91 |
| Tech Dir. (spring, sum '88, win '89) | Mark S. Dattar '90; MA - Finance; investment management; IT |
| AM Music Dir. | *John W. Stouffer III '90 |

**49. 1989-1990** (annc'd:  ; control spring 1989)

| | |
|---|---|
| General Mgr. | Tim Reynolds '91; TN - Interactive media (Meredith Broadcasting) |
| PD-WFRD (spring '89) | *Mark E. Wachen '89 |
| PD-WFRD (sum, fall '89, win '90) | Eric B. Wellman '91; NY - Radio; program director (NY) |
| PD-WDCR | Michael J. Gordon Jr. '91; FL - Financial advisor |
| PD-WDCR | John W. Stouffer III '90; CA - Television; public relations |
| News Dir. | ?Brett Haber '91; DC - TV sportscaster (ESPN, others) |
| News Dir. | *Eric C. Peterson '91 |
| Sports Dir. | Eric C. Peterson '91; PA - Administration (Del Monte); sports announcer |
| Business Mgr. | ?*Sarah E. Freitas (Waldman) '92 |
| Tech. Dir. (1990-  ) | *Marc O. Baptiste '91 |
| AM Music Dir. | *Brian R. Davis '89 |
| FM Music Dir. | Jeffrey R. Solomon '91, MBA '98; NV - Sports; management |

**50. 1990-1991** (annc'd:    )

| | |
|---|---|
| General Mgr. | I. Neel Chatterjee '91, JD '94; CA - Law; intellectual property, technology |
| General Mgr. (summer '90) | *Eric C. Peterson '91 |
| PD-WFRD | *Eric Wellman '91 |
| PD-WFRD (summer '90) | ?Geoffrey MacDonald '92, JD '95; VA - Law; attorney |
| PD-WFRD (summer '90) | Eric Klein '92, JD '98; CO - Law; attorney |
| PD-WDCR | *Michael J. Gordon Jr. '91 |
| News Dir. | T. "Fin" Repczynski '91, JD '96; VA - Law; attorney |
| Sports Dir. | Daryl Kessler '91, JD '95; NY - Law; attorney |
| Sports Dir. (summer '90) | J. Scott McBride '92, MED '94, JD '02; IL - Law; attorney; intellectual property |
| Business Mgr. | Kim Katzenberger '91, MBA '94; CA - Finance (GE, Fiji Water); CFO |
| Business Mgr. (temporary) | Beth Krakower '93; CA - Publicity; entertainment promotion (Cinemedia) |
| Business Mgr. (summer '90) | *Sarah E. Freitas (Waldman) '92 |
| Tech Dir. (first) | *Marc O. Baptiste '91 |
| Tech Dir. (second) | Amy Ertel '94, MA '99; NJ - Home manager |
| Production Dir. | *Tim Reynolds '91 |
| AM Music Dir. | *Brian R. Davis '89 |
| FM Music Dir. | *Jeffrey R. Solomon '91 |

**51. 1991-1992** (control spring 1991)

| | |
|---|---|
| General Mgr. | *Beth Krakower '93 |
| PD-WFRD | Christopher Frey '92, MS '97; PA - Architecture; historic preservation |
| PD-WF RD (summer '91) | Catherine E. Tucker '93, MS '95, JD '99; NH - Law; insurance fraud |
| PD-WDCR | Tracy A. Tysenn (MacDonald) '92; VA - Home manager |
| News Dir. | Sally A. Huntoon (Vitali) '93, MD '97; MA - Physician; critical care, pediatrics |
| Sports Dir. | Robert Simmelkjaer '93, JD '97; NY - Law; attorney, broadcasting executive, sportscaster (ESPN) |
| Business Mgr. (first?) | Tamara J. "Tammy" Fagell (Sloan) '93, MBA '99; NY - Home manager |
| Business Mgr. (second?) | Sara Fried (Ehrlich) '93, MBA '98; CA - Finance; hedge fund management |
| Tech Dir. | *Amy Ertel '94 |
| Tech Dir. (temporary) | Christine McGavran '94; CA - Software engineering |
| Tech Dir. (temporary) | Jon C. Ruiz '93; MN - Software |
| Promotion Dir. | *Geoff MacDonald '92 |
| AM Music Dir. | John Wolfe '93, BE '94, MS '11; NH - System administrator |
| AM Music Dir. | Andrew H. "Drew" Newman '92 - Consultant |
| FM Music Dir. | *Eric K. Klein '92 |

**52. 1992-1993** (control spring 1992)
| | |
|---|---|
| General Mgr. | *Sally A. Huntoon (Vitali) '93 |
| GM (summer '92) | Barry Cole '93?; NY - Music supervisor (film, soundtracks) |
| PD-WFRD | Andrew D. Kersey '94; CA - Artist manager |
| PD-WDCR | David S. Cohen '94, JD '97; PA - Law; staff attorney |
| News Dir. | Ann R. Koppel '94, JD '97; LA - Law; partner |
| Sports Dir. | *Rob Simmelkjaer '93 |
| Sports Dir. (summer '92) | Leonard C. "Len" Mead '94, MA '96; MA - Television; sports network program director |
| Business Mgr. | |
| Tech Dir. | *Amy Ertel '94 |
| Tech Dir. | Grant Bosse '94; NH - Radio reporter; political analyst (NH) |
| AM Music Dir. | *John Wolfe '93 |
| Public Affairs Dir. | Theodore "Ted" Schuerzinger '94; NY |

**53. 1993-1994** (annc'd:    )
| | |
|---|---|
| General Mgr. | *Amy Ertel '94 |
| GM (summer '93) | Brian K. Sward '95, MS '97, PhD '01; VA - Engineering; physical scientist |
| PD-WFRD | Nathan H. Saunders '94, JD '00; PA - Law; attorney; finance |
| PD-WFRD | *Andrew Kersey '94 |
| PD-WDCR | Charlotte Flower (Streidel) '95; MD - Marketing |
| PD-WDCR (fall '93) | William Bruce Sneddon '95, BS '85,MS '90,PhD '95; PA - Education; assistant professor |
| News Dir. (summer '93) | Adrienne Kim (Clarke) '95, MBA '00; IL - Marketing |
| News Dir. (fall '93, winter '94) | Philip S. Augur '95; CT - Insurance executive |
| Sports Dir. | *Leonard C. "Len" Mead '94 |
| Production Dir. | ?*David S. Cohen '94 |
| Business Mgr. | |
| Tech Dir. | |
| Tech Dir. (summer '93) | *Grant Bosse '94 |
| AM Music Dir. | R. Bradley "Brad" Byrd '95; CA - E-commerce; online marketing |
| Public Affairs Dir. | *Ted Schuerzinger '94 |
| Alumni Relations Dir. | Diem-Trang Do (Bloom) '94; NY |

**54. 1994-1995** (annc'd:    )
| | |
|---|---|
| General Mgr. | *Philip S. Augur '95 |
| GM (summer '94) | John M. Strayer '96, JD '02; DC - Law; attorney, public defender |
| PD-WFRD | Peter M. Jastreboff '96, MBA '05; CT - Information technology; finance |
| PD-WFRD (spring '94) | *Andrew Kersey '94 |
| PD-WDCR (rsg. Jan. '95) | Pammela Quinn (Saunders) '95, JD '00; PA - Education; asst. professor |
| PD-WDCR (Jan. 1995) | Keith A. Miles '96; CA - Sales manager |
| PD-WDCR (1995) | ?David J. Grelotti '96; CT - Research asst. |
| News Dir. | Sabrina Serrantino '95; CA |
| Sports Dir. | Brian A. Clark '95, MBA '11; CO - Business development, broadcasting, sports |
| Sports Dir. (summer '94) | C. Dean Maragos '96 (d. 11/17/99) - Sports production (ESPN); died in auto accident |
| Production Dir. | *Brian K. Sward '95 |
| Finance Dir. | Erik T. Wilson '95; TX - Real estate development, realtor |
| Tech Dir. | Katherine Wrisley (DeSimone) '95, BE '96, ME '97; AZ - Home manager; mechanical engineer |
| Alumni/ae Relations Dir. | Dana L. Brenner (Costello) '95, MS '99; CA - Education; teacher |
| AM Music Dir. | Jennifer L. Sekelsky '95; CT - Market research; imaging industry |
| FM Music Dir. | Steven K. Gord '95, MBA '01; PA - Finance; venture capital |

**55. 1995-1996** (annc'd:    )
| | |
|---|---|
| General Mgr. | April K. Whitescarver '96, JD '08; VA - Law; attorney, labor & employment |
| GM (summer '95) | Henry R. "Hank" Broaddus '97; VA - Dean of admissions (College of William & Mary) |
| PD-WFRD | *Keith A. Miles '96 |

| | |
|---|---|
| PD-WFRD (summer '95) | Jim Donnelly '97; CA |
| PD-WDCR (sum '95, win '96) | Cara Abercrombie '97; VA - Government; Defense Dept., policy analysis |
| PD-WDCR (fall '95) | David Avila '97, JD '01; DC - Law; trial attorney (U.S. Dept. of Justice) |
| PD-WDCR (winter '96) | *Adarsh Carter '97 |
| News Dir. | Vivian J. Lee '97, MBA '05; CA - Marketing; interactive media |
| News Dir. (winter '96) | Cheryl Chua '97; NY - Marketing, licensing |
| Sports Dir. | *C. Dean Maragos '96 |
| Production Dir. | Michael C. Henry '98, MBA '07; CA - Sales (Google) |
| Finance Dir. (fall '95) | Joanna C. Gibson '98, MA '08; NJ - Education; teaching assistant, music |
| Finance Dir. (winter '96) | *Dhruv Prasad '99 |
| Tech. Dir. | Jeremy Longinotti '96, MBA '04; CA - Sales; e-commerce |
| Career-Alumni Dir. (first) | *Peter M. Jastreboff '96 |
| Career-Alumni Dir. | James H. Muiter '98, BE '99, ME '00; MI - Engneering; mechanical, R&D (Ford) |
| Music-Finance Dir. (sum '95) | Dave Stefanowicz '97; GA - Insurance underwriter |
| AM Music Dir. | Jacob J. Waldman '97, JD '04; NY - Law; attorney |
| DEN Dir. | *Sabrina Serrantino '95 |

**56. 1996-1997** (annc'd: Apr. 1996)

| | |
|---|---|
| General Mgr. | *Vivian J. Lee '97 |
| GM (summer '96) | *Michael C. Henry '98 |
| PD-WFRD | *James Muiter '98 |
| PD-WDCR | ?*David Avila '97 |
| PD-WDCR (summer '96) | Adarsh Carter '97, JD '00; NC - Law, IT; attorney, Chief Technology Officer |
| News Dir. | Kathy Healy (Sucich) '97; MA - TV news producer, marketing, writer |
| News Dir. (summer '96) | Ted Huang '98; NY - Web projects, interactive marketing |
| Sports Dir. (rsg Feb '97) | Chris Emond '99, MD '03; PA - Physician; orthopedic surgery |
| Production Dir. | *Michael C. Henry '98 |
| Production Dir. (summer '96) | Jeffrey Wadlow '98; CA - Film director |
| Finance Dir. (first) | Laura Mannix '97, MA '01; MA - Human resources; training |
| Finance Dir. (second) | Dhruv Prasad '99, MBA '07; CT - Finance; radio group management |
| Finance Dir. (summer '96) | Gary Jan '98, MBA '05; CA - Finance; entertainment industry |
| Tech. Dir. | Phillip Cheung '97   MPL '05; CA - Software, product management |
| Tech. Dir (summer '96) | Brent W. Laffoon '98; CA - Writer |
| Tech. Dir.? | *James Muiter '98 |
| Career-Alumni Dir. | Patricia J. Wolfe '98, JD '04; NY - Law; finance |
| Career-Alumni Dir. (sum '96) | Gabriel G. Galletti '98, JD '04; NY - Law; finance, securities litigation |
| AM Music Dir. | *Jacob J. Waldman '97 |

**57. 1997-1998** (eff. Mar. 1997)

| | |
|---|---|
| General Mgr. | *Brent W. Laffoon '98 |
| GM (spring '97) | Chadd L. Kline '99; IL |
| GM (summer '97) | *Dhruv Prasad '99 |
| PD-WFRD | Kendra Kosko '99, JD '06; DC - Law; labor, employment |
| PD-WFRD (winter 1998) | *Michael C. Henry '98 |
| PD-WDCR | Zachary M. Lewis '99, JD '02; CA - Law; attorney, family, commercial |
| PD-WDCR | Dan Indelicato '99, MD '03; FL - Physician; radiation oncologist |
| News Dir. | Jonathan H. Flynn '00, JD '07; DC - Law; attorney; finance, securities |
| Sports Dir. | Josh Freeman '98; MA - Business consulting; healthcare |
| Production Dir. (first) | *Michael C. Henry '98 |
| Production Dir. (second) | Paul Schoenhard '00, JD '03; DC - Law; litigation, intellectual property |
| Finance Dir. | *Gary Jan '98 |
| Tech. Dir. | Sean N. Byrnes '00, ME '01; CA - Information technology, CTO |
| Career-Alumni Dir. | Robert Ristagno '00, MBA '05; MA - Marketing, strategic planning |
| Marketing-Research Dir. | Laura Guogas '98, PhD '04; NC - Biotechnology; research & development |
| AM Music Dir. | Vincent T. Cannon '99, MA '01, JD '07; CA - Law; corporate attorney |
| FM Music Dir. | *Chadd Kline '99 |
| Advertising Dir. | *Michael C. Henry '98 |

**58. 1998-1999** (annc'd: Feb. 26, 1998; control spring 1998)

| | |
|---|---|
| General Mgr. | *Jonathan Flynn '00 |
| GM (spring '98) | *Brent W. Laffoon '98 |
| PD-WFRD | Ryan Krauch '01; CA - Finance; investment management |
| PD-WFRD (summer '98) | Ryan Jones '00, MBA '07; MA - Internet marketing, entrepreneur |
| PD-WDCR | William Finnegan '00, MES '03; VT - Marketing; environmentalism; filmmaker |
| PD-WDCR (spring '98) | Brian Sleet '00, JD '05; IL - Law; attorney, family law |
| News Dir. | Timothy Wright '01; NY - Finance; investment management |
| News Dir. (summer '98) | Lisa H. Kahn '00, MED '04; DC - Education; administration (Johns Hopkins) |
| Sports Dir. | Casey Sixkiller '00; DC - Lobbyist; tribal law |
| Production Dir. | *Paul Schoenhard '00 |
| Business Mgr. | *Robert Ristagno '00 |
| Tech. Dir. | *Sean N. Byrnes '00 |
| Training Dir. | Mark Mullinix '00, MBA '06; *HK* - Marketing |
| Marketing & Alumni Relations | *Ryan Jones '00 |
| Marketing & Alumni Rel. (sum '98) | Jaime Dodge (Byrnes) '00, MA '04, JD '04; MA - Law; attorney |
| AM Music Dir. | Adam J. Greenwald '01; NY - Digital marketing |

**59. 1999-2000** (annc'd:    )

| | |
|---|---|
| General Mgr. | *Sean N. Byrnes '00 |
| General Mgr. (summer '99) | Abigail B. "Abbey" Nova '01, MA '10; NY - Publishing, public relations |
| PD-WFRD (spring '99) | *Ryan Krauch '01 |
| PD-WFRD (summer '99) | Kevin J. Stanhope '01; ME - Information services; systems business analyst |
| PD-WFRD (fall '99, win '00) | Dan S. King '02; DC - Education, high school teacher |
| PD-WDCR | *Abigail Nova '01 |
| PD-WDCR (summer '99) | Michelle Chui '01, JD '06; NY - Law; associate |
| News Dir. | Todd Piro '00, JD '03; CA - TV reporter |
| News Dir. (summer '99) | Marni Zelnick '01; NY - Filmmaker, writer, graduate student |
| Sports Dir. | Andrew Perlstein '00, MS '05; CA - Graduate student (China studies) |
| Sports Dir. (summer '99) | David Sherzer '02; TX - White House staff; spokesman for former Pres. George W. Bush |
| Production Dir. | David O. Lopez '02; NY - Marketing; financial services industry |
| Production Dir. (summer '99) | Michael Ringenburg '99, MS '01; WA - Software engineer |
| Finance Dir. | *Robert Ristagno '00 |
| Finance Dir. (summer '99) | Matthew Curro '01, JD '06; NY - Law; associate; corporate, finance |
| Tech. Dir. | Seth Hitchings '00; VA - Software engineer; executive |
| Tech. Dir. (summer '99) | Steve Magoun '00; MA - Software engineer |
| Training Dir. (sum, fall '99) | Sarah Honorowski (Mohr) '01, MA '03; MA - Home manager, teacher |
| AM Music Dir. | Suzanne Wrubel '01, JD '06; CA - Law; criminal |
| Marketing/ Alumni Rel. | *Lisa Kahn '00 |
| Marketing/Devel. (sum '99) | Catherine Curran (Kelly) '01; *HK* - Home manager |
| Comptroller | *Travis Escobedo '03 |

**60. 2000-2001** (control: spring '00)

| | |
|---|---|
| General Mgr. | *Dan S. King '02 |
| PD-WFRD | Justin "JT" Mohr '03, PhD '09; IL - Education, research; chemistry professor |
| PD-WDCR | Desmond Nation '02, MPA '04, MBA '09; MN - Marketing; finance |
| PD-WDCR (eff. Aug '00) | Michael F. O'Donnell '02; MA - Education; administrator, secondary schools |
| News Dir. | *Michelle Chui '01 |
| News Dir. (summer '00) | *Michael F. O'Donnell '02 |
| Sports Dir. | Kevin Allen '02; NY - Television; news producer (New York) |
| Production Dir. | *David O. Lopez '02 |
| Finance Dir. | Travis Escobedo '03; NY - Finance; investment banking |
| Tech. Dir. | Ben DeWitte '02; OR - Information technology; vineyard design |
| Tech. Dir. (fall '00) | *Roderick Beaton '03 |
| Marketing Dir. | Andrew Woodberry '02, MBA '09; CA - Internet services; sales |
| Marketing Dir. (fall '00) | Dan Sanner '02; CA - Finance; private equity fund |
| Training Dir. | Steve Dietz '02; MA - Finance; investment management |
| Training Dir. (fall '00) | *Kevin Stanhope '01 |

| | |
|---|---|
| Webmaster | *Keith Burdette '03 |

**61. 2001-2002** (annc'd:    )

| | |
|---|---|
| General Mgr. (spring '01) | *Dan S. King '02 |
| General Mgr. (eff Aug '01) | *Michael F. O'Donnell '02 |
| PD-WFRD | Kerrin B. Egalka '04, MA '05; NY - Sales; beverage industry, mixologist; |
| PD-WDCR | Eric S. McDonald '04, MBA '12; CT - Radio, program director, finance |
| PD-WDCR (summer '01) | Carl Burnett '03, MLIS '12; OR - Professional skiier; information services |
| News Dir. | Chris Bowen '02, JD '05; VA - Law; attorney, contracts |
| Sports Dir. | *Kevin Allen '02 |
| Production Dir. | *Justin "JT" Mohr '03 |
| Finance Dir. | *Travis Escobedo '03 |
| Tech. Dir. | *Ben DeWitte '02 |
| Tech. Dir. (summer '01) | *Roderick Beaton '03 |
| Webmaster | Adam Salem '03, MBA '07; NY - Information technology, finance |

**62. 2002-2003** (control: March '02)

| | |
|---|---|
| General Mgr. | *Eric S. McDonald '04 |
| PD-WFRD | Sebastian Miller '02; PA - Food production |
| PD-WDCR | Andrew "Drew" Van Ness '05, BE '08, ME '09; NY - Construction; engineer |
| PD-WDCR (summer '02) | Pedro Hernandez '04, JD '07; TX - Law; attorney, investigator |
| News Dir. (fall '02) | *Lynn Lee '05 |
| News Dir. (winter '03) | Alexander Taylor '04, M.Phil '09; NY - Finance; information technology |
| Sports Dir. | Keith Burdette '03, MS '12; CT - TV; producer (ESPN) |
| Production Dir. | *Justin T. Mohr '03 |
| Finance Dir. | Sandeep Ramesh '05, JD '08; NY - Law; corporate |
| Tech. Dir. | Roderick Beaton '03, MES '10; VT - Information technology |
| Marketing Dir. (fall '02) | *Danielle Ricci '05 |
| Marketing Dir. (winter '03) | *Daniel King '02 |
| Training Dir. (fall '02) | Mark D. Root '05; CA - Store manager |
| Co-Training Dir. (winter '03) | Danielle Ricci '05; VT - Marketing |
| Co-Training Dir. (winter '03) | Lynn Lee '05, MD; KS - Physician, pediatrics |
| Webmaster | Kimberly Siciliano (Salem) '03; NY - Computer programmer, photographer |

**63. 2003-2004** (annc'd: 2/21/03)

| | |
|---|---|
| General Mgr. | *Kerrin Egalka '04 |
| General Mgr. (summer '03) | ?*Danielle Ricci '05 |
| PD-WFRD | *Eric McDonald '04 |
| PD-WFRD | ?Mat A. Brown '05; NY - Software engineer (Ruby) |
| PD-WDCR | *Pedro Hernandez '04 |
| News Dir. | Nikhil V. Gore '06, JD '11; SG - Law; attorney |
| News Dir. (fall '03, rsg) | Adil Ahmad '05; IL - Finance; law student |
| Co-News Dir. (fall '03) | Vikash Reddy '05, MS '07; NY - Secondary school teacher; PhD candidate |
| Co-News Dir. (fall '03) | Scott Glabe '06, MS '08, JD '09 - Law; attorney, politics, author (*Dartmouth College: Off the Record*) |
| Sports Dir. (spring '03) | *Keith Burdette '03 |
| Sports Dir. (summer '03) | Tim Katz '05, MBA '11; CA - Marketing |
| Sports Dir. (fall '03, win '04) | *Alexander Taylor '04 |
| Sports Dir. | ?Justin Jack '03, JD '07; WV - Law; business litigation |
| Production Dir. (spring '03, win '04) | Myung-Hee Vabulas '06; MA |
| Production Dir. (sum, fall '03) | Noah Kekane Yuen '05; HI |
| Finance Dir. (rsg spring '03) | *Sandeep Ramesh '05 |
| Finance Dir. (fall '03) | *Keith Burdette '03 |
| Finance Dir. (eff. mid fall '03) | Erin Rumsey '06, MBA '13; IL - Marketing |
| Tech. Dir. | *Lynn Lee '05 |
| Marketing Dir. (rsg) | Jennifer Kosty '06, MD 12; TX - Physician; neurosurgery |
| Marketing Dir. (eff. fall '03) | Lavinia Weizel '04, JD '13; MA - Law; attorney |
| Training Dir. (spring '03) | *Sebastian Miller '02 |
| Training Dir. (eff. fall '03) | *Danielle Ricci '05 |
| Webmaster | Alex Middleton '06, JD '09; IL - Law; associate |

**64. 2004-2005** (annc'd:    )

| | |
|---|---|
| General Mgr. | *Noah Kekane Yuen '05 |
| PD-WFRD (part year) | Deborah E. Wassel '07, JD '10; NY - Law; criminal (Assistant D.A.) |
| PD-WFRD (part year) | *Mat A. Brown '05 |
| PD-WFRD (part year) | *Vikash Reddy '05 |
| PD-WDCR | Pamela Cortland (Brown) '06;  NY - Publishing; marketing |
| News Dir. | ?*Nikhil Gore '06 |
| News Dir. | Echo Brown '06; CA - Writing, editing, teaching |
| Sports Dir. | *Tim Katz '05 |
| Production Dir. | Daniel Moynihan '06; IL - Barista |
| Finance Dir. (spring '04?) | ?*Kerrin Egalka '04 |
| Finance Dir. | *Erin Rumsey |
| Finance Dir. (winter '05) | John Dominguez '05, MBA '12; CA - Marketing; entrepreneur |
| Tech. Dir. | *Lynn Lee '05 |
| Web Dir. | ?*Alex Middleton '06 |

**65. 2005-2006** (control: spring 2005)

| | |
|---|---|
| General Mgr. | *Nikhil V. Gore '06 |
| PD-WFRD | *Deborah E. Wassel '07 |
| PD-WDCR | *Pamela Cortland (Brown) '06 |
| News Dir. | *Echo Brown '06 |
| News Dir. (spring '05) | John "Tepp" Tepperman '08; VA - Middle East analyst |
| Sports Dir. (spring '05) | John Schriffen '06; DC - Television reporter (ABC) |
| Sports Dir. (fall '05) | Gino Beniamino '04, Ed.M '09; MA - Education; instructional technology (Harvard) |
| Sports Dir. (winter '06) | Alphonse D. Ramsey II '06; NY - Community services; administration |
| Production Dir. | *Daniel Moynihan '06 |
| Finance Dir. | John Milliken '07; NY - Finance |
| Finance Dir. (spring '05) | *John Dominguez '05 |
| Tech. Dir. | *Alex Middleton '06 |
| Marketing Dir. | Sonia Simmons '06;  GA - E-commerce; internet services |

**66. 2006-2007** (annc'd:    )

| | |
|---|---|
| General Mgr. (spring, sum '06) | Susannah R. Thompson '08; MA - Public relations, communications |
| General Mgr. (fall '06, win '07) | *Deborah Wassel '07 |
| PD-WFRD (spring '06, win '07) | Jacob L. "Jake" Schindel '09; NY - Publishing; editor |
| PD-WFRD (summer '06) | *Deborah Wassel '07 |
| PD-WFRD (fall '06) | Pavel A. Sotskov '09, BE '11; NH - Systems consultant; professional skiier |
| PD-WDCR (spring, sum '06) | Julio Gil '08; NY - Finance; investment analyst |
| PD-WDCR (fall '06) | John Ternovski '09; DC - Data analyst, econometrics |
| PD-WDCR (winter '07) | (vacant) |
| News Dir. | Chris Symeonides '07; OR - Law student |
| Sports Dir. | Dylan Higgins '09; AZ - Public relations; sports (baseball) |
| Production Dir. | Frederick "Trey" Roy '09, ME '11; VT - Product engineering |
| Finance Dir. (spring, sum '06) | *Nikhil V. Gore '06 |
| Finance Dir. (fall '06, win '07) | Karli Beitel (Erickson) '10; MT |
| Tech. Dir. (spring '06, win '07) | Ryan Wilson '09; AK - Health care; medical student |
| Co-Tech Dir. (fall '06) | Frederick C. "Rick" Tucker '09, BE '10; VA - Software |
| Co-Tech Dir. (fall '06) | Fruzsina Molnar '10 ; NY - Writer, editor |
| Marketing Dir. (spring, fall '06) | Carmen Kilpatrick '09; GA - Photography; retail sales |
| Marketing Dir. (sum '06, win '07) | RuDee Sade Lipscomb '08; CA - Actress, singer, producer |
| Recruitment Dir. (fall '06) | *RuDee Sade Lipscomb '08 |
| Recruitment Dir. (winter '07) | Christina Tjahjana '10; SG - Finance; investment analyst |
| Training Dir. (spring '06) | *Alex Middleton '06 |
| Music Dir. (fall '06) | *Chris Symeonides '07 |

**67. 2007-2008** (control: spring 2007)

| | |
|---|---|
| General Mgr. | *Susannah R. Thompson '08 |
| PD-WFRD | *Pavel A. Sotskov '09 |
| PD-WDCR | Robert Demick '10 |

| | |
|---|---|
| Sports & News Dir. | Schuyler S. "Sketch" Evans '10; CA - Television; literary manager |
| Production Dir. | Jannah "Tiger" Rahman '09; OH - Education; community service |
| Marketing Dir. (spring '07) | *RuDee Sade Lipscomb '08 |
| Marketing Dir. (fall '07) | *Christina Tjahjana '10 |
| Marketing Dir. (winter '08) | Andrew Sloan '09; IL - Video producer/editor |
| FM Promotions Dir. | ?*Jacob L. Schindel '09 |
| Recruitment Dir. | *Christina Tjahjana '10 |
| Recruitment Dir. (winter '08) | Olivia C. Snyder-Spak '10; CT- Television producer |
| Finance Dir. | *Karli Beitel '10 |
| Tech. Dir. | *Frederick C. "Rick" Tucker '09 |
| Tech. Dir. | *Ryan Wilson '09 |
| Training Dir. | Ji W. Yang '08; CA |
| Training Dir. | Sean A. Warnecke '10; CO |

**68. 2008-2009** (annc'd:    )

| | |
|---|---|
| General Mgr. | *Pavel A. Sotskov '09 |
| PD-WFRD | *Robert Demick '10 |
| PD-WFRD (spring, fall '08) | *Schuyler S. "Sketch" Evans '10 |
| PD-WDCR | Zach Mason '10; FL |
| News Dir./Production Dir. | *Schuyler S. "Sketch" Evans '10 |
| Sports Dir. | Jeremy A. Seidling '09; MO - Medical technology; neuroscience, IT |
| Finance Dir. | *Karli Beitel '10 |
| Tech. Dir. | *Ryan Wilson '09 |
| Marketing Dir. | *Andy Sloan '09 |
| Recruitment Dir. | *Olivia C. Snyder-Spak '10 |
| Training Dir. | ?Steven Elliott '11; NY - Marketing |

**69. 2009-2010** (annc'd:    )

| | |
|---|---|
| General Mgr. | *Schuyler S. "Sketch" Evans '10 |
| PD-WFRD (spring, sum '09) | David Kastner '12 |
| PD-WFRD (fall '09, win '10) | David Lumbert '12; DC - Healthcare; analyst |
| PD-WebDCR | Shirine Sajjadi '11; CA - Internet; analyst (Facebook) |
| News Dir. | Madison Rezaei '12; MA - Management consulting; analyst |
| Interim News Dir. (sum 09) | Ahra Cho '11; TX - Education; public school |
| Sports Dir. (spring '09) | Orli Kleiner '12; NY - Marketing; blogger |
| Sports Dir. (spring '09) | Beau Trudel '10; CA - Advertising; brand strategy |
| Sports Dir. | David Jiang '12; NH - Education; college administration |
| Production Dir. | Matthew Knight '11, BE '12; NY - Engineer; electronics |
| Finance Dir. | *Karli Beitel '10 |
| Tech. Dir. | Charles "Tony" Quincy '11; NY - Information technology; software, mobile |
| Marketing Dir. | Pierre T. Guo '12 ; VA - Financial services |
| Interim Marketing Dir. (sum '09) | Cindy Juarez '12; FL |
| Recruitment Dir. | Julia Cheng '10; MS |
| Training Dir. | Shinian Ye '10; NY - Finance; analyst |
| Internet Dir. | Ricky Melgares '11; TX - Internet security |
| Social Dir. | Philip L. Aubart '10; MN - Law; graduate student (Duke) |
| Interim Soc. Dir. (sum '09) | Jenny Juarez '12; FL |

**70. 2010-2011** (annc'd Jan. 22, control Feb. 5, 2010)

| | |
|---|---|
| General Mgr. (spring '10) | *Madison Rezaei '12 |
| General Mgr. (summer '10) | *Shirine Sajjadi '11 |
| General Mgr. (fall '10) | *Charles "Tony" Quincy '11 |
| Asst. GM (spring, fall '10) | *Shirine Sajjadi '11 |
| PD-WFRD | *David Lumbert '12 |
| Interim PD-WFRD (spring '10) | Jeff Ledolter '13; IA |
| PD-WFRD (fall '10) | *Shirine Sajjadi '11 |
| PD-WebDCR | *Pierre T. Guo '12 |
| PD-WebDCR (fall '10) | *Hannah Iaccarino '12 |
| News Dir. | Catherine Treyz '13; VA |
| Sports Dir. | *David Jiang '12 |

| | |
|---|---|
| Sports Dir. (fall '10) | *Christopher Zhao '13 |
| Production Dir. | Andrew Kim '12; CA |
| Finance Dir. | Mayuki Shimizu '12; NY - Management consulting |
| Tech. Dir. | *Charles "Tony" Quincy '11 |
| Tech. Dir. (fall 10) | *Ricky Melgares '11 |
| Marketing Dir. | *Ahra Cho '11 |
| Marketing-Brand Mgmnt (fall '10) | *Christopher Ryan Zehner '12 |
| Legal Dir. | Christopher Bachand Parente '11; NY - Law student |
| Recruitment Dir. | Richard Sunderland '11; NY - Management consulting |
| Training Dir. | |
| Social Dir. | *Richard Sunderland '11 |
| Social Dir. (spring '10) | *Ahra Cho '11 |
| Internet Dir. | *Ricky Melgares '11 |
| Promotions Dir. | Rosina Mummolo '12; MA |
| Music Dir.-FM | *Shirine Sajjadi '11 |

**71. 2011-2012** (annc'd: winter 2011)

| | |
|---|---|
| General Mgr. | Christopher Ryan Zehner '12; MA |
| Acting GM (summer '11) | *Christopher Zhao '13 |
| Asst. GM | *David Lumbert '12 |
| PD-WFRD | Christopher Zhao '13; NY |
| PD-WebDCR (spring, sum '11) | Hannah Iaccarino '12; MA |
| PD-WebDCR (fall '11) | Gregg Fox '13; MO |
| News Dir. | *Catherine Treyz '13 |
| News Dir. (fall '11) | Elizabeth Faiella '12; NH |
| Sports Dir. | Gilbert "Gil" Whalen '14 |
| Tech. Dir. | |
| Marketing Dir. | Huan He '13; IN |
| Legal Director | Ryan Tincher '12; MA - Management consulting; analyst |
| Music Dir-FM | *Shirine Sajjadi '11 |

**72. 2012-2013** (annc'd: spring 2012)

| | |
|---|---|
| General Mgr. | *Christopher Zhao '13 |
| Acting GM (summer '12) | Shane O'Neal '14 |
| Asst. GM | *Huan He '13 |
| PD-WFRD | Whelan Boyd '13; NH |
| PD-WFRD (summer, fall '12) | Geanette Foster '14 |
| PD-WebDCR | *Gregg Fox '13 |
| PD-WebDCR (summer '12) | Cooper Thomas '14 |
| News Dir. | Lawrence Anfo Whyte '13; *GB* |
| Sports Dir. | *Shane O'Neal '14 |
| Sports Dir. (summer '12) | Charlie Hetke '14 |
| Sports Dir. (fall '12) | Matthew Diephuis '14 |
| Finance Dir. | Kathryn MacNaughton '15 |
| Finance Dir. (summer '12) | Ruosi Zhou '14 |
| Tech./Web Master | Michael Urbach '14 |
| Marketing Dir. | *Gilbert "Gil" Whalen '14 |
| Legal Dir. | Michael Riordan '15 |
| Social Media Dir. (sum, fall '12) | Renee Lai '14 |

**73. 2013-2014** (annc'd March 2013)

| | |
|---|---|
| General Mgr. | *Shane O'Neal '14 |
| Acting GM (summer '13) | *Kathryn MacNaughton '15 |
| Asst. GM | *Gilbert "Gil" Whalen '14 |
| PD-WFRD | *Geanette Foster '14 |
| PD-WFRD (summer '13) | Sam Farid '15 |
| PD-WebDCR | *Cooper Thomas '14 |
| PD-WebDCR (summer '13) | Nick Pavlis '15 |
| News Dir. | Nick Zehner '15 |
| Sports Dir. | Blaine Steinberg '15 |

| | |
|---|---|
| Finance Dir. | Eric Siu '16 |
| Finance Dir. (summer '13) | Janice Tam '15 |
| Marketing Dir. | *Kathryn MacNaughton '15 |
| Marketing Dir. (summer '13) | Isabella Ford '15 |
| Tech. Dir. | |
| Social Media Dir. | *Renee Lai '14 |
| Web Dir. | Rennie Song '15 |
| Asst. PD-WFRD | Nick Duva '16 |
| Asst. PD-WFRD (summer '13) | Eileen Chen '15 |
| Asst. PD-WebDCR | Thomas Steventon '16 |
| Music Dir.-WFRD | Dan Shanker '16 |
| Training Dir.-WFRD | Alex Wasdahl '16 |
| Street Team Dir. | *Eileen Chen '15 |

# Appendix 2: Technical and Facility Timeline

1941: DBS begins broadcasting via telephone lines from two studios in Robinson Hall to 16 independent 0.8 watt "Deluxe Mystery Transmitters," located in dormitories. The tiny transmitters don't reach far, use different frequencies, and interfere with each other.

1942: The mini-transmitters are replaced with a surplus Army Signal Corps transmitter located in the basement of Middle Fayerweather dormitory, tuned to 640 kc, and patched into the College power lines. These then radiated the signal into dorm rooms. (Two smaller "booster" units are installed in Dick's House infirmary and the president's home.)

1947: The malfunctioning Army Signal Corps transmitter is replaced by a new homemade unit. Little improvement.

1949: First tape recorder placed in use (a Brush Soundmirror).

1949: New 20 watt transmitter built by Blanchard Pratt '47.

1950: First professional studio tape recorder acquired (an Ampex 400).

1951: New disc jockey studio 3X built, with homemade control board.

1957: Studios one (news) and two (production) and Master Control rebuilt, Gatesway control board (the station's first professional board) is installed.

1958: WDCR-AM goes on the air using RCA BTA 250w transmitter. Broadcasts from a tower erected at Chase athletic field.

1960: New Gates master control board installed.

1961: WDCR upgrades to 1000 w/daytime, 250 w/night, with a Gates BC-1T transmitter. The RCA transmitter is traded in.

1962: First remote unit (Marti 15w FM unit)

1966: WDCR named a regional Emergency Broadcast Station. "Bomb shelter" studio installed under Hopkins Center.

1966: First cartridge machines installed (Spotmaster), replacing reel-to-reel tape decks for commercials.

1967: Major studio reconstruction.

1969: WDCR acquires its first auto mobile unit, a Ford station wagon.

1975: FM master control and interview studio built.

1976: WFRD goes on the air with a Rockwell-Collins 831D2, partial solid-state transmitter. It broadcasts from a shared tower atop Craft's Hill in Lebanon.

1976: WDCR acquires a Gates BC-1F transmitter (built in 1949) as backup.

1982: WDCR acquires a Nautel Ampfet-1 solid state transmitter (serial #101) as primary transmitter. The Gates 1-T becomes backup, Gates 1-F is sidelined.

1982-84: AM and FM studios rebuilt.

1987: First CD player installed (a consumer unit).

1995-96: Major reconstruction of Robinson Hall; studios rebuilt. New studio equipment includes three Auditronics control boards.

2000: WDCR begins limited Internet streaming on campus using Quicktime. WFRD follows in 2005, and both go worldwide in 2006.

2004 (Nov.): Simian broadcast automation system installed, allowing voice tracking.

2006 (Nov.): WFRD switches to Nautel 6.0 kw transmitter, 1976 Collins becomes backup.

2008 (August): WDCR goes silent, except for brief period in August/September 2009. Programming continues to be streamed on the Internet as WebDCR.

2011: WDCR tower taken down. Nautel buys back historic Ampfet-1. Gates 1-T and 1-F transmitters are sold to collectors.

2013: Studios space rebuilt, upgraded, consolidated.

# Appendix 3: Alumni Testimonials

William Mitchel '42 (public relations) - DBS was a "major influence in selecting a career in public relations."

Stephen Flynn '44 (TV sales administration, NBC) - Said that Dartmouth radio led to his becoming "one of a small group that put together the NBC TV network."

Dick Hollands '50 (TV executive with NBC, NAB) - "Organizational experience at WDBS was helpful to me."

Bill Brooks '51 (marketing executive) - "Someone I respected a lot counseled me that 'Radio is a dying business. Get into something practical.' How wrong he was!"

Dave Dugan '52 (CBS news, professor) - "To all of you who were on the WDBS staff: I have never worked with a more talented or professional group of creative people. WDBS was my most satisfying and productive classroom. And we didn't have to pay for the education. I owe my career to Dartmouth Broadcasting."

Jim Rosenfield '52 (President, CBS-TV network) - He came to Dartmouth as pre-med to please his father, but WDBS introduced him to broadcasting, which became his obsession. Says WDBS was "certainly important" to him.

Richard Swicker '52 (TV producer, director, NBC) - "During freshman week I became involved in broadcasting, at WDBS--a career that lasted 40 years!"

John Kramer '56 (professor) - "The highlight of my Dartmouth career (aside from meeting my future wife) was broadcasting."

Robinson Brown '59 (radio promotion, general manager) - A self-described "WDCR radio nut," he reports that his "experience at a radio station as 'muscular' as WDBS and WDCR was *very impressive* to an important bunch of heavy hitters I sent my resume to. I got hired on sight in my first meeting with the general manager of (Midwest powerhouse) WCCO radio." Dartmouth broadcasting was "incredibly valuable - a wonderful experience."

Ron Kehoe '59 (Massachusetts Assistant Attorney General) - WDCR taught him a lot about speaking and elocution, got him his first job (in Boston radio), and was helpful in finding his career path too.

Robert Hager '60 (NBC news correspondent) - Says WDCR led to his news career.

Henry Goldsmith '62 (business) - He gained excellent experience as a manager.

David Shipler '64 (*New York Times* reporter, Pulitzer Prize winning author) - Says Dartmouth Broadcasting was a "vital experience," where he learned to manage people. Led to journalism school and thence to his career.

Allan Boyce '65 (railroad executive) - "I remember thinking, while at Dartmouth, that I could fill a very satisfying four years just working at WDCR and going on overnight DOC hikes. My best memories revolve around both."

Paul F. Klee '66 (filmmaker), "Working at the station was, for me, *the* outstanding activity of mine while at Dartmouth... [it] in no small way influenced my career as a documentary filmmaker."

Randy Odeneal '68 (radio station group owner) - "Dartmouth Broadcasting was a great proving ground."

Robert Reich '68 (U.S. Secretary of Labor, professor) - "I was enormously impressed with the talent and professionalism of the other undergraduates at the radio station, who not only took their jobs and responsibilities seriously but carried them out with enormous enthusiasm."

Arthur Fergenson '69 (attorney) - Says he learned presentation skills, effective advocacy at Dartmouth radio.

Wally Ford '70 (government, law) - Learned public speaking, how to convey a message. "And it was fun!"

Bill Moyes '70 (station owner) - "Radio's been very good to us Dartmouth guys!"

Stephen Zrike '71 (marketing at Colgate-Palmolive, elsewhere) - Dartmouth radio was "incredibly impactful" on his life, it was where he saw the power of radio news, learned to write, communicate.

Fred Frawley '73 (attorney) - Dartmouth radio "helped me get my first job" (at the FCC), was "the best year of my life." Helped him develop presence as a lawyer.

Charlie Smith '73 (sales and software executive, Microsoft) - "WDCR did more for me than my Dartmouth education." It got him his first jobs.

Scott McQueen '74 (multiple station owner) - Says Dartmouth radio got him started in the business.

Chris Davidson '76 (CBS program executive) - Where he learned how to lead a large organization, how to be diplomatic in difficult situations.

Kathy DeGioia-Eastwood '76 (professor) - Says it was good experience in making it in a man's world, helped her gain confidence, assertiveness.

Pam Gile '76 (health care) - Gave her experience working as a woman in a man's world.

Jeffrey Sudikoff '77 (financier, philanthropist) - A "great experience," led to his first job and later his career. "It had a direct impact on my career."

James Washington '77 (government official) - Dartmouth Broadcasting "broadened my horizons," "made Dartmouth a richer experience." He learned about public speaking, dealing with the administration, the importance of media in the community.

Rick Beyer '78 (writer/documentarian) - It was "of tremendous value to me," a seminal experience, started him on his career.

Walt Callender '78 (runs tech firm) - Calls it a great introduction to entrepreneurship, a valuable experience.

Jason Klein '82 (finance, president of a newspaper association) - Station heightened his interest in media, led him to stay in the field.

Bob Gray '83 (business) - "One of the best experiences of my life," "my fraternity" (better than the one he was actually in). Where he learned to be a "people person."

Jeff Shapiro '83 (station owner) - Led directly to buying his first station a couple of years after graduation (which he turned into Q106), and then a major career in group station ownership.

Dan Daniels '84 (attorney) - "Nothing I enjoyed more at Dartmouth," an "immensely positive experience," where he learned leadership, confidence.

Kate Mulligan '85 (school administration) - Calls it a great experience. Her first administrative experience (she was the first female General Manager), where she got a very diverse group - alternative rockers, classical fans, techies - to work together.

Jennifer Avellino '89 (newsperson) - Says it helped her get her first job.

Mark Wachen '89 (E-commerce, CEO) - Dartmouth Broadcasting had a "huge impact" on him. Invaluable management training, helped him get his first job.

Priscilla Huff '91 (news producer) - Although only one of her Dartmouth activities, it gave her valuable experience, "fearlessness" (in dealing with a male world), how to edit, meet deadlines.

Phil Augur '95 (insurance executive) - "I learned as much in Robinson Hall as in any of the academic buildings."

Dean Maragos '96 (sports production) - 99Rock sportscaster whose work at the station led to a dream job at ESPN, cut short by his untimely death.

April Whitescarver '96 (attorney) - "I found my home on campus" (at Dartmouth radio). Calls it a most positive experience, the best preparation for her military and business careers. Taught her how to lead.

Mike Henry '98 (sales, Google) - "Learned a ton from Dartmouth radio," learned negotiating skills. Got him his first job selling radio in San Francisco.

Brent Laffoon '98 (writer, physical trainer) - Had a great time, and Dartmouth Broadcasting was a "huge advantage" in getting his first job, in San Francisco radio.

Todd Piro '00 (attorney, local newscaster) - 'Learned to talk, learned about politics." His experience at the station was a great help in his career.

Deborah Wassel '07 (attorney, criminal law) - Was Dartmouth Broadcasting valuable? "Absolutely!" It provided invaluable experience in public speaking, management, negotiating, networking, managing expectations.

Pavel Sotskov '09 (professional skiier, sports commentator) - Where he learned how to run a real-world business, practice radio presentation. "No other student club like it.

# Notes

## Introduction

[1] Richard Krolik, founder of Dartmouth radio, speaking at the WDCR Banquet in March 1961.

[2] David Marston '74 introduced me to two useful books which bear on the subject. *The College Radio Handbook* by Billy G. Brant (Tab Books, 1981) is a somewhat generic primer for students on how to run a station, but it also contains a useful first chapter on the history of the medium. *The Gas Pipe Networks: A History of College Radio 1936-1946,* by Louis M. Bloch, Jr. (Cleveland: Bloch and Company, 1980) is a colorful reminiscence of the founding of early campus stations, especially Brown University's (1936), and of the Intercollegiate Broadcasting System.

[3] Carl Nolte, "A Forgotten Genius on Your Radio Dial," *San Francisco Chronicle*, April 5, 2009. **http://en.wikipedia.org/wiki/History_of_radio**, **http://en.wikipedia.org/wiki/Oldest_radio_station** .

[4] Brant, 12-13. Thomas H. White, "U.S. Special Land Stations, 1913-1921 Recap," October 7, 2000, at **http://earlyradiohistory.us/speclnd2.htm**. Jacob Larocca, "WRUC and the U: WRUC's Early Years," *Concordiensis*, October 6, 2011.

[5] D.J. Russell '35, letter to Dartmouth Broadcasting System, March 13, 1949 (in Rauner Archives).

[6] Brant, 12-17. S.E. Frost, Jr., *Education's Own Stations*, University of Chicago Press, 1937, 4 (reprinted in the series *History of Broadcasting: Radio to Television*, New York: Arno Press, 1971).

[7] Prior to 1960 the terms "megacyles" and "kilocycles" were used. These were replaced by megahertz (MHz) and kilohertz (KHz) in the 1960s.

[8] Brant, 18. *Broadcasting Yearbook*, 1950.

[9] Bloch, *The Gas Pipe Networks*. **http://en.wikipedia.org/wiki/LPFM** (and sources cited there).

[10] Delegates to the first IBS convention in 1940 were from Brown, Columbia, Cornell, Dartmouth, Harvard, M.I.T., Pembroke, Rhode Island State, University of Connecticut, University of New Hampshire, Wesleyan and Williams. See Bloch, 26-27.

[11] Alan G. Stavisky, Robert K. Avery, and Helena Vanhala. "From Class D to LPFM: The High-Powered Politics of Low-Power Radio." *Journalism & Mass Communication Quarterly* 78 (2001): 340–54.

[12] Martha Mitchell, "WBRU," *Encyclopedia Brunoniana*. Brown Broadcasting Service, Inc., 2011 IRS form 990.

[13] "The Original FM: The Columbia University Radio Club," at **www.studentaffairs.columbia.edu/wkcr/history**.

[14] Rebecca Harris, "Cornell Questions Status of WVBR on Campus," *The Cornell Daily Sun*, November 2, 2011. Cornell Radio Guild, Inc., 2010 IRS form 990. Correspondence with Bob Smith, former WVBR staffer, March 2012.

[15] "The Boston Radio Dial: WHRB(FM)," at **http://www.bostonradio.org/stations/26341**. Harvard Radio Broadcasting Co., Inc., 2010 IRS form 990.

[16] Dana Crum, "In Focus: WPRB Radio Station," at **www.princeton.edu/main/news/archive**. Princeton Broadcasting Service, Inc., 2010 IRS form 990.

[17] "WXPN-FM," University of Pennsylvania Records Center, at **www.archives.upenn.edu**. **www.xpn.org**. "WXPN," **www.wikipedia.org**.

[18] Interview with Sean Owczarek, Yale '11, former GM; Melissa DePetris, "Broadcasting the Rhythm of the City with WYBC," *Yale Herald*, Summer 1998. Meghan Glass, "Guide to the WYBC, Yale University, Records," Yale University Library, Manuscripts and Archives, July 2003. Yale Broadcasting Co., Inc., 2010 IRS form 990.

[19] **http://www.radio-locator.com/** (accessed September 8, 2012).

[20] According to the show's executive producer, Eric Conte, the name originated as a joke. Most of the Woodie awards recognize new cutting-edge artists, who instead of having gone gold or platinum in the commercial market "have gone wood." See Julie Tran, "Innovative Artists Honored at mtvU Woodie Awards," *Spartan Daily* (San Jose State University), March 4, 2012.

[21] *The Princeton Review's* questionnaire does not determine which station respondents are referring to in cases where there is more than one station on campus, so in the case of Emerson and Ithaca the award may be shared by those institutions' Internet-only student stations as well (WECB and Vic Radio, respectively). See **http://www.princetonreview.com/college-rankings.aspx**.

[22] There are several other college radio awards, among them the College Media Association "Pinnacle Award" for radio station of the year; the Broadcast Education Association "Signature Station" award; and the "Spirit of College Radio" award from College Radio Day. The last-named recognizes exceptional effort on behalf of College Radio Day. (Interview with Rob Quicke, October 2012.)

[23] Daniel de Vise, "College Radio Day: An S.O.S. for Student-Run Stations," *The Washington Post*, October 11, 2011; David Hinckley, "National College Radio Day Celebrates On-Air Talents, Undiscovered Artists and Up-and-Coming Deejays," (New York) *Daily News*, October 11, 2011; Kyle Spencer, "College Radio Heads: Off the Dial," *The New York Times*, November 4, 2011.

[24] "Vanderbilt Student Radio Station Sold, Pulled Off Air Hours Later," Student Press Law Center, June 8, 2011. At **http://www.splc.org/news/newsflash.asp?id=2234**. Jon Vorwald, "Waning Support for College Radio Sets Off a Debate, *The New York Times*, December 5, 2010. Jennifer Waits, "FCC Approves Sale of KTRU to University of Houston," *Radio Survivor*, April 15, 2011. Don Troop, "What's Eating College Radio?", *The Chronicle of Higher Education*, June 19, 2011. Jennifer Waits, "The Story Behind the KUSF Shut Down," *Pop Matters*, March 14, 2011. "KUSF Has Been Sold—Volunteers Seek Answers," on **www.youtube.com** (accessed September 18, 2012).

[25] According to Wikipedia the station was shut down abruptly and its assets sold by the administration of Dr. Peter Diamandopoulos, "due to a clash of philosophies between the university president and the student-run radio station." In 1997 Diamandopoulos and most of the University's trustees were removed by the state board of regents for financial mismanagement and allegedly lining their own pockets. The scandal led to a flurry of lawsuits that was resolved with restitution but no one admitting guilt. See David Halbfinger, "Lawsuits Over Ouster of Adelphi Chief Are Settled," *New York Times*, November 18, 1998.

[26] Spencer, "College Radio Heads: Off the Dial."

[27] Radio Business Report, August 12, 2010, "iPod, Online, Satellite Not Impacting Local Radio Listening," at **http://www.rbr.com/media-news/research/26668.html**. Kantar Media, U.S. Advertising Expenditure Report, September 13, 2010. At **http://www.kantarmediana.com/intelligence/press/kantar-media-reports-us-advertising-expenditures-increased-57-first-half-2010**.

[28] "The Video Consumer Mapping Study: Final Report," Council for Research Excellence, 2009, 32, 48. The study was conducted in 2008 among adults 18+ with a $3.5 million grant from The Nielsen Company. "Other audio" calculated as the difference between broadcast radio and "all audio" (90%). Details are at **http://www.researchexcellence.com/research/research.php**.

[29] Spencer, "College Radio Heads: Off the Dial."

[30] de Vise, "College Radio Day."

[31] As of this writing the top streaming college station in Shoutcast's ranking is KCRW, an NPR affiliate owned by Santa Monica College and run by professionals. However the top 10 college stations list also includes the student-run stations at Columbia, Princeton, the University of New Hampshire, Montana State, and the State University of New York campuses at Albany and Stony Brook. In August 2012 these ranged from 5,000 to 78,000

streaming listeners per month. **www.shoutcast.com**, accessed September 22, 2012. The top online station overall was IDOBI, an Internet-only punk rock station established in 1999 in Washington, D.C., which has promoted itself heavily through music industry tie-ins. It averages eight million listeners per month.

[32] Correspondence with Fritz Kass, IBS CEO, July 2012. Mr. Kass declined to be interviewed for this book, saying that IBS only deals with its member stations.

[33] Interview with Quicke, October 2012; de Vise, "College Radio Day"; Mary Beth Marklein, "College Radio Stations Fear Budget Cuts Could Silence Them," *USA Today*, October 11, 2011; Hinckley, "National College Radio Day"; Spencer, "College Radio Heads." Entry for Rob Quicke on **www.linkedin.com**. 585 student stations worldwide participated in College Radio Day 2012, and a 2013 event was in the works.

[34] "In the Beginning," at **www.collegeradioday.com** (accessed July 25, 2012).

[35] Dartmouth, founded in 1769, is one of nine Colonial colleges founded before the American Revolution.

[36] Confidential interview with a former general manager, September 2010.

[37] The Dartmouth Plan instituted a regular summer term and required that juniors and seniors spend at least one rotating term off campus, so that the entire student body would not be on campus at one time. This allowed the larger student body resulting from co-education to be accommodated in existing facilities.

[38] The Cornell station is owned by a student-run non profit corporation; Yale's by a non-profit overseen by students but with involvement by alumni and community representatives. Those of Columbia and Penn are, like Dartmouth's, owned by their universities.

**Chapter 1: 1920s**

[1] S.E. Frost, Jr., *Education's Own Stations*, University of Chicago Press, 1937, 81-82. (Reprinted as part of the *History of Broadcasting: Radio to Television* series, Arno Press, 1971.) *The Dartmouth*, March 24, 1917, 1, 4; *Dartmouth Alumni Magazine*, June 1923, 669 ("Dartmouth radio station to have 1300 meter range").

[2] *The Dartmouth,* October 14, 1924, 3.

[3] Letter from President Hopkins to Professor Hull, October 9, 1924.

[4] From the original license of operation granted to Dartmouth College by the Department of Commerce, October 18, 1924. The renewals of February 10, 1925, and September 23, 1925, had identical provisions except that the last one substituted "WDCH" for "WFBK."

[5] *The Dartmouth,* December 13, 1924, 4.

[6] *ibid.*

[7] *ibid.,* February 9, 1925, 4. According to alumni records Robert C. Saunders was actually class of 1925.

[8] Letter from D.J. Russell '35, *Dartmouth Alumni Magazine,* June 1942, 5.

[9] Manuscript by Dr. Hull, submitted on June 29, 1933 to S.E. Frost, Director of the National Advisory Council on Radio in Education in New York, and published in *Education's Own Stations*.

[10] Dick Dorrance '36, "Dartmouth on the Air," manuscript c.1936, provided by his son Sturges Dorrance '63.

**Chapter 2: 1941-1943**

[1] At one point in 1941 WKNE proposed setting up an FM station in Hanover, to rebroadcast its programs and recapture its lost Dartmouth audience.

[2] Dick Dorrance, "Dartmouth on the Air," manuscript c.1936.

[3] Hugh was the brother of Orville Dryfoos '34, longtime *New York Times* executive.

[4] Undated proposal by *The Dartmouth*, located (in 1964) in the Council on Student Organizations' "Radio Committee" file. Radio Council minutes indicate that it was formally submitted on February 22, 1941.

[5] "Survey of Opinion Regarding Intramural Radio System Sponsored by *The Dartmouth*," dated February 21, 1941, as of 1964 located in the aforementioned COSO file.

[6] Tom Jardine '41, Bill Mitchel '42, Fred Cassidy '42, and George Brickelmaier '42.

[7] Lincoln Diament, Chief Announcer of CURC, in an undated letter to Albert Goldman of *The Dartmouth* (in response to a questionnaire).

[8] "Teaneck Youth at Dartmouth Has His Own Radio Station," *Bergen (NJ) Evening Record*, November 6, 1941.

[9] Jerry Tallmer, "New Born DBS Broadcasts Clear, Crisp, Testing Programs to Five Dormitories," *The Dartmouth*, September 30, 1941.

[10] Interview with Tallmer, October 2012.

[11] A. Alexander Fanelli, "DBS and Players Join to Present Brilliant Drama," *The Dartmouth,* October 2, 1941.

[12] "DBS Opening - October 27, 1941," typescript in Rauner Archives.

[13] Reprinted in editorial "Busting Britches and DBS," *The Dartmouth*, February 3, 1942.

[14] John R. Williams, *This Was Your Hit Parade* (Camden, ME: self-published, 1973). Joel Whitburn, *Pop Hits 1940-1954* (Menomonee Falls, WI: Record Research Inc., 1994). Harrison B. Summers, ed., *A Thirty-Year History of Programs Carried on National Radio Networks in the United States, 1926-1956,* reprint edition (Salem, NH: Ayer Company, 1993). Each of these contains contemporary data on sales and popularity.

[15] Interviews with Richard Kanter and Paul Samek, both in September 2010.

[16] Letter to the Editor, *The Dartmouth,* November 8, 1941.

[17] *ibid.,* September 11, 1941.

[18] Correspondence with Hirschberg, December 2009. The attack commenced at approximately 8:00 a.m. Hawaiian time, with bulletins sent to the U.S. somewhat later; the time difference meant that most Americans heard the news in the afternoon or later.

[19] Franklin D. Roosevelt's death and the outbreak of the Korean War came while the station was off the air.

[20] "Busting Britches and DBS" (editorial).

[21] Dick Krolik, in a letter to Prof. Stearns Morse, March 26, 1942.

[22] Paul Samek, in a letter to Almon Ives, July 30, 1942.

[23] These are probable figures, listed on a rather unofficial-looking yellow sheet in COSO's "Radio Committee" file. Except for this and numerous expense "projections" (i.e., before the money was spent) of early and mid-1941, the author has been unable to find any financial records for the 1941-43 DBS.

[24] Legal radiation for such systems is determined by the formula 157,000/frequency (in KC), feet. The lower the frequency (to the bottom of the radio dial, at 550 KC) the greater the legally permissible coverage, which is why most college systems are on low frequencies.

[25] E.M. Jones, DBS Technical Department memo, September 11, 1942.

## Chapter 3: 1946-1951

[1] *The Dartmouth*, October 15, 1946.

[2] Interview with Richard A. "Rick" Kelly, September 2008.

[3] Letter from R.A. Schroth, in an October 1946, issue of *The Dartmouth.*

[4] From 1944, when its downtown theater burned, until 1950, the Nugget Theatre rented the facilities of the Webster Hall auditorium. *The Dartmouth*, May 6, 1947.

[5] "Report of President's Committee on Future Radio Policy," March 23, 1949.

[6] Ron Kehoe's description, ten years later.

[7] Letter from Alan Judson, *The Dartmouth*, May 19, 1948.

[8] *The Dartmouth,* October 17, 1947. The wording of the first paragraph has been slightly rearranged.

[9] *ibid.,* November 17, 1947.

[10] Lowell Thomas to Robert Shade, letter dated February 17, 1948.

[11] *Claremont Eagle,* March 25, 1948, 1.

[12] This and following quotes from *The Dartmouth* of March 25, 1948, or March 26, 1948, unless otherwise noted.

[13] *The Dartmouth,* May 1, 1948.

[14] Dick Hollands, "WDBS: Radio at Dartmouth, Less Than a Decade Old, Grows Into Potent Campus Force," *The Dartmouth Alumni Magazine,* May, 1950.

[15] *The Dartmouth,* December 2, 1948.

[16] John B. began his popular WOR morning news and talk program (later called *Rambling With Gambling*) in 1925, continuing until 1959, when he turned over the program to his son, John A. In 1991 John A. was succeeded by *his* son, John R., who is still on the air as of this writing.

[17] Believed to be from *The Dartmouth,* date unknown.

[18] "The Undergraduate Chair" (column), *Dartmouth Alumni Magazine,* January, 1949.

[19] Hollands, "WDBS," 11.

[20] "College Radio and the College Man," *Sponsor,* December 7, 1964, 47.

[21] *The Dartmouth,* May 14, 1949.

[22] *ibid.,* September 22, 1949.

[23] Lawrence Green, "Schedule Revamped, Features Two New Programs," *The Dartmouth,* an unknown May (?) 1949 issue.

[24] *ibid.*

[25] Letter from Robert J. Lyon , *The Dartmouth,* unknown October, 1949 issue.

[26] Quoted in Al Parson's "Once Over Lightly" column, *The Dartmouth,* October 3, 1949.

[27] *WDBS Newsletter,* March 20, 1950. Copies of most station newsletters could still be found buried in the Dartmouth College Archives at the time this was written, in the 1960s.

[28] Hollands, "WDBS," 12.

[29] All of these figures represent the "almost always listen" (four or more times a week in the case of daily shows) and "sometimes listen" (1-3 times weekly) categories lumped together. Other categories were "never or seldom" and (presumably) "no answer." Of those who did listen to a show, in virtually every case 35% to 40% did so "almost always." The major exception was *Music Til Midnight,* whose fans were unusually faithful.

[30] The identity of the White Mountain Ramblers is a bit of a mystery. They appear to have been related to a local country band by that name organized by young Canaan N.H. veteran John "Jack" Fiske, Jr. (1927-2011), immediately after he returned from service in World War II. His widow does not recall the band broadcasting on WDBS, however. Fiske was not a Dartmouth student and the band originated from a location outside of the studios. Obituary in *Manchester Union Leader,* July 21, 2011 (at **www.legacy.com**); correspondence with Dave Dugan, January 2013; interview with Mrs. Leona Fiske, September 2013.

[31] *The Aegis,* 1950 edition.

[32] Letter from Robert J. Lyon, *The Dartmouth,* unknown October, 1949 issue.

[33] Michael Heyman in a letter to George Mealy, technical director of Harvard's WHRV, February 20, 1950.

[34] *WDBS Newsletter,* January 14, 1951. It is not clear, incidentally, why turntables would have anything to do with surface noise, which is usually due to worn or damaged records.

[35] Hollands, "WDBS," 11-13. Slightly edited for length.

[36] *The Dartmouth,* February 23, 1951.

[37] *ibid.,* February 21, 1951.

[38] *ibid.,* March 7, 1951.

[39] Letter from Andrew Ashton, *The Dartmouth,* November 29, 1950.

[40] Letter from Irwin Freedberg, Thomas McConnor and Lawrence Mamlet, *The Dartmouth*, November 20, 1950.

[41] *The Dartmouth,* February 23, 1951.

[42] *ibid.*, December 15, 1950.

[43] Swicker was also known as "Rich" and "Swick."

[44] Kent Robinson, "Status Report of WDBS," May 19, 1952, 8.

[45] *WDBS Newsletter*, March 5, 1951.

[46] "Memorandum for the Radio File," May 1, 1950; "Summary Report of Information and Impressions Concerning Radio Station WTSL and its Relationship to WDBS," June 1, 1950.

[47] *The Dartmouth*, December 23, 1950.

[48] Gambling took advantage of his correspondence with the Hawaiian station mentioned earlier to look for a job in Hawaii. He stated his connection with WTSL as part of his qualifications. Gambling letter to station KPOA, December 10, 1950.

[49] Interview with Rosenfield, December 2010.

[50] *The Dartmouth*, April 28, 1951.

[51] Hollands, "WDBS," 14.

[52] *WDBS Newsletter*, March 12, 1951.

**Chapter 4: 1951-1955**

[1] *WDBS Newsletter,* October 15, 1951.

[2] The show was billed as "the only hour show brought to you in a half hour."

[3] *WDBS Newsletter*, November 5, 1951. Recordings of *Hunky-Dorey* provided by Bill Gitt, who engineered the show, April 2011.

[4] Correspondence with Buck Henry, September 2013.

[5] *The Dartmouth*, January 6, 1952.

[6] Kent C. Robinson, *Status Report of WDBS as of 1951-1952*, May 19, 1952. Mimeographed by WDBS.

[7] The semantic change from "production director" to "program director" was meant to avoid confusion of Solow with his production manager, a subordinate who had responsibility for pre-scripted "productions" like *Studio '52* and *The Co-Op Show*. "Program director" had previously been applied to staff producers in charge of individual programs or evenings. To add to the confusion, until 1955 Solow's department continued to be called the "Production Department."

[8] Barr was an engineer; Mitchel, strictly speaking, had no specialty.

[9] *WDBS Newsletter*, April 14, 1952.

[10] Swicker, letter to J. Edgar Hill, RCA representative for the region, March 21, 1952.

[11] *The Dartmouth*, March 25, 1952.

[12] The 1952 *Aegis.*

[13] Swicker, letter to J. Edgar Hill, November 1, 1951.

[14] *The Dartmouth*, May 6, 1952; *WDBS Newsletter*, April 14, 1952.

[15] *The Dartmouth*, April 17, 1952.

[16] Quoted by Lawrence Martz in an undated *Dartmouth* article, and in the *WDBS Newsletter*, May 19, 1952.

[17] Robert White, *The Dartmouth*, April 14, 1952.

[18] *The Dartmouth*, May 22, 1952.

[19] Robinson, *Status Report of WDBS*.

[20] *ibid.*, December 1, 1952.

[21] *ibid.*, January 2, 1953.

[22] *The Dartmouth*, May 9, 1953.

[23] *The Dartmouth*, January 7, 1953, elaborated in the 1953 *Aegis*.

[24] *The Dartmouth*, April 19, 1953.

[25] Roos in a year-end report to his successor, undated but presumably March, 1954.

[26] Roos in a typed Directorate Meeting report, September 29, 1953.

[27] *ibid.*, January 8, 1954

[28] Peter VonS. Stevens, *WDBS: A Study in Human Relations*, written in 1953 or early 1954.

[29] Correspondence with Russell, January 2010.

[30] *WDBS Newsletter*, April 13, 1954.

[31] *The Dartmouth,* undated 1953 article.

[32] WDBS Newsletter, May 16, 1954.

[33] *WDBS Handbook of Hand Signals,* March 1954. No one would admit authorship.

[34] Peter Roos, report of Directorate meeting, September 29, 1953.

[35] Donald Meltzer, "On the Air—16 Hours a Day," *Dartmouth Alumni Magazine,* May 1954, 21.

[36] Giden, in a letter to WRUV, the University of Vermont station, February 12, 1954.

[37] *The Dartmouth,* undated article (probably early 1954).

[38] Meltzer, "On the Air—16 Hours a Day."

[39] *The Dartmouth,* undated article of early 1955.

[40] John Sloan Dickey, in a letter to Station Manager Richard Harris, October 13, 1956, responding to Harris' proposal to resume the series.

[41] Report of Directorate meeting, October 13, 1954.

[42] WDCR Chief Engineer Robert Hargraves, "Re: Carrier Current Broadcasting," April 27, 1960. This six-page report was drawn up for the Tufts station and remained for years in the WDCR technical files under "Tufts University." It is probably the best overall summary of WDBS' sad experience with transmission during 1941-58.

[43] Quoted by Robinson in *Status Report of WDBS,* 7.

[44] Transcribed from a recording of the DBS re-inaugural broadcast of May 6, 1946.

[45] Undated sheet, probably compiled by Bill Tell.

[46] Stevens in a letter to the Ivy Network, February 5, 1955.

[47] Directorate meeting reports for February 28, March 13, and April 17, 1955.

[48] *The Dartmouth,* March 18, 1955.

**Chapter 5: 1955-1958**

[1] Ranney letter to Bill Gitt, December 11, 1955; Frank Spitzer of "The Satanic Six," quoted in *The Dartmouth,* March 21, 1956.

[2] Dave Miller, in the *WDBS Heeler's Manual,* fourth edition, 1955.

[3] *Billboard,* December 3, 1955. The Arnold record was a major pop hit at the time.

[4] *The Dartmouth,* October 19, 1955.

[5] Van de Kamp, in a Directorate meeting report (for the station files), November 11, 1955.

[6] *The Dartmouth,* December 2, 1955.

[7] These results are based on a rather skimpy, albeit scientifically pre-selected sample of 27 students. Since this was an Ivy poll, the results may have been padded somewhat to make the station look good.

[8] Van de Kamp in a general manager's report, November 11, 1955.

[9] Report of Executive Staff Meeting, October 6, 1955.

[10] Van de Kamp in a Directorate meeting report, January 15, 1956.

[11] *ibid.*

[12] Van de Kamp statement dated September 26, 1955, written in lieu of Directorate meeting report.

[13] Report of Executive Staff Meeting, October 6, 1955.

[14] Ranney in a letter to Bill Gitt, December 11, 1955.

[15] Assistant to the Treasurer Paul F. Young, letter to Ranney, February 10, 1956.

[16] Edward Wilder, Gates Radio Co. representative, letter to Ranney, February 7, 1956.

[17] Sauter's notes for station staff meeting, September 25, 1956.

[18] This is actually the schedule of John Long (Harris' successor), as Long described it in a May 16, 1957 letter to the Ivy Network. Only slight changes seem to have been made from Harris' original of October 1956, involving the 12:00 to 4:00 p.m. and 7:30 to 11:00 p.m. periods.

[19] 1957 *Aegis*. Although unsigned, this sounds very much like Harris' prose.

[20] Interviews with Ron Kehoe, December 2010, Rob Brown, August 2013.

[21] Bob Allen's report, in a letter to Frank Sauter, summer 1956.

[22] In a change of terminology, the term kilocycles (KC) was replaced by kilohertz (KHz) ca. 1960.

[23] Harris in a letter to Sauter, July 19, 1956.

[24] *The Dartmouth*, September 26, 1956.

[25] The proposal was contained in a letter from Rust to Bob Allen, October 5, 1956. Mimeographed copies were located in the WDCR files.

[26] WTSL, quoted in *The Dartmouth*, January 9, 1957.

[27] A more honest estimate of WTSL's potential Upper Valley audience: 25,000 to 30,000.

[28] Reprinted in *The Dartmouth*, January 8, 1957.

[29] *The Dartmouth*, January 9, 1957.

[30] *ibid.*

[31] Memo in Rauner Archive.

[32] *The Dartmouth*, January 23, 1957.

[33] Brown, letter to Al Pulsifer, March 31, 1957.

[34] Harris, in a duplicated letter to all station members, April 1957.

[35] Interview with Ron Kehoe, December 2010.

[36] Correspondence with Robert Hager, October 2010. Hager would later become an NBC News correspondent, while Kehoe would become Assistant Attorney General of Massachusetts.

[37] Interview with Kehoe, December 2010. *The Dartmouth*, February 17, 1958.

[38] *The Dartmouth*, November 26, 1957.

[39] Letter from Ivy Network president to all station members, November 1954.

[40] Letter from Ivy Network president to station members, undated but approximately 1960.

[41] *This Is College Radio* is nevertheless a fascinating behind-the-scenes look at a campus station in 1956. It was directed by James B. Sherwood and as of this writing can be viewed on YouTube.

[42] Display ad in *The Hanover Gazette* and *The Valley News*, October 24, 1957.

[43] *The Dartmouth*, November 19, 1957.

[44] Interview with Ron Kehoe, December 2010.

[45] The Injunaires was a quartet founded in 1946 as an offshoot of the Glee Club by Glee Club director Paul Zeller, and performed primarily pop and comedy tunes. It had grown to an octet by the 1950s. It changed its name to the "Aires" in the late 1970s.

[46] *The Dartmouth*, February 12, 1958.

[47] *ibid.*, February 17, 1958.

[48] Singer-songwriter Shelton T. "Chip" Fisher '59 later went into finance, and now lives in Denver.

[49] Kehoe letter to Jon Cohen, July 29, 1958 (station files).

[50] Dick Harris, quoted in *The Dartmouth*, February 17, 1958.

[51] Rev. George Kalbfleisch, letter in *The Dartmouth*, April 24, 1958.

[52] Kehoe letter to Jon Cohen, March 26, 1958.

[53] Kehoe memo to other Directorate members, June 16, 1958.

[54] Correspondence with Harris, February 2012.

[55] Kehoe, letter to Mr. Al Outcalt, December 27, 1958.

[56] Johnson, letter to the General Manager of WHUS, February 22, 1959.

[57] 1957 *Aegis*.

[58] *The Hanover Gazette*, February 27, 1958.

[59] *The Dartmouth,* February 17, 1958.

[60] *ibid.*

[61] Kehoe letter to Jon Cohen, July 29, 1958.

[62] Johnson, letter to the General Manager of WHUS, February 22, 1959.

**Chapter 6: 1958-1964**

[1] Sturges Dorrance, "A Station Has a Birthday: Twenty Years on the Air," *The Dartmouth,* October 26, 1961, 2.

[2] The producers of "Twenty Years," Messrs. Dorrance and Bob Gitt, found how little record their predecessors had left of the station's growth over the years. WDCR's "history files" were skimpy and chaotic; scrapbooks existed only for 1941-42 and a few months of 1956; no sound recordings at all existed for the important years prior to 1946, and there were few after that.

[3] Dorrance, "A Station Has a Birthday."

[4] Almon Ives, "To: Whom It May Concern, Subj: Problems in Program Policy at WDCR" (mimeographed memo). Undated, but probably early November, 1960.

[5] "Student-Operated WDCR Seeks New Image," *Broadcasting,* January 7, 1963.

[6] Cameron, letter to Ivy Network, October, 1959.

[7] Interviews with Bob Hager, August 2011, MacMillin, September 2012. Melvoin, a jazz pianist, later became a top Los Angeles studio musician, recording with Frank Sinatra, The Beach Boys, and others. For a feature story on him see Bonnie Barber, "Piano Man," *Dartmouth Alumni Magazine,* September/October 2004, 48-49. He died in February 2012.

[8] More on Walsh can be found at **http://www.timbrooks.net/PDFs/walsh70.pdf**. This episode (aka "From Cylinders to Stereo") appears to be the only surviving tape from the series (Rauner Archives).

[9] Mimeographed WDCR production schedule, Winter 1961.

[10] Feature story by producer Bob Cohn in WDCR's *Listener's Log,* June 3-9, 1963 (Vol. III, No. 9), 1.

[11] Correspondence with Gerbracht, December 2010. *WDCR Summer Newsletter,* August 1962, 5.

[12] Correspondence with Jones, September 2011; John Rockwell, November 2011. Interviews with MacMillin, 2011-2012.

[13] Paul A. Stein, "WDCR Protests College Trustees' Editorial Ban," *The Dartmouth,* May 7, 1958. Interview with Kehoe, December 2010.

[14] Correspondence with Levenson, September 2010.

[15] Despite this episode Radio Pulsebeat News continued to operate for many years thereafter. It is perhaps best known for interviews with The Beatles in early 1964, which were later released on LP.

[16] Correspondence with Whitehead, September 2010.

[17] The broadcast networks had begun using crude computer analyses on election night only four years earlier in 1956, using giant UNIVAC computers. See **http://www.wired.com/science/discoveries/news/2008/11/dayintech_1104**

[18] Sturges Dorrance, "WDCR Covers the Elections," *Dartmouth Alumni Magazine,* December 1962, 33,36.

[19] Burton C. Blanchard, Cornish Flat, NH, letter to program director of WDCR, February 20, 1961, 1.

[20] William Matthews, "WDCR Keeps Growing," *Dartmouth Alumni Magazine,* August, 1960. Correspondence with Henry Goldsmith, October 2010. The Cash interview is at **www.timbrooks.net**.

[21] The reports quoted were in the station files as of 1964.

[22] Correspondence and interview with Hager, October 2010, August 2011.

[23] Constitution of Dartmouth College Radio, March 1, 1960.

[24] *The Dartmouth,* May 14, 1962, 1.

[25] *Manchester (N.H.) Union Leader*, May 15 or 16, 1962, 1.

[26] *ibid.*, May 17 or 18, 1962, on editorial page.

[27] *WDCR Newsletter*, unmarked but probably No. 6, Fall, 1960.

[28] *ibid.*, No. 2, Winter, 1961.

[29] John W. Masland, "Television at Dartmouth College" (memo to Trustees), November 9, 1962.

[30] Sturges Dorrance, *WDCR Summer Newsletter*, August, 1962, 2.

[31] Correspondence with George Whitehead, September 2010, Goldsmith, October 2010.

[32] "Student-Operated WDCR Seeks New Image".

[33] This was my first broadcast survey, before embarking on a professional career in audience research, another example of the value of Dartmouth radio as a professional training ground.

[34] The telephone portion is technically called a "coincidental" survey, and is rather inefficient as it captures only those respondents who were listening to the radio at the moment they were called. Because many people will not be listening at that moment, it requires extremely large samples (much larger than that used by WDCR) to obtain data for individual programs or time periods.

[35] Ron Kehoe, letter to Richard Plummer, Dartmouth assistant business manager, February 4, 1959 (file).

[36] Tim Brooks, *Radio Listenership in the Upper Valley: 1963*, August 15, 1963.

## Chapter 7: 1964-1970

[1] "College Radio and the College Man," *Sponsor,* December 7, 1964, 42-48. *The Dartmouth,* November 3, 1964, 3. Correspondence with John Catlett, September 2010, and Panitt, January 2011.

[2] Robert Buck, "WDCR's 'Election—1966'," *WDCR Alumni Newsflash*, c.February 1967. Interview with Arthur Fergenson, February 2011.

[3] Paul Gambaccini, *Radio Boy: An Adolescent DJ's Story* (London: Elm Tree Books, 1986), 62. Correspondence with Prentice and Zrike, Oct. 2010.

[4] "WDCR Receives News Award," *The Dartmouth,* January 24, 1969, 1.

[5] *The Dartmouth,* October 28, 1968, 1. *Radio Boy*, 68-71. Interview with Fergenson, February 2011.

[6] *The Dartmouth*, January 28, 1966. Robert Buck, "Major Changes in WDCR's Program Schedule" and "WDCR Reports... The Comprehensive Newscast," *WDCR Alumni Newsflash*, c.February 1967.

[7] "Reich Radio Series to Start Wednesday," *The Dartmouth,* October 10, 1967, 1. *Radio Boy*, 76-77. Interview with Brylawski.

[8] *The Dartmouth*, November 12 and 25, 1965; April 12, 1966, 5; November 11, 1966, 1.

[9] *The Dartmouth,* February 3, 1965, 1, and April 2, 1965 (SNCC); February 22, 1965, 1 (Malcolm X); October 28, 1966, 1, and November 11, 1966 (Carmichael); May 4, 1967, 1 (Wallace). *Radio Boy*, 9-11.

[10] "Enmity in the North," *Time,* May 12, 1967. "Dartmouth Blacks Bar Physicist's Talk," *New York Times*, October 16, 1969, 37; *The Dartmouth*, November 11, 1969, 1; interview with Zrike, November 2010. The Shockley interview is on file at Dartmouth's Rauner Library.

[11] More popularly known as "The Summer of Love" due to media focus on events in the Haight-Ashbury district of San Francisco. *Sgt. Pepper* was released in June 1967 and subsequently spent more than three months as the number one best-selling album in the U.S.

[12] *Radio Boy*, 41. "Broadcast Disturbs Town," *The Dartmouth,* September 29, 1967, 1. Interview with Fergenson, February 2011. "College Launches Sweeping Drug Probe," *The Dartmouth,* January 19, 1968, 1.

[13] Interview with Fergenson, February 2011. Correspondence with Luehrmann, November, 2010, and Reich, February, 2011.

[14] *Radio Boy*, 111, interview with Fergenson, February 2011 (protests on green); *The Dartmouth*, April 17, 1968, 1 (survey); *The Dartmouth,* January 9, 1970 (Newton); "Radio Station to Cover Moratorium with Forum," *The Dartmouth,* October 7, 1969, 1, October 16, 1969, 1; *Radio Boy*, 124-127, *The Dartmouth*, October 29, 1969, 1, and November 17, 1969, 1 (march on Washington).

[15] *Radio Boy*, 124. Ryder continued her determined crusade until her death in 1981, when she was hit by a car. She is memorialized today on the web site **www.peacepilgrim.com**.

[16] *Radio Boy*, 121-124. Interview with Jack Beeler, July 2011. Correspondence with McKeever, December 2011.

[17] "300 Occupy a Hall in Dartmouth Sit-In to Protest ROTC," *New York Times*, April 23, 1969, 30; *The Dartmouth*, April 30, 1969, 1.

[18] "Sixty at Dartmouth Lock Themselves In, " *New York Times*, May 7, 1969, 32; "Anti-ROTC Dissidents Seize Parkhurst Hall; Yield to 90 State Troopers After 12 Hours," *The Dartmouth*, May 7, 1969, 1; Douglas Robinson, "Troopers Oust Protestors at Dartmouth," *New York Times*, May 8, 1969, 43. A full account, from Gambaccini's point of view, is in *Radio Boy*, 113-120. See also "Parkhurst Five Years After," (WDCR radio documentary narrated by Stephen Saglio);"The Storming of Parkhurst: 30 Years Later," *The Dartmouth,* May 6, 1999; "A Point of Protest," *The Dartmouth,* November 5, 2010. Also, interview with Fergenson.

[19] "Dartmouth Rebels Get 30-Day Terms in ROTC Protest," *New York Times*, May 10, 1969, 1, 14.

[20] *Radio Boy*, 29-43.

[21] *Radio Boy*, 73.

[22] Correspondence with Odeneal, November 2011.

[23] Correspondence with Gambaccini, July 2011; *Radio Boy*, 128; *The Dartmouth*, April 4, 1968; interview with Ford, January 2011.

[24] Interview with Ford, January 2011.

[25] Stephen Hill, "WDCR Starts All-Night Slate," *The Dartmouth,* October 3, 1969, 1.

[26] Allan Ryan, "Report from the General Manager," *WDCR Alumni Newsflash*, c.January 1966. *Radio Boy*, 46-48.

[27] "Judy Garland Visits Hanover," *The Dartmouth,* January 11, 1967, 1. Garland said she was going to marry the strapping Green "in the chapel at Dartmouth," but she soon dumped him. The autobiography was never published.

[28] Interview with David Marston, June 2009.

[29] Interview with Sandy Alderson, May 2013. "Far Away Listeners Follow Ivy League Champs," *WDCR Alumni Newsflash,* c.January 1966.

[30] Correspondence with Luehrmann, November 2010; Stephen Zrike, November 2010; Jack Beeler, July 2011; David Graves, July 2011.

[31] Articles in *The Dartmouth*, December 5, 1967, 1; January 11, 1968, 1; January 23, 1968, 1; January 31, 1968, 1; February 2, 1968, 1; February 23, 1968, 1; and April 2, 1968, 1.

[32] "WDCR Initiates Drive to Aid Vietnam Hamlet," *The Dartmouth,* November 17, 1967, 1. *Radio Boy*, 65. Robert Jeffe, "WDCR to Aid ABC," *The Dartmouth,* October 9, 1968, 1. Correspondence with Barnet, November 2011.

[33] Robert Jeffe, "WDCR to Aid ABC," *The Dartmouth,* October 9, 1968, 1. *Radio Boy*, 65-75.

[34] "Radio Starts 'Let's Help' Campaign," *The Dartmouth,* October 21, 1969, 1; "Noted Hanover People in Celebrity Day Roles," *Manchester Union Leader*, November 23, 1969; Mark Stitham, "Celebrities Aid WDCR Let's Help," *The Dartmouth,* November 24, 1969, 1-2; "'Let's Help' Funds Aid Center," *The Dartmouth,* January 19, 1970, 1-2. *Radio Boy*, 77-78.

[35] "WDCR Holds Second Annual Frisbee Contest," *The Dartmouth,* May 28, 1969, 2.

[36] Correspondence with Bill Moyes, November 2011.

[37] "Dartmouth Editors Given Provisional Course Reduction," *The Dartmouth,* January 21, 1965, 1; memo on summer operations (1971). "'Fred', 'Tony' on WDCR," *Dartmouth*

*Summer News,* July 26, 1965; Dian Lewis, "Summer Broadcast from a Feminine Point of View," *WDCR Alumni Newsflash,* c.January 1966.

[38] Memo from General Manager Owen Leach, May 3, 1966. "Proposal for Summer Broadcasting" (memo), December 6, 1966; memo on summer operations (1971); *Radio Boy,* 13-14.

[39] Correspondence with Henry Allen, October 2012, June 2013.

[40] "WDCR Advertising Revenue, 1958-1974" (file). The station's fiscal year ran from July to June, e.g. FY 1970 encompassed July 1969-June 1970.

[41] Correspondence with Zuckerman, November 2011. Steve Shechtman, "8 Ivy League Radio Stations Convene Here," *The Dartmouth,* April 30, 1965, 1; Robert Cohn, "WDCR Hosts Ivy Network Convention," *WDCR Alumni Newsflash,* c.January 1966"; WDCR's Grinnell Chairs Ivy Group," *The Dartmouth,* May 1, 1968, 1.

[42] Marshall (1919-1983) remained in the area for the rest of his life. He died at his desk at WNHV in 1983.

[43] "White River Station Soon WNHV," *The Dartmouth,* October 19, 1966, 1. Owen Leach, "Audience Survey for Tri-Town," *WDCR Alumni Newsflash,* c.February 1967.

[44] *Broadcasting Yearbook,* 1958 through 1967; Upper Valley Development Council, Inc., "Upper Valley Base Study," revised November 1967. According to the 1967 *Broadcasting Yearbook* WRLH began operation on July 26, 1966 on channel 49. The station is now known as WNNE. WENH: *The Dartmouth,* April 11, 1968, 1.

[45] Robert Sauer, "Who Listens to WDCR?", *WDCR Alumni Newsflash,* c.January 1966. Frederick F. Schauer, "Radio Listenership in the Tri-Town Area," for Amos Tuck School of Business Administration, December 1, 1967. This was a "telephone coincidental" study, the standard in the industry, in which respondents were asked what they were listening to at the moment they were called. It covered 7:00 to 9:00 a.m., a peak radio listening period. Owen Leach, "Audience Survey for Tri-Town," *WDCR Alumni Newsflash,* c.February 1967.

[46] *The Dartmouth,* November 10, 1965, 1; Robert Cohn, "Dartmouth Men - Never at a Loss in the Dark," *WDCR Alumni Newsflash,* c.January 1966.

[47] Christopher Kilgour, "Emergency!!", *WDCR Alumni Newsflash,* c.January 1966.

[48] Interview with Charlie Smith, November 2011. See also **http://stlradio.net/pages/ebsaccident.htm**.

[49] Henry Allen, "Technical Improvements - Greater Range, Fewer Errors," *WDCR Alumni Newsflash,* c.February 1967. Stephen Hill, "WDCR Starts All-Night Slate," *The Dartmouth,* October 3, 1969, 1. Correspondence with Tim McKeever, December 2011.

[50] "WDCR, Mags Offer Many Opportunities," *The Dartmouth,* August 1, 1967, 9. *Radio Boy,* 39-40.

[51] "WDCR Names New Officers," *The Dartmouth,* February 11, 1969, 1. Correspondence with Gambaccini and Zuckerman.

[52] Interview with Ford, January 2011.

[53] Correspondence with Aydelott, October 2010.

[54] "Dartmouth Editors Given Provisional Course Reduction," *The Dartmouth,* January 21, 1965, 1.

[55] Memo from Gilbert Tanis, assistant to President Dickey, to Members of the Staff (regarding establishment of Board of Overseers), March 15, 1966; interview with Bryant, August 2011; Board of Overseers Minutes, August 1972.

[56] Memo from Gilbert Tanis, March 15, 1966; interview with Bryant, September 2008.

[57] "WDCR Fetes Birthday," *The Dartmouth,* March 1, 1968, 4.

[58] "Seymour, Students to Present Touring Spring Variety Show," *The Dartmouth,* March 11, 1969, 1.

[59] Mike Mellin, "Class of 1969 Prepares to Bury Time Capsule," *The Dartmouth,* December 4, 1968, 3; Kent Foster, "'69 Plans Capsule for Green," *The Dartmouth,* April 21, 1969, 1; correspondence with Chip Elitzer, Norman Jacobs, Jeff Kelley and David Prentice, October 2010.

[60] Correspondence with Gambaccini, October 2010.

[61] Gambaccini, memo regarding an FM station (draft in file), May 13, 1969.

[62] Interview with Bryant, September 2008.

[63] Letter from John F. Meck to Gambaccini, re: FM Frequency, September 4, 1969; letter from Kirkland, Ellis (attorneys) to Bryant, September 9, 1969; Community Survey, October 1969.

[64] *The Dartmouth,* January 23, 1970. Correspondence with Martha Luehrmann, November 2010.

**Chapter 8: 1970-1976**

[1] Spring 1971 Mediastat Survey, at Rauner Archive.

[2] "WDCR Audience Profile," undated (c.1976) memo summarizing 1971-74 results.

[3] Memo from Sales Manager Thomas Lord, November 12, 1973 (file). Correspondence with John Donvan, October 2010, and Bob Kirkpatrick, December 2011.

[4] Interview with Smith, November 2011. This is J. Charles Smith '73, not Daniel Charles Smith '73 who was in the same class. Jeffrey McLaughlin, "Dartmouth Radio Station Tells It Like It Is," *The Boston Globe*, September 16, 1971

[5] Memo December 31, 1974; Board of Overseers report, February 1978 (file). Interview with Smith, November 2011.

[6] Memo from Yudkoff, undated but c.early 1974 (file).

[7] Correspondence with Chris Davidson, September 2010.

[8] "Sales Outlook" memo from Hunt, November 14, 1974 (file).

[9] Memo from Royce Yudkoff, undated but c.early 1974; Board of Overseers Minutes, February 19, 1974 (file).

[10] Interview with Davidson, October 2010.

[11] Alexander "Sandy" Macdonald, Jr. (1937-2006) had received a degree from Tuck School in 1973. According to his contract he operated as MacDonald Consulting Associates.

[12] Interviews with Davidson and John Bryant; memo on personnel, October 1975 (file).

[13] Interview with Davidson; station newsletter, October 20, 1975; Board of Overseers minutes, October 3, 1975.

[14] Board of Overseers minutes, April 9, 1976.

[15] Interview with Zrike, November 2010. Correspondence with Bill Downall, November 2011, and Jayne, December 2011.

[16] Interviews with Beeler, July 2011, and David Marston, June 2009; correspondence with Downall, Aydelott, Beeler, Sigward, November 2011; "Dartmouth Radio Station Tells It Like It Is," *The Boston Globe*, September 16, 1971; freshman recruiting letter, June 29, 1974; Jeffrey Sudikoff, "WDCR Forms Election Network" (press release), November 16, 1975.

[17] Correspondence with Sigward, November 2011.

[18] Interview with Beyer, September 2010.
**http://www.senate.gov/artandhistory/history/minute/Closest_election_in_Senate_history.htm**

[19] Frank Long, "Reagan Grilled by Panel, Protestors," *The Dartmouth,* February 6, 1976, 1; interview with Davidson, October 2010.

[20] Sudikoff press release, November 16, 1975; *Dartmouth Broadcasting Newsletter*, March 1977. Interviews with David Marston, June 2009, Rick Beyer, September 2010, Chris Davidson, October 2010, Sudikoff, February 2013. Correspondence with Richard Mark, various 2010. Articles in *The Dartmouth:* Thomas Mayer, "WDCR Covers Primary for Region," January 26, 1976, 1, 5; March 30, 1977, 2; Sherry Laprade, "WDCR - Twenty Years and Still Growing," April 11, 1978, 2; Diane Vogel, "Up to 10 Million Listeners Hear Dartmouth Election Network," February 28, 1980, 1, 5.

[21] "WDCR To Conduct Specials," *The Dartmouth,* May 5, 1970, 3. Interview with Zrike, November 2010. Correspondence with Richard Mark, September 2010.

[22] Richard Murphy, "Strikers Meet to Discuss Future Actions at College," *The Dartmouth*, May 14, 1970, 1.

[23] "Loeb Refuses to Speak with Wefers," *The Dartmouth,* January 21, 1971, 1, 3.

[24] Correspondence with Richard Mark, September 2010.

[25] *The Dartmouth*, May 8, 1974, 1.

[26] "WDCR Wins UPI Prize," *The Dartmouth*, April 2, 1971, 1.

[27] Freshman recruiting letter, June 29, 1974; interview with Davidson, October 2010; *The Dartmouth*, October 13, 1975, 7; *WDCR Weekly Newsletter*, May 9, 1974.

[28] Interview and correspondence with Davidson, October-November 2010, correspondence with Donvan, November 2010.

[29] Interview with Chris Davidson, October 2010. Bob Spitzfaden, "Beutel Claims Media Don't Provide Guidance to Public on News Value, " *The Dartmouth,* March 1, 1971, 1, 3; "Radio-Journalists on Dartmouth Panel," unidentified newspaper clipping, February 26, 1971.

[30] Correspondence with D'Auria, February 2011, John Donvan, November 2010. Interview with Davidson, October 2010. *WDCR Newsletter*, October 1974.

[31] Interviews with Koloff, Sudikoff, February 2013; correspondence with Mark, October 2010, Harway, September 2011. *WDCR Newsletter*, April 8, 1975. Some scripts survive in the station's files, and Harway kindly provided tapes of a few episodes.

[32] Interview with Sudikoff, February 2013; correspondence with Harway and Mark, October 2010; *WDCR Newsletter*, May 12, 1976.

[33] Correspondence with Donvan, November 2010. More on the venerable Omer & Bob's (founded in 1964) is at **http://www.t-n.com/magazine-summer09-omer.htm**.

[34] *WDCR Newsletter*, April 29, 1975; correspondence with Luehrmann, November 2010.

[35] Interviews with Jack Beeler, July 2011, Marston, June 2009, Kevin Koloff, February 2013; correspondence with David Graves, July 2011, Jayne, December 2011.

[36] Peter Gambaccini, "Miller Raps, Plays Oldies on DCR Visit," *The Dartmouth*, May 10, 1971, 2.

[37] Memo from Chris Davidson to Frank Smallwood, November 24, 1975; Board of Overseers minutes, June 1976.

[38] Articles in *The Dartmouth*: Keith Jordan, "WDCR 'Let's Help' To Assist Upper Valley Retarded Youth," October 21, 1970, 1, "WDCR Plans for 'Let's Help'," October 26, 1970, 1, Dave Sugarman, "Celebrities Take WDCR Mikes," November 12, 1970, 1; also January 4, 1971, 4, January 11, 1971, 1.

[39] Articles in *The Dartmouth*: "Home for the Aged to Benefit from WDCR," September 30, 1971, 3, "Aydelott, WDCR Staff Start Let's Help Drive," October 25, 1971, 2, "Aydelott Continues WDCR Marathon," October 28, 1971, 1, Drew Newman, "Aydelott Concludes Radio Vigil as 'Let's Help' Collects $3000," November 2, 1971, 1, "WDCR Completes 'Let's Help'," January 13, 1972, 1. WDCR Press Release, October 30, 1971.

[40] **http://www.radioworld.com/article/a-new-record-175-hours-on-air/18683**

[41] Frank Long, "WDCR Aids Aging Lebanon Opera House," *The Dartmouth,* January 28, 1974, 3. Interview with Chris Davidson, October 2010.

[42] Articles in *The Dartmouth:* April 9, 1965, 1, June 25, 1965, 1,4.

[43] *The Dartmouth*, January 22, 1969, 1. Arthur Fergenson, "Special Students at Dartmouth from 1968-72," essay posted in Linkedin.com Dartmouth alumni section, February 2011.

[44] Susan S. Perkins, "The Small Radio Station—Does It Meet Its Objectives?", Colby Junior College Independent Interim Project for 1972, January 25, 1972, 38.

[45] *The Dartmouth*, April 26, 1971, 1, November 22, 1971, 1. Correspondence with Tim McKeever, December 2011.

[46] Interviews with Beeler, July 2011, DeGioia, July 2011, and Gile, June 2011. Laurence "Al" Shepard was particularly well-liked; he died tragically in an auto accident in 1978.

[47] Interview with Harway, January 2011. David Hunt and seven others, "Confusion to Our Enemies," *The Dartmouth*, April 25, 1974, letters. *WDCR Newsletter*, April 30, 1974.

[48] In a 1954 survey nearly 90% of the student body favored the elimination of discrimination at fraternities, and in a celebrated 1956 case Delta Upsilon defied its national organization to admit its first black pledge. There were a few black staffers at WDCR over the years, including Technical Director Mike Lewis '65. However there were simply very few black students on campus. **http://dartmouthalumnimagazine.com/a-house-united/**.

[49] Interviews with Walter Callender, January 2011, Jack Beeler, July 2011. Correspondence with David Marston, July 2011. Perkins, "The Small Radio Station", 39.

[50] Ellen Cave, Monica Hargrove and Judi Redding, "Institutional Racism and Student Life at Dartmouth" (broadside), November 1974, republished by Afro-American Society, July 21, 1975. Directorate meeting notes, September 1, 1974.

[51] Interviews with Washington, January 2012, Callender, January 2011.

[52] Joseph Neuhaus, "Racism Charged, Denied at WDCR," *The Dartmouth*, February 17, 1976, 1, 5.

[53] Roberto "Bert" Ifill '76 is the brother of PBS Newcaster Gwen Ifill. He did not respond to requests to be interviewed for this history.

[54] Arthur W. Luehrmann, "The Inevitable Racism at WDCR," letter to the editor, *The Dartmouth*, February 24, 1976. Luehrmann clearly wanted WDCR to promote the interests of black students (as he saw them), and felt it must abandon its "naive commercial model" and be "directed to do so" by the College.

[55] Joseph Neuhaus, "Radio's Minority Relations Improve," *The Dartmouth*, April 16, 1976, 1,2; James Washington letter, April 12, 1976; memo from Jordan Baruch, April 15, 1976; interview with Baruch, January 2011.

[56] Interviews with Callender, January 2011, Washington, January 2012. *Reflections*, April 1977.

[57] Hunt, "The Indian Symbol," memo to all station members, October 29, 1974. Chris Davidson, memo to Sports Director Dave Cutler, February 7, 1976.

[58] Freshman recruiting letters, June 29, 1974, August 1, 1975. Rick Jones, fall 1973 questionnaire.

[59] Perkins, "The Small Radio Station", 33. C.H. Springer, "Havoc on Student Groups," *The Dartmouth*, April 17, 1975, 7. *WDCR Newsletter*, November 25, 1974.

[60] Interview with Jack Beeler, July 2011. "Rip Read Is Dead" (advertisement), *The Dartmouth*, April 10, 1970, 5.

[61] *WDCR Newsletter*, December 3, 1975. Correspondence with Chris Davidson, 2010. Davidson described Gregg as "a perfect example of well-to-do older Episcopal women. Passionately involved, unconditionally loving, sweet and funny. She was all about 'high hopes and abiding affection'." Her husband Abel Gregg was an official in the Red Cross, and her son Donald P. Gregg a U.S. ambassador who was deeply involved in the Iran-Contra controversy.

[62] *WDCR Newsletter*, March 3, 1975; "WDCR Announces 1976 Directorate," *The Dartmouth*, March 31, 1975, 1.

[63] Baruch (1923-2011) was at Dartmouth from 1974 to 1977. His obituary can be found in *The Washington Post*, November 4, 2011, and elsewhere. Interview with Baruch, January 2011.

[64] WDCR Directorate, "With Grateful Thanks for the Service, Guidance and Perseverance of Almon B. Ives," March 1, 1975. Message from Ives to those contributing letters, March 10, 1975.

[65] Board of Overseers minutes, February 1974. Correspondence with David Sices, January 2013. Sices was a Dartmouth graduate, class of '54, and had served as classical record director and classical d.j. for WDBS during his student years. He felt that WDCR and WFRD, as planned, misrepresented Dartmouth and should be programmed more along the lines of an National Public Radio station.

[66] Arthur Luehrmann, "Survey of Faculty Opinions About WDCR," March 1974; David Sices, "Statement for [Gonzalez] Programming Committee," c.1975.

[67] *WDCR Newsletter*, October 28, 1975, November 25, 1975. Joseph Neuhaus, "Radio Feud Sparks Faculty Petition," *The Dartmouth*, October 30, 1975, 1, 3.

[68] Paul Gigot, "WDCR Controls Rejected," *The Dartmouth,* January 20, 1976, 7. Interview with Davidson, October 2010.

[69] Stories in *The Dartmouth*: Stephen Cohen, "WDCR Relaxes After Faculty Vote," January 22, 1976, 1, 2; John B. McGrath, "Faculty Disagree on WDCR Vote," January 23, 1976, 1, 2; Luehrmann, "The Inevitable Racism at WDCR," February 24, 1976.

[70] Kevin Koloff, "Sices and Luehrmann Betray Foolish Philosophy" (letter), *The Dartmouth*, November 3, 1975. Interview with Bryant, August 2011.

[71] "End of an Era: WCAX-TV's Marselis Parsons," vermontbiz.com, November 2009 (at **http://www.vermontbiz.com/article/november/end-era-wcax-tvs-marselis-parsons**)

[72] Correspondence with Chris Davidson, September 2010. Interview with Jack Beeler, July 2011. *Broadcasting Yearbooks*, 1966-1974. *WDCR Newsletter* April 23, 1974. *The Dartmouth,* April 7, 1977, 1. There is much misinformation on the Internet about this ill-fated station. The account given here is the best I can reconstruct from original sources.

[73] Interviews with John Bryant, September 2008, Jack Beeler, July 2011, Davidson, October 2010. In addition this author recalls receiving the flyer, but cannot locate it now. Articles in *The Dartmouth*: Dan Wolpert, "TV Station Comes to Upper Valley by Labor Day," April 7, 1977, 1; July 19, 1977, 1; February 22, 1978, 1. Taft Broadcasting was owned by Paul E. Taft of Texas, and was unrelated to the larger Taft Broadcasting conglomerate headquartered in Cincinnati.

[74] Richard Yurko, "WDCR Applies for FM License, Enters into Competition with WTSL," *The Dartmouth*, May 2, 1972, 1. Correspondence with Tim McKeever, December 2011.

[75] "Construction Loan for WDCR-FM," summary memo from Overseers to President Kemeny, January 2, 1975.

[76] J.G. Dockum, "WDCR To Apply for FM License," *The Dartmouth*, April 5, 1972, 1. Memo from Charles Smith, "Recent Conversation with Jim Canto," c.1971.

[77] Marshall (1919-1983), "a sharply dressed, superbly well spoken, tall, elegant gentleman," suffered a heart attack at his desk on March 8, 1983, and died the next day. He was missed not only at WNHV but by the entire community. (**www.imdb.com**)

[78] Articles in *The Dartmouth*: Robert Lande, "FCC Will Reconsider Decision to Grant WDCR FM License," September 24, 1973, 1, 6; "FM For WDCR," September 25, 1973, 4; Robert Lande, "WDCR Obtains FM License, Awaits Further Decision By FCC," September 26, 1973, 1, 5; Howard Fielding, "Must Suffer Further Wait," November 12, 1973, 3.

[79] Interview with John Bryant, August 2011. Board of Overseers Minutes, February 18, 1974.

[80] Carey Heckman, "Dartmouth Radio and FM Acquisition," March 31, 1974 (with letter of transmittal to the Board of Overseers).

[81] Dan Nelson, "High on Your Dial: It's Worth the Trip as WDCR Spawns an FM Sister Station," *Dartmouth Alumni Magazine*, December 1975, 16-18. Jordan Roderick, "Putting in FM," *WDCR/WFRD Newsflash*, Summer 1977. Paul Gigot, "WDCR Gets FM License; Buys Out Two Competitors," *The Dartmouth*, September 20, 1974, 1, 11.

[82] Letter from Kemeny to David Hunt, February 27, 1975; "$56,000 Loan to WDCR FM Is Approved," *The Dartmouth*, March 27, 1975, 1, 5; [82] Nelson, "High on Your Dial," 17.

[83] Joseph Neuhaus, "WFRD Decides FM Programming," *The Dartmouth*, January 12, 1976, 1, 3; "Putting in FM," *WDCR/WFRD Newsflash*, Summer 1977.

[84] Correspondence with Davidson, September 2010.

[85] Nelson, "High on Your Dial," 16-18; "Putting in FM," *WDCR/WFRD Newsflash*, Summer 1977; correspondence with Mark, September 2010.

[86] Correspondence with Bardusch, June 2013.

[87] Stories in *The Dartmouth*: Mark Lennon, "WFRD Is Almost Here," September 25, 1975, 1; "WFRD Decides FM Programming," January 12, 1976, 1, 3.

[88] Correspondence with Chris Davidson, September 2010. Interview with Beyer, September 2010. Script for inaugural broadcast. Articles in *The Dartmouth*: Steve Peterson, "WFRD Starts Broadcasting Tonight," February 19, 1976, 3; Stephen Cohen, "WFRD Radio

Inaugurated," February 20, 1976, 1, 7. "An Introduction to WDCR/1340 AM [and] WFRD/99.3 FM," c. 1978.

[89] Articles in *The Dartmouth*: "Beyond the Call of Duty," February 27, 1976; "WFRD Starts Broadcasting Tonight," 3. *WDCR/WFRD Newsflash*, Summer 1977.

**Chapter 9: 1976-1984**

[1] The state of New Hampshire had strongly conservative governors during much of this period, in Meldrim Thomson, Jr. (1973-79) and John Sununu (1983-89).

[2] "Local Stations Unhurt by WFRD," *The Dartmouth,* April 13, 1976, 2.

[3] Joseph Neuhaus, "Radio Stations Get College Loans," *The Dartmouth*, November 1, 1976, 1, 7. The loan consisted of $60,000 in interest bearing and $20,000 in non-interest bearing debt, all to be repaid to the College out of future revenues. Dave Corey in *WDCR/WFRD Newsletter* No. 6, February 16, 1978.

[4] Interview with Koloff, February 2013; correspondence with Beyer, September 2010.

[5] I want to thank Beyer for sharing the audio clip, as well as his good humor about this event.

[6] *Dartmouth Broadcasting Newsletter*, November 5, 1976.

[7] *The Dartmouth*: "Election Coverage," February 26, 1980, 2, Diane Vogel, "Up to 10 Million Listeners Hear Dartmouth Election Network," February 28, 1980, 1, 5. Board of Overseers minutes, March 1, 1980. Interviews with David Marston, June 2009, Jeff Shapiro, September 2010. Correspondence with Farmer, December 2009.

[8] "The Dartmouth Election Network" (recap memo), November 4, 1980.

[9] "Election Experts," *The Dartmouth*, November 3, 1980, 2.

[10] John May, "1340 on Your Radio Dial," *Dartmouth Alumni Magazine*, April 1983, 41. John Boiney, "WDCR/WFRD Sets Plans for Primary Night Election Network," *The Dartmouth*, February 27, 1984, 10.

[11] "WDCR/WFRD Sets Plans for Primary Night," *The Dartmouth*, February 27, 1984, 1, 10.

[12] Correspondence with May, January 2012.

[13] John Kaliski, "Activities Planned for Election Night," *The Dartmouth*, November 5, 1984, 1, 10.

[14] *WDCR/WFRD Newsletter*, January 26, 1978. "Dial Dartmouth" ad, *The Dartmouth*, January 5, 1983, 7.

[15] Correspondence with John Landrigan, January 2012.

[16] David B. Fein, "Additional Verse of Alma Mater Reflects Changes in Student Body," *The Dartmouth*, June 27, 1980, 1, 5. Wikipedia entry for "Alma Mater (Dartmouth College)."

[17] For more on the *Review* see James Panero and Stefan Beck, eds., *The Dartmouth Review Pleads Innocent: Twenty-Five Years of Being Threatened, Impugned, Vandalized, Sued, Suspended, and Bitten at the Ivy League's Most Controversial Conservative Newspaper* (Wilmington, DE: ISI Books, 2006).

[18] Cole: *The Dartmouth*, January 19, January 31, March 2, April 5, September 28, 1983, April 6, 1984, May 7, 1985, others. Gay rights meeting: *The Dartmouth*, May 1, May 7, 1984. Chaplain: *The Dartmouth*, January 28, 1985.

[19] *Review* financing: *The Dartmouth*, October 17, 1984.

[20] Matthew Mosk, "View From the Bench," *Dartmouth Alumni Magazine*, Nov./Dec. 2008, 51.

[21] *The Review* obviously had a major presence on campus, being widely distributed, the subject of many stories in *The Dartmouth*, and giving rise to several anti-*Review* publications.

[22] Correspondence with May, January 2012.

[23] Interview with Dan Daniels, January 2012.

[24] Nancy Epifano, "Fans, Advertisers Like Rock Format," *The Dartmouth,* April 24, 1981, 7.

[25] Dave Goldberg, "WFRD Begins New Format," *The Dartmouth*, January 6, 1982, 1.

[26] Board of Overseers minutes, February 26, 1983; David Leitao, "Mulligan Named Head of WDCR/WFRD," *The Dartmouth*, November 16, 1983, 2.

[27] Mark Weiss, "FM Jock Quits Over Format," *The Dartmouth*, October 12, 1982, 1, 2.

[28] Greg Beasley, WDCR program director, *The Official WDCR Format Book*, August 1984.

[29] "WDCR Joins NBC News Network," *The Dartmouth*, May 18, 1981, 1. WTSL was affiliated with CBS and Mutual and WNHV with ABC Information. There have been quite a few affiliation changes by stations in the market over the years.

[30] "The Networks Come to Hanover," *WDCR/WFRD Newsflash*, Fall 1982; Board of Overseers minutes, November 13, 1982. *Broadcast Yearbooks*, 1982-1996. Interview with Jeff Shapiro, June 2012.

[31] In the early 1970s the station subscribed to both the Associated Press (AP) and United Press International (UPI) wire services. It dropped AP in 1976, then reinstated it and dropped UPI in 1980. Board of Overseers minutes, May 24, 1980. Mobile unit: interview with Jeff Shapiro, September 2010, WDCR/99Rock alumni newsletter, Summer 1993.

[32] Correspondence with John May, January 2012.

[33] "Radio Freebie," *The Dartmouth*, April 29, 1982, 2.

[34] Board of Overseers minutes, August 18, 1978, "An Introduction to WDCR/WFRD." *WDCR/WFRD Newsletter*, January 26, 1978. Dartmouth did ultimately lose, but by a respectable 64-78. The previous Dartmouth vs. Notre Dame contest had been in 1946.

[35] Memo from Joe Mannes to Seaver Peters, "DCAC Broadcast Proposal," July 24, 1979. "Hockey Airplay," *The Dartmouth*, March 26, 1980, 16.

[36] Brad Hutensky, "Dartmouth Fans Find Friends Over Airwaves," *The Dartmouth*, November 7, 1980, 11.

[37] Greg Fossedal, "WDCR Competes for Announcing Rights," *The Dartmouth*, July 31, 1979, 8.

[38] Board of Overseers minutes, August 9, 1980.

[39] *Dartmouth Broadcasting Newsletter*, October 15, 1976.

[40] Correspondence with Harway, January 2012.

[41] Board of Overseers minutes, November 21, 1981. Correspondence with Grindle, January 2012.

[42] "WDCR, WFRD Raise Money for Senior Citizens," *The Dartmouth*, August 19, 1977, 1. Directorate Report to the Trustees and Overseers, September 1977.

[43] "Saturday Is Kite Day!" (ad), *The Dartmouth*, May 7, 1976. Correspondence with Richard Mark, November 2010.

[44] Board of Overseers minutes, February 27, 1982.

[45] *The Dartmouth*, October 24, 1977, 1. *Broadcasting Yearbook*, 1979.

[46] *Broadcasting Yearbook*, 1979. *The Dartmouth*, May 19, 1977, 1.

[47] Marc Levine, "Maverick FM Station Airs Rock," *The Dartmouth*, February 2, 1977, 2.

[48] Mark S. Tomizawa, "Survey Sampling" (class project), June 1978. The campus survey (266 responses) was conducted by mail and the town survey (99) by telephone.

[49] "Results of Radio Listenership Survey for the Upper Valley Listening Area as Prepared by Radio Index" (sales brochure), week of 5/29/1981.

[50] Jean Butler et al, "WTSL Radio Listenership Survey, November 1978, Prepared for Mr. James Canto... in Connection with the Marketing Research Class at the Amos Tuck School of Business Administration, Dartmouth College," November 29, 1978. This was a telephone study with 626 responses, and was apparently one of a series of such studies.

[51] *Broadcasting Yearbook*, 1976-1985.

[52] *Dartmouth Broadcasting Newsletter*, April 7, 1977; Directorate Report to the Overseers and Trustees, June 1977; *Broadcasting Yearbook*, 1978-1990.

[53] Interviews with Rick Beyer, September 2010; Chris Davidson, October 2010; David Marston, June 2009 and September 2010. Marston has been extremely helpful in reconstructing the sequence of professional sales managers.

[54] Board of Overseers report, May 19-20, 1978.

[55] Marston; Board of Overseers minutes, August 18, 1978. Furman wound up at WCFR in Springfield, Vermont, where he stayed for almost 20 years

[56] Files; interviews with Jeff Shapiro, September 2010, Jason Klein, July 2011, Gerrett Conover, February 2012; correspondence with Margaret Smith, July 2009. Michael Berg, "On the Air," *Dartmouth Alumni Magazine*, December 1985, 40. The transition from Stanley to Canada took place in November 1984.

[57] Board of Overseers minutes, March 1, 1980.

[58] Interview with Kate Mulligan, January 2012.

[59] Board of Overseers minutes, May 19-20, 1978, February 25, 1984.

[60] Board of Overseers minutes, November 17, 1979, November 12, 1983, February 25, 1984.

[61] Board of Overseers minutes, August 18, 1978, November 13, 1982, November 12, 1983.

[62] "Studio 5," *WDCR/WFRD Newsflash*, Fall 1982; Board of Overseers minutes, Fall 1984; Matthew Garcia, "McLaughlin Speaks at FM Studio Opening," *The Dartmouth*, November 19, 1984, 1, 7.

[63] Correspondence with John May, January 2012.

[64] David Wachen, "An Argument for AM Stereo at WDCR" (prepared for a philosophy class), December 1, 1984. Correspondence with John May, January 2012.

[65] Advertisement, *The Dartmouth*, September 21, 1982, 8; interviews with Shapiro, September 2010, Jason Klein, July 2011, Gerrett Conover, February 2012.

[66] Board of Overseers minutes, November 17, 1979.

[67] Board of Overseers minutes, November 12, 1983. Andrew Dominus, "Radio Stations Will Give Grants," *The Dartmouth*, February 3, 1984, 1, 2. A 1982 memo indicated d.j.'s then were being paid $1.62 per hour for work during interims (about half the federal minimum wage at the time), which amounted to individual payouts of $3.00 to $80.00 according to the number of hours worked.

[68] Matthew Garcia, "Dartmouth Broadcasting Picks a New Directorate," *The Dartmouth*, November 12, 1984, 1, 7.

[69] Board of Overseers minutes, February 3-4, 1978.

[70] They may well have been in other directorate positions as well, but neither I nor the College have kept track of personnel by race.

[71] Interviews with Jeff Shapiro, September 2010, Gray, March 2012; Board of Overseers minutes, February 26, 1983.

[72] Directorate Report to Overseers and Trustees, June 1977.

[73] Kate Faunce, "Staff Problems Plague Radio," *The Dartmouth*, July 20, 1976, 1, 3.

[74] Richard Mark, "Five Objectives," March 30, 1976.

[75] "Objectives of Dartmouth Broadcasting," June 23, 1976, in Board of Overseers minutes, July 9-10, 1976. Approved by Executive Committee, Board of Trustees, August 6, 1976.

[76] *The Dartmouth*: "Radio 'Think-Tank' Seeks Solutions," October 31, 1977, 1; Carl Baum, "Radio To Seek Five-Year Plan," November 8, 1977, 3. Board of Overseers minutes, November 4-5, 1977.

[77] Board of Overseers minutes, February 3-4, 1978.

[78] Board of Overseers minutes, August 18, 1978.

[79] "An Analysis of Dartmouth Broadcasting Conducted and Prepared By the WRKO Management Team," October 9-10, 1978.

[80] Ann Munves, "Broadcasting Board May Lose Students," *The Dartmouth*, February 10, 1977, 1.

[81] "Guidelines for the Board of Overseers of Dartmouth Broadcasting," 1982.

[82] Dan Daniels, "Report to the Overseers: The Committee on the Future of the Stations," November 12, 1983; "Proceedings of the Committee on the Future of the Stations," October 7, 1983.

[83] At least I believe the 1977 *Newsflash* to have been the first since 1967; I have found none in between. Directorate Report to Overseers, September 1977.

[84] Interview with Jeff Shapiro, September 2010. Correspondence with Stu Zuckerman, July 2011. "Evelyn Lincoln Hutchins" (obituary), *Valley News*, July 13, 2011.

[85] Douglas Martin, "David T. McLaughlin, 72, Ex-President of Dartmouth, Dies" (obituary), *New York Times*, August 27, 2004. Interviews with John Bryant, August 2011, Jason Klein, July 2011

[86] *The Dartmouth*: Sherry LaPrade, "WDCR - Twenty Years and Still Growing," April 11, 1978, 1, 2; "40 Years Ago," September 30, 1981, 2.

[87] *The Dartmouth*: Christy Gherlein, "WDCR Plans for Silver Jubilee Celebration," May 13, 1983, 1; "Ethics in the Media" (ad), May 13, 1983, 6. May, "1340 on Your Radio Dial," 40-42. I received a nice letter from Dave Marston at the time indicating that the pocket history was been based in part on my 1964 history of the station, and hoping that a more detailed update could someday be published.

[88] Some of these concerns were raised by the previously discussed Committee on the Future of the Stations. Interview with Dan Daniels, January 2012.

[89] "Congratulations, Kids" (editorial), *The Dartmouth,* May 16, 1983, 4.

[90] Scott Cameron, "WDCR Gets Loan, TV, Copter," *The Dartmouth*, December 2, 1976, 7.

**Chapter 10: 1985-1990**

[1] The phrase "Winter of Discontent" appeared in the headline of an article about Dartmouth's troubles in *The Harvard Crimson*, February 12, 1986, and also in *The Dartmouth* and other media.

[2] Interview with Kate Mulligan, January 2012.

[3] "Program Change Proposal, WDCR/WFRD-FM," c.December, 1984. Interview with Gerrett Conover, February 2012.

[4] Board of Overseers minutes, January 12, 1985.

[5] Much of this is detailed in later letters and reports to the overseers.

[6] Matthew Garcia, "Radio Stations to Change Format: More Rock," *The Dartmouth*, January 22, 1985, 1.

[7] David Wheeler, *The Valley News*, February 9, 1985; *New Hampshire Times*, February 23, 1985, 15.

[8] *The Dartmouth*: Ingrid Nelson, "Format Changes Lead to Resignations," October 1, 1985, 1; Ingrid Nelson, "Radio Director Discusses Exit," October 2, 1985, 1, 2, 6; Margot Jacobs, "Rivalry Caused WFRD Resignations" (letter to editor), October 3, 1985, 4. Correspondence with Eric Overton, March 2012.

[9] Tim Rumberger, "Petition Critical of WFRD Programming," *The Dartmouth*, April 24, 1986, 1, 7.

[10] Mike Lee, "All We Hear Is Radio Gaga," *The Dartmouth*, August 25, 1987, 4, 5.

[11] Michael Berg, "On the Air," *Dartmouth Alumni Magazine*, December 1985, 38-41.

[12] Interviews with Gerrett Conover, February 2012 (Conover worked as a d.j. at the station during 1985), Shapiro, June 2012.

[13] "Birch Radio Survey, Hanover Trading Area," (attached to Board of Overseers minutes, May 3, 1986). Data reflects those who listened to station for at least five minutes, Monday-Sunday, 6:00 a.m.-Midnight. Rankings in average quarter hour listenership were similar. *Broadcasting Yearbook*, 1986.

[14] Alan Zarembo, "Q106 Bans G&R Tunes," *The Dartmouth*, January 25, 1990, 1.

[15] Eagle Glassheim, "Promos Make WFRD Popular," *The Dartmouth*, February 6, 1989, 1, 2.

[16] *The Valley News*, January 12, 1987; *Broadcasting Yearbook* 1988.

[17] Jeff Hoover, "Local News Grows Up," *The Dartmouth/Fortnightly*, January 29, 1988, 4, 5; *The Dartmouth*, April 18, 1989, 1, 2.

[18] Lisa Baker, "New Radio Officers to Continue Format," *The Dartmouth*, July 2, 1987, 2, 7.

[19] Board of Overseers minutes, November 9, 1985, November 4, 1986. Interviews with Seth Rosenblatt, November 2008, Mark Wachen, December 2010; correspondence with Bhavsar, January 2011.

[20] Correspondence with Bhavsar, January 2011; Interview with Wachen, December 2010.

[21] Carina Wong, "WFRD Goes 'Round the Clock," *The Dartmouth*, October 12, 1989, 1. Interview with Krakower, September 2010, correspondence with Seth Skolnik, January 2011.

[22] Anda Kuo, "WFRD Changes Format to Enhance Appeal," *The Dartmouth*, February 26, 1990, 1, 2.

[23] Interviews with Rosenblatt, November 2008, Mark Wachen, December 2010.

[24] Directorate reports, May 5, June 19, October 19, 1986.

[25] Correspondence with Rosenblatt, January 2011, Abdhish Bhavsar, January 2011, Andy Shapiro, January 2011, Interviews with Rosenblatt, November 2008, Huff, January 2011. Bhavsar remembers the first CD player as being a trade-out.

[26] Interview with Skolnik, February 2010.

[27] "Formation Proposal for the Dartmouth Radio Network," May 26, 1986.

[28] Dave Wachen, letter to station members, July 23, 1986; correspondence with Andy Shapiro, January 2011; interviews with Tim Reynolds, August 2008, Seth Rosenblatt, November 2008, Priscilla Huff, January 2011; Baker, "New Radio Officers to Continue Format"; Samuel Shukovsky, "Radio Station and SASC Dispute on Free Hooters Ads," *The Dartmouth*, May 5, 1988,1, 6. Alumni *News Flash*, Spring 1989.

[29] Glassheim, "Promos Make WFRD Popular," 1, 2.

[30] Joe Dever, "Radio Station, Parties Set to Mark Off Year Elections," *The Dartmouth*, November 4, 1986, 1, 2.

[31] Interview with Avellino, January 2012. Hart later tried to restart his campaign, and another story has him coming to the WDCR studios with his Secret Service detail, but this cannot be confirmed. Taylor, who has been known ever since for this one question, later agonized over whether his improper question (by 1987 standards) contributed to a "debasement of the political dialogue."

[32] Lisa Baker, "Radio Station Plans a Full Night of Primary Returns," *The Dartmouth*, February 16, 1988, 9. Interviews with Rosenblatt, November 2008, Seth Skolnik, February 2010, Avellino, January 2012. A story on Wikipedia claimed that the station made a false prediction that Dick Gephardt had won the Democratic primary (Michael Dukakis was the actual winner), but no one interviewed for this book could confirm this.

[33] "Station Will Cover NH and Vermont Live, National Elecs. via AP," *The Dartmouth*, November 8, 1988, 2.

[34] *The Dartmouth*, September 25, 1985, 1.

[35] "Winter of Discontent on the Big Green," *The Harvard Crimson*, February 12, 1986.

[36] Jeffrey Hart, "Shanties and Liberal Facism," King Features Syndicate, April 23, 1986.

[37] James Panero and Stefan Beck, eds., *The Dartmouth Review Pleads Innocent* (Wilmington, DE: ISI Books, 2006), 122-165. Quote from Dean Dwight Lahr, 143.

[38] Board of Overseers minutes, November 4, 1988. Interview with Avellino, January 2012. Alumni *News Flash*, Spring 1989.

[39] Interview with Adams, August 2008. David Wachen memo, July 2, 1986, Board of Overseers minutes, July 19, 1986.

[40] Board of Overseers minutes, November 4, 1988.

[41] Interviews with Tim Reynolds, August 2008, Beth Krakower, September 2010; correspondence with Wellman, May 2012.

[42] Interviews with Seth Rosenblatt , November 2008, Seth Skolnik, February 2010, Laura Daniels, April 2013 (Canada married in 1987 and changed her last name to Daniels). Various overseers and Directorate meeting reports. David Marston.

[43] *Broadcasting Yearbook*, 1986-90. Interview with Seth Rosenblatt, November 2008.

[44] Correspondence with George Whitehead, February 2012, Gerrett Conover, February 2012.

[45] *The Dartmouth*, January 3, 1984, 1, February 16, 1985, 1. Stephen Campbell, "Campus Email for Everyone: Making It Work in Real Life," Dartmouth College, February 1994; "Kevin Scofield's Weblog" at **http://radio-weblogs.com/0133184/2004/08/13.html** (2004); Kate Wooler, "The End Is Near," *Dartmouth Alumni Magazine*, November/December 2008, 25; interview with Rich E. Brown, May 2012; correspondence with Albert Henning and

Geoffrey Bronner, February 2012. Brown, David Gelhar '84 and Jim Matthews are given credit for designing the original BlitzMail and its associated name directory, although many others were involved in various aspects of the system.

[46] Interviews with Seth Skolnik, February 2010, Gerrett Conover, February 2012.

[47] Interview with Avellino, January 2012.

[48] Memo from Bruce Pipes to Ad Hoc Committee, September 8, 1985.

[49] Report of Ad Hoc Committee to Edward J. Shanahan, May 1, 1986; Board of Overseers minutes, May 3, 1986.

[50] Interview with Travis, September 2008.

[51] Interviews with Bryant, September 2008, Cary Clark, August 2011, Sateia, June 2012. Correspondence with Tim Hoehn, November 2011.

[52] *The Dartmouth*, April 25, 1985, 1. Douglas Martin, "David McLaughlin, 72, Ex-President of Dartmouth, Dies," *New York Times*, August 27, 2004.

[53] Karen Arenson, "James Freedman, Former Dartmouth President, Dies at 70," *New York Times*, March 22, 2006. "James O. Freedman," at **www.Wikipedia.com**. James O. Freedman, *Idealism and Liberal Education* (University of Michigan Press, 1996), 26 (recounting his famous "creative loner" speech). Interview with John Bryant, August 2011.

[54] *The Dartmouth*, October 13, 1989, 24, 25. Gambling retired in 1990 and died in 2004.

### Chapter 11: 1990-2000

[1] Jamie Yasnowitz '92, "WDCR: View from Afar," *The Dartmouth*, June 29, 1990, 4.

[2] Eric Wellman, "'WDCR: View from Afar' Hit Far Off the Mark," *The Dartmouth*, July 3, 1990, 4.

[3] Interview with Philip Augur, September 2011.

[4] WFRD, Hanover, NH Playlist, Week of 5/23/94; interview with Philip Augur, September 2011.

[5] Interview with Mike Henry, July 2009; Frederic J. Frommer, "The New and the Classic: A Radio Balancing Act," *The Valley News*, July 31, 1994.

[6] Pam Kunen, "Dartmouth Radio: The Students Are in Control," *The Dartmouth*, September 28, 1990, 4; interviews with Henry, July 2009, and April Whitescarver, April 2012.

[7] Brent Laffoon, "Letter from the General Manager," *Dartmouth Broadcasting: Signals*, [Spring] 1998, 5; Kathrin Weston, "WFRD Considers Format Change," *The Dartmouth*, October 8, 1997; WFRD entry in Wikipedia; interview with Tim Reynolds, August 2008.

[8] Interviews with Henry, July 2009, April Whitescarver, April 2012; *News from Dartmouth Broadcasting*, Fall 1995/Winter 1996, 5, 6; *Dartmouth Broadcasting Signals*, Summer/Fall 1996, 5, 1997, 6; Directorate minutes, March 31, 1996.

[9] Interviews with Vivian Lee, October 2010, Tim Hoehn, October 2011; Sarah Rubenstein, "Laffoon Calls the Plays, Plays the Hits on 99 Rock," *The Dartmouth*, November 4, 1997.

[10] Rini Ghosh, "WFRD Rated Number One Radio Station for Past Two Years," *The Dartmouth*, July 31, 1995.

[11] *Dartmouth Broadcasting Signals*, 1997, 3.

[12] Board of Overseers minutes, August 2, 1990, 10; interview with Mike Henry, July 2009.

[13] Interviews with Tim Hoehn, October 2011, June 2012.

[14] Interview with Augur, September 2011.

[15] Jack Vaitayanonta, "Gov. Dean Declares Month 'Rocktober'," *The Dartmouth*, October 4, 1994; *Dartmouth Broadcasting Alumni Newsletter*, c.fall 1994.

[16] Interview with Tim Hoehn, October 2011.

[17] *Dartmouth Broadcasting Signals*, Summer/Fall 1996, 3; interview with Tim Hoehn, October 2011.

[18] Board of Overseers minutes, July 30, 1999; correspondence with Tim Hoehn, April 2012.

[19] Ed Ballam, "Haverhill Prepares to Rock," *Valley News*, August 13, 1998, 1, A6. The other bands included the Lisa Guyer Band and Red Telephone.

[20] Liability for such events is of course covered by insurance.

[21] Interview with Tim Hoehn, October 2011; correspondence with Sean Byrnes, December 2009.

[22] Correspondence with Brian Hughes, Dartmouth webmaster, December 2010; interview with Tim Hoehn, October 2011.

[23] Interview with Mike Henry, July 2009; Correspondence with Cheung, September 2010; *News from Dartmouth Broadcasting*, Fall 1995/Winter 1996, 2, 3.

[24] *Signals: News from Dartmouth Broadcasting*, Summer/Fall 1996, 4; Board of Overseers minutes, July 30, 1999; **www.dartmouth.edu/community/broadcast**, as of February 16, 2000 (archived at **http://web.archive.org**).

[25] "1340 WDCR Statement for Board of Overseers Meeting," February 23, 1996 (unsigned). "WDCR AM Survey," undated but Spring 1995.

[26] *The Dartmouth*: Adrienne Kim, "DJ to Address Riots on Radio," May 7, 1992, 1; Steve Larson, "Radio Station Plays Through It All," February 10, 1992, 9; Alex Perez, "Keeping It 'Real' in the Upper Valley," November 5, 1997.

[27] *Dartmouth Broadcasting Signals*, 1997, 3.

[28] Neil Desai, "Robinson '24 Spins Classic Tunes," *The Dartmouth*, August 20, 1996.

[29] Erika Patrick, "Steve and Doug Bring Insight, Innuendo to Tuesdays on DCR," *The Dartmouth*, April 29, 1997.

[30] *Dartmouth Broadcasting Signals*, 1998, 4; Josephine Huang, "Success of Up All Night Sets New Party Standard," *The Dartmouth*, April 14, 1997;

[31] Stephen Costalas, "WDCR Extends Election Coverage," *The Dartmouth*, October 31, 1990, 1, 10.

[32] *The Dartmouth*: Adrienne Kim, "'Rock the Vote' Tries to Drum Up Interest," January 9, 1992, 1, 8; Dawn Conner, "'Rock the Vote' Registers Hundreds," February 14, 1992, 10; interview with Krakower, September 2010.

[33] Interview with Hoehn, October 2011.

[34] Interview with Tim Hoehn, October 2011; Jeffrey Giuffrida, "Radio Covers N.H. Primary," *The Dartmouth*, February 16, 1996; Vivian Lee, "With N.H. Primary Ahead, Exciting Time for News," *News from Dartmouth Broadcasting*, Fall 1995/Winter 1996, 1, 5.

[35] Brad Russo, "Midterm Elections Hit College," *The Dartmouth*, November 3, 1998.

[36] Interview with Piro, April 2012.

[37] Board of Overseers minutes, February 21, 1991; interview with Hoehn, October 2011.

[38] *The Dartmouth*: Matthew Berry, "WDCR Censors Conservative Opinions," October 11, 1993; Pamm Quinn, "Maintain Diverse Programming," January 27, 1995.

[39] *News from Dartmouth Broadcasting*, Fall 1995/Winter 1996, 5; Erik Tanouye, "'Dialectic' Promotes Political Discussion," *The Dartmouth*, November 15, 1995.

[40] *Dartmouth Broadcasting Signals*, 1997, 5; 1998, 2.

[41] Peggy Grodinsky, "DJ Marathon Aids LISTEN," *Valley News*, c.December 1992; "99 Hour Marathon" (WFRD press release), c.December 1992. Interview with Tim Hoehn, October 2011; correspondence with Whitescarver, April 2012, Wellman, May 2012, Krakower, May 2012.

[42] Tom Zawistowski, TRZ, letter to Kathy Slattery, Dartmouth Athletic Dept., December 6, 1996. TRZ has since migrated to a web-based service, although Dartmouth games are no longer carried.

[43] Board of Overseers minutes, August 2, 1990. Interview with Sateia, June 2012. In 1987, shortly before leaving, Canada had married and become Laura Daniels.

[44] Interviews with Hoehn, October 2011, June 2012, Laura Daniels, April 2013. Hoehn, a Chicago native, was previously a d.j. or program director at stations in Randolph, VT, Newport, NH, and Stowe, VT.

[45] Interviews with Hoehn, June 2012, Sateia, June 2012.

[46] Brian Sward, *From The General Manager* (station newsletter), Summer 1993. Hanover-Lebanon are in Grafton County, White River Junction and environs are in Windsor.

[47] *Dartmouth Broadcasting Alumni Newsletter*, c.Summer/Fall 1994; Frederic J. Frommer, "The New and the Classic: A Radio Balancing Act," *The Valley News*, July 31, 1994.

[48] Ghosh, "WFRD Rated Number One Radio Station for Past Two Years." Interviews with Henry, July 2009, Brent Laffoon, July 2009, Phil Augur, September 2011.

[49] There are numerous references to this case on the Internet. See for example **http://www.antennazoning.com/docs/success-koor-nerw.htm**

[50] *The Dartmouth*: January 23, 1991, 1; William Scott, "DTV! Hits the Airwaves at Dartmouth," May 16, 1991, 1, 7.

[51] Maggie Fritz, "DNN Airs Show," *The Dartmouth*, January 11, 1994; *Dartmouth Broadcasting Alumni Newsletter,* c.Summer/Fall 1994.

[52] Letter from Philip Augur to Board of Overseers, December 14, 1994; from Augur to Dartmouth Broadcasting members, December 20, 1994.

[53] Letter from Rick Adams to Augur and others, December 22, 1994.

[54] *The Dartmouth*: Nathaniel LeClery, "Turmoil at WDCR," January 26, 1995; Pamm Quinn, "Maintain Diverse Programming," January 27, 1995.

[55] "WDCR AM Survey," undated but Spring 1995.

[56] Interviews with Augur, September, 2011; Tim Hoehn, October, 2011.

[57] According to one history, "the building was donated by Boston businessman Wallace Fullam Robinson to be a home for student organizations and an antidote to the influence of athletics." See **http://www.dartmo.com/buildings/qrsbldg.html#robinsonhall**.

[58] *The Dartmouth*: James Hunnicutt, "Robinson Renovations Slated," January 19, 1995; Michael Posey, "College Station Will Stay," January 19, 1995. *News From Dartmouth Broadcasting*, Fall 1995/Winter 1996.

[59] *The Dartmouth*: Neil Desai, "Equipment Worth $5,000 Stolen From Robinson Hall," November 21, 1995, David Pichler, "Renovated Robinson Hall Opens Tomorrow," August 8, 1996. Interview with Tim Hoehn, October, 2011.

[60] Interviews with Mike Henry, July 2009, Vivian Lee, October 2010. *Signals: News from Dartmouth Broadcasting*, Summer/Fall 1996, 5.

[61] Cara Abercrombie, "Radio Days," *The Dartmouth*, April 17, 1996.

[62] Interviews with Beth Krakower, September 2010, Vivian Lee, October 2010, Mike Henry, July 2009, Brent Laffoon, July 2009, Piro, April 2012, Hoehn, October 2011, Sateia, June 2012.

[63] *The Dartmouth*: Scott Anthony, "Strayer Stands By His Words," July 14, 1994, Maggie Fritz, "Grelotti '96 Enters Assembly Race," April 10, 1995.

[64] "1340 WDCR Statement for Board of Overseers Meeting," February 23, 1996 (unsigned).

[65] Interview with Hoehn, October 2011.

[66] *The Dartmouth:* John Strayer, "Recent Suicides Lead to Questions about Dartmouth," October 25, 1995; Justin Steinman, "Sarah Devens '96 Dies in Apparent Suicide," July 12, 1995. Gerry Callahan and Sonja Steptoe, "An End Too Soon," *Sports Illustrated*, July 24, 1995. The high profile sports suicide was that of hockey captain Sarah Devens.

[67] Robert Isaacs, "Some Students Turn to Matchmaking This Valentine's Day," *The Dartmouth*, February 14, 1996.

[68] Kendra Kosko, "Love and Passion, Robinson Style," *The Dartmouth*, August 4, 1997.

[69] Interview with Huff, January 2011. *The Dartmouth*: Pamm Quinn, "Maintain Diverse Programming," January 27, 1995; Maggie Lockwood, "New Group Unites Female Broadcasters," April 25, 1994.

[70] Holly Sateia, "A Note from the Dean," *Dartmouth Broadcasting Alumni Newsletter*, c.Summer/Fall 1994.

[71] Pamm Quinn, "Fighting Sexism an Unnecessary Sacrifice," *The Dartmouth*, November 17, 1994

[72] Pam Quinn, "Maintain Diverse Programming," *The Dartmouth*, January 27, 1995.

[73] Jack Vaitayanonta, "Women Assess Leadership," *The Dartmouth*, November 23, 1994. Interviews with Whitescarver, April 2012; Lee, October 2010.

[74] Diem-Trang Do, letter to alumni, c.March 26, 1993. *Dartmouth Broadcasting Signals*, 1997, 2.

[75] Pam Kunen, "Dartmouth Radio: The Students Are in Control," *The Dartmouth*, September 28, 1990, 4.

[76] Kunen, "Dartmouth Radio: The Students Are in Control," 4.

**Chapter 12: 2000-2006**

[1] Correspondence with King, October 2010, Mike O'Donnell, January 2011. Interviews with Tim Hoehn, October 2011, Beth Krakower, September 2010.

[2] Timothy W. Grinsell, "Dartmouth Radio Sells Out," *Dartmouth Free Press*, Issue 3.14 (2003), posted to the Internet on August 1, 2003.

[3] Interview with Laura Daniels, April 2013. Ms. Daniels divorced in 1997 and was once again known as Laura Canada.

[4] Ginsell, "Dartmouth Radio Sells Out."

[5] Board of Overseers reports, May 9, 2003, 6,18.

[6] Board of Overseers reports, May 9, 2003, 16,17.

[7] William Meland, "Change the Channel," *The Dartmouth*, January 28, 2003.

[8] Dan King and members of the Dartmouth Broadcasting Directorate, "Dartmouth Radio Responds," *The Dartmouth*, February 3, 2003. See also Neha Narula, "Don't Change the Channel," and Danielle Ricci, "College Radio," both in *The Dartmouth,* February 4, 2003.

[9] *The Dartmouth*: Jacques P. Hebert, "Armed with $400, DTV Battles to Find Audience," April 28, 2005, Deborah Wassel, "99 Rocks," April 29, 2005.

[10] Board of Overseers reports and minutes, February 21, 2003, May 9, 2003. The Electra Night Club closed in 2010, and a year later its burly co-owner, Louis Fucci, was arrested for hiring a hit man to kill his ex-business partner and ex-girlfriend. (Christian Avard, "Plea Deal Reached in Murder-for-Hire Plot Case," *Vermont Today*, March 28, 2012.)

[11] Interview with Deborah Wassel, June 2012.

[12] Board of Overseers reports, February 21, 2003, May 9, 2003.

[13] Board of Overseers reports, November 14, 2003.

[14] **http://dartreview.blogspot.com/2003_04_01_archive.html**.

[15] Board of Overseers report, February 25, 2006. Astrid Bradley, "Prescott to Lead Sexual Abuse Awareness Program," *The Dartmouth*, November 1, 2005.

[16] Board of Overseers report, February 21, 2003.

[17] Neil Desai, "Robinson '24 Spins Classic Tunes," *The Dartmouth*, August 20, 1996.

[18] From an obituary provided by the Robinson family. Correspondence with Chris Robinson, October 2010.

[19] Robinson is often cited as dying at age 99, but according to the obituary provided by his family he was born on May 11, 1903 and died on March 3, 2002.

[20] Julia Levy, "Media Competes for Your Vote," *The Dartmouth,* November 7, 2000.

[21] Board of Overseers minutes, November 8, 2002.

[22] Interviews with Tim Reynolds, August 2008, Tim Hoehn, October 2011.

[23] Board of Overseers report, May 9, 2003.

[24] Correspondence with Burdette, February 2011.

[25] Correspondence with Burdette, June 2012, Beniamino, June 2012.

[26] Board of Overseers reports, February 25, 2006.

[27] Board of Overseers reports, February 19, 2005.

[28] Board of Overseers reports and minutes, February 24, 2007.

[29] Board of Overseers minutes, July 30, 1999.

[30] Based on an analysis of Dartmouth Broadcasting websites 2000-2006, captured by **www.archive.org** and accessed through its Wayback Machine. Board of Overseers minutes, February 21, 2003. Interview with Heath Cole, June 2012. According to Cole many radio

stations began streaming in 2000 but stopped shortly thereafter to wait for the legal dust to settle.

[31] Board of Overseers reports, August 11, 2006.

[32] Interviews with Deborah Wassel, June 2012, Cole, June 2012.

[33] Board of Overseers reports, May 9, 2003. Interview with Shapiro, September 2010.

[34] Board of Overseers reports, November 14, 2003.

[35] Board of Overseers reports, November 14, 2003, February 19, 2005.

[36] Interview with Jeff Shapiro, June 2012; Board of Overseers minutes, February 21, 2003.

[37] Board of Overseers reports, May 9, 2003.

[38] Board of Overseers reports, February 21, 2003.

[39] Board of Overseers reports, November 14, 2003.

[40] Board of Overseers reports, February 21, 2003.

[41] Board of Overseers reports and minutes, November 14, 2003.

[42] Interview with Heath Cole, June 2012.

[43] Board of Overseers reports, February 19, 2005.

[44] Interviews with Shapiro, June 2012, Heath Cole, June 2012. Great Eastern owned a station in Concord, N.H., but this was too distant to be packaged with WFRD.

[45] Board of Overseers reports, February 25, 2006.

[46] KISS was used for a time as a identifier by WZRT, before it reverted to its more familiar Z97. Correspondence with Heath Cole, November 2012.

## Chapter 13: 2006 to Date

[1] "Eye Toward the Future," *The Voice of Dartmouth Broadcasting* [newsletter], [Spring] 2007, 4; interviews with Cole, June 2011 and June 2012.

[2] Board of Overseers reports, May 19, 2006. Interview with Cole, June 2012.

[3] Interviews with Wassel, June 2012; Cole, June 2012; Pavel Sotskov, July 2012.

[4] Board of Overseers reports, November 7, 2006.

[5] Board of Overseers reports, November 2, 2007.

[6] "99Rock WFRD-FM Playlist for 8/29/11-9/4/11." Interviews with Zhao, August 2011, Pavel Sotskov, July 2012.

[7] Interview with Pavel Sotskov, July, 2012; Board of Overseers report, February 1, 2010.

[8] Interview with Pavel Sotskov, July, 2012.

[9] Board of Overseers reports, May 5, 2008.

[10] Board of Overseers reports, April 16, 2011.

[11] Correspondence with Cole, July 2012; Schuyler Evans, "National Recognition," *Greetings from Dartmouth Broadcasting* (alumni newsletter), c.June 2009; Board of Overseers reports, November 2, 2009.

[12] Joe Debonis, "Dartmouth Radio Locally Popular But Has Few Student Listeners," *The Dartmouth*, November 7, 2006. David Corriveau, "Patience, Diplomacy Are Keys to This Car," *Valley News*, undated clipping (c.May 23 or 24, 2007), A1, A7.

[13] Board of Overseers reports, November 2, 2007.

[14] Board of Overseers reports, May 5, 2008.

[15] "The Student Experience," The *Voice of Dartmouth Broadcasting*, Fall 2008, 2. Interview with Julie Kaye and Heath Cole, January 2009.

[16] Board of Overseers reports, November 2, 2009.

[17] Board of Overseers reports, April 16, 2010.

[18] Board of Overseers reports, February 23, 2008.

[19] Board of Overseers reports, October 23, 2010.

[20] Interview with Cole, June, 2012.

[21] Interviews with Deborah Wassel, June 2012, Gregg Fox, June 2012.

[22] Board of Overseers reports, May 16, 2006.

[23] Debonis, "Dartmouth Radio Locally Popular."

[24] Board of Overseers reports and minutes, February 24, 2007, May 18, 2007.

[25] Board of Overseers reports, November 2, 2007, February 23, 2008, May 5, 2008..

[26] Correspondence with Heath Cole, July 2012. Board of Overseers reports, May 5, 2008.

[27] Board of Overseers reports and minutes, April 16, 2010.

[28] Board of Overseers reports, October 23, 2010.

[29] Spring 2012 Programming Guide; Interview with Fox, June 2012.

[30] Board of Overseers reports, November 7, 2006.

[31] Board of Overseers reports, February 24, 2007.

[32] Board of Overseers reports, May 5, 2008.

[33] Board of Overseers reports, November 2, 2009.

[34] Board of Overseers reports, November 2, 2009.

[35] Jonathan Li, "Valley Voices Brings Culture-Focused Program to Upper Valley Radio," **www.dartbeat.com**, November 9, 2012. (Daily blog of *The Dartmouth*.)

[36] Correspondence with Stu Zuckerman, October 2008. Interview with Evans, February 2011.

[37] Correspondence with Heath Cole and Ryan Zehner, October 2011; Board of Overseers reports, October 29, 2011.

[38] Board of Overseers reports and minutes, February 24, 2007.

[39] Correspondence with Heath Cole, July 2012.

[40] Elisabeth Lubiak, "'The Big Green Scene' Adds Commentary to Dartmouth Sports," *The Dartmouth,* February 2, 2011. Board of Overseers reports, April 16, 2011.

[41] **http://www.askcbi.org/?page_id=1822**

[42] Interviews with Heath Cole, June 2011, Schuyler Evans, February 2012, Pavel Sotskov, July 2012. Board of Overseers reports, May 18, 2007. According to College records Belser did not graduate.

[43] *Greetings from Dartmouth Broadcasting* (newsletter), undated but c.June 2009.

[44] Interview with Pavel Sotskov, July 2012; Board of Overseers reports, February 23, 2008.

[45] Board of Overseers reports, November 2, 2009.

[46] Board of Overseers reports, May 18, 2007.

[47] Steve Smith, "Dartmouth Broadcasting Helps Bring Holiday Gifts to Local Children," *Dartmouth Now*, December 7, 2011.

[48] "WFRD-FM/New Hampshire," NAB Broadcasters Public Service, at **www.broadcastpublicservice.org/story.asp?id=1313**. "Pauline 'Polly' Robbins-Loyd 1976-2008." at **www.legacy.com/Obituaries.asp?Page=LifeStory&PersonId=101210880**. Interview with Heath Cole, June 2011.

[49] **http://www.nhabblog.org/2011/10/2011-granite-mikes-held-by-new-hampshire-association-of-broadcasters/**

[50] Board of Overseers reports, February 23, 2008.

[51] Interviews with Cole, June 2012, Sotskov, July 2012.

[52] Board of Overseers reports, April 16, 2010.

[53] Interview with Heath Cole, June 2012. Various Board of Overseers reports.

[54] Board of Overseers reports, November 7, 2006.

[55] Board of Overseers reports, February 23, 2008.

[56] *Greetings from Dartmouth Broadcasting* (newsletter), undated but c.June 2009 and Fall 2009. Board of Overseers reports, April 16, 2010.

[57] Board of Overseers reports, October 13, 2012, correspondence with George Whitehead, October, 2012. The student Directorate had no involvement in these plans.

[58] "WDCR AM 1340 - Celebrating 50 Years!", at **http://webdcr.com/WDCRs50thAnniversary/tabid/124/Default.aspx**.

[59] "A Reunion Dinner at the Norwich," *The Voice of Dartmouth Broadcasting*, Fall 2008. "WDCR's Golden Oldies!", *'72 News* (Class of '72 newsletter), December 2008.

[60] Correspondence with and documents from Whitehead, March 2012.

[61] Board of Overseers reports, November 2, 2009.

[62] Correspondence with George Whitehead, February 2012.

---

[63] Correspondence with George Whitehead, August 2011. Whitehead happened on the scene just after the tower came down, and memorialized the scene in pictures and a written reminiscence.

[64] Interviews with Heath Cole, June 2012, Gregg Fox, June 2012.

[65] Board of Overseers reports, October 29, 2011.

[66] Interview with Kate Burke, April 2013.

# Index

# About the Author

TIM BROOKS was born in New Hampshire and attended Dartmouth in the 1960s as an economics major—although his true major was WDCR, where he was a disc jockey, administrative director, and served on the Directorate. Like many station staffers he planned on a career in radio, but after military service (as a Signal Corps officer in Vietnam) his first job was writing copy at a local television station. He earned a master's degree at Syracuse University (where he revived his *Pick of the Past* show on WAER-FM), and then landed at NBC-TV in New York where he rose through the ranks. His 1963 WDCR listenership survey had lit a spark of interest in audience research, and he eventually became a director of research for NBC, and then the top research executive at a major ad agency, USA Network, The Sci-Fi Channel (which he helped launch), and Lifetime Television. He has also been quite active in industry organizations, serving as chairman of the Advertising Research Foundation and of the Media Rating Council, and on the boards of other organizations. He was a founding member of the Council for Research Excellence in 2005. He is frequently quoted in the press on audience matters.

Concurrently he pursued a career in writing, starting with the highly successful *Complete Directory to Prime Time Network and Cable TV Shows, 1946-Present* (1979), which has published nine editions. Other books include *The Complete Directory to Prime Time TV Stars* (1987) and *Lost Sounds: Blacks and the Birth of the Recording Industry, 1890-1919* (2004). His books have won numerous awards, and *Lost Sounds* led to a *Lost Sounds* double-CD which won a Grammy Award. He is also president of the Association for Recorded Sound Collections and director of the Historical Recording Coalition for Access and Preservation, which seeks to reform overly restrictive U.S. copyright laws in order to preserve historical recordings and make them accessible to the public.

Since 2008 Tim has been an active consultant to the TV industry, including work as an expert witness. The suggestion in 2008 that he finish his history of Dartmouth radio turned into quite an adventure, but he is glad that he agreed to do it. More than nostalgia, it has been a journey of discovery about the fascinating world of college radio.